Learning to Live Naturally

Learning to Live Naturally

Stoic Ethics and its Modern Significance

CHRISTOPHER GILL

OXFORD
UNIVERSITY PRESS

OXFORD
UNIVERSITY PRESS

Great Clarendon Street, Oxford, OX2 6DP,
United Kingdom

Oxford University Press is a department of the University of Oxford.
It furthers the University's objective of excellence in research, scholarship,
and education by publishing worldwide. Oxford is a registered trade mark of
Oxford University Press in the UK and in certain other countries

© Christopher Gill 2022

The moral rights of the author have been asserted

First Edition published in 2022

Published in the United States of America by Oxford University Press
198 Madison Avenue, New York, NY 10016, United States of America

British Library Cataloguing in Publication Data
Data available

Library of Congress Control Number: 2022941735

ISBN 978–0–19–886616–9

DOI: 10.1093/oso/9780198866169.001.0001

Printed and bound in the UK by
Clays Ltd, Elcograf S.p.A.

To my four sons, their partners and children.

To all those scholars, students, and 'modern Stoics' with whom I have discussed Stoic ideas and from whom I have learnt so much.

Contents

III. STOIC ETHICS AND MODERN MORAL THEORY

Preface

As explained in the Introduction, this book offers a reading of key distinctive themes in Stoic ethics and explores their significance for modern thought, especially contemporary virtue ethics. Although I have been working on Stoic philosophy for some time, this project is a new one for me, in its objectives and scope; however, there are some salient points of connection with my previous writings. The book draws on a longstanding interest in the interface between ancient ethics and psychology, as well as the relationship between ancient and modern ideas, including ethical ones. Also, my interpretation of Stoic ethics underlines the importance given to interpersonal and social engagement, an aspect of Stoicism sometimes overlooked. This emphasis reflects the weight I have elsewhere given to this dimension of Greek and Roman thought and its significance for modern thought. I have sometimes presented this dimension as the idea of 'the self in dialogue' or the 'objective-participant' conception of personality.

During the period of work on this book, I have become closely involved in the public presentation of Stoic ideas for a broad audience through a project ('Modern Stoicism') outlined at the end of Chapter 8. It is striking and positive to see how much resonance Stoic ideas have for so many people at present. This book is not framed as life-guidance for a general audience; it is a sustained academic study of Stoic ethics and its implications, especially for modern moral philosophy. However, I have set out to explore in depth the Stoic ethical ideas on which contemporary life-guidance is based. Also, I have aimed to convey this exploration in clear, non-technical language, and to support my interpretation by extensive reference to the ancient evidence, with quotations in English translation. So I hope the book will be accessible and useful to some of those whose primary concern is with Stoicism as life-guidance, as well as to scholars and students of ancient and modern philosophy, and other types of reader drawn to the topic. Part II of the book, especially Chapters 5, 7, and 8 may be of most interest to such readers.

Like anyone working in this area, I have benefited greatly from the upsurge of research and scholarly publication on Stoicism in recent decades. Also, composition of the book was substantially helped by a Leverhulme Emeritus Fellowship (2014–2016). This award enabled me to organize in autumn 2016 a pair of two-day workshops, at Yale and Cambridge, in which groups of scholars discussed a first draft of parts of the book (about 60,000 words). Participants included, at Yale, Julia Annas, David Charles, Stephen Darwall, Verity Harte, Brad Inwood, Daniel Russell, and Katja Vogt, as well as several graduate students. At Cambridge, the participants consisted of Gábor Betegh, Rae Langton, M. M. McCabe, Onora

O'Neill, Malcolm Schofield, David Sedley, and Raphael Woolf. This provided an exceptional, and highly valuable, opportunity to have detailed, expert, comments at a stage in the composition of the book when I could take full account of these responses, and both workshops have made a material difference to my approach and presentation. I am extremely grateful to all those who gave their time and attention to the book in this way, and especially to Brad Inwood and Gábor Betegh, who helped me to organize the workshops. In addition, Julia Annas and Brad Inwood kindly commented on subsequent drafts of certain chapters. I would also like to thank anonymous readers for the Press, who reviewed the book at preliminary and final stages, for their constructive and perceptive observations. I am very grateful to Peter Momtchiloff for his advice and support, and all those in the Press who have helped the book through the stages of production.

All scholarly research constitutes a kind of dialogue between oneself and others exploring the material, and I am deeply conscious of learning much on Stoic ethics from fellow-scholars as well as students and those with whom, in recent years, I have been engaged in modern (applied) Stoicism. My life has also been enriched immeasurably by loving involvement in the lives of my four sons, their partners, and their children. The book is dedicated to both these groups.

Note on Conventions

The abbreviations for ancient authors and their works cited or noted are given in full form in the Index of Ancient Passages. All scholarly works cited by author and date are given in full form in the References. All quotations in Greek and Latin are translated. In most cases, a published translation is cited; where there is no citation, the translation is mine. When a published translation is cited, there may be minor stylistic modifications to the published version (these are not marked). Any significant change or addition to the published translation is noted. Where an ancient passage is cited as LS (an abbreviation explained shortly), their translation is used unless otherwise indicated.

There are numerous cross-references in footnotes, designed to highlight connections within the argument of the book and to avoid repetition of content. The cross-references take this form: 'see text to nn. 3–4', referring to the same chapter; or 'see Ch. 3, text to nn. 3–4', referring to a different chapter (all instances of capitalized Ch., are cross-references); or 'see 3.4 and 4.5' referring to sections within chapters. References of this type ('see 3.4, 4.5') not linked with abbreviated references to ancient authors and works are cross-references. In addition to the standard abbreviations such as 'e.g.' and 'i.e.': I also use 'esp.' for 'especially'.

These abbreviations are used throughout the book:

D.L. Diogenes Laertius, *Lives of Eminent Philosophers*. References are to book and chapters, usually to the '*Life of Zeno*', Book 7 (e.g. D.L. 7.88).

IG B. Inwood and L. Gerson, *The Stoics Reader: Selected Writings and Testimonia*, Indianapolis, 2008. References are to page numbers (e.g. IG: 135).

LS A. A. Long and D. N. Sedley, *The Hellenistic Philosophers*, 2 vols., Cambridge. References are mostly to section and paragraph (e.g. 59 D) or subdivision of paragraph (e.g. 59 D(3)). Page references are to the commentaries following each section in vol. 1 (e.g. LS, vol. 1, p. 156).

Stob. Stobaeus or John of Stobi. Most references are to the summary of Stoic ethics regarded as derived from Arius Didymus and sometimes ascribed to him. References to this summary cite the relevant section number (e.g. 5 or 5a). This is followed by a reference to the standard edition of Stobaeus, cited by volume (usually 2), page number, and lines in the page. So, a typical reference is 'Stob. 5a, 2.143.6–7'. A few references to Stobaeus are not to the ethical summary and have no initial section number (e.g. 5.111.6–7), The standard ancient edition is:

C. Wachsmuth, and O. Hense (eds.), *Ioannis Stobaei: Anthologium*, 5 vols. Berlin (1884–1912, reprint 1958). When quoting from Stobaeus, the translation cited is generally IG.

SVF H. von Arnim (ed.), *Stoicorum Veterum Fragmenta*, 4 vols., Leipzig 1903–5 (reprint Munich, 2004). References are to volume and section, e.g. '*SVF* 3.295'.

Main thinkers discussed and their dates are as follows.

Stoics (heads of the school) all dates BC:

Zeno of Citium (founder) (334–262); Cleanthes (*c.* 331–230, head from 262); Chrysippus (*c.* 280–*c.* 206, head from 230); Zeno of Tarsus (flourished *c.* 210); Diogenes of Babylon (*c.* 228–*c.* 152); Antipater (*c.* 200–*c.*130, head from *c.* 152–*c.* 130); Panaetius (*c.* 185–*c.* 110, head from *c.* 130).

Other Stoics:

Aristo (3rd cent. BC); Posidonius (*c.* 133–*c.* 51 BC); Seneca (AD *c.* 1–65); Epictetus (AD *c.* 50–*c.* 130); Marcus Aurelius (AD 121–80); Hierocles (flourished *c.* AD 120).

Other thinkers:

Socrates (469–399 BC); Plato (427–347 BC); Aristotle (384–322 BC); Antiochus (*c.* 130–*c.* 68 BC); Cicero (106–43 BC); Arius Didymus (late first cent. BC); Plutarch (AD *c.* 45–125.), Galen (AD 129–*c.* 216).

Relevant periods of antiquity (in broad terms):

Classical Greece, 6th–4th cent. BC; Hellenistic period, 3rd–1st cent. BC; Roman Imperial period, AD 1st–5th cent. ('Post-Hellenistic' period is an overlapping category, indicating the continuation of Hellenistic ideas over a long period and usually taken as being 100 (or 200) BC–AD 200.)

Introduction

Aims

In this book I have two main aims. In the first two parts, I offer a reading of core
distinctive themes in Stoic ethics, centred on the idea of happiness as the life
according to nature and on ethical development as learning to live this kind of life.
In the third part, I suggest that Stoic ethics has more to contribute to modern
moral theory, especially in virtue ethics, than it has done so far. These two aims are
closely interconnected. My account of Stoic ethics is designed to bring out its
coherence and strengths, as I see them, which are linked with (but not limited to)
its coherence. The combination of the coherence and strengths underlie the main
claim of the final chapters, that Stoicism can serve as an especially valuable
contributor to modern virtue ethics, as a supplement or alternative to the standard
ancient prototype, Aristotle.

I begin by a general statement of these claims, which are explained further in
the following outline of chapters. I see Stoic ethics as a coherent combination of an
innovative theory of value with a credible conception of nature, both human and
universal, and of ethical development or education. The Stoic theory of value is
ethically rigorous in seeing virtue as the sole basis for happiness, as contrasted
with the main ancient alternative, that happiness is based on a combination of
virtue and other kinds of good things. However, this ethical rigour is explained,
and justified, in three main ways. It is justified, in terms of value theory, by the
distinction between the special value (goodness) of virtue and the value of other
things normally regarded as good, which the Stoics call 'indifferents'. This is
linked, in turn, with a conception of virtue as expertise in selecting between
indifferents and in leading a happy life. This value theory is further supported
by reference to ideas of nature and ethical development. Both virtue and happiness
are analysed as expressing nature at its best, either human or universal (that of the
world or universe) or both. This supports the claim that virtue constitutes the sole
basis for happiness. Stoic value theory is also closely linked with, and supported
by, its account of ethical development, the main distinctive features of which are
the ideas of 'appropriation' (*oikeiōsis*) and emotional development (or 'therapy').
The theory of development centres on the ideas that the movement towards virtue
and virtue-based happiness forms an integral part of a life expressing human (or
universal) nature at its best and also that the capacity to develop in this way falls
within the scope of all human beings. A further, correlated, feature of Stoic ethical

Learning to Live Naturally: Stoic Ethics and its Modern Significance. Christopher Gill, Oxford University Press.
© Christopher Gill 2022. DOI: 10.1093/oso/9780198866169.003.0001

theory is stress on the social and other-benefitting dimensions of human life. This is conveyed especially in the ideas that human beings are constitutively rational and sociable and that the motive to care for others is a primary, in-built motive alongside the motive to care for oneself.

In all these respects, I see the Stoic ethical theory both as exceptionally coherent, and as strong, in its combination of a rigorous ethical theory with a credible form of naturalism and approach to ethical development. This interpretation, set out in the first two parts of the book, forms the basis for the claim, in the third part, that Stoic ethics has a special, and so far not fully realized, contribution to make to modern moral theory, especially in virtue ethics.

More precisely, Stoicism can contribute most effectively to the combination sometimes found in modern theory, of virtue ethics, eudaimonism, and ethical naturalism. Aristotle has served as the main ancient model for this kind of modern theory. However, I argue that, even if one assumes a broadly Aristotelian theoretical framework, Stoicism offers a stronger and more internally coherent version of this framework. The Stoic approach avoids the internal tensions or problems that arise in Aristotle's thinking about the relative contribution of virtue and other goods to happiness and about the relation between the practical and theoretical dimensions of a happy life. As a result, Stoicism offers a more coherent paradigm for the virtue-happiness relationship. In particular, it provides a better framework for accommodating two, seemingly competing ideas, that virtue is intrinsically valuable and that happiness is the overall goal of life. The combination of these two ideas is seen as desirable in certain strands of modern, as well as ancient, ethical theory. Stoicism also offers an approach to self-other relations (notably in the idea that care for others is a primary human motive) that offers an effective defence against the criticism that eudaimonistic virtue ethics is inherently egoistic.

Further, I argue that Stoic ethical ideas about human and cosmic nature can enhance modern thinking (especially in modern virtue ethics) on human nature and the environment. Stoic and Aristotelian ethics converge in presenting virtue or happiness as the realization of human nature at its best. However, Stoicism, by linking human virtue and happiness with universal nature, provides ideas which can be used to support modern environmental ethics, especially regarding our response to climate breakdown. Finally, I suggest that Stoic thinking on development and guidance has a distinctive and important contribution to make to modern thinking on these subjects. Stoicism can inform modern virtue ethical theory on these subjects in ways that go beyond Aristotle. Also, the recent upsurge of modern 'life-guidance' books and courses based on Stoicism and the positive public response to these bring out the continuing resonance for modern audiences of Stoic ethical ideas.

How does this book relate to its broader scholarly context? The increase of research and publication on Hellenistic philosophy in recent decades, especially Stoicism, has greatly enhanced our understanding of Stoic ethics. Even so, there are rather few specialized book-length studies of Stoic ethics, taken as a whole, in English; and some of these have rather specific concerns.[1] Hence, a further aim of this book is to present, for a relatively broad readership, the core concepts of Stoic ethics and their relationship to each other, and to display the evidence on which any general account of Stoic ethics is based. This book, in its first two sections, discusses all the main ethical topics recognized in ancient summaries (virtue, happiness or the goal of life, indifferents, appropriate actions, appropriation, emotions), along with 'nature', an important idea, though not a distinct topic, in Stoic ethics.[2] It also explores the interplay between these concepts within Stoic ethics as a whole, and, at certain points, connections between ethics and other branches of knowledge, especially theology (part of Stoic physics). As well as building on previous scholarly work, I sometimes refer to areas of scholarly debate, for instance on the role of cosmic nature in ethics. However, in general, I have been rather sparing in scholarly references, and have concentrated on offering my own interpretation of the evidence and bringing out what I see as the main strengths of the Stoic framework.[3]

In the third part of the book, I argue that Stoic ethics offers an alternative, or better, ancient prototype (compared with Aristotelian ethics) for modern virtue ethics; and this argument is innovative in its overall character.[4] However, my discussion in Chapter 6 builds on philosophically informed discussions of the rival merits of the Stoic and Aristotelian ethical positions by scholars such as Julia Annas and Terry Irwin. A further suggestive parallel is Daniel Russell's comparative assessment of the competing strengths of Stoic and Aristotelian concepts of happiness, viewed as potential contributors to modern (virtue ethical) ideas of happiness.[5] The discussion of Chapter 7, centred on Stoic and modern ideas about human nature and the natural environment, breaks largely new ground. So too, in a different way, does the treatment in Chapter 8 of Stoic thinking on ethical development and guidance and modern theory and practice. Overall, the aim of this part of the book is to give Stoic ethics a new prominence in modern theoretical debate.

I have described my discussion as a 'reading' or 'interpretation' of Stoic ethics: why present it in this way? Why do I not just summarize Stoic theory, offer a

---

[1] Brennan 2005 and Jedan 2009 offer relatively comprehensive accounts of Stoic ethics, though Brennan also treats psychology and fate; Jedan focuses on virtue, appropriate actions, and the religious dimension of Stoic ethics. Inwood 1985 is centred on the relationship between ethics and action theory. Inwood and Donini 1999 provide a useful (book-chapter) overview; Annas 1993 contains valuable discussion of Stoic ethical themes, as does Long 1996. On Becker 1998/2017, see n. 4; for books on Stoic ethics and life-guidance, see Ch. 8, n. 91.

[2] See Long and Sedley 1987 (=LS) 56 A (D.L. 7.84); also Schofield 2003: 237–8.

[3] A full treatment of all topics of scholarly controversy in Stoic ethics would have made this book much longer and less generally accessible.

[4] Becker 1998/2017 also aims to present Stoic ethics (or at least a modernized version of this) as a prototype for virtue ethics; see Ch. 6, text to nn. 20–2.

[5] See Annas 1993: chs. 19–21; Irwin 2007: ch. 13 (also 1986); Russell 2012.

'consensus' scholarly account, and then go on consider more complex questions such as the relationship to modern ethical theory? Doing so is not as straightforward as it might seem. For anyone working on Stoic ethics, a rather pressing question arises: *where is it?* The treatises of the Hellenistic Stoics, on ethics and other subjects, are lost, except for later quotations and references.[6] For our knowledge of their ideas, we are largely reliant on three summaries of Stoic ethical theory, taken from Cicero, Diogenes Laertius, and Stobaeus (the latter apparently based on Arius Didymus).[7] Though composed later than the Hellenistic era, these summaries present themselves as, and are generally taken to be, reliable accounts of the ideas developed by a series of Stoic thinkers from the founder Zeno onwards, especially those of Chrysippus, the major theorist and systematizer of the theory.[8] These summaries, along with discussions, sometimes critical, by other ancient thinkers, represent our core evidence for Stoic ethics.[9] In addition, there are surviving complete works or parts of works from the late Roman Republic and Imperial period, which present Stoic ethical theories and related topics, including theology. The main relevant authors or thinkers are Cicero, who was not a Stoic but a highly informed presenter of their ideas, and Seneca, a prolific Stoic author writing in a number of genres. In addition, we have reports of ethical discussions by Epictetus and the philosophical notebook of the emperor Marcus Aurelius.[10]

Given the nature of our evidence, any account of Stoic ethics, or any other aspect of their theory, inevitably, involves reconstruction and interpretation. A subsidiary aim of this book is to bring out the exploratory nature of this process of reconstruction.[11] Some scholarly treatments are presented as accounts of 'early' or 'old' Stoic theory, generally meaning the ideas of the first three heads of the school, Zeno, Cleanthes, and Chrysippus, in so far as these can be securely identified.[12] Also, some (especially earlier) scholarship, subdivides Stoicism, like other ancient theories, into 'early', 'middle', and 'late' periods, although this subdivision is not made in ancient sources. I too am especially interested in reconstructing Stoic ethical theory in the Hellenistic era, especially that of Chrysippus, and I take as the core evidence for this theory the three summaries

---

[6] See Mansfeld 1999a, 3–13.

[7] Cicero, *On Ends* (*De Finibus*) (*Fin.*) 3; Diogenes Laertius 7.84–131; Stobaeus *Anthology* 2.5–12, generally thought to be based on an account by Arius Didymus, and often referred to as the summary of Arius Didymus; apart from Cicero, all those mentioned are writers of handbooks. On these summaries see 3.3.

[8] See Schofield 2003: 236–9; on Stobaeus, see Long 1996: ch. 5.

[9] For the main ancient sources in English translation, see LS vol. 1, sections 56–67 (with commentary); Inwood and Gerson 2008 (= IG): 113–76; also Inwood and Gerson 1997: 190–260. The most complete collection of Greek and Roman sources is von Arnim 1903–5 (*SVF*).

[10] On Cicero, see Powell 1995; Woolf 2015; Schofield 2021 (political philosophy); on Seneca, Inwood 2005; on Epictetus, Long 2002; on Marcus Aurelius, Gill 2013a: introduction; Sellars 2021. For extracts on ethics from later Stoics, see Inwood and Gerson 2008: 177–205.

[11] See esp. 1.3 and Ch. 3.

[12] On main thinkers and dates (also periods referred to), see 'Conventions', p. xii. On the history of Stoic philosophy, see Sedley 2003 and Gill 2003.

of ethical doctrines. However, my subject here is 'Stoicism', and not specifically 'early Stoicism'; and I draw extensively on the evidence of Cicero and, to a lesser extent, the Imperial Stoic thinkers, where this seems to be consistent with previous Stoic thought. I make fuller use of Cicero's *On Duties* than is often done, as well as Cicero's summary of ethical doctrines in *On Ends* 3, and, for theology, *On the Nature of the Gods* 2, which are normally regarded as good evidence for Stoic thought.[13] In general, and especially for readers whose main interest is modern ethics, these discussions of Cicero offer a valuable point of access to Stoic ethics. They provide continuous exposition and analysis and not just handbook summary; and they correlate the distinctive features of Stoic thought, as Cicero sees them, with other ancient theories. To some extent, these works, along with those of Seneca, compensate modern readers for the loss of Hellenistic treatises, and offer material that can be compared with the more readily available writings of Plato and Aristotle.

At various points in my book, I juxtapose Stoic ethical thought to that of Aristotle, especially the *Nicomachean Ethics*, his best-known ethical work. The question how far Stoic thinkers had detailed knowledge of Aristotle's school-texts, which we describe as his 'works', is a rather complex one. Some evidence suggests that these school-texts were generally not available throughout much of the Hellenistic period.[14] However, it is likely that Stoic thinkers in this period had a broad knowledge of his main ideas, although, given the nature of our sources for Stoicism, specifying the extent of their knowledge is not easy. In any case, my concern here is not with identifying Stoic responses to Aristotle but with comparing and contrasting Stoic and Aristotelian ideas, especially (in Chapters 6–7), considered as ancient prototypes for modern virtue ethics. The texts of Plato were widely available throughout the Hellenistic and Imperial periods. However, my focus here, again, is on correlation of Stoic and Platonic ideas and not Stoic responses to Platonic (or Socratic) thought.[15]

Outline of Chapters

The book is subdivided into three parts, though these are closely interconnected. In the first part ('Living Naturally'), I discuss, in the first two chapters, what have been seen, since antiquity, as central Stoic ethical claims, regarding virtue, happiness, and 'indifferents', and in the third chapter, another major theme of Stoic ethics, the role of nature. In the second part ('Learning to Live Naturally'),

---

[13] On Cic. *Fin.* 3, see esp. Ch. 4; on Cic. *Off.*, see Ch. 2 (also 4.3); on Cic. *N. D.* 2, see 1.3, 3.4.

[14] See Barnes 1997: Nielsen 2012; also Sedley 2003: 12; and Gill 2006: 20–2.

[15] On Stoic responses to Socrates, see Long 1996: ch. 1; on Stoic responses to Plato, see A. G. Long 2013a.

I discuss Stoic thinking on ethical development, preceded by an Introduction to Part II, on distinctive features of the Stoic approach to this subject. I focus on the theory of development as 'appropriation' (*oikeiōsis*) in Chapter 4, and on emotional development and the 'therapy' of emotions in Chapter 5. The third part of the book ('Stoic Ethics and Modern Moral Theory') explores the significance of the Stoic ideas discussed in Parts I and II for contemporary moral philosophy, especially in virtue ethics. Chapter 6 is centred on Stoic ideas on the virtue-happiness relationship, viewed as a basis for engagement with modern thinking on this topic. Chapter 7 suggests ways in which Stoic thinking on human and cosmic nature can contribute to modern debate on the ethical significance of the idea of human nature and on environmental questions, notably the ethical response to climate breakdown. Chapter 8 discusses ways in which Stoic thinking can inform current thinking on ethical development and guidance, and takes note of one area where Stoicism has already made a major impact on modern thought, namely in 'life-guidance'.

In Chapters 1 and 2, I examine two central and distinctive Stoic ethical claims: that virtue constitutes the sole basis for happiness, and that other things normally regarded as good, such as health and prosperity, are 'matters of indifference', compared with virtue, though they have positive value and are rightly seen as 'preferable'. In considering these claims, I focus, initially, on the conception of happiness as the life according to nature. For at least one major Stoic thinker (Chrysippus), this signifies the life according to human and universal nature (the latter meaning nature as a whole or cosmic nature). Human nature is often conceived, in Stoic theory, as a combination of rationality and sociability. Universal nature is, typically, characterized in terms of structure, order, and wholeness (overall, consistency). It is also characterized, at the cosmic level, in terms of the exercise of providential care for everything in the universe; at the human level, this providential care is expressed in the in-built motives of care for oneself and for others of one's kind. Happiness, or the life according to nature is understood, I suggest, as a life that expresses most fully these features of human and universal nature. This account of happiness represents an interpretation, rather than a standard ancient formulation; however, it is based on well-defined and central Stoic ideas, going back at least to Chrysippus (1.3). This set of ideas underpins other important aspects of Stoic thinking, including their understanding of virtue, indifferents, and ethical development as 'appropriation'. This complex of themes forms the basis for the notion of 'Living Naturally' that I have taken as the title of this part of the book.

Virtue is conceived in Stoic ethics as a form of knowledge or expertise, by contrast with happiness, which is seen as a form of life. However, this expertise is often characterized in terms similar to those of happiness, namely as expressing human nature, understood as rational and sociable, or universal nature, associated with the themes of structure, order, and wholeness and of care for oneself and others. The structural similarity between the conceptions of happiness and virtue does much to explain the Stoic claims that virtue constitutes expertise in living a happy life and that virtue forms the sole basis for happiness (1.4).

In Chapter 2, I examine evidence both on the virtue-indifferents relationship and on practical deliberation (in Stoic terms, performing 'appropriate actions'). Although Stoic thinking on the value-status of indifferents has sometimes been regarded as problematic, in antiquity and modern scholarship, I suggest that it makes good sense if viewed in the light of this framework of thinking about virtue and happiness. Things such as health and prosperity are potentially positive factors in a human life and are naturally 'preferred' by human beings; but they do not make the difference between living a happy life or not, as virtue does, and are 'indifferent' in this sense. Virtue, on the other hand, understood as expertise in leading a happy life (a life according to nature) does make this difference. Virtue is conceived as expertise in selecting between indifferents in a way that reflects the recognition of the positive or negative value of indifferents but bases the selection on what makes for the happy life (2.2–3). I interpret Cicero's *On Duties*, the only surviving extended Stoic study of practical deliberation, as expressing this conception of the relationship between virtue, indifferents, appropriate acts, and happiness (2.3–4). Although the type of deliberation advocated there recognizes the positive value of preferable indifferents, the main criterion of properly conducted deliberation is what is right, that is, in line with the virtues, sometimes combined with ideas about what counts as natural, meaning, in this context, what is consistent with human nature at its best. All three books of *On Duties*, in different ways, offer guidance on developing skill in practical deliberation which reflects this understanding of the relationship between virtue, happiness, indifferents, and appropriate actions; in this way, this work offers a good illustration of Stoic thinking on these topics.

The set of ideas considered so far, especially the idea of happiness as the life according to nature, provides a new point of access to a question much debated in recent scholarship, the ethical significance of the idea of nature in Stoic philosophy. In Chapter 3, I review this debate, re-examine the main evidence, and offer a partly new account. Scholars have disagreed about whether Stoic ethics is grounded on the idea of universal nature presented in Stoic physics or is seen as independent but supported by ideas of nature, both human and universal. The three ethical summaries, our core primary evidence for this topic, present the Stoic framework in various ways: in purely ethical terms (those of value theory) or with reference to human nature, universal nature, or a combination of these ideas (3.3). Some ancient evidence seems to state that ethical principles are grounded on universal nature or god as presented in physics, specifically, theology. However, I suggest that this evidence, taken with that for Stoic theology generally, points to a reciprocal relationship between these branches of knowledge. Theology provides an authoritative account of the types of nature relevant for ethics, while ethical theory is authoritative in its analysis of the moral ideas deployed both in ethics and theology. This view matches the collaborative or reciprocal (rather than hierarchical) relationship between the branches of Stoic knowledge suggested by other evidence (3.4). Finally, I examine the Stoic idea of 'harmonizing' yourself to universal nature or god, especially in Stoic writings on practical ethics. Although, on the face of it, this theme presupposes that ethical principles are grounded on universal nature, I suggest that the evidence, more closely examined, points to a more complex, and mutually supporting, relationship between ethical principles and universal nature or god (3.5). Overall, this discussion illustrates that the idea of universal nature, alongside that of human nature, plays a major role in Stoic ethics, but casts doubt on the supposition that this relationship is best characterized in terms of 'grounding'.

In the second part of the book ('Learning to Live Naturally'), the focus moves to ethical development. A separate introduction to this part explores in two ways the rather paradoxical idea of *learning* to live naturally. First, I examine the links between the main distinctive features of Stoic thinking on ethical development (appropriation and the therapy of emotions) and the Stoic ideal of living naturally (according to nature). Second, I explore other ways in which, in the Stoic view, ethical development is conceived as being natural. These include the capacity of all human beings to develop ethically, to do so at any stage in their lives, and to do so in any socio-political or intellectual context. These features are defined, in part, by contrast with an alternative ancient pattern found in Plato and Aristotle, in which ethical development depends on the combination of a special kind of inborn nature, social habituation, and intellectual education. For partly related reasons, the Stoic approach focuses on ethical development within adult life, rather than on childhood and youth viewed as a preparation for adulthood; it also stresses the idea of adult life as ongoing (uncompleted) progress towards virtue and happiness. These general characteristics of Stoic thinking on development are illustrated in the two subsequent chapters by well-known Stoic innovations: their theories of ethical development as 'appropriation' (*oikeiōsis*) and of emotional development, sometimes presented as the 'therapy' of emotions.

The theory of appropriation (Chapter 4) is closely interconnected with other central aspects of their ethical framework, their ideas about virtue and happiness and about human and universal nature. While taking account of the full range of evidence, I focus on that of Cicero, in On Ends 3 (16–22, 62–8), taken in conjunction with relevant parts of On Duties (especially 1.11–15, 50–9). The process of appropriation is sometimes subdivided into two strands, leading towards ethical understanding and properly conducted relationships, respectively (for instance, in Cicero, On Ends 3).These two strands, taken together, reflect what the Stoics see as salient characteristics of human and universal nature: rationality and sociability, on the one hand (marks of human nature); and care for oneself and others of one's kind, on the other hand (features linked with universal nature).

The first strand of appropriation also culminates in the formation of internal order and wholeness, another idea linked with universal nature. The growth of ethical understanding is analysed in ways that reflect and support Stoic thinking on the relationship between virtue, indifferents, and happiness. This strand of development consists in acquiring expertise in selecting between indifferents in a way that brings about happiness understood as the life according to nature (*On Ends* 3.20–1; see 4.4). In interpreting the theory of appropriation, I stress the interplay and interconnections between these two strands, a feature which is particularly evident in Cicero's *On Duties* (4.3, 4.5). In the second (sociable) strand, I underline that, in most surviving evidence, the development of engagement in specific and localized relationships with individuals and one's own community is presented as compatible with recognizing the fundamental community of humankind (4.6).

The Stoic theory of emotions (Chapter 5) has often generated criticism, though it is viewed more positively in most recent scholarship. It is important to interpret it as, crucially, a theory of emotional development, if we are to understand the rationale for the distinction between bad emotions (or 'passions') and 'good emotions'. Also, this dimension of Stoic thinking is closely interconnected with the theory of appropriation. Although Stoic thinking on emotional development (or the therapy of bad emotions) forms a distinct topic in Stoic ethical writings, emotional development is seen as dependent on the two strands that make up appropriation. The aim of the Stoic therapy of emotions is sometimes seen by scholars as the production of a, fundamentally egocentric, self-sufficiency that depends on detachment from other people. I argue that this view runs counter to most Stoic evidence on this subject, which presents emotional development as a corollary of ethical progress, including development of fully engaged social relationships. The one passage (in Epictetus) which seems, at first glance, to support the view I am challenging forms part of a discussion whose overall objective is in line with standard Stoic thinking on ethical and emotional development. The passage advocates that committed interpersonal engagement should be combined with recognition of the fact that relationships can be ruptured by death, a position which is quite different from advocating detachment from other people.[16]

On the basis of this reading of central Stoic ideas, I turn in the third part of the book ('Stoic Ethics and Modern Moral Theory') to the question what Stoic ethics, distinctively, can contribute to contemporary moral philosophy. The scope for engagement between Stoicism and current approaches is greatest in modern virtue ethics, especially in theories which combine virtue ethics with eudaimonism and ethical naturalism. Aristotle has often been taken as the main ancient prototype for modern virtue ethics. However, I argue (Chapter 6) that Stoicism offers an

---

[16] The controversial passage is Epictetus, *Discourses* (*Diss.*) 3.24.84–8, summarized (in more problematic form) as *Handbook* 3; see 5.3.

ethical theory that is both more coherent, and in some ways more cogent, than Aristotle's, while sharing his overall framework of thinking, which is also adopted by much modern virtue ethics. Stoic ethics can be seen as a coherent combination of an innovative theory of value with a credible conception of nature, both human and universal, and of ethical development or education. The Stoic theory of value is ethically rigorous in presenting virtue as the sole basis for happiness, as contrasted with the Aristotelian position, that happiness is based on a combination of virtue and other kinds of good things. However, this ethical rigour is explained, and justified, in several ways. It is justified, in terms of value theory, by the distinction between the special value (goodness) of virtue and of other things normally regarded as good, which the Stoics call 'indifferents'. This is linked, in turn, with a conception of virtue as expertise in selecting between indifferents and in leading a happy life. The Stoic position is further supported by its thinking on nature (human and universal) and ethical development.

The Stoic theory has several advantages, compared with Aristotle, as a basis for engagement with modern virtue ethics. The ethical rigour of the Stoic position (that virtue is the sole basis for happiness) has advantages in meeting modern expectations in modern moral theory, both within and outside virtue ethics. This point also applies to the Stoic conception of 'indifferents', as contrasted with Aristotelian thinking about bodily and external goods. Also, Stoicism offers a more coherent and fully worked-out framework which can inform modern virtue ethical thinking on several major topics. For instance, the Stoic account of the virtue-happiness relationship is more internally consistent than Aristotle's. The Stoic account of the relationship between virtue, happiness and preferred indifferents provides a more coherent framework of thinking about value than Aristotle's discussion of the contribution of goods other than virtue to happiness (*Nicomachean Ethics* 1.8-10). Stoic theory also avoids the internal tensions that arise in Aristotle's account of the respective contributions of practical and theoretical wisdom to happiness (*NE* 10.7-8, see 6.2). It also provides a stronger and more coherent explanatory framework for the combination of two ideas which figure in both Aristotelian and Stoic theory and which some modern theories are also disposed to adopt. These are (1) that virtue is intrinsically valuable and desirable and (2) that happiness is the overall goal of a human life. The Stoic version of these ideas makes good sense in the light of the links between virtue, happiness, and human and universal nature discussed in Chapter 1 (6.3). Also, although both Aristotle and the Stoics recognize fully the social, and other-benefiting, dimensions of both virtue and happiness, the Stoics do so in a more straightforward and thoroughgoing way, that makes for closer engagement with modern ethical concerns (6.4).

In these respects, Stoic theory can inform any modern version of virtue ethics and eudaimonism. However, if these approaches are also combined with ethical naturalism, as they are in some modern theories, Stoic ethics is well placed to make a further contribution, brought out in Chapter 7. For instance, Anscombe, Foot, and Hursthouse have argued that we should understand ethics as, distinctively, *human* ethics. Aristotle and the Stoics both adopt versions of a similar view, notably in conceiving happiness as the realization of human nature at its best. However, the Stoic version, because it is more coherent and more fully worked out, enables closer engagement between Stoic and modern thinking on this subject (7.1–2). Also, the Stoics extend the ethical framework in giving a central role to universal nature and the place of human beings in the universe. This feature enables Stoic thinking to contribute positively to a new and pressing modern ethical concern, namely responding seriously and effectively to the looming threat of climate breakdown and environmental collapse. For instance, the Stoic view of the natural universe as inherently valuable, or, more strongly, good, as ordered and exercising providential care, offers the basis of what is known in modern environmental theory as an 'ecocentric' view. The Stoic linkage between virtue, happiness, and universal nature provides a framework that facilitates the recognition of action directed at repairing the natural order as an integral part of virtuous activity (7.3–4).

Finally (Chapter 8), I consider in two ways the contribution of Stoic thinking on ethical development and guidance to contemporary thought. First, I explore ways in which Stoic ideas on these topics can inform modern virtue ethical thinking, which has so far been mainly influenced by Aristotle, as in other respects (8.1). Second (8.2), I consider one area of modern thought where Stoic ideas on development and guidance have already had a major impact, that is, in offering 'life-guidance' through books and on-line courses, referring especially to a project ('Modern Stoicism') in which I have been closely involved. I suggest that the positive public response to Stoic ethical ideas, as presented in these courses, supports the general thesis of the third part of this book. It suggests that the Stoic ethical framework not only is highly cogent and coherent at the theoretical level but also has powerful resonance for modern thought.

PART I
LIVING NATURALLY

1

Virtue and Happiness

1.1 Preliminaries

The first three chapters of this book explore the core concepts and claims of Stoic ethics. The main concepts discussed are virtue, happiness, 'indifferents', and nature. The central claims are that virtue forms the sole basis needed for happiness; that things other than virtue generally considered good are only 'preferable indifferents'; that happiness constitutes 'the life according to nature'; and that nature, in various senses, supports the ethical framework. The present chapter focuses on Stoic thinking on virtue and happiness and aims to explain their claim that virtue is the sole basis for happiness (this explanation continues in Chapter 2). The explanation centres on the idea that happiness consists in the life according to nature. This idea is explicated in terms of a combination of human and universal nature; and these features are further analysed in terms of a combination of rationality and sociability, structure, order, wholeness, and providential care. These are characteristics both of happiness and virtue; and these shared characteristics explain, in part at least, why virtue is presented as the sole basis for happiness in Stoic ethics.

The chapter takes this form. First (1.2), I place Stoic ideas on the relationship between virtue and happiness within ancient Greek philosophical thinking on this subject. Second (1.3), I discuss Stoic thinking on happiness, conceived as the life according to nature. Third (1.4), I consider Stoic ideas on virtue, focusing on the idea that virtue is expertise in leading a happy (natural) life.

1.2 Stoic Ideas in Their Greek Philosophical Context

I begin by locating Stoic ideas about the virtue-happiness relationship in the context of Greek philosophical debate on this topic. The salient point is that Stoic thinking forms part of a broader philosophical movement, running from Socrates to Aristotle and beyond, designed to challenge and revise conventional Greek thinking about the virtue-happiness relationship. The revision takes the form of maintaining that virtue is fundamental for happiness: it is either (on the stronger view) the sole basis for happiness or (on the weaker view) the main factor in happiness.[1]

---

[1] For discussions covering parts of this survey in much greater depth, see Annas 1993: chs. 1–2, 18–20; Irwin 2007: chs. 2, 5, 8–9, 13; Russell 2012: parts 2 and 3.

Learning to Live Naturally: Stoic Ethics and its Modern Significance. Christopher Gill, Oxford University Press. © Christopher Gill 2022. DOI: 10.1093/oso/9780198866169.003.0002

How do these philosophical claims relate to conventional Greek thinking, as far as this can be established? From at least Plato's *Symposium* onwards, ancient philosophers present as widely accepted the idea that all human beings, as their overall goal in life, want to be happy. This is combined with the recognition that different people have different views about what constitutes happiness. In *Nicomachean Ethics* 1.4, Aristotle summarizes popular beliefs as being that happiness consists in pleasure, wealth, or honour. We also find the idea that different conceptions of happiness shape people's dominant life-projects or objectives. Aristotle, for instance, presents certain ideas of happiness (as pleasure, honour, or theoretical activity) as the basis for three kinds of life (ordinary, political, and philosophical). Similarly, Plato's *Symposium* depicts different forms of life as pathways to different conceptions of happiness or the good, analysed in terms of types of desire (*erōs*).[2] What about virtue? Where does this fit in conventional Greek thought? Aristotle, in a summary of widely held ideas of happiness in his society (in the *Rhetoric*), presents virtue as one, but only one, possible component, alongside a wide range of other things considered as good:

> Let happiness then be said to be doing well together with virtue, or self-sufficiency of life, or the most pleasant life together with security, or affluence in possessions and slaves, together with the power to protect and make use of them...If happiness is something like this, then its parts must necessarily be good birth, having many friends, having good friends, having good children, having many children, a good old age, further, the bodily virtues, such as health, beauty, strength, size, competitive power, and reputation, honour, good luck and virtue.[3]

It is noteworthy that, in this summary, the various factors are presented as, in themselves, 'parts' of happiness. In other words, happiness is presented in what we might call 'objective' terms, as constituted by these factors, rather than as a subjective response to such factors. This matches the etymology of *eudaimonia*, which suggests having a good *daimōn*, or guardian-spirit, and thus gaining specific advantages in one's life.[4] In modern English, where happiness typically conveys a mood-state ('I feel happy'), we might more readily see happiness as a subjective response to these factors. However, the list of items included in *eudaimonia* often includes pleasure, or 'the most pleasant life', so the subjective dimension of enjoyment figures as part of this complex of ideas.

---

[2] Pl. *Smp.* 204e–205a, 206a–b, 208e–209e; Arist. *NE* 1.4–5. On Pl. *Smp.*, see also Sheffield 2012: 122–7.
[3] Arist. *Rh.* 1.5, 1360b14–23, trans. Annas 1993: 364. For Aristotle's summary of conventional ideas on virtue, see *Rh.* 1.9.
[4] This 'objective' view is common in conventional Greek thought, according to Dover 1974: 174.

How does the idea that virtue is central for happiness emerge in Greek thought? It seems to arise as the outcome of a sustained movement by a series of Greek philosophers, designed to challenge and revise conventional Greek thinking. Some of these thinkers, notably Socrates, Plato, and the Stoics, maintain that virtue is the sole basis for happiness, while others (Aristotle and his followers) argue that virtue is the most important element, even though other factors make a significant contribution. To judge from Plato's early dialogues, standardly used as the main source for Socratic thought, Socrates does not, necessarily, frame his challenge to conventional thought in terms of happiness (*eudaimonia*). But he, certainly, claims that virtue, typically conceived as a form of knowledge or expertise, is the only essential or fundamental source of a good life.[5] He also combines this claim with revisionist accounts of what should count as good. We find a number of arguments to the effect that the only thing that is good is virtue or wisdom, and that other so-called 'goods', that is, bodily or external advantages, do not merit this status. A version of this argument in Plato's *Euthydemus* is widely taken to have helped to shape the Stoic thesis that such advantages do not count as goods but only 'preferred indifferents'.[6] Socrates also repeatedly claims that people are only harmed (that is, suffer bad things) as the result of their own wrongdoing or vice, and are not harmed by loss of external advantages.[7] Socrates' most explicit formulation of this line of thought in terms of happiness comes in Plato's *Gorgias*, at a point in the dialogue where Socrates is confronting the 'immoralist' Callicles, who maintains that a happy life is one of maximal self-indulgence or vice. Socrates argues, by contrast, that happiness derives from the virtue of moderation or self-control, understood as psychological order, thus prefiguring a theme in Plato's *Republic*.[8]

Plato's *Republic*, generally taken as reflecting Plato's mature thought, constitutes a sustained argument that virtue (more precisely, justice, though broadly conceived)[9] constitutes the sole basis for happiness. Plato's Socrates is challenged, early in Book 2, to show that justice in itself benefits the just person, regardless of any external rewards she receives;[10] and the whole argument represents a defence of this claim. The argument is a complex one, combining psychological and political strands, and incorporating an elaborate two-stage educational

---

[5] See Pl. *Ap.* 30a–b, 48a–b; for virtue as knowledge (and unified), see Pl. *Meno* 88c–d, *Euthd.* 281a–e; *Prt.* 349a–361c.

[6] Pl. *Euthd.* 281d–e; also Ch. 2, text to nn. 40–1.

[7] Pl. *Ap.* 30c–d, 41d; *Grg.* 508c–e. See also Russell 2012: 141–4, 148–51.

[8] Pl. *Grg.* 492c, 507c, 508b. (In 508a, Socrates anticipates Stoicism in linking psychic and cosmic order.) See also Long 2002: 70–4. On Socrates as a pioneer in maintaining the idea of virtue as sufficient for happiness, see Russell 2012: 135–55, including arguments (148–51) against the competing view of Vlastos that Socrates' position prefigures Aristotle's.

[9] Although centred initially on justice, the argument progressively becomes one about virtue as a whole, see *Rep.* 427e–435a, 441d–443e; also Kosman 2007.

[10] Pl. *Rep.* 360e–362c, 367b–e.

programme, which amounts to an account of ethical development.[11] In this way, justice is analysed at two levels or phases. At the first stage or level, justice is defined as a form of psychological harmony, in which the two lower parts of the psyche (appetite and spirit) are dominated by the rational part. This harmony is presented as one that can be established by a properly conducted social pro- gramme of education, though one falling short of full-scale intellectual enquiry and knowledge.[12] The second stage of education is described as providing this kind of knowledge, culminating in dialectically based understanding of the good.[13] It is implied, at least, that this stage produces justice as psychic harmony in a yet deeper and more firmly grounded form.[14] At both levels, Plato's Socrates claims that the form of psychological harmony (or inner justice) created benefits the person concerned and constitutes happiness.[15] In this way, Socrates provides the defence required that justice, in itself (in the psyche), represents the best possible and most happy state.[16] Although the argument focuses on the advantages of psychological harmony, Socrates also maintains that inner justice brings with it the best possible form of pleasure[17] and other benefits.[18] So the argument, though centred on the benefits of inner justice, also makes reference to factors, notably pleasure, which are conventionally seen as parts of happiness,[19] though these parts are reconceived in terms of the main argument.

Aristotle's position on the virtue-happiness relationship is, significantly, differ- ent from that of Socrates, Plato, and the Stoics. However, Aristotle is crucial for this question. This is partly because he was the first thinker to designate ethics as a distinct area of enquiry. In addition, his analysis of the core ethical concepts (virtue and happiness) influenced the whole framework of thinking in the Hellenistic and post-Hellenistic eras, even if thinkers in this period did not necessarily adopt Aristotle's own ethical positions. Even though Aristotle's lectures to his students on ethics (that is, what we call the *Eudemian* and *Nicomachean Ethics*) seem not to have been widely available during the Hellenistic period, his ideas were propagated by his followers, starting with his successor Theophrastus. Aristotle's ideas were also sometimes combined with

---

[11] On the form of the argument, see Annas 1981: 59–71; on the educational programme and ethical development, see Gill 1996: 260–307.

[12] Pl. *Rep.* 441c–443e, based on a combination of cultural and athletic education (441e; see also 401d–402a).

[13] Pl. *Rep.* 518b–519c, 531c–534c.

[14] This seems to be implied in Pl. *Rep.* 485d–e, 486a–b, 586e–587a; see Gill 1996: 294–7, 1998b: 210–14.

[15] Pl. *Rep.* 444c–445b, 588e–592c; the term 'happiness' (*eudaimonia*) does not figure in these passages, but appears in related passages, 580b, 621d.

[16] Pl. *Rep.* 444e–445b, 588a–b; and 580b–c. See also Annas 1981: 153–69, 305–20.

[17] Pl. *Rep.* 580d–588a.

[18] Pl. *Rep.* 612d–613e (rewards for justice given by other people or gods); 614a, 618b–619a, 621c–d (rewards given after death).

[19] See text to n. 3.

those of Plato (or his successors) by later thinkers including Polemo, one of the teachers of Zeno, founder of Stoicism.[20]

Aristotle formalizes the widespread idea, in conventional and preceding philosophical thought, that happiness (*eudaimonia*) is the overall or ultimate goal (*telos*) of purposeful human action. He specifies certain criteria for a credible account of happiness, namely, being complete and self-sufficient, as well as constituting an end in itself.[21] He recognizes the existence of divergent views about what constitutes happiness; but he offers his own account of happiness, which is presented as universally valid and incorporating other views (*NE* 1.5–8). In formulating his account of happiness, Aristotle presents it as an analysis of what is distinctive of human beings, by contrast with other animals (the human function or work, *ergon*, specified as rationality). Happiness is defined as the best expression of what is distinctively human, namely 'an activity of the psyche according to virtue, or, if there is more than one virtue, the best and most complete (or perfect, *teleiotatē*) virtue'.[22] Subsequently, Aristotle analyses the concept of virtue (*aretē*), using a part-based model of the psyche apparently based on Plato's. He subdivides virtues between intellectual (purely rational) ones and ethical ones, that is, virtues based on *ēthos*, 'character', which is non-rational but shaped by reason.[23] In the practical sphere, ethical virtues function in conjunction with practical wisdom (which is one of the intellectual virtues).[24] Aristotle also identifies a separate, purely theoretical or 'contemplative', type of wisdom.[25] Virtues are described as stable states or 'dispositions' (*hexeis*). Ethical virtues are defined as dispositions to make choices in a certain (correct) way; more precisely, an ethical virtue is 'a disposition concerned with choice, lying in a mean relative to us, this being determined by reason and in the way a person of practical wisdom would determine it'.[26] Virtuous actions are also said to be chosen 'for their own sake' or 'for the sake of the fine' (*to kalon*), these being presented as the same.[27] Aristotle recognizes a wide range of ethical and intellectual virtues; they are not systematized under the heading of the four cardinal virtues (wisdom, courage, moderation, and justice). However, Aristotle sometimes presents the ethical virtues as unified or interdependent, because they all involve the exercise of practical wisdom (*phronēsis*).[28]

---

[20] See Introd., text to n. 14: a third ethical work, *Magna Moralia*, is generally seen as written by a later follower of Aristotle. On Polemo as a teacher of Zeno, see Sedley 2003: 10; Gill 2006: 17–18.

[21] Arist. *NE* 1.1, 1.7. On these criteria, see Annas 1993: 34–42; Russell 2012: 73–9.

[22] Arist. *NE* 1.7, esp. 1097b22–1098a18 (a16–18 quoted).

[23] Arist. *NE* 1.13, *EE* 2.1. On the linkage with Platonic psychology, see Gill 1996: 245–50.

[24] Arist. *NE* 6.12, esp. 1144a6–1144b1; also 3.14, 1119b15–18 and 6.2, 1139a22–6.

[25] Arist. *NE* 6.7, 6.12.   [26] Arist. *NE* 2.6, 1106b36–1107a2.

[27] *NE* 2.4, 1105a32, 3.7, 1115b11–13.

[28] *NE* 6.13, 1144b33–1145a2; see also Annas 1993: 76–8; Russell 2009: 335–8. On Aristotle's theory of virtue overall, see Annas 1993: 48–61, 66–8, 73–7; Russell 2009: 4–34 (esp. on *phronēsis*).

How, more exactly, does Aristotle understand the relationship between happiness and virtue; does he also believe that virtue forms the sole basis for happiness? In the first instance (*NE* 1.7), as just noted, Aristotle defines happiness purely by reference to virtue.[29] However, he subsequently qualifies his definition, maintaining that other kinds of factors, such as bodily health, possessions and the welfare of one's family, are 'goods' and that they make a substantive contribution to happiness, even if virtue remains the key factor.[30] Aristotle's discussion in *NE* 1.8–10 is nuanced and dialectical; and he acknowledges the appeal of the idea that virtue can enable someone to surmount any situation, however appalling, although his conclusion does not reflect that recognition.[31] At different times he refers both to the idea that bodily goods are valuable only as far as they enable the exercise of virtue and the idea that they contribute to happiness in their own right.[32] However, the second idea plays a decisive role in his argument. This point seems to underlie the significance he attaches to the case of Priam, who, in the course of his life, lost almost all his great family, wealth, and political power. Aristotle suggests that someone who has experienced losses on this scale cannot be considered 'happy' (*eudaimōn*), even if he retains his virtue.[33] In reaching this conclusion, he seems to see the losses as ones that are bad in themselves (and which have an impact on Priam's happiness) and not only as ones which disable him from performing virtuous actions. Hence, finally, Aristotle reaches the conclusion that happiness requires not just virtue but also 'an adequate supply of external goods' as well as 'a complete life' (*NE* 1.10, 1101a14–16). To this extent, Aristotle, while stressing (like Socrates and Plato) the central importance of virtue for happiness, retains the conventional Greek view that other advantages count as 'parts' of happiness.[34]

Subsequent Peripatetic (Aristotelian) thinkers adopt the final position reached in *NE* 1.10. From Theophrastus onwards, they maintain that, although virtue is the most important factor in determining happiness, other factors, treated as types of 'good', make an independent contribution to our happiness.[35] A version of this position is adopted by Antiochus, an independent-minded Academic (Platonic) thinker, whose views are pitted against those of the Stoics by Cicero in *On Ends*, Books 4–5. Antiochus maintains that virtue is sufficient to make someone happy

---

[29] See text to n. 22.

[30] For the idea of three kinds of goods (psychological, bodily, and external), see *NE* 1.8, 1098b12–16.

[31] See *NE* 1100b12–22, 1100b30–1101a6.

[32] See *NE* 1.8, 1099a31–1099b8. 1.10. See Annas 1993: 378–84; Russell 2012: 108–17.

[33] On Priam, see *NE* 1.9, 1100a5–10, 1.10, 1100b32–1101a8. The second passage is sometimes seen as suggesting that the virtuous person who experiences great disasters will remain 'happy' (*eudaimōn*) but ceases to be 'blessed' (*makarios*), i.e. marking two grades of happiness; but this does not seem to be the point Aristotle is making; see Russell 2012: 127–30. See also *NE* 1.5, 1095b31–1096a2, 7.13, 1153b17–21, where Aristotle rejects as paradoxical the claim that a virtuous person who experiences great sufferings is still happy (*eudaimōn*).

[34] See text to n. 3–4.

[35] See Sharples 2010: ch. 18; Russell 2012: 117–30; Inwood 2014: chs. 1–3.

(*beatus*), but that the most happy, or perfectly happy, life is one which also contains bodily and external goods.[36]

How does the Stoic position relate to this philosophical background? The Stoics maintain in a strong, explicit, and elaborated form the thesis that happiness is based solely on virtue and does not depend on other things widely regarded as goods. In Hellenistic and post-Hellenistic debate, their position is regarded as the classic statement of this position, and is, correspondingly, subjected to criticism from Academic sceptics such as Carneades and followers of the Aristotelian approach, such as Antiochus.[37]

I consider the Stoic position, first in relation to the other Greek thinkers whose views have just been outlined, and then in more analytic terms. Since we have lost the works of the Hellenistic Stoics and only know their ideas indirectly, it is difficult to say for certain how far the Stoics were consciously adopting, or reacting against, earlier ideas, though we have some evidence bearing on this question. It is particularly difficult to gauge the Stoic response to Aristotle, given the uncertainty about how far his school-texts were available in the Hellenistic era (text to n. 20), though the writings presenting the ideas of Socrates and Plato were widely accessible. In any case, my main concern here is to compare and contrast the Stoic position with earlier Greek philosophical ideas, with a view to bringing out its distinctive features, rather than to try to reconstruct the history of Stoic responses to other thinkers.

Obviously, the Stoic position is closer to that of Socrates and Plato's *Republic* than to Aristotle's final statement in *NE* 1.10. Indeed, the Stoic view can be understood as a more fully worked out version of Socrates' approach; and in general Socrates seems to have served as an influential prototype for the Stoics.[38] The Stoics adopt the Socratic idea that virtue is a mode of knowledge or expertise, that it is one or unified,[39] and that it determines happiness or its opposite, as maintained by Socrates in Plato's *Gorgias*, a text cited repeatedly by Epictetus, for instance.[40] The Stoic presentation of virtue (or wisdom) alone as good, by contrast with bodily and external advantages, is widely seen as based on Socrates' argument to this effect in Plato's *Euthydemus*.[41] However, the Stoic formulation of these ideas is much more elaborated and theorized than the Socratic one; and their elaborations can be defined partly by reference to Platonic and Aristotelian thinking on this topic.

The Stoic response to Plato's *Republic* seems to have been quite complex. Our evidence suggests that they reacted strongly against several important features of

---

[36] See Cic. *Fin.* 5.77–86, *Tusc.* 5.21–3; also Gill 2016a: 240–7. Antiochus may have interpreted Aristotle as distinguishing two grades of happiness (see n. 33); see Annas 1993: 419–23.
[37] See LS 58, 60, 63–4; also Annas 1993: 388–411; Irwin 2007: 321–41; Russell 2012: 178–96.
[38] See Long 1996: 1–34.   [39] See LS 61, and text to nn. 132–4.
[40] See Long 2002: 68–74; Russell 2012: 141–4, 148–51.
[41] See text to n. 6; also Ch. 2, text to nn. 40–1.

Plato's argument there. These include the theory of Forms; the idea that the psyche is subdivided into three separate parts or sources of motivation; and the conception of the ideal state as subdivided into three distinct classes.[42] However, Plato's *Republic* remains a significant part of the background for Stoic ethical thinking. The Stoics seem to have given some thought to the question how far how far Plato's work prefigured the 'hard' Stoic thesis, that virtue alone is good and is the sole basis for happiness. Apparently, Chrysippus, the major Stoic theorist, criticized Plato's formulations on this point, as not going far enough in this direction, referring especially to Book 1 of the *Republic*. However, a later Stoic head, Antipater, took a more positive view, claiming that, according to Plato, only the 'fine' (*kalon*), that is, what is in line with virtue, is good, though not necessarily referring to the *Republic*.[43]

On other relevant points, though rejecting the Platonic division between rational and non-rational parts of the psyche, they seem to have adopted aspects of Plato's analysis that prefigure their own unified or holistic conception of human psychology.[44] While they do not accept Plato's two-stage or two-level conception of virtue (first as psychological harmony and then as knowledge), they maintain that virtue constitutes knowledge or expertise and that it carries with it psychological harmony or unity. They also adopt Plato's framework of the four cardinal virtues (wisdom, courage, moderation, and justice), though in a reconceived and more closely integrated form.[45] Although they do not take over the Platonic two-stage programme of education and ethical development, they share the idea that reaching virtue in the full sense is a difficult, and probably (at best) a life-long process, and also a rare achievement.[46] Further, while not following Plato in claiming that the achievement of virtue brings with it the best kind of pleasure, they maintain that it confers emotional benefits, namely freedom from damaging emotions or 'passions' and the development of 'good emotions'.[47]

In the case of Aristotle, it is more difficult to reconstruct Stoic responses to his thought, though we can certainly use Aristotle to define the distinctively Stoic approach. Like most other Hellenistic thinkers, the Stoics adopt Aristotle's view that human life is organized around an overarching 'goal' (*telos*), which can be identified with happiness (*eudaimonia*). Also, they sometimes adopt the

[42] On Forms see LS 30; on political theory, see Schofield 1991: 22–6, 2000: 443–6; on psychology, see text to nn. 60–2.

[43] See Plu. *Sto. Rep.* 1040 A, D; Clement, *Stromateis* 5.14 (*SVF* vol. 3, Antipater: 56); also A. G. Long (2013b): 126–7. Antipater's move, assimilating Plato's view to the Stoic position, may form part of polemical debate in this period between Stoics and Academics.

[44] See Gill 1998a: 130–7, 2006: 304–22.

[45] On Plato's two-level conception of virtue, see text to nn. 11–14; on Stoic thinking on virtue, see 1.4. On the four cardinal virtues, see Pl. *Rep.* 428b–435a, 441c–444a; for analogous Stoic ideas, see LS 61 C–D and text to nn. 141–6.

[46] On the Platonic educational programme (for the philosopher-ruler), see *Rep.* 534d–541b; on relevant features of Stoic thinking on ethical development, see Introd. to Part II, text to nn. 53–5.

[47] On Plato, see n. 17; on Stoic thinking on this topic, see LS 60 J–L, esp. K(1), 65 F; more broadly 5.1.

Aristotelian move of referring to distinctively human nature, by contrast with that of other animals, to define what constitutes happiness.[48] More precisely, they combine this idea with a version of the standpoint taken up in Plato's *Timaeus*, of viewing human beings in the broader framework of the universe as a whole.[49] As regards virtue, they adopt a much more unified or holistic conception than Aristotle does; the Stoic conception incorporates elements that in Aristotle are subdivided between character and intellectual virtue and between practical and contemplative wisdom.[50] Like Aristotle, the Stoics think that the virtuous person is marked by a high degree of consistency between his ethical judgements and his emotions and desires.[51] On the virtue-happiness relationship, they emphatically reject Aristotle's final position, in *NE* 1.10, that happiness depends on a combination of virtue and (what Aristotle calls) bodily and external goods. However, their position can be seen as similar to the view on the virtue-happiness relationship stated by Aristotle *NE* 1.7, *before* the qualifications and reservations added in 1.8–10.[52] As with Plato's *Republic*, the Stoics share Aristotle's claim that virtue (and virtue-based happiness) carries with it positive affective states, but they conceive this idea in terms of 'good emotions', rather than pleasure.[53]

The distinctive features of the Stoic position on this topic can also be characterized in more analytic terms. Describing the Stoic approach in this way brings out the philosophical interest of their ideas, considered both in relation to other ancient approaches and modern ethical theory. Three lines of argument are most relevant for this topic: what one might call an 'anthropological' or, more broadly, naturalistic approach, ideas related to value, and psychological ideas. These lines of argument overlap and are mutually reinforcing.

A standard Stoic definition of happiness (the goal) is 'the life according to nature' or 'the natural life'. Although this formulation may have been understood differently by different thinkers, Chrysippus, the most important Stoic theorist, seems to have conceived this in terms of a combination of human and universal (or cosmic) nature (D.L. 7.89 = LS 63 C(5)). As explained shortly, the distinctive mark of human nature, in Stoic thought, is the pairing of rationality and

---

[48] Arist. *NE* 1.1–2, 1.7. On the pervasive presence of the Aristotelian framework in Hellenistic thought, see Annas 1993: ch. 1. On human nature (among other conceptions of nature) as an ethical ideal, see LS 63 C–E; also 3.3.

[49] On the Stoic combination of human and universal nature, see 1.3. On the influence of the *Timaeus* on Stoicism, see Betegh 2003; Gill 2006: 16–20, 283–4. Relevant Platonic themes include those of divine providence and cosmic order as a paradigm for human beings (Pl. *Ti*. 30a–c, 90a–d).

[50] See LS 61 and 1.4.

[51] See Aristotle's distinction between the moderate (*sōphrōn*) and self-restrained (*enkratēs*) person (*NE* 1.13, 1102b26–8, and 7.9, 1151b34–1152a6); on the psychological unity of the virtuous person in Stoicism, see Ch. 5, text to nn. 9–17.

[52] See text to n. 22 and nn. 30–4. Another Aristotelian qualification they do not add is the requirement for a complete life (Arist. *NE* 1.7, 1098a18–20); on the Stoic view that happiness is not increased by length of life, see Gill 2006: 88, referring to Cic. *Fin*. 3.46, 76.

[53] On Plato and Aristotle, see n. 17 and Arist. *NE* 1.8, 1099a7–31. For the Stoic view, see n. 47.

sociability. The relevant features of universal nature are (again) rationality, but manifested especially in structure, order, and wholeness, or, overall, consistency; and also in exercising providential care for all elements of nature. Human beings are seen in Stoic thought as, constitutionally, capable of expressing these features of universal nature; in the case of providential care, this takes the form of expressing the best possible form of care of oneself and others of one's kind. Virtue, in Stoic thought, is understood in similar terms; that is, as a combination of rationality and sociability, structure, order, and wholeness (overall, consistency), and as the best possible form of care for oneself and others of one's kind. More precisely, virtue (or the four cardinal virtues, conceived as a matched set) constitutes expertise in leading a happy life, that is, the life according to nature, characterized by these features. Ethical development, understood in Stoic terms as appropriation of one's nature and of others who are one's own, constitutes a progressive movement towards virtue and happiness in this sense. This set of ideas raise many conceptual and interpretative questions, considered in the course of this book. But one point that emerges clearly is that there is a structural similarity between virtue and happiness, as thus understood. This similarity goes a long way towards explaining and justifying the Stoic claim that virtue constitutes the sole basis for happiness. This similarity also explains why the Stoics see virtue, in part at least, as expertise in leading a happy life.[54]

Before turning to the second main line of Stoic thought on this topic, two distinctive features of Stoic thinking on this subject are worth underlining. One is that the analysis of virtue and happiness is formulated in terms of universal (or cosmic) nature as well as human. This aspect of Stoic thinking has generated much scholarly interest and competing interpretative views; it is discussed fully in Chapter 3. The second aspect has received much less attention, though it is important both in its own right and in relation to modern ethical theory. Greek philosophical theory on virtue and happiness, like conventional Greek thought in general, gives a substantial role to the social, other-benefiting dimension of human life.[55] However, in certain respects, Stoic thought accentuates this dimension and provides an especially strong theoretical basis for it. Human nature is sometimes defined not just in terms of rationality, as is common in Greek thought, but also the combination of rationality and sociability.[56] Reference to universal nature supports not just the idea of the naturalness of concern for oneself but also for others of one's kind. This set of ideas underlies the Stoic conception of ethical development as appropriation, which has clearly designated rational and sociable

[54] For the ideas in this paragraph, see 1.3–4.
[55] On this dimension in Greek philosophical ethics, see Annas 1993: chs. 10–12; in Greek culture more generally, Gill 1996, esp. chs. 2–3, 5.
[56] In Arist. *NE* 1.7, the distinctive human feature is presented as rationality (1098a3–17), though sociability is cited in connection with one of the requirements for happiness (self-sufficiency) (1097b8–11).

strands, and which presents as natural the disposition to care for others of one's kind as well as to care for oneself. Stoic thinking on practical deliberation, as presented in one major source (Cicero's *On Duties*), underlines the combination and integration of rational and social strands, and also that of care for others as well as oneself. This is a significant, and sometimes under-appreciated, dimension of Stoic thought, which plays an important role in their thinking on virtue and happiness and in other areas too.[57]

The second Stoic line of thought relevant for this question relates to the theory of value. The Stoics reserve the category of goodness for virtue and (virtue-based) happiness, and for things dependent on virtue, arguing that these things alone benefit unequivocally. They deny that other things commonly regarded as good, such as health, prosperity, and the welfare of our families and friends (bodily and external goods, according to Aristotle)[58] confer benefit in this way. What confers benefit is the expert use of such things by virtue; more precisely, use of such things in a way that enables us to lead a happy (natural) life, with the connotations of this idea outlined earlier. Hence, the Stoics categorize these other things as 'matters of indifference', which are neither good nor bad, and which do not determine whether we live a happy life in the way that virtue does. However, at least in mainstream Stoic thought, such things are recognized as having real or natural value and as providing grounds for action. Hence, they are characterized as 'preferable' things, or, in an alternative phraseology, 'things according to nature' or 'natural things'. The Stoic theory of value is, thus, quite complex and subtle (more so than is sometimes recognized). It provides further support for the Stoic claim that virtue constitutes the sole basis for happiness. It also provides a framework for the analysis of virtuous practical deliberation as expert selection between indifferents, with a view to living a happy life. This line of thought is discussed in Chapter 2.[59]

These two lines of thought, taken together, provide the main support for the Stoic thesis that virtue constitutes the sole basis for happiness. However, a third line of thought is relevant for understanding the Stoic conception of virtue and happiness and the relationship between them. The Stoics evolve a distinctive psychological framework which reflects features of earlier ancient thought but also incorporates certain new features. One aspect of this framework is a new analysis of action, framed in terms of impression, assent, and motive, rather than of belief (or reason) and desire, as in Platonic and Aristotelian accounts.[60] The Stoics, like Plato and Aristotle, regard human beings (at least human adults) as distinctively rational, by contrast with other animals. However, unlike Plato and Aristotle, the Stoics do not subdivide the psyche into rational and non-rational 'parts', sometimes seen as independent source of motivation. The Stoics see all

---

[57] See 1.3–4, 2.4–5, 4.2–3, 4.5, 5.2–3, 6.4.   [58] Arist. *NE* 1.8, 1098b12–16.
[59] See also LS 58, 60.   [60] See LS 53 Q–T; also Inwood 1985: ch. 3.

adult human functions as informed by rationality, even though such functions, typically, fall short of the perfect exercise of rationality, that is, virtue and happiness. Hence, emotions are classified in Stoic theory according to the quality of the rationality which informs them, either as misguided 'passions' or as well-judged 'good emotions'. The virtuous and happy person does not experience passions; and, because passions carry with them internal conflict and tension, this is another respect in which the virtuous person is internally consistent and unified. However, she does experience good emotions, which are based on a correct, and correctly applied, understanding of what counts as a happy (natural) life.[61] Happiness is not defined, primarily, in Stoicism, in terms of the emotional state, but in terms of the life according to nature. However, freedom from misguided passions and experience of good emotions count as secondary markers of the virtuous and happy person. To this degree, as in Plato and Aristotle, the Stoic theory refers to the affective state of the virtuous and happy person.[62] These three lines of thought in Stoicism support, in different ways, their thesis that virtue provides the sole basis for happiness. They also constitute cogent and original ethical ideas, to be examined and correlated with modern ideas later in this book.

1.3 Happiness as the Life According to Nature

> They [the Stoics] say that being happy (*eudaimonein*) is the goal (*telos*), for the sake of which everything is done and which is itself done for the sake of nothing else; and this consists in living according to virtue, living in agreement [or 'consistently'], and again (which is the same thing) living according to nature.[63]

A striking feature of our evidence for Stoic thought is that we are offered numerous formulations for key notions, notably for happiness or the goal of life. This variation, apparently, reflects the history of the Stoic school. Zeno, the founder, laid the foundation for the theory; but he seems to have done so in the form of compressed arguments and definitions inviting further analysis and debate.[64] Subsequent heads of the school at Athens, and other leading Stoics, added their own glosses, explanations, and variations. Chrysippus, the third head, played a particularly important role in elaborating the theory, and wrote many treatises which formed a crucial basis for subsequent study of Stoic ideas.[65] However, the process of debate and reformulation continued after his time, provoked and sharpened by criticism from outside the school. Even so, Stoics seem to have regarded themselves as presenting and

---

[61] See LS 65 A–J; Gill 2006: 244–66; Graver 2007; chs. 2–3, 6–8; also 5.1.   [62] See text to n. 53.
[63] Stob. 6e, 2.77.16–19, trans. IG: 133 (also LS 63 A(1)).   [64] See Schofield 1983.
[65] See Sedley 2003: 15–18.

developing a single body of theory, with certain central doctrines, one of which was the idea that virtue is the sole basis for happiness. The passage just cited encapsulates three formulations of the Stoic goal: life 'according to virtue', 'according to nature', and living 'consistently' (sometimes presented as shorthand for 'living consistently with nature').[66] Other versions, ascribed to later Hellenistic Stoics, focus on the idea of appropriate or consistent 'selection' between 'things according to nature' (or 'preferred indifferents').[67]

Of these various formulations, I focus in the first instance on the idea of living according to nature, while bearing in mind the equivalence with living according to virtue. What kind of nature is involved? The two relevant senses seem to be human nature and nature as a whole, that is, universal or cosmic nature. In the most informative source for this topic, we are told that Zeno simply spoke of 'agreement with nature', though apparently meaning human nature.[68] However his successors elaborated the point. It seems that Cleanthes, the second Stoic head, specified only universal nature, whereas Chrysippus, the third head, referred both to human nature and nature as a whole.[69] In what seems to be a quotation from Chrysippus, *On Ends* 1, we are told:

> Therefore, the goal becomes 'to live consistently with nature', i.e. according to one's own [i.e. human] nature and that of the universe, doing nothing which is forbidden by the common law, which is right reason, penetrating all things, being the same as Zeus, who is the leader of the administration of things. And this itself is the virtue of the happy person and a smooth flow of life, whenever all things are done according to the harmony of the *daimōn* in each of us with the will of the administrator of the universe.[70]

This passage raises many interpretative questions, taken up later in this book.[71] However, certain points emerge clearly and are confirmed by other sources. One is that living according to human nature and according to universal nature are taken to be identical or, at least, consistent with each other. Another is that consistency

---

[66] According to Stob. 6a, 2.75.11–76.3 (LS 63 B(1–2)), Zeno's original formula was just 'living consistently', meaning 'living according to one harmonious reason, since those who live in conflict are unhappy'; and it was his successors who expanded the formula to 'living in agreement with nature'. But D.L. 7.87 (LS 63 C(1)) attributes the second formula to Zeno. See Striker 1996: 222–4; Sellars 2021: 107–110.

[67] On *telos*-formulas, see Stob. 6a–e, D.L. 7.87–9, Cic. *Fin.* 3.21–2, 26; also 63 A–C; and criticisms in LS 64. On the later Hellenistic formulas, see LS 58 K, and Ch. 2, text to n. 60.

[68] See D.L. 7.87–9 (LS 63 C), esp. 7.87 (LS 63 C(1)). The comment is ascribed to his work, *On Human Nature*.

[69] D.L. 7.89 (LS 63 C(5)).

[70] D.L. 7.88, trans. IG: 114; for an alternative translation, see LS 63 C(3–4). For the latest text of D.L. see Dorandi 2013. 'Smooth flow of life' (*eurhoia tou biou*) is another formulation for happiness: see Stob. 6e, 2.77.22 (LS 63 A(2)).

[71] See Ch. 3, on nature in Stoic ethics, esp. 3.5 on possible interpretations of Chrysippus' definition.

with cosmic nature involves some kind of 'harmony' or agreement between an element in us (the *daimōn* or 'guardian-spirit', generally taken here to mean 'mind') and the central animating principle of the universe (or Zeus). Thirdly, life in accordance with both human and cosmic nature is identical with life according to virtue, and all these also constitute happiness.

In exploring the meaning of this definition, I start with the significance of human nature. Modern accounts of what Stoics see as distinctive of human nature often focus solely on rationality,[72] and there is much evidence to support this focus. However, we sometimes find an alternative formulation: human beings are distinctively rational and social (or sociable). This formula occurs three times in Stobaeus' summary of Stoic ethics.[73] In Marcus Aurelius' *Meditations*, the combination 'rational and social' occurs repeatedly.[74] Seneca also presents reason (*ratio*) and 'sociability' or 'fellowship' (*societas*) as distinctively human features.[75] In Stoic writings on ethical development understood as 'appropriation' (*oikeiōsis*),[76] which is presented as a natural process, there is a good deal of evidence linking rationality and sociability. For instance, the summary treatment in Cicero's *On Duties* 1.11–15 marks a close link between rationality, as a distinctive human quality, and sociability. The two longer accounts of appropriation in Cicero, *On Ends* 3.16–22 and 62–8 subdivide the rational and the social sides of ethical development. However, closer inspection shows that the social strand also highlights the special role of human rationality and the first strand also presupposes social engagement.[77] A similar coupling is suggested in Hierocles' account of appropriation, in which (despite its fragmentary state) we can see that the course of human development gives an explicit and significant role to both the rational and the social sides of human nature.[78]

Before looking more closely at the evidence, let me suggest two possible ways of interpreting this line of thought in Stoicism. One possible view would be that human beings are distinctively rational and social. In other words, what is unique about human beings is the combination of rationality and sociability, whereas other animals are in some sense sociable but not rational.[79] Also, it might be

---

[72] See e.g. Sen. *Ep.* 76.9–10 (LS 63 D); also Inwood 1985: ch. 2; Gill 1991: 184–93, 2006: 138–45.

[73] Stob. 5b1, 2.59.6: 'a naturally social (*politikon*) and rational animal'; 6, 2.75.7–8 ('a rational, mortal, animal, social (*politikon*) by nature'); 11m, 2.109.16–18: '[the wise person] will marry and have children since these things follow on the nature of the rational and social (*koinōnikou*) and philanthropic (*philallēlou*) animal' (trans. IG: 125, 132, 148).

[74] M. A. 3.74, 5.16.3–4, 5.29.2, 6.14.2, 6.44.5, 7.68.3, 7.72, 8.2, 10.2.3.

[75] Sen. *Ben.* 4.18.2; also Griffin 2013: 27.

[76] There is no satisfactory English equivalent for this notion: I use 'appropriation' (like LS); other terms used by scholars include 'familiarization', 'affinity', 'endearment', and 'conciliation'.

[77] See refs. in n. 82.

[78] LS 57 D: 'The appropriate disposition...to one's kindred is affection (*sterktikou*), and...to things which contribute to the needs of its constitution, selection (*eklektikōs*)'; for an alternative translation, see Ramelli 2009: 25.

[79] For animal sociability, see Cic. *Fin.* 3.62–3, Cic. *N. D.* 2.123–4. God (Zeus) or the gods are also seen as rational animals (see text to nn. 84–9, 94), but I leave that factor out of account for the moment.

implied that some of the characteristic manifestations of rationality and sociability are interconnected and interdependent. One might take this view, for instance, about the capacity for using languages and forming communities. On the one hand, language can be seen as requiring a social context and, on the other, the formation of communities requires some rational functions, including, again, that of language use. So, one might argue, the distinctively human features are rationality-plus-sociability. Although this is a credible suggestion (which might be supported by Cicero, *On Duties* 1.11–15),[80] an alternative view is more persuasive, and matches the fuller accounts of appropriation in Cicero, *On Ends* 3. On this view, as is standardly supposed, the feature that makes human beings unique among animals is rationality, which signifies a range of capacities including language use and inferential reasoning.[81] The two parallel accounts of appropriation in *On Ends* 3 demonstrate how the emergence of rationality, in its various dimensions, informs and transforms two primary animal motives. One of these motives is self-preservation or, more precisely, the motive to maintain one's 'constitution' (*sustasis*) as a human being (3.16–22). The second is the motive, seen as common to all animals, including human beings, to care for others of one's kind, a motive expressed, paradigmatically, in the form of parental love (3.62–8, esp. 63–4). In the second strand of appropriation, what is presented is the development of sociability informed by rationality. In the first strand in *On Ends* (3.16–22), I think a social context is also presupposed; and so here too, implicitly, we have rationality at work in a social context.[82] On this alternative view, rationality is indeed the distinctively human feature; but its development and operation in a human life only makes sense if we see this as closely, indeed inseparably, linked with sociability. In this sense, the connection between the two features highlighted by Stobaeus, Marcus Aurelius, and Seneca is an intelligible one. In what follows, I take the combination 'rational and social' to be presupposed widely in Stoic ethics, though if we are being more precise, the relationship between rationality and sociability is the one I have just traced.

What about the idea that happiness consists in living a life 'according to nature' in the sense of nature as a whole (cosmic or universal nature)? Although we have ancient evidence stating that this idea formed part of Stoic thinking,[83] we lack any ancient discussion explaining in a discursive way how this idea was worked out, and so we have to reconstruct this explanation for ourselves.[84] Outside Stoic ethics the most relevant source seems to be their thinking on theology (which falls under

---

[80] This passage combines rationality and sociability in several different ways in 1.11, 12, 13, and 14.

[81] On these and other rational capacities in Stoicism, including belief-based action and emotion, see Gill 2006: 140–5. On the scope of reason (*logos*) in Greek philosophy in general, see M. Frede 1996: 5–19, esp. 17, discussed in Gill 2006: 252–4.

[82] See further on these points, 4.3, 4.5, text to nn. 202–15.

[83] As well as D.L. 7.87–9, partly cited in text to n. 70, see Plu. *Sto. Rep.* 1035 C–D (= LS 60 A).

[84] On this feature of Stoic thought and scholarly interpretations of it, see Ch. 3, esp. 3.1, 3.4.

Stoic 'physics' or the philosophy of nature); an especially useful text is the general account of Stoic theology in Cicero, *On the Nature of the Gods* (*N. D.*), Book 2. We can trace connections between this source and Stoic writings on ethics, especially on appropriation.

One idea that is strongly marked in Stoic theology is the claim that the universe as a whole is rational and is, indeed, the paradigm of rationality.[85] Is there also evidence for the idea that the universe is also a paradigm of sociability or community, perhaps linked with the theme of rationality? We do find the idea of the universe as a community of gods and humans, both seen as animals (living beings) which share the possession of rationality. We also find the more restricted idea of the community of the wise, that is, gods and wise humans, who possess rationality in the highest degree.[86] We may take such ideas as implying that there exists at a cosmic or universal level an equivalent for the idea that human beings are distinctively rational and sociable. As at the human level (see text to nn. 81–2), we might analyse this idea as being that rationality, in some sense, pervades the universe and that community between gods and humans (or at least wise humans) is an important expression of this pervasive presence.

Although this suggestion has some plausibility, I think there is an alternative one which can take us further, and which may incorporate elements of the first. The Stoics offer various arguments for the rationality of the universe as a whole. But a particularly important one is that the universe is rational because it embodies structure, order, and wholeness. The clearest expression of this is taken to be the regular and ordered movements of the sun, moon, and planets, that is, what we would consider to be the solar system, but conceived by the Stoics in geocentric terms.[87] These can be recognized as expressions of structure and order. 'Structure' and 'order' are terms which are close in meaning; but I take 'structure' to imply, simply, organization, whereas 'order' implies organization of an especially excellent kind, for instance, as being symmetrical or internally coherent and consistent. As regards wholeness, the universe is, obviously, whole in the sense that it includes everything else. But the Stoics have in view a wholeness which not only includes the examples of structure and order just noted but is itself also structured and ordered *as a whole*.[88] The linkage between these features and rationality or reason (*logos*) may seem puzzling, especially if we take 'reason' to consist in a certain kind of (human) psychological function, which is the obvious sense. However, it is surely relevant that Stoics understand

---

[85] See LS 54 E–G.

[86] See e.g. Cic. *Fin.* 3.64, Cic. *N. D.* 2.34, 153–4, and LS 67 L; for full discussion, see Vogt 2008a: chs. 2–3.

[87] See Cic. *N. D.* 2.15, 43, 49–50, 54–6, 97. A similar idea appears in Pl. *Tim.* 30a–c, 34a–b, 38b–40b.

[88] See Cic. *N. D.* 2.37–9 (= LS 54 H). On 'holism', or a tendency to think in terms of 'structure', rather than 'composition', as a recurrent feature of Stoicism, see Gill 2006: 4–14; Gill 2010a: 14–17, 181–9.

rationality as an ordered and complex set of capacities or skills, and one which constitutes a coherent whole.[89]

Second, in Stoic theology, the universe constitutes the highest embodiment or paradigm of providential care. This feature is very strongly marked in Cicero's account. It is manifested not only in nature's providential care for human beings, but for all types of living entities, including plants, fish, and non-human animals, and for all aspects of the natural order, including the sea, air, land, and heavenly bodies.[90] One indicator of this providential care is that all animals are naturally equipped with the capacities and means of self-defence and self-preservation. This is built into their bodily structure and the instinctive awareness of how to use these bodily means of self-maintenance. Another indicator is that all animals are naturally equipped for procreation and the perpetuation of their kind by their bodily form and by having an instinctive desire to take care of their young (Cic. N. D. 2.122–9).

This pair of features, while not identical with the combination of rationality and sociability, can be seen as parallel to it. The linkage between structure, order, and wholeness and rationality has just been discussed. Providential care and sociability have in common an other-related dimension (though providential care can also be directed at oneself).[91] Thus, we might infer, one set of features (structure and providential care) in nature as a whole parallels and underlies the other set of features (rationality and sociability) in human beings. However, a further question raised by this topic is this: what links these two features (structure and providential care) and makes them a natural or logical combination? If we think about this question in abstract terms, certain possible answers present themselves. We might suggest that the achievement of wholeness, structure, and order brings with it the motive to promote these qualities in other forms; for instance, the achievement of maturity in human beings and other animals brings with it the desire to procreate offspring. Alternatively, we might see the production of structure, order, and wholeness in some form other than oneself as a natural expression of providential care (for others).

However, in the context of Stoic theology, a different, though related, idea seems more plausible. Although I have been talking about the characteristics of nature as a whole, the topic being discussed in Stoic theology is, strictly speaking, god (or gods, or the divine, ideas treated as equivalents). The Stoic conception of

---

[89] E.g. in Cic. Off. 1.11–14, these are specified as the capacities for logical reasoning, language, the formation of community, learning about truth, and recognizing the presence of order in things; see also Gill 2006: 140–1.

[90] Cic. N. D. 2. 75–153, esp. 2.83 (plants), 100–1 (sea and air), 122–30 (non-human animals); not all the material is Stoic in origin but the general claim is Stoic. On providential care for human beings see Cic. N. D. 2.154–67. On providential care in Stoic theology, see also D. Frede 2002: 95–115.

[91] Thus, the providential care of universal nature can also be seen as self-directed, in so far as the universe constitutes the totality of things. Also, the expression of (nature's) universal care at the animal level consists of care for oneself as well as for others of one's kind.

god is complex and many-sided;[92] but it is clear that, for the Stoics, god is conceived neither as the transcendental divine person and creator of the Judaeo-Christian universe nor as the autonomous craftsman of Plato's *Timaeus*.[93] The Stoic god is an immanent agency or force within nature as a whole, and constitutes the 'active', rather than 'passive', cause in things. The Stoic god is also conceived as mind and rationality, and as an inner creative force. The following characterization is typical:

> The Stoics made god out to be intelligent, a designing fire...and a breath pervading the whole world...god is an animal which is immortal and rational or intelligent, perfect in happiness, not admitting of any evil, provident towards the world and its occupants...[94]

The two features of the universe under discussion can be seen as interconnected aspects of the agency of god, as so conceived. The operation of the divine mind (or the active cause in things) naturally expresses itself in enabling things to emerge as structured and ordered wholes and in exercising providential care for them. This activity can be seen, as the Stoics suppose, in the universe as a whole; and it can equally be seen in the relationship between god and the component parts of the universe, including human beings.[95] On this view, then, structure, order, and wholeness, on the one hand, and providential care, on the other, are both to be understood as natural expressions of the activity of god as in-built mind and agency.

What reason do we have to think that the Stoics themselves saw a connection between these features of the universe or god and human happiness, understood as 'the life according to nature'? The clearest indications, again, come in accounts of appropriation. Two parallel passages invite us to see the core motives of the two strands in appropriation (self-preservation and care for others of one's kind) as expressions of nature's providential work. The repetition of a similar phraseology for these two motives (a repetition which may go back to Chrysippus), underlines this linkage:

> For nature was not likely either to alienate the animal from itself, or to make it and then neither alienate it nor appropriate it (*oikeiōsai*). So it remains to say that in constituting the animal, nature appropriates it to itself [i.e. to the animal itself] ... But it could not be consistent for nature both to desire the production of offspring and not to be concerned that offspring should be loved.[96]

---

[92] See Cic. *N. D.* 2.45–72, and criticisms on this ground in 3.20–64.

[93] This point is compatible with the fact that Plato's divine craftsman (and the *Timaeus* in general) was probably a powerful influence on Stoic theology: see Betegh 2003; Gill 2006: 16–20.

[94] LS 46 A, 54 A; also, more broadly, LS 44, 46, 54. See also D. Frede 2002: 95–109; Bénatouïl 2009.

[95] Cic. *N. D.* 2.57–8, 75.

[96] D.L. 7.85 (LS 57 A(2)), Cic. *Fin.* 3.62 (LS 57 F(1)). The first passage is presented as taken from Chrysippus, *On Ends* 1; and the same may be true of the second. On the similarity in phraseology, see Schofield 1995: 196–7 (also Ch. 4, text to nn. 61–2). For evidence that Chrysippus linked these two kinds of 'appropriation' closely, see LS 57 E.

During development, animals, including humans, extend this starting-point by 'appropriating' themselves and others of their kind in ways that are suitable to their species. The implication, then, is that nature's providential care is exercised in enabling, and motivating, animals to exercise care on their own behalf and those of others of their kind (at least).[97] Put differently, animals express nature's providential care, by taking care of themselves and realizing their nature, and by enabling others of their kind to do the same. What this care consists in depends on the species involved; but in human beings, this is informed by the distinctively human capacity (shared with gods) of rationality. The fullest surviving account of human appropriation, in Cicero's On Ends 3, shows this process leading, in one strand, to the complete development of virtue and happiness, and, in the other strand, to the expression of virtue in relationships with other human beings of different kinds, who are recognized as being 'our own' or of our kind. These two strands represent the highest possible exercise, by human beings, of the two motives of care for oneself and for others of one's kind. They can also be seen, in another way, as an expression of the providential care of nature or god as an active cause in nature.[98]

What about links between appropriation and the other feature of cosmic nature stressed in Stoic theology, namely, structure, order, and wholeness? There is nothing which quite corresponds to the explicit linkage just illustrated between divine (or universal) care for animals and animals' care for themselves and others of their kind.[99] However, the idea of order makes a prominent appearance at a crucial moment in the first strand of appropriation, as Cicero presents this, which culminates in the understanding of the good. The good is characterized partly in terms of standard formulations for happiness or the goal of life, such as 'consistency'. It is also described in terms which indicate virtue ('right action and the right itself', honeste facta et honestum). The good is also characterized as 'the order (ordinem) and, as it were, harmony (concordiam) of actions', evoking the themes of structure, order, and perhaps wholeness (Cic. Fin. 3.21). The preceding account of increasingly appropriate 'selection' between indifferents also suggests a process of emerging structure.[100] This process is also closely linked with the operation of advanced forms of rationality.[101] As brought out shortly, Stoic characterizations of virtue also stress the presence of structure, order, and wholeness.

In summing up the implications of the points made so far, it may be useful to refer back to Chrysippus' formulation of happiness (or the life according to

---

[97] Cic. Fin. 3.63 highlights the idea that some species of animals exercise care for other species (see also Cic. N. D. 2.123); but Fin. 3.67 confines human care to other human beings.

[98] See Cic. Fin. 3.16–22, 62–8: also Cic. Off. 1.11–15; and Ch. 4.   [99] See text to n. 96.

[100] Cic. Fin. 3.20: such selection is made first 'with appropriate action' (cum officio), then this kind of selection is 'continuous' (perpetua), finally 'consistent' (constans) and in line with nature.

[101] See e.g. Cic. Fin. 3.21: '[the person] infers by intelligence and reason that…'; also ennoia ('conception'). See further on Cic. Fin. 3.21–2, Ch. 4, esp. 4.4.

nature) in terms of the combination of human and universal nature, illustrated at the start of this section in a passage referring to the 'harmonization' of human and divine will.[102] The material discussed in this section raises substantial conceptual and interpretative questions, regarding the role of nature, especially universal or cosmic nature, in Stoic ethical thought, discussed later (Chapter 3). However, the preceding discussion enables us to offer one possible interpretation, at least, of Chrysippus' passage,[103] and thus to illuminate Stoic thinking on the idea of happiness as the life according to nature. Happiness, as the goal of life, can be understood as the highest expression of human nature, as encapsulating the chief markers of humanity at its best, namely rationality and sociability (more precisely, sociability shaped by rationality). Alternatively, or in addition, happiness can be understood as an expression (the highest manifestation among terrestrial animals) of cosmic or universal nature. This is because happiness encapsulates, at the human level, two key features of cosmic nature, namely structure, order, and wholeness, and providential care, both of which can also be seen as expressions of rational mind or agency. Against this background, we can offer an interpretation of what is meant by 'the harmony (sumphōnia) of the daimōn ["guardian spirit"] in each of us with the will (boulēsis) of the administrator of the universe' (D.L. 7.88). As indicated earlier, rationality or mind is presented as the underlying element or agency which underlies the combination of structure, order, and wholeness, and providential care at the human and the universal level.[104] In so far as appropriation, in human beings, represents the realization of these two salient features of universal nature, underpinned by the exercise of rational mind, this constitutes the harmonization of human mind and understanding with the mind pervading and shaping the universe. (I am taking daimōn, as in effect, 'mind' or understanding, at the human level, and 'will' as the operation of the cosmic mind.) To restate the point, human beings harmonize themselves, at the deepest level, with the core principles of nature as a whole by achieving virtue and happiness, of the kind open to human beings. In this way, we can make sense of the idea of happiness as being the life 'according to nature' (human and cosmic) in ways that are consistent with, among other evidence, Stoic accounts of appropriation and treatments of virtue considered shortly.

1.4 Virtue as Expertise in Leading a Happy Life

How do the Stoics understand the relationship between virtue and happiness? As brought out in the preceding survey of Greek philosophical views (1.2), the Stoics, like Socrates and Plato, in the *Republic*, but unlike Aristotle and his followers, hold

---

[102] D.L. 7.88 (LS 63 C(3–4)); see text to n. 70.
[103] On other possible interpretations of this passage, see 3.5.   [104] See text to nn. 94–101.

that virtue constitutes the sole basis for happiness, or, as it is often put, that virtue is necessary and sufficient for happiness. What underlies this claim? Put differently, why do the Stoics not adopt the Aristotelian position, often seen as more intuitively appealing, that happiness consists in a combination of virtue and other things widely seen as goods? There are a number of possible ways of analysing the rationale for the Stoic position. However, the one stressed here is the idea that virtue constitutes knowledge or expertise in leading a happy life, that is, a life according to nature, with the connotations of that idea just discussed. Happiness depends on virtue precisely because it depends on the exercise of this expertise. This idea does not, admittedly, explain the Stoic claim that virtue *alone* constitutes this basis. To reconstruct the argument in full, we need to examine the Stoic thesis that things other than virtue normally considered good, such as health and property, do not determine happiness (as I do in 2.2–3). This explains why the Stoics do not conceive happiness as a combination of virtue and (what are often considered to be) other goods. However, the idea of virtue as expertise in leading a happy life merits examination on its own. Also, this idea grounds a second important role for virtue in Stoic thought, namely virtue as expertise in selecting between indifferents (also discussed in Chapter 2).

First, I discuss certain general comments in our ancient sources on the virtue-happiness relationship. In considering this material, I highlight certain qualifications to two ideas often held to be fundamental to the Stoic position; these are the ideas that virtue is identical with happiness and that virtue is the only good. Second, I discuss evidence for the idea that virtue is a form of expertise or knowledge. Third, I underline links between the Stoic conception of virtue and the connotations of human and universal nature considered in connection with happiness, that is, the combination of rationality and sociability and of structure, order, wholeness, and care for oneself and others of one's kind. These links, I suggest, make sense of the idea that virtue is expertise in leading a happy life, and hence of the claim that virtue provides the essential basis for happiness.

Ancient accounts of Stoic ethics standardly present the goal or end of virtue as being to live happily. These comments are typical:

> The goal of all these virtues is to live consistently with nature... Each of the virtues, by acting in concert and by its own particular properties, enables human beings to live consistently with nature... all the virtues make it their goal to be happy, which consists in living in agreement with nature, but each [virtue] attains this in its own way.[105]

---

[105] Stob. 5b3, 2.62.7–8, 12–14, 5b5, 2.64.9–12, trans. Pomeroy 1999.

A second recurrent theme is that virtue enables one to live well over a whole life, thus evoking the idea of happiness as a certain kind of life (the life according to nature). We are told that 'virtue is a disposition (*diathesis*) of the psyche in harmony (*sumphōnon*) with itself concerning one's whole life', and that virtue 'is expertise concerned with the whole of life'.[106]

It is clear from these comments that virtue plays a crucial role in bringing about happiness. But how, more precisely, should we conceive the relationship between virtue and happiness? This relationship is presented as very close; indeed, some comments suggest that the relationship is that of identity. For instance, as just noted, we are told that 'happiness consists in virtue',[107] and that the life according to virtue and according to nature are one and the same.[108] However, it is made clear elsewhere that the relationship between them is not quite that of identity. For instance, virtue has happiness as its 'end' (*telos*), whereas happiness does not have virtue as its end.[109] Similarly, 'the virtues are both instrumental and final goods. For they both generate happiness and they complete it, since they are parts of it'.[110] Virtue is 'instrumental', in the sense that it brings happiness about; indeed, it is the only thing that is indispensable for happiness.[111] Happiness, on the other hand, as the goal of life, is a purely final good.[112]

What features differentiate virtue from happiness, despite their close relationship? One is that they are conceived as entities of a different kind. Virtue is a property of the agent, whereas happiness is a property of the agent's life. As Plutarch puts it: 'virtue is a certain character (*diathesis*) and power (*dunamis*) of the controlling centre (*hēgemonikon*) of the psyche'.[113] Happiness, by contrast, is characterized as a mode of life, typically, the life 'according to nature' or 'according to virtue'. The characteristic Stoic formulation of happiness (but not virtue) is in terms of living (*to zēn*) in a certain way.[114] The distinction is one that Aristotle also drew: between virtue as a dispositional property of agents (at any one time), and happiness as a property of lives, that is, of a series of activities and experiences lived over time.[115] However, the contrast is narrowed, in the Stoic case at least, by certain salient features. The Stoics stress the permanence of virtue, once

---

[106] Stob. 5b1, 2.60.7–8, trans. Pomeroy 1999, and 5b10, 2.66.20–67.1, trans. LS 61 G(2). For similar ideas, see also text to nn. 109–11.

[107] D.L. 7.89 (LS 61 A(2) trans.); more literally, 'happiness exists in virtue' or 'lies in virtue'.

[108] Stob. 6e, 2.77.18–19 (LS 63 A(1)). See also D.L. 7.87, 88 (LS 63 C(1 and 4)), Sen. *Ep.* 92.3 (LS 63 F).

[109] 'The goal (*telos*) of all these virtues is to live consistently with nature', i.e. to be happy, Stob. 5b3, 2.627–8; see also Stob. 5b5, 2.64.8–12 (LS 63 G(3)); Sen. *Ep.* 76.9–10 (LS 63 D): perfected reason (i.e. virtue) realizes the human end (i.e. happiness).

[110] Stob. 5g, 2.72.4–6, (LS 60 M).

[111] D.L. 7.127 (LS 61 L(3)): 'virtue is sufficient for happiness'.   [112] Stob. 6b, 2.76.16–23.

[113] Plu. *Virt. Mor.* 441 B–C (LS 61 B(8)).

[114] See e.g. LS 63 A(1), B, C; also 58 K. In Greek, *to zēn* is a definite article plus infinitive, signifying 'to *x*' or '*x*-ing'.

[115] Arist. *NE* 1.7, 1098b30–1099a7; also *NE* 2.5, on virtue as a disposition (*hexis*).

developed, and sometimes use a special term for 'disposition', *diathesis*, rather than the Aristotelian term, *hexis*, to denote this.[116] They present consistency as a mark both of virtue, as a mode of character, and the life of happiness.[117] Also, the consistency of the happy life, in Stoicism, is not subject to the loss of bodily and external goods ('preferred indifferents') in the way that Aristotelian happiness is.[118] This point partly explains why virtue and happiness are sometimes presented as virtually identical, as in this passage: 'Happiness consists in virtue since virtue is a psyche which has been fashioned to achieve consistency in the whole of life'.[119] Even so, the shared consistency belongs to entities which are different in kind.

A second difference is that, although virtue is the only thing that is essential for happiness, happiness can include things other than virtue.[120] Put differently, the class of things that count as 'good' in Stoic ethics, and thus potentially part of the good or happy life, is wider than just virtue, in the sense of the virtues proper, that is, the four cardinal virtues and their subdivisions, conceived as forms of knowledge or expertise. This wider class of goods does not include what the Stoics call 'preferred indifferents', such as bodily health and material prosperity, although these are recognized as objectively valuable.[121] However, it does include a range of other types of entity, falling (broadly speaking) into the psychological sphere.[122] These entities include (1) features such as psychological health, strength or beauty, which are also classed as 'virtues', though distinguished from virtues proper, which are forms of knowledge.[123] They also include (2) 'pursuits' or 'practices' (*epitēdeumata*), such as the practice of, or expertise in, of music, letters and horsemanship, which may become quasi-virtues under certain conditions (explained shortly).[124] These two types of good are relatively permanent or stable conditions.[125] Goods can also include (3) occurrent actions (actions performed on a specific occasion) by a virtuous person,[126] and (4) the so-called 'good emotions' (*eupatheiai*), of which the main generic types are wish, joy, and caution.[127] The

---

[116] See LS 47 S, 60 J, 61 A; this terminology reverses Aristotle's usage, as noted in LS 47 S (also Inwood 1985: 39–40). See also LS 61 I on Stoic debate about whether virtue (once gained) can be lost. However, Aristotle also stresses the permanence of virtue (*NE* 2.4, 1105a32–3).

[117] See D.L. 7.89 (LS 61 A), and Stob. 6a, 2.75.11–76.8 (LS 63 B). On virtue and consistency, see also Jedan 2009: 58–64.

[118] See Arist. *NE* 1.10, and text to nn. 32–4.

[119] D.L. 7.89 (LS 61 A). See also D.L. 7.89: 'the virtue of the happy person and his good flow of life [=happiness] are just this, always doing everything [according to nature]' (LS 63 C(4)).

[120] The wise (also happy) always have virtue but only sometimes have these other goods: Stob. 5c, 2.68.24–69.10.

[121] See LS 58 and 2.2–3.

[122] However, we also sometimes find reference to 'external' goods such as (virtuous) friends, though their goodness depends on virtue (Stob. 5e, 2.70.8–20, also LS 60 G); also 'psychological', means, strictly, psychophysical in Stoic thought (Stob. 5b7, 2.64.18–65.6, and LS 61 E).

[123] See Stob. 5b, 2.58.7–8, 13–14.   [124] Stob. 5b11, 2.67.5–12.

[125] On these and other types of good, demarcated from each other by reference to their permanent or temporary status, see LS 60 J–L, and LS, vol. 1, p. 376.

[126] See e.g. 'prudent action' (*phronimeuma*), Stob. 5f, 2.71.5.

[127] On 'good emotions', see D.L. 7.115, Stob. 5b, 2.58.8–9; also Ch. 5, text to nn. 22–7.

common characteristic of all these types of good thing is that they depend, for their existence, on the presence and exercise of virtue, that is, the virtues proper, conceived as forms of knowledge or expertise. Hence, the entities in the first category (psychological health or beauty) are presented as 'supervening' (*epigenesthai*) on the virtues proper.[128] Also, the pursuits or practices in the second category become 'quasi-virtues', when they 'are transformed in the virtuous person by his virtue and become unchangeable'.[129] It is worth noting too that the language of supervenience is also sometimes used to describe the relationship of happiness to virtue. Happiness is said to 'supervene' on a life when the performance of 'appropriate acts' (*kathēkonta*) 'acquires the additional properties of firmness and tenor and their own particular fixity', that is, when they are performed by someone who has the virtues proper.[130] Taken as a whole, these other types of good are classified, like happiness, as final goods (that is, goods which are also 'ends'), whereas the virtues proper are both instrumental, because they produce happiness, and final goods, because they form part of happiness.[131] Thus, happiness, which may include these other goods, is in this respect a broader class of entity than virtue (the virtues proper); however, happiness depends (solely) on virtue, in the sense that virtue is the only factor that is required for happiness and that happiness depends directly on virtue.

I now develop the suggestion that virtue is conceived in Stoic ethics as knowledge of how to lead a happy life. First, I discuss the idea of virtue as a form of knowledge or expertise, and then explore the linkage between virtue and happiness, understood as 'the life according to nature', in the senses discussed in 1.3. The virtues proper, as distinct from the broader class of secondary goods, are consistently described as forms of knowledge (epistēmē), expertise, or skill (technē).[132]

Is virtue understood as a unified form of knowledge or a plurality? By the time of Stoicism, there had been much debate about whether virtue should be conceived as a single entity or a plurality. Socrates, as presented by Plato, argues that virtue is one,[133] and that it is knowledge.[134] Plato, by contrast, in the *Republic*, for instance, maintains that there are four cardinal virtues, though one of them, wisdom, has a special, leading role.[135] Aristotle recognizes a large number of virtues, subdivided into ethical and intellectual, but sees the ethical virtues as unified by the exercise of practical wisdom.[136] The Stoic position is intermediate, in this respect, between the Socratic and Platonic views. On the one hand, the Stoics adopt the framework of the four cardinal virtues, seen as generic virtues,

---

[128] Stob. 5b4, 2.62.15–63.5, cited in text to n. 196.   [129] Stob. 5k, 2.73.7–12, IG: 131.
[130] The comment is ascribed to Chrysippus: Stob. 5.906.18–907.5 (LS 59 I).
[131] D.L. 7.94, Stob. 5g, 2.71.15–72.6 (LS 60 M).   [132] Stob. 5b5, 2.63.6–7.
[133] See Pl. *Prt.* 349a–361c.   [134] See Pl. *Meno* 88c–d, *Euthd.* 281a–e.
[135] Pl. *Rep.* 428b–434c, 441c–444a.   [136] See text to nn. 23–8.

with many subdivisions;[137] they also give wisdom a special, leading role. On the other hand, they sometimes underline, in various ways, that the virtues form a unified set (for instance, they are interdependent); and all the cardinal virtues, and not just wisdom, count as forms of knowledge.[138] In addition, the virtues are conceived in terms of the Stoic unified or holistic psychological framework. All the psychological functions of the adult human being are seen as informed by rationality; by contrast with Plato and Aristotle, the Stoics do not see the psyche as subdivided into rational and non-rational parts.[139] Hence, different virtues are not linked, as in Plato's *Republic*, with different parts of the psyche; nor do we find the Aristotelian distinction between 'ethical' and 'intellectual' virtue, based on the subdivision between rational and non-rational parts.[140] Knowledge or expertise is seen as informing the motives of the virtuous person, including desires and emotions. So we should not suppose, from the Stoic use of the term 'knowledge' to characterize virtue, that this is conceived as a function of a Platonic-Aristotelian rational part, rather than being a function of the psyche as a whole.

Zeno and Chrysippus, the two main early Stoic thinkers, offer different, but closely related, versions of this line of thought. Zeno recognizes four main virtues, 'wisdom (*phronēsis*), courage, moderation (or temperance, *sophrosunē*), and justice, on the grounds that, although inseparable, they are distinct and different from each other'.[141] However, he also presents wisdom as the leading virtue and the other three virtues as modalities of wisdom: 'he defines wisdom in matters requiring distribution as justice, in matters requiring choice as moderation, and in matters requiring endurance as courage'.[142] One of the standard accounts of Stoic virtues begins in this way:

Wisdom is knowledge of what one is to do and not to do and what is neither or the knowledge in a naturally social and rational animal of good things, bad things, and what is neither (and they say that this [definition] is to be understood [to apply] in the case of the rest of the virtues too). Temperance is knowledge of what is to be chosen and avoided and what is neither. Justice is knowledge of the distribution of proper value to each person. Courage is knowledge of what is terrible and not terrible and what is neither.[143]

---

[137] Stob. 5b2, 2.60.18–62.6.

[138] See also Annas 1993: 79–83; Jedan 2009: 66–74; Vogt 2017: 184–6.

[139] LS 61 B, 65 A–J; Graver 2007: chs. 1–2. See also Ch. 5, text to nn. 9–17.

[140] Contrast Pl. *Rep.* 441c–444a; Arist. *NE* 1.13: see also Gill 1996: 245–60.

[141] Plu. *Sto. Rep.* 1034 C (LS 61 C(1)).

[142] Plu. *Virt. Mor.* 441 B (LS 61 B(5)). It does not seem that Zeno allocates a specific sub-area of activity for prudence (Schofield 2013: 12–17; Vogt 2017: 191), despite the role supplied by a textual supplement in LS 61 C(2).

[143] Stob. 5b1, 2.59.4–11, IG: 125, their additions in square brackets: I have translated *phronēsis* as 'wisdom' in place of IG's 'prudence'.

This definition is probably based on Chrysippus' thought, like much else in standard accounts of Stoic ethics.[144] This formulation also reflects Zeno's view, except that the four cardinal virtues (and subdivisions of these) are presented as modalities of knowledge, rather than wisdom. Wisdom retains its leading role, with a sphere of action that is more general than that of the other virtues. A further feature of Chrysippus' thinking is elaboration of the idea that the virtues, while distinct, are also inseparable and interdependent. All four cardinal virtues have their own primary 'topics' or 'headings' (*kephalaia*), but each virtuous act also involves, in a secondary way, the topics of the other three cardinal virtues. Thus:

> ...the topics of wisdom (*phronēsis*) are, in the first instance, considering and doing what is to be done, and in the second instance, considering what one should distribute [topic of justice] and what one should choose [topic of moderation] and what one should endure [topic of courage], for the sake of doing so without error. The topic of moderation (or temperance, *sōphrosunē*) is, in the first instance, to make the motives stable and to consider them and, in the second instance, [to consider] the topics of the other virtues for the sake of acting without error in one's motives.[145]

Although Chrysippus' theory can be interpreted in various ways, I take it that what is involved is interdependence of a strong kind. Each virtuous act involves all four cardinal virtues (or some subdivision of these), although one virtue will be primarily relevant to any given situation.[146]

A further point made in this passage is worth exploring more fully, since it sheds light on the role of virtue as knowledge of how to live a happy life. The passage begins: 'All the virtues which are forms of knowledge and expertise have common (or "shared", *koina*) theorems (*theorēmata*) and the same goal [to live consistently with nature], as was said, and consequently they are inseparable'.[147] As just noted, the contents of the specific topics (*kephalaia*) are specified explicitly, but that of the shared theorems are not. Can we work out what is meant, and also how knowledge of these theorems enables the virtues to have the shared aim of living consistently with nature?

---

[144] See also Schofield 2013: 22–4.

[145] Stob. 5b5, 2.63.11–19, IG: 127, with my additions in square or round brackets.

[146] For this view, see Gill 2006: 153–4, based on Cooper 1999: 96–104. For a rather weaker version (the virtues are not inconsistent with each other), see LS, vol. 1, p. 384. See also Jedan 2009: 77–80.

[147] Stob. 5b5, 2.63.6–8, IG: 127, with my additions in square or round brackets. This point is confirmed by D.L. 7.125, citing several Stoic thinkers, including Chrysippus. For the continuation of the passage, see Stob. 5b5, 2.63.10–25 (LS 61 D). D.L. 7.126 presents similar ideas but less clearly (see also Schofield 2013: 24–5).

It may be useful to consider the implications of a passage cited earlier:

Wisdom is knowledge of what one is to do and not to do and what is neither or the knowledge in a naturally social and rational animal of good things, bad things, and what is neither (and they say that this [definition] is to be understood [to apply] in the case of the rest of the virtues too).[148]

Although the opening items in the passage (what one is to do and not, and good and bad or what is neither) are allocated here only to wisdom (*phronēsis*), we are also told that this definition also applies in the case of the other virtues. So we can infer that the shared theorems of the later passage (5b5) consist in knowledge of what one ought to do and not, and of good and bad things or neither (that is, the 'indifferents'). Some other evidence points in the same direction. We are told that the early Stoic Aristo defined virtue as a unitary kind of knowledge, namely, knowledge of good and bad things. The cardinal virtues constitute the application of this single kind of knowledge to different areas. Aristo was subsequently regarded as a dissident in the Stoic tradition.[149] However, Zeno also presented the other cardinal virtues as modalities of wisdom in different spheres of action; and he may also have regarded wisdom as knowledge of good and bad and what one ought to do and not.[150] Seneca also presents knowledge of good and bad things as the culmination of wisdom and as what underlies all the virtues.[151] So we have a recurrent pattern in which, although the different virtues have different sub-fields, they have a shared understanding of what is good and bad and what is to be done.

However, it is still not clear how knowledge of good and bad things and what is neither is related to knowledge of happiness, understood as the life according to nature. The phrase, 'what is good and bad and neither', can be taken as summing up the core principles of Stoic ethics. Central to their theory is the distinction between virtue (a good) and the indifferents (neither good nor bad). Happiness or the life according to nature is also a good; indeed, it is the final good, that is, the goal of human life; and virtue and happiness, as goods, are defined in relation to each other. These points provide the organizing framework for Stobaeus' summary of Stoic ethics (the most systematic of the three summaries), and they are also clearly marked in those of Diogenes Laertius and Cicero, though they are rather differently structured.[152] So to

---

[148] Stob. 5b1, 2.59.4–7, IG: 125, their brackets; for the whole passage, see text to n. 143.

[149] Gal. *PHP* 7.2.1–3 (*SVF* 1.374); LS 61 B(2–3); on Aristo, see Sedley 2003: 14.

[150] See text to nn. 143–4. See also S. E. *M.* 11.170 (*SVF* 3.598), and 11.246: (Stoic) wisdom is defined as 'knowledge of good and bad things and what is neither, which constitutes expertise as regards one's life'; also Spinelli 2012: 103–5.

[151] Sen. *Ep.* 88.28–30.

[152] Stobaeus' account begins with an analysis of good things, centred first on virtue (5b–5b8), and then on happiness (6–6e), before proceeding to indifferents (7–7g). Diogenes Laertius introduces happiness early in the account (7.87–9), before moving on to virtue (90–104, including discussion of what is good, 94–101), and then indifferents (104–7). Cic. *Fin.* 3 gives a central place to the thesis that

have knowledge of 'what is good and bad and neither' is, in effect, to have a grasp of the core ethical principles, as understood in Stoicism, including the conception of happiness as the life according to nature and virtue.

The idea that virtue constitutes knowledge of how to live a happy life is also confirmed by a large number of passages in Stoic ethical writings. This evidence connects virtue both with the characteristic features of human nature (rationality and sociability) and with those of universal nature (structure, order, and wholeness, and providential care). The links with the idea of human nature as rational and social are brought out with special clarity in Stobaeus' summary of Stoic ethics, a version sometimes seen as reflecting most closely Chrysippus' thought.[153]

These links are stated explicitly in this general statement: 'Since a human being is a rational, mortal animal, social [or "political", *politikos*] by nature, they [the Stoics] say that all human virtue and happiness constitute a life which is consistent and in agreement with nature'.[154] The link between virtue as a form of knowledge and human nature (as rational and social) is also stated in a passage just cited. We are told that wisdom is knowledge of what one is to do and not to do and what is good and bad 'in a naturally social and rational animal', and similarly with the other virtues.[155] Here, the linkage between virtue and human nature is made at a general level. However, another passage in the same context presents the four cardinal virtues as the expression of four core human motives or inclinations (*aphormai*).

> The goal of all these virtues is to live consistently with nature. Each virtue through its individual properties enables the human being to achieve this. For from nature a human being has initial inclinations (*aphormai*) for the discovery of what is appropriate [wisdom], for the balancing of his motives [moderation or temperance], for acts of endurance [courage], and for acts of distribution [justice]. Each of the virtues, by acting in harmony (*sumphōnōn*) and by its own particular properties, enables the human being to live consistently with nature.[156]

The passage expresses two relevant ideas. One is that the virtues, as a matched set, cover the four main sectors of human action and experience, both as regards one's own activities and one's relations to others. The other is that each of the cardinal virtues represents the fullest expression of certain fundamental human

---

virtue (by contrast with indifferents) is good and forms the sole basis for happiness (3.21–34), and indifferents are discussed later (50–7). On the organization of these accounts of Stoic ethics, see Schofield 2003: 236–46.

[153] For the last point, see Long 1996: 130; also Ch. 3, text to nn. 78–86.

[154] Stob. 6, 2.75.7–10. See also Stob. 11m, 2.109.16–18, also noted in n. 73.

[155] Stob. 5b1, 2.59.4–7.

[156] Stob. 5b3, 2.62.7–14, trans. based on Pomeroy 1999, names of the four cardinal virtues added in square brackets.

inclinations. These inclinations are not identical with the two basic or core human (and animal) motives that underpin the Stoic theory of 'appropriation', though they build on these basic motives. The basic motives are to preserve and maintain one's own constitution and to care for others of one's kind.[157] The four inclinations highlighted in the passage just cited are all distinctively human ones, in the sense that they presuppose the (distinctively human) combination of rationality and sociability. This applies both to the four inclinations taken separately, each of which presuppose advanced rational and social functions, such as determining what is appropriate or distributing what is valuable. The virtues, which are forms of knowledge or expertise, enable people to express and realize fully these four core inclinations, and also to co-ordinate or harmonize them (*sumphōnon*) with each other. The combination of these two aspects of virtue enables the person to 'live consistently with nature', that is, to realize the best qualities of human beings as rational and social.

The pattern of ideas conveyed, rather briefly, in this passage is confirmed by a fuller treatment in Cicero's *On Duties*. This work constitutes Cicero's independent version of a late Hellenistic treatise by the last Stoic head, Panaetius. Panaetius has sometimes been seen as rather unorthodox in his approach, compared with earlier Stoic thinkers. However, the main lines of his thinking on virtue are close to that in Stobaeus' summary of Stoic ethics, usually seen as orthodox, although there are some distinctive or innovative features in Panaetius' treatment.[158] In Book 1 of *On Duties*, Cicero sets out an account of the four cardinal virtues, presented as a basis for ethical decision-making.[159] This account is preceded by a short section (1.11–15), explaining that the virtues are rooted in core human motives. The section begins by stating the idea, fundamental for the Stoic theory of appropriation, that human beings share with other animals two basic motives (the desire to preserve and maintain themselves and to procreate and care for others of their kind), the development of which is informed, in adult humans, by the possession of reason.[160] This idea serves as the starting-point for describing four natural human inclinations which provide the basis of the four cardinal virtues.[161]

The first inclination is presented as an extension of the second basic motive, in its human (rational) form: namely, the desire for involvement in family and communal life, conducted through language, as a way of expressing care for

---

[157] For these basic motives, see LS 57 A(1), F(1); also 4.2.

[158] Tieleman 2007 argues, convincingly, that Panaetius' approach has much in common with earlier Stoic thought. The main distinctive features of Panaetius' thinking on this topic are his replacement of courage with magnanimity and moderation with 'fittingness' (*decorum*).

[159] In Stoic terms, a basis for determining 'appropriate actions' (*kathēkonta*); on the aims and organization of *Off.*, see 2.4–5.

[160] Cic. *Off.* 1.11; for this idea, see also D.L. 7.85–6, Cic. *Fin.* 3.20–2, 62–3 (also Ch. 4, esp. 4.2–3).

[161] Cic. *Off.* 1.11–15, esp. 1.11, can be connected with Panaetius' reported definition of the goal of life as 'living according to the starting-points (*aphormai*) provided by nature', Clement of Alexandria, *Stromateis* 2.21.129.1–5. See also Striker 1996: 253–5.

others as well as oneself. This serves as the basis for the virtue of justice.[162] Thus, the description of this inclination underlines both rationality and sociability. In the other three inclinations, emphasis is placed on the influence of rationality, without explicit reference to sociability. However, the three inclinations are characterized in ways that suggest a natural tendency towards social involvement, and this prepares the ground for an analogous emphasis in the presentation of each of the virtues. Thus, greatness of spirit (*magnanimitas animi*), the Panaetian equivalent of courage, expressed in indifference to adversity and the desire to do great (socially beneficial) actions, is derived from the inclination to 'pre-eminence' or leadership (*principatus*). This is described as leading one to disregard anyone whose advice or orders are not just or legitimate, that is, to exercise moral leadership or independence from corrupting influences.[163] The virtue of 'fitting-ness' (*decorum*), the Panaetian equivalent of 'moderation' (*sōphrosunē*), is derived from the natural human recognition of, and attraction to, order and beauty. This is presented as shaping one's pattern of decisions and actions, including social behaviour, a theme elaborated in the account of the virtue.[164] The social dimension is least obvious in the case of wisdom, characterized here as an extension of the natural (rational) desire to learn for its own sake. However, this desire also leads one to understand that 'what is simple and true (*sincerum*) is most fitted to human nature' (1.13). In a parallel discussion in Cicero's *On Ends* (2.45–7), this inclination is presented as leading one to hate things that are false and deceptive, such as cheating, perjury, malice, and injustice (2.47).[165] The implicit reference to human nature as social as well as rational, reinforced by much emphasis on this dimension later in *On Duties* Book 1, confirms that these four inclinations are seen as based on the idea of human nature as social as well as rational, as indicated in *Off.* 1.11–12.

This set of ideas is reinforced later in Book 1 of *On Duties*, following Cicero's introduction of the fourth virtue, namely 'fittingness' (*decorum* in Latin, *prepon* in Greek). This quality is presented as having a two-fold character, as a specific virtue, and as an aspect of all the virtues. In its latter role, fittingness is constituted by the combination of beauty and order that is a shared feature of all the virtues.[166] In this connection, Cicero makes several points relevant to the linkage between virtue and nature. First, using a metaphor based on drama, he states that the

---

[162] Cic. *Off.* 1.12. Initially, this chapter seems to continue the description of the two core motives in 1.11; but it becomes clear that it presents the first of the four inclinations set out in 1.12–14 and summarized in 1.15.

[163] Cic. *Off.* 1.13. This presentation of the human inclination underlying magnanimity seems, at first sight, rather odd. But there are clear links with the characterization of the virtue of magnanimity in *Off.* 1.66, and with the parallel discussion in Cic. *Fin.* 2.46 (part of 2.45–7, outlined shortly).

[164] Cic. *Off.* 1.14; on *decorum* in social behaviour, see I.99–100, 103–4. 122–40.

[165] In *Fin.* 2.45–7, we find again the four virtues (here unnamed) seen as expressions of the same four natural inclinations, and as exhibiting human rationality (and by inference sociability); see also Dyck 1996: 85.

[166] Cic. *Off.* 1.93–6.

virtues represent a role (*persona*) given to us (all) by nature; the earlier discussion of the natural motives and inclinations underlying the virtues helps to support this assertion.[167] Second, he suggests that the fittingness that forms a dimension of each virtue gives every virtuous act a beauty and order that are inherently appealing to other people, and that should provide a standard for us in the way we try to express each of the four virtues. It should also give us a standard in the sphere of the fitting, considered as a specific virtue, that is, in the management of emotions and desires and in appropriate behaviour as participants in society.[168] Underlying these ideas, especially the second, is the claim made earlier (1.14) that the virtue of fittingness derives from the natural human inclination to love beauty and order. This point is restated with emphasis in connection with the fourth virtue. The natural or intrinsic love of beauty and order are presented as distinctively human characteristics, not shared with other animals, and are linked here with the human capacity for exercising rationality and enjoying doing so for its own sake (1.97–8, 105–6). This passage reinforces the theme that the virtues constitute a developed expression of natural human inclinations (here, the inclination towards order and beauty), which in turn reflect the constitutive human character as rational and sociable.

A further suggestive, and rather unnoticed, feature of Cicero's presentation of the virtues in *On Duties* 1 is relevant here. Each of the virtues is presented as having two aspects. The first constitutes the core qualities of the virtue, and the second adds a more actively benevolent and other-directed focus. The characterization of courage (conceived as magnanimity) can serve as an example.

A brave and great spirit is in general seen in two things. One lies in disdain for things external, in the conviction that one should admire, should choose, should pursue nothing except what is right and fitting, and should yield to no one, nor to agitation of the spirit, nor to fortune. The second is that you should, in the spirit I have described, do actions which are great, certainly, but above all useful, and you should vigorously undertake difficult and laborious tasks which endanger both life itself and much that concerns life.[169]

The pattern found here also applies in different ways to the other virtues. Justice is subdivided into the core quality of giving what is due to others and a more active quality of beneficence, kindness, or liberality.[170] In the presentation of the fitting,

---

[167] Cic. *Off.* 1.97–8; also 1.14, 17; this prepares the way for the theory of the four roles (1.107–15).

[168] Cic. *Off.* 1. 98–103.

[169] Cic. *Off.* 1.66, trans. Griffin and Atkins 1991; for text of *Off.*, see Winterbottom 1994. In fact, after an introduction centred on the first aspect (1.66–9), Cicero focuses on the second (1.69–91). On Cicero's presentation of this virtue, and its relationship to Stoic thinking in general on this virtue, see Gill 2019b.

[170] Cic. *Off.* 1.20; on justice, see 1.20–41 on justice and 1.42–59 on generosity.

the Panaetian equivalent of moderation, although there is no formal subdivision, we find a combination of internal restraint and management of emotions and desires, on the one hand, and appropriate behaviour towards other people, on the other.[171] In the case of wisdom, we have a short discussion, at the start of the series of virtues, centred on the idea of learning and discovery of truth as natural inclinations, though also raising the question of the proper use to which learning should be put.[172] At the end of the review of virtues, Cicero returns to the second question, emphasizing the importance of the use of reason for practical purposes and for social benefit and the idea that sociability is natural to human beings and should be given priority over the pursuit of knowledge for its own sake.[173] The last discussion, in particular, seems to reflect Cicero's own views, though some of the points he stresses to support the priority of sociability have a Stoic basis.[174] However, the two-fold characterization of the virtues is firmly embedded in the structure of the whole treatment and almost certainly reflects Panaetius' approach.[175] The idea that human beings are constitutively rational and sociable, rather than simply rational, is prominent in other accounts of Stoic ethics, including Stobaeus' treatment of the virtues.[176] So we might see Cicero's account as reflecting this two-fold emphasis in Stoic ethical thinking, focusing first on the virtue in question as an expression of human rationality and then as expressing sociability, informed by rationality. An alternative explanation is that Panaetius, followed by Cicero, organizes his account of the virtues in this way to underline the role of the virtues in promoting social, or other-directed actions, often thought to be a key Panaetian theme.[177] However, on either reading, this feature of the account brings out the central role of sociability, closely interconnected with rationality, in Stoic ethical thinking, even if this role is especially emphasized in this Ciceronian discussion.

It is clear, from the evidence reviewed so far, that Stoics recognized a close relationship between virtue and nature in the sense of human nature. What about the relationship between virtue and universal or cosmic nature? There is, certainly, evidence supporting a close linkage in Stoic thought between virtue, as well as happiness, and universal nature. For instance, a passage of Chrysippus, cited

---

[171] Cic. *Off.* 1.93. 100–2, on the one hand, and 99–100, 103–4, on the other.

[172] Cic. *Off.* 1.18–19 (on the underlying natural inclination, see also 1.13, 16).

[173] Cic. *Off.* 1.153–8.

[174] See e.g. Cic. *Off.* 1.153 (community of gods and humans), 157 (sociability as an inherent human motivation, not merely instrumental to individual benefit); see also 1.12, 1.50, Cic. *Fin.* 3.62–6. On *Off.* 1.152–61 as a Ciceronian addition to the argument (and a rather maladroit one, despite the presence of genuinely Stoic motifs), see Dyck 1996: 338–40.

[175] The two-fold character of each of the virtues is especially marked in *Off.* 1.20 (justice/generosity), 66–7 (magnanimity/great actions), and implicit in 1.102–4 (management of emotions and appropriate social behaviour), even if 1.18–19 and 1.152–61 (on wisdom) reflect, rather, a Ciceronian view. See also Dyck 1996: 106, 183–5.

[176] See text to n. 73, and nn. 153–4.

[177] For this Panaetian emphasis, see Dyck 1996: 106, 183–5.

earlier, presents 'the virtue of the happy person and his good flow of life [happiness]' as consisting in agreement with 'the will of the administrator of the whole'.[178] Chrysippus is also reported as saying that 'there is no other or more appropriate way of approaching the theory of good or bad things or virtues or happiness than from universal nature and from the administration of the world'.[179] These comments, taken on their own, offer little precise indication about the nature of the connection between virtue, happiness, and universal nature. Two remarks by Cicero support this linkage, though again without being elaborated fully in their immediate context. Near the end of *On Duties* 1, Cicero refers to one of the standard Stoic definitions of wisdom, namely as 'knowledge of all things human and divine'.[180] This knowledge, he says, includes the idea of the universe as a community of gods and humans; and he uses this idea to support his main thesis in this passage, that is, the fundamental importance of human sociability, and hence the priority of justice over (pure) learning.[181] In *On Ends* 3, again near the end of the discussion, Cicero gives a rather fuller account of the ethical significance of knowledge of nature as a whole. One point he makes is that such knowledge enables us to answer the question whether human nature is or is not in harmony or agreement (*conveniat*) with that of the universe as a whole. Another is that this knowledge enables us to understand the power of nature in promoting justice and properly conducted social relationships and in making sense of piety and gratitude to the gods.[182]

In considering the connection made in Stoicism between happiness, understood as 'the life according to nature', and universal nature, I have pointed out that we have no extended ancient theoretical account of this relationship and so we need to construct a rationale for ourselves. I have suggested that Stoic theology, especially as presented in Cicero's *On the Nature of the Gods* 2, is an especially useful resource for doing so. This text highlights characteristic features of the universe as a whole, which also constitute salient marks of human happiness, namely structure, order, and wholeness, on the other hand, and providential care, on the other. The same point applies in the case of virtue, as one would expect, given the very close relationship between virtue and happiness presupposed in Stoicism.

I start with structure, order, and wholeness. This complex of ideas is suggested, in the first instance, by two significant features of Stoic thinking about virtue. One, already illustrated, is that the virtues form a unified or interdependent set. This

---

[178] D.L.7.88 (LS 63 C(4)); see also text to n. 70.

[179] Plu. *Sto. Rep.* 1035 C, also D–E (LS 60 A, B). See also 3.4, esp. text to n. 116 on this passage.

[180] For this definition, see Aëtius 1, *Preface* 2; also Brouwer 2014: 8–41.

[181] Cic. *Off.* 1.153; see also n. 174. Cicero seems not to be following Panaetius closely at this point, and the line of argument is not wholly in line with Stoic thinking, despite the reference to the Stoic idea of the community of gods and humans.

[182] Cic. *Fin.* 3. 73; the third (less significant) point is that natural philosophy helps us to interpret the ancient ethical maxims of wise people. On this passage, see also 3.4, esp. text to n. 119.

idea is not unique to Stoic theory,[183] but it is supplemented there by the idea that the four cardinal virtues derive from four natural tendencies and that in this way they map the main areas of human action and experience.[184] This point consolidates the idea that virtue constitutes a coherent structure and whole. A second striking feature is the idea that virtue is characterized by consistency, inner coherence, and stability, whereas absence of virtue, which gives rise to defective emotions or 'passions', is marked by inconsistency, internal incoherence, and instability. Again, there are partial parallels to this contrast in some other theories;[185] but the Stoic version is more systematic and fully worked out and is reinforced by the distinctive Stoic unified or holistic psychological framework.[186]

The linkage between Stoic thinking on virtue and the ideas of structure, order, and wholeness is accentuated by a series of striking features of terminology or thought.[187] One such idea is that virtue 'perfects' or 'completes' (and thus brings wholeness); hence, virtue is sometimes defined as a kind of 'perfection' (*teleiōsis*).[188] In an arresting image, Cleanthes compares most people to 'half-lines in iambic verse; hence, if they remain incomplete [that is non-wise] they are bad, but if they are completed [or perfected, *teleiōthentas*], they are virtuous'.[189] The virtues, taken as a whole, are said to constitute 'a complex system of craftsman-like knowledge, which provides its own stability'.[190] An associated idea is that the four virtues, as a matched set, are 'perfectly symmetrical' (D.L. 7.100). A related notion is that a perfectly correct act (*katorthōma*), which is performed by someone with virtue, by contrast with an appropriate act (*kathēkon*), 'has all the numbers', meaning it is in a state of complete harmony.[191] A similar idea is that a person does not achieve virtue and happiness simply by performing 'appropriate acts' but only when those actions 'acquire the additional properties of firmness and tenor and their own particular fixity' by the addition of virtue.[192]

This pattern of thinking helps to explain why the ideas of structure, order, and wholeness appear prominently in Stoic discussions of the virtues. For instance, the climactic stage of Cicero's account of a major strand in ethical development consists in the recognition of the good (conceived as both virtue and happiness)

---

[183] Aristotle, for instance, presupposes the unity of the virtues (*NE* 1.13, 1144b43–1145a1), see also Russell 2009: ch. 11. But the ideas of structure, order, and wholeness are not given such a central place in his thinking about the virtues.

[184] See text to nn. 156–7.

[185] On parallels with the presentation of defective psychological conditions in Pl. *Rep.* 8–9, see Gill 2006: 318–21.

[186] See 5.1, text to nn. 8–9, 56–8, 69–77; also Gill 2006: 254–62.

[187] On this point, see also Gill 2006: 154–6.

[188] See D.L. 7.90, also 94 (*teleion*), and Stob. 5b4, 2.62.15–17, discussed shortly.

[189] Stob. 5b8, 2.65.9–11, IG: 128. A series of iambic dimeters was regarded as metrically incomplete till closed by a catalectic dimeter.

[190] Stob. 5l, 2.73.23–74.1, IG: 131.

[191] Stob. 11a, 2.93.14–16; see also Long 1996: 210–13. On the contrast between appropriate action and perfectly correct action, see LS 59 B.

[192] Stob. 5, 906.18–907.5 (LS 59 I).

as being inherently and uniquely valuable. The good is characterized as 'order and...harmony (*ordinem et...concordiam*) of actions', and as 'consistency' (*homologia*).[193] This way of understanding virtue helps to explain Panaetius' replacement of the standard cardinal virtue of moderation or temperance with 'fittingness' (*prepon* or *decorum*), and his characterization of this virtue as the recognition of order and beauty. These connotations are evident in one striking comment:

> Just as the eye is aroused by the beauty of a body, because of the appropriate arrangement of the limbs, and is delighted just because all its parts are in graceful harmony so this quality of fittingness (*decorum*), shining out in one's life, arouses the approval of one's fellows, because of the order (*ordo*) and consistency (*constantia*), and moderation of every word and action.[194]

Another revealing passage is Seneca's description of the kind of character and actions that help us to form an understanding of virtue.

> We grasped moderation, courage, prudence, justice, and gave to each its due. From whom then did we perceive virtue? That person's orderliness (*ordo*) revealed it to us, his fittingness (*decor*), consistency, the mutual harmony (*concordia*) of his actions, and his great capacity to surmount everything. From this we perceived that happy life which flows on smoothly, complete in its own self-mastery.[195]

Seneca here suggests that our ability to understand the virtues as a matched set depends on recognizing these qualities in other people, who display order and harmony in their character and actions and thus enable us to develop our understanding of what the virtues involve. The use of the term 'fittingness' (*decor*) is significant, in the light of Cicero's attribution of these qualities (beauty, symmetry, harmony) to the fourth virtue in *On Duties* 1.

We also find the same ideas used in connection with one of the secondary types of good noted earlier, namely health, strength, and beauty of psyche. These are described as virtues, though their status as virtues, and goods, derives from the fact that they express the virtues proper, that is, the virtues that constitute forms of knowledge or expertise.

---

[193] Cic. *Fin.* 3.21 (LS 59 D(4–5)); see also Ch. 4, text to nn. 114–22.
[194] Cic. *Off.* 1.98, trans. Griffin and Atkins 1991. See also 1.95: *decorum* is a characteristic of all the virtues, and is no more separable from them than beauty is from health.
[195] Sen. *Ep.* 120.11 (LS 60 E(8)); also Inwood 2007: 327.

...those virtues just listed [the cardinal virtues] are perfect in our lives...but others supervene (*epigenesthai*) on them, which are no longer forms of expertise but rather certain capabilities that come as a result of practice, for example, health of the psyche and its soundness and strength and beauty. Just as the health of the body is a good blend (*eukrasia*) of the hot and cold and wet and dry elements in the body, so too the health of the psyche is a good blend of the beliefs (*dogmata*) in the psyche. Similarly, just as strength of the body is a sufficient tension in the sinews, so too the strength of the psyche is a sufficient tension in judging and in not doing so. Just as beauty of the body is a symmetry (*summetria*) of its limbs constituted with respect to each other and to the whole, so too the beauty of the psyche is a symmetry of reason and its parts with respect to the whole of it and to each other.[196]

This passage, which is based on Chrysippus' thinking, refers to the idea, common in Hellenistic medicine, that health and strength derive from 'a good blend' of elements, as well as the Stoic idea of beauty as symmetry.[197] It may also allude to the Stoic theory that psychological states are also physical ones, that is, what one might call their 'psychophysical holism'.[198] However, the focus here is on the psychological analogue of these qualities. Health, strength, and beauty of psyche are presented as derivative qualities that 'supervene' on the underlying virtues (forms of knowledge) on which they are based. Just as those virtues are characterized in terms of structure, order, and wholeness, so too are the secondary virtues described here. These secondary virtues, like the primary ones, consist in ordered sets of 'beliefs' and 'parts of reason'.[199] However, they are presented not as forms of expertise or knowledge but as 'capabilities' that result from practice. Their presence reflects the Stoic view that knowledge informs and shapes the personality as a whole, in this case by extending the structure of virtue to these secondary forms of human goodness.[200]

It is clear, then, that the ideas of structure, order, and wholeness play a significant role in Stoic thinking on the virtues, just as they do in their thinking on the best qualities of the natural universe. What about the other main point of connection between universal nature and ethics, namely, in universal nature, providential care for all elements in nature and, in human beings and other animals, an in-built instinct to care for oneself and others of one's kind? The most obvious indication of this linkage, as with happiness, is the Stoic idea of

---

[196] Stob. 5b4, 2.62.15–63.5, IG: 126.   [197] On the latter idea, see Čelkytė, 2017, 2020: ch. 6.

[198] On this feature of Stoicism, see Gill 2006: 29–46. On interpretation of this passage, see Tieleman 2003: 148–57; Gill 2010a: 229–42.

[199] For parallels to the idea of 'parts of reason', see Gal. *PHP* 5.2.47, 49 (*SVF* 3.471a), 5.3.1 (*SVF* 2.841).

[200] On these qualities as derivative goods, see text to nn. 120–31; on the idea of reason as shaping the personality as a whole, see Gill 2006: 141–5.

development as appropriation. This is presented as a process in which animals express universal nature's providential care by exercising care for themselves and others of their kind, a process which is informed, in human beings, by rationality. This process of development gives a key role to the formation of the virtues, based on the shaping of these core human (and animal) motivations by reason.[201]

In Cicero's discussion of development in *On Ends* 3, the process of appropriation is subdivided into two strands.[202] As suggested earlier, it is plausible to see this subdivision as corresponding to the two features sometimes highlighted in Stoic thought as characteristic of human nature, namely rationality and sociability. We can interpret the first strand as centred on rationality and the second on sociability, though with very close interconnections between these two strands.[203] We can also see these two strands as the development of the two core motives underlying appropriation, that is, exercising care for oneself and for others of one's kind, though these two processes are, again, closely interlinked. In the account in *On Ends* 3, the first strand culminates in the recognition of virtue (as distinct from the 'preferred indifferents') as constituting the good; as just noted, the good is characterized in terms of structure and order.[204] This presentation implies that the fullest expression of care for oneself (the primary motive of this strand) is realized by developing a proper understanding of virtue. In the second strand, centred on care for others of one's kind, the development of virtue is not, in Cicero's presentation, stressed in the same way. The main focus is on two kinds of social engagement, namely involvement in family and communal life and recognition of the idea that human beings (and gods), as rational agents, form a single community.[205] However, Cicero also underlines that the development of social engagement forms a context in which virtue can be developed and expressed, thus reinforcing the linkage between the two strands of appropriation.[206] Also implied in Cicero's account, by the repeated emphasis on the 'naturalness' of the processes described, is the idea that these two strands (including, crucially, the development of virtue) lead towards happiness, understood as 'the life according to nature'.[207] The idea that this process of development is linked with universal nature is explicit at the start of this section, in the idea that nature implants in animals the instinct to take care of others of one's kind and also the idea of the universe as a home for the community of human beings and gods.[208]

Thus, we can see in Stoic writings on virtue, as well as happiness, reference to the two principal features highlighted as being the best qualities of the universe as

---

[201] See also text to nn. 96–8.   [202] Cic. *Fin.* 3.16–22, 62–8 (selections in LS 59 D, 57 F).

[203] See text to nn. 75–8; on the linkage between the two strands of appropriation, see 4.3, and 4.5, text to nn. 202–15.

[204] Cic. *Fin.* 3.21 (LS 59 D(4–5)). See text to n. 193.   [205] Cic. *Fin.* 3.64, 68 (LS 57 F(3, 8)).

[206] Cic. *Fin.* 3.66 (justice and benevolence), 68 (the wise person's involvement in family and communal life). See also 4.5, text to nn. 205–10.

[207] For this theme, see Cic. *Fin.* 3.62–3, 65–6, 68.

[208] Cic. *Fin.* 3.62, 64 (LS 57 (1, 3)). See also 4.4, text to nn. 189–95.

a whole, namely structure, order, and wholeness, and providential care.[209] The fact that these accounts refer to key features of human nature as well as nature as a whole, and present these as consistent with each other is unsurprising. Although some Stoic thinkers, we are told, accentuated one or other kind of nature in this connection, Chrysippus, the major theorist of the movement, saw both as relevant,[210] and is likely that the writings reviewed reflect his approach to this topic. In this section, I have considered the Stoic view that virtue constitutes a form of knowledge or expertise, and also discussed evidence linking virtue with 'the life according to nature', both in the sense of human nature and universal nature, as in the case of happiness. If we combine these two points, it yields the conclusion that virtue consists in knowledge or expertise in living a happy life, conceived as the life according to nature.[211]

---

[209] See text to nn. 87–90.   [210] See D.L. 7.87–9 (LS 63 C); also text to nn. 69–71.
[211] At least, it yields the conclusion that this is a primary function of virtue, though it may have others, including expertise in guiding selection between indifferents (Ch. 2).

2

Virtue, Indifferents, and Practical Deliberation

2.1 Preliminaries

A notable feature of Stoic ethics, though one shared with Socrates and Plato, is the claim that virtue constitutes the sole basis for happiness (1.2). This thesis depends partly on the idea that virtue consists in expertise in living a happy life, often understood in Stoicism as 'the life according to nature' (1.3–4). However, this idea does not, on its own, explain why virtue is presented by Stoics as the sole basis for happiness, or, as it is often put by scholars, as both necessary and sufficient for happiness.[1] This claim also rests on a second idea, that happiness does not depend on what are often described as 'bodily and external goods', such as health, wealth, and the well-being of our families and friends. Aristotle, by contrast, maintains that happiness depends on a combination of virtue and these other goods.[2] The Stoics deny this; they also deny that such things (by contrast with virtue) count as good, and characterize them as 'indifferents', meaning that they do not make the difference between happiness and its opposite. Even so, the Stoics recognize that such things have positive value, are naturally desired by human beings, and often, though not always, form part of a happy human life.

The Stoic idea of indifferents has sometimes been seen as a problematic feature of their ethical thought. From antiquity onwards, critics have questioned the consistency of the Stoic move of attributing positive value to things such as health, while denying that they determine happiness and that they count as good. Critics have also questioned the psychological credibility of the claim that happiness is not affected by loss of such things.[3] I think Stoic thinking on indifferents is consistent with their thinking on virtue and happiness in general. I also think it is psychologically credible, particularly in the light of their ideas about ethical development, including emotional development, considered later in this book. Indeed, I think that Stoic ideas about indifferents, as well as about virtue and

---

[1] See Russell 2012: 178–96. For reservations about this formulation and an alternative: 'virtue is that without which it is not possible to be happy', see Vogt 2017: 192–4.

[2] See Arist. *NE* 1.8–10, esp. 1101a14–16; also Ch. 1, text to nn. 29–34.

[3] On modern criticisms of the idea of indifferents and a defence against them, see Vogt 2014.

Learning to Live Naturally: Stoic Ethics and its Modern Significance. Christopher Gill, Oxford University Press.
© Christopher Gill 2022. DOI: 10.1093/oso/9780198866169.003.0003

happiness, constitute a potentially valuable contribution to modern ethics.[4] In considering Stoic thought on indifferents, we need to take into account their conceptions of virtue and happiness. The Stoic position is that achieving happiness or the life according to nature depends solely on the exercise of virtue as expertise in leading a happy life. Virtue can also be analysed as expertise in selecting between indifferents. This selection has regard to the positive and negative value of relevant indifferents; but the decisive factor for the virtuous person is not preferability, taken on its own, but whether or not the selection promotes a happy life (a life according to nature) or not. As so interpreted, I think Stoic thinking on indifferents, while complex, is coherent and psychologically credible.

I begin (2.2) by summarizing key features of their theory, in particular, the combination of these two beliefs: (1) that certain indifferents, such as health and property, have positive value and (2) that the presence or absence of such things does not determine happiness or its opposite. I then examine certain questions raised by the Stoic theory, referring to the ancient debate aroused by their theory (2.3). I consider whether the Stoic position is coherent in combining these two beliefs. I also discuss the question of the form of virtuous deliberation, on a Stoic view, including the criteria employed. The second part of the chapter consists of an extended discussion of Cicero's *On Duties*, treated as exemplifying Stoic thinking on soundly conducted practical deliberation (2.4–5). I suggest that this work reflects the Stoic ideas about virtue and indifferents discussed in 2.2–3. It also shows how the Stoic theory can provide a coherent and powerful framework for shaping actions in specific situations.

2.2 The Virtue-Indifferents Relationship

I start with the central feature of the Stoic position, the belief that things such as health and property have positive value in human life but that, none the less, they do not count as good and do not determine happiness or its opposite. This combination of ideas forms part of mainstream Stoic ethical thinking from Zeno onwards.[5] However, while all Stoics accepted that happiness is determined by virtue, they did not all accept that things such as health have positive value and therefore count as 'preferred', rather than 'dispreferred', indifferents.[6] Aristo, an

---

[4] On indifferents and ethical development, see 4.4; on indifferents and emotional development, see 5.1, esp. text to nn. 28–35. On indifferents as an integral part of a coherent set of ideas on virtue and happiness that constitute a potential contribution to modern virtue ethics, see 6.2, esp. text to nn. 90–1 and 6.3, text to nn. 117–20.

[5] See LS 58, esp. A–E, I; for a thorough analysis, probing conceptual questions raised by the topic, see Klein 2015.

[6] Alternative terminology for this distinction is 'preferable' (and 'dispreferable') or 'promoted' (and 'demoted') indifferents.

early Stoic and younger contemporary of Zeno, stressed, like other Stoics, the crucial role of virtue, or wisdom, in determining happiness, and the point that the wise person can be happy even in what are normally considered unfavourable circumstances. However, by contrast with Zeno, he argued that this means that there is no valid basis for the distinction between preferred and dispreferred indifferents; indeed, he defined happiness, exceptionally, in terms of 'indifference' to circumstances:

> Aristo of Chios... said that the end [goal of life] is to live with a disposition of indifference (*to adiaphorōs zēn*) towards what is intermediate between vice and virtue, not retaining any difference within that class of things [indifferents], but being equally disposed towards them all. The wise person is like a good actor who, when he puts on the mask of Thersites or Agamemnon, plays either part in the proper way.[7]

In response, Chrysippus claimed that adopting Aristo's view would mean that 'no function or task for wisdom [or virtue] could be found, since there would be no difference at all between the things that concern the living of life, and no choice between them would have to be made'. Chrysippus also asked, 'What am I to begin from, and what am I to take as the foundation of appropriate action and the material (*hulē*) of virtue if I pass over nature and what accords with nature?'[8] As often in Stoic ethics, Chrysippus' view became the standard one, and the distinction between preferred and dispreferred indifferents is prominent in all the main summaries of Stoic ethics.[9] Aristo's position on this question was not generally adopted within the school, although Epictetus and Marcus Aurelius de-emphasize the distinction between preferred and dispreferred indifferents.[10]

How, then, should we understand the relationship between virtue and indifferents, assuming the mainstream (Chrysippean) view? The Stoic view is that preferred indifferents have intrinsic value and can make a positive contribution to a happy life, understood as the life according to nature. Indeed, practical deliberation, in such a life, gives a central role to selecting between indifferents, both preferred and dispreferred. However, the preferred indifferents do not count as goods because they do not consistently confer benefit, which is the mark of goodness. The virtues, by contrast, consistently confer benefit, and so count as goods. Why should the virtues be considered as good in this respect, rather than the preferred indifferents? This derives primarily from the character of the virtues

---

[7] D.L. 7.160 (LS 58 G); also S. E. *M.* 11.64–7 (LS 58 F). See also LS, vol. 1, pp. 358–9; and Sedley 2003: 14.

[8] Cic. *Fin.* 3.50 (LS 58 I), Plu. *Comm. Not.* 1069 E (LS 59 A); also Cic. *Fin.* 4.68.

[9] See D.L. 7.104–5 (LS 58 B); Stob. 7a, 2.79.18–80.13 (LS 58 C(1–3)); Cic. *Fin.* 3.50–4.

[10] On Epictetus, see Long 2002: 182–5, 201–2; on Marcus Aurelius, see Gill 2013a: xxxviii–xl. See also Roskam 2005: 112–24, 131–5, on both thinkers.

as forms of knowledge or expertise. The virtues, as brought out in the preceding chapter (1.4), are conceived as modes of expertise in leading a happy life. They are also understood, as we see later, as modes of expertise in selecting between indifferents. In this respect, they consistently confer benefit and count as goods. This is the core of the difference in value between virtues and preferred indifferents. The virtues *make the difference* between happiness and its opposite, whereas the preferred indifferents do not; hence, their characterization as 'indifferents'. Although preferred indifferents normally contribute positively towards a happy life, they do not determine whether or not the life is happy, whereas the virtues do; and it is possible to be happy, the Stoics believe, even in the absence of preferred indifferents.

I now set out their view in more detail. What kind of things are 'indifferent'? Here is one ancient list: 'for instance, life, health, pleasure, strength, wealth, reputation, noble birth, and their opposites, death, disease, pain, ugliness, weakness, poverty, low repute, ignoble birth and the like'.[11] On the face of it, the category is similar to the Aristotelian one of bodily and external goods and the corresponding bad things.[12] However, our sources also include some psychological qualities. Indifferents are sometimes subdivided into (1) psychological: including natural ability, (ethical) progress, good memory; (2) bodily: including health and sense-perception; and (3) external: including parents, children, possessions in due measure, and acceptance by other human beings.[13] Lists of indifferents are subdivided between positive and negative ones. These are analysed as 'things according to nature' (or 'natural things') and 'things contrary to nature' (or 'unnatural things'). Alternatively, they are categorized as 'preferred' or 'promoted' (*proēgmena*) and 'dispreferred' or 'un-promoted' (*apoproēgmena*) indifferents. Sometimes, we find further subdivisions, for instance, between primary natural things, such as health, and things which are valuable only incidentally, such as money or fame.[14] However, the positive items are characterized generically as preferred or preferable indifferents or things according to nature. A related terminological distinction is drawn by the Stoics between the kind of response we should make towards indifferents and towards things that are good. We should exercise 'selection' or 'rejection' (*eklogē, selectio* or *apeklogē, reiectio*) in the case of indifferents and 'choice' (*hairesis*, or, Latin infinitive, *expetere*) in the case of what is good. This contrast indicates that our motivational attitude towards the good should be more whole-hearted and unqualified than towards indifferents, reflecting our recognition of the contrast between the two kinds of value involved.[15]

---

[11] D.L. 7.102 (LS 58 A(4)).   [12] See Arist. *NE* 1.8, 1098b12–14.

[13] Stob. 7b, 2.80.22–81.6. The items included are positive ones, but they have negative equivalents. For a similar list, including psychological qualities, see D.L. 7.106.

[14] Stob. 7c–d, 2.82.5–19, D.L. 7.107, Cic. *Fin.* 3.56–7.

[15] Stob. 5o, 2.75.1–6, 6f, 2.78.7–12, 7, 2.79.1–17, Cic. *Fin.* 3.20–1; also Inwood 1985: 201–15, 238–40.

A key Stoic thesis is that the preferable indifferents have positive value (*axia*).[16] This value is inherent and objective. The indifferents (positive and negative) also play a role in Stoic ethics as 'the material of virtue'.[17] But they are not valuable only because they have this latter role but in themselves, as suggested by their designation as 'things according to nature' or 'natural things'.[18] The significance of describing them as 'natural' can be brought out by referring to the Stoic theory of development as appropriation (*oikeiōsis*).[19] The Stoics believe that human beings, like other animals, are instinctively drawn towards things that maintain their nature or 'constitution' (*sustasis*) and are repelled by things that damage this. Correspondingly, the factors towards which they are drawn are characterized as 'things according to nature' and those by which they are repelled are 'things contrary to nature'.[20] In the process of human development, the emergence of rationality converts instinctive attraction and repulsion into 'selection' and 'rejection', a process based, in the first instance, on the same criterion of things being 'according' or 'contrary' to nature.[21] This point helps us to see why preferable indifferents, such as those listed earlier, are presented as naturally valuable. They are valuable because they enable us to realize our nature as human beings. I think this helps to explain why the list of preferable indifferents includes not merely basic needs such as life and health, but also features that promote our nature as rational and social animals, including family relationships and reputation or acceptance by other human beings.[22] In other words, preferable indifferents constitute many of the things that, on a conventional view, and also on a Stoic view, make for a rich and inclusive (and indeed happy) human life,[23] apart from virtue and the things that derive from virtue.

However, while stressing the natural value of preferred indifferents, the Stoics insist that they do not count as goods, unlike virtue and the things that derive from virtue. Here, the contrast with the Aristotelian view comes out most clearly. For Aristotle and those following him, the three types of 'good' include the kind of items classed by Stoics as preferred indifferents. By the same token,

---

[16] For 'value' (*axia*) and 'disvalue' (*apaxia*), see Stob. 7f, 2.83.10–84.3 (LS 58 D).

[17] See Plu. *Comm. Not.* 1069 E (LS 59 A).

[18] On this point, see LS vol. 1, pp. 357–9; Vogt 2014: 61–2; Klein 2015: 246–8.

[19] On this theory, see LS 57 and 59 D; also Ch. 4. For the link between this theory and the concept of 'natural things', see LS, vol. 1, p. 357.

[20] These responses are sometimes distinguished as 'motives (towards)' (*hormai*) and 'motives away from' (*aphormai*) things, though the latter term is also sometimes used to signify (in-built) inclinations; see Inwood 1985: 45, 224–30.

[21] See Cic. *Fin.* 3.16, 20 (LS 59 D (1–2)).

[22] See refs in nn. 11–13. For human beings as naturally rational and social, see Ch. 1, text to nn. 72–82.

[23] For the idea that preferables can contribute to happiness, while not determining it, see D.L. 7.105 (IG: 117–18); on this passage, see Klein 2015: 242–5. On the 'parts' of happiness in conventional Greek thought, see Ch. 1, text to n. 3.

although virtue is consistently seen by Peripatetics as the key basis of happiness, the other kinds of good are still regarded as helping to determine whether or not one has a happy life.[24] Admittedly, Peripatetic thinkers also stress the idea that virtue constitutes a much more important factor in producing happiness than the other goods.[25] However, for them, the difference between virtue and other goods is, in the end, one of degree not of kind. The Stoic position is sharply contrasted in this respect. The innovation in terminology, 'preferred indifferents', marks the fact that the difference is one of kind and not just of degree. The indifferents are not a sub-class of things that are good or bad but a distinct, intermediate category: things that are neither good nor bad.[26] Correspondingly, they are 'indifferent' as regards human happiness and its opposite; they do not *make the difference* between happiness and its opposite, whereas virtue and vice do. This remains true although the positive value of preferable indifferents provides a sound basis for adopting them. As one source puts it: '[preferable indifferents] are indifferent relative to a well-shaped life (*euschēmonōs zēn*), in which happiness consists, but not—by Zeus!—relative to being in accordance with nature or stimulating motivation towards or away from [something]'.[27] The Stoics sometimes go further in stressing that happiness does not depend on preferred indifferents: 'it is possible to be happy even without these [preferable indifferents], though the manner of using them is constitutive of happiness or unhappiness'.[28]

But can the Stoics really have it both ways, claiming that preferred indifferents have objective value but denying that they are good and that they determine happiness or its absence? Their ancient critics thought not.[29] For instance, it was claimed that 'preferred indifferents' were, in effect, equivalent to Aristotelian bodily and external goods, though dressed up as a new idea with its own terminology.[30] A related criticism was that the Stoic theory, though presented as an alternative to the Aristotelian one, was a much less convincing one, which ignored the fact that people in fact treat 'preferable indifferents' as determining happiness or its opposite.[31] Another objection was that the Stoic theory is inconsistent, in attaching positive value to the preferred indifferents, while denying that they form

---

[24] See Cic. *Fin.* 3.41–4; Sharples 2010: ch. 18; also Ch. 1, text to nn. 35–6.

[25] See Cic. *Tusc.* 5.50, 76–7, *Fin.* 5.71–2. The Peripatetics accept that virtue greatly 'outweighs' other goods; those other goods 'lie prostrate on the ground' compared with virtue; they are 'eclipsed' by the light of virtue.

[26] Stob. 5a, 2.57.18–58.4, 7, 2.79.4–5.

[27] Stob. 7a, 2.80.9–13, LS 58 C(3); see also Stob. 7, 2.79.15–17. For the idea of a 'well-shaped life' as a happy one, see Ch. 1, text to nn. 99–101.

[28] D.L. 7.104 (LS 58 B(1)). This passage illustrates Vogt's formulation of the Stoic position (2017: 192–4); see n. 1.

[29] On the debate between the Stoics and their ancient critics aroused by the distinction, see Annas 1993: 395–411; Striker 1996: 239–48, 298–315; Klein 2015: 226–7, 239–40; also 2.3.

[30] See Cic. *Fin.* 4.2, 20–1, 56–60, 72–3.   [31] See Cic. *Fin.* 4.29–31, 5.71–2.

part of happiness or the goal of life.[32] The prevalence of such criticisms reflects the intensely dialectical character of ancient philosophical debate, which is also the source of much of our evidence for Stoic ethics. But the ancient criticisms articulate questions or concerns that modern scholars and thinkers may also have, when confronted with the Stoic theory on this topic.[33] However, the Stoics provide a set of reasons for holding this view, which are, I think, coherent and credible. These reasons centre on three ideas, those of benefit, right use, and knowledge or expertise, which, taken together, can be seen as justifying their position on this subject.

I take the idea of benefit (ōpheleia) first. Goodness is sometimes defined in Stoicism in terms of benefit: what is good is, by that very fact, beneficial. Virtue is offered as the paradigm case of what is beneficial (and good). Thus:

> Good is in general that from which there is something beneficial. Hence virtue itself and the good, which participates in it, are spoken of in these three ways: (1) the good is that *from which* being benefited is a characteristic result; (2) it is that *according to which* [being benefited] is a characteristic result, for example action according to virtue; (3) it is he *by whom* [being benefited is a characteristic result]; and 'by whom', means, for example the virtuous person who participates in virtue.[34]

The rather cumbersome formulation spells out the point that what is good characteristically or constitutively confers benefit; this is not an incidental or occasional feature. Virtue is not presented as the only thing that is good (happiness is also good, and so is god or the universe);[35] but virtue is the standard example. This feature is also presented as a salient point of difference between virtue and indifferents: 'Just as heating, not cooling, is a property of the hot, so benefiting, not harming is a property of the good; but wealth and health do not benefit any more than they harm'. Again: 'they [indifferents] neither benefit nor harm'.[36]

So far, this point simply restates the categorical distinction between virtue and indifference in terms of 'benefit', as well as 'good', without explaining it further. However, the second point takes the matter further. Virtue is characterized in terms of right use, whereas indifferents are presented as things that can be used either well or badly.

---

[32] See Cic. *Fin.* 4.24–6, 39, 47–8, 78. Cic. *Fin.* 4 constitutes a catalogue of such objections; see Bénatouïl 2016a, esp. 198–9, and Brittain 2016: 26–8.

[33] See Vogt 2014: 56–7, which identifies a series of objections modern thinkers may have to the Stoic theory.

[34] D.L. 7.94, IG: 115, their italics and square brackets. For similar ideas, see S. E. *M.* 11.22–6 (LS 60 G). For goods as virtues or things deriving from virtue, see LS 60 J.

[35] See LS 60 I; also LS 54 E–F, H. On the scope of goods in Stoic ethics, see Ch, 1, text to nn. 120–31.

[36] D.L. 7.103, and 7.102, IG: 117; see also LS 58 A(4, 5).

...wealth and health do not benefit any more than they harm; therefore, neither wealth nor health is good. Again, they say that what can be used [both] well and badly is not good; but it is possible to use wealth and health [both] well and badly; therefore, wealth and health are not good.[37]

Two principal ideas seem to underlie this passage. One is that preferable indifferents do not *consistently* benefit us, whereas virtue does. A rather straightforward example is provided by the early Stoic Aristo: 'For instance, if healthy people had to serve a tyrant and be destroyed for this reason, while the sick people had to be released from the service and therefore also, from destruction, the wise person would rather choose sickness in this circumstance than health'.[38] Aristo cited this kind of case as an objection to the idea that some indifferents were naturally 'preferred' or 'preferable', a view on which he departed from mainstream Stoic thinking; but this example also brings out how indifferents in general do not invariably benefit people, on a conventional understanding of what 'benefit' means.[39]

The second idea underlying this passage takes us further in making sense of the Stoic view that benefit is conferred by virtue and not indifferents. The point is that preferable indifferents do not *constitutively* benefit us; what benefits us (what brings about our happiness) is the right use of indifferents, not the indifferents themselves. Right use of indifferents is a salient function of virtue, as is implied, for instance, in Diogenes' definition of happiness as 'reasoning well in the selection and rejection of things in accordance with nature'.[40] As we have just seen, the idea that virtue, because it is good, benefits constitutively, is firmly embedded in Stoic thinking; and right use of indifferents is part of the characteristic work of virtue. It is widely supposed that, on this subject, the early Stoics were influenced by an argument in Plato's *Euthydemus*. According to this argument, since things other than wisdom, such as health, possessions, and social status, may produce either harm or benefit, they are only beneficial if they are controlled by wisdom. The conclusion of this argument is ambiguously phrased in the *Euthydemus*. Initially, the claim is that these things are 'greater goods', if controlled by wisdom, and 'greater bads' (bad things), if not. However, the final statement is that 'of the other things, none is either good or bad, but of these two things, wisdom is good, and the other—ignorance—is bad'. It is the concluding view that the Stoics adopt,

---

[37] D.L. 7.103, IG: 117 (their additions in square brackets); see also LS 58 A(5).

[38] S. E. *M.* 11.64–7 (LS 58 F(4)).

[39] The Stoic idea of benefit is outlined in D.L. 7.104: 'to benefit is to change or maintain something in accordance with virtue', IG: 117. Aristo's example presupposes a more conventional view, that one is benefited by gaining preferred indifferents (life rather than health), though this is rather surprising, given his rejection of this category (text to n. 7).

[40] Stob. 6a, 2.76.9–10 (LS 58 K(1)). Although this is a definition of happiness (see text to n. 60), the implication is that reasoning well is a function of virtue, which leads to happiness. See also Sen. *Ep.* 92.11–13 (LS 64 J).

maintaining that things other than wisdom (or virtue) are neither good nor bad, or no more good than bad, and that benefit depends on right use of these other things by virtue.[41]

This point is, clearly, crucial for the Stoic position. We are benefited not by preferable indifferents but by *right use* of indifferents, which must mean effectiveness in selecting between indifferents, both preferable and dispreferable, as indicated in Diogenes' definition of happiness, just cited. What justifies the claim that virtue provides the basis for right use of indifferents? On this point, it makes sense to refer to the Stoic definition of virtue as knowledge or expertise, examined earlier (1.4). The virtuous person knows how to make right use of indifferents and how to select between them because of this expertise. As in the *Euthydemus* argument just cited, knowledge or wisdom makes the decisive difference and so (in the Stoic version of this argument, at least), it is knowledge, that is, virtue, that benefits, and counts as good, rather than the preferred indifferents. As we also saw earlier, virtue is expertise in leading a happy life; its goal is achieving the life of happiness, understood as the life according to nature. Virtue is conceived as a unitary mode of expertise, or an interconnected set of forms of expertise, which guides us towards the happy life.[42] This explains why virtue is seen as making the difference between happiness and its opposite, whereas the indifferents, preferred and dispreferred, do not make this difference, despite having objective value or disvalue.

These features of Stoic thinking, taken together, explain why the Stoics believe that the virtues, constitutively, benefit us, whereas the indifferents do not (more precisely, they neither benefit us or harm us).[43] The virtues are crucial expressions of human agency; they determine our judgements, character, motivation, our actions, and relationships to other people. More precisely, they constitute forms of knowledge or expertise and thus shape our agency in a way that constitutes 'right use' of indifferents and leads towards happiness, conceived as the life according to nature. Analogously, the vices harm us by preventing us from doing so. The indifferents, as a category, do not have this central role in our agency, in shaping our life and happiness or its opposite. The preferred indifferents constitute, one may say, the basic conditions or framework of a good human life: having life, good health, material goods and a certain kind of social context. Even the psychological ones, such as natural ability or good memory, only provide the basis for constructing a happy life.[44] This explains the Stoic view that the indifferents no more benefit us than they harm us. The preferred indifferents are, none the less, things that, if circumstances permit, all of us would naturally want

---

[41] Plato, *Euthd.* 281d–e. On this passage and its probable influence on Stoic thought, see Annas 1994; Long 1996: 22–32; Striker 1996: 316–24; Gill 2000a: 133–7; McCabe 2002; Russell 2012: 144–8, 190.
[42] See 1.4, esp. text to nn. 105–12, 133–46.   [43] See D.L. 7.102 (LS 58 A(4)).
[44] See text to nn. 11–13.

to form the fabric or material of our life. But they do not constitute central structuring expressions of our agency in the way the virtues do, and so they are not essential to leading a good human life; hence, it is possible to be happy without preferred indifferents.[45]

2.3 The Virtue-Indifferents Relationship Re-Examined

The preceding section sets out an overall statement of the virtue-indifferents relationship that is, I think, credible and consistent with the main evidence. In this section, I probe the theory more closely, taking account of criticisms and questions raised by ancient opponents and modern scholars, and considering possible responses to these challenges. Overall, I suggest that the Stoic theory is coherent and strongly supported and that it constitutes a powerful alternative to Aristotle's view on the contribution of goods other than virtue to happiness.[46]

The question on which I focus is this. The Stoics present the value of preferred indifferents as real and objective ('natural', as they put it). This value is also presented as distinct and independent of the use made of indifferents by virtue. The distinction between 'preferred' and 'dispreferred' is not based on whether the indifferents are used (or 'selected') virtuously or not. Thus, although Chrysippus presents indifferents as the 'material' of virtue, their value (positive or negative) is not defined by reference to this role but by reference to their intrinsic desirability as elements in a normal human life.[47] This point, taken on its own, seems clear enough from our evidence. However, this raises a potential problem for Stoic theory. We seem to have two independent standards, 'goodness' (applying to virtue, and happiness) and 'value', applying to indifferents. It is not entirely clear how these two standards are to be correlated, and what weight is to be given to each standard. As a result, it is unclear how to reconstruct the Stoic view of the practical deliberation of the virtuous person, and the role of the two kinds of factor in her considerations.[48]

Before considering possible responses to this problem, I highlight evidence suggesting that there is, indeed, a puzzle here that needs to be explained. In his account of Stoic ethics in On Ends 3,[49] Cicero makes two comments that underline the point that preferability constitutes an independent criterion of action and does so for the virtuous person. In On Ends 3.21–2, Cicero describes a process of ethical

---

[45] See D.L. 7.104 (LS 58 B(1)).

[46] On the contrast with Aristotle's view, see text to nn. 29–34, 48–52; also Ch. 6, text to nn. 80–91.

[47] See text to n. 8 and nn. 16–23. This aspect of Stoic thinking on indifferents is stressed by LS, vol. 1, pp. 357–9; Vogt 2014: 61–2; Klein 2015: 242–5.

[48] Klein 2015: 245–58 underlines this point.

[49] Like most scholars, I assume Cic. *Fin.* 3 is a broadly reliable account of Stoic ethics; for a different view, see Schmitz 2014, who sees the book as strongly shaped by Peripatetic ideas, transmitted through Antiochus.

development which leads someone to recognize the fundamental difference in value between virtue and happiness, on the one hand, and preferred indifferents, on the other, namely the difference between goodness and preferability.[50] However, he adds that preferability or its absence remains a valid ground of action, by inference, even for the virtuous person, who has completed the process of ethical development just described. As he puts it, 'all appropriate actions are aimed at our obtaining the primary objects of nature [preferable indifferents]'.[51] Later in his account, Cicero accentuates the same idea. He highlights the Stoic view that wise people sometimes rightly consider it appropriate to take their own lives in cases such as terminal or extreme illness. In such cases, as Cicero underlines, the wise act in line with the preponderance of preferable or dispreferable things. They decide that life is not worth living when there is more pain, illness or injury in prospect than good health.[52] It is, on the face of it, paradoxical that the wise or virtuous are presented as right to end their lives in this kind of situation, despite being happy, when the foolish would not be right to end their lives, under other circumstances, despite their folly and therefore their unhappiness.[53] However, the example brings out again the point that estimation of preferability and dispreferability provides a valid ground of action, and does so for those are virtuous.[54] By the same token, Cicero's comments raise the questions posed earlier, about how we should correlate the two standards of preferability and virtue and how we should conceive virtuous deliberation, on a Stoic view.

This question is also accentuated by one of the criticisms directed at Stoic thinking on the virtue-indifferents relation by their ancient philosophical opponents. There were several criticisms, most of which seem to go back to Carneades, a second-century BC Academic Sceptic, but which were perpetuated by later Platonic and Aristotelian thinkers.[55] One criticism is particularly relevant to the present topic. The kernel was a dilemma posed for the Stoic view: *either*, on their

---

[50] On this account, see 4.4.

[51] Cic. *Fin.* 3.22, trans. Annas and Woolf 2001; see Barney 2003: 312–13. Cicero's comment here is somewhat simplified or overstated, but the core point is valid. On 'appropriate actions', see 2.4, text to nn. 100–4.

[52] Cic. *Fin.* 3.59–61. On Stoic thinking on suicide, see also Sen. *Ep.* 58.35, Olympiodorus, *Commentary on Plato's Phaedo* 1.8.19–39. Stoics also recognize other (more socially directed) grounds for suicide; see D.L. 7.130, Cic. *Off.* 1.112 (also Reydams-Schils 2005: 45–8).

[53] Cic. *Fin.* 3.61; for this point (made from a more critical standpoint), see also Plu. *Sto. Rep.* 1042 D. The problem (or criticism) is that considerations of virtue (and happiness) and preferability seem to be running counter to each other.

[54] Cic. *Fin.* 3.60: 'From [indifferents] all appropriate actions proceed; and so it is with good reason that all our deliberations are said to be directed at them, including the question of our departing from life and remaining alive', trans. Annas and Woolf 2001. On Cic. *Fin.* 3.59–61, see also Cooper 1999: 534–6; Barney 2003: 313–14; Brennan 2005: 194–6, stressing the weight placed in this passage on preponderance of preferred indifferents.

[55] Other critics included Plutarch (1st–2nd cent. AD Platonist) and Alexander of Aphrodisias (Aristotelian commentator, flourished *c.* AD 200). For the main sources, see LS 64. On the debate, see Annas 1993: 395–403; Striker 1996: 239–48, 298–315; also (on 'Carneades' division), Annas 2007a. On these criticisms, see text to nn. 29–32 and n. 53 as well as the following discussion.

account, there are two overall goals in life (preferable indifferents and happiness, however defined) *or* the overall goal in life (happiness) differs from the reference-point (the explicit objective) of all purposive action.[56] Both of these options, as presented by the critics, were unacceptable to the Stoics. The Stoics posited only one overall goal in life, though one which could be characterized in different ways, for instance, as the life according to nature or as reasonable and consistent selection between indifferents.[57] Nor would they want to accept the idea that this overall goal was distinct from the reference-point of all purposive action, which Carneades, at least, presented as securing preferable indifferents. The object of criticism was the Stoic claim that preferable indifferents have intrinsic value and are appropriate objects of selection, without therefore being good (beneficial) or determining happiness.

This criticism could be directed at any formulation of mainstream (Chrysippean) Stoic thinking on virtue and indifferents.[58] However, it seems to have been directed especially at certain definitions of happiness or the goal of life offered by second-century BC Stoic thinkers, including two successive heads of the school, Diogenes and Antipater:

> And Diogenes: 'to be reasonable in the selection and rejection of things according to nature'...And Antipater: 'to live invariably selecting things according to nature and rejecting things contrary to nature'. He often defined it thus as well: 'invariably and unswervingly to do everything in one's power for the attainment of naturally preferable things'.[59] (Archedemus): to live 'selecting the greatest and most important things in accordance with nature...'[60]

These definitions of happiness were probably intended as clarifications of the more standard ones, such as 'life according to nature (or virtue)', and not as replacements of them.[61] Cicero, summing up the Stoic position, combines both formulations:

> We are left with the conclusion that the final good is a life in which one applies knowledge of those things that happen by nature, selecting those in accordance with nature and rejecting those contrary to nature, that is, a life in agreement and consistent with nature.[62]

---

[56] Plu. *Comm. Not.* 1070 F–1071 B (LS 64 C(1–6)); Cic. *Fin.* 3.22. See also Striker 1996: 241–2, 301–4.

[57] On Stoic formulations of the goal in life, see Ch. 1, text to nn. 63–7.

[58] The criticism would not, however, apply to Aristo's non-standard version of Stoic ethics (text to n. 7).

[59] Stob. 6a, 2.76.9–15, IG: 132 (see also LS 58 K).

[60] Archedemus was another 2nd-cent. Stoic. Clement, *Stromateis* 2.21 (*SVF* 3.21), trans. Barney 2003: 305.

[61] Striker 1996: 305–6, argues that they are not properly regarded as definitions of happiness but statements about it, which presuppose the standard definitions.

[62] Cic. *Fin.* 3.31 (LS 64 A). The first phrase incorporates a definition of happiness ascribed to Chrysippus: 'living in accordance with experience of what happens by nature' (Stob. 6a, 2.76.5–6).

However, the second-century definitions seem to have been innovative in including reference to selection of indifferents in their accounts of the goal of life; and this feature especially gave rise to the objection that the Stoics operate with two conceptions of the goal: happiness and indifferents.

How cogent is this criticism? One could argue that it misses its target in certain respects, and that the definitions already incorporate features which, in effect, meet these objections.[63] This is so especially if we assume that these accounts presuppose the older definitions and their connotations. The Stoics might have replied, in response to the first criticism, that the goal of life was not securing preferred indifferents, as Carneades assumed, but selecting between indifferents 'reasonably' (Diogenes' definition) and 'invariably' (both of Antipater's definitions). In effect, these definitions restate the standard Stoic view that happiness is constituted not by securing preferred indifferents but by 'right use' of indifferents.[64] The terms 'reasonable' and 'invariable' (or 'consistent') can be seen as referring to ideas which are either standard formulations of happiness or are typical attributes of happiness defined as the life according to nature or virtue.[65] Hence, the response might have been that Carneades' criticism is misdirected at the Stoic definition, both in its standard and second-century versions. There are not two Stoic goals but one, which combines the characteristics which Carneades subdivides. As stated by Diogenes, and by Antipater in his first formulation, the single goal is selecting indifferents *in a certain way*, that is, reasonably or invariably,[66] and so the criticism of having two goals misreads the theory. A response of this kind is suggested by a comment which seems to come from Antipater: 'the wise (*phronimōs*) selection and acceptance of these things is the goal in life, whereas the [preferred] things themselves and the obtaining of them are not the goal but are given as a kind of material having selective value'.[67]

How far does this response address the ancient criticism that the Stoics operate with two goals and the modern concern that Stoicism operates with two independent standards, goodness and 'value'? The response clarifies the Stoic position to some extent. It underlines the point that acting virtuously and selecting indifferents are not two, distinct, activities, even if the two aspects are conceptually

---

[63] It is generally supposed that the definition of Diogenes and the first definition of Antipater preceded and aroused the criticisms of Carneades and that Antipater's second definition responded to his criticisms. See LS, vol. 1, pp. 408–9, Striker 1996: 301–2. (Diogenes died *c.* 152, and Antipater was head *c.* 152–*c.* 129; Carneades was active mid-second century and retired in 137; all dates BC.)

[64] See text to nn. 40–1. For a later statement of this view, see Sen. *Ep.* 92.11–13 (LS 64 J).

[65] For 'living consistently' as the goal, see Stob. 6a, 2.75.11–12 (LS 63 B(1)); also 'consistency' (*homologia*) in Cic. *Fin.* 3.21; on rationality as characteristic of human and cosmic nature (and thus of 'the life according to nature'), see Ch. 1, text to nn. 72–86.

[66] For this characterization of the Stoic conception of virtue, see Inwood and Donini 1999: 729.

[67] Plu. *Comm. Not.* 1071 B, trans. Cherniss 1976; the idea of 'selective value' is ascribed to Antipater in Stob. 7f, 2.83.10–84.2. The distinction between 'selecting' (or 'doing everything in your power') and 'obtaining' also evokes Antipater's second definition (text to n. 60; also Cic. *Fin.* 3.22, taken with LS, vol. 1, pp. 408–9, Striker 1996: 301–2).

distinguishable. Acting virtuously consists, in part at least, in selecting between indifferents in an appropriate way, that is, 'reasonably' or 'consistently'. The expertise of virtue consists, again in part, in correct selection of indifferents. Presumably, it is for this reason that Stoic thinkers describe indifferents as providing the 'material' of appropriate action and virtue (and happiness).[68] However, this response takes us only so far in making sense of the Stoic view. It still leaves open the question of the criteria to be applied in making a correct or virtuous selection between indifferents. Should we suppose that the only relevant criteria are supplied by the preferability and dispreferability of the indifferents involved in any situation?

I think it is reasonable to think that the virtuous person has regard to the preferability and dispreferability of the indifferents involved in any situation. This, after all, is what is stated, emphatically, by Cicero, in the passages cited earlier in *On Ends* 3; and this is also suggested by other passages in the ancient ethical summaries.[69] Indeed, it seems likely that the expertise of the virtuous person consists (in part again) in giving the correct weight to the preferability and dispreferability of the relevant indifferents; this is also implied by Cicero's discussion of the wise who decide (correctly) to end their lives. However, does it follow that this is the *only* criterion applied by the virtuous person? This suggestion has been made, by Rachel Barney; indeed, she proposes that the virtuous person, in Stoic ethics, is the one who focuses, correctly, on maximizing her own stock of preferable indifferents (health, property, and so on).[70] Tad Brennan also considers, at least, the same idea.[71] However, both Barney and Brennan, while making this suggestion, also acknowledge that it runs counter to some other prominent strands in Stoic ethics.[72] I have to say that I do not consider it at all plausible to think that the virtuous person is conceived in this way in Stoic ethics (as aiming, exclusively, to maximize preferable indifferents for herself), though it is reasonable to see the virtuous person as making a correct estimate of the preferability of indifferents (for others as well as herself) in her situation at any one time. However, on my view, the question arises of the other criteria drawn on by the virtuous person. What other considerations are brought in and how do they relate to those of preferability and dispreferability? And, if the virtuous person deploys criteria other than preferability, does this not land us back with the problem originally posed, that of Stoic ethics having two standards, one of goodness and another of 'value'?[73]

---

[68] See text to nn. 8 and 67. On the other part of virtuous deliberation, see text to nn. 74-5.

[69] See Cic. *Fin.* 3.22, 59-61 (text to nn. 50-4); also Stob. 7c, 2.82.20-83.9 (LS 58 C(3-4)), 8a, 2.86.12-14.

[70] Barney 2003: 321-5, also 304-19.   [71] Brennan 2005: 194-8.

[72] E.g. the virtuous surrender of one's own preferable indifferents by Stoic figures such as Regulus (Cic. *Off.* 3.99-115); see Barney 2003: 319-20; Brennan 2005: 203-4.

[73] See text to n. 48.

In responding to this question, the first move, I think, is to recall the Stoic accounts of virtue as a form of expertise, discussed in Chapter 1. Virtue is defined, generically, in terms of knowledge of what is to be done and not done (or what is good and bad, and neither); the cardinal virtues are defined as exercising this knowledge in the four main areas relevant to each virtue. Virtue is also defined as knowledge of how to lead a happy life, that is, a life according to nature, both human and universal. In Stoic accounts of virtue as well as happiness, we find indications of the main connotations of human nature (namely rationality and sociability) and of universal nature (namely, structure, order, and wholeness, and care for oneself and others of one's kind).[74] The idea of virtue as knowledge or expertise in selecting indifferents is less prominent in Stoic accounts of virtue, though it is implied in the definitions of happiness or the goal of life by the second-century Stoics discussed earlier. Also, Cicero, summing up Stoic ideas on happiness, brings together knowledge of how to select between indifferents and how to realize the life according to nature.[75] How should we understand the relationship between these two conceptions of virtue as knowledge or expertise? What makes the best sense of this evidence, I think, is the idea that virtue as knowledge of how to realize a happy life shapes or informs knowledge of how to select between indifferents. The virtuous person needs to have a correct under-standing of preferability and dispreferability, and to be able to weigh this factor, as it affects herself and the other people involved, in the specific situation in which she finds herself. But what determines her selection of which indifferents to allocate to herself and others is her judgement about what course of action is right under the circumstances. Her judgement about what is right is shaped by an understanding of what kind of actions are in line with the virtues, and, more broadly, what kind of actions contribute to living a happy life (a life according to nature), with the connotations already outlined.

This account of the Stoic conception of virtue as expertise may seem, in broad outline, a credible one. But it raises certain questions. First, what evidence supports this account? More precisely, what evidence supports the account just offered of the relationship between virtue as expertise in living a happy life and expertise in selecting indifferents? Second, this picture of Stoic thinking raises certain conceptual questions. How, for instance, should we reconstruct the delib-eration or decision-making process of a virtuous person, on this view? Should we suppose that ideas about virtue, happiness, and indifferents form part of her conscious thought-processes in planning or carrying out actions? Or do these considerations figure in a distinct process of reflection about how to shape one's

---

[74] See 1.3–4.
[75] 'We are left with the conclusion that the final good is a life in which one applies knowledge of those things that happen by nature, selecting those in accordance with nature and rejecting those contrary to nature, that is, a life in agreement and consistent with nature' (Cic. *Fin.* 3.13, (LS 64 A); see also text to n. 62).

life that informs practical deliberation, regardless of the form that deliberation itself takes? Alternatively, do these categories provide ways of analysing a deliberative process which is conceived by the person concerned in more specific and localized terms?[76] The second set of questions have been much debated in connection with Aristotelian ethics. Scholars have considered whether ideas about happiness as the goal of life form part of the virtuous person's deliberative processes or whether these ideas constitute ways of analysing forms of practical deliberation conceived by the person in more specific ways.[77] These questions also arise in connection with Stoic accounts of deliberation.

In addressing these questions, I focus initially on the evidence for Stoic thinking on indifferents already considered, and then discuss them in connection with the guidance on practical deliberation offered in Cicero's On Duties.[78] Support for the view I am proposing can be found in the second-century BC formulations of happiness discussed earlier. I have suggested that these formulations, which refer to indifferents as part of the account of happiness, are designed to bring out two key features of (mainstream) Stoic thinking. They underline that preferability constitutes a valid ground for action (more precisely, for 'selection') by the virtuous person. At the same time, they also stress that the overall goal in life is not simply maximizing preferable indifferents, for oneself or others, but doing so 'reasonably', 'wisely', or 'invariably' (or 'consistently'), that is, in a way that is characteristic of the virtuous and happy person.[79] Antipater seems especially to underline these two points, accentuating the significance for the happy life of gaining preferable indifferents, while also stressing the importance of doing so in a certain way ('invariably and unswervingly').[80] The latter point was also reinforced, it seems, by drawing a distinction between the localized aim of a specific action (gaining indifferents) and the ultimate goal (doing so virtuously, and in a way that realizes the life according to nature).[81] This reading is strengthened if we assume that the second-century formulations presuppose, rather than replace, the older definition of happiness as the life according to nature.[82] The virtuous person selects between indifferents in a way that is shaped by her understanding of how to bring about a life according to nature, that is, by performing right actions in line with virtue. On this interpretation, the second-century definitions indicate how Stoic accounts of virtue as expertise recognize the significance of preferability

---

[76] For 'split-level' interpretations of Stoic ethical deliberation, see text to n. 92.

[77] See Price 2005; 2011: 189–250.

[78] For discussion of these questions in connection with On Duties, see text to nn. 86–93; also text to nn. 143–55, 161–5, 245–8.

[79] See text to nn. 64–6.

[80] Antipater's definitions: 'to live invariably selecting things according to nature and rejecting things contrary to nature' and 'invariably and unswervingly to do everything in one's power for the attainment of naturally preferable things' (Stob. 6a, 2.76.11–15, IG: 132; also LS 58 K).

[81] See Cic. Fin. 3.22 (LS 64 F(2–4)).

[82] For this suggestion, see Striker 1996: 304–6. See also text to n. 61.

as a factor in virtuous decision-making, but without introducing two, competing standards.[83]

Although I think the second-century formulations can be interpreted in this way, I recognize that the evidence is limited in extent and open to various interpretations;[84] hence, I focus for the remainder of this chapter on Cicero's *On Duties*. This text has several advantages for considering the question of the criteria of virtuous decision-making. As explained shortly, it is the only surviving, extended Stoic-style discussion of practical deliberation (in Stoic terms, performing 'appropriate action').[85] Also, both the overall framework and the specific guidance offered illustrate the general approach outlined here. In providing criteria for decision-making, and for determining what is 'right' (*honestum*), in specific circumstances, Cicero refers primarily to accounts of the virtues and the kind of actions characteristic of the virtues. He does not explicitly take up the question of the relationship of virtue to happiness. However, the discussion highlights repeatedly several of the main connotations of the Stoic idea of happiness as the life according to nature and of virtue as expertise in bringing about such a life. As discussed in Chapter 1, *On Duties* refers, in several ways, to the idea of human nature as a combination of rationality and sociability. It also alludes to the idea that virtue is marked by a combination of structure, order, and wholeness, that is, one of the main connotations of universal nature in Stoic thought.[86] A notable feature of *On Duties*, especially in Books One and Three, is prominent use of the idea of nature as an ethically significant one, in ways that can be linked with the standard Stoic connotations of this idea. Thus, the discussion builds into the consideration of what is right not only the criterion of what is in line with the virtues but also the idea that exercise of the virtues constitutes a means of bringing about the life according to nature.[87] The work also incorporates, in all three books, in different ways, consideration of indifferents as a factor in practical deliberation. The discussion assumes the mainstream Stoic distinction between preferable and dispreferable indifferents and the idea that preferability constitutes, in principle, a ground for action. However, it also assumes that, in selecting between indifferents, the salient criterion for a virtuous person is what is right, that is, what counts as an action characteristic of the virtues. This criterion is reinforced by other ideas, notably, reference to ideas about what is 'natural', in one of several ethically significant senses.[88] Thus, overall, *On Duties* both confirms and illustrates the conception of virtuous decision-making proposed here. The framework gives scope for applying the criterion of preferability, in ways that affect both oneself

---

[83] For the 'two-standards' criticism of Stoic theory, see text to nn. 56–7.

[84] See LS 58 K and 64. For divergent readings, see Striker 1996: 241–8, 298–315; Annas 1993: 399–403; Barney 2003: 304–19.

[85] See text to nn. 112–17.

[86] See 1.4, esp. text to nn. 160–77, 194. See also text to nn. 161–5 in this chapter.

[87] See text to nn. 121–3.   [88] See text to nn. 156–65, 211–16.

and others. However, in virtuous decision-making, the central focus lies in determining the allocation of indifferents which is correct or right, that is, which is characteristic of the virtues and, more broadly, which promotes the life according to nature.

As well as offering a general framework for ethical decision-making, *On Duties* also offers insights into the thought-processes of the person deciding. This work does not set out to offer a theoretical analysis of virtuous decision-making; however, it offers guidance for someone aiming to make progress towards virtue, and in doing so indicates the kind of considerations that should inform virtuous deliberation.[89] What indications does it offer about the thought-processes involved? On the one hand, it suggests that, in many cases, the focus is on specific features of the relevant situation and on the indifferents involved. For instance, the guidance on performing generous acts urges close and detailed consideration of which indifferents should be allocated to the people involved on the basis of their claims and relationship to the person concerned. This guidance assumes that the person involved should assess the (objective or natural) preferability or disprefer-ability of different elements in the situation. It is also suggested that the person concerned should take account of more general factors which bear on the situ-ation. These may include an understanding of what is involved in exercising the virtue of generosity, conceived as a subdivision of justice, and also of the nature and basis of human sociability, which underpins the various kinds of relationships we form with others.[90] Reference to these factors, along with other features in the discussion noted earlier, evokes the yet broader idea of aiming to live a happy life, in the sense of the life according to nature and virtue, as conceived in Stoic ethics.[91] The implication is that these more general considerations should inform the specific decision-making, including the selection between indifferents, whether these considerations are taken into account in advance or at the time. Thus, the presentation of practical deliberation in *On Duties* does not support the 'split-level' analysis of Stoic decision-making sometimes offered, in which the agent gives attention only to specific factors, without reference to broader con-siderations. It also does not bear out the further idea sometimes maintained, that the agent focuses solely on selection of indifferents, based on their preferability, without reference to consideration of questions of right and wrong, the virtues, or 'nature', in one of several ethically significant senses.[92] I think the picture offered

---

[89] On the type of guidance offered and the idea of ethical progress, see text to nn. 126–8, 163–77.

[90] See discussion of Cic. *Off.* 1.42, taken with 1.50–9, in text to nn. 136–47, 156–60.

[91] See text to nn. 161–5.

[92] For 'split-level' accounts, see Cooper 1999: 534; Barney 2003: 317–19. For a view of Stoic (virtuous) deliberation as focused solely on (maximizing) preferable indifferents, see Barney 2003: 304–19, 321–5. However, Barney elsewhere in her discussion highlights the idea of nature as ethically significant (2003: 332–6). See also text to nn. 76–7; and text to nn. 143–55, 208–11.

by *On Duties* can be confirmed by other evidence for Stoic ethical guidance, including that of Seneca, considered later.[93]

This view of the picture of ethical deliberation given in *On Duties* is presented in full in the following two sections. I close this section by returning to the broader questions about the virtue-indifferents relation raised here. This discussion has taken its starting-point from the criticism that the Stoic ethical framework operates with two distinct standards (goodness and 'value') or two distinct conceptions of the goal in life (virtue-based happiness or preferred indifferents) which are not effectively integrated or correlated with each other. My response has been to maintain that, as regards standards, there are, indeed, two distinct standards; but that Stoic ethics offers a clear account of how these are correlated or integrated with each other. The expertise of the virtuous person includes correct assessment of preferability and dispreferability, as a factor taken on its own. But her expertise also includes the ability to consider which allocation of indifferents (to oneself and others), in a given situation, counts as right, in line with the virtues, and such as to promote the life according to nature. (Cicero's *On Duties* is designed to help someone learn how to develop this expertise.) In this respect, Stoic ethics does not operate with two conceptions of the overall goal in life. There is one goal (happiness understood as the life according to nature or virtue), and the indifferents selected form the 'material' deployed to achieve this goal.[94] Hence, although the idea of nature functions in, at least, two senses in this framework, namely as things according to nature or preferred indifferents and the life according to nature, these senses, while distinct, are coherently related.[95]

The criticisms sometimes directed at the Stoic theory seem, in fact, to be more appropriately levelled at Aristotle's ethical framework. As outlined earlier, Aristotle in the *Nicomachean Ethics* initially defines happiness by reference to virtue, but then adds the further requirement of an adequate level of bodily and external goods. Aristotle's final position is clear enough, and was generally adopted by his later ancient followers; but he reaches this conclusion through a nuanced and balanced reflection that leaves several salient points open.[96] For instance, at different times, he presents these other goods as valuable both as instruments of virtuous action and as independent contributors to happiness, without explicitly distinguishing these types of value or their significance for his conclusion. Also, while presenting the other goods as independently valuable, at least sometimes, he does not make it clear how this kind of value is integrated or correlated with that of virtue. He does not offer a further, distinct, scale of value, which would enable the two types of value to be assessed in relation to each other.

---

[93] See Sen. *Ep.* 94–5, and text to nn. 166–77.

[94] See text to nn. 48, 55–7, for the broad question addressed; see text to nn. 8, 68, on the idea of indifferents as the 'material' of virtue.

[95] On the various senses of 'nature' as a significant notion in Stoic ethics, see Ch. 3, esp. 3.3.

[96] See 1.2, text to nn. 29–34.

The Stoic position is, I think, clearer on all these points. Preferred indifferents ('things according to nature') have independent value; they are not valuable only as instruments of virtue, though they are properly used in this way. On the other hand, they do not determine happiness or its opposite; the designation of 'indifferents' is based on this point.[97] There is a clear contrast, on this point, with virtue, understood as expertise in selection of indifferents and in leading a happy life, which does determine happiness or its opposite. In this respect, virtue, like happiness, but unlike preferred indifferents, counts as good. Hence, the question of how to weigh virtue against (in Aristotelian terms) bodily and external goods does not arise in Stoic ethics. On all these points, the Stoic position is clear and determinate, where the Aristotelian one is left open. Indeed, although we do not know exactly how far the early Stoics responded directly to Aristotelian writings or ideas,[98] it is possible that the Stoic position might have been designed specifically to avoid the ambiguities or gaps of the Aristotelian treatment.

2.4 Practical Deliberation: Cicero, *On Duties* 1

I now focus on Cicero's *On Duties*, taken as illustrating Stoic thinking on virtue and indifferents. However, the formal subject of this work is not indifferents but 'appropriate actions' (*kathēkonta* in Greek and *officia* in Latin). What does this idea involve and how is it related to 'indifferents'? In ancient summaries of Stoic ethics, these two notions are coupled with each other and discussed after the central ideas of virtue and happiness (or the goal of life).[99] The two ideas are rather different in kind: one (appropriate actions) consists of acts that human beings, and other animals, characteristically perform, and the other (indifferents) consists of conditions of life that have positive or negative value.[100] However, they have in common the fact that they express typical patterns of human (and animal) action and motivation and that their ethical quality depends on the exercise of virtue.

Appropriate actions are defined, generically, as actions which have 'a reasonable justification'.[101] Indifferents are defined as things which are neither good nor bad, but which, according to most Stoic thinkers, have positive or negative value (LS 58). Both ideas can be used in connection with human beings and other animals, though they are worked out in their complete form only in the case of adult human beings, conceived as rational and sociable animals.[102] The term 'appropriate actions' (*kathēkonta*) can be applied to non-human animals, and

---

[97] See further on this point, Ch. 6, text to nn. 78–91.   [98] See Introd. text to n. 14.
[99] See D.L. 7.102–9 (following 7.87–101); Stob. 7–8 (following 5–6); Cic. *Fin.* 3.50–61 (following 3.26–39, 42–9).
[100] On this conception of indifferents, see text to n. 44.   [101] Stob. 8, 2.85.14–15 (LS 59 B(1)).
[102] On the Stoic distinction between non-human animals (and human children) and adult humans, see Inwood 1985: 66–91; Gill 1991: 184–92.

even plants, as well as human beings, both children and adults. In all cases, the actions (or behaviour or processes) are those which are characteristic of these forms of life; for this reason, Long and Sedley translate this term as 'proper functions'.[103] In the case of adult humans, this category includes social actions such as 'honouring parents, brothers and country, spending time with friends', and self-related actions such as 'looking after one's health, and one's sense-organs'.[104] The category of indifferents is, normally, subdivided into 'preferred' or 'preferable' indifferents (or 'things according to nature'), such as health and property, and 'dispreferred' or 'dispreferable' indifferents (or things 'contrary to nature'), such as illness and poverty.[105] Like appropriate actions, this idea is deployed in connection with non-human animals and children as well as adult humans. Hence, in the Stoic theory of development as appropriation, animals and humans (both children and adults) are presented as instinctively drawn towards 'things according to nature' and away from 'things contrary to nature'.[106] The category of 'things according to nature' (or 'preferred indifferents') includes all the elements typically regarded as contributing to a rich and inclusive human life, apart from virtue and happiness.

A further, and crucial, point of similarity between indifferents and appropriate actions concerns their relation to virtue. Whereas virtue (and happiness) count as good in Stoic ethics, indifferents, even preferred ones, and appropriate actions are classified as being neither good nor bad.[107] Whether or not they contribute to a good (happy) life is determined by virtue, as a form of expertise. It is the exercise of virtue that converts an appropriate action into a 'perfectly correct action' (*katorthōma*).[108] It is also the exercise of virtue that ensures that indifferents, both preferred or dispreferred, contribute to a good life overall.[109] Hence, although preferred indifferents (and, by implication, appropriate actions) have positive value, there is no attempt in Stoic ethics to systematize their value or to calculate their contribution to a good life *regardless* of whether they are exercised in a virtuous way.[110] Thus, as regards appropriate actions:

> The virtuous person's function is not to look after his parents and honour them in other respects but to do so on the basis of wisdom. Just as the care of health is

---

[103] See LS 59, esp. 59 B (Stob. 8, 2.85.13–86.4) and 59 C (D.L. 7.107).
[104] D.L. 7.108–9 (LS 59 E(1–2)).
[105] See LS 58 A–E; for a variant view (that of Aristo) see LS 58 F–G and text to n. 7. See also 2.2.
[106] See Cic. *Fin.* 3.16, 20 (also text to nn. 19–23).
[107] See D.L. 7.101–3 (LS 58 A) (indifferents); LS 59 F and H (also LS, vol. 1, pp. 366–7) (appropriate actions).
[108] See Stob. 8, 2.85.18–86.4 (LS 59 B(4)); Stob. 11a, 2.93.14–18 (LS 59 K).
[109] Hence, famously, the Stoic wise person can be happy even 'on the rack' (of torture), i.e. without preferred indifferents (other than life) (Cic. *Fin.* 3.42, also 5.84).
[110] Barney's 'deliberative sufficiency' or 'maximizing' interpretation of Stoic ethics (2003: 323–5) would involve this kind of systematization; however, for criticism of this interpretation, see text to nn. 69–72, 144–7.

common to the doctor and the layman, but caring for health in the medical way is peculiar to the expert, so too the honouring of parents is common to the virtuous and non-virtuous person, but to do so on the basis of wisdom is peculiar to the wise person.[111]

In exploring Stoic thinking on virtue, indifferents, and appropriate actions, I focus on Cicero's *On Duties*. Why turn to Cicero's *On Duties* for this topic, rather than *On Ends* 3, which is Cicero's most authoritative summary of Stoic ethics. The reason is that *On Duties* is directly focused on the question being examined here (the relationship between appropriate actions, indifferent, and virtue), whereas this topic is treated in a more generalized way in *On Ends* 3 and the other summaries of Stoic ethical doctrine.[112] Also, as brought out here, the approach taken to this topic in *On Duties* is consistent with the overall Stoic ethical framework.

Cicero's *On Duties* is, in fact, the only surviving extended Stoic-style ancient discussion of appropriate actions.[113] Books 1 and 2 are presented as closely based on a three-book work by the last Stoic head Panaetius, *peri tou kathēkontos* (*On Appropriate Action*). (Like other Hellenistic Stoic treatises, this work no longer survives.) Book 3 is presented as Cicero's own composition, though completing a task Panaetius set himself.[114] Can we take *On Duties* as a reliable indicator of mainstream Stoic ethical thinking? Although it is obvious that Cicero has elaborated the material, especially in Book 3, the main lines of theory seem to reflect Panaetius' work. Panaetius himself has sometimes been seen as rather unorthodox; but I follow some recent scholarship in seeing his ethical approach as largely in line with earlier Stoic thought, going back to Zeno and Chrysippus.[115] *On Duties*, like the Panaetian work, it would seem, is not framed as a survey of the key Stoic categories, as the ethical summaries are, but as a work of guidance, designed to inform practical deliberation and the shaping of one's life. Like other writings on Stoic guidance, it is intended to promote what the Stoics call 'progress' towards ethical understanding (that is, towards virtue or wisdom and happiness).[116] Specifically, it is addressed to Cicero's son, then studying philosophy in Athens,[117] and it draws extensively on Cicero's own knowledge and experience of practical life. However, I think the approach adopted by Cicero also reflects Stoic thinking in general on appropriate actions, indifferents, and virtues.

---

[111] S. E. *M.* 111.200–1 (LS 59 G(1–2)). For an analogous point as regards indifferents, see text to nn. 34–42.
[112] See refs. in n. 107.
[113] Hence, the work figures prominently in discussions of this topic, e.g. Inwood 1999: 112–27; Brennan 2005: 203–32.
[114] See *Off.* 1.6–10, 3.7–12; Dyck 1996: 17–24; Gourinat 2014; Veillard 2014.
[115] See Tieleman 2007.
[116] On Stoic thinking on ethical progress, see Inwood and Donini 1999: 724–36; and Roskam 2005.
[117] See Cic. *Off.* 1.1.–4.

The main lines of approach to this topic are set out in Book 1, and are then extended, in different ways, in Books 2–3. In offering guidance on performing appropriate actions the main reference-point, used to structure the whole work, is the idea of the virtues, specifically the four cardinal virtues. Brief general accounts of the virtues are combined with more extended illustrations of specific actions presented as characteristic of the virtues.[118] Although the virtues provide the main structural framework, this is linked with a second theme. This is nature, particularly human nature, conceived as rational and sociable, and potentially ordered and structured. This theme is developed with reference to appropriation, social relations, and the theory of the four roles (*personae*).[119] In connection with this theme too, general statements are combined with specific illustrations. What scope does this framework offer for consideration of indifferents (preferred and dispreferred) and selection between them? In a summary of the work, Cicero suggests that the first book centres on what is *honestum* (right), the second on 'advantages' (*utilia*, that is, 'preferred indifferents'), and the third on cases of (apparent) conflict between the two.[120] In fact, the theme of the relationship between virtue and indifferents figures in different ways in all three books, more or less explicitly. In Book 1, for instance, guidance on determining what is right (in line with the virtues) involves selection between indifferents. More precisely, it involves selection regarding the type and level of indifferent to be allocated to each person affected by the action, including the agent herself.

I discuss shortly the approach taken in Book 1, and subsequently applied in the two other books. But first I raise the question how, in broad terms, this approach is related to Stoic thinking more generally, on appropriate actions and indifferents and, to some extent, on virtue and happiness. As highlighted earlier, in Stoic ethics, there is no attempt to provide an evaluative framework for assessing appropriate actions *irrespective* of the virtue (or vice) being exercised. Appropriate actions, like preferred indifferents, are only, as one might put it, 'in principle' contributors to a good or happy life, depending on whether or not virtue is exercised in connection with them.[121] Thus, it makes sense, that, in offering guidance on performing appropriate actions, Cicero (like Panaetius) cites the virtues and actions characteristic of the virtues as the primary indicators of appropriate actions that can form part of a good life.[122] Stoic thinking on virtue and happiness, discussed in Chapter 1, also explains why *On Duties* incorporates the theme of nature, alongside that of the virtues. Virtue is standardly presented as

---

[118] See Cic. *Off.* 1.18–19 (wisdom); 20–60 (justice); 60–92 (greatness of spirit, the Panaetian version of courage); and 93–151 (the fitting, *decorum*, the Panaetian version of moderation). As brought out in the synopsis in Griffin and Atkins 1991: xlviii–li, the four virtues provide the main structure for the whole work.

[119] See text to n. 133, and nn. 156–60, 212–16 (also Ch. 1, text to nn. 158–68).

[120] Cic. *Off.* 1.9–10, cited in text to n. 135, and *Off.* 3.7.   [121] See text to nn. 107–11.

[122] See LS, vol. 1, p. 368 on the consistency of this feature with Stoic ethical thinking more generally.

the expertise that brings about the happy life, conceived as the life according to nature, with the characteristics of nature brought out in *On Duties* 1, especially the combination of rationality and sociability (1.4). The references to nature in *On Duties* 1 have the function, in part at least, of indicating the kind of human life that is shaped by the exercise of virtue.[123] How does the further theme of indifferents relate to this framework? Preferred indifferents (and indeed dispreferred ones) contribute to the good life to the extent to which they are deployed with virtue, as shown in the idea of virtue making 'right use' of indifferents. Put differently, virtue as expertise in leading a happy life determines correct selection between indifferents.[124] Hence, in *On Duties* 1, appropriate actions informed by virtue involve selection between indifferents and (correct) allocation of preferred and dispreferred indifferents to those involved in the actions. These points, of course, require further specification with reference to *On Duties*. However, they show how the approach of *On Duties* is linked with the wider theoretical framework of Stoic ethics.

There is one further preliminary point to be made. It should not be supposed that, in presenting actions characteristic of the virtues, Cicero thinks that he is offering a definitive or authoritative specification of such actions. In Stoic terms, he does not claim to be specifying 'perfectly correct actions' (*katorthōmata*), which only the wise person can determine in any given situation. Cicero is explicit that he does not operate at this level; he neither claims to be wise nor claims to write for those who are wise. He is writing for those (such as his son, he hopes) who aim to 'make progress' towards gaining the expertise of virtue.[125] This is a stance, it seems, that Panaetius also, typically, adopted.[126] Of course, Cicero, like Panaetius and other Stoic thinkers writing on this subject, is likely to have thought that the specific 'appropriate actions' presented as right have a good prima facie chance of being what a wise person might have done in the relevant circumstances. But a debate presented by Cicero in *On Duties* 3 shows that different Stoic heads (Diogenes and Antipater) might disagree about what actions should count as right in a specific situation, even when applying the same criterion of consistency with virtue.[127] This does not mean that Stoic guidance on this subject is pointless. But it does mean that Stoic guidance differs from, at least, some modern moral theoretical discussions which purport to establish precise rules or formulas for determining which actions are right in a specific kind of situation.[128]

I now set out the approach of *On Duties* 1 more fully and illustrate the method with reference to Cicero's discussion of the virtue of generosity, the

---

[123] See text to nn. 161–5.   [124] See text to nn. 40–1, 80–8.
[125] See Cic. *Off.* 1.4, 1.7–8, 1.46, 3.13–16. On the distinction between 'appropriate actions' and 'perfectly correct actions', see LS 59 B.
[126] See Sen. *Ep.* 116.5; also Gill 1988: 170–1.   [127] See Cic. *Off.* 3.50–7; also text to nn. 229–33.
[128] See Inwood 1999: 98–104, 107–110, 120–7. On rules, right action, and virtue ethics (ancient and modern), see Hursthouse 1999: ch. 1; Russell 2009: part 1; Annas 2011: 41–51.

actively benevolent dimension of justice. The project of Book 1 is to help someone to deliberate on whether a course of action under consideration is 'right' (*honestum*).[129] How, broadly speaking, does the book do this? After introducing the idea of the four cardinal virtues, it is explained that specific duties (appropriate actions) can be derived from each of these virtues in turn, although the interdependence of the virtues is also recognized: 'Although these four [virtues] are bound together and interwoven, specific kinds of duty [appropriate action] have their origin in each [virtue] individually'.[130] The exposition typically takes this form. There is a brief general statement of the main character of each of the virtues; this corresponds to what is sometimes presented as the 'heading' or 'topic' (*kephalaion*) of each virtue, in the accounts of the virtues found in the summaries of ethical doctrines.[131] As pointed out in Chapter 1, each of the four cardinal virtues is subdivided in *On Duties* 1 between the core quality of the virtue and a second characteristic, which is more socially directed.[132] Cicero then discusses the kind of actions in which the virtue is expressed, referring to the salient features of the virtues. He illustrates the discussion by referring to specific people and situations from Greek and Roman history and his own experience, providing particularized instances of the kind of actions discussed. A further dimension of Book I, also illustrated in Chapter 1, is reference to several general ideas of nature which are relevant to the virtues and the actions typical of them. The exposition starts with a short account of development conceived as appropriation, based on the idea of human nature as constitutively rational and sociable, and identifying four in-built human motives underlying the four cardinal virtues (1.11–15). A second idea, discussed more fully shortly, is that all human beings, as rational and sociable, form a single fellowship or community, which underpins more limited, though closer, forms of human association, such as family, friendship, and political bond (1.50–9). A third is the idea that human life should be lived in the awareness that we have four, interconnected roles (*personae*). These are our common human character (as rational and sociable), our individual talents, inclinations and character, and our specific social context in life, both that in which we find ourselves, and that which is chosen, if we are able to choose our role in life. If we are to realize the fourth virtue, presented as doing what is 'fitting', in the Panaetian scheme, or indeed any of the virtues, we need to harmonize all these roles to each other, including the two types of 'nature', universal and individual (1.107–15). The idea of nature, as presented in these various forms, provides a

---

[129] Cic. *Off.* 1.9–10, 3.7.

[130] Cic. *Off.* 1.15, trans. Griffin and Atkins 1991, with my addition in square brackets; the point is restated near the end of Book 1 (1.152).

[131] See Stob. 5b5, 2.63.6–24 (LS 61 D); also Stob. 5b1–2, 2.59.4–60.2, 60.9–24 (LS 61 H); also Ch. 1, text to n. 145.

[132] Ch. 1, text to nn. 169–77, suggesting a link between this pattern and the Stoic characterization of human nature as rational and sociable.

broader theoretical background for the discussion of the virtues and the actions characteristic of the virtues.[133] Also, this idea is sometimes used as a further means of specifying and illustrating the kind of actions presented as characteristic of one or other virtue. Thus, taken as a whole, Book 1 combines salient features of Stoic theory, relating to the virtues and human nature, with illustrative specification of actions in line with these normative ideas. In this way, the approach consists of a combination of what Stoics sometimes called 'doctrines' (*decreta*) and 'instructions' (*praecepta*), a point developed later.[134] The overall aim of the approach is to provide guidance on the kind of appropriate actions that can reasonably be seen as 'right' (*honestum*) and thus to inform practical deliberation and the shaping of one's life.

What about the selection of indifferents: how does this theme fit into the approach of Book 1? In the introduction to this book, Cicero, reporting Panaetius, sets out three questions that can arise in practical deliberation:

> In the first place, people may be uncertain whether the thing that falls under consideration is a right (*honestum*) or wrong (*turpe*) thing to do...Secondly, they investigate or debate whether or not the course they are considering is conducive to the convenience and pleasantness of life, to opportunities and resources for doing things, to wealth and power, all of which enable them to benefit themselves and those dear to them. All such deliberation falls under reasoning about what is advantageous (*utile*). The third type of uncertainty arises when something that seems to be advantageous appears to conflict with what is right.[135]

It is implied that the three books of *On Duties* correspond to the three questions posed; and, roughly speaking, these questions form the main themes for these books. However, this summary does not go on to analyse the approach taken to these topics, which is more complex than it appears here. For one thing, all three books, in different ways, and not just Book 3, involve the relationship between what is right and what is advantageous, that is, in more technical Stoic terms, what counts as a preferred indifferent. For another, in approaching all three questions, the primary reference-point is constituted by the virtues, sometimes coupled with ideas of nature. In Book 1, for instance, which provides the framework for the whole discussion, what is right (*honestum*) is determined, primarily, by reference to one or other virtue, supported by the idea of nature, in various forms. Also, the specification of what is right involves, explicitly or implicitly, what is called in Stoic theory, 'selection of indifferents', in the form of deliberation about the proper allocation of preferred and dispreferred indifferents to oneself and others.

---

[133] See also Ch. 1, text to nn. 160–8; and text to nn. 161–5.   [134] See text to nn. 166–77.
[135] Cic. *Off.* 1.9, trans. Griffin and Atkins 1991. See also *Off.* 3.7.

This approach can be illustrated by reference to Cicero's discussion of generosity, the actively benevolent aspect of justice. Justice, in Stoic accounts of the virtues, is, typically, defined as 'knowledge in allocating what is due (*axia*) to each person'.[136] Cicero's first general statement of this virtue is this: 'Of justice, the first function is that nobody should harm anyone else unless he has been provoked by injustice, the next that one should treat common goods as common and private one's as one's own' (1.20). Subsequently, he supplements this account in this way:

> . . . we ought in this to follow nature as our leader, to contribute to the common stock the things that benefit everyone together, and, by the exchange of dutiful services [or 'appropriate actions', *officia*], by giving and receiving expertise and effort and means, to bind fast the fellowship of human beings with each other.[137]

As noted earlier, each virtue is presented as having a core, distinctive character and a benevolent, other-benefiting aspect. In the case of justice, the second aspect is indicated in the comment just cited and subsequently examined in detail, characterized as kindness (*benignitas*) or generosity (*liberalitas*).[138] Cicero's opening statement of advice on how to act in line with this second aspect of the virtue is particularly suggestive for interpreting his overall approach in Book 1.

> First one must make sure that kindness (*benignitas*) harms neither the very people whom one seems to be treating kindly, nor others; next that one's kindness does not exceed one's capabilities; and then, that kindness is bestowed upon each person according to his standing. Indeed, that is fundamental to justice (*iustitia*), to which all these things ought to be referred. For those who do someone a favour (*gratificantur*) in such a way that they harm the person whom they appear to want to assist, should be judged neither beneficent nor generous, but dangerous flatterers. Those who, in order to be generous towards some, harm others, fall into the same injustice (*iniustia*) as if they had converted someone else's possessions to their own account.[139]

One point that is obvious here, and, indeed, throughout the whole account of virtues in Book 1, is that the exercise of virtue involves what Stoic theory characterizes as selection between indifferents, and that virtue constitutes expertise in such selection. Generosity is expressed in allocating preferable indifferents ('advantages', *utilia*) such as material goods or social status or support for the welfare of family to a specific person or persons. The generous person (the donor)

[136] Stob. 5b1, 2.59.9–10; see also Stob. 5b5, 2.63.21–2 (LS 61 H(3) and D(5)).
[137] Cic. *Off*. 1.22, trans. Griffin and Atkins 1991, with my additions in square brackets.
[138] The two-fold division is made in Cic. *Off*. 1.20; the first aspect is explained in 1.21–41, and the second in 1.42–60; see also Ch. 1, text to nn. 169–77.
[139] Cic. *Off*. 1.42, trans. Griffin and Atkins 1991.

has to determine what benefit or favour, such as material goods or social status, is to be conferred on which recipient and on what grounds. The assumption made by donor and recipient is that the objects conferred (preferable indifferents) have positive value. Correspondingly, in the passage cited, 'benefit' and 'harm' carry their conventional senses of giving or taking away preferable indifferents rather than the strictly Stoic sense of promoting virtue or vice.[140] In Cicero's elaboration of this general account, assessment of the value of indifferents and correlation with grounds for generosity both play significant roles in the practical reasoning of the generous person.[141] This discussion thus illustrates ideas closely associated with Chrysippus, namely that discrimination between indifferents forms a central part of the 'function of wisdom' and that indifferents constitute the 'material of virtue'.[142]

What form does such assessment of indifferents take, as indicated by Cicero's account? In considering this question, I refer to two models for Stoic deliberation put forward in recent scholarship, noted earlier.[143] Although I have reservations about both these models, as accounts of Stoic theory, they provide a means of defining, partly by contrast, what I see as a more credible interpretation of the Stoic framework illustrated here.[144] It is clear, I think, that what Cicero describes does not match the idea that virtuous deliberation can be analysed *purely* in terms of assessment of preferability of indifferents (the 'deliberative sufficiency' model put forward by Rachel Barney). It is yet clearer that it does not reflect the idea that virtuous deliberation aims, specifically, at maximizing preferable indifferents for the agent.[145] The generous donor in Cicero's account is not aiming to maximize her own preferable indifferents (otherwise she would not be a donor at all).[146] Nor is she aiming, simply, to maximize those of the intended recipient, taking this factor in isolation. The passage cited alludes to the case of someone who, in being generous to one person, harms others, presumably by taking away gifts or resources to which they are entitled. What the generous donor is aiming to do is to determine the level of preferable indifferents that is right (*honestum*) for achieving the aims of the donation. Those aims, as indicated in the passage cited, centre on conferring a benefit (*beneficium*) on someone (voluntarily), that

---

[140] On these two senses, see n. 39.   [141] See Cic. *Off.* 1.45, 47–9.

[142] Cic. *Fin.* 3.50 (LS 58 I), Plu. *Comm. Not.* 1069 E (LS 59 A). See also text to n. 8.

[143] See text to nn. 92; also text to nn. 208–11.

[144] These scholarly discussions are not designed to analyse Cicero's approach; their aim is to uncover early Stoic ideas about deliberation, which are seen by them as, in some respects, different from those of Cic. *Off.* (and Panaetius). See Barney 2003: 303–4, 334–6; Brennan 2005: chs. 12–13. However, I think Cicero's discussion is largely in line with earlier Stoic thought, and so it is reasonable to consider these scholarly analyses in connection with Cic. *Off.*

[145] Barney 2003: 322–4; also 304–19. Cic. *Off.* 1 raises the question of what counts as 'right' (e.g. in line with the virtue of generosity) and not simply what is preferable or not.

[146] The further question whether virtuous action (such as that prompted by generosity) yields preferable indifferents for the agent (as well as the person benefited by the virtuous action) is pursued in Cic. *Off.* 2, discussed in 2.5.

is, doing her a favour (*gratificare*) and thus expressing kindness (*benignitas*). But they also include doing so in a way that matches the requirements of justice, in giving each person her due, which avoids being unjust to those not receiving the donation. What Cicero has in mind, when he speaks of giving 'according to standing' (*pro dignitate tribuere*, 1.42) is indicated slightly later in his account of the virtue:

> ... one should when exercising beneficence make choices according to standing. Here we should look at the conduct of the person on whom we are conferring a benefit (*beneficium*), and at the spirit in which he views us, at the association and fellowship of our lives together, and at the dutiful services (*officia*) he has previously carried out for our advantage (*utilitates*).[147]

'Standing' (*dignitas*) is one of the factors to be considered (one with several strands, as indicated here); another is the recipient's need for the benefit (1.49, 59). What is required, as Cicero stresses, is to take all these factors into account and make the assessment of preferables and dispreferables that is 'right', given the whole situation. Thus, what this passage indicates is that selecting between indifferents and determining which action is 'right' or not are not two separate activities, even if they are conceptually separable. They are two aspects of the same process, or two ways of characterizing it. The expertise of virtue (in this case, generosity) lies in determining the kind and level of preferable indifferent that is appropriate for donor and recipient in the specific situation in which they find themselves.

Reference to another recent interpretation of Stoic deliberation can serve to define Cicero's approach further, though again largely by contrast.[148] Brennan considers various possible ways of interpreting Stoic thinking on deliberation, all of which have in common the assumption that, in performing appropriate acts, the virtuous person is primarily motivated to maximize his own preferred indifferents.[149] In the option which he finally adopts (characterized as 'no-shoving'), the maximization of preferables is qualified or constrained by considerations of what is required by just treatment of other people. Hence, Brennan identifies what he regards as a standard procedure for sound ethical deliberation. This consists in a three-stage process: (1) maximizing preferred indifferents, but (2) avoiding injustice to other people, and (3) taking account of the interests of the community

---

[147] Cic. *Off.* 1.45, trans. Griffin and Atkins 1991.

[148] As noted earlier (n. 144), Brennan, like Barney, aims to uncover early Stoic ideas about deliberation, but, in doing so, he draws heavily on Cic. *Off.* 3, so it seems reasonable to see if his approach matches this text, taken as a whole.

[149] The options considered, but not adopted, are (1) 'indifferents-only' (based especially on Cic. *Fin.* 3.59–61); and 'seek indifferents *salva virtute* (except when virtue prevents this)' (based especially on Cic. *Off.* 3.13). On (1), see Brennan 2005: 194–8; on (2) see Brennan 2005: 184–94 (also Barney 2003: 330–2).

or state. In his view, this provides a model of Stoic deliberation which gives a central place to maximization of indifferents but also takes into account the justified claims of other people.[150] Brennan's account is based on a number of passages, mostly taken from Book 3 of Cicero's *On Duties*: one of these passages, attributed to Chrysippus, provides the label, 'no-shoving':

> Runners in a race ought to compete and strive to win as hard as they can, but by no means should they trip up their competitors or give them a shove (*manu depellere*). So too in life; it is not wrong for each person to seek after the things useful for life; but to do so by depriving someone else is not just.[151]

Brennan presents this as a general pattern in Stoic deliberation and not just a feature of the argumentation of Cicero's *On Duties* 3.

Brennan's pattern goes some way towards defining the kind of deliberation we find in this work; his account gives room both for selecting indifferents and for taking account of considerations of justice. However, his account requires considerable modification to match what we find in *On Duties*. For one thing, Brennan's pattern is adversarial in form: the agent's natural desire for preferable indifferents is checked or restrained by reference to indications of justice.[152] In Cicero's discussion, the pattern is not adversarial in form. The agent positively wants to select the preferable indifferents (for someone else) that are in line with the criteria of generosity and justice (giving what is due to all those affected by the donation). The agent's motive (*hormē*, in Stoic terms) or intention, as a generous person, is, specifically, to confer the benefit that matches these criteria and is thus appropriate or right (*honestum*). This feature is also marked in Seneca's treatment of generosity in *On Benefits*, which is strongly shaped by Stoic thinking.[153] A second point of difference is that Brennan limits the virtuous person's considerations (other than maximizing preferable indifferents) to indications of justice or the interest of the community. There is no reference, in his account, to indications of the other virtues (despite the Stoic thesis of the interdependence of the virtues); he also rejects the idea that the deliberating person might reflect more generally on what the virtues involve.[154] However, Cicero's whole discussion, as noted earlier, is premised on the idea that, in determining what is right, we should take account of all four cardinal virtues and their interconnection. Cicero's

---

[150] See Brennan 2005: ch. 13, esp. 204–6, 210–14.

[151] Cic. *Off.* 3.42. Griffin and Atkins 1991: 116 print the last sentence as Cicero's comment on Chrysippus' comment. Other passages cited by Brennan (2005: 206–8) include *Off.* 3.26, 28, 30, 32, 35.

[152] Brennan 2005: 206–14.

[153] On Seneca's (Stoic) stress on the generous donor's intention or motivation, rather than (just) the gift conferred, see Inwood 2005: 84–9; Griffin 2013: 105–7. On Stoic influence on Sen. *Ben.* In general, see Griffin 2013: 19–29. See also Griffin 2013: 194–5, linking Cic. *Off.* 1.42 and Sen. *Ben.* 2.15.3–17.

[154] Brennan 2005: 216–18. For a similar view, see Barney 2003: 317–19, 330–2.

discussion also assumes that we should consider the virtues in more general terms, as well as reflecting on the kind of actions characteristic of each of the virtues.[155]

In specifying the motivation and practical reasoning that are characteristic of generosity, what contribution is made by the idea of what is 'natural', which figures prominently in Book 1?[156] There is a rather substantial treatment of nature (specifically, the social dimension of human nature), which is inserted by Cicero into his discussion of generosity. The starting-point is the distinctive Stoic idea that all human beings form a kind of community or fellowship, an idea also highlighted at the start of Book 1 and linked in both passages with the point that human beings are constitutively sociable as well as rational (1.11–12, 50). This fellowship of humanity is presented, first, as underpinning the generalized bond we have with all other human beings, which obligates us to help those such as travellers and strangers whom we can assist. It also underpins successively narrower circles of relationship (reaching by degrees to the family), which are presented, initially, as increasingly limited expressions of the fundamental fellowship of humanity (*Off.* 1.50–3). In a second phase of exploration of this theme (1.54–9), Cicero presents the more extended forms of relationship, such as political community, as derived from the familial bond, which expresses the primary instinct to care for others of one's kind in parental love. Although the two phases of discussion of this theme go in opposite directions (towards and from the narrower social bond), both phases evoke ideas about human sociability found elsewhere in Stoic treatments of this theme.[157]

How does this discussion of natural human sociability contribute to our understanding of the virtue of generosity and the kinds of appropriate actions in which this is expressed? The main explicit link is with the idea presented in both phases that our natural sociability is expressed in different 'circles' of relationship, which are more or less close to us (1.53, 54–7). This is presented as enabling us to determine more accurately what is due to the different kinds of people with whom we are connected, as regards generous actions, and thus helping us to become 'good calculators (or "reasoners", (*ratiocinatores*) of our duties [appropriate actions])', though only if we also pay attention to the needs of those involved in the specific situation (1.59). In this way, the discussion amplifies the preceding treatment of the different strands of 'standing' or 'worth' (*dignitas*), that we should hold in view in calibrating the benefits we confer (1.45–9). Hence, though framed in general terms (in 1.50–7), this idea contributes to providing relatively specific

[155] See text to nn. 129–32. The role of the four virtues in structuring the argument of *On Duties* emerges very clearly in the synopsis of the work in Griffin and Atkins 1991: xlviii–li. For the virtues as the basis of specifying appropriate actions, see Jedan 2009: 147–51.
[156] Both Barney (2003: 332–6) and Brennan (2005: 218–26) recognize the significance of the idea of nature as a factor in Stoic deliberation, but do not interpret its significance in the way suggested here.
[157] For the fellowship of humankind, see also Cic. *Fin.* 3.64; for the family as the basis of this larger community, see Cic. *Fin.* 3.62–3. See further on *Off.* 1.50–9 (taken in conjunction with *Fin.* 3.62–8), 4.5, text to nn. 170–82.

and particularized guidance on actions that are characteristic of the virtue of generosity.

However, there are two further ways in which this discussion enables us to form a better grasp of generosity. For one thing, it provides a broader conceptual framework for making sense of the motive or intention underlying generous actions. As indicated in the opening account of the virtue, cited earlier, this motive consists in wanting to express special kindness (*benignitas*) or to do a favour (*gratificare*) to certain people with whom we are in some way connected, while also acting justly (giving what is due) to all those affected by our donation (1.42). When juxtaposed to the discussion of 1.50–9, this motive can be understood as one expression of the sociability (more precisely, the combination of rationality and sociability) that is natural to us as human beings. It is worth recalling that, at the start of *On Duties* 1, two primary instincts are identified, and presented as common to all animals, namely to care for themselves and others of their kind; in the case of human beings, these motives are shaped by our distinctive rationality, which issues in the four primary motives underlying the four cardinal virtues.[158] The motive of justice (and generosity) is concerned 'with preserving fellowship among human beings, with assigning to each his own, and with faithfulness to agreements he has made'.[159] The formation and realization of the different social relationships, both broad and narrow, presented in 1.50–9, constitute the expression of this motive. Generous actions to a particular person, performed in the context of one's whole nexus of relationships, express this motive in a more specific way. Hence, we can see virtuous motivation not just (as in Brennan's 'no-shoving' pattern) as directed towards gaining preferable indifferents for ourselves, while also taking account of indications of justice.[160] The motivation is directed precisely and positively towards generous actions that are also consistent with principles of justice; and the motivation is explained, in a broad sense, by reference to our human nature as rational and sociable.

There is one further implication of the discussion of nature in connection with generosity. More precisely, this is an implication of all the references to nature, when taken in conjunction with the account of the virtues and the actions typical of the virtues, which forms the main structural framework for *On Duties* Book 1. This combination of themes evokes one of the central ideas of Stoic thinking on virtue and happiness discussed in Chapter 1. This is the idea that the virtues constitute modes of knowledge or expertise in leading a happy life, conceived as 'the life according to nature', with the connotations already discussed, namely, being rational and sociable, ordered, structured and whole, and exercising care for

---

[158] Cic. *Off.* 1.11–15; see also Ch. 1, text to nn. 159–65.
[159] Cic. *Off.* 1.15, trans. Griffin and Atkins 1991. See also *Off.* 1.22, which also locates the origin of justice (characterized in similar terms to 1.15) in the natural fellowship of humanity.
[160] See Brennan 2005: 206–14.

oneself and others of one's kind.[161] This idea is not expounded systematically in *On Duties*; however, it underlies the work and the strategy adopted there for explaining how to perform appropriate actions. Appropriate actions are presented, in effect, as those which are typical of someone who exercises the virtues and thus has expertise in leading a life according to nature. It is also implied, as the discussion of generosity illustrates, that this expertise in leading a happy (natural) life shapes selection between indifferents. The generous person allocates preferable indifferents in a manner that matches her desire to confer material or social favours on another person or persons in a way that is just to all those affected by the gift. In a broader sense, doing so enables her to express the underlying desire to lead the best possible human life (the happy life), which is marked by a combination of rationality and sociability, structure, order, and wholeness, and care for oneself and others of one's kind. It does not follow, of course, that the generous person will necessarily conceive her act, on each and every occasion, under this very broad description (as expressing the desire to live the life according to nature). It is much more likely that practical deliberation will be framed in terms of the relevant specific features of the person concerned, such as his relation to the donor, his claims, or needs, the donor's own resources, and the effect of the gift on other people.[162] However, Cicero's inclusion of the more general ideas (the accounts of the virtues and of 'nature', in various senses) implies that they form part of a framework on which the deliberating person can draw during the deliberative process or in ethical reflection designed to inform deliberation.[163] Cicero (like Panaetius, presumably) includes this broader framework of ideas in a work designed to enable an ethical learner to make progress in performing appropriate actions; and this suggests that the framework is designed to be useful for such a person when engaging in practical deliberation.[164] Bearing this framework in mind can help someone to deliberate better on specific occasions and to correlate features of her situation with the guidance offered. Cicero's presentation runs counter to the idea proposed by some scholars that Stoic ethics operates with a 'split-level' theory, in which deliberation is framed wholly in terms of indifferents, and the idea of 'virtue' (or 'happiness') belongs wholly to third-personal analysis of virtuous deliberation.[165]

The combination of general ideas and specific guidance found in *On Duties* 1 can be linked with another well-marked feature of Stoic thinking on ethical guidance. Two of Seneca's letters (94 and 95) provide access to Stoic debate on

---

[161] See 1.4, esp. text to nn. 158–77, 194, on points in Cic. *Off.* which reflect this framework of thinking about virtue and happiness.

[162] For these factors, see Cic. *Off.* 1.45, 58–9.

[163] On the question of the relationship between deliberation and reflection as one which is raised by Stoic (and other) ethical theories, see text to nn. 76–7.

[164] See text to nn. 90–1.

[165] For 'split-level' views of Stoic ethics, see Cooper 1999: 534; Barney 2003: 317–18; also text to n. 92.

this topic, which centres on the question of the respective roles of *decreta* ('doctrines') and *praecepta* ('instructions' or 'precepts').[166] Aristo, a dissident early Stoic thinker, argued that doctrines alone constitute the basis of ethical guidance, and that without a proper grasp of the significance of doctrines, more specific instructions or advice on how to live your life are useless.[167] Mainstream Stoics from Zeno onwards took a different view, and supplemented treatises on core ethical doctrines with works offering more specific kinds of guidance, on appropriate acts or types of life or what is required by specific social roles.[168] Seneca offers what is probably a representative Stoic view: that doctrines provide the basis for shaping your life as a whole, whereas instructions help you to translate this basis into practice, by correlating it with the specific forms and contexts of your life. Both kinds of guidance have their usefulness, but they need to be properly integrated with each other to carry out this role.[169] I share Brad Inwood's view that neither *decreta* nor *praecepta* are best understood as codified rules (general or specific).[170] Seneca's discussion confirms the prevalence in Stoic thought of the two-fold framework for ethical guidance, based on a combination of broad, theoretical ideals and the translation of those ideals into specific illustrations.

Several features of Cicero's *On Duties* can be linked with Seneca's approach. The two examples of doctrines that Seneca cites are the community of humankind (and the implications of this idea for our treatment of others), and the nature of the virtues and their interdependence.[171] Both of these topics figure prominently in *On Duties* and they are connected with each other.[172] Cicero also illustrates, especially in Book 3, how we can draw on these ideas to provide practical guidance, notably guidance about how to make specific decisions where there are factors making it difficult to translate these ideas into action.[173] Cicero's treatment is also evocative of the views of Posidonius, a leading first-century BC Stoic, who recommends discussing the general features of each virtue (and vice) and also offering specific exemplification of these features (*ēthologia*).[174] Seneca develops this last point by citing Cato as an exemplar of courage; this matches Cicero's extensive use of exemplification, notably in the case of Regulus.[175] Seneca does not refer here explicitly to the theory of the four roles, though he does refer to

---

[166] See also Inwood 1999: 112–27, which combines discussion of Cic. *Off.* with that of Sen. *Ep.* 94–5.

[167] Sen. *Ep.* 94. 1–17; on Aristo, see LS 58 F–G and text to n. 7.

[168] Sen. *Ep.* 94, 3–4, 11, 35. For indications of what this advice involves, see Cic. *Off.* 1.122–5, Epict. *Diss.* 2.10; also LS 66 and 67 W. See also Griffin 1976: 341–2; Gill 1988: 175; Brunt 2013: chs. 1, 4.

[169] Sen. *Ep.* 94. 21, 31, 45; 95. 10–12, 37–8, 44, 64.

[170] See Inwood 1999: 113–20; also 105–12, arguing against scholars who maintain that 'natural law' in Stoicism constitutes a set of determinate rules.

[171] Sen. *Ep.* 95. 52–5.

[172] For the interdependence of the virtues, see Cic. *Off.* 1.16, 63, 94, 153, 2.18, 35. On the community of humankind, see *Off.* 1.50–2, 3.21–8, 3.53.

[173] See Cic. *Off.* 3.20–2, discussed in 2.5; also Inwood 1999: 121–2.   [174] Sen. *Ep.* 95.65–6.

[175] Sen. *Ep.* 95.69–72; also Cic. *Off.* 1.112 (on Cato), 3.99–111 (on Regulus).

it in other contexts,[176] and Seneca's contemporary Epictetus deploys a similar framework. However, this theory is used by Cicero, and Epictetus, to carry out the procedure that Seneca recommends in letters 94–5, namely connecting the broader ideals of Stoicism with the specific features of one's character, social context and chosen role in life.[177] Seneca's evidence thus confirms that the kind of ethical guidance offered by Cicero in *On Duties* 1 falls squarely within Stoic thinking and practice.

2.5 Practical Deliberation: Cicero, *On Duties* 2–3

In Books 2–3, Cicero applies the approach worked out in Book 1 to a new set of questions: deliberating about what is advantageous or not and deliberating about cases where what is right clashes (or seems to clash) with what is advantageous. This is, perhaps, not quite what we might have expected from Cicero's summary of his project.[178] We might have anticipated that, in Book 2, Cicero would have examined the various advantages (or 'preferred indifferents') and actions consistent with them in the same way that he examines the virtues and actions consistent with them in Book 1. We might also have supposed from this summary that in Book 3, Cicero would have constructed a two-fold system of criteria for action, based on the virtues and the advantages, respectively, and offered advice on how to assess each set and weigh them against each other. However, neither book is organized in this way. Book 2 is centred on a single theme, the relationship between the virtue of generosity and gaining the advantage of social approval. The focus is on the point that the only reliable way to gaining the latter is by acting in line with the virtues, especially generosity. In Book 3, the argument, as in Book 1, is structured around the virtues, especially justice, sometimes supplemented by reference to ideas of nature. The main objective is providing guidance on determining what counts as right action and carrying this out, even in cases where there are, apparently, greater advantages to be gained by not doing so.[179] In effect, then, *On Duties* as a whole deploys a single approach, based on aiming to perform actions that are right, taken to be in line with the virtues. Each of the books explores in a rather different way what this approach involves for gaining or surrendering advantages; but none of the books offers a rival system of deliberation, based on maximizing advantages, taken in isolation from the exercise of virtue.

---

[176] See Griffin 1976: 341–3, referring to Sen. *TA*, ch. 6; Griffin 2013: 194–5, referring to *Ben.* 2.15.3–17.

[177] On Cic. *Off.* 1. 107–15 and Epict. *Diss.* 1.2, 2.10, see Gill 1988; also Tieleman 2007: 130–40; Jedan 2009: 145–7, linking the four–roles theory with evidence for earlier Stoic thought.

[178] Cic. *Off.* 1.9–10, cited in text to n. 135, and *Off.* 3.7. Book 2 is based on Panaetius' work and Book 3 is independently constructed by Cicero.

[179] Again, the synopsis in Griffin and Atkins 1991: l–li clarifies the structure of the two books.

In Book 2, as just noted, Cicero focuses almost entirely on one advantage, namely social support and approval, taken to include both the support of family and friends and public reputation or glory.[180] He emphasizes that the most effective, indeed only reliable, way to gain social support is to exercise the virtues, which in turn stimulates other people to give us their support:

> I count it as the special property of virtue to win over people's hearts and to enlist them in its own service... it is the wisdom and virtue of outstanding persons that inspire other people to be prompt, ready and devoted in assisting our advancement... A vigorous love is aroused in the masses, however, by the very reputation and rumour of liberality, of beneficence, of justice, of keeping faith, and of all the virtues that are associated with gentleness and ease of conduct (*mansuetudinem morum ac facilitatem*). For, because the very thing we call right and fitting (*decorum*) pleases us in itself, and moves the heart of all by its nature and appearance, shining out brightly, so to speak, from the virtues that I have mentioned—because of that, when we think people possess these virtues, we are compelled by nature to love them.[181]

In fact, although Cicero does discuss other virtues, including magnanimity (2.37–8), the focus in Book 2 is on justice or generosity, treated, as in Book 1, as aspects of a single virtue.[182]

Cicero's emphasis on social support, especially public reputation, expresses his own concerns, as a leading Roman politician, though it seems also to reflect a similar emphasis in Panaetius' treatment.[183] How far does this presentation of the relationship between virtue and preferred indifferents (advantages) match Stoic thinking in general? Let us take a comment made in connection with magnanimity and the reputation produced by this virtue:

> But as for those who look down with a great and elevated mind upon prosperity and adversity alike (*excelso animo magnoque despiciunt*), especially when some great and right actions (*ampla et honesta*) are before them, which draws them wholly towards these things and engages them, who can fail to admire the splendour and beauty of virtue? Therefore, a mind contemptuous in this way arouses great admiration.[184]

---

[180] There is a brief discussion of other advantages (health and money) in 2.86–7.

[181] Cic. *Off.* 2.17, 32, trans. Griffin and Atkins 1991. See also 2.9–10, 16–18, 32–8.

[182] Cic. *Off.* 2.38–40 (justice), 2.52–85 (generosity); see also 1.20–60 on justice (including generosity, 42–59).

[183] See Long 1995: 228; also Dyck 1996: 353–60, 416–17.

[184] Cic. *Off.* 2.37–8, trans. Griffin and Atkins 1991; on magnanimity, see also 1.66. The following two and a half paragraphs are based on Gill 2019b: 64–6.

How consistent with Stoic ethics is the presentation of a virtue (here, magnanimity) as valuable, at least in part, because it produces an advantage, namely admiration or, more broadly, honour and reputation? It is not problematic that someone should want to obtain advantages; after all, it is standard Stoic doctrine that preferred indifferents, which include reputation, have a real and positive value and that human beings naturally go for them.[185] What is more questionable, in Stoic ethics, is the idea, which seems to be implied here, that virtue is of value *because* it brings about advantage, rather than because it is good and choiceworthy for itself.[186]

Cicero, at one point, addresses this problem explicitly, though what he says is not wholly reassuring: 'Therefore justice should be cultivated and maintained by every means, both for its own sake (otherwise it would not be justice) and for the sake of enhancing one's honour and glory' (2.42). The first point represents orthodox Stoic thinking, but the second is more questionable. The comment is compatible with some features of Stoic ethical doctrine. As just noted, advantages (preferable indifferents) have positive value and constitute grounds for action; hence, virtue, as expertise in selection between indifferents, can, in principle, aim to produce preferable indifferents for the agent.[187] Also, indifferents (preferable or dispreferable) constitute 'the material of virtue' in the sense that selection between them is the means by which virtue is exercised.[188] Hence, as A. A. Long points out, Cicero's comment would have been more consistently phrased as being that 'justice is both desirable for its own sake and as the *only* [justifiable] means of securing glory'.[189] In other words, the weight needs to fall on the idea that one should aim, first and foremost, to act rightly (in line with the virtues), even while recognizing that doing so also, typically, produces advantages for oneself, as well as others. In fact, in his exposition as a whole, this is where Cicero does place his emphasis, rather than suggesting that virtuous action is only desirable as a means of securing advantages. Cicero also stresses that a good reputation, earned as a result of exercising virtue, enables one to achieve socially beneficial results; and, as emphasized throughout Book 1, achieving such results is a characteristic function of all the virtues.[190] In elaborating this line of thought in Book 2, Cicero's concern is especially with the way things work in Roman society, when they are working well; but the points he makes are also compatible with Stoic doctrine.[191]

It is worth noting here a debate, among Stoic thinkers, regarding the value-status of honour. Cicero himself provides in *On Ends* (3.57) the main evidence:

---

[185] See text to nn. 16–23.

[186] See 2.2 for a summary of standard Stoic thinking on the virtue-indifferents relationship.

[187] This does not mean we have to adopt Barney's principle of 'maximization' (text to nn. 144–5).

[188] Plu. *Comm. Not.* 1069 E (LS 59 A).   [189] Long 1995: 232; I have supplied 'justifiable'.

[190] For the idea that each of the cardinal virtues, as presented in *Off*. 1, has a socially directed and other-benefiting dimension, see Ch. 1, text to nn. 169–77.

[191] Cic. *Off*. 2.36–50; also Long 1995: 230–2.

As far as good reputation is concerned (what they call *eudoxia*...), Chrysippus himself and Diogenes [of Babylon] used to say that, aside from any instrumental benefit (*utilitas*) it may have, it was not worth lifting a finger for, and I agree with them strongly. But their successors... declared that a good reputation is preferable and worthy of adoption in its own right.

This comment assumes a three-fold distinction within the category of preferable indifferents: (1) those preferable in themselves, such as good appearance; (2) those preferable instrumentally, such as money; and (3) those preferable for both reasons, such as health.[192] As Cicero indicates here, he favours the idea that honour falls under the second of these options, on theoretical grounds, while later Stoic thinkers—this might include Panaetius—adopt the first, or perhaps third.[193] In *On Duties* 2, Cicero presents the idea that the role of glory or honour is instrumental with reference to social practice current in Roman aristocratic political life. Glory or social approval, including electoral and public support, enables someone to engage effectively in political action and in this way to benefit the community as a whole. This fits in with the point made earlier about magnanimity (2.37–8) and the other virtues discussed in Book 2. The virtues arouse admiration (a preferred indifferent), in part, because they promote social benefit; admiration or honour reinforces this process, in an instrumental way, by oiling the wheels of social and political process. The point can be put more broadly, in a way which brings out more clearly the link with Stoic doctrine. Virtue, while choiceworthy in itself, is also instrumental, in that it produces the happy life, conceived as 'the life according to nature', that is, in part at least, the best possible life for human beings as rational and sociable animals. Indifferents can also contribute to the happy life in a number of ways: preferable indifferents are valuable in themselves; also indifferents constitute 'the material' of virtue, conceived as expertise in selection.[194] In addition, preferable indifferents such as good reputation can promote the exercise of virtue (including the socially beneficial dimension of virtue), and thus enable a life according to human nature as rational and sociable. Hence, overall, Cicero's presentation of the virtues as effective in producing glory or honour fits not only with his overall theme in Book 2 but also with Stoic ethics in general.

Cicero's project in Book 3 is also, I think, in line with the approach of Book 1 (and with Stoic ethics more generally). Here, Cicero takes up the third question, which Panaetius planned in his programme for the work but did not complete. This is presented by Cicero as being how to determine the right course of action

---

[192] See Cic. *Fin.* 3.56; also Stob. 7d–e, 2.82.11–83.9, D.L. 7.107.

[193] See Long 1995: 232–3; of course, none of these thinkers places honour in the same class as virtue (which is not only choiceworthy in itself but also good, rather than a preferable indifferent).

[194] For these points, see Ch. 1, text to nn. 105–12, 148–56, and 2.3, esp. text to nn. 17–23, 37–42.

when acting rightly and gaining advantage conflict—or rather, when they seem to do so.[195] Cicero insists that, properly understood, there can be no such conflict, only the appearance of conflict, and that his advice is based on this assumption. Why does Cicero, seemingly following Panaetius, maintain that there can be no such conflict, only the appearance of conflict?[196] It is, in fact, perfectly possible, in Stoic theory, for the pursuit of one's own advantage (preferable indifferents) to conflict with adopting a course of action in line with virtue. Indeed, many of the cases discussed by Cicero in Book 3 are, precisely, cases of such conflict. What, then, is the rationale for Cicero's insistence on this point, and what does it tell us about Cicero's approach to the question of what counts as virtuous deliberation?

There is no attempt in Book 3 to restate the general thesis of Book 2, that gaining advantages, or at least some of them, such as public support, derives from exercising the virtues, and to argue that, therefore, there can be no conflict between virtuous action and gaining advantage. Cicero does allude to the standard Stoic idea, that virtue, by contrast with the preferable indifferents, is wholly good, and so there is no conflict, or comparison, between virtue and indifferents in terms of value.[197] However, it is compatible with this thesis that the virtuous agent might find herself in a situation where acting virtuously (though this is, ultimately, beneficial for her), runs counter to gaining preferable indifferents for herself.

What Cicero is ruling out of consideration is the idea that a virtuous person (or someone aiming to act virtuously) could recognize a conflict between acting rightly and gaining advantages and still be in doubt what to do, or—even worse—decide to follow the more advantageous course of action, rather than the right one. Of course, it is psychologically possible for people to do this; indeed, Cicero provides several examples of people acting in this way.[198] But acting in this way is wrong; it shows a complete misunderstanding of what ethical behaviour involves. Throughout *On Duties*, Cicero frames advice directed at someone whose aim is to gain a better understanding of how to act rightly (*honeste*), that is, how to carry out appropriate actions in line with the virtues. He does not mount arguments for someone who recognizes a conflict between right and advantageous action and is still uncertain what to do, or who deliberately adopts the advantageous course, rather than the right one.[199] However, it is entirely possible, in the Stoic framework, that an ethical learner or progressor might be in doubt about which course of action is right, particularly when one of the possible options involves substantial loss of advantages.[200] So, in Book 3, Cicero focuses on cases where determining the right course of action is difficult, particularly cases where

---

[195] Cic. *Off.* 3.7–10; also 1.9–10.   [196] Cic. *Off.* 3.11–12.

[197] See 2.2. See Cic. *Off.* 3.20, also 3.11, 33, 35.   [198] Cic. *Off.* 3.36, 75, 79–83, 87–8.

[199] Cicero is not aiming to mount arguments to confront the 'immoralist' position, like Plato, in *Gorgias* and *Republic* (especially Book 1); on such arguments, see Williams 1985: 22–9.

[200] The wise person, by contrast, is seen as having infallible knowledge in all such cases; for Cicero's focus here on advice for those aiming to make progress, see Cic. *Off.* 1.8–9, 3.13–18.

what seems to be right runs counter to maximizing one's own advantages (preferable indifferents). Drawing primarily on Stoic teaching, he provides guidelines which can help people to establish the right course of action in such situations, assuming that this is their aim.[201]

What kind of material does he offer for this purpose? In the absence of a single Stoic prototype, of the kind he uses in Books 1–2, Cicero draws on a range of Stoic writings, as well as supplementing these, here as elsewhere, with Roman historical examples and his own experience and comments. However, overall, his advice represents a version of the guidance provided in *On Duties* 1. He refers to accounts of the virtues or offers illustrations of actions typical of those exercising the virtues. He also deploys ideas about what is natural, of a kind that reflect Stoic thinking about what constitutes the life according to nature, such as the idea that human beings are naturally rational and sociable, or that they are members of different types of human community (local or universal). As in Book One, these two themes (virtue and nature) are presented as integrally linked; this presentation reflects the close linkage between virtue or happiness and nature brought out in Chapter 1.[202] Cicero also draws on Stoic casuistry (that is, discussion of ethically difficult cases), and mounts arguments for and against specific courses of action based on Stoic assumptions. Cicero, like the Stoic thinkers on whom he draws, presupposes that people are naturally disposed to gain preferable, rather than dispreferable, indifferents, and that virtuous deliberation will take into account the probable consequences of one's actions as regards indifferents both for oneself and others affected by one's actions. However, there is no attempt, in Book 3 or the preceding books, to present the maximizing of preferable indifferents, taken in isolation, as the criterion of virtuous deliberation. The focus, in Book 3, is on enabling the person addressed to form a better understanding of what should count as the right (*honestum*) course of action. A further premise is that the person addressed, like the exemplary figures, such as Regulus, discussed in the work, is positively motivated towards doing what is right, that is, in line with the virtues and towards what is 'natural', in Stoic terms, once this has been determined, even when this results in reduction of advantages for oneself.

Book 3 begins with a preliminary statement, and application to specific cases, of a 'rule of procedure' (*regula*) that Cicero presents as generally valid for providing the kind of advice he has in view. He then adopts the approach outlined in connection with cases grouped under each of the cardinal virtues (as in Book 1).[203] I focus here on three elements in Book 3 that, taken together, illustrate Cicero's approach and bring out the linkage to Stoic theory more generally. These elements are (1) the opening discussion of the rule of procedure (3.19–32); (2) the report of Stoic

---

[201] Cic. *Off.* 3.33–4.   [202] See text to nn. 86–8, 121–4 (in this chapter).
[203] Cic. *Off.* 3.40–74 (justice and wisdom, taken together, see 96), 97–115 (magnanimity), 116–20 (moderation or what is fitting).

casuistic debate on business ethics (3.50–7, falling under the heading of justice); (3) the discussion of Regulus (3.99–115, illustrating magnanimity).

Cicero's presentation of his rule of procedure begins in this way:

> Now then: for one person to take something from another and to increase his own advantage at the cost of another's disadvantage is more contrary to nature than death, than poverty, than pain, and anything else that may happen to his body and external possessions. In the first place, it destroys the common life and fellowship of human beings; if we are so minded that any one person will use theft or violence against another for his own profit, then necessarily the thing that is most in accordance with nature will be shattered, that is, the fellowship of the human race.[204]

The term 'rule of procedure' (*regula*) is taken from Roman legal practice; the employment of this term in connection with Stoic ethics seems to be Cicero's own innovation, as is the formulation of the rule. However, the ideas deployed in this way are consistent with the Stoic ethical framework adopted throughout *On Duties*. The opening formulation strongly evokes Cicero's account of the virtue of justice in Book 1. In both contexts, Cicero's statement combines two themes: (1) not harming anyone without proper reason; (2) helping other people or our community as a way of contributing to the fellowship of human beings in general. As formulated in Book 1:

> Of justice, the first duty [appropriate action] is that no one should harm another unless he has been provoked by injustice. (1.20) ... we ought to follow nature as our leader, to contribute to the common stock the things that benefit everyone together, and by the exchange of dutiful services, by giving and receiving expertise and effort and means, to bind fast the fellowship of human beings with each other (1.22).[205]

The evocation in Book 3 of the earlier account of justice is reinforced by repeated references to the idea that acting justly, and in line with the other virtues, is 'according to nature' in one of the senses of nature seen as significant in Stoic ethics. The main idea stressed in Book 3 is that humanity as a whole, or the political or social community that forms a distinct subdivision of humanity, constitutes a single, organic 'body' (a shared or common fellowship), governed by a single 'natural law'.[206] Cicero also underlines the point that acting in

---

[204] Cic. *Off.* 3.21, trans. Griffin and Atkins 1991.

[205] Trans. Griffin and Atkins 1991. See also text to nn. 136–7.

[206] See Cic. *Off.* 3.21 (common fellowship); 3.22 (organic body); 3.23 (natural law); 3.26–7 (shared human fellowship); 3.28 claims of our own political community and also foreigners. See also *Off.* 1.12, 50–9, 155–8.

accordance with nature, in these senses, and acting in line with the virtues (the virtues in general and not only justice, despite the strong evocation of justice in 1.21) are integrally linked.[207]

Cicero's presentation of the rule of procedure also refers to the role of indifferents in deliberation. Before offering my own interpretation, it is worth considering how far Cicero's treatment matches the scholarly accounts of Stoic deliberation discussed earlier. On Duties 3 provides little or no support for Barney's hypothesis that virtuous deliberation is framed wholly in terms of assessment of preferability of indifferents, or that it is designed to maximize preferable indifferents ('advantages') for the agent. The latter policy is treated by Cicero, rather, as a target for ethical criticism.[208] Brennan's 'no-shoving' interpretation is closer to the Ciceronian approach; indeed, the passages that Brennan cites in support of this view are mostly taken from Book 3 and reflect the project of considering cases where right action and gaining preferable indifferents conflict (or seem to conflict, as Cicero puts it).[209] However, as suggested earlier, Brennan's interpretation is rather narrowly conceived, notably in focusing on indications of justice or the needs of the community, while excluding consideration of the other virtues or general accounts of the virtues.[210] As regards motivation, Brennan concentrates on the desire for preferable indifferents (though he sees this as one that can be checked by considerations of justice); he does not consider the idea that the agent might be positively motivated towards acting virtuously. Both Barney and Brennan recognize that Cicero, in On Duties, gives a prominent role to the idea that acting 'according to nature' can play a part in virtuous deliberation. Barney treats this as an alternative model of virtuous deliberation to the one she proposes. Brennan sees this as a supplement or reinforcement of his 'no-shoving' model: the agent is discouraged from 'shoving' (pursuing his own interests) by seeing this as more contrary to nature than taking account of considerations of justice.[211] However, neither scholar connects this theme in On Duties with Stoic thinking on virtue and happiness (conceived as the life according to nature).

In elaborating his rule of procedure in 3.21–8, Cicero refers repeatedly to the idea of nature, in a way that illustrates Stoic thinking on virtuous deliberation and bears on the question of how to interpret their theory. First, Cicero maintains that it is natural for human beings to pursue advantages for themselves, rather than others, though it is not natural (in another sense, according to the principles of human fellowship) for them to maximize their own advantages at the expense of others. He then comments that communal laws are designed to prevent someone

---

[207] Cic. Off. 3.24, 28.
[208] See Cic. Off. 3.36, 75, 79–83, 87–8. See Barney 2003: 322–4; also text to nn. 144–7.
[209] See Brennan 2005: 204–14, referring to Cic. Off. 3.13, 3.42, 3.63, 3.70.
[210] See text to nn. 148–55.   [211] Barney 2003: 332–6; Brennan 2005: 218–20.

from harming another for his own advantage and in this way undermining social bonds. However, he adds that following natural law achieves the same objective much more fully: 'Whoever is willing (*velit*) to obey it (everyone will obey it who wants (*volet*) to live in accordance with nature) will never act so as to seek what is another's'. He also claims that 'loftiness and greatness of spirit, and, indeed, friendliness, justice, and liberality, are far more in accordance with nature, than pleasure, than life, than riches'.[212] He supplements this point by pointing to Hercules (one of two heroes sometimes presented by Stoics as candidates for the status of being wise people)[213] as one who 'undertook extreme toils and troubles in order to protect and assist all human races', and maintaining that it is 'more in accordance with nature to imitate him in this' than to live in solitude, even if this carried with it many advantages.[214] He then attributes to someone who acts violently to secure his own benefit the belief that doing so is more 'according to nature' than acting rightly (3.26). Further, he claims that 'all human beings should have this one object (*propositum*), that the benefit of each individual and the benefit of all together should be the same'.[215] Finally, he stresses, again, that anyone who pursues his own advantage at the expense of others, will 'tear apart the common fellowship of the human race' and that, when this happens, 'kindness, liberality, goodness and justice are utterly destroyed'.[216]

The line of thought developed here is consistent with the ideas on virtues, the indifferent, and nature that are presented in Books 1 of *On Duties*, and, more broadly, with Stoic ethical theory in general. However, this approach differs, in some respects, from the interpretative models offered by Barney and Brennan, notably as regards the motivational attitude attributed to the virtuous agent and encouraged in the person addressed in the work. What deters such a person from exploiting others (from 'shoving', in Brennan's terms) is not just a recognition of considerations of justice and the claims of community, though it includes such recognition. What Cicero also stresses is the presence of a positive motive to benefit others[217] by conferring preferable indifferents on them, even if, as for Hercules, this involves reduction in one's own acquisition of preferable indifferents. This stress on the positive motive to benefit others matches the second strand in the account of justice in Book 1, as well as the desire to confer benefits on others that is characteristic of generosity, as Cicero present this.[218] This positive motive is, under one description, the desire to act in line with the virtues and to perform actions characteristic of them, especially those which contribute to human

---

[212] Cic. *Off*. 3.23-4, trans. Griffin and Atkins 1991.
[213] See Brouwer 2014: 111-12 (the other is Odysseus); see also Cic. *Fin*. 3.66.
[214] Cic. *Off*. 3.25, trans. Griffin and Atkins 1991.
[215] Cic. *Off*. 3.26, trans. Griffin and Atkins 1991.
[216] Cic. *Off*. 3.28, trans. Griffin and Atkins 1991.
[217] See the stress on 'wanting' (*volere*), 3.23-4, and forming the objective (*propositum*), 3.28, to act in this way.
[218] See Cic. *Off*. 1.22, 42; and text to nn. 137-9, 152-5.

fellowship. It is also, under another description, the desire to act in a way that is in accordance to nature, meaning, especially, to express one's own (human) nature as rational and sociable by promoting human fellowship through one's own actions, as these affect family or friends, one's community, or strangers. Given the very close relationship between virtue and happiness (the life according to nature), discussed in Chapter 1, and between virtue and nature in *On Duties* 1, these two descriptions can be seen as identifying integrated aspects of a single pattern of motivation. This does not mean that the virtuous person has ceased to want to have preferable indifferents (for herself) or to regard this as a natural motive. But this motive is subsumed under the broader desire to lead the life according to nature, which includes selecting between indifferents correctly or expertly, that is, in line with virtue.[219] This point is, presumably, what Cicero has in mind in saying that acting in line with nature (meaning acting in line with human fellowship) is *more* natural than acting in a way that (simply) secures preferable indifferents for oneself.[220]

Cicero's rule of procedure is presented as designed to help someone reach the right decision in situations where there is scope for debate about what this is, notably in cases where the right action conflicts (or seems to conflict, as he puts it) with securing preferred indifferents. Does Cicero, then, envisage the person concerned deploying the line of thought just outlined in the course of her deliberations? Or should we suppose that Cicero's guidance is designed, rather, to help preliminary reflection (or, that it constitutes an analysis of the main relevant considerations), and that the actual deliberation is framed in different terms? As suggested earlier, in connection with Cicero's discussion of generosity, we do not have to assume that, on each and every occasion, the virtuous person rehearses the full set of considerations presented by Cicero, and here, offered as a rule of procedure (*Off.* 3.21–8).[221] It is plausible to think that the person focuses, primarily, on specific features of the situation and on alternative, concrete plans of action. However, I do not think we should adopt the 'split-level' model of decision-making proposed by Cooper and Barney, according to which the deliberating person thinks in one set of terms (for instance, maximization of preferable indifferents for herself), which are analysed from the outside in quite different terms (those of virtue, or 'nature', in one or other sense), and that the analysis has no direct impact on the deliberation.[222] Cicero's rule of procedure is designed to inform decision-making, and especially to enable someone to determine which

---

[219] This point is put in general form in *Off.* 3.13: 'when the Stoics say that the greatest good is to live in agreement (*convenienter*) with nature, this means, in my view, the following: always to concur with virtue; and as for the other things which are according to nature [preferable indifferents], to choose them if they do not conflict with virtue' (trans. Griffin and Atkins 1991). For discussions of this passage, though based on different interpretative assumptions from mine, see Barney 2003: 334; Brennan 2005: 182–94, 206.

[220] Cic. *Off.* 3.24–5; on this striking formulation, see also Barney 2003: 334; Brennan 2005: 206–7.

[221] See also text to nn. 162 on this point.   [222] See text to nn. 92, 163–5.

specific factors need to be considered, and how they should be understood, both in preliminary reflection and in the immediate situation. He is aiming to enable someone to determine the course of action that is right (*honestum*), in cases where this is not clear or where it runs counter to securing one's own advantages. The discussion of accounts of virtues such as justice and of actions characteristic of these virtues and the consideration of relevant ideas of nature are presented as helping someone to determine what is right in specific (especially complex or ambiguous) situations.

Cicero's account of the rule of procedure is followed by two case-studies where the rule is applied; and this application reinforces the view that the rule is intended to provide ideas which are deployed in actual deliberation. The first question is whether 'a wise person, if he is dying of hunger, would steal food from someone else'; the second is whether such a person 'would steal the clothes of Phalaris (a cruel and monstrous tyrant), to prevent himself from dying of cold'.[223] In the first case, as Cicero presents the matter, the right decision depends partly on the question of motive. The theft is justified if (and only if) 'you are the kind of person who, if you were to remain alive, could bring great benefit to your political community, and to human fellowship, and if *for that reason* (*ob eam causam*) you deprive someone else of something', the act is not reprehensible. Indeed, it is just and in accordance with the law of nature for this transference of resources to take place; but not if the act is based on 'self-esteem or self-love'.[224] The second case study is presented as much more straightforward. Tyrants are described as having excluded themselves from human fellowship or the organic body of humankind, and thus it is legitimate to 'amputate' them; hence, 'it is not contrary to nature to rob someone whom it is right to kill'.[225] Cicero here applies the same ideas that form part of his account of the rule of procedure, including the claim that acting justly and in a way that benefits one's community (and in this sense promoting the fellowship of humanity) is according to nature, and that the opposite principle also holds good. In the first case, as in the rule of procedure, he stresses the importance of motive, specifically the motive to benefit other people; indeed, in the case study, the question of motivation is partly criterial of rightness or wrongness.[226] These similarities strongly suggest that Cicero's guidance, as formulated in the rule of procedure and throughout *On Duties*, is taken to correspond to considerations employed by the person deliberating. In fact, apart from *On Duties*, we have ample evidence, especially from Cicero's letters, that educated Romans in Cicero's time regarded philosophical principles, taken from various

---

[223] Cic. *Off.* 3.29. These case studies seem to be based on existing Stoic casuistry (Dyck 1996: 532), though the treatment of the second one is likely to reflect Cicero's own views.

[224] Cic. *Off.* 3. 30-1, trans. Griffin and Atkins 1991.   [225] Cic. *Off.* 3.32.

[226] On the first point, see Cic. *Off.* 3.21-2 (including the idea of the community as an organic body), 26-7; on the second, see 3.23-4, 26. On the importance of motive, in determining what is right, see also text to nn. 153-5, 212-20.

theories, as directly relevant to deliberating about difficult questions, including that of the rightness of assassinating Julius Caesar in 44 BC, to which Cicero alludes in the second case study.[227] It is, actually, much more open to question than Cicero suggests, whether this assassination can be justified on Stoic grounds.[228] However, the idea that such considerations could reasonably be deployed in dealing with problematic cases seems to be entirely in line with Stoic thinking.

In 3.50–7, Cicero reports what he presents as a debate between two successive Stoic heads of the Stoic school, Diogenes and Antipater, about the ethics of business dealings. The debate centres on cases (relating to trading in corn and selling a house) where you can increase your profit by keeping silent about facts which are materially relevant to the price you can ask. In both cases, the two heads are presented as taking opposed positions: Diogenes advocates keeping silent, in line with normal business practice, while Antipater urges going beyond normal practice in revealing all the facts relevant to the sale, though unknown to the buyer. The two thinkers do not disagree that one should always do what is right, whether or not it is more advantageous. As Cicero points out: 'in the whole of this debate the following is never said: "Although this is wrong (*turpe*), I will do it, because it is expedient", but rather, "It is expedient without being wrong"'.[229] Their disagreement is about the course of action that matches these specifications. In the first case, Antipater argues for his policy of openness on these grounds:

'What are you saying? You ought to be considering the interests of human beings and serving human community (*humanae societati*); you were born under a law, and have principles of nature, which you ought to follow, to the effect that your advantage (*utilitas*) is also the common benefit, and conversely, the common benefit is yours. Will you conceal from human beings the material goods and resources that are available to them?'[230]

However, Diogenes, while accepting the relevance of this consideration, argues that, on Antipater's view, private property has no validity, and that, if this is so, 'then nothing can be sold at all, but must be given'.[231] This exchange is not continued, though Antipater could have replied that, even allowing for the

---

[227] See also Cic. *Off.* 3.19 (on the rightness of the assassination), and Long 1995: 219–33. See Sedley 1997 on evidence for applying philosophical principles to the question of Caesar's assassination; and Griffin 1995, on applying them in other contexts.

[228] Stoicism did not, typically, validate one type of constitution rather than another (Sedley 1997: 49–50); opposition to imperial rule by Roman Stoics was based on judgements of wrong action rather than objection to sole rule as such (Griffin 1976: 360–6).

[229] Cic. *Off.* 3.53, trans. Griffin and Atkins 1991.

[230] Cic. *Off.* 3.52, trans. Griffin and Atkins 1991. For similar ideas, see Cic. *Off.* 3.26, Cic. *Fin.* 3.64.

[231] Cic. *Off.* 3.53, trans. Griffin and Atkins 1991. However, Chrysippus, like Antipater, seems to have argued for the compatibility of the community of humankind with the validity of private property (Cic. *Fin.* 3.67).

legitimacy of private property, and of buying and selling, the community of humankind requires openness in the way this process is conducted. In the second exchange, Antipater, in the second phase of the debate, cites the obligation, where resources allow, to give to strangers, which is presented elsewhere in *On Duties* as derived from the community of humankind.[232] Diogenes again disputes its applicability to buying and selling. Although Cicero may have misrepresented the original dialectical context of this debate,[233] it is likely that this report reflects accurately the kind of ideas put forward by these Stoic thinkers. The approach taken is similar to that presented by Cicero in his rule of procedure and elsewhere in *On Duties*. Both Stoic thinkers, as reported here, aim to offer guidance on what should count as right, assuming that deliberation should be centred on this aim, and they also seek to correlate general ideals (notably those of human fellowship and natural law) with specific actions in concrete situations. This confirms the impression formed so far, that considerations of this kind are seen as informing valid deliberation, and do not simply provide the basis for analysing such deliberation.

The final discussion in Book 3 (3.99–111) considered here is that of Regulus, a Roman general captured in the First Punic war (third century BC). As presented by Cicero,[234] he was sent back to Rome to arrange his own exchange for a number of younger Carthaginian prisoners, but he argued strongly in the Senate against this exchange, as not benefiting Rome. Having sworn to the enemy that he would return to Carthage if he did not arrange this exchange, he did so, though knowing that this meant return to torture and death (3.99–100). This case study plays a climactic role in Book 3 and is clearly regarded by Cicero as highly significant.[235] What does it contribute to the overall project of Book 3 and how does it illuminate Stoic thinking on virtue and indifferents, and appropriate actions? Regulus is consistently presented by Cicero as having made the right (*honestum*) decision in a situation where it was difficult to determine what this was.[236] Also, the decision was one that conferred no advantages on Regulus himself;[237] so it represents an extreme as regards 'selection between indifferents'. The case is more striking because Regulus could have secured advantages by taking different decisions which were open to him; he takes the initiative, and goes beyond what might be

---

[232] Cic. *Off.* 3.55, also 1.51–2.

[233] For some suggestions on this, see Striker 1996: 265–6; Annas 1997: however, Inwood 1999: 122–4 takes it as a credible presentation of Stoic thinking.

[234] Cicero's presentation is highly selective, to judge from other reports of the incident (Dyck 1996: 619, 622–3).

[235] A letter from Cicero on 6/7 November 44 BC (*ad Atticum* 16.11.4) highlights the role of Regulus in his planning of *Off.* 3. See also Dyck 1996: 484–5, 620–1.

[236] See Cic. *Off.* 3.99–100, 101, 110.

[237] The advantages he gives up include 'remaining in his own country, being at home with his wife and children, maintaining his rank and standing as an ex-consul' (3.99,), rather than returning to 'death through enforced wakefulness' (3.100, trans. Griffin and Atkins 1991). Cicero also notes in 3.101 that all human beings are naturally drawn towards preferable, rather than dispreferable, indifferents.

expected of him, in adopting the course of action he did.[238] However, he is not presented by Cicero as acting in a way that is extreme or perverse. On the contrary, he is depicted as expressing the virtue of magnanimity, as described in Book 1, and justice, in his maintenance of the oath sworn to enemies.[239] Regulus thus fulfils a number of important roles in Cicero's exposition of Stoic ethics. He is an exemplar of the virtues; hence, he contributes significantly to illustrating appropriate actions characteristic of them. He illustrates what is involved in making the right decision in an ethically problematic situation (one where right and advantage 'seem to conflict', as Cicero puts it). He also shows that, under certain circumstances, the correct decision may involve giving up all preferable indifferents (advantages), even life itself.[240]

As Cicero recognizes, the effectiveness of this case study depends on showing that Regulus did indeed reach the correct (that is, the right, *honestum*) decision. Cicero highlights this point in a dialectical way, by presenting objections to Regulus' actions and by offering counterarguments to those objections. He maintains that Regulus did not act 'foolishly' (*stulte*) in arguing (against his own self-interest) in the Senate that the Carthaginian prisoners should not be returned, but that his act was right because it was advantageous to the Roman state (3.101). Cicero also argues that Regulus' insistence on honouring his oath reflected a proper understanding of the rules of warfare as well as the significance of swearing oaths in Roman public life.[241] Clearly, Cicero frames his argument in his own terms here (terms which would have weight with a Roman readership) and is not drawing on Stoic casuistry. Also, here, by contrast with his account of the rule of procedure (3.21–8) and his report of the debate between Diogenes and Antipater (3.50–7), he does not couch his argument in terms of what is 'natural', as understood in Stoic ethics. However, the features Cicero accentuates in Regulus' actions corresponds to ideas that also appear in those earlier discussions and which are significant in Stoic ethics. In taking the initiative in arguing against returning the prisoners, Regulus combines exercising a virtue, magnanimity, with showing a positive desire to benefit his state, rather than himself, and to contribute to human fellowship in this way.[242] Similarly, in insisting on maintaining his oath to the enemy, when he would not have been criticized for setting it aside,[243] he acted justly towards those falling outside his community, who are also members of the community of humankind, at the same time as maintaining proper standards

---

[238] That is, in arguing against returning the prisoners and in insisting on maintaining his oath: see 3.99–102, 110–11.

[239] Regulus acted from 'greatness of spirit and courage': 'it is characteristic of these virtues to fear nothing, to disdain anything human, and to think nothing can happen to a human being that is unendurable' (3.100, trans. Griffin and Atkins 1991; see also 1.66). He showed 'justice and good faith' in maintaining his oath (3.104, also 107).

[240] For the idea that happiness is possible even without preferred indifferents, see text to n. 28.

[241] Cic. *Off.* 3.107–9, also 104.   [242] Cf. Cic. *Off.* 3.99–101, 110, and 3.24.26–8, 52–3.

[243] Cicero presents (but does not endorse) arguments for setting the oath aside in 3.102, 104.

of warfare and oath-keeping within his community.[244] So we can see connections between the discussion of this specific case and the general ethical framework set out earlier in *On Duties*.

What are the broader implications of the discussion of Regulus for the question of the nature of virtuous deliberation, as conceived in Stoic ethics? This case study confirms the overall view offered here, rather than in some other recent inter-pretations. As Barney acknowledges, the presentation of Regulus, which she accepts as being in line with Stoic thinking, runs counter to the idea that virtuous deliberation centres on maximizing preferable indifferents for the agent.[245] The depiction of Regulus strongly supports the idea that virtuous deliberation depends, at least sometimes, on positive motivation to benefit others (for instance, one's state, or humankind as represented in some specific group or person), and not only on recognition of indications of justice as a constraint on one's own legitimate pursuit of advantage, as in Brennan's 'no-shoving' model.[246] The presentation of the incident, especially the statement of arguments for and against his action, seems designed to bring out considerations that Regulus himself might have deployed in reaching his decision, rather than those which only make sense as part of an analysis conducted from outside.[247] Although these considerations are framed, in Regulus' case, in relatively specific terms, they correspond to those discussed elsewhere in terms of 'nature', and they could have been formulated in that way here too.[248] Overall, despite the strongly Ciceronian, and Roman, character of this case study, it confirms the general picture of Stoic virtuous deliberation already given here, including the role of indifferents.

[244] On the force of oaths given (sincerely) to enemies, see 3.107–8; on ethical obligations to those outside one's community, see 1.51–2, 3.28.

[245] Barney 2003: 319–20.

[246] The definition of justice in Cic. *Off*. 1.20, 22 combines both elements; see text to nn. 136–7 (on justice); 148–51, 208–11 (on Brennan's approach).

[247] See *Off*. 3.100–8; on 'split-level' theories, see text to nn. 92, 164–5, 222.

[248] See nn. 206–7, 218–20, 230–2.

3

Ethics and Nature

3.1 Preliminaries

It is evident from the previous two chapters that the idea of nature plays a highly significant role in Stoic ethics. The characterization of happiness as 'the life according to nature' and of preferred indifferents as 'things according to nature' constitutes a strong indication of this point. However, it is less clear how, exactly, we should understand this role. Some scholars have claimed that the idea of nature or the Stoic worldview is foundational for Stoic ethics. Others have challenged this claim, maintaining that Stoic ethical principles are seen as being independently grounded, even if they are supported or complemented by the Stoic conception of nature. The debate between different versions of these two positions has been one of the major sources of controversy among Stoic scholars in recent years. This question is also an important one for our understanding of the relationship between Stoic and modern ethics. The question of the relationship between ethical theory and nature is a highly significant—and evolving—one in modern philosophical debate.[1] Hence, the view we form of Stoic ethics in this respect has implications for the scope of Stoicism to contribute to modern moral theory.

After outlining recent debate on this question (3.2), I review a wide range of relevant evidence in Stoic writings. I focus initially on the main ancient summaries of ethical doctrines (3.3); and then on ancient evidence that seems to present physics (specifically theology) as foundational for ethics (3.4). Finally, I consider the role of universal nature in Stoic writings on practical ethics, notably in Epictetus and Marcus Aurelius (3.5). At each stage, and especially the end of the chapter, I consider the implications of this evidence for the scholarly debate on the role of nature in Stoic ethics.

3.2 Scholarly Debate about Ethics and Nature

First, I locate Stoic ideas on this subject in the broader context of ancient thought. We should note that traditional Greek thinking does not presuppose a worldview in which nature as a whole (or dominant powers in nature, such as gods), provides

---

[1] See Ch. 7.

Learning to Live Naturally: Stoic Ethics and its Modern Significance. Christopher Gill, Oxford University Press.
© Christopher Gill 2022. DOI: 10.1093/oso/9780198866169.003.0004

a foundational, or even supportive, basis for human ethics. Major and influential Greek poems, such as Homer's *Iliad* and *Odyssey*, Hesiod's *Theogony*, and the fifth-century BC Athenian tragedies, underline what is ethically problematic in divine actions and their effects on human beings. Plato, in the *Republic*, maintains that traditional poetic presentation of gods runs counter to the aim of promoting sound ethical standards and argues for a radically revised view of divine character and action.[2] There is a marked contrast in this respect with modern Western culture, especially in the medieval and early modern periods, in which Christian religion and the associated worldview were widely seen as underpinning morality.[3] In the later fifth century BC, the idea of nature was appropriated by thinkers arguing that there was a fundamental conflict between natural human desires and conventional ethical standards. The *nomos-phusis* (or 'convention' versus 'nature') debate, as it is generally known, also gave rise to opposing views, defending the validity of normal ethical principles. However, in the fifth century at least, among the so-called 'sophists', this defence was not, typically, couched in terms of 'nature'. The claim was rather that human societies could only survive and protect their members by framing legal rules and promoting ethical attitudes; this view was sometimes presented as the idea that ethics constitutes a 'social contract'.[4]

The stronger claim that ethical principles are actually in line with nature, in some sense, emerges in the fourth century, in Plato and Aristotle. In the *Republic*, for instance, we find the argument that the four cardinal virtues constitute forms of structured relationship between the parts of the psyche, and that these relationships express the real nature of the psyche.[5] In Plato's *Timaeus*, a work widely regarded as influential on the Stoic worldview, the universe is seen as a coherent and ordered whole, reflecting the objectives of a benevolent and providential craftsman-god. The universe is seen as teleologically organized, and at least some of its parts, notably human beings, are presented as having distinctive natural purposes. We also find the idea that human beings are capable of becoming more virtuous and 'orderly' (*kosmios*) by patterning themselves on the order of the universe (*kosmos*).[6] Aristotle, as usually interpreted, adopts a form of natural teleology in which the focus is on the realization by specific life-forms of their in-built nature, rather than on the idea of overall cosmic purpose.[7] Consistently with this view, Aristotle stresses, in the ethical context, the idea that happiness, for

---

[2] See Pl. *Rep.* 377b–385c; Gill 1995: 67, 70.
[3] On Christianity as ethically foundational, see text to nn. 123–5.
[4] On this debate, see, in outline, Gill 1995: 72–3; also Guthrie 1969: chs. 4–5; Kerferd 1981: ch. 10.
[5] Pl. *Rep.* 434d–444e (esp. 444c–d), 588c–591e.
[6] Pl. *Ti.* 29c–30c, 39e–40a, 41b–d, 44d–47e, 90a–d. This teleological worldview is anticipated in Pl. *Phd.* 96a–99c; it is sometimes seen as based on Socratic thinking (Xen. *Mem.* 1.4, 4.3). See Sedley 2007: chs. 3–4. On Plato's *Timaeus* and Stoicism, see Betegh 2003; Gill 2006: 16–20.
[7] For this view, see Rocca 2017: 12–13, summarizing scholarly opinion (also Johnson 2005: 1–11, chs. 7, 9); however, Sedley 2007: 194–203 argues for a type of cosmic teleology in Aristotle.

human beings, represents the fulfilment of the distinctive human function or 'work'. However, he also suggests, in a much discussed further move, that the *highest* happiness is constituted by philosophical or theoretical activity, presented as marking a 'divine', and not simply 'human', level of happiness. The second move, as well as the first, can be seen as correlating ethical value with 'nature', in a broad sense.[8]

The Stoic position on this topic, as on others, was independently formulated.[9] However, their thinking on this subject is much closer to Plato and Aristotle than to any of the positions in the earlier, fifth-century, debate. The idea of human beings as having a distinctive, in-built, nature (as rational and sociable) plays a substantial role in their ethical thinking.[10] In physics, especially theology (which falls under 'physics', for them)[11] the Stoics adopt a worldview that has both Platonic and Aristotelian prototypes.[12] The Stoics conceive the natural universe as a unified organic entity, which is rational and benevolent or providentially caring. It is seen as teleologically structured, and its component parts, including human beings and other animals, have their own specific natural purposes.[13] This worldview was sharply divergent from that of the Epicureans, their contemporaries and main rivals in Hellenistic thought. For the Epicureans, the universe was the product of purely mechanical processes (the fortuitous interaction of atoms) without any in-built purposive structure or aims. The Epicureans, like the Stoics, sometimes stress the value for ethics of understanding nature; but, in the Epicurean case, this value is not based on a recognition of a teleological worldview in which human beings have a determinate place.[14]

In addition to these Stoic ideas about human and cosmic nature, a second distinctive feature of their thought is the adoption of a series of 'hard' or rigorous positions on topics of ancient ethical debate. These positions are those discussed in Chapters 1 and 2 (virtue as the sole basis for happiness and the virtue-indifferents distinction). These are linked, as brought out later, with key features of Stoic thinking on appropriation and emotions, all marking differences from Aristotelian views.[15] The presence of these two distinctive features (the Stoic teleological worldview and the 'hard' ethical theses) is recognized by all scholars of Stoicism; and everyone, I think, acknowledges the existence of some relationship between them. However, the precise character and extent of this relationship

---

[8] See Arist. *NE* 1.7, 1097b22–1098a; 10.7–8; also Johnson 2005: 217–22 on the relationship between the ethical idea of the human function and Aristotelian natural teleology. See also on nature and ethics in Aristotle, Ch. 6, text to nn. 92–9, Ch. 7, text to nn. 168–72.

[9] See Sedley 2003: 9–13; Gill 2006: 20–2.   [10] See Ch. 1, text to nn. 72–82.

[11] On the Stoic branches of knowledge, and the place of theology, see LS 26 A–E (especially C); also 3.4.

[12] The Stoic worldview combines a Platonic-style cosmic teleology with the Aristotelian idea that the component forms of life have their own specific natural purpose.

[13] See LS 54; also Sedley 2007: ch. 7.   [14] See LS 13, 25, esp. B; also Gill 2006: 187–90.

[15] See 4.4 and 5.1.

is disputed. According to a longstanding view, the first feature, the worldview, provides the grounding or foundation for Stoic ethics.[16] The worldview is seen as offering a teleological context for mapping and explaining the capacities and in-built tendencies of different natural kinds, including human beings.[17] Also, the Stoic ethical theses are analysed and explained by reference to the Stoic providential worldview. The interpretative claim, made with varying degrees of explicitness, is that the credibility of the Stoic ethical theses depends on, and needs, the support of, the Stoic worldview. This approach has been applied especially in connection with the theory of development as appropriation, an idea often seen as providing a link between the Stoic account of the cosmos, with its structured mapping of natural kinds, and ethics. In particular, the main distinctive feature of Stoic appropriation, the idea that ethical development leads to recognition of the special value of virtue, as distinct from preferred indifferents, is seen as dependent on links with the Stoic worldview. For instance, the motivational shift, linked with the recognition of the radical difference in value between virtue and indifferents, is sometimes regarded as based on assimilation of oneself to the order built into the cosmos.[18] Also, the devaluation of preferred indifferents, as a result of development, and the associated emotional response (freedom from 'passions') is sometimes regarded as dependent on recognizing the providential power of cosmic nature, which underlies the shaping of events.[19] In a further version of this approach, the value of indifferents, as a source of guidance for the virtuous person, is taken to depend on the fact that, if properly interpreted, they communicate the will of Zeus or the providential order built into the cosmos and the unfolding series of events.[20] These interpretative moves by scholars are seen as confirming the rather widely held belief that the Stoic worldview provides the basis for its 'hard' ethical theses.

However, not all scholars adopt this position. Julia Annas and Terence Irwin, for instance, have maintained that Stoic ethical claims are, typically, formulated and supported within the standard framework of ancient ethical categories and arguments.[21] Annas has highlighted the significance of the fact that, in ancient discussions such as Cicero's *On Ends*, theses such as the sufficiency of virtue for

[16] On the idea of 'grounding' or 'foundations', see n. 122.
[17] See White 1979, 1985; Inwood 1985, esp. chs. 2, 6; Menn 1995; Long 1996: ch. 6; Inwood and Donini 1999: 675–87; Jedan 2009: 103–9. D.L. 7.85–9 is taken as a prime source for this view.
[18] See White 1979: 162–70, 1985: 61–3; Striker 1996: 224–31; M. Frede 1999: 80–94; On the motivational shift, see Cic. *Fin.* 3.20–2; also 4.4, text to nn. 133–9, questioning the extent of the shift.
[19] See White 1985: 58–63; Cooper 1995: 594–6.
[20] See Klein 2015: 258–70; also Brennan 2014, discussing Klein's approach. This point is taken to apply both to cases where 'the will of Zeus' coincides with gaining preferred indifferents and to cases where it coincides with giving them up (or being deprived of them). Klein's view that the ethical significance of indifferents is underpinned by divine (cosmic) providence is broadly similar to that of Striker 1996: 228–31 and M. Frede 1999: 80–94.
[21] See Irwin 1986, 2007: ch. 13; Annas 1993: ch. 5. See also Engberg-Pedersen 1990: 64–100 (discussed in Gill 2006: 157–8, 360–70).

happiness are maintained, and attacked by their opponents, without explicit reference to the Stoic worldview.[22] Annas has also challenged the widespread view that Stoic ethics presupposes the foundation of the Stoic worldview and needs this support to render its main claims credible.[23] Annas does not dispute that ideas about nature form a standard part of ancient ethical discourse (in Aristotle, for instance);[24] and she gives a significant role to Stoic ideas about human nature in her interpretation of Stoic ethics. For instance, she explains the motivational shift within ethical development (the recognition of the value of virtue rather than indifferents) by referring to the Stoic conception of human beings as constitutively rational.[25] Indeed, she also accepts that Stoic thinkers regard the Stoic worldview as providing a broad framework for their account of Stoic ethics. But she thinks that reference to the worldview belongs to a second stage of ethical reflection, when the main distinctive claims have been independently established. Stoic ethical ideas are placed in a wider perspective by reference to the picture of human nature offered by physics (study of nature).[26] However, the ideas thus presented do not depend, primarily, for their credibility and cogency on this worldview but on the ethical arguments offered on their behalf.[27]

Annas's challenge has proved highly controversial and has generated substantial debate; most of the responses have been critical, restating the importance of cosmic nature in Stoic ethics,[28] though some have been more even-handed.[29] The debate might seem to have led simply to an impasse, in that neither side in the debate has decisively altered the approach taken. However, several significant new points have been made; and, overall, I think we have moved towards a clearer understanding of the relationship between these two distinctive features of Stoic thought (the teleological worldview and the 'hard' ethical theses). For instance, an exchange of views between Annas and John Cooper clarified the key point at issue. What is disputed is not whether Stoic ideas about universal nature are combined and, in some way, integrated with the distinctive ethical theses, but whether the cogency and credibility of the ethical theses *depend* on distinctively Stoic thinking about universal nature.[30]

Annas has herself contributed to ongoing debate on this topic; and she has refined and developed her position in certain respects. For instance, she withdrew at an early stage the suggestion that reference to universal nature, in any form, was a non-standard feature in Stoic ethics, though she did so without revising the main

---

[22] See Annas 1993: 166; 1995: 599–600, 608–9.
[23] Annas 1993: ch. 5, especially 160–3; 1995: 600–2, 608–9.   [24] See Annas 1993: chs. 3, 4, 9.
[25] Annas 1993: 168–72.   [26] Annas 1993: 163–6; 1995: 603–4.
[27] Annas 1993: 178: for detailed discussion of the (ethical) arguments offered by Cic. *Fin.* 3, see Annas 1993: 388–411.
[28] See Inwood 1995: 653–61; Cooper 1995; Boeri 2009.
[29] Gill 2004b, 2006: 148–66; Brüllmann 2015: ch. 2.
[30] See Annas 1995: 606–9; Cooper 1995: 591–6; also Annas 2007b: 68–72. See also 3.4, esp. text following n. 122, on this point.

lines of her approach.[31] In a subsequent discussion (2007b), she made two further significant points. She argued that it is mistaken to try to identify a single authoritative Stoic approach to the question of the role of nature in ethics. As brought out shortly, our sources differ importantly between themselves on this point. However, she maintains, in none of the summaries is it clearly stated and argued that the core ethical claims *depend* on the Stoic account of universal nature.[32] A second point made by Annas concerns the relationship between the main branches of knowledge in Stoicism, that is, logic, ethics, and physics. She acknowledges the presence of ancient evidence maintaining that the Stoic world-view (falling within physics and especially theology) provides the basis for Stoic ethics. Some of this evidence is supplied by Plutarch in a rather unhelpful form designed to show Stoic self-contradictions.[33] However, Annas also stresses that this evidence is in tension with other indications that the three branches of knowledge in Stoic ethics are seen as reciprocal and mutually informing rather than hierarchically related.[34]

A substantial contribution to the debate has been made by Philipp Brüllmann (2015). Brüllmann offers a more philosophically searching examination of the idea of nature as an ethical norm in Stoicism than any previous treatment. He identifies significant strengths and weaknesses in both sides of the debate. His main criticism of Annas, directed especially against her first discussion (1993: ch. 5), is that she seriously understates the importance of cosmic or universal nature in Stoic ethical writings.[35] However, he endorses her principal challenge to more orthodox (one might say, 'naturalist'), interpreters, namely, that they have failed to demonstrate the connection claimed between the distinctive features of the Stoic worldview and the Stoic ethical claims. While asserting repeatedly *that* universal nature is, in some sense, authoritative or normative, they have failed to explain precisely *how* this norm operates, and how the content of Stoic ethical ideas is shaped by reference to this idea. Brüllmann develops this criticism by distinguishing two senses in which universal nature might, in principle, play this role, namely as a standard of value and as a source of normativity, and by asking if universal nature does in fact play either role in Stoicism.[36]

His conclusions are negative or at least qualified. On the first point, he argues that, if universal nature were seen as a standard of value, in a strong sense, ethical judgements would be based, consistently, on conformity with this standard. However, he argues that this is not maintained in Stoic theology, as presented,

---

[31] See Annas 1995: 604–5, n. 13; contrast 1993: 160–1, 175–6.
[32] Annas 2007b: 80–7, also 73–9.
[33] See Plu. *Sto. Rep.* 1035 C–D (LS 60 A); Cic. *Fin.* 3.73; a similar view may be implied in D.L. 7.88; on these passages, see 3.4. On Plutarch's unhelpful presentation, see Annas 2007b: 79–84.
[34] Annas 2007b: 60–3, referring to Sen. *Ep.* 89 1–2, D.L. 7.39–41 (LS 26 B) (see also LS 26 A, C–E).
[35] As noted in text to n. 31, Annas subsequently qualified this claim.
[36] Brüllmann 2015: ch. 2.

for instance, in Cicero's *On the Nature of the Gods* 2. The claim is not that the universe is *ipso facto* good, and that all other things are good in so far as they resemble the universe. The Stoic view is that the universe is good *in virtue of* certain good-making features, notably being rational and beneficial; these features also make other things good, notably human beings. The universe is seen as a paradigm of goodness because it exhibits these good-making qualities to a very high degree; to this extent, the universe is a standard of value in a weak sense. But it falls short of being a standard in the strong sense of being good by definition. Brüllmann also examines critically the view that the idea of nature functions as a source of normativity and provides criteria for right and wrong action, in Stoic ethics. As he points out, the characterization of being 'according to nature' (*kata phusin*) is ascribed to different types of value in Stoic ethics; both 'preferred indifferents' and virtue-based happiness are described in this way, and in one account of appropriation, that in Cicero's *On Ends* 3.16–22, both types of value are characterized in these terms.[37] The fact that they share the same designation is not, in itself, problematic; however, it means that the category of being 'according to nature' is not used, by itself, to discriminate between levels of value.[38] These points do not, by themselves, settle—and are not presented by Brüllmann as settling—the disagreement about the ethical significance of nature between Annas and 'naturalist' interpreters. However, they suggest that the question whether the idea of nature (especially universal nature) functions as an ethical standard or norm requires further examination than it has so far received. These points also indicate that the idea of nature is used in varied and flexible ways in Stoic ethics, an inference drawn by Brüllmann from its usage in, for instance, Cleanthes' 'Hymn to Zeus' and Epictetus' *Discourses*.[39] Different Stoic thinkers elaborate in different ways the view that ethical ideas can be defined in terms of nature (human or universal or both) or in purely ethical terms. They are neither presupposing nor deflecting from a single authoritative Stoic account of the relationship between universal nature and ethics.

I think Brüllmann's analysis is largely convincing, and that, taken with the two main points made by Annas (2007b), this opens up a more credible picture of Stoic thinking on the relationship between the distinctive worldview and the ethical claims. It is not plausible to suppose that there was, at any given time, *one* definitive Stoic account of this relationship.[40] To judge from what are generally recognized as the three main ancient summaries of ethical ideas,[41] there were

---

[37] On Cicero's account of appropriation, see 6.4 (also Brüllmann 2015: 135–7).

[38] Brüllmann 2015: ch. 3, esp. 99–138.   [39] Brüllmann 2015: ch. 3, esp. 141–50.

[40] In fact, this is agreed by many scholars, even if they take sharply different views on the main points at issue: see Long 1996: 155; Schofield 2003: 236–46 (also Schofield 1995 191–9); Inwood 2009: 206–7.

[41] That is, D.L. 7.84–131, Stob. 5–12, 2.57–116, Cic. *Fin.* 3; these are presented in translation in IG: 113–57 (Cic. *Fin.* 3 in shortened form).

various possible ways of presenting ethics. The core ethical ideas could be pre-sented entirely in their own terms (as they are, to a large extent, in all three summaries);[42] alternatively, they can be combined or supported with references to 'nature', whether human, universal, or both. For instance, they can be presented as incorporating conceptions of human nature, as they are in Stobaeus (and also in Cicero's *On Duties*).[43] They can also be formulated in a way that locates views of human nature in a broader picture of natural animal behaviour and motives, especially in connection with the theme of development as appropriation; this formulation can be found in Diogenes Laertius, Cicero's *On Ends* 3 (and *On Duties* 1).[44] They can also be presented as supported by, or incorporating, ideas about universal nature, framed either in terms of Zeus' direction or plan, as they are near the start of Diogenes' summary or, in rather broader terms, at the end of Cicero, *On Ends* 3.[45]

It is not entirely clear why we find this degree of variation. Some of the differences reflect broader differences between the three accounts. Diogenes' version is, very much, a 'handbook' (or doxographical) version, which combines different elements without attempting to provide an overall synthesis. His account begins (like Cicero's in *On Ends* 3) by locating human motivation in a larger natural pattern, and then by citing a definition of happiness (or the goal of life) which refers to human and universal nature. Subsequently, it shifts to a more classificatory style, and discusses the typical ethical topics in much the same (purely ethical) terms as the other accounts.[46] The version in Stobaeus is the most systematic and detailed and is classificatory throughout; it is organized consistently around categories of value (good, bad, and neither good nor bad, that is, indifferent).[47] It is also consistent in excluding explicit reference to universal nature or appropriation (a theory which, typically, places human nature in a broader picture of natural behaviour and motivation), and in focusing wholly on the role of human nature in ethics.[48] However, the rationale for these two distinctive features of Stobaeus' account is not obvious.[49] Cicero's account in *On Ends* 3 differs from the other two versions in that the book forms part of a

---

[42] See text to nn. 62–77.

[43] Stob. 5b1, 5b3, 6; Cic. *Off.* 1.11–15, 50–9, 3.21–32, 52–3. See text to nn. 78–91; also Ch. 1, text to nn. 72–82, 154–79. Cic. *Off.* is not a summary of Stoic ethics as a whole but it is closely related on certain key points to these summaries, esp. that of Stobaeus.

[44] See D.L. 7.85–7, Cic. *Fin.* 3.16–22, 62–8; also Cic. *Off.* 1.11–12, 50–4. See also text to nn. 92–7.

[45] D.L. 7.87–9; Cic. *Fin.* 3.73. See also text to nn. 98–107.

[46] See D.L. 7.85–9, Cic. *Fin.* 3.16–21; also Schofield 2003: 238–9.

[47] See Long 1996: 110–22, 130–3.

[48] See Stob. 6a–e, 2.75.11–78.6, on the goal; also 5b3, 2.62.7–14, on basic human motives (replacing appropriation). On human nature, typically described as rational and sociable, see 5b1, 2.59.4–7, 5b3 again, 6, 2.75.7–10 (also text to nn. 78–91). On Stobaeus' selective treatment, see Long 1996: 124; Inwood 1995: 254–5. On the single phrase that refers, by implication, to universal nature, see n. 82.

[49] Stobaeus' account (very late, probably 5th cent. AD) is usually ascribed to Arius Didymus (late 1st c. BC); but this is not certain, and in any case this does not, in itself, explain his emphases (see Long 1996: 107–10, 122–30).

connected review of ethical ideas in Hellenistic philosophy, those of the
Epicureans, Stoics and Antiochus (who is, broadly, Platonic-Aristotelian in
approach). In this respect, Cicero's is the most independently and dialectically
shaped of the three accounts. Some of Cicero's emphases (on appropriation, and
on Stoic, as opposed to Aristotelian, views about the scope of what is really good)
are, clearly, correlated with this aim.[50] Conceivably, his de-emphasizing of universal nature (which is confined to a parenthetical final comment, *Fin.* 3.73) may
reflect the fact that this idea is not relevant for comparison and contrast with
Antiochus, which is the overall aim of Books 4–5. However, this variation between
the summaries in the treatment of the idea of nature, which is combined with a
high degree of consistency in the formulation of the core ethical ideas, carries a
clear overall implication. What is suggested is that there was no single, authoritative Stoic way of presenting the relationship between the core ethical ideas,
including the 'hard' ethical theses noted earlier,[51] and the concept of nature, even
though all three accounts include some reference to nature, human or universal or
both. It is striking that some of these different forms of presentation seem to be
derived from Chrysippus, the most influential Stoic theorist. Diogenes' opening
summary of appropriation and his formulation of the goal of life (including
reference to universal nature) are ascribed to Chrysippus.[52] However, the systematic and value-centred treatment found in Stobaeus, combined with deployment
of the idea of human nature, is also thought by scholars to reflect Chrysippus'
approach.[53] Thus, it seems that Chrysippus may have treated the theme of nature
in ethics in at least two different ways, perhaps in different works (he wrote
numerous ethical works).[54]

This presentation runs counter to the view of some scholars that the Stoic
worldview provides the authoritative basis for ethics.[55] On this view, one would
expect the linkage with universal nature to be a consistent feature of Stoic ethics,
or at least acknowledged in some way in each version.[56] The presentation of Stoic
ethics suggests, rather that, if any element is indispensable, it is discussion of the
core ethical ideas (good and bad, the end, virtue, indifferents, appropriate actions),
couched in those terms. The other elements (appropriation, human and universal

---

[50] See Cic. *Fin.* 3.16–22, 26–31, 41–50. These topics are also central, from an opposed position, in
Cic. *Fin.* 4–5. On the shaping of the argument of *Fin.* 3, see Annas 1993: 392–411; on *Fin.* 4–5, see
Bénatouïl 2016a; Gill 2016a.

[51] See text to nn. 15–16.

[52] See D.L. 7.85–9 (the ethical significance of the references to universal nature, is stressed, for
instance, by Long 1996: ch. 6).

[53] See Long 1996: 124, 130; Schofield 2003: 236–8.

[54] On Chrysippus' numerous ethical works, see D.L. 7.199–202. Also D.L. 7.89 reports that
Chrysippus stressed the ethical significance of both human and cosmic nature, unlike Cleanthes who
only stressed cosmic nature.

[55] See text to nn. 17–20.

[56] Cic. *Fin.* 3.73 does acknowledge the significance of universal nature (not elsewhere evident in
Cic. *Fin.* 3); but there is no such acknowledgement in Stobaeus' account.

nature) could be drawn on or not, as seemed appropriate, in order to deepen or enhance the significance of those ideas.[57] This picture runs counter to the claim that Stoic ethical ideas, especially the distinctive 'hard' ethical theses, were derived from, or dependent on, the specification of universal nature.[58] The point comes out by contrast with, for instance, Kantian or Utilitarian theories, where ethical principles are presented as directly and explicitly derived from certain fundamental or grounding ideas: namely the 'Categorical Imperative' or the greatest happiness of the greatest number.[59] However, the presentation of Stoic ethics is quite compatible with the view that their ethical claims are consistent with, or informed by, ideas of universal, as well as human, nature.

In contributing to this subject here, I take as my starting point the stage that the debate has now reached. The substantive conflict, it seems to me, is no longer between what one might call 'ethicist' or 'naturalist' scholarly approaches or between those who stress the importance of *either* human *or* cosmic nature in ethics. I take it as obvious that nature, both human and universal, plays a significant role in Stoic ethics; the problem is to determine precisely what this role is. The main interpretative challenge, in my view, is to reconcile the presentation of Stoic ethics in the three ancient summaries with other ancient evidence, which suggests that the Stoic worldview, as depicted in Stoic theology, in some sense grounds ethical principles. Whereas the overall implication of the summaries is that Stoic ethics can be presented in different ways with equal validity, this other ancient evidence seems to give authoritative weight to the ethical role of universal nature or god. Hence, I examine the presentation of nature in the three ancient summaries (3.3), before considering the competing evidence which suggests that Stoic theology, which gives a central place to universal nature, is authoritative for ethics (3.4). Finally, I consider indications from Stoic writing in practical ethics of the different roles played there by universal nature (3.5). I think that a credible overall picture of the role of the idea of nature, including universal nature, in Stoic ethics emerges, though it is a complex and nuanced one.

3.3 The Presentation of Ethics in the Three Ancient Summaries

I begin by exploring the varied presentation of the role of nature in the three ancient summaries of ethical doctrine, found in Diogenes Laertius, Stobaeus, perhaps derived from Arius Didymus, and Cicero (*On Ends* 3). The view of Stoic ethical theory and its presentation that, I think, has emerged from scholarly

[57] This is also Brüllmann's conclusion, 2015: 161–2.
[58] On these theses and the question of the relationship with ideas of nature, see text to nn. 15–16.
[59] On this contrast, see also Annas 1993: ch. 22. See further text to nn. 127–9.

debate is this. The core principles of Stoic ethics can be presented in four different, but related, ways, each of which has its own validity, though each is consistent with, and in some way supported by, the other modes of presentation. (1) These principles can be presented in terms of the standard concepts of Greek ethical theory (virtue, happiness, good and so on), though modified in the light of the distinctive claims of Stoic ethics. (2) They can be presented in ethical terms (those of type (1)), combined with reference to human nature. (3) They can be presented in ethical terms, along with a mode of analysis (notably the theory of development as appropriation) which conceives human nature as part of a broader natural pattern of forms of life. (4) They can be presented in ethical terms, together with reference to universal or cosmic nature (or god). The three ethical summaries illustrate these four forms of presentation. In all three cases, the bulk of the discussion consists of type (1) presentation, though each of the summaries also contains one or more of the other types. For instance, Stobaeus' summary combines type (1) and type (2) presentation. In the summaries of Diogenes Laertius and Cicero, we find a combination of type (1) and type (3) presentation, in the accounts of appropriation which play a prominent role in their treatments. Diogenes Laertius also provides a clear example of the combination of type (1) with type (4) presentation, which also appears in Cicero's On Ends 3, in the form of a statement about physics (or theology) and ethics.[60] A clear implication of this overall pattern of presentation is that each of these modes, including type (1), is regarded by Stoics as constituting a valid way of stating core ethical principles. A second implication is that the additional elements in types (2)–(4) (the idea of 'nature' in one or other form) provides explanation or support for the claims made in type (1). Whether this support should be described as providing grounding or foundations for the type (1) claims, as some scholars maintain, is considered in the following section (3.4).[61]

I now illustrate these types of presentation in the three ethical summaries. All three summaries present a specific set of topics (the core ethical doctrines of Stoicism) and do so in similar terms;[62] it is sometimes supposed that their accounts derive, ultimately, from an ethical compendium by Chrysippus.[63] The list of topics, as treated by Stobaeus, for instance, consists of: good and bad things, especially virtue and vice, the goal of life, indifferents, appropriate actions, and

---

[60] On these variations, see also text to nn. 41–54.

[61] The 'grounding' or 'foundational' view is characteristic of the 'naturalist' approach to ethics outlined earlier (text to nn. 17–20).

[62] All the summaries include the goal of life, good and bad, virtues, indifferents, appropriate actions. See D.L. 7.87–9 (goal), 90–3 (virtue), 94–102 (good), 104–7 (indifferents), 108–9 (appropriate actions); Stob. 5b–5b7 (virtue), 5c–5m (good), 6–6e (goal), 7–7g (indifferents), 8–8a (appropriate actions). Cic. Fin. 3 is presented more dialectically and less as a series of topics; but most of 3.10–50 centres on the claim that virtue is the only good and basis for happiness (or the goal); then follows discussion of indifferents (51–4, 56–7) and appropriate actions (58–61).

[63] See Long 1996: 122–4; Schofield 2003: 236–9.

motive, including the emotions.[64] This list of topics reflects the ideas central to previous Greek ethical theory, especially that of Plato and Aristotle, such as virtue and happiness or the goal of life, good and bad, and also psychology (in the form of 'motive', including emotions).[65] There is also a substantial role in the summaries for social ethics, which is not evident from the list of contents.[66] The topics also reflect the key innovations of Stoic theory, notably through the appearance of the topics of 'indifferents' and 'appropriate actions', and, implicitly, in connection with 'virtue' and 'good'. In all three summaries, the bulk of the discussion is formulated in terms of type (1) presentation, although all of them also deploy, in addition, the idea of nature. In this, purely formal, sense, type (1) presentation forms a distinct mode of formulating Stoic ethical theory, and is, indeed, the predominant mode.

Also, and more importantly for this question, all the summaries offer explanation and argument for the distinctive claims of Stoic ethics framed in terms of presentation (1), even if they also do so in other terms. The central Stoic thesis is that virtue constitutes the sole basis for happiness, and that other things generally considered good are only 'matters of indifference', while they are also naturally 'preferable'. In this sense, virtue, along with virtue-based happiness, is the only good, and the only inherently choiceworthy object. A salient argument for this claim (formulated in type (1) presentation) is that the virtues, by contrast with the preferred indifferents, are forms of knowledge or expertise which enable the person concerned to lead a happy life. This thesis, in turn, underlies the argument that virtue as knowledge constitutes 'right use' of indifferents and thereby consistently benefits the person involved (as well as others affected), whereas the preferred indifferents do not consistently benefit those people.[67] All three summaries give a central place to these ideas, articulated in type (1) presentation, though couched in different ways that reflect the overall style of each summary. The summary of Diogenes Laertius is the most straightforward and unelaborated; points are set out and explained one by one. The claim of the sufficiency of virtue for happiness (and its goodness) is formulated in this way, as is the distinction between virtue, conceived as right use, and indifferents.[68] Cicero's version is the most analytic and dialectical in style. The thesis of the sufficiency of virtue for happiness is highlighted from the start, and explained and defended in a number

---

[64] See Schofield 2003: 238: for a similar list, see D.L. 7.84 (LS 56 A). For a detailed outline of Stobaeus' topics, correlated with those of D.L. and Cicero, see Long 1996: 130–3. A further topic sometimes included in the ancient lists, 'encouragement and discouragement', is found in works of practical ethics, such as Epictetus' *Discourses*, but does not appear in the ethical summaries.

[65] On Stoic ethical psychology and the idea of 'motive' (*hormē*), see 5.1, text to nn. 9–17. The category of 'motive' is seen as including the topic of appropriation (see LS 57).

[66] See D.L. 7.120–4, 129–31, Stob. 11b–11d, 11i, 11m, 11p–s (in connection with characterization of the wise person, in both accounts); also Cic. *Fin.* 3. 62–8.

[67] On these claims, framed in terms of type (1) presentation, see Ch. 1, text to nn. 132–52, Ch. 2, text to nn. 34–45.

[68] See D.L. 7.89, 92–103.

of ways (some of which fall under type (1)).[69] This is followed by a defence of the Stoic thesis by contrast with the Aristotelian one, framed again in terms of type (1).[70] Subsequently, Cicero discusses the ideas of indifferents and appropriate actions, underlining the link with the core Stoic claim about virtue, again couched in terms of type (1).[71] Stobaeus' version is systematic and classificatory, rather than dialectical, and, on the face of it, contains rather little in the way of argument for the core theses. However, the argument is expressed in the overall structure and the definitions and subdivisions of the summary. The distinction between good things, bad things, and indifferents forms the basis for the organization of the whole account. Ideas crucial for the Stoic position, including that of the virtues as forms of knowledge or expertise, by contrast with indifferents, are central for the analysis. The concept of good is carefully defined and the rationale for its limitation of scope to virtue, and corollaries of virtue, and happiness, is brought out clearly.[72] The predominant mode of presentation in the three summaries is type (1), and this mode is deployed to explicate and support the core Stoic claims in the ways indicated.

A further, suggestive, feature of the summaries is worth noting. We find in all three accounts versions of a specific kind of argument, based on the meaning of ethical terms and the interrelationship between those meanings. These arguments are used to substantiate the Stoic claims about the special status of virtue as good. In Stobaeus, for instance, the general claim of the goodness of virtue is supported by reference to its possession of a series of related or co-ordinate qualities, such as being praiseworthy, useful, and self-sufficient.[73] A similar argument is deployed by Diogenes Laertius, designed to show that what is good (paradigmatically, virtue) is also beneficial, because it is useful, praiseworthy, and worth choosing.[74] Cicero cites a similar argument, based on the claim that what is good is thereby praiseworthy and right.[75] This style of argument is strongly reminiscent of the characteristic idiom of the early (supposedly Socratic) dialogues of Plato.[76] Cicero characterizes the mode as 'syllogistic', thus highlighting a link with the expository style typical of Zeno, founder of Stoicism; so this form of argument should not be

---

[69] See Cic. *Fin.* 3.10–14, 22–9, 30–4, 36–9 (however, 3.16–22 is couched in terms of type (3)).
[70] See Cic. *Fin.* 3.41–50; this debate is continued throughout *Fin.* Books 4–5. See also Annas 1993: 391–5.
[71] Cic. *Fin.* 3.50–61.
[72] See Stob. 5a, 5b–b6, 5d–n, 6d–f, 7–7g. For analysis of the structure of the summary, see Long 1996: 107–33, esp. the synopsis on 130–3.
[73] Stob. 11h, 2.100.15–101.4.
[74] D.L. 7.99; see also Stob. 5d, 2.69.11–70.7. arguing for a necessary link between the ideas of goodness and benefit.
[75] Cic. *Fin.* 3.27.
[76] See e.g. Pl. *Grg.* 474c–475e, 476e–477d. On Socrates as a key influence on Stoicism, see Long 1996: ch. 1.

taken as a feature only of later Stoicism.[77] The presence of this type of theme in the summaries indicates that argumentation based solely on considerations of value is regarded as a valid part of Stoic ethical theory, without reference to the idea of nature.

The second type of presentation consists in the standard Stoic ethical claims, combined with reference to human nature. In the three ethical summaries, this type occurs only in Stobaeus, although the combination of human and universal nature is prominent in the other two summaries. However, the features found in Stobaeus are similar to ideas found in Cicero's *On Duties*, which, while not a summary of Stoic ethical doctrines, is based on a Hellenistic Stoic ethical treatise and is closely related in content to the summaries.[78] The main relevant points are discussed in Chapter 1 and are summarized here. Early in the account, Stobaeus presents wisdom and the other virtues as 'knowledge in a naturally social and rational animal of good and bad things, and what is neither [that is, indifferents]'.[79] Slightly later, the statement that 'the goal of all these virtues [listed earlier] is to live consistently with nature' is supported by reference to four primary, in-built human inclinations (*aphormai*) underlying the four cardinal virtues: 'to discover what is appropriate and to stabilize his motives and to stand firm and to distribute [fairly]'.[80] The section on the goal of life (or happiness) begins with this statement: 'Since a human being is a rational, mortal animal, sociable by nature, they [the Stoics] say that all human virtue and happiness constitute a life which is consistent and in agreement with nature'.[81] Subsequently, Stobaeus' review of Stoic formulations of happiness, though including 'the life according to nature', fails to clarify whether this means universal or human nature, by contrast with a comparable review in Diogenes Laertius.[82] By inference, then, the idea of 'the life according to nature' signifies, for Stobaeus, the life according to human nature, characterized as rational and sociable. It is not obvious why Stobaeus' summary does not refer explicitly to universal nature.[83]

---

[77] Cic. *Fin.* 3.27 (and Annas 1993: 390–1). On Zeno's syllogisms, see Schofield 1983; LS 54 D, G–G for Zeno's syllogistic style applied to theology; also LS vol. 1, pp. 189–90.

[78] See Ch. 1, text to nn. 154–77; Ch. 2, text to nn. 156–7, 161–5.

[79] Stob. 5b1, 2.59.5–7, IG: 125; see also Cic. *Off.* 1.11 (also the presentation of each of the virtues as rational and sociable in *Off.* 1, Ch. 1, text to nn. 169–77).

[80] Stob. 5b3, 2.10–12, IG: 126; i.e. the inclinations underlying wisdom, moderation, courage, and justice. See also Cic. *Off.* 1.11–15.

[81] Stob. 6, 2.75.7–10, IG: 132. See also 11m, 2.109.16–18: the wise person will marry and have children, in line with his/her 'nature as a rational and sociable and co-operative animal'.

[82] Stob. 6a and 6e; contrast D.L. 7.87–9. On this omission, see Inwood 1995: 654–5. Stobaeus (6a, 2.76.8, IG: 132) does include a Chrysippean formulation ('to live according to experience of the things that happen by nature'), which, in D.L. 7.87, is explained as referring to universal nature ('for our natures are parts of the nature of the whole', LS 63 C(2)). But, as Schofield 2003: 245, n. 29, points out, the meaning of this phrase, taken on its own, is far from self-evident; 'experience' (*empeiria*) is not an obvious term to use in describing knowledge of cosmic nature (*theōria*, 'theory', might seem more appropriate). So, without the gloss provided in D.L. 7.87, the phrase may be taken as referring to human nature or nature in general (covering all types of nature).

[83] See text to nn. 48–9.

Some scholars see a focus on human nature, rather than cosmic, as an indication of Aristotelian (or Platonic-Aristotelian) influence on Stoic writings.[84] However, in general, Stobaeus' summary is seen as closely reflecting Chrysippus' approach;[85] and we know that Chrysippus defined happiness both in terms of human and universal nature.[86] The accounts of Stoic ethics presented in type (3) attach significance to human nature, though seen in a broader, universal, context. So, overall, it seems that Stobaeus' focus on human nature represents one of several valid Stoic ways of defining happiness (and virtue), rather than being non-standard.

What does type (2) presentation add to type (1)? The answer seems relatively straightforward. This formulation supports the Stoic accounts of virtue and happiness by linking them with a determinate, and recognizable, conception of what is distinctively human, namely the combination of rationality and sociability. The validity of the Stoic claims does not depend on this form of presentation, since they can be formulated independently, in terms of type (1). However, their validity is reinforced in this way; both virtue and happiness are depicted, in this formulation, as expressing what is central to being human. Also, more particularly, this formulation supports the key, distinctive Stoic ethical claim: that virtue, by contrast with the preferred indifferents, is necessary and sufficient for happiness. This claim is reinforced by the idea that virtue constitutes knowledge or expertise in leading a human life and, in this respect, gives the sole basis needed for living a happy life, understood as the best possible human life.[87] That this is the intended function of this formulation is indicated by the fact that, in Stobaeus' version, reference to the idea of human nature is closely integrated with the argument for this core Stoic claim. The idea of human nature is linked first with the definition of virtue as expertise or knowledge, and then with the idea that virtue enables one to lead the life according to nature, understood as human nature.[88] This prepares the ground for the close linkage between virtue and happiness, as functions of a human being, characterized as rational and sociable, made at the start of the section on happiness or the goal of life.[89] It also paves the way for the claim of the equivalence of the ideas of living according to virtue and living according to nature (that is, by implication, human nature), which closes the main part of this section.[90] Stobaeus' summary seems to reflect a decision (made by Arius Didymus or Chrysippus himself)[91] to focus, in this context, on reinforcing this central Stoic claim by reference to human nature. This focus has been selected, it

---

[84] See White 1979, contrasting the (Platonic-Aristotelian) approach of Antiochus to that of the early Stoics, as he interprets this; also Striker 1996: 225–31.

[85] Long 1996: 130; Schofield 2003: 236.   [86] D.L. 7.89 (LS 63 C(5)).

[87] For this line of thought, see 1.4; this claim also depends on the virtue-indifferents distinction (2.2).

[88] Stob. 5b1, esp. 2.59.4–7; 5b3, 2.62.7–8.   [89] Stob. 6, 2.75.7–10.

[90] Stob. 6e, 2.78.1–6; see also 6d on the claim that only virtue is needed for happiness (and not the other types of good, such as good emotions, which depend on virtue).

[91] On the background of Stobaeus' summary, see Long 1996: 107–10, 122–30; Schofield 2003: 236–9.

seems, as one of the possible ways of supporting this central claim, even though there are other possible ways, which involve the idea of universal nature, or the combination of human and universal nature.

The distinctive mark of presentation type (3) is reference to the combination of human and universal nature. We are told that Chrysippus' formulation of happiness or the goal of life (or, at least, one of these) is framed in terms of presentation (3).[92] However, the fullest expression of this type appears in the accounts of development as appropriation that are placed at the start of the summary of Diogenes Laertius and near the start and end of the version of Cicero, On Ends 3.[93] Type (3) presentation incorporates type (2) in the sense that it includes reference to human nature, typically understood in the same way as in type (2), namely as a combination of rationality and sociability.[94] However, there are at least two important additions. Human nature is located, along with (non-human) animal nature in a broader natural framework, conceived teleologically. Also, going along with the first addition, are two further points, which, by implication at least, place human nature in the context of the universe or nature as a whole. The first is the idea that human motivation in general is derived, ultimately, from certain in-built primary motives, shared, in their basic form, with other animals. One motive is to preserve oneself (more broadly, to maintain oneself in one's nature or 'constitution'); the other is to care for others of one's kind, a motive expressed most obviously in parental love for offspring. In human beings, these motives are, during development, progressively informed by rationality (or the combination of rationality and sociability).[95] The second point is that advanced human development, shaped by a combination of rationality and sociability, leads towards the formation of structure, order, and wholeness, in understanding, character, and pattern of living. As highlighted in Chapter 1, both these features are presented in Stoic theology as points of connection between human nature at its best and universal or cosmic nature. This connection is, at least, implicit in some Stoic accounts of appropriation, and certain key ideas are also spelled out in Stoic theology.[96] Hence, type (3) presentation introduces another, and rather complex, layer of ideas about nature, both human and universal.

---

[92] D.L. 7.89 (also 7.88) (LS 63 C(3, 5)). In Stobaeus' summary, however, also thought to derive from Chrysippus, happiness is presented solely in terms of human nature: so it may be that there is no single Chrysippean formulation.

[93] D.L. 7.85–6, Cic. Fin. 3.16–22, 62–8. Cic. Off. 1.11–15, and to some extent 1.50–7, are also accounts of appropriation (see 4.3, 4.5), but framed solely in terms of human nature.

[94] The short account in D.L. 7.86 brings out only rationality. Cic. Fin. 3 presents separately rationality (3.16–22) and sociability (3.62–8), but implies connections between them (see Ch. 4, text to nn. 202–15). Cic. Off. 1.11–15 brings out the combination of rationality and sociability (see also 1.50–7).

[95] On the basic motives, see 4.2; on the development of these two motives, involving both rationality and sociability, see 4.3–5.

[96] See Ch. 1, text to nn. 99–101, 183–95, esp. n. 193.

What does type (3) presentation add to type (1)? In my view, the answer is similar to that given for type (2). The core Stoic ethical claims, which are independently argued for (in type (1) presentation), can also be supported by reference to the distinctive features of human nature, viewed in the context of nature as a whole. More precisely, they can be supported by reference to the Stoic account of natural human (and animal) development, conceived as development in motivation. The clearest instance of this form of argument comes in a section of Cicero's *On Ends* 3 (20–2), where Cicero presents as natural the process by which human beings develop from instinctive attraction to 'things according to nature' (preferred indifferents) to rational selection of them. Next, human beings develop to the point of recognizing that what counts as good, and choiceworthy, is not the preferred indifferents themselves but proper (virtuous) selection of them, and that this forms the sole basis for the happy life (the life according to nature). This process of development (or progressive shift of motivation) is presented as natural, in the sense of matching human nature at its best, viewed in the context of nature as a whole. This presentation thus supports the thesis about the relationship between virtue and happiness which is central to Cicero's account of Stoic ethics in Book 3. The discussion of appropriation supports the distinctive Stoic claim that virtue, and not the preferred indifferents, constitutes the sole basis needed for happiness, by contrast with the competing Aristotelian view on virtue and happiness.[97]

The distinctive feature of type (4) presentation is that universal nature is presented as providing a pattern for human beings to follow. In presentation (3), by contrast, the focus is on the idea that human beings should act according to human nature, viewed within the framework of nature as a whole. Although type (4) presentation is well represented in Stoic writings generally, it is not prominent in the three ethical summaries. In fact, the idea is only stated twice there. The first passage is given a prominent place, near the start of the summary of Diogenes Laertius. It is presented as Chrysippus' definition of the goal of life, or happiness:

> Therefore, the goal becomes 'to live consistently with nature', i.e. according to one's own [i.e. human] nature and that of the universe, doing nothing which is forbidden by the common law, which is right reason, penetrating all things, being the same as Zeus, who is the leader of the administration of things. And this itself is the virtue of the happy person and a smooth flow of life, whenever all things are done according to the harmony of the *daimōn* in each of us with the will of the administrator of the universe.[98]

---

[97] Cic. *Fin.* 3.20 (more broadly, 3.16–22) thus plays a pivotal role in the argument of Book 3, and is followed by further arguments, framed in terms of type (1) presentation, for the same thesis: 3.23–34, contrasted with the Aristotelian approach in 3.30, 41–8. On Aristotle's competing view, see Ch. 1, text to nn. 29–34. On interpretative questions raised by Cic. *Fin.* 3.16–22, see 4.4; also Gill 2006: 145–66.

[98] D.L. 7.88, IG: 114; see also LS 63 C(3–4). This passage is also cited in Ch. 1, text to n. 70.

It is worth noting, first, that this account of the goal involves a combination of acting according to human and universal nature, and in this respect matches the distinctive feature of Chrysippus' definition of the goal noted by Diogenes Laertius just after this passage.[99] In this respect, this passage can also be taken as illustrating presentation type (3), stressing the combination of human and universal nature. However, the idea of taking universal nature as a norm (and 'harmonizing' oneself to it) is a further feature; and this is the salient mark of presentation (4). However, specifying what it means to take universal nature as a norm is far from simple; and this, rather intricately formulated, passage indicates some of the complexity involved. As presented in Diogenes' summary, without further elaboration, the significance is rather open-ended. However, in the final section of this chapter (3.5), I offer three possible interpretations of the passage, drawing on the later Stoics Epictetus and Marcus Aurelius, who make extensive use of the idea of universal nature, or Zeus or god, as a norm. The second passage in the ethical summaries in which we find presentation (4) comes towards the end of Cicero's treatment. Cicero presents knowledge of universal nature as providing the basis for understanding what is good and bad and for living the life according to nature. I discuss this passage, along with related ones in other sources, in 3.4.[100]

As with the other types of presentation, the question arises, what does type (4) add to type (1)? In broad terms, the answer is similar to that given for types (2) and (3). This mode of presentation lends support to the key concepts and claims of Stoic ethics, by reference to an account of universal or cosmic nature. How does it provide this support? Answering this question is more difficult than in the case of types (2) and (3), in part because the passages presenting this idea are not closely integrated with the summaries as a whole in which they are located.[101] By contrast, the ideas of human nature (in Stobaeus) and appropriation (at least in Cicero's account) are much more closely linked with their context and with the core Stoic ethical claims.[102] Hence, in Chapter 1, in exploring the links between Stoic thinking on happiness, virtue, and universal nature, I have gone outside Stoic ethical writings and drawn on Stoic theology, especially Cicero's *On the Nature of the Gods* 2,[103] including points of connection linked with the theory of appropriation.[104] I have suggested that both virtue and happiness can be seen as the fullest possible realization, in human beings, of two prominent features of universal nature in Stoic thinking. One of these is the combination of structure,

---

[99] D.L. 7.89 (LS 63 C(5)).   [100] Cic. *Fin.* 3.73; see 3.4, esp. text to n. 119.

[101] D.L. 7.88 can be read as continuing the teleological survey of animal and human motives in D.L. 7.85–6 (see Long 1996: 145–52), but also as part of a new section, on 'the goal' (7.87–9), as distinct from 'motive'. In any case, the remainder of D.L.'s summary is similar in content to that of Stobaeus and Cicero (see also Schofield 2003: 238–9). Cic. *Fin.* 3.72–3 has no obvious link with the preceding account.

[102] See text to nn. 88–91, 97.   [103] See Ch. 1, text to nn. 83–94.

[104] The theory of appropriation is included in Cic. *N. D.* 2. 127–9, as well as the ethical summaries; on links between the two treatments of appropriation, see Ch. 1, text to nn. 96–8.

order, and wholeness (or overall consistency). The other, in human beings, is the expression of the two primary animal motives of taking care of oneself and others of one's kind, which is presented as an expression of universal nature's providential care for all elements within nature. In human beings, conceived as rational and sociable animals, the fullest realization of these motives consists in the development and exercise of the virtues, as modes of expertise, and in the happy life (the life according to nature) which derives from the development and exercise of the virtues. The overall effect of these ideas, articulated in various ways in Stoic ethical writings as well as theological ones, is to support or reinforce the core distinctive Stoic claim, that virtue constitutes the sole basis needed for happiness, as distinct from the preferred indifferents.[105] This point is implied, at least, in Chrysippus' statement, in the passage just cited, that living according to (human and) universal nature 'is itself the virtue of the happy person and a smooth flow of life [i.e. happiness]'.[106] The virtual equivalence of virtue and happiness here, as elsewhere in Stoic ethics,[107] underlines this point. Hence, we can see how presentation (4) lends support to presentation (1) of the key Stoic ethical thesis, although this connection between the two modes of presentation is not fully spelled out in the three ethical summaries.

If we supply this line of interpretation for presentation type (4), the overall implication of the presentation of nature in the ethical summaries is quite clear. There are at least four different, and valid, ways of presenting Stoic ethical doctrines, including the distinctive and controversial claims about virtue, happiness, and indifferents. In all three summaries, most of the exposition is framed in purely ethical terms, and this constitutes the core content of the accounts. However, each of the summaries also supports these ideas, including the distinctive Stoic ethical claims, by reference to ideas about nature, either human or universal or both. The ethical doctrines themselves and the various ideas about nature are consistent with each other and with the formulations offered in other summaries. But there is no single, definitive characterization of the role of nature in Stoic ethics. This conclusion runs counter to the widespread, though not unanimous, view that the distinctive Stoic ethical claims depend on ideas about universal nature, and that those ideas have a unique role as the foundation or grounds of ethics.[108] Also, this conclusion is at odds with some ancient evidence that seems to give universal nature precisely this grounding role. Hence, in the next section, I focus on this evidence, asking how far it can be seen as consistent with the ethical summaries on this question.

---

[105] See 1.3–4.

[106] D.L. 7.88, IG: 144, with my addition in square brackets; for 'a smooth flow of life' as one of Zeno's definitions of happiness, and one retained by later Stoics, see Stob. 6e, 2.77.20–7.

[107] See Ch. 1, text to nn. 107–12.   [108] See text to nn. 17–20.

3.4 Is Stoic Theology Foundational for Ethics?

The main topic here is the ancient evidence suggesting that Stoic theology, which gives a central role to universal or cosmic nature, is authoritative or foundational for ethics. This evidence needs to be located in the context of Stoic thinking in general on the main branches of knowledge, which points to a co-ordinated, rather than hierarchical, relationship between these branches. In the course of this discussion, I argue that the co-ordinated view also applies to the relationship between Stoic theology and ethics. I also suggest that, on closer examination, the passages on the relationship between theology and ethics are consistent with the view of the role of universal nature in Stoic ethics provided by the ancient ethical summaries.

The Stoics subdivide philosophy into physics, ethics, and logic, which they see as having distinct objectives and topics. Thus: 'physics is practised whenever we investigate the world and its contents, ethics is our engagement with human life, and logic, which they also call dialectic, is our engagement with discourse'.[109] However, the Stoics also stress that these branches of knowledge can be combined to make up a coherent and organic unity.[110] They deploy various similes to convey this point, likening the branches of knowledge to different parts of a single entity, such as a living being, an egg, a fertile field, and a well-fortified city. For instance, in the living body, logic is compared to bones and sinew, ethics to flesh, and physics to the psyche. We are also told that, on some Stoic views, 'no part is given preference over another but they are mixed together' and transmitted in this mixed form. Also, in a distinct but related point, we are told that Stoic thinkers adopted various orders or sequences for the different branches of knowledge. The orders adopted seem to be for pedagogical purposes, rather than constituting a conceptual or epistemological ladder of types of knowledge.[111]

Why is this feature of Stoic thinking relevant to the present question? What is striking is that, in these passages, the Stoics do *not* arrange the branches of knowledge in an epistemologically hierarchical way, in which, for instance, ethics is subordinate to physics. Although there are various pedagogical orders for the branches of knowledge, we find different orders in different thinkers. Also, the branches of knowledge are sometimes taught in a mixed form. This implies that the order of instruction is, ultimately non-significant, provided that it

---

[109] Aëtius I, preface 2 (LS 26 A, trans. slightly rearranged). A further, rather puzzling, idea in this passage, is that there are three types of virtue corresponding to the three branches of knowledge; on this idea, see also D.L. 7.83, Cic. *Fin.* 7.83; and Jedan 2009: 84–90; Vogt 2017: 187–90.

[110] See Cic. *Fin.* 3.74; also Sen. *Ep.* 89.1–2. Inwood 2013 doubts that this view was widely held in Stoicism; but LS 26 B–D point towards this view. This view is also compatible with variations in Stoic ways of understanding the relationship between branches of knowledge (the existence of such variations is stressed by Inwood 2009).

[111] See D.L. 7.39–41 (LS 26 B), especially D.L. 7.40 (LS 26 B(3)), cited. See also Ieradiakonou 1993; Brouwer 2014: 19–24.

yields, eventually, a unified framework of knowledge.[112] The contrast with the famous philosophical curriculum in Book 7 of Plato's *Republic*, leading step-by-step from mathematics to meta-mathematics and then dialectic, and culminating in dialectically based knowledge of the form of the good, is stark. There, by contrast, the pedagogical order coincides with the epistemological order.[113] The precise way in which the Stoic branches of knowledge work together to provide a unified framework is not spelled out in this kind of ancient evidence. However, it is not suggested, in this context, that this unified view is achieved through an epistemological hierarchy, as in the Platonic picture. Rather, the obvious inference is that the Stoic branches of knowledge are on the same conceptual or epistemological level. Hence, it seems that the unified picture is achieved by the compatibility or consistency of the different branches of knowledge or by their being mutually or reciprocally supporting in certain respects. This implication runs counter to the widely held scholarly view that an understanding of universal or cosmic nature is authoritative for ethics and thus that physics is placed on a different epistemological level from the other branches.[114] The variations in the role of nature in the ethical summaries just discussed (3.3) match the non-hierarchical view of the relationship between the three main branches of knowledge. The core Stoic ethical doctrines are sometimes (in presentation type (4)), but not always, supported by the idea of universal nature. However, we would expect the doctrines to be consistently supported in this way if knowledge of universal nature were standardly seen as authoritative for ethics.

However, there are other passages which, on the face of it, do seem to give an authoritative status to physics or, more specifically, theology, which falls within Stoic physics.[115] Three relevant comments are ascribed to Chrysippus:

... [from *On the Gods*]: It is not possible to find another starting-point (*archē*) or another origin for justice other than the one from Zeus and from universal nature; it is from this that every such thing must have its starting-point, if we are going to say anything about goods and evils. [from *Physical Theses*]: There is no other or more appropriate way of approaching the accounts of goods and evils, or virtue and happiness, than from universal nature and the organization of

---

[112] See also LS vol. 1, pp. 160–1. The significance of the various orders of knowledge has been much discussed, though without reaching any clear or definitive conclusion; see Gill 2006: 161–2.

[113] See Pl. *Rep.* 522b–540b. On the role of mathematics in this curriculum, see Burnyeat 2000 and Gill 2007.

[114] On this point, see Annas 2007b: 58–65. For the scholarly view, see text to nn. 17–20. For some suggestions about ways in which ethics and theology (part of Stoic physics) are *partly* reciprocal or mutually supporting, see text to nn. 151–62.

[115] See Plu. *Sto.* 1035 C (LS 26 C). Although these passages sometimes refer to 'physics', rather than theology, they also refer to 'Zeus' or 'the gods', indicating that it is theology that is intended. Theology seems to have been the context in which the providential worldview was presented by the Stoics, as indicated in Cic. *N. D.* 2 and S. E. *M.* 9.13–137. Also, Plutarch explicitly links his comments with theology, as a sub-branch of physics (*Sto. Rep.* 1035 A–E).

the universe.... There is no better starting-point or reference-point [for goods and evils], nor is physical theory taken up for the sake of anything other than the discrimination of goods and evils.[116]

These passages are taken out of their original contexts by Plutarch in a work explicitly designed to bring out contradictions in Stoic thought. The contradiction identified by Plutarch is not with the comments on the branches of knowledge just discussed (LS 26 B) or the idea that these branches are on the same level and co-ordinated, rather than related in a hierarchical way. Instead, Plutarch claims, rather unconvincingly, that these passages are in conflict with Chrysippus' deci-sion, in a quite different work (*On Ways of Life*), to adopt the pedagogical order of logic, ethics, physics, rather than placing physics first.[117] Plutarch cites in the same context Chrysippus' practice of prefacing ethical works with the words: 'Zeus, Destiny, Providence, and the statement that universe, being one and finite, is held together by a single power'.[118] Cicero, near the close of *On Ends* 3, makes a similar statement:

The same honour is bestowed upon physics, with good cause. The starting-point (*proficiscendum est*) for anyone who is to live in accordance with nature is the universe as a whole and its government. Moreover, one cannot make correct judgements about good and evil unless one understands the whole system of nature and indeed the life of the gods, as well as the question whether human nature matches (*conveniat*) universal nature.[119]

It is passages of this kind, especially, that underpin the widespread scholarly view that Stoic ethics is grounded on the Stoic worldview.

How, and how far, can these passages be interpreted in a way that renders them consistent with other Stoic evidence on the ethical role of nature? They are compatible with Stoic thinking on the branches of knowledge (LS 26 B) in suggesting that the different areas of Stoic theory are consistent with, and support, each other. Also, as highlighted in Chapter 1, we can discern significant connec-tions between Stoic thinking on virtue and happiness and the Stoic worldview, as presented in Stoic theology.[120] So there is nothing odd in the idea found in these passages of tracing links between physics, especially theology, and ethics. However, there are two remaining puzzles in these passages. One is that the standpoint of physics seems to be presented as authoritative for ethics in a way

---

[116] Plu. *Sto. Rep.* 1035 C, trans. Annas 2007b: 79; see also LS 60 A.
[117] Plu. *Sto. Rep.* 1035 A–B, also D–F. Annas 2007b: 77–80 suggests that Chrysippus may have adopted different pedagogical orders in different contexts.
[118] Plu. *Sto. Rep.* 1035 B. trans. Cherniss 1976.
[119] Cic. *Fin.* 3.73, trans. Annas and Woolf 2001.
[120] See Ch. 1, text to nn. 84–101, 178–99; also text to nn. 103–7 in this chapter.

that does not square with other evidence (however, for another possible reading of these passages, see text to nn. 152–6). The branches of knowledge are not elsewhere described in this way; and, within the ethical summaries, there is no obvious priority given to the type of presentation (4) that refers to universal nature. Second, there is a problem in the way that the Stoic worldview is described as authoritative. The passages just cited seem, at first glance, to suggest that Stoic theology provides a foundational analysis of goods and evils, or virtue (including justice) and happiness, and that we need to take account of this analysis if we are to understand the significance of these concepts in Stoic ethics. However, this impression does not match what we find in our evidence for Stoic theology, in ways brought out shortly. This does not mean that these passages can simply be set aside, although they are in some ways unsatisfactory as evidence for this question.[121] The interpretative challenge is to understand the meaning of these passages in a way that does justice to their precise content, while taking account of other evidence on Stoic ethics and theology.

This evidence, especially, seems to lend support to the scholarly view that Stoic ethics is 'grounded' on physics or that the worldview provides the 'foundations' of ethics.[122] The Stoics, certainly, see close links between their worldview and ethics; but is that linkage best described in these terms? To place this question in a broader perspective, it may be useful to point to some modern examples, both religious and philosophical, which clearly exemplify ethical foundationalism. The first example is the Judaeo-Christian framework, which has exercised great, though complicated, influence on modern moral thinking. In this framework, God,[123] or God as mediated by Jesus, is seen (to use Brüllmann's terms, discussed earlier),[124] as the ultimate standard of value and source of normativity. God's goodness is the ultimate reference-point for goodness in general. God's love for the world, shown above all in the sacrifice and resurrection of Jesus, represents the definitive paradigm for human love. In this respect, God is the ultimate standard of value. God is also the ultimate source of normativity, framed as rules, laws, or guidance. These are expressed in Judaeo-Christian writings, in forms such as the Ten Commandments or Jesus' version of these commandments.[125] Hence, moral

---

[121] The quotations from Chrysippus are taken out of context by Plutarch and are cited for polemical purposes (see Annas 2007b: 77–84); the Ciceronian passage is not obviously linked with, or explained by, the preceding discussion in *Fin.* 3.

[122] 'The foundations of Stoic ethics are to be sought...in cosmology or theology' (Striker 1996: 231). 'The Stoics' eudaimonism is principally grounded in their beliefs about the relation in which human beings stand to a determinate and providentially governed world' (Long 1996: 195). See also text to nn. 17–20.

[123] Normally in this book I use the lower-case 'god(s)' in connection with Greco-Roman thought; but I use the upper-case 'God' to signify the (systematically monotheistic and transcendent) Judaeo-Christian personal deity. Although the Stoic god is sometimes presented in a monotheistic way, their deity can be expressed as 'gods', and is also identified with the active cause (or immanent force for animation or structure) in the universe; see also Ch. 1, text to nn. 92–4.

[124] Brüllmann 2015: ch. 2; also text to nn. 36–9.   [125] Exodus 20; Matthew 22: 35–40.

principles (right and wrong) are derived, ultimately again, from statements or commands from God or Jesus.

There are also prominent and clear-cut examples of ethical foundationalism in modern moral philosophy. A famous and influential example is found in Kant's work, *Groundwork* (or *Foundations*) *of the Metaphysics of Morals*. Here, moral obligations or duties are presented as grounded on 'the Categorical Imperative', namely, 'Act only on that maxim through which you can at the same time will that it should become a universal law'.[126] Similarly, in Utilitarianism, human benefit, sometimes formulated as the greatest happiness of the greatest number, is taken as a foundational principle. Actions are classed as right or wrong in so far as they promote benefit or harm. In this account, moral judgements (about what is good and bad or right and wrong) are seen as grounded on, and explained by, the idea of human benefit.[127] In *The Sources of Normativity*, Christine Korsgaard reviews a whole series of modern Western theories, in which the force of moral judgements is regarded as grounded on universal or underpinning principles of this kind.[128] Stephen Darwall maintains that this way of framing ethics, as the derivation of moral obligations from certain grounding principles, is characteristic of modern, by contrast with ancient, theory.[129]

In these examples of ethical foundationalism, there are two features that, I think, are crucial. One is the idea that the foundation is essential or indispensable: the moral force of the rules or norms validated *depends* on the underlying authority of the grounding principle (God, the Categorical Imperative, or human benefit). Second, moral judgements and rules (about what is right or wrong) are, explicitly and systematically, *derived* from the underpinning foundation. There are, of course, many specific differences between these modern frameworks and Stoic thinking, both theological and ethical. However, these two features, and the modern examples on which they are based, provide criteria which can help us to determine whether or not Stoic thinking is appropriately characterized in terms of ethical foundationalism. I raise this question first with reference to Stoic ethics, as expressed in the summaries discussed in 3.3, and then Stoic theology, as presented, for instance, in Cicero *On the Nature of the Gods* 2. I then explore the relationship between these two types of Stoic theory.

In both types of Stoic theory, I think that the evidence falls short of meeting these criteria for ethical foundationalism, though it still provides support for a close relationship between universal nature and ethics. The Stoic worldview, or the idea of universal nature, is not presented as essential or indispensable for the core

---

[126] Kant, *Groundwork*, Prussian Academy edition, vol. 4, 421 (cited from Paton 1948: 84).
[127] See Mill 1993: 7; also Gill 2005a: 18–19; Broadie 2005: 42–5.
[128] See Korsgaard 1996: chs 1–4.
[129] Darwall 2012, discussing philosophy from the seventeenth century onwards, and arguing against Irwin 2007–8, who sees continuity of thought between ancient and modern theory in this respect.

Stoic ethical claims, as is brought out in the preceding discussion of the ethical summaries (3.3). Although these claims are *sometimes* supported by reference to universal nature, or by an account of human nature viewed in a larger natural framework (presentation types 3 and 4), this is not *always* the case, as it would need to be if universal nature constituted the indispensable foundation. Also, even when there is reference to universal nature, the core Stoic ethical claims are not derived from this idea in the way that, in these modern examples, moral rules or norms are, systematically, derived from God, the Categorical Imperative, or the principle of human benefit. The summary of Diogenes Laertius, often taken as offering strong support for the foundationalist interpretation, provides a particularly striking case. The opening pages locate human motivation in a broader natural pattern (type 3 presentation) and go on to define human happiness in terms of universal nature (type 4). However, instead of deriving the core ethical claims from these ideas or using them to analyse these claims, the account then discusses them in the same (ethical) terms as the other summaries mostly do (type 1 presentation).[130] So both the criteria for ethical foundationalism highlighted earlier are missing from the ethical summaries.

In our evidence for Stoic theology,[131] the two criteria for foundationalism are also missing. This comes out if we correlate the Stoic material, first, with the modern philosophical examples and then Christianity. By contrast with Kantian and Utilitarian theory, Stoic theology does not purport to offer a foundational analysis of what should count as good, or what underpins right or wrong. Indeed, Stoic theology does not actually provide a theoretical analysis of good and bad at all, although it deploys the notion of good in its claims about god or universal nature.[132] Similarly, it does not analyse the notion of virtue, although this concept is used in connection with god.[133] The Stoic analysis of ideas such as good and virtue is provided in ethical writings, typically formulated in all three summaries in terms of presentation type (1). It is there that the key distinctions are made, such as that between virtue and indifferents, and core distinctive claims are made, such as that happiness depends on virtue and not indifferents.[134] If we turn to the comparison with Christian theological ethics, there are also relevant differences. In Christianity, God's goodness is taken as a primary fact or postulate and as the ultimate reference-point for human goodness. The Stoics also claim the goodness

---

[130] See D.L. 7.85–9 (taken as providing the physical basis for ethics in Long 1996; ch. 6). On the marked shift in mode of presentation (between 7.85–9 and 7.90–110), see Schofield 2003: 238–9.

[131] For this evidence, see Cic. *N. D.* Book 2. S. E. *M.* 9.13–37; selections in LS 54, IG 60–85; also Mansfeld 1999b, esp. 457–62, 464–9; Algra 2003; Jedan 2009: 21–30.

[132] On the perfection of god (or the divinely informed universe), see D.L. 7. 147 (LS 54 A), Cic. *N. D.* 2.37–9 (LS 54 H); also Mansfeld 1999b: 458–60; Algra 2003: 162, 166. See also text to nn. 36–9.

[133] See Cic. *N. D.* 2.39; S. E. *M.* 9.88; and (from a critical standpoint), S. E. *M.* 9.152–77: also Mansfeld 1999b: 459, 461, 476.

[134] See text to nn. 62–76.

of god or the universe (of which god is the animating source).[135] However, this is not taken to be a primary fact or postulate,[136] but something that needs to be argued for, at some length, and demonstrated by reference to specific good-making qualities, including rationality, order, wholeness, coherence, and providential care for all aspects of nature.[137] Hence, as Brüllmann points out, god or universal nature is not treated by Stoic thinkers as good by definition; goodness is ascribed to god or universal nature in the same way and on the same basis as it is ascribed to other things or to people.[138] In this respect, the goodness of god or universal nature is not taken as primary and foundational for ethics in the same way as in Christianity. Stoic theology also does not present god or nature as a source of normativity in the sense of presenting commands, rules or laws which constitute the basis of right or wrong in human action.[139] Although we sometimes find the idea of the will or plan of Zeus, in ethical writings,[140] this does not reflect the presence of an articulated set of commandments in Stoic theology. Thus, comparison with these modern examples brings out the absence in Stoic theology of the two criteria highlighted earlier. Reference to universal nature is not an essential or indispensable basis for goodness, and goodness or rightness is not, systematically, derived from the properties of universal nature.

How do these conclusions square with the ancient passages cited earlier, from Plutarch and Cicero?[141] These are passages which, on first reading at least, seem to ascribe to Stoic theology or the idea of universal nature precisely the ethically foundational role that I am calling into question. However, we can identify a credible function for Stoic theology that falls short of presenting it as ethically foundational, while still allowing that it plays an important part in supporting core ethical claims. Also, a careful reading of the ancient passages shows that they are consistent with this view. The evidence points to two ethically significant roles for Stoic theology. First, theology sets out, in a comprehensive way, the various types of nature relevant for Stoic ethics, especially human and universal nature, and the

---

[135] It is important to distinguish the claims (1) that god is the animating source of the universe and (2) that both god and the universe are good from the claim (3) that god is the primary and foundational source of goodness as such.

[136] Long 1996: 186 (also 186–9) ascribes the 'theocratic postulate' to the Stoics; but it seems more appropriately ascribed to Judaeo-Christian thought.

[137] This is a central, reiterated theme in Stoic theology: see D.L. 7.147 (LS 54 A), Cic. N. D. 2.15–16, 18–21, 29, 34–6, 43, 79–80, 86–7, 132; also Mansfeld 1999b: 458–61; Jedan 2009: 25–8.

[138] Brüllmann 2015: 115–17. Hence, the Stoics often argue (controversially) that the goodness of the universe is shown in the possession of qualities, such as rationality, that are (uncontroversially) also possessed by human beings. See Cic. N. D. 2.16, 18–19, 20, 22, 29–30, 35 and S. E. M. 9.104, 108–9 (LS 54 G); also Algra 2003: 168.

[139] The idea of 'natural law' does form part of Stoic ethics (LS 67 R–S), but this idea does not figure in our evidence for Stoic theology. On the problems raised by trying to find determinate, articulated rules in Stoic ethics that are derived from the idea of natural law, see Inwood 1999; however, for a more positive view of this project, see Jedan 2009: 121–35.

[140] See (in ethical writings), D.L. 7.88, Epict. Diss. 1.17.13–15; see further on this idea 3.5.

[141] See text to nn. 116–19.

relationship between those types. Second, theology considers, at least in broad terms, the ethical significance of these types of nature and their relationship. The combination of these features explains the description of the relationship between theology and ethics given in the passages cited. However, the combination of these roles does not render theology ethically foundational in the sense just discussed. Stoic theology does not offer a foundational analysis of ethical principles or derive value and norms from god or nature.[142] The analysis of core ethical notions falls into the sphere of Stoic ethics, which thus has a distinct and independent role, as well as informing Stoic theology in this respect. This explains why, elsewhere (in LS 26 B, for instance), the areas of ethics and physics (and logic) are presented as compatible and co-ordinated or mutually supporting, rather than related hierarchically.[143]

The four main topics of Stoic theology, as presented, for instance, by Cicero, in *On the Nature of the Gods* 2, are (1) the existence of the gods, (2) their nature, (3) providential government of the world, (4) providential government on behalf of human beings.[144] Cicero's discussion, which in this respect seems typical of Stoic theology, combines the two features just highlighted. It offers a comprehensive account of the different types of nature in the universe (especially divine or universal and human nature), and it discusses the ethical quality or significance of these natures and their relationship. Central arguments, within this framework, include the claim that god, or the universe shaped by divine action, is good. The goodness of the universe (or god) is taken to be shown by its rationality (as manifested by unity, cohesion, order and structure), and also by its providential care for everything within the universe.[145] Another claim, made in part (4) of this scheme, is that human beings have a special status within the universe because they share the rationality of god and the universe as a whole, which in turn explains their special role as beneficiaries of divine (or natural) providence.[146] A further theme is that animals, including humans, instantiate divine providential care by expressing the in-built motive to care for themselves and others of their kind.[147] These are all claims about the nature of the universe and the relationship between its parts, and thus match the description of the scope of theology offered by the passages in Plutarch and Cicero cited earlier. However, they are also ethical claims, in the sense that they express the general thesis that the universe as a whole and its providential organization of the parts of the universe are good. In addition, they are ideas which play an important supporting role in Stoic ethics. As brought

---

[142] See text to nn. 132–40.   [143] See text to nn. 109–12; also text to nn. 151–61.

[144] See Cic. *N. D.* 2.3; also the synopsis in Walsh 1998: xlvii–iii; D. Frede 2002: 96–7. This four-fold set of topics seems to be typical of Stoic theology (for some qualifications to this view, see Algra 2003: 159–60).

[145] See Ch. 1, text to nn. 85–95. These features also appear in S. E. *M.* 9.13–137, another important source.

[146] Cic. *N. D.* 2.133, 147–9, 153–4.

[147] Cic. *N. D.* 2.128–9. See also D.L. 7.85–6, Cic. *Fin.* 3.16–17, 62–3.

out in Chapter 1, these ideas, along with that of human nature, give determinate content to the Stoic definition of happiness or the goal as 'the life according to nature'. They also support the distinctive Stoic conception of ethical development as appropriation, especially the idea that human beings, like other animals have an in-built motive to care for themselves and others of their kind, and to do so, in the case of human beings, in a rational way.[148] This ethically supporting role explains why the ancient ethical summaries are sometimes framed in terms of presentation type (3) and (4) as well as types (1) and (2).

The combination of these two features explains the characterization of the role of theology (or accounts of universal nature) in the comments of Plutarch and Cicero. These comments accentuate the ideas of presenting a comprehensive account of types of nature and of bringing out the ethical significance of those natures and their relationship. This is very clear in the Ciceronian passage. The point that is made repeatedly is that, in order to lead a happy life ('a life according to nature'), or to make correct judgements about good and bad, we need to understand the universe as a whole (universal nature), or 'the whole system of nature', and 'the question of whether or not human nature matches that of the universe'. Subsequently, Cicero states that physics (meaning, I think, theology) is needed to 'reveal the power of nature to foster justice and preserve friendship and other bonds of affection'; also that in order to promote piety and gratitude towards the gods, we need 'an explanation of the natural world'.[149] Similarly, in the passages cited by Plutarch, we are told that, to gain proper understanding of good and bad things, or virtue and happiness, we need to know about 'Zeus and universal nature', or 'universal nature and the organization of the universe' or 'physical theory'.[150] These points correspond precisely with the two relevant features that, I have suggested, we find in Stoic accounts of theology such as Cicero's.

How far are these passages consistent with the usual Stoic view of the relationship between the branches of knowledge?[151] On the face of it, the passages imply a relationship that is hierarchical, and in which theology is authoritative over ethics, rather than the co-ordinated and mutually supporting relationship suggested by other evidence. However, closer examination of the passages can help to correct this impression. The Plutarchean passages, repeatedly, use the term *archē*, or cognates such as *anaphora* ('reference-point'). The term *archē* is sometimes used in Greek philosophy to denote a fundamental explanatory principle,[152] a meaning which would fit the reading of Stoic theology as ethically foundationalist. However, it can also mean 'starting-point' or 'point of access';[153] and this meaning

---

[148] See Ch. 1, text to nn. 83–101; also text to nn. 103–7 in this chapter.
[149] See Cic. *Fin.* 3.73, partly cited earlier (text to n. 119).
[150] Plu. *Sto. Rep.* 1035 B–D (cited in text to n. 116).   [151] See text to nn. 109–13.
[152] Aristotle uses the term often in this sense, in *Phys.* 1.1–6.
[153] Note also 'starting-point' (*proficiscendum est*) in Cic. *Fin.* 3.73, cited in text to n. 119.

fits better with Plutarch's concern, which is the pedagogical order in which the Stoic branches of knowledge are taught. Plutarch's (polemical) aim is to show that the order advocated in these passages (physics, specifically, theology, followed by ethics) is inconsistent with the order (logic, ethics, physics, with theology as the final element or 'culmination', *teletai*) advocated by Chrysippus in another work. Hence, Plutarch claims, Stoic physics (or theology) is both 'before' and 'behind' ethics. Plutarch's criticism presupposes that there must be a single pedagogical order, perhaps on the model of the famous philosophical curriculum in Plato's *Republic*.[154] However, as suggested earlier, what is implied by this and other evidence for Stoic practice is that there was no fixed order for teaching the branches of knowledge, although there were certain conceptual advantages offered by different orders.[155] Significantly, although one of Plutarch's quotations states that there is no order other than the one mentioned here (physics preceding ethics), the remaining two passages say there is no other order that is 'more appropriate' or 'better'. The latter two phrases can be taken as implying that other orders are possible in other contexts and that different orders are more 'appropriate' or 'better' for different purposes.[156] What, then, are the conceptual advantages of the different orders?

I have already highlighted the ways in which theology can be seen as informing ethics, the point stressed in the passages cited. What are the conceptual advantages of the alternative order cited by Plutarch, that is logic, followed by ethics and physics? This order matches our evidence for Stoic theology in several important ways. First, regarded as a sub-branch of physics, theology includes certain key features of the Stoic worldview, notably the conception of god as active cause and as the (immanent) shaping force within the universe.[157] Second, we have ample evidence that the arguments for the goodness, as expressed in the rationality, of god(s) or of the divinely informed universe, are framed in the syllogistic (logical) style that goes back to Zeno and is adopted and elaborated by his immediate successors.[158] In this sense, logic plays a key role in providing a conceptual basis for theology; and the same applies to ethics. It is not only that, as noted earlier (text to nn. 132–8), the Stoic arguments for the goodness of god(s) deploy standard ethical concepts such as 'good' and 'virtue'. Also, these ethical notions have specifically Stoic ethical connotations, as becomes clear from the contrasting use of such terms in Stoic and Epicurean theology. Both theories present gods as

---

[154] Plu. *Sto. Rep.* 1035 A–F. For 'before and after', see 1035 D; for close (critical) reading of Plutarch's claims, see Annas 2007b: 79–84. For Plato's ideal curriculum, see text to n. 113.

[155] See text to nn. 112–13.

[156] See Plu. *Sto. Rep.* 1035 C–D (text to n. 116); also Annas 2007b: 82–4.

[157] See Aëtius 1.7.33 (LS 46 A), D.L. 7.147 (LS 54 A), Cic. *N. D.* 1.39 (LS 54 B). On god as active cause, see LS 44 B, F.

[158] See LS 54 D–G; also Schofield 1983: 34, 38, 42–8; Mansfeld 1999b: 457–61; Algra 2003: 162–5.

happy or blessed. However, for Epicureanism, this means happiness marked by absence of pain or distress and, indeed, freedom from work and trouble, since Epicurean gods are conceived as playing no active role in the world or universe. The happiness of the Stoic gods is characterized, first, by virtue (reflecting the close linkage between virtue and happiness in Stoic ethics), and second, by virtue conceived as actively beneficent. This virtuous beneficence is expressed in providential care for all aspects of the universe, including human beings. Thus, theology is informed by ethics conceived in specifically Stoic terms.[159] In this respect, the methodology of Stoic theology matches this alternative pedagogical order in that theology, while falling within physics and expressing its overall aim of presenting the world and its contents, is informed by both Stoic logic and ethics. However, there is no reason why, from another standpoint, or in a different pedagogical context, theology cannot be seen as using the conclusions reached by this route to inform ethics. What we have is not a failed attempt at a hierarchical relationship, which is what Plutarch implies, but a mutually supporting, and overlapping, one.[160]

I now sum up the implications of the preceding discussion of the relationship between Stoic theology and ethics. Theology, in its role as the 'culminating' dimension of physics, is equipped to offer an authoritative account of nature, including the types of nature (human and universal) most relevant for ethics. Also, theology, viewed as physics informed by ethics, and logic, is equipped to provide an authoritative statement of the ethical character and significance of these types of nature, especially the goodness of the universe as a whole (or god) and the relationship between this goodness and that of human beings. Although Stoic theology is authoritative in these respects, it is not foundationalist in the way explained earlier, by contrast with the types of foundationalism exemplified by Christianity and Kantian or Utilitarian philosophy. Stoic theology does not set out to show how ethical concepts such as good, virtue, and happiness, can be derived from more fundamental ethical ideas such as the Categorical Imperative or human benefit. Nor does it present god as the ultimate standard of value or source of normativity, though it does ascribe goodness to god and human beings in virtue of shared good-making features. By contrast, the analysis of ethical concepts, including that of good and virtue, which are employed in Stoic theology, falls into the

---

[159] On the contrast between Epicurean and Stoic conceptions of god, in this respect, see Mansfeld 1999b: 459–60, 464–6; also (Epicureanism) LS 23 B, D, 22 B(1–2); (Stoicism) Plu. *Sto. Rep.* 1051 E–F, Cic. *N. D.* 2.38–9, 73–5, 79–80, S. E. *M.* 9.88, 91. Brüllmann 2015: 155, also suggests that Stoic ethics informs theology. As Mansfeld 1999b: 460 points out, 'Cleanthes...explicitly integrates theology and ethics'.

[160] See text to nn. 112–13. Theology can be described as an 'interface' discipline in this respect, falling within physics but informed by logic and ethics. As pointed out in D.L. 7.40 (LS 26 B(4)), the branches of knowledge are sometimes presented by Stoic thinkers in a 'mixed' form.

sphere of ethics, and so ethics is authoritative in this respect. Ethics is also authoritative in determining whether or not the idea of universal nature should be deployed within ethics, and if so, how it should be used, as is clear from the discussion of the ethical summaries in 3.3. The branches of knowledge, therefore, are conceived as consistent with each other and mutually supporting, and not as steps on a single (hierarchically arranged) epistemological ladder as in Plato's ideal curriculum in the *Republic*.

This picture of the relationship between the Stoic branches of knowledge matches the framework suggested by LS 26 B, according to which the relationship between the branches of knowledge is co-ordinated or reciprocal, rather than hierarchical. In using the term 'reciprocal' here, I am assuming partial reciprocity, not reciprocity in a more comprehensive sense. I assume that the three main Stoic branches of knowledge, while independently formulated and organized, inform each other in certain respects. Thus, as just illustrated, ethics informs theology, as regards the arguments for the goodness of god. Also, theology (which is informed by ethics and logic) informs ethics, in offering a comprehensive framework of the types of nature relevant for ethics and clarifying the ethical relationship between those types of nature. Theology presents a comprehensive picture of what one might call the 'nature-related' aspects of ethics, though it does not attempt to analyse the meaning or interrelationship of the core ethical ('value-related') concepts, which is the work of ethical theory.[161] I am not assuming that ethics informs theology as a whole, let alone physics as a whole; or that physics, as a whole, informs all aspects of ethics. This view of the relationship between ethics and theology, as well as supported by the evidence reviewed earlier, matches the variations in the presentation of ethics in the summaries of Stoic ethics, discussed in 3.3, in which ethical claims are sometimes, but not always, presented as informed by reference to universal nature. Hence, despite the initial impression given by the Plutarchean and Ciceronian passages, they do not support the view often maintained that physics (especially theology) is foundational for ethics. However, they do support the weaker, but more plausible, claim that ideas from Stoic theology can be used, along with the idea of human nature, to support and inform distinctive and central ethical claims. These passages are also consistent with the idea that the three main branches of Stoic knowledge, while having their own areas of authority, can be combined with each other in a co-ordinated and partly reciprocal way in order to yield the theoretical unity and cohesion at which the Stoics aim.[162]

---

[161] See text to nn. 142–50, 159.

[162] On the three branches of knowledge in Stoicism, see text to nn. 110–14; the question of the relationship between these branches is often linked with debate about the role of nature in Stoic ethics (3.2). See Gill 2006: 161–6; Annas 2007b, referring to competing views on this subject.

3.5 Harmonizing with Universal Nature: Three Versions

So far in this chapter, I have approached the question of the role of nature in Stoic ethics by considering ancient texts which are theoretical in character. In this final section, I turn to evidence of a different kind, namely Stoic writings on practical ethics, especially the written reports of Epictetus' oral discussions on ethics and the philosophical notebook of Marcus Aurelius.[163] This kind of material offers several advantages for this question. For one thing, these texts enable us to recognize how the idea of nature is deployed in practical contexts, especially as part of the project of promoting ethical development, which is the main focus of Stoic writings on practical ethics.[164] Cicero's *On Duties* is another practically oriented Stoic text; however (like Stobaeus' summary), this work only deploys the idea of human nature,[165] whereas Epictetus and Marcus refer, extensively, to universal nature as an ethical idea, alongside human nature.[166] These numerous references supplement the limited use of the idea of universal nature (type 4 presentation) in the ethical summaries. Hence, Epictetus and Marcus offer a broader range of material for understanding the role of the idea of universal nature and for assessing how far this idea is seen as grounding Stoic ethics.[167]

I explore this question with reference to a text which has already figured prominently in this book, namely Chrysippus' account of happiness as harmonizing oneself to universal nature, or Zeus' plan.[168] This passage seems to have been regarded as an important one in Stoic ethics in antiquity and is sometimes evoked by both Epictetus and Marcus.[169] I cite again Chrysippus' account:

> Therefore, the goal becomes 'to live consistently with nature', i.e. according to one's one own [i.e. human] nature and that of the universe, doing nothing which is forbidden by the common law, which is right reason, penetrating all things, being the same as Zeus, who is the leader of the administration of things. And

[163] On the overall style and character of these writings, see (on Epictetus), Long 2002, esp. ch. 2: (on Marcus), Gill 2013a: xxi–xlix; Sellars 2021: ch. 2.

[164] On Stoic practical ethics and its aims, see Gill 2003: 40–4. On the project of ethical development taken forward in this context, see (on Epictetus), Long 2002: chs. 2, 4; (Marcus) Gill 2013a: xxxiv–xlix; (on both thinkers) Hadot 1995: 179–205, 1998: chs. 3, 5.

[165] See Ch. 2, esp. text to nn. 113–19, 156–65. On the similarity in this respect to Stobaeus' ethical summary, see text to n. 78, and Ch. 1, text to nn. 154–65.

[166] As regards universal nature, Epictetus tends to emphasize god and Marcus 'the whole' (Long 2002: 177–8), but this emphasis is not systematic in either case. On human nature, see Epict. *Diss.* 1.6.12–22, 2.9.1–12, 2.10.–1–6; M. A. 5.1; 5.16.3, 6.14.2, 7.68.1–3, 9.42.13.

[167] See text to nn. 244–53, which addresses this issue directly.

[168] D.L. 7.88 (LS C(3–4)); see Ch. 1, text to n. 70; also 3.3, text to n. 98.

[169] Its importance is indicated by the prominence in the ethical summary of D.L. (7.88). See Long 1996: 141–52; also Long 2002: 163–8 (on Epictetus); Gill 2013a: lxiv-lxv, 90–1 (on Marcus). The importance of Chrysippus as an authoritative source of Stoic doctrine is less obvious in Marcus than Epictetus (on Marcus' knowledge of Chrysippus, see Sellars 2021: 10–11); but Marcus seems to have regarded this passage as a key Stoic text and often evokes it.

this itself is the virtue of the happy person and a smooth flow of life, whenever all things are done according to the harmony of the *daimōn* in each of us with the will of the administrator of the universe.[170]

As explained earlier, this passage offers a statement of the standard Stoic defin-ition of happiness or the goal as 'the life according to nature'; here, at any rate, this is understood as being according to a combination of human and universal (cosmic) nature.[171] Although this passage was regarded as a highly significant one for Stoic ethics, it is, in some respects, a rather ambiguous or open-ended one. The final phrase is particularly enigmatic: 'according to the harmony of the *daimōn* in each of us with the will of the administrator of the universe'. What kind of 'harmonizing' process is involved? Put differently, what does it mean to 'follow' nature, or more precisely, god or Zeus and his will (*boulē*)? I consider three alternative interpretations, each of which brings out at least one aspect of the significance of universal nature in Stoic ethics. These are three possible (modern scholarly) interpretations of the passage. They are also ideas which, I think, we find expressed in ancient Stoic writings, which are, sometimes at least, linked with the Chrysippean passage.

All three interpretations centre on the idea that the achievement of the goal of life consists in the establishment of a special kind of connection ('harmony', *sumphōnia*) between the mind or rationality (*daimōn*) of the human being[172] and core principles of nature. Also, in all three cases, I think, we can supply the connotations of human and universal nature already discussed; that is, in the case of human nature, the combination of rationality and sociability, and in universal nature, the combination of structure, order, and wholeness, and providential care. So, 'harmonizing' oneself with the administrator of the whole means realizing the best qualities of both human nature and universal nature, in so far as they can be expressed at the human level.[173] However, assuming this interpretative frame-work, there are three main ways of specifying what it means to harmonize yourself in this way. (4a) Following universal nature is identical with acting virtuously ('the virtue of the happy person and his good flow of life are just this . . .').[174] This is the case whether or not the person concerned conceives the virtuous and happy life as

---

[170] D.L. 7.88, IG: 144; for other references to this passage, see n. 168.

[171] For this combination, presented as Chrysippus' conception of the goal of life, see D.L. 7.89 (LS 63 C(5)).

[172] On 'mind', rather than 'guardian-spirit', in a more literal sense, as the meaning of *daimōn*, see Long 2002: 163–4; Betegh 2003: 286–8.

[173] See Ch. 1, text to nn. 70–104.

[174] It does not matter, for this interpretation (or the other two), whether, at the semantic level, one reads Chrysippus as saying that virtue consists in following nature or that following nature constitutes virtue. As Long 2002: 163 points out, the two descriptions are a 'hendiadys', i.e. they signify the same thing. (Such statements of equivalence are common in Stoic formulations for happiness, e.g. Stob. 6a, e.) The interpretative challenge, however, lies in determining what the two formulations mean and in what sense they are equivalent.

one in which she follows universal nature. (4b) Following universal nature is consciously and explicitly taken by the person concerned as an ideal and a source of guidance for her actions and aspirations and one which can enable her to make progress towards living a virtuous and happy life. (4c) Harmonizing oneself with universal nature in a full-hearted way and accepting its ethical significance for the virtuous and happy life enables one to accept with equanimity seemingly unfavourable features of one's life, such as illness and death. This third interpretation is also sometimes linked with accepting the fated sequence of events, as being an expression of the providential care of universal nature or god. The last formulation goes beyond the literal meaning of Chrysippus' passage. However, it certainly represents a well-marked strand in Stoic thought, and the passage was sometimes taken by Stoic writers as expressing this idea.[175]

Before exploring these three interpretations, I spell out certain patterns of thought which underlie all three types, though in somewhat different ways. These patterns relate to points of resemblance and analogy between the universal or cosmic and human levels (that is, between cosmic order and providential care and human virtue and happiness). There are two main types of qualities operating at both levels, and the relationship between them is expressed in different ways. One type of quality is rationality, seen as expressed especially in the combination of structure, order, and wholeness. At the cosmic or universal level, these qualities are exhibited in features such as planetary and seasonal regularity. At the human level, they are exhibited in features such as the unity or interdependence of the virtues, and in the consistency and coherence found in the understanding, character, actions, and relationships of the virtuous person.[176] The relationship between the two levels can be conceived in various ways. One such pattern (a longstanding one in ancient Greek thought) is that of analogy of structure or organization, and specifically analogy between microcosm (the smaller unit) and macrocosm (the larger unit).[177] The pattern can also be conceived in terms of the relationship between inner and outer versions of these qualities. 'Inner' signifies qualities of human understanding and character, actions, and relationships with others, that is, features involving psychological agency. 'Outer' signifies qualities of operations at the cosmic or universal level, such as planetary or seasonal regularities or other large-scale natural patterns. The relationship between human and cosmic order can also be characterized in terms of part and whole. However, I think, that this pattern needs to be conceived in a way that enables the part

<hr>

[175] There are echoes of the Chrysippus passage in these texts on this theme: Epict. *Diss.* 1.6.37–40, 3.5.7–11; M. A. 2.13.1–2, 2.17.4. 3.7.2–4.

[176] See Ch. 1, text to nn. 85–101, 183–200.

[177] On these patterns in Greek thought, see Lloyd 1966, part 2, esp. (on microcosm-macrocosm) 235–6, 252–3, 295–6.

(order at the human level) to have its own integrity and significance and not to depend entirely on the value of the whole (order at the cosmic level).[178]

A similar set of patterns can be identified in connection with the second main relevant feature of the cosmic-human relationship, namely providential care at the universal level and care for oneself and others of one's kind at the human level, especially as expressed in development as appropriation.[179] Human care for oneself and others can be seen as analogous to the providential care of universal nature or god for the whole universe and its parts (as microcosm to macrocosm). Human care can also be conceived in terms of the part-whole relationship, as part of the universal motive of providential care, though a part which has its own distinct integrity and significance, as is brought out in the Stoic accounts of appropriation. Alternatively, care for oneself and others can be seen as that which 'internalizes' the motive of providential care expressed in the (outer) relationship between universal nature (or god) and the component parts of the universe.[180] Taking these patterns into account, we can see that 'harmonizing' oneself with the direction of the universe or Zeus can be understood as developing those qualities (virtue and happiness) which correspond to goodness at the cosmic level. An advantage of this approach is that it matches the Stoic practice of identifying goodness both at the human and universal level, without presenting the human type of excellence as valuable only because it is derived from the universal type.[181]

I now explore these three interpretations (4a–c) more fully. The distinctive feature of the first interpretation is this. The achievement of virtue and happiness is, in itself, identical with harmonizing one's mind with nature's will. If someone develops virtue and gains happiness, this very process is what it means to follow nature or the plan of Zeus. The person concerned expresses in her character, understanding, and life the best possible qualities of human nature and universal nature, in so far as these can be realized by human beings. In this sense, she meets all the requirements of the will of nature; she fulfils in the highest degree the excellences in-built in human nature or the universe. The person concerned does not need to conceive her own character, understanding, and life under this description, provided that she does indeed instantiate the kind of virtue and happiness involved. In other words, the characterization of 'harmonizing' her

---

[178] On this point, see n. 181.

[179] See Ch. 1, text to nn. 90–8, 201–8. On the Stoic theory of appropriation, see Ch. 4.

[180] In summary, the three patterns identified are those of (1) analogy of structure, (2) part-whole relationship (as understood here), and (3) inner-outer relationship, as set out in the preceding paragraph.

[181] I take it that this point is implied by the discussion of 3.3, which shows that the Stoic core ethical claims about value can be stated and argued for in terms of presentation type (1) and not only in terms of presentation type (4), as they would need to be if they were, systematically, dependent on the idea of universal nature.

daimōn with Zeus' will is a third-personal analysis of her state or activity, and not one that she needs to apply to herself in order for it to be valid.

This is the interpretation of Chrysippus' passage I have offered in Chapter 1, discussing the implications of the Stoic definition of happiness as 'the life according to nature'.[182] The patterns of thought about virtue and universal nature or god just outlined are ones which can be found in Epictetus and Marcus, in connection with interpretation 4b, which involves the conscious and explicit use of the idea of universal nature.[183] However, one might call into question whether 4a constitutes a credible interpretation of Chrysippus' passage and a determinate strand in Stoic thinking. Is there any reason to think that the ancient Stoics themselves recognized this conceptual possibility? The fact that the theme does not, obviously at least,[184] appear in practical ethical writings is not an objection to this possibility, because such writings take the form of ethical guidance couched explicitly in Stoic ethical terms, including those of universal nature. However, one could argue that 4a fills a conceptual space in Stoic theory, whether or not the ancient Stoics refer to it explicitly. If we assume that the Stoic analysis of happiness, for instance, as formulated by Chrysippus, is meant to apply universally (as we surely must), 4a is applicable to any fully virtuous and happy person, even if he is not a Stoic philosopher or someone who thinks in terms of Stoic categories. An indication of Stoic thinking on this question is that, in offering possible candidates for the ideal state of wisdom, the Stoics do not cite the heads of the school, who have studied Stoic philosophy to the fullest possible extent, but rather non-Stoic thinkers such as Socrates or Diogenes the Cynic, or non-philosophers such as Heracles and Odysseus.[185] It follows then that, there are (or could be)[186] people who have achieved the state of character and understanding described in Chrysippus' passage but who do not conceive this in terms of 'harmonizing' themselves to the plan of Zeus, interpreted with the conceptual connotations just outlined, namely expressing the best qualities of human and universal nature.[187] These people, then, meet the conditions for the first interpretation; they embody virtue and happiness, but do not, or do not necessarily, conceive them in Stoic terms.

There is at least one passage in Epictetus which might be taken as implying interpretation 4a. *Discourse* 1.17 is a rather intricate discussion which explores the relationship between the three branches of knowledge (starting with logic), or

---

[182] See 1.3–4, esp. text to nn. 102–4, 178–211.   [183] See text to nn. 194–209.

[184] However, see discussion of Epict. *Diss.* 1.17 in text to nn. 188–93.

[185] See Brouwer 2014: 106–12.

[186] It is open to question whether any specific individual has reached the ideal level of the wise person, though this is, in principle, a possibility for all human beings; see Brouwer 2014: 97–112.

[187] A further possibility is that such people recognize the relevant ideas, including that of universal nature or god, but do not formulate them in terms of Stoic doctrine.

rather the implications of this relationship for practical ethics.[188] In the relevant part of this discourse, Chrysippus is presented as an interpreter of nature and compared to a soothsayer or diviner, that is, someone who interprets divine will or plans by observing the entrails of sacrificial animals.[189] The idea that needs to be interpreted is 'the will (*boulēma*) of nature', one which seems to evoke the Chrysippean definition of happiness (D.L. 7.88–9).[190] According to Epictetus, Chrysippus' understanding of this idea has nothing to do with predicting the future course of events by signs. Epictetus explains this idea by reference to one of his recurrent themes, that each of us (human beings) has, ineluctably, the capacity for rational agency and choice (*prohairesis*). We can all, in principle, exercise this capacity in a way that is not constrained by our situation, and can disregard the motivating pressure of the potential loss of preferred indifferents (for instance, the threat of death) by aiming to act rightly and in line with virtue. At least, we can all exercise the in-built human capacity to make progress in this direction.[191] Thus, it turns out, what is needed to interpret 'the will of nature' is not so much expertise in Stoic ethical theory, of a kind that Chrysippus had, and that Epictetus' students focus on gaining, but grasping, and putting into practice, the core ethical message conveyed by this idea, that is, our in-built human capacity for moral choice.[192] Hence, by implication, anyone who puts this message into practice is, by that very fact, interpreting and embodying (or 'harmonizing' himself to) 'the will of nature'. Although this passage is striking for its apparent echo of the Chrysippean passage, the key point is that what really matters in human life is acting in line with the ethical principles analysed by Stoic theory, and not—or not just—understanding the theory (including its idea of universal nature); and this is one of Epictetus' most common themes.[193] To this extent, Epictetus in this passage and elsewhere can be taken as underlining the line of thought I have characterized as interpretation 4a.

The second interpretation is similar in most respects to the first. The salient difference is that the person concerned conceives her own state of mind or activity under this description. She not only has achieved virtue and happiness but also understands this condition as constituting the best possible expression of human and universal nature, and, in that sense, as 'harmonizing' her *daimōn* with Zeus' will. I think this interpretation is more commonly adopted by modern scholars

---

[188] Epict. *Diss.* 1.17.1–12; the role of logic, or clear rational thinking, as a basis for ethics, or living well, is a recurrent theme in Epictetus (e.g. 1.7).

[189] Epict. *Diss.* 1.17.13–29, esp. 15–19, 29. Stoics discussed divination in connection with their theory of determinism (LS 38 E, 42 D–E; also Bobzien 1998a: 87–96); but this is not the idea pursued by Epictetus.

[190] Epict. *Diss.* 1.17.14–15, 17, 28.

[191] Epict. *Diss.* 1.17.20–7; the need for progress is not explicit here but is underlined often elsewhere (e.g. 1.4). See also (on *prohairesis* and what is 'up to us' in Epictetus), Inwood 1985: 240–2; Bobzien 1998a: 330–6; Long 2002: ch. 8.

[192] Epict. *Diss.* 1.17, 13, 19, 28–9.

[193] Epict. *Diss.*1.4.14–17, 2.17.34–6, 3.21.7–9, 4.4.11–18. See also on this theme, Gill 2006: 382–9.

than the first; and some of the scholars whose approach is characterized earlier as 'naturalist' adopt this interpretation, though they do not generally distinguish it from the first.[194] The fullest evidence for the second type of interpretation comes from writings on practical ethics by Seneca,[195] Epictetus, and Marcus Aurelius. None of these thinkers presents himself as having achieved virtue and happiness; their writings (or reported teachings, in Epictetus' case) are protreptic or aspirational in aim, and designed to enable others, or the thinker himself, to make progress towards virtue and happiness.[196] They sometimes deploy the language and ideas of the passage of Chrysippus under discussion (D.L. 7.88) to promote ethical development.

For instance, prominent in Epictetus is the idea that Zeus has built into us (human beings as rational animals) a *daimōn* or inner god, and that we should show proper respect for this *daimōn* by acting virtuously. The underlying thought, explored in different ways in different discourses, is that god or nature exercises providential care for human beings, as rational animals, by implanting this *daimōn*, that is, our capacity for rational agency, and thus conferring the capacity for taking care of ourselves (by virtuous action) in ways that non-rational animals cannot do.[197] In some cases, we are encouraged to improve ourselves by patterning ourselves on god or Zeus, taken as a model of rationality or providential care.[198] In other cases, emphasis falls on the idea that we should realize in ourselves capacities for rationality directed at virtue or for thoughtful self-care in a way that other non-rational animals cannot.[199] Both these types of response can be seen as 'harmonizing' ourselves (or our *daimōn*) to god or Zeus conceived as the shaping organization of the natural universe as a whole.[200] The Chrysippean passage is also one of those most often evoked by Marcus Aurelius in his *Meditations*, with a similar range of connotations.[201] Themes specially linked with this passage include the idea that we (human beings) have a rationality (*daimōn*) in us that is parallel to that in the universe, and we should show proper respect to this fact by exercising our rationality and self-care in a proper way.[202] This is sometimes specified as acting virtuously in ways that affect ourselves and others; this theme is also

---

[194] See e.g. Long 2002: ch. 6, esp. 163–75.

[195] In Seneca, see *Ep.* 41; also references in Long 2002: 176–7.   [196] See refs in n. 164.

[197] See Epict. *Diss.* 1.14, esp. 11–14, centred on the idea of providential care; and 2.8.12–14, 23; also Long 2002: 163–8 on 'the internal deity'.

[198] See Epict. *Diss.* 2.14.10–13 (imitating divine virtues) and 1.6.37 (imitating divine or cosmic order). This idea evokes in a Stoic way the Platonic ideal of ethical aspiration as 'likening oneself to god'; see Pl. *Tht.* 176a–b, *Tim.* 90a (also Long 2002: 164–5, 170). The presence of this theme in Stoic writing on practical ethics does not, I think, carry the theoretical implication that god or the universe is the sole paradigm of goodness or the ultimate source of goodness (on this question, see 3.4).

[199] See Epict. *Diss.* 1.6.12–22, 3.5.10. See also Long 2002: 173–5.

[200] See Long 2002: 163–4, underlining the influence on Epictetus' thinking of the Chrysippean passage.

[201] See Gill 2013a: lxiv–lxv, 90–1, and Gill's 2013a commentary on the passages cited in the following notes.

[202] M. A. 5.21, 5.27, 6.40. 6.58.

sometimes linked with the idea of accepting events with equanimity (the third interpretation, 4c, examined shortly).[203] Respecting our inner *daimōn* is also identified with exercising proper care for ourselves, again implying acting virtuously.[204] So, for Marcus too, the Chrysippean passage is taken as encouraging us to harmonize ourselves to the universe as a whole (or god) by activating in ourselves, at the human level, qualities also ascribed to the universe, such as rationality or providential care. Acting in this way is presented as a specifically human (rational) capacity and is also characterized by Marcus as doing the proper work of a human being or exercising the distinctively human expertise, under-stood as combining rationality and sociability.[205] So, in both Epictetus and Marcus, the Chrysippean passage conveys the idea of parallelism between human and cosmic levels, specifically, harmonizing oneself to the organization of the universe by acting virtuously and achieving happiness, but doing so with this parallel explicitly held in mind.

In the treatment of this theme by Epictetus and Marcus, we find the patterns of thinking about the relationship between human and universal levels outlined earlier. This relationship can be conceived in terms of analogy between the human and universal levels (as microcosm to macrocosm),[206] or as part to whole (though on the assumption that the part has its own integrity and signifi-cance). It can also be understood in terms of the relationship between internal and external, and as involving the internalization of features (such as structure or providential care) also found at the cosmic level.[207] In both themes 4a and 4b, the same principle applies, that the value or significance of the human level does not consist only in linkage with the universal. What is highlighted is the presence of goodness at two distinct but correlated levels.[208] The reference to universal nature, then, represents one possible way of supporting the project of ethical improve-ment, which is the overall aim of these works. It does not carry the implication that reference to universal nature is the only proper way of promoting ethical development, or that Stoic ethical principles depend for their validity solely on derivation from universal nature or god.[209]

The third interpretation incorporates aspects of the first two; but it also introduces two new elements. One element is a focus on acceptance (typically, full-hearted acceptance), rather than action or aspiration, though in some cases, the attitude of acceptance is presented as influencing one's actions. Specifically,

---

[203] M. A. 2.13, 2.17. 4, 3.12. On the link between these two themes, see text to nn. 237–40.

[204] M. A. 3.6.2, 3.7.2, 3.7.4.

[205] See M. A. 5.1, 5.15, 6.19, 6.33; (human expertise) 5.1.5, 6.35; on human nature as rational and sociable, see M. A. 3.7.4, 5.29, 6.44.5 (also Ch. 1, text to nn. 72–8, esp. 74).

[206] The microcosm-macrocosm analogy is particularly prominent in Marcus: see *Med.* 2.9, 5.10.6–7, 5.21, 6.58.

[207] See text to nn. 176–80.   [208] See text to n. 181.

[209] For this point, discussed in connection with Stoic theory (rather than practical ethical writings), see text to n. 108. For scholarship which does assume this view of Stoic ethics, see text to nn. 17–20.

the focus is on accepting the current course of events as fated and, therefore, providentially shaped, and as, in some sense, working out for the best. The second new element is the idea that the recognition of the providential nature of events counteracts, or helps to counteract, negative judgements or emotions we might otherwise be inclined to have. These, then, are additional elements in this strand in what is involved in harmonizing oneself (or one's *daimōn*) to Zeus' plan. This third interpretation corresponds to one of the most widely recognized themes in Stoic ethics; the theme is taken by some scholars to demonstrate that Stoic ethics depends, in a strong sense, on convictions about universal nature.[210] It is also a response that is often, in conventional thought, seen as 'stoic'.[211] There are numerous expressions of this theme in Epictetus and Marcus Aurelius, sometimes presented as evocations of the Chrysippus passage and sometimes in other formulations.[212] There is also some evidence that the theme goes back to early Stoic thought.[213] However, despite the prominence of the idea in Stoic writings, the theoretical basis for this theme is less obvious than with the other two interpretations and requires some unpacking.

A passage often cited in support of this idea comes in Epictetus:

So Chrysippus did well to say: 'As long as the consequences remain unclear to me, I always hold on to what is best fitted to secure such things as are in accordance with nature; god himself made me capable of selecting (*eklektikon*) these things. But if, in fact (or at least, *ge*), I knew that it was now fated (*katheimartai*) for me to be ill, I would be positively motivated (*hōrmōn*) towards this. In the same way, the foot, if it had a mind, would want to be covered with mud [if its owner found that necessary]'.[214]

Although this passage is often cited in support of this theme, its implications are rather ambiguous. The response actually commended by Chrysippus, in the first clause, is that the person concerned should determine her actions on the basis

---

[210] See White 1985: 58–61, 2002: 313–14; Cooper 1995: 595–6; also (summarizing this view) Gill 2006: 199–200.

[211] I use the lower case 'stoic' to denote conventional, rather than scholarly, uses of this notion.

[212] Evocations of the Chrysippus passages are marked by 'C': Epict. *Diss.* 1.6.37–43, 2.6.11–19, 2.8.11–29, especially 27–8 (C); 3.5.7–11 (C); M. A. 2.3, 2.13 (C), 2.4.2 (C), 2.17.4–5 (C), 3.7.2–4 (C), 5.8.9–11 (C).

[213] One relevant passage, cited most fully in Epictetus, *Handbook* 53, is a hymn attributed to Cleanthes. See also the more well-known 'Hymn to Zeus' by Cleanthes (LS 54 I (*SVF* 1.357). However, Bobzien (1998a: 345–57) argues, convincingly, that this passage, like the 'dog and cart' simile attributed to Zeno and Chrysippus (LS 62 A), is problematic, in terms of Stoic theory; so I focus on the Chrysippean passage discussed shortly.

[214] Epict. *Diss.* 2.6.9–10, my trans.; for similar ideas and for the final image, see also 2.5.24–6, 2.10.5–6. The passage plays a prominent role in Brennan 2014: 54, 61; Klein 2015: 266–8, though differently interpreted from here.

of what seems best to her. The response advocated under normal human conditions is to select things 'according to nature' or 'preferable indifferents'.[215] The response linked with the theme under discussion (interpretation 4c) is presented counterfactually, as what one should do if one actually knew what was fated to happen, which human beings do not normally know. In this response, one accepts, or is positively motivated towards, things that are contrary to nature, such as illness or death. Although this response is here presented counterfactually, it is one that is recommended, on various grounds, in actual situations in Stoic ethical discussions. These grounds include a sense of social or political obligation, or, in the case of terminal illness, the judgement that death involves a reduction in 'things contrary to nature' such as pain and prolonged infirmity.[216] Such factors, at least terminal illness, may be implicitly assumed here. However, we have, in addition, the thought that the 'dispreferable' outcome involved is fated and should be adopted for this reason, presumably on the grounds that this outcome is providentially shaped.

What, exactly, in Stoic thinking, is this theme based on and how does it relate to the other two interpretations? In addressing this question, I focus on ideas that can reasonably be traced to Chrysippus, rather than earlier Stoic thinkers.[217] I consider first why fated events should be regarded as being, for that reason, good and worthy of arousing positive motivation. In the first instance, it is relevant that Stoics are determinists or, more precisely, compatibilists, who see determinism as compatible with the exercise of choice by adult humans, regarded as rational animals. The form of determinism adopted by Chrysippus is sometimes called universal causal determinism; the course of events is conceived as a seamless web of causes, without causal gaps.[218] The exercise of rational agency and choice by human adults is seen as part of this seamless causal web; rational choice constitutes a specific kind of cause.[219] The course of events is also seen as providentially shaped by Zeus or god, understood as an immanent agency at work in all parts of the universe and in everything that happens within it.[220] The course of events, as thus conceived, is regarded as good or working out for the best, in what might call

---

[215] The focus in the first clause on seeking things 'in accordance with nature' is contrasted, implicitly, with the second clause, which recommends being motivated towards things that are, typically, 'contrary to nature' (though fated to occur). This does not necessarily imply that virtuous practical deliberation is limited to selecting between indifferents and adopting on each occasion what is more 'preferable' (on this point see Ch. 2, text to nn. 69–73, 145–6; also Klein 2015: 273).

[216] For death chosen as a political obligation, see (on Regulus), Cic. *Off.* 3.99–115 (also Ch. 2, text to nn. 234–48), and (on Cato), Cic. *Off.* 1.112. On death chosen on the basis of the preponderance of things 'according' or 'contrary' to nature, see Cic. *Fin.* 3.60–1. See also Griffin 1986; Cooper 1999: 515–41, esp. 532–6.

[217] On points of difference regarding determinism between Chrysippus and earlier Stoics, see LS, vol. 1, pp. 392–4. However, this claim about difference of view within Stoic thinking on this subject is challenged by Jedan 2009: 31–48.

[218] See LS 55; also Bobzien 1998a: chs. 1, 4; Meyer 2009.

[219] See LS 62, C–D; also Bobzien 1998a: ch. 6, 1999; D. Frede 2003.

[220] See LS 46 A–B; also Bénatouïl 2009.

a thin or weak sense. Events are good in the sense that, as a seamless web of causes, that is, without causal gaps or random events, they constitute a cohesive, structured, and ordered whole.[221] This view makes more sense if one considers the main opposing ancient theory, that of Epicureanism. According to Epicureans, events are random or fortuitous, in various senses. They are the product of mechanical laws of movements of atoms, on the one hand, and of random 'swerves' by atoms, on the other, which, in some way, explain the human capacity for 'free will'. There is no idea of in-built purpose or rationale in the overall course of events.[222] This is one sense in which Stoics see the unfolding course of events as good; as indicated, one could see it as a rather weak sense; is there a stronger sense in which events are seen as good?

In addressing this question, it is worth noting that, in a number of respects, Stoics do *not* see the course of events as good. Although they see the universe or world as well-suited for enabling all forms of life (a point discussed shortly), they acknowledge fully the presence of periodic events which are disadvantageous for the existence or well-being of human beings or other animals and plants. Thus, for instance, they do not ignore the occurrence of intermittent floods, fires, earthquakes, and other such disasters, which have a damaging effect on large or small groups or individuals.[223] They also accept the existence of more permanent or structural features which are damaging to human beings, but which are seen as necessary concomitants of a framework that is, overall, favourable to human life or well-being, such as the thinness of the bones around the brain, leaving human beings more liable to injury than other animals.[224] These are features which, in terms of Stoic ethics, would be classed as 'things contrary to nature' or 'dispreferred indifferents'.[225] However, the Stoics, including Chrysippus, also acknowledge the existence of things that are 'bad' in the Stoic sense, that is ethical defects or vices.[226] Indeed, they could hardly fail to do so, since Stoics regard as bad, in the strict sense, anyone who falls short of perfect wisdom or virtue, which means virtually everyone. The Stoics also believe that, of the two main sources of ethical corruption, one lies in 'the nature of things', as they put it, namely in the natural tendency of human beings to overvalue preferred indifferents rather than things that are genuinely good, namely virtue and virtue-based happiness.[227] These features of their thought were seen by critics of Stoicism as incompatible with

---

[221] See LS 54 A–B, 55 J–N; Bobzien 1998a: 45–58.

[222] See LS 13, 20; also Morel 2009; O'Keefe 2009. 'Free will' (indeterminist libertarianism) is a key idea for Epicureanism, though not for Stoicism: see Bobzien 1998b, 1998a: 276–90.

[223] See e.g. Seneca, *Natural Questions*, Book 2 (thunder and lightning), Book 3 (effects of water, including flooding), Book 6 (earthquakes); see Inwood 2005: ch. 6, esp. 170–3, 178–81.

[224] See LS 54 Q (Gellius 7.1.1–13), esp. Q(2); for this example, see also Pl. *Tim.* 75.

[225] Hence, Seneca de-emphasizes their negative effect in *On Providence* 2.1–2, 2.7, 4.1, 5.9; see Inwood 2018: 58–61.

[226] See LS 54 Q (Gellius 7.1.1–13), esp. Q(1). The Stoic argument is that goodness requires the co-existence of (balancing) badness.

[227] See 5.1, text to nn. 44–55.

their belief in divine providence, though they were defended in various ways by Stoic thinkers.[228] However, their presence, along with the acknowledgement of the existence of natural disasters and 'necessary concomitants' of a favourable natural framework, show that the Stoics are far from promoting a naïvely optimistic view of the natural universe and the unfolding course of events.

In fact, given these points, it may seem puzzling why the Stoics maintain that the universe and course of events are providentially shaped for the best, apart from the rather 'thin' sense noted earlier, that of universal, causal determinism. However, it seems most likely that, in so far as they identify a stronger sense of providential shaping for the best, it depends on the features noted earlier in this book as providing evidence of the providential care of the universe (or Zeus or god, conceived as an in-built organizing force) for all elements within it. The Stoics see human beings, especially, as recipients of this providential care, but also to some extent, non-human animals, plants, and other elements in nature such as air and sea.[229] In the case of human beings and other animals, this providential care is shown not just in the provision of an environmental context which, in general (if not in each and every case)[230] enables life and well-being. It is also shown in the implanting of natural instincts which promote the life and well-being of human beings and other animals, and also which dispose them to procreate and take care of others of their kind.[231] These are the basic motives which activate natural development, conceived as 'appropriation' (oikeiōsis) in animals, and which, in the case of human beings, underlie the development of the virtues, conceived as forms of expertise in producing happiness.[232] Another benefit conferred on human beings is the capacity for resilience in coping with what are normally seen as disasters.[233] This is closely tied to the capacity for ethical development, since this development involves recognizing the radical distinction in value between virtue and 'preferred indifferents' and between vice and 'dispreferred indifferents'.[234] Also, as brought out later, it also involves a correlated change in emotional register, as the person changes from experiencing misguided 'passions' or bad emotions to having well-judged 'good emotions'.[235]

---

[228] See LS 54 O–U, and LS vol. 1, pp. 332–3; also Mansfeld 1999b: 466–7; Algra 2003: 170–2.

[229] See Cic. N. D. 2.73–168; objects of care include plants (83), sea and air (100), non-human animals (122–30), as well as human beings (154–68). See also D. Frede 2002: 103–16, who stresses that this generalized care represents the main theme of Stoic thinking on providence even if there is also evidence for the idea of providential care for individual human beings. See also Ch. 1, text to n. 90.

[230] Note the qualifications in text to nn. 223–8. The focus on the main structural features of universal nature is implied in Chrysippus' concession that 'some things are neglected . . . even if the overall housekeeping is good' (Plu. Sto. Rep. 1051 B–C (LS 54 S)).

[231] See Cic. N. D. 2.121–7 (means of self-preservation), 128–30 (means of procreation and care of offspring).

[232] See LS 57 A, D, E–F, 59 D; also Ch. 4, esp. 4.2.

[233] This is a recurrent theme in Epictetus: see Diss. 1.6.37–43, 1.12.30–5, 1.14.11–17, 3.5.7–11, 4.1.108–9; see also M. A. 2.13.1–2, 4.49, Seneca, On Providence 2.1–2, 2.7.

[234] See Cic. Fin. 3.20–2; also 4.4.   [235] See 5.1.

These features of the universe, or world, are surely the ones which make it most reasonable for Stoics to see the natural course of events as providentially shaped for the best, particularly for human beings as rational and sociable animals. These features promote not only human physical and social well-being, that is, 'things according to nature' or 'preferables'. They also enable human beings to develop the highest forms of human excellence, that is, the virtues and virtue-based happiness (the life according to nature). By the same token, they enable human beings to develop the capacity to respond with resilience to the temporary or permanent removal of things advantageous to their life and well-being, as a result of natural disasters, or illness and death, or the prospect of these, in their own lives or the lives of those who with whom they are concerned. This connection between these Stoic ideas partly explains why the themes of responding with resilience to (what are normally seen as) disasters and accepting with equanimity the fated and providentially shaped course of events are closely linked, as in the Epictetus passage cited earlier.[236] The connection also explains why the capacity for virtuous action is closely linked with this kind of acceptance, since both types of response form integral parts of ethical development.[237] The response commended in this complex of ideas is that of coping with adversity—in part, at least[238]—by recognizing that events are providentially shaped (they form part of the 'plan of Zeus'). The providential plan in-built in universal nature and in the course of events includes the capacity for developing the virtues and, as a result, showing resilience in adversity.

What, exactly, is the response recommended in this theme? On the face of it, the answer is quite clear: recognition of the fact that events, even if adverse, form part of the fated course of events (the will of Zeus) renders them more acceptable to the person concerned. In this sense, the person 'harmonizes' herself (or her *daimōn*) to the will of the administrator of the universe, in terms of the Chrysippus passage which forms the basis of this discussion.[239] However, as Epictetus points out several times, there is no reason to think that this recognition, taken on its own, will be enough to produce this acceptance. Epictetus highlights the fact that, in the absence of virtue, people regularly curse or dismiss Zeus and his will and bitterly resent the fact that their wishes are not being fulfilled in reality.[240] In other words, as Brennan suggests, what is needed is not only the recognition of divine action but also that of the radical distinction in value

---

[236] See Epict. *Diss* 2.6.9–10 (text to n. 214). See also Epict. *Diss*. 1.6.37–43, 3.26.28–38, 4.1.99–106, M. A. 2.11, 2.17.4–5, 5.8.

[237] Epict. *Diss*. 1.6.37–43, 2.8.11–29, esp. 23, 27, 28, 3.5.7–11, 14; this is linked with Epictetus' recurrent stress on the importance of distinguishing between what is and is not 'up to us' (within our power), *Handbook* 1. See also M. A. 2.5, 2.13.2, 2.17.4–5, 3.6.1, 3.7.

[238] A second element is identified in the following paragraph.   [239] D.L. 7.88.

[240] Epict. *Diss*. 1.22.13–16, 1. 27. 12–14, 2.22.15–17.

between virtue and preferred indifferents.[241] This in turn implies that, for this recognition to take place and to have the desired effect, what is required is not just a certain way of understanding nature or the course of events but also ethical development, as presented in Stoic thought, involving both development in beliefs (about what is really good) and the correlated change in emotional response. Put differently, the recognition presented in this theme is not separate from ethical development, as described elsewhere in Stoic theory, but forms part of this process of development.

This point also comes out in a slightly different way in the *Meditations*. Marcus, repeatedly, combines acting correctly and accepting the fated unfolding of events, and presents both responses as objects of aspiration, towards which he urges himself through his reflections. He also links both responses closely with exercising the virtues, including the four Stoic cardinal virtues, towards whose development and expression Marcus urges himself throughout the work.[242] Thus, although Marcus' comments presuppose that, in his view, events work out in a providential way, he also brings out that *recognizing* this providential role depends on developing virtue and the associated attitudes and actions. In other words, for him too, the understanding of the ethical significance of nature is inseparable from ethical development more generally.

This point clarifies another question raised by this theme, namely the relationship between this theme (4c) and the two previous themes discussed (4a–b), all of which can be seen as interpretations of the Chrysippus passage taken as the starting-point. This theme, obviously, introduces additional elements, but it also has points in common with both preceding ones. In the first theme (4a), achieving virtue and happiness is, by itself, equivalent to harmonizing oneself to the will of Zeus. As just pointed out, the recognition of these events as providentially shaped by Zeus or universal nature, even when they are adverse, depends on the development of virtue as well as on interpreting events in the appropriate way. In this respect, theme three (4c) presupposes theme one (4a), or at least presupposes the achievement of virtue and happiness which is central for theme one. Theme two (4b) also presupposes theme one (4a), in that that the overall aim of theme two is to promote ethical development by referring to features of universal nature analogous to those associated with virtue and happiness, notably order and providential care. Themes two and three (4b-c) have in common the fact that the person concerned conceives his response under the description of harmonizing his *daimōn* with the will of Zeus, instead of this idea being implicit or a third-personal analysis. However, the focus of the response differs, being centred on

---

[241] Brennan 2005: 237–8. See also M. A. 3.6, 3.11, which highlight the importance of combining an understanding of the difference between goods and indifferents with a recognition of divine providential care for human beings, if we are to respond appropriately to adversity; see also text to n. 242 on this point.

[242] M. A. 3.6.1, 3.11.3–4, 3.12.1, 10.8.2, 10.11.2, 12.3.3. On Marcus and virtue, see Gill forthcoming b.

action or aspiration in theme two and on acceptance of events in theme three. Despite this difference of focus, there is much in common between all three themes. All of them presuppose that the universe forms a teleologically structured set of natural entities and that Zeus (or god or the universe) exercises providential care in enabling these entities to fulfil their nature.[243] All these themes presuppose (and encourage progress towards) the achievement of virtue and happiness, that is, the state of understanding, character, and life presented in theme one. So, although the three themes have shades of difference, they also represent overlapping aspects of the same set of ideas.

I conclude by considering the implications of this discussion of possible interpretations of the Chrysippus passage for the scholarly debate reviewed earlier about the role of nature, especially universal or cosmic nature, in Stoic ethics (3.2). Although there is no doubt that the idea of universal, as well as human nature, is an important one in Stoic ethics, I have questioned one common scholarly belief on this subject, namely that the Stoic worldview is consistently regarded as authoritative for ethics, and that ethical ideas, including the distinctive 'hard' ethical theses, are systematically presented as dependent on this worldview.[244] I have maintained that the evidence of three main ancient summaries of Stoic ethics point to a more complex and flexible situation, in which ethical ideas can be presented independently, or supported by ideas about human or universal nature or both, and in which each of these forms of presentation is regarded as valid (3.3). Also, in discussing Stoic ideas about the relationship between branches of knowledge, I have argued for a division of authority between theology and ethics (3.4). Stoic theology is authoritative in its presentation of types of nature, including universal and human nature, and in highlighting the ethical significance of these types of nature. However, ethics is authoritative in its analysis of ethical concepts and in framing arguments for the distinctive ('hard') ethical claims. In addition, ethics informs theology, regarding its use of the notion of 'good', while theology informs ethics, regarding nature-related ideas and their ethical significance; and in this respect their relationship is a reciprocal one.[245] Hence, overall, there is scope for variation, evident in the ethical summaries, in the extent to which the resources of theology (that is, the Stoic worldview) are drawn on for the purposes of ethical theory and in the specific aspect of nature (human, human and universal, or universal) which is accentuated in ethical discussion on any one occasion.

How far do the three ideas presented here as interpretations of the Chrysippus passage on the goal of life (4a-c) support this way of understanding the role of nature in ethics or point to a different one? This question is particularly pertinent

---

[243] For these ideas, see Cic. *N. D.* 2.73–168, also 2.33–9 (on the teleological structure or *scala naturae*).

[244] For versions of this view, see text to nn. 17–20; also refs. in n. 122.

[245] On this point, see text to nn. 151–62.

since the Chrysippus passage and some others noted in my discussion are often seen as lending decisive support to the view that ideas about cosmic nature provide the fundamental basis for Stoic ethics.[246] Of course, the material reviewed here is rather different in character from that discussed in the preceding two sections (3.3–4). I have drawn on Stoic writings on practical ethics, where the focus is on using ideas to promote ethical development rather than on summarizing or analysing ethical doctrines. However, this material also carries implications about the theoretical ideas and assumptions which underpin the practical objectives; hence, it is relevant for the question of the role of universal nature, and other kinds of nature, in Stoic ethics.

In the first interpretation (4a), the Chrysippean passage is taken as offering an analysis, in terms of harmonizing oneself with Zeus' plan, for a process, ethical development, that is not necessarily conceived by the person concerned under that description. Clearly, in this case, harmonizing oneself with Zeus' plan is one possible way of describing ethical development and its outcome. But we know from other sources that this process can be conceived and described in different ways, which do not involve reference to the idea of 'harmonizing' yourself to universal nature or Zeus' will or plan. This idea does not figure, for instance, in the account of the final stages of ethical development in Cicero, On Ends 3.20–2, although, in Cicero's account and elsewhere, appropriation is sometimes placed in a broader framework of human and animal motivation.[247] A similar point can be made about the second interpretation of the Chrysippus passage (4b). In this version, the person sees herself as harmonizing herself to Zeus' plan or will; cosmic nature is regarded as an explicit object of ethical aspiration and provides a framework for defining ethical aims. However, again, this is only one possible Stoic way of characterizing ethical aspiration. In Cicero's On Duties 1, the targets of ethical aspiration are analysed differently, in terms of the virtues as a matched set and types of action characteristic of the virtues. Cicero's framework in On Duties also involves reference to nature, but human nature, in various forms, rather than universal or divine nature.[248] Neither of these forms of analysis invalidate the other; indeed, both may well have their basis in the thinking of Chrysippus, who defined happiness in terms of both human and universal nature.[249] However, the implication is that these are alternative, but valid, ways of characterizing the goal of life, rather than that one way, involving universal

[246] Long 1996: ch. 6, gives a central place to D.L. 7.85–8, including 7.88; see also Long 2002: 163–8; Inwood and Donini 1999: 682–7. Epict. Diss. 2.6.9–10 is given a key role in Brennan 2014.

[247] For references to this broader natural framework (presentation type 3 in terms of 3.3), see D.L. 7.85–6 (LS 57 A), and Cic. Fin. 3.16, 3.62–3. Although the idea of 'harmonizing' oneself to Zeus' plan does not figure in Cic. Fin. 3.20–1, implicit reference is sometimes seen to qualities, notably order, shared with universal nature (see Ch. 1, text to nn. 99–101, also 4.4, text to nn. 127–32).

[248] See Ch. 2, text to nn. 156–65. Stobaeus' summary, sometimes seen as closely based on Chrysippus (Long 1996: 130), shares this focus on human nature with Cic. Off.; see 3.3, text to nn. 78–91.

[249] D.L. 7.87–9 (LS 63 C(2–5)).

nature, is definitive or authoritative and that all other accounts are secondary or derived from this one.

What about the third interpretation (4c) and the ideas in Stoic ethics linked with this theme? As just noted, these ideas are often cited as lending decisive support to the claim that Stoic ethics is grounded on Stoic thinking on universal or cosmic nature. Certainly, the theme that all events are providentially shaped and work out for the best provides a new layer of significance to the idea of harmonizing oneself to Zeus' will or plan. However, it is open to question whether this new element radically alters the overall position. For one thing, as highlighted by Epictetus and Marcus (and Brennan), the force of this consideration still depends on the ethical state of the person concerned, and on whether or not she has developed ethically in a way that enables her to see Zeus' plan as one to which she wishes to harmonize herself.[250] There is also the question, reviewed earlier, of the various senses in which it can be credibly claimed that, on the Stoic view, events do indeed work out for the best. The strongest ground for this claim, as I have suggested, is that universal nature provides the basis for forms of life to realize their in-built capacities and motives; in the human case, this means, above all, the capacity for developing virtue and happiness, understood as the life according to nature. Exercising this capacity involves developing the kind of resilience that enables one to accept what are normally seen as disasters as being part of a providentially shaped course of events.[251] The Stoics, of course, offer grounds for forming this view of the natural universe and of the sequence of events that typically take place within the universe. However, one can reasonably argue that forming this view depends not just on considerations marshalled about cosmic nature or determinism but also on the ethical attitudes one brings to bear in taking account of these considerations. The Stoic worldview is only likely to be convincing for someone who has made substantive progress in developing virtue and happiness of the kind that this worldview is presented as supporting. Thus, we find here an equivalent at the practical level for the idea discussed earlier, that the Stoic worldview (as presented in theology) and ethical theory inform each other in leading to conclusions relevant for ethics.[252] In other words, the relationship between these two branches of knowledge is co-ordinated and, in the relevant respects, mutually supporting, rather than hierarchical.[253]

---

[250] See text to nn. 240–2.   [251] See text to nn. 232–8.   [252] See 3.4, text to nn. 151–62.
[253] On this contrast, see text to nn. 109–14, also nn. 161–2.

PART II
LEARNING TO LIVE NATURALLY

Introduction to Part II

So far in this book, I have examined core Stoic ethical concepts and the central, distinctive claims about virtue, happiness (understood as 'the life according to nature') and 'indifferents'. In this second part, I turn from the Stoic ideal life ('living naturally') to the process of development by which we move towards this life ('learning to live naturally'). I consider what are widely recognized as two notable features of their thought on this subject, their idea of development as 'appropriation' (*oikeiōsis*) and their conception of emotions. In the main introduction to this book, I have outlined the principal themes of these two chapters and their role within my overall argument.[1] In this further introductory section, I explain what is meant by the rather paradoxical idea of *learning* to live naturally: if this process is natural, why do we need to learn it and what form does such learning take? I do so, first, by explaining how the discussion of appropriation and emotions in Chapter 4–5 is related to the Stoic ideas about nature already considered in Chapters 1–3. Second, I locate Stoic thinking about ethical development within a broader picture of ancient ideas on development and explain their stress on naturalness in that context. In this way, I prepare the ground for the claim (in Chapter 8) that the Stoics offer an original and distinctive view on ethical development that can contribute significantly to modern thought, notably contemporary virtue ethics.

First, how does the discussion of Chapters 4–5 fit in with the reading of core themes in Stoic ethics given in Chapters 1–3? It is worth noting, first, that the two topics covered here, appropriation and emotions, appear regularly, alongside other key themes, in the three main ancient summaries of Stoic ethics.[2] However, this raises the further question, why are these two themes given this significant role? The answer is more obvious in the case of appropriation than emotions. In broad terms, the theory of appropriation shows how the

---

[1] See pp. C1P17–18.
[2] See D.L. 7.85–7 (appropriation), 110–17 (emotions); Stob. 10–10e (emotions), no section on appropriation but a short section (5b3) on primary motives; Cic. *Fin.* 3.16–22, 62–8 (appropriation), 3.35 (emotions), also Cic. *Tusc.* Books 3–4 give a leading role to Stoic thinking on emotions. On the standard topics of ethics, including 'motive' (including appropriation) and 'emotions', see D.L. 7.84 (LS 56 A), also Schofield 2003: 336–9.

development of virtue and virtue-based happiness forms a central part of a good human life and also, to some extent, how this life fits in with broader patterns in nature as a whole. The link between emotions and other central Stoic ethical themes is less evident. However, I stress here that Stoics see good or bad patterns of emotional response as the expression of success or failure in ethical develop- ment; in this respect, like appropriation, the topic of emotions is integrated with other ethical themes. I now explain more fully how Chapters 4–5 bring out the significance of these two themes and thus contribute to understanding the sense in which the good life, according to Stoicism, that of virtue-based happiness, con- stitutes a 'natural' life.

In considering appropriation (Chapter 4), I focus on sources which are closely linked with core Stoic ethical claims (about virtue, happiness, and indifferents) and which illustrate advanced human ethical development. These sources are, primarily, Cicero's *On Ends* 3.16–22, and 62–8, supported by reference to *On Duties* 1.11–15, 50–9. These treatments are more relevant for this concern than some other Stoic discussions of appropriation, whose aim is to locate human motives and behaviour in a broader natural framework, or which centre on infant and other basic forms of development.[3] In considering these Ciceronian texts, I bring out how they show the realization of 'the life according to nature', in both the main relevant senses, that is, human and universal nature. I presuppose here the connotations of these ideas discussed earlier, namely the combination of rationality and sociability, on the one hand, and of structure, order, and whole- ness, and care of oneself and others of one's kind, on the other hand. My discussion accentuates the importance of the sociable and other-directed aspects of appropriation, and the way that these are closely integrated with accounts of ethical learning. For instance, I explore the conceptual and thematic links between the two strands of appropriation in Cicero's *On Ends* (3.16–22, 62–8), which are centred on ethical learning and sociability, respectively, as well as highlighting analogous features of *On Duties* (esp. 1.11–15), where these two aspects of appropriation are closely connected with each other.[4] In these ways, I bring out how appropriation is presented as the progressive realization of human nature, as rational and sociable, and as the rational expression of the basic human (and animal) motives to take care of oneself and others.[5] Another point about human sociability explored here is the combination, and integration, in Cicero's treatment and some other Stoic texts of two central Stoic themes: recognizing the commu- nity of humankind as a whole and full-hearted engagement in localized family and social relationships (4.5–6). I also highlight the inclusion, in Cicero, *On Ends*

---

[3] For these other aspects of appropriation, see D.L. 7.85–6, Sen. *Ep.* 121, Hierocles, *Elements of Ethics* (selections in LS 57 A–C), texts often given emphasis in scholarly discussions of appropriation.

[4] See 4.3, 4.5, text to nn. 202–15.

[5] On basic motives, see 4.2; on the development of human beings as rational and sociable see 4.3–5.

3.20–2, of selection between indifferents as an integral part of the progress towards ethical understanding and as a continuing part of the exercise of this understanding. This illustrates the central role of selecting 'things according to nature' as part of the progress towards, and realization of, 'the life according to nature'.[6]

It is not unusual to see close links between Cicero's presentation of appropriation in *On Ends* 3.16–22, at least, and core Stoic ethical claims about virtue and happiness. This is less common in the case of the Stoic theory of emotions, which is more often examined from a psychological standpoint. However, my treatment here underlines in various ways how this theory is integrated with Stoic thinking about ethical development and with what counts as 'the life according to nature', especially human nature. I stress that the Stoic theory is not only about defective emotions or 'passions' but also about 'good emotions', which form part of the virtuous and happy life. I also emphasize that the Stoic theory, including their ideas about the therapy of (defective) emotions, is, centrally, about successful and failed ethical development. The Stoics see our pattern of emotional reactions as reflecting our overall ethical state and the extent to which we have or have not made progress in learning to live 'the life according to nature'.[7] In particular, I underline the close connection between Stoic thinking on emotions and the social strand of ethical development as appropriation. I discuss a set of texts, in Seneca, Marcus, and Epictetus, which bring out the idea that our pattern of emotional reactions is correlated with progress (or lack of progress) in learning how to form well-judged and committed interpersonal and communal relationships. I also challenge the view sometimes put forward by scholars that the aim of Stoic therapy is a kind of self-sufficiency produced by emotional detachment from other people.[8] Thus, overall, I bring out the connections between the Stoic theory of emotions and their thinking about development towards the 'life according to nature', especially our human nature (as both rational and sociable), and towards the proper exercise of care for others as well as for ourselves.

So far, it may seem that the Stoic presentation of ethical development as 'natural' depends entirely on accepting their specialized characterization of virtue and happiness in terms of 'naturalness'. However, the Stoics also claim that such development is natural in several more familiar senses of this term. For instance, they claim that all human beings have a constitutional (natural) capacity to develop ethically. They also present ethical development as a process that can occur (naturally) in any given family or social context, as well as being one that does not, necessarily, depend on philosophical expertise. Further, they see ethical development as a process that can occur at any point in an adult life and one that

---

[6] See 4.3 and 4.4, text to nn. 104–13.

[7] The Stoic presentation of defective emotions as 'contrary to nature', as well as 'irrational, in certain senses, reflects this view (see LS 65 A(1, 6–8), J). Note also Epictetus' argument with the father of a sick daughter in *Diss.* 1.11 about what counts as a 'natural' response to this illness (Ch. 5, text to nn. 124–6).

[8] See 5.2–3.

is not decisively shaped, or prevented, by earlier forms of character formation. A further distinctive feature of Stoic thought, correlated with these ideas, is their focus, especially in practically oriented ethical works, on guidance designed to help anyone, at any stage of their lives, to make progress towards virtue and virtue-based happiness. Another relevant idea is that, given Stoic high expectations about what counts as virtue, a Stoic life is, for almost everyone, likely to be a life of progress towards virtue rather than successful completion of a developmental process followed by the exercise of virtue. This view might seem to run counter to Stoic claims about the 'naturalness' of ethical development. However, the Stoics maintain that this conception of ethical development falls within a credible and cogent conception of what counts as a good life, viewed in terms of human nature and the larger natural framework.

These claims about naturalness form key points in the Stoic theory of ethical development. I outline this theory, defined, in part, by contrast with another important ancient pattern of thinking on this subject; both approaches are described in broad terms, in line with the introductory aim of this discussion. As well as explaining in this way Stoic ideas about naturalness, I also clarify why the Stoic theory is, predominantly, a theory of development within adult life. This is particularly important because the alternative ancient pattern, like much modern thinking, gives a central role to childhood development.

The alternative ancient pattern is, in certain salient respects, shared by Plato's *Republic* and *Laws* and by Aristotle's ethical writings and *Politics*. This pattern differs from some other ancient approaches, including that associated with Socrates in the early Platonic dialogues, which prefigures the Stoic view.[9] The Platonic-Aristotelian pattern, as I call it, was regarded as a standard or 'consensus' view by some later thinkers, including Plutarch and Galen, who sometimes use it as the basis for criticizing the Stoic view.[10] A well-marked theme in the Platonic-Aristotelian framework is that ethical development depends on the combination of a special kind of inborn nature, social habituation in beliefs and practices, and philosophical education. These factors are sometimes formalized as 'nature' (*phusis*), 'habit' (*ethos*), and 'reason' (*logos*) or 'education' (*paideia*). Another shared feature of this pattern is the idea that ethical development can be divided into two, relatively distinct, stages, one of socially based emotional habituation, especially in childhood, and another of intellectual education, in adult life. In Plato's *Republic*, Books 2–4 and 6–7, these correspond to the two stages of the educational programme, first for the guardian class as a whole, and then, for those selected for the élite

[9] Socratic ideas prefiguring the Stoic view include the idea that progress towards virtue is 'up to us' (and in principle open to anyone), coupled with the idea that virtue is knowledge and a unified conception of human psychology. See Gill 2006: 85–8; also 177–83, on shared Epicurean and Stoic ideas on development.

[10] On Plutarch, see Gill 2006: 231–2, 414–5; on Galen, Gill 2010a: 221–9, referring esp. to Gal. *PHP*, Book 5, and *QAM*, ch. 11.

group of philosopher rulers.[11] In Aristotle's ethical thought, this idea is expressed as the contrast between acquiring the 'facts' (or 'the that') of ethical life and understanding the 'reason' (or the 'why').[12] This subdivision is also framed in psychological terms. The first, habituative stage is conceived as the shaping of emotion and desire in line with rational norms, whereas the second stage is seen as wholly rational, though it may contribute to a further shaping of emotion and desire.[13] A further assumption of the Platonic-Aristotelian approach is that the scope for successful ethical development depends on the nature of the socio-political context in which it occurs. This is explicit in Plato's *Republic* and *Laws*, which are both exercises in framing the kind of constitution in which the citizens (or a subgroup of them) can develop virtue and achieve happiness. This is also part of the project of Aristotle's *Politics*, which is seen by Aristotle as a sequel to his study of ethics.[14] Hence, by implication at least, the success of the programme of ethical development sketched in Aristotle's ethical works depends on whether this is carried out in societies which can, effectively, provide 'the that' or social habituation, which serves as a basis for the reflective enquiry into the 'why' of ethics. A further shared Platonic-Aristotelian assumption is that ethical development is only completed by the achievement of philosophical understanding, supported by a prior basis in habituative training in attitudes and emotions.[15]

This Platonic-Aristotelian pattern can serve to define, by contrast, salient features of Stoic thought on ethical development. Although the Stoics sometimes refer to the idea of distinctive inborn character,[16] they also maintain that, regardless of this, all human beings are constitutively capable of achieving (complete) virtue and happiness. They claim that: 'All human beings have the starting-points (*aphormai*) of virtue by nature', and that, 'Virtue is teachable ... as is evident from the fact that inferior people become good'.[17] One idea, underlying this claim, is the belief that all human beings have the in-built capacity to form an understanding of the good. In more technical terms, human beings have 'preconceptions'

[11] For these two stages, see Pl. *Rep.* Books 2–3, centred on training in poetry and athletics, esp. 400c–402a, Book 7, education through mathematics and dialectic, esp. 518d–519b, 525b–c, 535a–537c, 539d–540c; also Gill 1996: 266–87, 2006: 134–6. In Pl. *Leg.*, on emotional habituation, see 653a–c, 654c–d, 655d–656b, 658e–660a; also 643e–645c, 649a–650b. The second stage in *Leg.* is provided by the account of the dialectical education of the 'nocturnal council' (961d–968a) and by Book 10, giving a philosophical framework for the ethical and religious belief-set of the community.

[12] See Arist. *NE* 1.4, 1095b4–8, also 10.9; also Burnyeat 1980; Gill 1996: 273–5.

[13] See, in Pl. *Rep.*, refs. in n. 11, also 485d–486b, 500b–d, 586e–587a; Arist. *NE* 1.13, 2.1, 2.3. See also Gill 1985b, 1996: 245–60, 268–75, 292–7; 1998b: 196–214.

[14] On this point in Pl. *Rep.*, see Gill 1996: 279–87. See also Arist. *NE* 10.9, linking ethics and politics in this respect, and referring to the three key factors in ethical education (nature, habituation, and education), *NE* 10.9, 1179b20–1180a24. For the link between ethics and the political framework, see Arist. *Pol.* 7.13, esp. 1332a28–b11 (again citing these three factors); on childhood education in the political context, see *Pol.* 7.17, 8.1–7.

[15] On this contrast between Platonic-Aristotelian and Stoic approaches to development, see also Gill 2006: 85–8, 134–6 (Platonic-Aristotelian pattern), 136–45 (Stoic pattern).

[16] See Gal. *QAM* ch. 4, Kuhn 784, Cicero, *On Fate* 8. See also Gill 2006: 178–9; Graver 2007: 170–1.

[17] Stob. 5b8, 2.65.8–9, D.L. 7.91 (LS 61 L and K).

(*prolēpseis*) for grasping the notion of good; and the development of these preconceptions into a full understanding of what is good is especially associated with the process of appropriation.[18] Accordingly, as brought out in Chapter 4, appropriation, for instance, in Cicero's *On Ends* 3 and *On Duties* 1, is presented as stemming from motives that belong to human beings as such. These motives are to realize one's nature or constitution (as human) and to care for others of one's kind (other human beings). These motives are sometimes characterized as reflecting human nature conceived as constitutively rational and sociable.[19] The achievement of complete ethical understanding, including recognition of the good and its special value-status, is, certainly, presented as an exceptional one, and as the outcome of a complex and demanding process, as is stressed in the account of appropriation in Cicero's *On Ends* 3.16–22. However, this recognition is still presented as being 'according to nature',[20] which implies, among other things, that it falls within the scope of human nature, as such. Achieving this knowledge is not, in principle, confined to an élite subsection of humanity, characterized by a specific kind of inborn nature, habituative upbringing, and intellectual education, in the way we find in the Platonic-Aristotelian pattern.[21]

This point goes along with a further difference between the Stoic and Platonic-Aristotelian patterns. In Plato and Aristotle, as just noted, there is great emphasis on the idea that complete ethical development requires a specific type of social context, which can provide the right kind of habituation of beliefs and emotional responses (what Aristotle calls 'the that') as a basis for full ethical understanding.[22] The Stoics do not ignore the possibility that ethical development can be disrupted by poor upbringing and corrupting social influences.[23] Stoic thinkers also indicate how our relationships with other people can contribute positively to progress in ethical understanding. Seneca, in Letter 120, for instance, discusses the human capacity to form a conception of virtue and happiness by extension from the qualities of the people we observe in our lives.[24] Analogously, Marcus Aurelius, in his autobiographical Book 1 of the *Meditations*, shows how his observation of the qualities of those encountered at each stage of his life has contributed to his ethical understanding of core Stoic ethical ideas, including that of 'the life according to nature', though he does not suggest that any of the people observed (or he himself)

---

[18] See Plu. *Sto. Rep.* 60 B and D.L. 7.53 (LS 60 C–D). See also Jackson-McCabe 2004: Inwood 2005: 271–301; I. Hadot 2014.

[19] See Cic. *Fin.* 3.16, 62, *Off.* 1. 11–12; also Ch. 1, text to nn. 96–8; 4.2.

[20] The recognition is 'according to nature', and stimulates us to desire it far more strongly than we are stimulated by all the earlier objects [the things 'according to nature', or 'preferred indifferents']. Cic. *Fin.* 3.21 (LS 59 D(6)). See 4.4, esp. text to n. 105.

[21] See Gill 2006: 131–8, 178–82.   [22] See text to nn. 14–15.

[23] See Ch. 5, text to nn. 44–55.

[24] Sen. *Ep.* 120.5–9 (LS 60 E3–6); also, more puzzlingly, Seneca seems to suggest we have had actual experience of complete virtue and virtue-based happiness (120.10–11 (LS 60 E(7–8)). See Inwood 2005: 284–91, 2007: 324–27.

have achieved complete virtue or wisdom.[25] These comments reflect the Stoic analysis of the acquisition of knowledge, which gives a key role to 'inference' or 'analogy' and allows the possibility of building on, but going beyond, empirical observation of one's experiences.[26] However, the Stoics recognize the positive or negative consequences of social involvement without making the further Platonic-Aristotelian move of stipulating that a certain kind of family or community upbringing is a prerequisite for ethical development. The Stoic accounts of appropriation, including the advanced, rational stages, are presented in terms of activities, such as 'selecting' between indifferents and forming family and communal relationships, that can occur in any social or political context.[27] This presentation reflects their belief that all human beings have, by nature, the starting-points and 'preconceptions' that provide the basis for ethical understanding.

These points bring out certain structural differences between Stoic thought and the Platonic-Aristotelian pattern of thinking on development; they also support the Stoic claim that ethical development is 'natural' in two respects that do not apply in the alternative framework. Another point of difference relates to the question whether completing the process of ethical development requires expertise in philosophy or not. In Plato's *Republic* and, in a different way, *Laws*, the completion of ethical development involves a programme of philosophical enquiry, following a prior stage of social habituation.[28] Aristotle's 'that-why' distinction implies a similar picture; also, his presentation of the highest human happiness as based on philosophical understanding matches this view.[29] In Stoic thought there are, on the face of it, competing indications on this question. On the one hand, the virtues are defined as forms of knowledge or expertise.[30] Wisdom, the leading virtue, is regularly defined as 'knowledge of human and divine things', which suggests a form of knowledge based on philosophy.[31] Also, as highlighted in an earlier chapter, philosophy is subdivided into three broad areas, namely logic, physics, and ethics, and philosophical understanding as a whole is presented as combining or synthesizing these three branches.[32] The implication seems to be that wisdom (or 'knowledge of matters divine and human') depends on this

---

[25] M. A., Book 1, esp. 1.9.1, 1.17.11 ('life according to nature'); also Gill 2013a: lxxxi–iii.
[26] See Cic. *Fin.* 3.33–4 (LS 60 D), Sen. *Ep.* 120.3–5 (LS 60 E 1–4).   [27] See 4.3–5.
[28] See Pl. *Rep.* 521d–534c, on this second, philosophical, stage, and, on the necessity of the prior, habituative first stage, see *Rep.* 400c–402c, 412a–414a, 535a–537d; also nn. 11, 13, referring also to Plato, *Laws*.
[29] On the 'that-why' distinction, see n. 12; on philosophical contemplation (*theoria*) as the highest form of human happiness, see Arist. 10.7–8 (Ch. 6, text to nn. 92–9).
[30] On the virtues as forms of knowledge or expertise, see LS 61 B–D; also Ch. 1, text to nn. 133–46.
[31] See Brouwer 2014: 8–18, citing the main evidence and defending the view that this idea is Stoic in origin.
[32] On this theme, see LS 26 A–E; also Brouwer 2014: 19–29; see also Ch. 3, text to nn. 109–14.

unified or holistic grasp of the main ideas of the three branches of philosophy.[33] Indeed, in some sources, the virtues are presented as three-fold (physical, ethical, and logical) and as corresponding to the three-fold division of philosophy.[34] This is a rather puzzling idea; but one possible implication is that wisdom (conceived by Stoics either as co-extensive with the virtues or as the leading virtue)[35] depends on philosophical understanding of these areas, taken as a whole. These points, taken together, might seem to suggest that, for the Stoics, as well as Plato and Aristotle, the advanced or final stage of ethical development consists in, or depends on, philosophical understanding.

On the other hand, the presentation of the development of virtue (in Cicero's *On Ends* and *On Duties*), is framed in general terms without explicit reference to philosophical enquiry or understanding.[36] Other features of Stoic thought, including some noted earlier in this book, point in the same direction. Candidates for the role of the ideal Stoic wise person include the non-philosophers Heracles and Odysseus as well as the politician Cato. By contrast, the Stoic heads, who have studied Stoic philosophy to the highest possible level, are not presented as wise people or as regarding themselves as wise.[37] The many illustrative pictures of the wise person in the ancient ethical summaries present this figure as engaged in practical and social activities as much as intellectual ones.[38] The Stoics also repudiate the Platonic-Aristotelian dichotomy between the lives of practice and (philosophical) theory, and distance themselves from the idea that happiness depends on philosophical activity.[39] The overall implication seems to be that, although philosophical activity constitutes one, valid, form of the exercise of wisdom, it is not the only one and does not have the special, authoritative status that it does in the Platonic-Aristotelian framework. By the same token, it follows that philosophical expertise is not a prerequisite for the achievement of virtue and virtue-based happiness, or the life 'according to nature', which marks the culmination of ethical development. If so, this marks a further point of difference between the Stoic and Platonic-Aristotelian patterns and is another feature reflecting the idea that the capacity to develop ethically belongs to human beings as such and is in this sense a 'natural' one.

A further distinctive feature of Stoic thought also bears on the question of 'naturalness' and ethical development. In the Platonic-Aristotelian pattern,

---

[33] On the linkage between wisdom, as so defined, and philosophy (without reference to the three branches), see Sen. *Ep.* 89.4–5 (LS 26 G).

[34] See LS 26 A; and Cic. *Fin.* 3.72–3, D.L. 7.83; also Jedan 2009: 84–90; Vogt 2017: 187–90.

[35] See LS 61 B–D.   [36] See 4.3–4.

[37] See Brouwer 2014: 114–34 (on the Stoic heads), 104–5 (on Cato), 110–12 (Heracles and Odysseus); other possible candidates are the pre-Stoic thinkers, Socrates and Diogenes the Cynic (Brouwer 2014: 107–9). See also Ch. 3, text to n. 184–7.

[38] See Stob. 11m, D.L. 7.117–25; also Inwood and Donini 1999: 720–2 on the function of these exemplary pictures.

[39] See LS 67 W–X, and Ch. 6, text to nn. 123–9.

habituative training is conceived as instilling certain types of emotion and desire, along with beliefs.[40] This is linked with the view that the human psyche consists of a combination of rational and non-rational 'parts', understood, in some cases at least, as separate and independent sources of motivation. The idea that the human psyche, in adults as well as children, is constituted in this way underlies certain central features of Platonic and Aristotelian ethical psychology. It forms the basis of the idea, in Plato's *Republic*, that the cardinal virtues can be analysed in terms of the relationship between the three psychic parts. It also underpins Aristotle's distinction between ethical or 'character' virtue, a type of virtue that involves the co-operation of the rational and non-rational or partly rational part, and 'intellectual' virtue, wholly situated in the rational part.[41] The Stoics do not subdivide the human psyche into distinct, and potentially conflicting, motivational parts in this way. They distinguish between the psychological state of non-human animals (and human children) and adult humans, regarding the former as non-rational (or pre-rational in the case of human children) and the latter as rational. Adult human psychological processes are seen as uniformly rational, in certain senses at least. While non-human animals, human children, and human adults share the same basic psychological processes, those of human adults are shaped by the development of rationality, for instance in the form of language-acquisition, concept-formation, logical inference, and judgement. This point applies to all adult human psychological processes, including emotions as well as actions, and practical activities as well as intellectual ones. These are all equally 'rational', in the sense that they involve the application of one or more forms of rationality of this type. The Stoics also sometimes use 'rational' in a different (normative) sense, signifying, in effect, virtuous or wise, but this additional sense presupposes the more basic sense.[42]

This difference is widely recognized as a major, substantive point of contrast between the Stoic and Platonic-Aristotelian frameworks. It bears centrally on the Stoic theory of emotions, discussed in Chapter 5; and it also has implications for their view of the distinction between adult human and childhood motivational responses, as brought out in Chapter 4. However, there are further, wide-ranging implications for Stoic thinking on development which are less often recognized. For one thing, Stoic accounts of development have no equivalent for the preliminary stage of habituation in attitudes and emotions (especially in childhood) that plays such an important role in the Platonic and Aristotelian accounts.[43] A related point is that Stoic interest in emotional development, from an ethical standpoint,

---

[40] See Pl. *Rep.* 2–3, esp. 400d–402a; Arist. *NE* 2.1,2.3; also text to nn. 11–13.

[41] See Pl. *Rep.* 441e–442d, Arist. *NE* 1.13, esp. 1103a4–10; also Gill 1996: 245–60, 2006: 134–6.

[42] See LS 33 C, I, and LS 53, esp. A, Q, S–T; also Inwood 1985: ch. 3; Brennan 2003: 265–9; Gill 2006: 138–45, 251–3. See also Ch. 5, text to nn. 10–17.

[43] See text to nn. 11–13. Epictetus refers to the role of habit as part of ethical training (*Diss.* 2.18); but he does not presuppose the Platonic-Aristotelian view of the role of childhood emotional habituation.

including their ideas on the therapy of defective emotions, centres very largely on adults, rather than children. A further implication of this focus is that, despite recognizing that adults are likely to have been corrupted by their earlier life-experience and social influences,[44] they do not see them as disabled by this from ethical development in adult life, in principle leading to complete ethical understanding. This marks a difference, particularly from Aristotle's view.[45] In one notable passage on moral responsibility (*NE* 3.5), Aristotle suggests that a mature adult can reach a point in his ethical development where he is no longer capable of becoming a good person, even if he now wants to do so. What seems to underlie this suggestion is the view that the non-rational part of the psyche has been so badly habituated that the option of change of character to the better is no longer possible.[46] The Stoics also recognize that people have naturally, or develop during their lives, tendencies or dispositions towards one or other type of defective emotion (*euemptosiai*), and that, in some cases, these tendencies can become 'ingrained' or 'callused'.[47] None the less, they insist that adults retain, in principle, the capacity for change, and improvement, in the ethical quality of their attitudes and emotions, as well as their pattern of actions. A striking exemplification of this point, discussed in Chapter 5, is the figure of Medea, as presented by Euripides, and as interpreted by Chrysippus and Epictetus. Even Medea, despite her appalling earlier history of murder, recognizes that her plan to kill her own children is 'bad' for her as well as the children; and she is torn by psychological conflict between her (natural human) love for her children and her self-activated desire for vengeance on her husband. Hence, she is, in principle at least, open to the therapy of emotions that the Stoics advocate, as well as serving as a cautionary example for other people more open to change and improvement.[48] What underlies the Stoic view of Medea and their emotional therapy in general is the set of ideas reviewed here, including their unified or holistic psychological framework, and their belief that all human beings, as such, have the in-built capacities and motives for becoming good people. This Stoic stress on the scope for ethical improvement in adult life is a further distinctive feature of Stoic thought, linked both with certain differences from Platonic or Aristotelian thought and with Stoic ideas about what is 'natural' for human beings.

The Stoic focus on ethical development in adults, rather than on social habituation of children, can also be linked with a further notable feature of their thought. This is the prominence in their ethical writings of guidance for the management of

---

[44] On Stoic thinking on sources of corruption, see Ch. 5, text to nn. 44–55.

[45] In Plato, an analogous idea to the Aristotelian one noted shortly is that even 'great natures' can be so corrupted by bad education that they are disabled from realizing their natural potential; see *Rep.* 491b–495b, a theme taken over by Plutarch (Gill 2006: 415).

[46] See Arist. *NE* 3.5, esp. 1114a3–21; also Gill 2006: 104–5, 2010a: 222.

[47] Cic. *Tusc.* 4.24–33, Stob. 10e, 2.9.1–13; also Gill 2006: 261–6; Graver 2007: 164–7.

[48] See Ch. 5, text to nn. 63–73.

living, especially guidance directed at enabling people to make progress in their own attempts at ethical improvement. The emergence of genres or types of practical ethics (including the categories of protreptic, therapy, and advice) is a rather general feature of Hellenistic and post-Hellenistic ethics. However, the Stoics give special attention to this aspect of ethical teaching and writing; the topic of 'encouragements and discouragements' is presented as a standard one in Stoic ethics.[49] A particularly striking feature is the emergence of three-fold programmes of practical ethics, directed at promoting self-improvement. Thus, for instance, we find in Seneca a programme based on (1) assessment of value, (2) adjustment of motive to the assessment made and (3) consistency between motive and subsequent actions. In Epictetus, a (much-noted) programme is centred on (1) examining desires and aversions, (2) shaping motives directed at actions and social interactions, and (3) exercising care and achieving consistency in the judgements reached.[50] These programmes relate in several ways to the Stoic framework of thinking ethical development. They reflect the Stoic unified or holistic (or, in modern terms, 'cognitive') psychological framework, according to which emotions and actions are shaped by beliefs and assumptions and are thus open to change by changes in belief. They also express the Stoic focus, in ethical development, on seeking to influence adults, in this case by promoting considered self-management regarding attitudes, motives and emotional responses. These programmes also assume that the adults addressed are, in principle, capable of making significant progress in ethical development, in a way that is not pre-empted by character formation in childhood or earlier adult life. Thus, they assume the framework of assumptions about the universal human capacity, and motivational basis, for ethical development outlined so far here, by contrast with certain features of the Platonic-Aristotelian pattern.[51]

Finally, I note what might seem to be a problem for Stoic thinking on ethical development. On the one hand, the Stoics stress the natural human capacity for development, and spell out, in some detail, the stages of a complete process of development, both in connection with appropriation and the therapy of emotions.[52] On the other hand, they sometimes accentuate (more than other ancient philosophical approaches) the gap between the ideal wise person and even someone who has completed most of the steps towards this ideal level of

---

[49] See, on 'encouragements and discouragements', D.L. 7.84 (LS 56 A). More broadly, on the Stoic emphasis on guidance in the Hellenistic period as well as later, see LS 66, Gill 2003: 40–4; Schofield 2003: 253–6; Brunt 2013: chs. 1, 3, 4.

[50] See Sen. *Ep.* 89.14, Epict. *Diss.* 3.2.1–5 (LS 56 B–C); see also Cic. *Off.* 2.18; Stob. 2.47.7–2.45.6 (the programme of Eudorus, a 'Middle Platonist' influenced by Stoicism). The programme of Epictetus has been much discussed: see P. Hadot 1995: 191–5, applied to M. A. *Med.* in P. Hadot 1995: 195–202; P. Hadot 1998: 43–7; Gill 2006: 380–91.

[51] See further on this feature and its influence on, and significance for, modern thought, 8.1, text to nn. 24–6, 55–7 and 8.2.

[52] See Cic. *Fin.* 3.20–2 (LS 59 D) (also 6.4); Sen. *Ep.* 75.8–18; also Inwood and Donini 1999: 726–31.

understanding and character.[53] The combination of these two features carries the implication that, even for the most committed and ethically advanced follower of Stoicism, one's life is likely to be, at best, that of an ongoing journey towards virtue and virtue-based happiness. This conclusion may seem problematic (as ancient critics of Stoicism suggest) or, at any rate, demotivating. However, this negative implication is counteracted by certain ways in which the Stoics present the process of making progress towards the Stoic ideal, as well as the completion of this process, as a natural one. For instance, the process of appropriation, in Cic. *Fin.* 3.16–22, is presented, at each stage, as one that realizes the capacities and motives characteristic of human nature, sometimes viewed in a broader natural framework. Also, the completion of the process constitutes simply the highest level of the same kind of activities (notably, selection between indifferents and performing appropriate actions) that also form part of the progress towards virtue, and not a qualitatively different activity or state. Similarly, in the social strand of appropriation (in Cic. *Fin.* 3.62–8), both the actions ascribed to virtuous and wise people and those ascribed to people in general moving towards this level are presented as expressing motives and qualities characteristic of human nature, sometimes viewed in a broader natural framework.[54] In the case of emotions, the therapy of emotions, designed to counteract the effect of earlier corruption, is presented as the removal of features of human behaviour that are 'unnatural', and out of line with human nature at its best as well as generating internal conflict and disturbance.[55] Hence, although the achievement of perfect virtue and wisdom marks a substantive 'step-change', by comparison with which all other levels are incomplete and defective, the movement towards this level is also inherently worthwhile, and expresses distinctively human ('natural') capacities and motives, sometimes viewed within a broader natural framework.

---

[53] See LS 59 I, N, LS 61 S–U. See Inwood and Donini 1999: 714–26; Roskam 2005: 9–10, 15–32; Brouwer 2014: 57–61, 68–70, 93–8. Other such ideal figures include Socrates, Diogenes the Cynic, Epicurus, and Pyrrho the Sceptic (see Long 1999: 618–32).

[54] See 4.4–5, esp. text to nn. 133–48, 199–201. Contrast the more sharply differentiated levels in the educational programme and associated images (notably the 'myth of the cave'). In Pl. *Rep.* 6–7.

[55] See Ch. 5, text to nn. 57–80; also Gill 2006: 254–60.

4

'Appropriation': Ethical Development as Natural

4.1 The Theory of Appropriation

A salient feature of Stoic thinking about ethical development is that this is seen as a natural process, in various senses, rather than one that depends on a combination of specific types of inborn nature, social habituation, and intellectual education (the contrasting Platonic-Aristotelian view).[1] A central expression of this view is the theory of development as appropriation; although this became a widespread way of conceiving ethical development in Hellenistic and post-Hellenistic thought, it seems to be a Stoic innovation and one that reflects broader features of their ethical approach.[2] The term 'appropriation' (*oikeiōsis*) suggests the notion of making something 'one's own' (*oikeios*); development consists in making oneself (or one's nature or constitution or other people of one's kind) 'one's own' in some way.[3] The underlying motive is best understood as expressing care or concern for oneself or others.[4] A further feature of the theory, shared with other theories in the period, is that ethical development, seen as an advanced human function, is placed in a broader pattern of natural motives and behaviour and correlated with those of other animals.[5] Although I take account of this broader natural framework (particularly in 6.2), my main interest is in those sources, especially Cic. *Fin.* 3.16–22, 62–8, and *Off.* 1.11–15, 50–9, which show advanced human ethical development and bring out links between the theory and the core Stoic ethical ideas discussed in Chapters 1–3. I am less concerned with Stoic texts which address only the broader natural framework or are focused on basic, especially childhood, development.[6] The theory of appropriation has

---

[1] See Introd. to Part II.
[2] See Gill 2017, esp. 111–12. On later Aristotelian versions of appropriation, see Sharples 2010: ch. 17.
[3] The term *oikeiōsis* is not easily rendered in English: other possible translations include 'attachment', 'endearment', 'familiarization', and 'orientation'.
[4] See 4.2; also Inwood 1985: 184–5; Schofield 1995: 196; Klein 2016: 149–50.
[5] For the main sources, see LS 57 and 59 D. See also (on both strands of the theory), Pembroke 1971; Engberg-Pedersen 1990; Annas 1993: 262–76; on self-appropriation only, Inwood 1985: ch. 6; Gill 2006: 129–66; Klein 2016; on appropriation of others, Blundell 1990; Reydams-Schils 2005: ch. 2.
[6] Texts centred on these other aspects of appropriation include D.L. 7.85–6, the fragments of Hierocles, *Elements of Ethics*, and Sen. *Ep.* 121 (for extracts, see LS 57 A–C); see also on these aspects Gill 2006: 36–46; Klein 2016.

Learning to Live Naturally: Stoic Ethics and its Modern Significance. Christopher Gill, Oxford University Press.
© Christopher Gill 2022. DOI: 10.1093/oso/9780198866169.003.0005

already figured prominently in previous chapters of this book.[7] Here, I examine the theory in more detail and with closer reference to the most relevant texts. After discussing the overall aim of the theory in this section, I consider how it is used to explain the basic motives (care for oneself and others) shared by human beings and other animals (4.2). I then consider the advanced stages of human development, referring both to Cicero, *On Duties*, especially 1.11–15, which combines appropriation of oneself and others in a single account and *On Ends* 3 (16–22, 62–8), which discusses them separately (4.3–5).[8]

What is the overall aim of the theory of appropriation, viewed in the context of Stoic ethics as a whole? Like most other scholars, I see it as providing support for the Stoic conception of the goal of life (happiness) as 'the life according to nature', supplying what is sometimes described as an 'argument' for this conception.[9] But how does the theory provide this support? This is not done by mounting formal arguments for the Stoic, as distinct from other, ancient accounts of the goal of life. Rather, the theory describes, typically in narrative form, the process of development towards the (Stoic) goal and presents this as being, in some sense, natural.[10] How is the case made? What we find is a three-fold pattern, used to analyse human behaviour both at a basic level, shared with other animals, and at an advanced, rational (purely human) level. Thus, in the first instance, the theory appeals to human and animal behaviour that is widespread and readily observable, and presents this behaviour as best explained by reference to certain basic motives, that is, self-preservation and parental love. These motives are, in turn, analysed by reference to two core dispositions, namely appropriation of oneself (or one's constitution) and of others of one's kind. It is also maintained that these dispositions are in-built in human (or animal) nature and that they reflect broader patterns in nature as a whole.[11]

The same pattern can be found at more advanced stages of ethical development, though the working out of this pattern is much more complex. The best available texts for this purpose are Cicero's *On Ends* 3.20–2 and 3.62–8.[12] The functions accentuated by Cicero in *On Ends* 3.20–2 are, first, rational selection of things

---

[7] See Ch. 1, text to nn. 96–8, 153–7, 201–8; Ch. 3, text to nn. 80, 95–7.

[8] On the relationship between these two versions and the reason for the divergence of approach, see 4.3.

[9] Striker 1996: 281–97, examines closely whether the theory provides an argument for the Stoic goal. Her conclusion, like mine, is that the theory offers 'an account of psychological development that shows how man could come to adopt accordance with nature as his only goal' (293), rather than providing an argument grounding the conception of the goal.

[10] See Gill 2017: 202–8, which also sees this as characteristic of accounts of appropriation in the period.

[11] On this three-fold pattern. See also 4.2, text to n. 30; 4.4, text to n. 95; 4.5, text following n. 173.

[12] D.L. 7. 85–6 (LS 57A) is sometimes regarded as the key text for appropriation, both non-rational and rational. But, although it gives a clear illustration of the three-fold pattern of ideas linked with appropriation (see 4.2, text to nn. 31–46), it is much less explicit in its account of advanced rational functions than Cic. *Fin.* 3.20–2, and simply highlights the role of reason in transforming motivation as the distinctive feature of human beings (or rational animals) (D.L. 7.86 (LS 57 A(5)).

according to nature; and, second, recognition that the things according to nature are of a radically lower order of value than virtue (or virtue-based happiness). A third function is continuing selection of indifferents in the light of fully achieved virtue. These functions are also characterized in terms of motives; and these motives are explained, by implication at least, by reference to appropriation of oneself. This process is also presented, again implicitly, as the realization of human nature at its best and of the good-making qualities of universal nature. Hence, we have a more complex equivalent of the three-fold pattern present at the basic level.[13] Separately, in *On Ends* 3.62–8, Cicero appeals to various kinds of rational and social behaviour by human beings and presents this as expressing motives which reflect the disposition to appropriate others of one's kind, that is, other human beings. He also indicates ways in which appropriating others expresses the virtues, while also reflecting the best features of human and universal nature. I suggest that, although these two strands (appropriation of oneself and others) in *On Ends* are presented separately, they imply each other, and that both strands need to be combined and integrated, as they are in *On Duties* 1.11–15, to provide a complete and credible picture of ethical development.[14] So, overall, the theory of appropriation, as presented in this text, supports the Stoic account of the goal of the life, that is, happiness conceived as the life according to nature, by showing that the movement towards this goal expresses two dispositions (to appropriate oneself and others of one's kind) that reflect the best features of human nature and also of nature as a whole. The Stoic theory shows that this development is natural in the sense that it expresses these core, in-built, natural human and animal dispositions and does so to the highest possible degree. In this way, the theory of appropriation supports the Stoic account of the goal of life.[15]

The question of how to interpret Cicero's account of appropriation in *On Ends* 3 (especially 3.20–2) is complex and much debated. In arguing for the view outlined here, I also refer to the treatment of analogous topics in Cicero's *On Duties* (6.3). Cicero's treatment there contains a shorter presentation of appropriation in 1.11–15, as well as a discussion of social relationships (1.50–9) which is comparable in some respects with *On Ends* 3.62–8 (4.5). Cicero's version of the Stoic theory of appropriation differs in certain respects in the two works. However, I suggest that *On Duties* has implications for the interpretation of *On Ends* 3 (3.16–22 and 3.62–8), both as regards the virtue-indifferents relation and the interplay between self-related and other-related aspects of ethical development. Taken together, these two texts offer a good basis for making sense of Stoic thinking on the advanced stages of appropriation of oneself and others and showing how they relate to the three-fold pattern outlined here.

---

[13] See 4.4, esp. text to nn. 123–48. [14] See 4.3, 4.5, text to nn. 202–14.
[15] See further 4.4, text to nn. 149–65.

I close this introductory section by considering another general question about the Stoic concept of appropriation. Is there just one form of appropriation, appropriation of oneself or one's constitution,[16] or are there two forms, appropriation of oneself and others of one's kind?[17] And, if there are two forms, should we suppose, as has sometimes been claimed, that appropriation of oneself was the original form and that appropriation of others was a (conceptually derivative) addition?[18] The answer, at least to the first question, is not obvious, because the ancient sources offer material for both views. There are some, quite prominent, treatments of the topic which are centred solely on appropriation of oneself or one's constitution.[19] There are also accounts, notably Cicero, *On Ends* 3.16–22, 62–8, which present the two kinds of appropriation separately.[20] In fact, it seems clear that both kinds of appropriation go back to Chrysippus (who may well have been the originator of the whole theory),[21] as is clear from this comment of Plutarch:

> Why then in heaven's sake in every book on physics and ethics does he [Chrysippus] weary us to death in writing that we are appropriated (*oikeiou-metha*) to ourselves, as soon as we are born, and our parts and our offspring?[22]

This source, I think, invalidates the idea that there was only one original form of appropriation (appropriation of oneself), since it identifies both appropriation of ourselves and our offspring, referring to parental love, the paradigm of appropriation of others.[23] However, the passage also, perhaps, explains why the theory is presented in different ways in our surviving sources. Chrysippus' comment can be read as referring to one theory, embracing all aspects of appropriation, or two theories or strands, or, indeed, three theories or strands (appropriation of ourselves, our parts—that is, our body[24]—and our offspring).

Thus, it seems that in this area of Stoic thinking, as well as the ethical role of nature,[25] there is more scope for valid variation than is always recognized, at least

---

[16] For different versions of this view, see Inwood 1985: ch. 6; Klein 2016.

[17] For this view, see Blundell 1990; Annas 1993: 275–6; Schofield 1995: 195–9; Reydams-Schils 2005: 55–9.

[18] Inwood 1983: 195–201. On this suggestion, see text to n. 23.

[19] See D.L. 7.85–6, Cic. *Fin.* 3.16–22, Sen. *Ep.* 121. Most of Hierocles' *Elements of Ethics* focuses on appropriation of oneself (for extracts, see LS 57 C); but Hierocles also recognizes social appropriation as a separate strand (LS 57 D).

[20] See 4.4–5.

[21] Evidence for a theory of appropriation going back to Zeno is very limited; see Radice 2000: 247–62, referring esp. to *SVF* 1.197–8.

[22] Plu. *Sto. Rep.* 1038 B (LS 57 E(1)).

[23] This evidence thus runs counter to the proposal that social appropriation was a later addition, as suggested by Inwood 1983.

[24] Appropriation to one's own body is an important theme in the Stoic texts, notably in Hierocles and Seneca (see LS 57 B–C); see also Gill 2006: 37–46.

[25] See 3.2, text to nn. 41–54, 3.3, first para.

as regards the subdivision of the topic. Hence, appropriation of oneself might be presented on its own, or coupled with a separate account of appropriation of others, or the two kinds could be combined, without this being regarded as inconsistent or unorthodox.[26] However, any complete discussion of this topic in Stoicism needs to take account of both kinds of appropriation, and of the possible relationship between the two strands.

It may seem conceptually rather puzzling that we find this degree of variation; does not appropriation of oneself point in a competing, even opposite, direction to appropriation of others? However, the answer to this question is, surely, 'no'. Appropriation of oneself and others are not seen as, fundamentally, opposed but as aspects of a larger, overall pattern. It is significant that, when appropriation of oneself (or one's constitution) is discussed on its own, the 'constitution' appropriated sometimes includes a social, other-directed dimension.[27] Also, even when the social dimension is not explicitly mentioned, it may be implied in the account of appropriation of oneself (or one's constitution); and I suggest that this is the case in Cicero, *On Ends* 3.16–22, even though the social dimension is also discussed separately later in Book 3.[28] In considering this question, it is important not to assimilate the two kinds of appropriation to the modern 'egoism-altruism' contrast (though scholars sometimes do this). Appropriation of oneself is not egoism or selfishness (that is, an ethically defective attitude), nor is appropriation of others properly identified with altruism (taken to be an ethically good attitude). The Stoic motives or dispositions are, in themselves, ethically neutral; their quality depends on whether or not they develop into virtues or vices. They are also not seen as opposed motives but as compatible parts of human (or animal) motivation.[29] Hence the variation we find in Stoic sources for appropriation as regards self-appropriation and appropriation of others does not raise the ethical problems that would be generated in the case of egoism and altruism.

4.2 Basic Motives

I now consider Stoic accounts of basic motives, shared by human beings and animals; their basic character is supported by reference to human children and young animals. These accounts indicate a shared pattern of ideas, with three main elements. (1) Widely observed forms of behaviour in animals and human beings

---

[26] For these variations, see D.L. 7.85–6 (appropriation of oneself on its own); Cic. *Fin.* 3.16–22, 62–8 (appropriation of oneself and others presented separately); Cic. *Off.* 1.11–15 (the two types combined).
[27] For this point, see Klein 2016: 161–2, esp. n. 42, 166, esp. nn. 53–4, 186. Passages cited include Hierocles 2.5–9, 3.23, Cic. *N. D.* 2.123–4, Epict. *Diss.* 1.2.30–1, M. A. 11.18.1. In a distinct, though related, move, Epictetus claims that self-appropriation involves other-directed motives: Epict. *Diss.* 1.9.11–15, 2.22.19–21; see also Magrin 2018: 322–31.
[28] See 4.3, text to nn. 79–81, 87–90, 4.5, text to nn. 202–5.
[29] On the modern egoism-altruism contrast and Stoic thinking, see 6.4.

are explained in terms of two types of basic motive: self-preservation and parental love. (2) These motives are interpreted, in turn, as expressions of two underlying dispositions, to appropriate oneself (or one's 'constitution') and to appropriate others of one's kind. (3) It is maintained that these dispositions are in-built in human (or animal) nature and that they reflect broader patterns in nature generally.[30]

This pattern of ideas can be illustrated by reference to two well-known ancient passages, both centred on appropriation of oneself, in Diogenes Laertius and Cicero:

> [The Stoics] say that an animal has self-preservation as the object of its first motive, since nature from the beginning appropriates it, as Chrysippus says in his *On Ends* Book 1. The first thing appropriate (*prōton oikeion*) to every animal... is its own constitution (*sustasis*) and the consciousness (*suneidesis*) of this. Nature was not likely to alienate (*allotriōsai*) the animal itself, or to make it and then neither alienate it nor appropriate it (*oikeiōsai*). So it remains to say that in constituting (*sustēsamenen*) the animal, nature appropriated it to itself [that is, nature appropriated the animal to the animal itself]. That is why the animal rejects what is harmful and accepts what is appropriate.[31]

> [The Stoics] hold that as soon as an animal is born ... it is appropriated to itself (*ipsum sibi conciliari*) and led to preserve itself and to love its constitution (*suum statum*) and those things which preserve its constitution, and to be alienated from its death and from those things that lead to death. They prove that this is so from the fact that, before either pleasure or pain has affected them, infants seek what preserves them and reject the opposite, something which would not happen unless they loved their constitution and feared death. But it cannot be the case that they desire anything unless they have a sense of themselves (*sensum sui*) and therefore love themselves. Hence, it must be realized that the principle (*principium*) has been drawn from self-love.[32]

Both passages bring out the first element in the pattern just outlined. The behaviour of young humans and animals is explained in terms of the motive of self-preservation, more broadly, of rejecting what is harmful (things that lead to death) and seeking what promotes life and well-being. In the second, Ciceronian, passage, this explanation is contrasted with the main competing ancient view that, from birth onwards, infant animals and humans go for pleasure, thus supporting

---

[30] On the distinction between motives and dispositions (which are long-term motives), see Inwood 1985: 189–91 (also 39–40 on dispositions in Stoic psychology); LS, vol. 1, p. 351.

[31] D.L. 7.85 (LS 57 A(2)), LS trans. with my addition in square brackets. On this passage, see also Inwood 1985: 186–94.

[32] Cic. *Fin.* 3.16, trans. Brunschwig 1986: 128.

the Epicurean account of the goal of life.[33] In another Stoic discussion of appropriation of oneself, Seneca also cites infant behaviour in support of the claim that humans and animals are naturally inclined to realize their natural capacities rather than to seek pleasure.[34]

Both passages also bring out the second element in the pattern of ideas. The motive of instinctive self-preservation is analysed as an expression of a more fundamental, life-long, disposition, namely appropriation of oneself.[35] This disposition is also presented in these passages as appropriation of one's 'constitution' (*sustasis, status*).[36] The constitution is defined elsewhere as 'the ruling centre (or mind, *hēgemonikon*) in a certain relation to the body'.[37] Bearing in mind that the Stoics are physicalists in their psychological assumptions, and in general,[38] the 'constitution' is one's nature, conceived as a psychophysical state. This constitution includes, in adult humans, rationality and sociability.[39] The animal and human instinct for self-preservation is, thus, interpreted as showing the in-built disposition to maintain one's constitution, meaning, in the first instance, one's body and its life. This self-appropriation is mediated by self-consciousness or self-awareness, characterized elsewhere, by the Stoic Hierocles, as self-perception.[40] What is involved here is not Cartesian-style self-consciousness or subjective awareness, but an instinctive awareness of one's own body as a psychophysical unit and of its in-built resources for self-defence and self-preservation, and, more broadly, for doing the things natural to one's kind.[41] In the Ciceronian passage, exceptionally in Stoic texts, this relationship to oneself also involves self-love.[42] As becomes clear, appropriation to oneself is not expressed only in the basic motive of self-preservation. However, this motive (self-preservation) applies on a life-long basis, though informed in adult human beings by rationality.

The third element in this set of ideas consists in the idea that appropriation to oneself is in-built in human or animal nature and reflects broader patterns in nature as a whole. One aspect of this has already been noted. The in-built character of the disposition to appropriate oneself is taken to be shown by the instinctive awareness among animals of their bodies, their resources for

---

[33] For the Epicurean claim, see Cic. *Fin*. 1.30 (LS 21 A(2)); on these competing 'cradle-arguments', see Brunschwig 1986.

[34] Sen. *Ep*. 121. 8 (LS 57 B(2)): infants struggle, even while crying with pain, to stand up after falling down and so to realize their natural capacity to walk upright.

[35] See Inwood 1985: 189–91; also Klein 2016: 155–6.

[36] Appropriation of oneself and one's constitution are normally treated as equivalent ideas, though distinguished in Sen. *Ep*. 121.16 (appropriation of oneself is life-long, though the human constitution changes, in becoming rational); see Gill 2006: 44–5.

[37] Sen. *Ep*. 121.10.   [38] See LS 45, 53; also Gill 2006: 29–46.

[39] Sen. *Ep*. 121.14–16 (rationality); on in-built sociability, see text to nn. 57–64.

[40] Hierocles 4.38–53 (LS B(5–9)). See also Ramelli 2009: 5.

[41] See Gill 2006: 38–43; also Long 1996: ch. 11.

[42] Schmitz (2014: 16–41) sees Cicero as influenced in this respect by Aristotle's thinking on self-love, mediated by Antiochus, who stresses self-love in his version of development as appropriation (Cic. *Fin*. 5.24); on Antiochus' theory see Gill 2016a: 222–9.

self-defence, and for certain distinctive ways of moving, such as standing upright (in human beings). Hierocles especially emphasizes instinctive awareness of oneself as a psychophysical unit, presented as a kind of self-perception; but the overall line of thought is shared with other Stoic thinkers.[43] The other aspect is the presentation of self-appropriation as reflecting a broader pattern in nature generally. This idea is especially marked in Diogenes Laertius' account, ascribed to Chrysippus:

> Nature was not likely to alienate (*allotriōsai*) the animal itself, or to make it and then neither alienate it nor appropriate it (*oikeiōsai*). So it remains to say that in constituting (*sustēsamenen*) the animal, nature appropriated it to itself [that is, nature appropriated the animal to the animal itself].[44]

The framework of ideas implied in this passage, set out in Cicero's *On the Nature of the Gods* 2, has already been discussed here (in Chapter 1). Nature as a whole, as an active force, sometimes identified as 'god', is presented as providential and benevolent in the sense that it enables all elements within the world to take care of themselves, and others of their kind, as brought out shortly. As formulated in this passage, nature 'appropriates' the animal (which is, of course, part of nature as a whole) by 'constituting' it, that is, implanting a 'constitution', *sustasis*, in such a way that the animal is appropriated to itself. Put differently, the animal's in-built disposition to appropriate itself reflects a broader tendency present in nature as a whole to preserve and maintain itself. The animal expresses this broader natural tendency in a form appropriate to its constitution.[45] These two strands of Stoic thinking, about in-built instinctive animal motives and about nature's providential workings, represent co-ordinated ways of making the same point, that appropriation of oneself is firmly in-built in the animal's make-up, including the human make-up, and is in this sense 'natural'.[46]

A similar pattern of ideas can be found regarding appropriation of others of one's kind; indeed, the parallelism between these two dispositions is marked in Stoic treatments of this topic, going back to Chrysippus. The one major difference between the two types of disposition is that the standard example of the expression of appropriation to others, at a basic level, is parental love. By contrast with self-preservation, this is not a motive that is present from birth, and it belongs only to adult life. However, we should not suppose that parental love is the only possible expression of appropriation of others, or is a necessary prerequisite for this; rather,

---

[43] See Sen. *Ep.* 121.6–15 (LS 57 B); also refs in nn. 40–1.

[44] D.L. 7.85 (LS 57 A(2)), LS trans. with my addition in square brackets. For the full passage, see text to n. 31.

[45] See Ch. 1, text to nn. 90–8. See also Inwood 1985: 86–94.

[46] See Schofield 1995 on (social) appropriation and divine providence as co-ordinated Stoic ways of approaching the question of the basis of justice.

like self-preservation, parental love is a motive that explains much, widely observed, behaviour among humans and other animals, and thus serves as a marker for this kind of appropriation.[47] Hence, these two basic motives are sometimes presented as parallel, in explaining commonly observed behaviour (the first element in this pattern of ideas), as in this passage from Cicero's *On Duties*:

> From the beginning nature has assigned to every type of creature the tendency to preserve itself, its life and body, and to reject anything that seems likely to harm them, seeking and obtaining everything necessary for life, such as nourishment, shelter and so on. Common also to all animals is the impulse (*appetitus*) to unite for the purposes of procreation and a certain kind of care (*cura quaedam*) for those that are born.[48]

A similar point is made in the section on social appropriation in Cicero's *On Ends*:

> Even among animals nature's power can be observed; when we see the effort they spend on giving birth and on rearing, we seem to be listening to the actual voice of nature. As it is evident therefore that we naturally shrink from pain, so it is clear that nature drives us to love those we have engendered.[49]

The reference to pain indicates an instinctive avoidance of harmful things (things contrary to nature), and not adherence to the Epicurean view that animals (including humans) instinctively seek pleasure and avoid pain.[50]

The first element in this set of ideas is thus closely parallel in the two kinds of appropriation. We also find an analogue for the second element, though it takes a slightly different form in the two types of appropriation. In the case of appropriation of oneself, the motive of self-preservation is analysed as an expression of a fundamental, life-long disposition, appropriation of oneself, or one's constitution, a relationship mediated by special kinds of self-awareness.[51] In the case of appropriation of others, parental love and the instinctive drive to procreate are closely linked with a broader range of other-directed relationships, typically involving (human) rationality. Although Cicero, for instance, sometimes presents parental love or the instinctive desire to procreate as the 'starting point' (*initium*) of the other relationships,[52] the core idea seems to be that parental love is an obvious and basic expression of care for others, and not that it provides in each

---

[47] See Reydams-Schils 2005: 56.   [48] Cic. *Off.* 1.11, trans. Griffin and Atkins 1991.
[49] Cic. *Fin.* 3.62 (LS 57 F(1)).
[50] For avoidance of harmful things as natural, see D.L. 7.85; for the contrast with Epicurean ideas, see text to n. 33.
[51] See text to nn. 40–2.
[52] Cic. *Fin.* 3.62 (also 3.63, cited shortly); *Off.* 1.54 ('seed-bed', *seminarium* of political community).

case the motivational basis for these other forms of caring relationship. These relationships fall into two main types. One type is direct involvement in family life (of course, parental love figures centrally in this relationship), and also friendship, and communal or political engagement.[53] The other is concern for other human beings as such, who are seen as constituting a kind of fellowship, 'brotherhood' or 'co-citizenship'.[54] For instance, Cicero states: 'From this [parental love] there originates a form of natural concern (*commendatio*), shared by human beings among human beings: that simply because he is human, one human being should be thought to be not alien to another'. Although this form of appropriation is presented as, in some sense, originating from parental love, it is also presented, independently, as natural by analogy with other natural bonds, namely connections between parts of the same body and associations between non-human animals.[55] What this pattern seems to imply is that, as in the case of self-appropriation, the basic motive (here, parental love) is an expression and a prime example of a more broadly conceived, and prevalent, disposition, namely appropriation of others of one's kind. This point is also implied in a passage in Hierocles. First, we have the standard analogy between self-preservation and parental love as basic motives: 'Just as our appropriate disposition (*oikeioumetha*) to our children is affection...so an animal's appropriate disposition to itself is self-preservation, and to things which contribute to the needs of its constitution, selection'. Then Hierocles adds this comment: 'We are an animal, but a gregarious one which needs someone else as well. For this reason too we inhabit cities... Secondly, we make friendships easily'.[56] So, again, parental love serves as a prime example of a more general type of motivational disposition, that of forming relationships with other human beings and expressing care for them in these contexts.

We also find in this form of appropriation the third element, that is, the idea that the disposition is in-built in human (or animal) nature and that it reflects broader patterns in nature generally. Both ideas are brought out in Cicero's discussion of social appropriation in *On Ends* 3:

> This [the naturalness of parental love] must be clear from bodies' shape and limbs, which make it plain by themselves that reproduction is a principle possessed by nature. But it would not be consistent (*congruere*) for nature both

---

[53] Cic. *Fin.* 3.63 (end), 64, 65, 68; *Off.* 1.12, 54–8.   [54] Cic. *Fin.* 3.62, 63–6, 51–2; *Off.* 1.51.

[55] Cic. *Fin.* 3.63, trans. based on Schofield 1995: 197. See also Schofield 1995: 197–8, esp.: '[human beings] are the social animals *par excellence*, naturally given to a greater and more ambitious variety of forms of congregation than any other species' (p. 198). For fuller discussion of this passage, see 6.5, text to nn. 176–9.

[56] Hierocles 9.3–10, 11.14–18 (LS 57 D); see also Ramelli 2009: 25, 29.

to desire the production of offspring and not to be concerned that the offspring should be loved.[57]

The configuration of male and female bodies, to some extent at least, from birth, is taken as indicating that parental love (expressing the disposition to appropriate others of our kind) is in-built in the psychophysical make-up.[58] The passage also expresses the idea that this feature of animal bodies reflects a pattern prevalent in nature as a whole. This is formulated, as in the passage on appropriation to oneself ascribed to Chrysippus,[59] as reflection about the operation of nature's providential care. In Stoic theology, an indication of nature's providential care is that it builds into its components (at least, animals, including human beings) the disposition both to care for themselves and to reproduce and care for others of their kind.[60] The second sentence in the Cicero passage just cited refers to the second of these ideas. The formulation of this idea, inferring what would be 'consistent' with nature's wishes about the production of offspring, evokes the phrasing used in the passage in Diogenes Laertius (7.85, ascribed to Chrysippus) about what nature is 'likely' to have done, as regards attachment to oneself.[61] The implication is that both forms of appropriation are fundamentally built into animal nature.[62] The same idea seems to underlie a claim, cited earlier, which was made repeatedly by Chrysippus, that 'we are appropriated (*oikeioumetha*) to ourselves as soon as we are born and our parts and our children'.[63] The claim is paradoxical, and even seems absurd; although appropriation to our own bodies ('our parts') goes back to birth, how can this also apply to our own children? However, the comment makes more sense, in the light of the Stoic idea, just noted, that we are constituted for reproduction by bodily make-up, 'as soon as we born'. This reflects, in turn, the broader idea that appropriation to others of our kind, as well as to ourselves, is a disposition built into our nature.[64]

4.3 Rational Appropriation: Alternative Patterns

So far, I have been concerned with appropriation as this applies to human beings, children and adults, and other animals; from now on, my concern is only with the advanced (rational) stages of development as appropriation, restricted to human

---

[57] Cic. *Fin.* 3.62 (LS 57 F(1)).
[58] For this idea, see also Cic. *N. D.* 2.127–8.
[59] D.L. 7.85, cited in text to n. 44.   [60] Cic. *N. D.* 2.122–9.
[61] On this similarity of phrasing and idea, see also Schofield 1995: 196–7; Inwood 2016: 152, 158–9.
[62] On the conceptual basis for this linkage, see Ch. 1, text to nn. 91–8.
[63] Plu. *Sto. Rep.* 1038 B (LS 57 E(1)). See also text to nn. 22–4.
[64] See also Reydams-Schils 2005: 55.

adults.[65] The emergence of rationality, in human adults, is marked as a significant stage in all Stoic writings on this subject. It is presented as a transition that occurs regularly, as part of a normal human life-cycle, to some extent at least, although completing the full scope of rational development, including the development of virtue and virtue-based happiness, is an exceptional achievement. Rationality is presented as informing, and to some extent transforming, the two basic motives common to humans and other animals. It also reshapes the two primary dispositions underlying the basic motives, the desire to appropriate one's constitution or nature and to appropriate others of one's kind.

The most important source for this topic (at least for appropriation of oneself) is Cicero, *On Ends* 3.20-2, discussed in detail in the following section (4.4). However, before doing so, I juxtapose this treatment to another Ciceronian discussion of this topic (*On Duties* 1.11–15), along with certain other relevant features of *On Duties*. Both discussions are based on Hellenistic Stoic materials, and both express different, but valid, Stoic ways of conceiving ethical development.[66] The most obvious difference between the two treatments is that *On Duties* consistently integrates the themes of appropriation of oneself and others, whereas *On Ends* 3 discusses appropriation of oneself in 3.20-2, and appropriation of others in 3.62–8. This raises the question of the reason for these different approaches. Primarily, I think this reflects the different aims of the two treatments within the works in which they occur. *On Duties* provides an outline treatment of appropriation (1.11–15), which is designed to set the scene for a programme of guidance on practical deliberation (or performing 'appropriate acts').[67] The introductory treatment of appropriation, like the programme of guidance which follows, gives an inclusive picture of ethical life, which combines self-related and other-related motives and actions. *On Ends* 3.20-2 has a more specific, and narrower, focus. The overall aim is to give a picture of 'natural' human development in support of the Stoic conception of the goal of life, which is the main topic in the first half of *On Ends* 3.[68] In doing so, *On Ends* 3.20-2 focuses solely on appropriation of oneself (at least explicitly), and thus concentrates attention on the ideas concerning the value of indifferents and virtue which the account of appropriation is designed to illustrate.[69] However, the discussion in *On Ends* 3.20-2 elides the fact that lived human experience includes both kinds of

---

[65] Adulthood is taken to occur at fourteen (with an earlier transition at seven); see Inwood 1985: 72–4. On Stoic ideas about rationality and human development, see Inwood 1985: 66–91; Gill 1991: 184–93; Gill 2006: 138–41.

[66] *On Duties* is, explicitly, based on a treatise by Panaetius (see Ch. 2, text to nn. 113–17); the sources of *On Ends* 3 are less obvious; but Cicero refers to the ideas of Diogenes and Antipater, the two heads of the school before Panaetius (*Fin.* 3.22, 33, 50).

[67] See Ch. 1, text to nn. 161–8, on appropriation in *Off.*, and Ch. 2, text to nn. 118–20, on the programme of guidance.

[68] The account of appropriation in *Fin.* 3.16–22 leads directly into arguments for the distinctive Stoic claim on good (3.23–9, 32–4, 36–40), juxtaposed to competing ancient positions in 3.30–1, 41–4.

[69] On these ideas, see para including n. 72.

appropriation (intertwined with each other), as certain parallels in *On Duties* bring out. Hence, Cicero returns to the topic of appropriation of others later in *On Ends* 3 (62–8), thereby covering the side of rational appropriation omitted in 3.20–2. As brought out later, both discussions of appropriation in *On Ends* 3 presuppose the dimension of ethical life treated in the other one.[70] Thus, Cicero's focus on appropriation of oneself in *On Ends* 3 does not signal a deliberate exclusion of the other dimension of appropriation (as not being relevant to Stoic theory). Indeed, the account of appropriation in 3.20–2 and the support provided for the core Stoic ethical claims only make full sense if we assume that both forms of appropriation are involved, albeit implicitly.[71]

I now summarize the discussion of *On Ends* 3.20–2, before highlighting relevant features of *On Duties*. Cicero's treatment takes its starting point, in 3.16–17, from the basic phase, shared by human children and other animals (discussed in 4.2). In this initial phase, human beings, like other animals, have an instinct to go for things, such as health, which preserve and maintain their constitution, rather than pleasure, as the Epicureans claim (3.16–17). The rational stages of appropriation are then set out in three main steps.[72] (1) Human beings, unlike other animals, naturally develop rationality and exercise this function in making a selection between things that do or do not maintain their constitution, that is, things according to nature or contrary to nature, or preferred and dispreferred indifferents (3.20). (2) This process of selection and rejection is also closely linked with the performance of appropriate acts; and these activities form the means by which human beings recognize what is really good, that is, virtue (or virtue-based happiness), and, increasingly, embody this in their actions and lives (3.20). (3) This, in turn, leads to the understanding that virtue, or happiness based on virtue, described as 'right actions and the right itself', and also as 'consistency' or 'order and harmony of actions', constitutes the only real good and the proper object of choice. The things towards which humans were previously drawn (things according to nature), while they are still seen as having positive value, and as providing a valid basis for selection, are recognized as being of a qualitatively lesser order of value (that is, as preferred indifferents) (3.21–2). Cicero's account brings out clearly how the whole sequence of activities and the motivation underlying them are internally linked, with the later stages building on, but also modifying or transforming, the earlier ones. It is the whole sequence that conveys what is involved in appropriation of oneself as a rational animal, and that also provides support for the Stoic conception of the goal of life.

---

[70] See text to nn. 202–14.   [71] On this point, see text to nn. 14–15.

[72] LS vol. 1, p. 368, identifies five steps, followed by Inwood and Donini 1999: 728–30. For translations of this important passage (Cic. *Fin.* 3.20–2), see LS 59 D(3–6) and IG: 152–3. For more detailed analysis of this passage, see 4.4.

I now outline salient features of Cicero's alternative treatment of appropriation and related themes in *On Duties*, indicating in each case how they supplement, and have implications for, Cicero's account of appropriation in *On Ends* 3.20–2. I have already discussed this material in Chapters 1 and 2,[73] and focus here on the points that are most relevant for the comparison with the three-stage process set out in *On Ends* 3.20–2. *On Duties* 1.11–15 begins with a statement of the two basic motives of appropriation, highlighting both self-preservation and self-maintenance and parental love (1.11). It is then pointed out that, in human beings, these motives are informed by rational functions. This is followed by an account of four primary inclinations, which seem to be the product of combination of the basic motives, shaped by rationality. These four inclinations are very similar to the 'starting points' (*aphormai*), underlying the four virtues, identified in Stobaeus' summary of Stoic ethical doctrines; in Cicero's version, they form the basis for justice, wisdom, courage (or magnanimity), and moderation (or the fitting).[74] It is worth noting that these four inclinations are characterized in a way that involves reference both to their rational and their sociable dimensions. This is also a feature of the full-scale account of the virtues offered later in *On Duties* 1.[75] In this respect, the discussion reflects the conception of human beings as, constitutively, sociable as well as rational, which is also a marked feature of Stobaeus' summary.[76] This, relatively brief, but suggestive, presentation of appropriation shares certain features with the treatment in *On Ends* 3.16–22. Both discussions start from basic motives and proceed to the formation of virtue. In both treatments, we find virtue, or at least one virtue (in *On Duties*), characterized in terms of order.[77] However, one difference is that, in *On Duties*, the virtues are more directly linked with the basic motives, by way of the four primary inclinations, which have no obvious equivalent in *On Ends* 3.20–2. In *On Ends*, by contrast, virtue emerges out of the selection of preferables and performance of appropriate acts, rather than from basic or primary motives more directly.[78] Second, the opening account of appropriation in *On Duties* combines association of oneself and others (or the rational and sociable strands of human nature) whereas *On Ends* 3.16–22 focuses on self-appropriation.

The second point, the combination of self-related and other-related strands, is a very consistent feature of the ethical framework presented in *On Duties* 1 as a whole. I illustrate three aspects, highlighting the contrast with *On Ends* 3.20–2, and then discuss the overall implications for interpreting the latter text and

---

[73] See Ch. 1, text to nn. 158–68, Ch. 2, text to nn. 139–47.
[74] Cic. *Off.* 1.12–15; see also Stob. 6, 2.75.7–10 (cited in Ch. 1, text to n. 156).
[75] See Ch. 1, text to nn. 158–77.   [76] See Ch. 1, text to nn. 153–5; also Ch. 3, text to nn. 79–90.
[77] See *Off.* 1.14 (the inclination underlying moderation or 'the fitting'; also 1.98); and *Fin.* 3.21.
[78] See *Fin.* 3.20–1. However, these activities are presented as a rational extension of the basic motive of self-preservation and self-maintenance (3.16). Also, the themes of selection and appropriate action figure prominently in *Off.* 1 generally, so the contrast should not be overstated.

making sense of Stoic thinking on ethical development. In *On Ends* 3.20, the first stage in the developmental schema outlined earlier, rational selection of things according to nature, is presented only in terms of appropriation of oneself:

> With the principles thus established that those things which are in accordance with nature are to be taken for their own sake, and that their opposites are to be rejected, the first 'appropriate act' (this is my term for *kathēkon*) is to preserve oneself in one's natural constitution, the second is to seize hold of the things that accord with nature and reject their opposites.[79]

The account of appropriation in *On Duties* 1.11–15 is not organized according to the same developmental schema; but there is a parallel between stage 1 in *On Ends* 3.20–2 and the account of the primary inclinations characteristic of human beings as rational animals in *On Duties*.[80] Also, in *On Duties* 1.12, Cicero highlights a process that is analogous to the selection of things according to nature, that is, things that maintain one's human constitution. However, there are two salient differences: in *On Duties* this process falls within the account of the primary inclination to social association, and it combines self-related and other-related actions, as highlighted in the words in italics:

> The same [human] nature, by the power of reason, unites one human being to another (*conciliat*) for the fellowship both of common speech and of life, creating above all a particular love for offspring. It drives him to desire that people should meet together and congregate, and that he should join them himself; and for the same reason to devote himself to providing *whatever may contribute to the comfort and sustenance not only of himself, but also of his wife, his children, and others whom he holds dear and ought to protect.*[81]

The version in On *Duties* gives a fuller and more credible picture of what is involved, in lived human experience, in selecting things according to nature, namely that one does so both for oneself and for others for whom one cares. The processes of appropriating oneself and appropriating others are combined and interconnected in human development, as described here. I take up later the question of the rationale for the difference and the implications for the interpretation of *On Ends* 3.20–2.

---

[79] Cic. *Fin.* 3.20 (LS 59 D(3), modifying their translation of *kathēkon* as 'proper function'). On this category, see also Ch. 2, text to nn. 99–111.

[80] Both stages are intermediate between the identification of a basic motive or motives and the full development of virtue.

[81] Cic. *Off.* 1.12, trans. Griffin and Atkins 1991, with my added square brackets and italics.

A similar point emerges if we compare the account of stage 2 in *On Ends* 3.20 with an analogous feature of the discussion in *On Duties*. Here is Cicero's presentation of this stage:

The first (i) appropriate action (this is my term for *kathēkon*) is to preserve oneself in one's natural constitution; the second (ii) is to seize hold of the things that accord with nature and to banish their opposites. Once this procedure of selection and rejection has been discovered, the next consequence (iii) is selection exercised with appropriate action (*cum officio selectio*); then (iv) such selection performed continuously; finally, (v) selection which is absolutely consistent and in full accordance with nature. At this point, for the first time, what which can truly be called good begins to be present and understood.[82]

In fact, this outline covers virtually the whole developmental schema in *On Ends* 3.20–2; but I focus on the process outlined in (iii–iv), leading up to (v). This consists in selection of indifferents in a form that is linked with performance of appropriate acts and which constitutes a pathway towards the understanding and exercise of virtue. This is similar in general type to the procedure on which Cicero offers guidance in Book 1 of *On Duties*. As illustrated in Chapter 2, this consists in deliberation about performing appropriate acts, a process which also involves selection between indifferents. The person deliberating is conceived as deploying her ideas about what the virtues involve with a view to determining what counts as 'right' (*honestum*) in performing appropriate acts; the whole process can also be conceived as making progress towards the complete understanding of virtue (and happiness).[83] The feature of this presentation I want to emphasize here is that, again, *On Duties* combines and integrates self-related and other-related dimensions. This comes out clearly in the guidance on generosity or kindness, discussed at length in Chapter 2:

First one must make sure that kindness (*benignitas*) harms neither the very people whom one seems to be treating kindly, nor others; next, that one's kindness is bestowed upon each person according to his standing. Indeed, that is fundamental to justice (*iustitia*), to which all these things ought to be referred.[84]

As brought out here, and in the surrounding context, finding the appropriate act that is right is seen as a matter of determining what benefit or favour (what

---

[82] Cic. *Fin.* 3.20, trans. and numeration based on Inwood and Donini 1999: 728, which is based in turn on LS 59 D(3–4). See also the commentary in Inwood and Donini 1999: 728–30.

[83] See Ch. 2, text to nn. 121–4.

[84] Cic. *Off.* 1.42, trans. Griffin and Atkins 1991, cited more fully in Ch. 2, text to n. 139.

preferred indifferent) should be allocated to which people and on what grounds. Reflecting on one's pattern of relationships with the people affected by the decision, and the claims they have on us, forms an integral part of the process of deliberation. Hence, in this context, Cicero includes a general discussion of the natural principles of human association (*On Duties* 1.50–9), which is similar in content to the account of appropriation of others in *On Ends* 3.62–8.[85] Thus, again, reference to *On Duties* illustrates that appropriation of oneself is, in lived human experience, integrally linked with appropriation of others. Hence, stage 2 of the developmental schema of *On Ends* 3.20–2, though presented only in terms of self-related activities, identifies a process that, in normal human life, is linked with relationships with others. The development that occurs at this stage is not just rational but also sociable, and the two aspects are bound up with each other.

A third and related point arises in connection with stage 3 in the developmental schema of *On Ends* 3.20–2. This is the emergence of virtue, along with understanding the fundamental difference in value between virtue and preferred indifferents, though this is coupled with the recognition that preferred indifferents still constitute grounds for selection. This stage is described in *On Ends* 3.20–2 in terms that make no reference to other-related actions and attitudes, and as the final stage in appropriation of oneself or one's constitution. However, again, *On Duties* 1 provides a fuller, and more recognizable, picture of what virtue involves, and brings out the fact that it constitutes the completion of the developmental process of appropriation of others as well as of oneself. As noted earlier, the description of the four primary inclinations which underlies the formation of the four cardinal virtues integrates self- and other-related (or rational and sociable) dimensions; and so do the accounts of the four cardinal virtues and of the actions characteristic of the virtues later in Book 1. Of special interest here is the fact, discussed in Chapter 1, that each of the four virtues is characterized in a two-fold way, identifying both the core qualities of the virtue and the actively benevolent and other-related dimensions. It is also noteworthy that, in discussing appropriation of others in *On Ends* 3.62–8, Cicero also emphasizes other-benefiting action, and presents this as characteristic of the virtues (citing benevolence, justice, and wisdom), and as the fulfilment of appropriation of others.[86] My point is not that, for the Stoics, 'virtue', by itself, necessarily constitutes other-related virtue, as it tends to do in modern virtue ethical discussions. For the Stoics, as for other ancient theories, virtue has self-related and other-related dimensions. The point is that Cicero's linkage of the development of virtue only with appropriation of oneself in *On Ends* 3.20–2 does not reflect a specifically Stoic conception of virtue. Other Stoic discussions, notably *On Duties* 1 and *On Ends* 3.62–8, show that the

---

[85] See Ch. 2, text to nn. 156–7; also 4.5, text to nn. 170–3.

[86] See text to nn. 206–10; and on the two-fold characterization of the virtues in Cic. *Off.* 1, see Ch. 1, text to nn. 169–77.

achievement of virtue is, typically, conceived as marking the completion of appropriation of others as well as oneself, and that ethical development, taken as a whole, includes both aspects.

This raises the question why, in *On Ends* 3.20–2, Cicero, presumably following an earlier Stoic source, presents his account of the rational stages of development solely with reference to appropriation of oneself. He does not restate this developmental account in connection with appropriation of others, in 3.62–8, though I think it is implied there too.[87] Cicero's main aim in 3.20–2, it seems, is not to provide a complete picture of ethical development, but to support the distinctively Stoic ethical claims about virtue, happiness, and indifferents, which are argued for subsequently in *On Ends* (3.23–40).[88] The account of self-appropriation can be conceived as doing service for both aspects of development, that is, for appropriation as a whole. I think there are other ancient accounts in which appropriation of oneself or one's constitution does service for appropriation as a whole and is used as the basis for setting out a developmental schema.[89] This feature may explain the view of some scholars that self-appropriation is the sole, or at least primary, form of the theory, and that appropriation of others is a secondary or derivative version. As already stated, I do not hold this view.[90] However, I accept that, in certain sources, and for specific purposes, self-appropriation stands in for appropriation as a whole; and this is the form of presentation that Cicero adopts in *On Ends* 3.20–2. More precisely, Cicero focuses on aspects of development, notably, selection of 'things according to nature' and recognition of the superordinate value of virtue, which apply equally to the appropriation of oneself and others. Thus, Cicero describes appropriation in a 'stripped-down' form that elides the distinctively self- or other-related aspects of the process. *On Duties*, by contrast, which is designed to give a more practically directed version of Stoic ethics, characterizes appropriation (in 1.11–15) and practical deliberation (in Book 1 as a whole) in a fuller way that refers to both self-related and other-related actions and attitudes. As shown by *On Ends* 3.62–8, this more inclusive view of appropriation forms part of the overall picture of Stoic ethics offered in *On Ends* Book 3, though this is not made explicit in 3.20–2.

There is a second possible reason why Cicero adopts this 'stripped-down' version in 3.20–2, which does not make explicit reference to appropriation of others. The Stoic claim that virtue is the sole basis for happiness, as brought out in

---

[87] On this point, see text to nn. 211–15.

[88] On the nature of this support, see text to nn. 149–65.

[89] D.L. 7.85–6 (LS 57 A); Sen. 121 (extracts in LS 57 B); the earlier parts of Hierocles, *Elements Of Ethics* (extracts in LS 57 C), but not the later ones (LS 57 D). But there may be other factors at work, notably the fact that all three accounts begin from birth when the salient marks of appropriation of oneself are more evident than those of appropriation of others.

[90] For the view that appropriation of others is derivative of appropriation of oneself, see Inwood 1983. Klein 2016 sees social appropriation as subsumed within self-appropriation; see text to nn. 16–28, esp. nn. 18, 27.

Ch. 1, can be seen as an elaboration of Socratic or Platonic versions of this claim. These earlier versions include the thesis of the *Republic*, that justice (in the psyche) constitutes happiness, because it is the best possible state of the psyche, namely inner harmony and health.[91] The Platonic versions include arguments, directed at 'immoralist' critics (or their more moderate spokesmen), who maintain that virtue is not beneficial for the agent herself but is forced on her by social pressure or, at least, by the ethical demands of other people or our community.[92] The Stoic ethical claim is not, typically, framed in this form (as a response to 'immoralists'); the rival positions addressed in *On Ends* 3, for instance, are (broadly, Aristotelian) views which are closer to Stoicism on this point.[93] However, the Stoics, like Plato in the *Republic*, would resist the claim that virtue is not beneficial for the agent but is forced on her by social pressure or purely other-benefiting demands. It may be for this reason that Cicero, in the presentation of appropriation in *On Ends* 3.20–2, avoids explicit reference to appropriation of others, since this might suggest that development towards virtue is beneficial only for this purpose (for meeting others' claims), and not also for the agent herself. This may be a further reason for Cicero's adoption of the neutral presentation of appropriation found in 3.20–2, which can accommodate reference to both kinds of appropriation, but which does not render them explicit or refer to their interplay in the way we find in parallel passages in *On Duties*.

4.4 Rational Appropriation of Oneself
(Cicero, *On Ends* 3.20–2)

I now discuss in more detail the form and function of the presentation of rational appropriation in *On Ends* 3.20–2. Earlier, I set out a three-stage outline of ethical development, as described in 3.20–2, which I restate briefly here. Following the basic stage of instinctive attraction to things according to nature, we have: (1) rational selection of 'things according to nature'; (2) increasingly consistent selection; (3) the emergence of virtue, the recognition of the difference in value between virtue and indifferents, and virtue-based selection of indifferents.[94] In the introduction to this chapter (4.1), I suggest that this developmental process can be explained in terms of the three-fold pattern of appropriation applied earlier in

---

[91] See Pl. *Rep.* 443c–445b, 588b–592a; also Ch. 1, text to nn. 9–19.

[92] See Pl. *Rep.* 357a–368b (Glaucon and Adeimantus taking up the case of the 'immoralist' Thrasymachus, presented in 338b–c, 343b–c, 348b–d); Pl. *Grg.* 482c–484c (Callicles, another 'immoralist'). See further text to nn. 149–65 on the function of the theory of appropriation (esp. as presented in Cic. *Fin.* 3.20–2) within Stoic ethics.

[93] See Cic. *Fin.* 3.30, 41–4, referring to those who think that virtue forms the basis of happiness but only when combined with bodily and external goods.

[94] See para. including n. 72 for a fuller summary.

connection with basic motives.[95] (1) The rational functions in all three developmental stages are presented as widespread (or at least, highly recognizable) features of human behaviour. (2) These functions are characterized in terms of motives; and these motives are explained, by implication at least, in terms of appropriation of oneself. (3) This process is also presented, implicitly again, as the realization of human nature at its best and of the good-making qualities of universal nature. Here, I discuss how, and how far, this three-fold framework provides a convincing rationale for the developmental schema presented in 3.20–2. I also consider the way in which Cicero's account of ethical development provides support for the distinctive Stoic ethical claims about virtue and happiness.

I begin with the first point in the three-fold pattern, which is closely linked with the second point. This is straightforward in the first, and to some extent second, stage of the developmental schema but is much more complex in the third stage. In the basic stage, widespread forms of human and animal behaviour are cited as indicating the motive of self-preservation, or maintenance of one's nature or 'constitution', at a basic level. This, in turn, is taken as expressing the core (human and animal) disposition of appropriation of oneself or, again, one's constitution.[96] The first rational stage closely mirrors the basic one, but with the addition that the rational functions associated with adulthood in Stoic thought inform motivation and action. The developing person is not only attracted, instinctively, to things that maintain her constitution ('things according to nature') and repelled by things that damage this ('things contrary to nature'). She 'selects' and 'rejects' them on this basis, and this is presented as the first or primary 'appropriate act' for a human adult or rational animal. Although this stage is not explicitly presented as expressing the core motive or disposition of self-appropriation, the points of similarity with the basic stage imply this point, with the further corollary that this is now appropriation of oneself as a rational animal.[97] The idea that appropriation of oneself (or one's constitution) is a constant feature of one's life but that the constitution one appropriates develops with the growth of rationality is explicated by Seneca in Letter 121, and is implied here.[98]

The second stage is more complex. Cicero's account, cited earlier, is worth repeating here:

The first (i) appropriate action (this is my term for *kathēkon*) is to preserve oneself in one's natural constitution; the second (ii) is to seize hold of the things that

---

[95] See text to n. 11; also, for this pattern applied to appropriation of others, see para. following n. 173. The pattern is presented here in a modified form to reflect the emergence of rationality.

[96] See D.L. 7.85–6 (LS 57 A(1–3)); Cic. *Fin.* 3.16–17; also 4.2.

[97] Cic. *Fin.* 3.20 (LS 59 D(3), start), cited in text to n. 82. See also D.L. 7.86, 'reason supervenes as the craftsman of motive' (LS 57 A(5)). On this stage and the preceding one, see Inwood 1985: 194–205. On the Stoic psychological model assumed here, see also Ch. 5, text to nn. 11–17.

[98] Sen. *Ep.* 121.15–16.

accord with nature and to banish their opposites. Once this procedure of selection and rejection that been discovered, the next consequence (iii) is selection exercised with appropriate action (*cum officio selectio*); then (iv) such selection performed continuously; finally, (v) selection which is absolutely consistent and in full accordance with nature. At this point, for the first time, what which can truly be called good begins to be present and understood.[99]

This stage is clearly marked as transitional. On the one hand, there is an explicit link to the previous stage, especially regarding the criteria of selection (selecting things according to nature and rejecting things contrary to nature). On the other hand, new and distinct characteristics of (advanced) selection are also brought out: selection 'with appropriate action', 'continuous', 'consistent and in full accordance with nature'. Since some at least of these terms have connotations of virtue (and virtue-based happiness) in Stoicism,[100] it is reasonable to see here the progressive emergence of the kind of 'selection' characteristic of virtue. What this is, exactly, is left rather open. However, the third stage, considered shortly, suggests what this might be. This is the kind of selection which, while recognizing the objective (or natural) value of 'things accordance to nature', selects between these on the basis of what is 'right' (*honestum*) or 'appropriate', given the ethical claims of those, including oneself, to whom such things are being allocated. This is the kind of selection which is presented in Book 1 of *On Duties*,[101] and it makes sense to see it indicated here too (and in stage 3), as brought out shortly. Virtue is also presented in Stoic ethics as expertise in achieving happiness, that is, in living the life according to nature, with the connotations of this idea explored in Chapter 1 of this book. Selecting 'rightly' between indifferents and doing so in a way that realizes happiness understood as the life according to nature are, typically, seen as two, correlated, functions of virtue.[102] The reference in this passage to selecting 'consistently and in full accordance with nature' (both connotations of happiness) may indicate the role of virtue as expertise in living a happy life, which is brought out more explicitly in stage 3.

The passage also raises the question whether what is described is still presented as self-appropriation. I think this description still applies, in two ways. First, the passage suggests at the start that this stage incorporates the kind of selection found in stage 1 (based on preferability). This kind of selection is presented in stage 1 as a continuation of the self-appropriation found in the basic stage.[103] However, the

---

[99] Cic. *Fin.* 3.20, trans. and numeration based on Inwood and Donini 1999: 728. See also text to n. 82.

[100] For consistency and 'according to nature', see LS 63 A, B, C; also Ch. 1, text to nn. 63–70. On appropriate actions, see LS 59, and Ch. 2, text to nn. 99–106.

[101] See Ch. 2, text to nn. 88–93, 139–42.

[102] On virtue as expertise in living a happy life, see 1.4. On virtue as combining expertise in selection between indifferents and in living a happy life, see Ch. 2, text to nn. 42–5, 74–5, 86–94.

[103] Shared features are maintaining one's constitution and going for things according to nature; see Cic. *Fin.* 3.16 and 3.20 (LS 59 D(1), (3)).

language in the second part of the passage also implies a more complex kind of self-appropriation, one also indicated in stage 3. By making this kind of selection (continuous, consistent, according to nature) one appropriates oneself as an advanced rational animal capable of the kind of ethical expertise involved in virtue. Selection of this kind does not, necessarily, focus solely on things according to nature for oneself, and in this way does not promote the maintenance of one's constitution in the sense found in stage 1. However, it promotes the maintenance of one's constitution in a more complex sense, as someone capable of developing virtue, which is why it is marked as a further stage of ethical development.[104]

Cicero's account of the third and final stage raises similar questions in a more complex form, but it also provides more material for answering them.

> A human being's first affiliation (*conciliatio*) is towards those things which are in accordance with nature. But as soon as he has acquired understanding, or rather the conception which the Stoics call *ennoia*, and has seen the regularity and, so to speak, the harmony of things to be done, he comes to value this far higher than all those objects of his initial affection; and he draws the rational conclusion that this constitutes the highest human good, which is worthy of praise and desirable for its own sake. (5) Since that good is situated in what the Stoics call *homologia* ('agreement' will be our term for this if you don't mind) – since it is in this, then, that that good consists which is the standard of all things, right actions and the right itself, which is reckoned the only good, though later in origin, is the only thing desirable through its intrinsic nature and value, whereas none of the first objects of nature is desirable for its own sake. (6) But since those things which I called appropriate acts originate in nature's starting points [things according to nature], it must be the case that the former are the means to the latter; so it could be correctly said that the end of all appropriate acts is to obtain nature's primary requirements, but not that this is the ultimate good, since right action is not present in the first affiliations of nature. It is an outcome of these, and arises later, as I have said. Yet it is in accordance with nature, and stimulates us to desire it far more strongly than we are stimulated by all the earlier objects.[105]

I discuss first what is suggested here about value, and then turn to the question of self-appropriation, and, subsequently, human and universal nature. First and most obviously, the passage illustrates the distinctive Stoic claim that, by contrast with virtue, or happiness based on virtue, other things classed as 'goods' by other schools are not properly regarded as good, but as (relatively) matters of indifference.[106]

---

[104] See again Sen. *Ep.* 121. 15–16, on appropriation of a constitution that develops along with rationality; also Inwood 2007: 339–42; Klein 2016: 160–2.

[105] Cic. *Fin.* 3.21–2 (LS 59 D(4–6)), my addition in square brackets.   [106] See 2.2.

Virtue, or happiness,[107] is 'the only thing desirable through its own nature and value, whereas none of the first objects of nature', such as health and property, 'is desirable for its own sake'. This description explains the understanding towards which the developing person is moving in stage 2. The person is moving towards the expertise that enables her to select between indifferents in a way that is 'right' (*honestum*) and to do so 'continuously' and 'consistently'. This idea is central for the passage and is sometimes the only one accentuated by scholars.

However, the latter part of the passage also highlights a seemingly contrasting idea. Despite the point just made, it remains the case that people, reasonably, continue to engage in practical deliberation (perform appropriate actions) in a way that recognizes that preferability provides grounds for action.[108] In this sense, 'the end of all appropriate acts is to obtain nature's primary requirements', that is, things according to nature or preferables. However, this is not 'the ultimate good since right action is not present in the first affiliations of nature'. This suggests that performing right action does not consist simply in securing preferables, though it properly takes account of preferability, for oneself and others affected. The last point is indicated in the comment that right action, while it 'arises later' than selection of preferables, is an outcome (*consequens*) of such selection.[109] Implicit here, perhaps, is the idea that virtue can be conceived, in part at least, as expertise in selection between indifferents, an expertise which develops through the process of selection. Virtue can also be conceived as expertise in living a happy life (a life according to nature), a form of expertise which can inform the selection of indifferents made.[110] In accentuating these two ideas (the superordinate value of virtue and the continuing value of preferability), Cicero's account of the final stage might seem to point in two different directions. Indeed, Cicero, implicitly acknowledges this point, denying that his account means that Stoicism operates with two (rival or competing) conceptions of good, virtue and preferred indifferents.[111] I think that the picture presented here is self-consistent and also in line with Stoic thinking on value as discussed so far in this book. Virtue, as expertise, and the happiness that depends on this, constitute kinds of good that are superordinate and distinct in kind from other things classed as good by other schools.[112] However, this is compatible with the fact that the wise or virtuous person, as well as those making progress towards virtue, rightly takes account of preferability as a basis for action. Hence, virtue is sometimes characterized in Stoic ethics as

---

[107] On the question which one is referred to here, see text to nn. 114–22.

[108] For this idea, see Ch. 2, text to nn. 17–23, 50–4.

[109] The importance of this second point (about the continuing significance of preferability for virtuous deliberation) is stressed also by Barney 2003: 312–4 (though I do not share her view about the 'deliberative sufficiency' of preferability); see Ch. 2, text to nn. 69–75, 145–6, 208, 245–7.

[110] See refs. in n. 102.

[111] Cic. *Fin.* 3.22: on this criticism of the Stoic conception of the end, see Ch. 2, text to nn. 48–62.

[112] See Ch. 1, text to nn. 105–31, Ch. 2, text nn. 24–8.

expertise in selection between indifferents of a kind that takes account of preferability.[113]

One other question about value arises in the passage cited. Is the 'good' whose superordinate value is recognized virtue or happiness? Different phrases imply different answers: 'right actions and the right itself' suggests virtue (as expertise in right action);[114] *homologia* ('agreement' or 'consistency') is a standard formula for happiness or the end;[115] 'regularity and... harmony of things to be done' evokes both virtue and happiness.[116] In fact, given the very close relationship between the two concepts and the fact that both are regularly seen as good in Stoic ethics, this ambivalence is unsurprising, and unproblematic. Ethical development culminates in the achievement of virtue (as a quality of the agent), which is sufficient, in itself, to confer happiness (as a quality of the agent's life).[117] Does the passage, also, suggest the idea of the 'life according to nature', along with the connotations of human and universal nature that are standard in Stoic ethics, and which are also linked with their conception of virtue?[118] The whole developmental sequence is presented as the unfolding exercise of human rationality, and the role of rationality in gaining ethical understanding and informing motivational response is accentuated in the final stage.[119] There is no corresponding emphasis here on sociability, the other normal marker of human nature, though, of course, sociability (along with rationality) is treated fully in *On Ends* 3.62–8, and the sociable, other-related dimension of virtue (and happiness) may be implied here.[120] The phrases 'regularity and... harmony of things to be done' and 'agreement' (or 'consistency') have been seen as evoking the idea of cosmic regularity and order; and this connotation has also been ascribed to the progress described in stage 2, moving towards selection that is 'consistent and in full accordance with nature'.[121] Given that these phrases are also applied to (human) virtue and happiness, without reference to universal nature, it is difficult to say for certain whether universal nature is implied here. However, as brought out in Chapter 1, linkage between human virtue and happiness and the best features of universal nature is a standard theme in Stoic ethics and may be implied here.[122]

Taking all three stages together, how far does the developmental sequence match the pattern outlined earlier? Should we see the whole sequence as

---

[113] See Ch. 2, text to nn. 40–2, 58–75.

[114] See Stob. 8, 2.85.20–86.4 (LS 59B(4)); also LS 59 G, L.   [115] See LS 63 A(1), B(1), C(1).

[116] See D.L. 7.89 (LS 61 A); Sen. 120. 11 (LS 60 E(8)), LS 59 I–J. See also Ch. 1, text to nn. 87–9, 100–1, 183–200; Gill 2006: 150–7.

[117] See Ch. 1, text to nn. 105–19.

[118] That is, rationality and sociability, structure, order, and wholeness (1.3–4).

[119] Thus, 'as soon as he has acquired understanding... and has seen the regularity... he draws the rational conclusion' (Cic. *Fin.* 3.21 (LS 59 D(4)).

[120] On virtue and happiness as expressing human nature as rational and sociable, see Stob. 5b1, 2.59.4–7, 6, 2.75.7–10. On Cic. *Fin.* 3.20–2 as implying both kinds of appropriation, see 4.3, text to nn. 87–93.

[121] See text to nn. 127–31.   [122] See 1.3–4, esp. text to nn. 70, 87–95, 100–1, 178–200.

constituting appropriation of oneself (or one's constitution)? Is it also presented as the realization of human nature at its best and of the good-making qualities of universal nature? Points already made here, in connection with the three stages, suggest a positive answer to both these questions. However, since both questions have been the subject of extensive scholarly debate, I take account of this debate here, and in this way clarify my view.[123] This scholarly debate reflects, in part, the dispute between 'ethicist' and 'naturalist' interpretations of the significance of nature, especially universal or cosmic nature, in Stoic ethics discussed in Chapter 3.[124] Both sets of scholars assume that there is a major motivational shift in stage 3, as the developing person recognizes the superordinate value (goodness) of virtue or happiness, as contrasted with the value of preferred indifferents (a point I return to shortly). The question that has been addressed is how, in Cicero's account, this shift is explained; the answers differ on the scope and role of appropriation and on whether the process represented gives a key role to human or universal nature.

Some scholars, writing from what one might call an 'ethicist' standpoint, think that the whole sequence can be explained by reference to the idea of self-realization or appropriation of oneself. The final stages (2-3) are taken to represent a progressively deeper understanding of one's nature or constitution as a rational agent and of what rational consistency involves for such an agent, namely the achievement of virtue and happiness.[125] In one version of this view, Annas takes it as significant that Cicero's account of stage (3) does *not* explicitly offer an explanation for the motivational shift. The passage presupposes that it is natural for human beings to develop to the point of recognizing the absolute primacy of virtue. In so far as the account (including stage (2)) implies an explanation, it is seen as based on a developing understanding of what rational consistency implies.[126] Overall, then, the whole process is seen as appropriation of one's constitution as embodying human nature, understood as rational.

By contrast, other scholars, writing from a 'naturalist' standpoint, think that the idea of self-realization (appropriation of oneself) only applies in the initial stage of the developmental process, and that Cicero's account of the final stage marks a contrast with this stage. What then explains the final shift in assessment of value and motivation? These scholars appeal to the order, rationality and providentiality of nature, especially cosmic or universal nature. Nature's providentiality, as we have seen, is regularly invoked in Stoic writings in connection with the idea that the basic motives linked with the appropriation of oneself and others are in-built

---

[123] On this debate, see also Gill 2004b: 103-5, 2006: 146-50, 157-9.

[124] See Ch. 3, text to nn. 16-27.

[125] For different versions of this approach, see Pohlenz 1940: 1-47, 1959: 116-18 (summarized in White 1979: 144-6); Engberg-Pedersen 1990: 64-11 (discussed in Gill 2006: 360-70); Annas 1993: 169-72.

[126] Annas 1993: 166-8; see also Gill 2006: 148-9.

in human beings and other animals.[127] Providential care is taken to be implied in the first stage, in the fact that human beings are naturally disposed to select things that promote their constitution ('things according to nature').[128] Although the idea of cosmic nature as ordered and providential does not appear explicitly in Cicero's account of the final stages of rational development,[129] some scholars think it is implied there. Cosmic order is seen as implied in the final stage, in the phrase 'regularity and... harmony of things to be done'.[130] The developing person is regarded as recognizing in her own life and actions (notably in her selection of things 'according to nature') an emerging pattern of ordered behaviour which reflects cosmic nature's providential care and provides a paradigm for understanding what goodness consists in.[131] Thus, overall, on this view the idea of appropriation of oneself is seen as applying only to the basic stages and the first rational stage, while stages (2–3) of the sequence are seen as marking a shift to a different explanatory framework, based on assimilating oneself to universal nature.[132]

As just indicated, both parties to this dispute share the assumption that there is a sharp, even radical, shift in valuation and motivation in stage (3), as the superordinate value of virtue, as contrasted with preferred indifferents, is recognized.[133] This is also assumed by some ancient critics of the Stoic theory.[134] Certainly, Cicero does underline a substantial change in the understanding of value, which has implications for motivation.[135] However, as stressed earlier, he also insists that, even when this is recognized, it remains the case that preferability remains, in principle, a valid ground for action (or 'selection').[136] This point is reinforced later in Book 3 when Cicero stresses that the preponderance of 'things according to (or contrary to) nature' can, under certain circumstances, constitute, for the wise person, a reason for committing suicide.[137] Similarly, virtue is regularly understood in Stoic ethics as expertise in selecting between indifferents, a view adopted especially by the second-century heads of the schools, Diogenes and Antipater, whose ideas Cicero alludes to in 3.22.[138] Taking all this into account, the evaluative and motivational shift presented in 3.20 should not be seen as a 'blanket' shift

---

[127] See text to nn. 44–6, 57–64.   [128] See White 1979: 156–7; M. Frede 1999: 79–81.
[129] As highlighted by Annas 1993: 170, n. 46.   [130] Cic. *Fin.* 3.32 (LS 59 D(4)).
[131] Striker 1996: 230–1; M. Frede 1999: 78–81. Cic. *Fin.* 3.20 (LS 59 D(3)), cited here in connection with stage (2) (text to n. 99), is seen as describing this process.
[132] See White 1979: 155–9; Striker 1996: 225–31.
[133] On this point, see also Klein 2016: 156–7, who rejects this assumption.
[134] See Cicero's criticism (made from an Antiochean standpoint), in *Fin.* 4.26–39, esp. 26–8; also Gill 2006: 168–9, 2016a: 229–30.
[135] Cic. *Fin.* 3.21 (LS 59 D(4)), cited in text to n. 105; see also *Fin.* 3.23 (start).
[136] See Cic. *Fin.* 3.22, and text to nn. 108–10.
[137] Cic. *Fin.* 3.61 (on this point, see Barney 2003: 314).
[138] See Cic. *Fin.* 3.22 (referring to the 'two ends' criticism directed at Diogenes and Antipater; on which see Ch. 2, text to nn. 55–7). See also Stob. 6a 2.76.9–15, and Ch. 2, text to nn. 60, for the definitions of Diogenes and Antipater.

from valuing and seeking 'things according to nature' to valuing and seeking virtue. The transition is, rather, towards valuing and selecting between indifferents *correctly*, that is, with the expertise that constitutes virtue and leads towards happiness. This shift brings with it, as Cicero's account suggests in 3.21, the recognition that it is virtue (expertise in selection) that forms the sole basis of happiness, by contrast with the things selected. Hence, under certain circumstances (though not normally), the virtuous person could achieve happiness even in the absence of all preferred indifferents.[139]

This point has implications for the question whether the whole developmental sequence should be seen as appropriation of oneself (or one's constitution) or only the basic phase and the first rational stage, as supposed by some 'naturalist' interpreters. On the view I am suggesting, valuation of, and motivation towards, 'things according to nature', that is, things that maintain one's constitution, persist throughout the whole sequence, though in the final stage these are informed (and, in a sense, transformed) by ethical understanding and virtue. So self-appropriation in the sense of maintenance of one's constitution through things according to nature runs through the process.[140] However, in the final stage, there is a new level of self-appropriation and maintenance of one's constitution, as the person realizes her nature as a rational animal fully by achieving complete ethical understanding (3.21). This interpretation matches the formal presentation of the rational stages (and to some extent the whole process) as a continuous process of self-appropriation, though with progressive deepening in the level achieved. The term 'conciliare', Cicero's standard word for 'appropriating', figures prominently at the start of the basic phase; the idea, if not the term, is signalled strongly in connection with rational stage (1); and the term is repeated at the start of the third stage.[141] Also, just after completing the sequence, and referring to the outcome of the process, he uses an image which suggests the appropriation of one's nature, as an embodied but also rational animal (3.23):

> Just as our limbs were given to us in such a way that they seem to have been given to us for a certain way of life, similarly the motivation of our mind (*appetitio animi*, in Greek *hormē*) seems not to have been given for any old type of life but for a certain kind of living; and the same applies in the case of reason and perfected reason.[142]

---

[139] On virtue as expertise in selecting indifferents, see also text to nn. 108–113. For the idea that happiness can be achieved, if need be, without preferred indifferents, see Ch. 2, text to n. 28; also Cic. *Fin.* 3.29, 3.42.

[140] See Cic. *Fin.* 3.16, 20, 22.   [141] See Cic. *Fin.* 3.16, 20 (LS 59 D(3)), 21 (start) (LS 59 D(4)).

[142] The idea that self-appropriation involves appropriation of our body is a standard Stoic theme (LS 57 B–C, E); on the body as providentially shaped to enable appropriation (of others), see Cic. *Fin.* 3.62 (LS 57 F); here this idea is extended to the mind and motivation, when shaped by reason.

All these points indicate that the developmental sequence as a whole, and not just the first stages, constitute self-appropriation.[143]

Assuming this view about appropriation, how far does the account also suggest that this constitutes the realization of human nature at its best and of the good-making qualities of universal nature, that is, the third point in the pattern outlined earlier?[144] As already indicated, scholarly discussions of appropriation have tended to stress one side or other, that is, realization of human nature or the significance of universal nature.[145] However, throughout this book I stress that Stoic ethics combines both ideas, and sees them as both valid and compatible, going back, at least to Chrysippus' idea of happiness as 'harmonization' with the best qualities of human and universal nature.[146] In connection with the third stage, I have highlighted indications that the completion of the developmental sequence realizes the distinctively human characteristic of rationality, while also (at least by implication) achieving the structure, order, and wholeness that marks the natural universe as a whole.[147] Also, the start of the developmental process presents self-preservation, the basic marker of self-appropriation, as the expression of the providential care of universal nature.[148] The comment just after the sequence, just cited, indicates that appropriation of our rational nature (the shaping of motivation by 'perfected reason'), like the appropriation of our embodied nature through self-preservation, constitutes a similar expression of nature's providential care. Therefore, the account, taken as a whole, suggests that ethical development, conceived as appropriation of oneself, represents the realization of the best qualities of human and universal nature. When combined with 3.62–8, discussed shortly, Cicero's treatment suggests that it is the combination of appropriation of oneself and others of one's kind that constitutes this realization of human and universal nature at its best.

I close by considering the overall aim of the account of rational appropriation offered in *On Ends* 3.20–2, both in its context in Book 3, and in the broader framework of Stoic ethics. Earlier, I have suggested that the account of appropriation, taken as a whole, supports the core Stoic ethical claims (notably the claim that virtue forms the sole basis for happiness) by showing that it is natural to develop towards virtue and happiness, as conceived in Stoicism.[149] But what kind of support, exactly, is offered by the account and in what sense is ethical development, as understood in Stoic theory, presented as natural? In addressing this question, I begin by ruling out two possible views. I do not think the Stoic theory of appropriation (to use Bernard Williams's term) is 'Archimedean' in aiming to prove to *anyone*, even an immoralist, that it is natural, and therefore desirable, to

---

[143] For this view, see also Klein 2016 (summarized in his 160–2), based on a wide range of texts.
[144] See text to n. 95.   [145] See text to nn. 123–4.
[146] D.L. 7.88–9 (LS 63 C); also Ch. 1, text to nn. 68–70.   [147] See text to n. 118–22.
[148] Cic. *Fin.* 3.16, taken with D.L. 7.57–8 (LS 57 A).   [149] See 4.1, text to nn. 9–11.

develop towards virtue as understood in Stoic terms.[150] It is true that the theory sometimes appeals to certain basic motives, self-preservation and parental love, as indicators of appropriation of oneself or others, whose status as natural can be widely accepted by people of widely differing ethical beliefs and attitudes. However, accounts of the theory also go on to suggest that the status of being natural can be extended to other forms of motivation, notably the desire to achieve a proper understanding of virtue (conceived as a special, superordinate kind of goodness) and to exercise this in action.[151] This is a claim that no immoralist is likely to accept. Indeed, even to accept the proposition that ethical development, as so understood, is, in some sense, natural seems to presuppose an acceptance of the core ethical claim (about the virtue-happiness relation) being presented.[152] Cicero, in *On Ends*, underlines this point by his criticism in Book 4 of the naturalness of the account of development, a criticism framed from an alternative ancient (Antiochean) standpoint.[153]

A second possible line of explanation for stressing the naturalness of the process is that the account of development as appropriation provides grounding or foundations for Stoic ethical principles (above all, the claim that virtue is the sole basis for happiness) by showing that they are rooted in nature. This view assumes an addressee who is prepared, in principle, to accept this ethical claim (not an immoralist); the theory of appropriation provides the necessary basis for doing so by showing that ethical development, as understood in Stoic theory, has a natural grounding, in features of human or universal nature. This is a more plausible view; it is argued for by some scholars, at least as regards universal nature;[154] and my view may seem close to this one. However, I do not think this interpretation is quite right, for reasons discussed at length in Chapter 3, on the role of the idea of nature in Stoic ethics. I argue there that Stoic ethics is not structured as a foundationalist theory, in the way sometimes supposed; more specifically, Stoic ethics is not grounded on an account of nature or of natural development, as is sometimes claimed. If this were the case, Stoic ethical principles would always, and systematically, be presented as grounded in this way, whereas this is not the case.[155] As shown here, the theory of development as appropriation plays a prominent role in Cicero's account of Stoic ethical thinking in *On Ends* 3, and it appears at the start of the summary of Stoic ethics in Diogenes Laertius

---

[150] Williams 1985: 22-9, esp. 28-9. On 'Archimedean' arguments and Greek philosophy, see Gill 1996, index under 'Archimedean role'. On the questions considered in this and the following paragraph, see also Ch. 7, text to nn. 13-23, on Williams and Aristotle. On Plato as addressing 'immoralists', see text to n. 92.

[151] See Cic. *Fin.* 3.21-2 (LS 59 D(4-6)).   [152] For this view, see also Gill 1990: 145-8.

[153] See Cic. *Fin.* 4.26-39, esp. 26-8; also Gill 2006: 168-70; Bénatouïl 2016a: 215-17.

[154] See e.g. Long 1996: ch. 6, based on D.L. 85-8; and Striker 1996: 225-31, based mainly on Cic. *Fin.* 3.16, 20-2; also text to nn. 127-32.

[155] See Ch. 3, text to nn. 51-9, referring to claims that Stoic ethics is grounded on a conception of universal nature.

(though its role there is less clear).[156] However, the theory does not figure in Stobaeus' summary, even though there is a partial parallel.[157] Also, and more importantly, even in the account of Stoic ethics where the theory of appropriation is most central, Cicero's On Ends 3, its role is better interpreted as supporting, rather than grounding or foundational, for the distinctive Stoic claims. Following the account of appropriation, the Stoic ethical claims are argued for, in dialectical mode, without referring back to the theory of appropriation or to ideas of nature.[158] This reflects a general feature of Stoic ethics, underlined in Chapter 3: that ethical principles are presented, standardly, in their own terms in all three summaries, even if they are also supported by reference to ideas of human or universal nature or accounts of natural development.[159] This fits a picture of Stoic theory, in which the different branches of knowledge are seen as mutually supporting and as having different but complementary spheres of authority rather than one in which ethics is seen as grounded on physics or the study of nature, including the study of natural development.[160]

What, then, on my view, is the role of the account of appropriation vis-à-vis the core Stoic ethical claims? The account does indeed support the claims, and it does so by referring to ideas about nature, either human or universal, or both. Both in On Duties 1.11–15 and On Ends 3 (16–22, 62–8), appropriation is presented as natural, and part of the thesis is that the motive of appropriation (of oneself or others) is in-built in nature and reflects broader patterns of human nature or nature as a whole.[161] The theory of appropriation helps to make sense of the key Stoic ethical ideas (especially that virtue is the sole basis for happiness) by correlating them with a credible conception of nature and natural development. In this respect, the presentation of ethical development (conceived as appropriation of oneself and others) as natural does real philosophical work in supporting the distinctive Stoic ethical ideas. It is relevant for this point that the core Stoic ethical ideas about virtue and happiness are themselves often formulated in terms of 'nature'. Notably, happiness or the goal is, standardly, defined as the 'the life according to nature', with the connotations of this term explored in Chapter 1.[162] Hence, reference to the theory of development as appropriation serves, in part, as a way of spelling out these connotations of their conception of happiness, both regarding human and universal nature. More precisely, the theory serves as a way of spelling out those connotations in a certain respect, namely in terms in

---

[156] D.L. 7.85–6 gives an account of appropriation, and 7.87–9 summarizes Stoic views on the goal of life; and sometimes these are seen as making up a single argument (see Long 1996: ch. 6; Striker 1996: 228–31); but it is not clear how far the two passages form an integrated whole.

[157] See Stob. 5b3, for the idea of *aphormai* ('starting points') for the four cardinal virtues, which can be taken together with the stress in Stobaeus on human nature (as rational and sociable), rather than universal nature; see Ch. 1, text to nn. 155–7.

[158] Cic. *Fin.* 3.24–34, 36–9.   [159] See Ch. 3, text to nn. 41–5, 51–9.

[160] See Ch. 3, text to nn. 109–14, 151–62.   [161] See Cic. *Off.* 1.11, *Fin.* 3.16, 21–3, 62–4.

[162] See 1.3.

development, especially development in human motivation.[163] The theory of appropriation, then, is not merely a rhetorical flourish added to the distinctive Stoic ethical claims.[164] However, the theory is also not, as just argued, foundational for those claims; indeed, the credibility of the account of appropriation, in its advanced stages, depends not just on the picture of what is in line with nature but also on the ethical credibility of the claims made about the relationship between virtue and indifferents or virtue and happiness.[165] Otherwise, the attempt to correlate those two elements through the theory of appropriation will not work. On this view, the appeal to naturalness in the Stoic theory of appropriation has substantive content, and is also, I think, credible.

4.5 Rational Appropriation of Others
(Cicero, *On Ends* 3.62–8)

On Ends 3.20–2 is our most important surviving discussion of rational appropriation. However, as highlighted earlier, there is one, very conspicuous, gap. The whole sequence of ethical development is traced with reference to appropriation of oneself, with no (explicit) reference to appropriation of others.[166] This is in spite of the fact that, as brought out in *On Duties*, in lived human experience the two kinds of appropriation are thoroughly intertwined and both form an integral part of ethical development as expressed in practical deliberation.[167] In what seems to be an implicit acknowledgement of this gap, Cicero returns to the topic of appropriation later in *On Ends* 3, but now focuses wholly on appropriation of others (3.62–8). The second discussion does not refer explicitly back to the first one and presents itself as a free-standing treatment.[168] However, I suggest later that 3.62–8 identifies a series of (other-related) features which complement the developmental sequence of 3.20–3.[169] Hence, the two discussions, taken together (and also taken with related treatments, such as *On Duties*), suggest that, in Stoic ethics, a

---

[163] For this view, see also Gill 2017: 102.

[164] The phrase 'rhetorical flourish' is taken from McDowell 1980: 371, which describes in this way Aristotle's use of the idea of the human function in *NE* 1.7; on the point at issue, see Ch. 7, text to nn. 13–23, and Gill 1990: 142–3.

[165] Also, the credibility of the account depends on the addressee having made at least some progress in the ethical development presented; for a similar point regarding the development of virtue and the recognition of divine providence, see Ch. 3, text to nn. 239–42, 250.

[166] Some other Stoic accounts, though centred on self-appropriation or appropriation of one's constitution, incorporate reference to social engagement as part of the constitution; see n. 27.

[167] See 4.3, esp. text to nn. 79–86.

[168] Cicero's inclusion of this topic here may reflect the tendency in Stoic ethical summaries to provide a section on social action, covering practical ethics and illustrative pictures of the wise person in social situations (see Ch. 3, text to n. 66).

[169] See text to nn. 211–15.

complete account of ethical development needs to combine and co-ordinate the themes of appropriation of oneself and others.

On Ends 3.62–8 is the fullest surviving ancient discussion of appropriation of others.[170] However, in certain respects, the line of thought is not easy to follow.[171] Hence, I correlate this discussion with a partly parallel treatment of social relations in On Duties (1.50–9), thus enabling comparison with another Stoic treatment. I also use the three-fold framework for appropriation deployed so far to explain some of the moves made by Cicero. A feature shared by On Ends 3.62–8 and On Duties 1.50–9 is that the idea of the community of humankind is seen as wholly compatible with ethical engagement in specific and localized forms of community. This runs counter to the impression sometimes formed that cosmopolitanism, in Stoic ethics, replaces localized involvement. After discussing On Ends 3.62–8, I consider how far Cicero's view on this point is reflected in other Stoic sources on social relations (4.6).

I start by summarizing On Ends 3.62–8 and On Duties 1.50–9. Although the latter discussion has a different overall aim, it deploys a similar set of Stoic ideas for this purpose. On Ends 3.62–8 begins by presenting certain motives as natural, namely parental love and human sociability, as expressed in various forms of social group, including the community of humankind and that of humans and gods (3.62–4). The claim of the naturalness of these motives is also supported by reference to widely practised, or at least highly recognizable, types of human action. These include actions on behalf of one's community or state, making a will for one's heirs, performing heroic actions to benefit humankind, and engaging fully in family, communal, and political life (3.64–8). Cicero's On Duties 1.50–9 is an excursus within the main topic of Book 1 (guidance on performing 'appropriate acts' in line with the four virtues); the aim of this section is 'to examine more thoroughly what are the natural principles of human fellowship and community'.[172] The examination moves in two opposite directions, though these are presented as linked. The first part begins with the idea of humankind as a community (1.50–2), before proceeding by degrees to more limited forms of social association, including city-state and family (1.53). The second part moves from the family, the terminus of the previous part, to progressively larger and more diverse forms of social association. These are, first, the extended family, then friends (especially in friendships based on the shared possession of virtue), and, finally, country or state (1.54–7). On the basis of the second part, especially, Cicero considers which of these relationships, in principle, justifies 'appropriate acts' (officia) on other people's behalf, and outlines a spectrum of claims owed to

---

[170] See LS 57 F, and IG: 156–7, for translations of extracts of this discussion.
[171] E.g. on the nature of the link between basic and rational motives or between cosmopolitanism and localized social engagement. Inwood 2016: 158–66, identifies several problems.
[172] Off. 1.50, trans. Griffin and Atkins 1991.

various kinds of person (1.58, also 1.45). The excursus informs in this way the discussion of actions characteristic of generosity (the actively benevolent aspect of justice).[173]

In considering the implications of *On Ends* 3.62–8 as an account of appropriation of others, I use as a starting-point the three-fold framework deployed elsewhere to analyse appropriation, though modified slightly to fit this topic. (1) The discussion begins by identifying two motives, one basic and one advanced, both of which are treated here are as primary human motives, namely parental love and human (rational) sociability (3.62–3). (2) Both motives are presented as expressing the underlying disposition to appropriate others of one's kind, an idea which is also supported by reference to a series of types of other-benefiting actions discussed later (3.64–8). (3) The two primary motives are described both as in-built in human nature and as reflecting the providence of universal nature (3.62–4). I take these points in turn.

In Stoic writings on appropriation, a typical move is to refer to widely observable patterns of behaviour among animals, including human beings, to support the idea that there are certain basic (natural) motives, namely, self-preservation and parental love. This feature appears at the start of *On Ends* 3.62–8, in support of the idea that parental love constitutes a basic motive in animal life: 'Even among animals nature's power can be observed; when we see the effort they spend on giving birth and on rearing, we seem to be listening to the actual voice of nature'.[174] However, in this context, this basic motive is coupled with a second one, which is restricted to human beings as rational animals. There is a parallel to this move in *On Duties* 1.50–9: Cicero there presents two motives as fundamental for human society, namely the sense of community among all human beings as such (1.50–1) and the desire to procreate and care for one's children (1.54). In *On Ends* 3.63, particularly, the presentation of the rational motive raises certain interpretative questions. For one thing, Cicero's initial formulation of this motive is ambiguous; the Latin words can be taken as referring either to the community of humankind or to the human disposition to sociability, as expressed in in the formation of communities.[175] Cicero's phrases his point in this way: 'From this starting-point [parental love] we can follow the development of the shared society which unites the human race'.[176] Cicero's meaning has been interpreted in different ways by recent translations.[177] In fact, Cicero refers to both these ideas in his subsequent elaboration of this point in 3.63: 'From this [parental love], it

---

[173] See *Off.* 1.42–65. Each virtue is examined in *Off.* in its core character and in its social, other-benefiting character (see Ch. 1, text to nn. 169–77).
[174] *Fin.* 3.62 (LS 57 F(1)), also cited earlier (text to n. 49).
[175] Cic. *Fin.* 3.62: 'communem humani generis societatem'.
[176] *Fin.* 3.62, IG: 156 (with my addition in square brackets).
[177] LS 57 F(1) opt for 'the universal community of the human race'; Annas and Woolf 2001 for 'the development of all human society'; IG's translation, cited in text to n. 176, preserves the ambiguity of the Latin.

develops naturally that there is among human beings a common and natural affinity of people to each other, with the result that it is right for them to feel that other humans, just because they are humans, are not alien to them [community of humankind] ... So we are naturally suited to living in gatherings, groups, and states [natural tendency to form communities]'.[178] Similarly, in 3.64, having presented the idea of human beings (and gods) as forming a kind of cosmic city or state, Cicero illustrates this idea by referring to the willingness of human individuals to act on behalf of their state (meaning their own, specific state), and if need be to die for it. The implication is that Cicero has both these ideas in mind and that he sees them as compatible and mutually supporting. To participate fully in specific communities is, in a sense, also to express a sense of the community of humankind as a whole; and the idea of the community of humankind underpins the formation of specific communities.[179] The parallel passage in *On Duties* 1.50–9 presents these ideas somewhat differently. Although the community of humankind is seen as, in a generalized way, forming a framework for more specific and localized groups, the broader conception is especially associated with acting on behalf of those outside one's own community or social circle, for instance in performing acts of charity for strangers, travellers, and those in need (51–2).

A second interpretative question is raised by Cicero's presentation of these two primary motives in the two discussions. In *On Ends* 3.62–3, as just illustrated, parental love is twice described as the source of the community of humankind (or of the desire of human beings to form communities).[180] In what sense it is the source? Two main options present themselves. One is that parental love constitutes the motivational basis, though perhaps in a diffused or indirect form, for the second, communal, motive. This is an idea which we encounter in *On Duties* 1.50–9. In 1.54–5, the family is described as the first instance of a series of types of relationship which are derived from the instinct to procreate, starting with the family ('the first fellowship'). The family, in turn, is presented as 'the starting-point' (*principium*) of a city and the 'seed-bed' (*seminarium*) of a political community, an idea supported by the role of marriages and kinship ties in building up the community and its shared practices.[181] In *On Duties*, the other primary motive (for fellowship among human beings as such) is not presented as based on parental love but as a distinct and independently grounded one (based on shared reason and communication, 1.50–1). In *On Ends* 3.63–4, there is no equivalent for the idea found in *On Duties* 1.54–5 that parental love helps to build up families that, in turn, serve to construct communities. Rather, Cicero offers a

---

[178] *Fin.* 3.63, IG: 157, my additions in square brackets.
[179] For other possible ways of conceiving the relationship between these two ideas, see 4.6.
[180] See Cic. *Fin.* 3.62 (start); end of 3.62 and start of 3.63 (text to nn. 176, 178).
[181] Cic. *Off.* 1.54, trans. Griffin and Atkins 1991.

distinct set of grounds for seeing the community of humankind (or the desire to form communities) as a fundamental or primary motive.[182] This raises the question of the role of parental love in *On Ends* 3.62–3. Earlier, I suggest that, in Stoic theory in general, parental love is taken as the paradigm case of appropriation of others, rather than as the necessary basis for all other expressions of this disposition.[183] Correspondingly, in *On Ends* 3, parental love serves as the starting point for understanding the naturalness of appropriation of others,[184] and not as the motivational source of the more complex forms of social relationships. Parental love is the starting-point because it is the basic motive shared by all animals, including human beings. The community of humankind (or the desire to form communities) is a second primary motive, at least for human beings, as rational animals, and one that, in a more direct way, grounds the other, more specific, types of relationships referred to in *On Ends* 3.64–8. Hence, for human beings, as rational animals, there are two primary motives, one basic and shared with other animals, and one restricted to human adults, a view presented in both *On Ends* 3.62–8 and *On Duties* 1.50–9.

   This point leads to the second feature of the framework outlined earlier. In Stoic writings on appropriation, the basic motives (self-preservation and the desire to procreate and care for one's offspring) are not presented simply as fundamental features of animal life, including human life. They are also seen as expressions of two underlying natural dispositions, namely to appropriate oneself (or one's constitution) and to appropriate others of one's kind. In the case of human beings, one's constitution develops with the emergence of rationality;[185] this has profound implications for what it means to appropriate oneself fully, as we have seen in connection with *On Ends* 3.20–2, and also for what it means to appropriate others. (There are also implications for the understanding of the scope of those who are 'of one's kind' or 'one's own' (*oikeioi*, in Greek), and for the way in which we carry out this appropriation.)[186] These points are indicated at the start of Cicero's discussion (*On Ends* 3.62–3). Cicero begins by underlining the naturalness of parental love, the standard indicator of the second strand in appropriation. At the same time, as just discussed, he presents parental love as the starting-point for understanding a much more broadly conceived, and specifically human, form of attachment (what I am calling the second primary motive). This is attachment to human beings as such, linked with (or expressed in) the formation of 'unions, assemblies, and states',[187] that is, specifically human forms of association. This

---

[182] Cic. *Fin.* 3.63–4; see text to nn. 178–9.   [183] See text to nn. 47–9.

[184] This point is implied in the translation of Annas and Woolf 2001: 'From this starting point we trace (*persequimur*) the development of human society' (*Fin.* 3.62).

[185] For this point, see Sen. *Ep.* 121.15–16 (LS 57 B(3)); also Inwood 1985: 194–7.

[186] The core activity of appropriation is making something 'one's own' (*oikeios*), in the case of others, making them 'one's own'. See Pembroke 1971: 115–16, 121–2.

[187] *Fin.* 3.63 (*coetus, concilia, civitates*).

idea is then supported by the discussion of types of other-benefiting motivation and action linked with these various forms of association in 3.64–8. The implication is that the two primary motives and the various forms of other-benefiting action constitute expressions of the same underlying natural human disposition, to appropriate others of one's kind.[188]

The third feature of the framework for appropriation is this. In the case of basic motives, their naturalness is supported by the claims that they are in-built in human (and animal) nature and that they express the providential care of universal nature. Although these two features are sometimes seen as distinct, or competing, elements in Stoic theory, I have suggested that they are understood by Stoic thinkers as compatible and mutually supporting.[189] Both these features figure here in connection with the basic motive of the desire for procreation and parental love: '...the form and organs of the body...show that nature has a rational scheme for reproduction; but it would be inconsistent for nature to want offspring to be born and yet not to see to it that they are loved once they are born'.[190] Cicero also makes an analogous claim regarding the second primary motive, restricted to human adults (or rational animals), that is, the attachment of human beings to each other as human and their inclination to form communities. He refers first to the idea that individual human beings constitute integral parts of a single body (that is, the human race).[191] Although, as he allows, certain animal species also function as naturally co-operative units in this way (or engage in regular cross-specific assistance), 'the ties between human beings are far closer', presumably because their capacities for reason and communication mean that 'they are fitted by nature to form unions, assemblies, and states'.[192]

The idea that human beings form an integral part of a universe shaped by natural teleology (or divine providence) also underlies the further point made here about the second primary motive. Cicero refers to the common Stoic idea that human beings (along with gods) make up a cosmic or universal city or community.[193] Hence: 'Each of us is a part of this universe. It follows naturally from this that we value the common good more than our own'.[194] Cicero's line of thought here is very compressed. However, I think he is (1) assuming the links

---

[188] On the place of *Fin.* 3.64–8 in the overall discussion, see text to nn. 196–8.

[189] See text to n. 46.

[190] See *Fin.* 3.62, IG: 156–7. The form of argument is similar to that found in D.L. 7.85 (LS 57 A(2)); see text to nn. 57–62; also Schofield 1995: 196–7; Inwood 2016: 158–9.

[191] For this idea, see also Cic. *Off.* 3.21–2.

[192] *Fin* 3.63. For reason and communication as distinctively human capacities, see Cic. *Off.* 1.12, 1.50 (also Inwood 1985: 72–84). On Cicero's argument in *Fin.* 3.63, see also Schofield 1995: 197–8.

[193] See LS 67 L; Cic. *N. D.* 2.133, 154; also Schofield 1991: ch. 3; Vogt 2008a: ch. 3.

[194] *Fin.* 3.64; *mundus* can mean either 'universe' or 'world'.

between Stoic natural teleology and ethics discussed elsewhere in this book,[195] and (2) using these links to support the idea of the human community (or the inclination of human beings to form communities) just stated. Our in-built human nature, as rational and sociable, and as disposed to care for others as well as ourselves, leads us to view ourselves as integral parts of social wholes, such as states, and, when appropriate, to value the common good of these wholes above our own. Put differently, like the sociable animals he has just cited (ants, bees, and storks), we see ourselves as integral parts of a larger whole or body, but we do so in ways that reflect our distinctive rationality or our being sociable in a distinctively rational way. Hence, our readiness to act on behalf of our homeland and, if necessary, die for it is presented as an expression of our appropriating others of our kind in a way that reflects characteristically human forms of reasoning and social engagement.

A further feature in *On Ends* 3.62–8 is the citation of a series of other-benefiting actions (3.64–8) presented as expressing the primary motives described as natural (3.62–4), and thus the underlying disposition to appropriate others of one's kind. This feature does not appear in writings on the basic motives, since what is involved consists of rational, deliberate actions, rather than the instinctive behaviour shared by humans and animals. On the face of it, these actions might seem to play the same role in this passage as the 'appropriate acts' (*officia*) based on social relationships in *On Duties*, directed either at strangers and travellers or at those with whom one has familial, friendly, or communal relationships.[196] The actions listed in *On Ends* 3.64–8 are similar in kind, and they could also be characterized as appropriate acts correlated with various types of social relationship. However, the role of these actions in *On Ends* is different from that in *On Duties*; they are presented as illustrating the primary motives set out in 3.62–4, especially the second motive, and the disposition to appropriate others which these motives express. As highlighted earlier, the second motive is broadly formulated in 3.63–4, embracing both fellow-feeling for other human beings as such and the desire to express one's sociability by forming and engaging in communities; and the illustrative actions reflect this dual focus. Some actions, especially those carried out by people with exceptional ability, are described as motivated by the desire to benefit humankind in general or at least as many people as possible.[197] Other actions are directed towards specific people with whom we have close relationships; however, these too are, typically, characterized as expressing a broader sense

---

[195] Certain key ideas found here, e.g. that certain animals regularly help other species (Cic. *Fin.* 3.63), and that human beings are distinctively rational and sociable and hence disposed to form communities, also occur in Cic. *N. D.* 2.123–4, 133, 147–8. 153. On links between Stoic theology and ethics, see Ch. 1, text to nn. 84–101; 3.4.

[196] *Off.* 1.51–2, 56–7, 59.

[197] *Fin.* 3.65: 'we are naturally driven to want to help as many people as possible'; 3.66, 'those with great talent... have a natural inclination to help the human race', trans. Annas and Woolf 2001.

of human community.[198] The implication, in the latter case, is that one aims to benefit humankind through benefiting the specific people affected by one's actions.

Cicero stresses that such actions illustrate the naturalness of these motives, especially the second primary motive, and they are sometimes explicitly described as natural.[199] In what sense are they natural? In some cases, they express widespread, highly recognizable, patterns of human activity. The readiness to obey the city's laws, and work for (if need be, even die for) one's homeland and to make provision for one's children after one's death matches this pattern (3.64). Actions of this kind play a role in the theory like the readily observable and regularly performed actions cited elsewhere to support the naturalness of basic motives,[200] although they are, of course, rational actions reflecting rational motives. In other cases, the actions (the exceptional benefactions of heroic figures) show that such outstanding people 'have a natural inclination to help the human race' (3.64). The wise person's readiness to involve himself in family life and politics is also presented as 'consistent with human nature' (3.68). In effect, the claim is that these actions express human nature at its best, rather than marking behaviour which is commonly found in human life. However, the discussion appeals to (what can plausibly be presented as) recognizable expressions of natural human feeling; in this way, it supports the general claim of the 'naturalness' of the primary motives illustrated, and also the idea that we have an underlying disposition to appropriate others of our kind.[201] Taken overall, I think On Ends 3.62–8 constitutes a largely coherent presentation of Stoic ideas about appropriation of others, underpinned by the three-fold pattern of thinking about appropriation.

Cicero's two discussions of this topic in On Ends 3 are important pieces of evidence for Stoic thinking on the two aspects of appropriation; however, he gives no explicit indication how we are to understand the relationship between them. Even so, I think the two treatments can be seen as complementary, so that, taken together, they give a more complete picture of appropriation than either treatment does on its own. I take, first, the implications of the second discussion for the first, and then, those of the first for the second.

In On Ends 3.16–22, Cicero provides an analysis, in narrative form, of ethical development that runs from the basic stage of human life to the final outcome, the

---

[198] *Fin.* 3.64: 'we value the common good more than our own' ... 'it is undoubtedly true that we must consider on its own account the interests of those who will one day come after us', trans. Annas and Woolf 2001.

[199] See refs. in n. 197; also 3.68, cited shortly.

[200] See Cic. *Fin.* 3.62: 'When we observe the effort they devote to breeding and rearing, it is as if we hear nature's very own voice', trans. Annas and Woolf 2001; see also Cic. *Fin.* 3.16–17, D.L. 7. 85–6 (text to nn. 31–2).

[201] The focus on actions expressing (distinctively) human sociability (or the community of humankind) partly explains the (rather awkward) digression in 3.67, excluding non-human animals from the scope of justice. See also Cic. *N. D.* 2.133, 154, 158–60; Ch. 7, text to nn. 119–21.

achievement and exercise of ethical understanding, virtue, and happiness. He presents this as the unfolding realization of one form of appropriation, that of oneself or one's constitution. I have suggested that the developmental sequence is presented there in a 'stripped-down' form, which largely avoids reference to specifically self- or other-related aspects and does service for appropriation as a whole.[202] However, the categories used in this account, potentially, have distinctly social connotations. For instance, the account refers to three notions (things according to nature or preferred indifferents, appropriate actions, and virtues) each of which can have a social or other-related dimension. Among standard lists of preferred indifferents, we find 'parents and children', among appropriate acts 'honouring parents, brothers, and country',[203] and among virtues justice and courage, though all the virtues, conceived as a unified or interdependent set, have a social dimension.[204] Hence, any complete account of the developmental process set out in 3.16–22, running from instinctive attraction towards 'things according to nature' to ethical understanding and valuation of virtue for its own sake, needs to conceive the developing person as, in part at least, an engaged participant in social relations. This point is, indeed, brought out in several ways in the presentation of Stoic ethics in *On Duties*, as illustrated earlier (4.3). It is also indicated in *On Ends* 3.62–8 in a way that bears more directly on 3.16–22.

The key point that emerges strongly from 3.62–8 is that other-directed motivation is a fundamental part of our human make-up, and as fundamental a part as self-directed motivation. From 3.16–22, one might conclude that ethical development consists simply in enlarging and deepening one's understanding of one's own constitution, conceived as that of a rational agent who is capable of virtue and happiness. One might also suppose that the social dimension of human life could be adequately acknowledged by treating it as one aspect of the human constitution, and there are, indeed, some Stoic writings which seem to take this view.[205] However, 3.62–8 suggests that a more substantial addition is needed. The disposition to care for others is as fundamental a part of human nature as that of the disposition to care for ourselves or our constitution; thus, ethical development, when fully described, embraces the progressive unfolding and realization of both dispositions. Hence, 3.62–8 presents the basic motive of parental love as an integral a part of human (and animal) nature, like the basic motive of self-preservation. Also, in human beings, the discussion presents this basic motive as the index of a more pervasive, but still primary, human motive, namely the desire to form, or engage in, communities or a sense of shared humanity. This motive is presented as underpinning a wide variety of widely recognizable human actions,

---

[202] See text to n. 90.   [203] See Stob 7b, 2.81.6; D.L. 7.108.
[204] On the cardinal virtues as unified or interdependent, and as, for each virtue, having a social or other-benefiting dimension, see Ch. 1, text to nn. 133–46, 169–77.
[205] For these ideas, see, respectively, text to nn. 140–3 and text to n. 27.

including those which express virtues such as wisdom and justice. Thus, 3.62–8 underlines that each of the stages of ethical development presented in 3.16–22 may not just have a social dimension but may also be positively motivated by other-concern. Put differently, the second discussion implies that the analysis of the sequence of ethical development in 3.16–22 is incomplete unless other-directed motivation is taken into account. This point applies to all three stages of the rational sequence: selection of things according to nature, selection moving progressively closer to virtue, and the selection of indifferents that expresses the understanding of what virtue involves and of its superordinate value in relation to preferred indifferents.

I have presented this idea about the significance of the second discussion for the first one simply as an implication, rather than something that Cicero himself highlights. However, there are at least some parts of 3.62–8 where this implication is made virtually explicit. These are texts which seem to be very closely based on Stoic thinking, going back to Chrysippus, and are thus especially significant. In 3.66, Cicero points out that we describe gods such as Zeus as defenders in recognition of their providential role in protecting us. However, he adds that 'it is hardly consistent' (*minime convenit*) for us to expect the gods to do this if we fail to protect and defend each other. He continues:

> We use the parts of our body before we have learned the actual reasons why we have them. In the same way it is by nature that we have gathered together and formed ourselves into civil societies. If things were not that way, there would be no place for justice or benevolence (*bonitas*).[206]

The claim here is that, just as we have an instinctive awareness of our bodily capacities for self-preservation and self-maintenance (the basic motive of self-appropriation), we also have an in-built (natural) desire to form communities, that is, to express the second primary motive linked with appropriation of others (3.62–4). Cicero adds the point that, without the desire to appropriate others in this way, there would be no scope for the virtues of justice or benevolence. This complex of themes evokes ideas we can trace back to Chrysippus.[207] We also know that Chrysippus considered appropriation of others as part at least of the basis of

---

[206] *Fin.* 3.66, trans. Annas and Woolf 2001.
[207] We have here (1) the combination of appropriation of oneself and others (Plu. *Sto. Rep.* 1038 B, LS 57 E); (2) expression at the human level of divine providential care; and (3) and the claim that 'consistency' (typically that of divine providential care but here that of human action modelled on divine care) supports the idea of social appropriation (see Cic. *Fin.* 3.62, LS 57 F(1); D.L. 7.85, LS 57 A(1)). These are all themes associated with Chrysippus (see text to nn. 22–4, 60–3; also Ch. 1, text to nn. 96–8).

justice.[208] This suggests that the view that the achievement of the virtues depends not just on appropriation of oneself (or one's constitution) but also on appropriation of others also goes back to Chrysippus. Slightly later we find a closely related idea:

> ... since we observe that humans are born to protect and defend each other, it is consistent with human nature for the wise person to want to take part in the business of government, and, in living according to nature, to take a spouse and to wish to have children.[209]

Here too, we have the idea that it is natural for human beings to want to defend others and that involvement in social groups (the family and political community) represents a way of doing this.[210] This motive is said to be characteristic of the wise person (the Stoic ethical paradigm), who is also described as wanting to live a life 'according to nature' (*e natura*), a phrase which may evoke the standard Stoic formulation of happiness. Thus, in effect, again, virtue and virtue-based happiness are presented as dependent on carrying to its completion appropriation of others as well as the appropriation of oneself which forms the subject matter of *On Ends* 3.16–22.

The same overall point emerges if we consider the relationship between the two accounts of appropriation from the other direction and explore the implications of *On Ends* 3.16–22 for 3.62–8. Just as the process of development described in 3.16–22 (towards virtue and happiness) is incomplete unless we incorporate the other-directed aspect of appropriation, so the appropriation of others presented in 3.62–8 is incomplete unless we presuppose the developmental sequence set out in 3.16–22. In fact, the account of the second strand already has a broadly developmental character: it begins with the basic motive of parental love (3.62) and moves towards presenting paradigms of (other-directed) virtue (justice or benevolence) such as Hercules and the Stoic ideal wise person (3.66, 68). The discussion also incorporates features (such as making a will for one's heirs or benefiting others by teaching) which could have been presented as (socially directed) 'appropriate actions', or as the selection of indifferents, and thus as characteristic of stage 2 of the developmental schema of 3.16–22.[211] To this degree, the second discussion contains features which evoke the sequential account of ethical development set out

---

[208] 'In his *On Justice* book 1 [Chrysippus] says that even the beasts are appropriated to their offspring in harmony with their needs' (Plu. *Rep.* 1038 B (LS 57 E)). For reconstruction of Chrysippus' thinking on justice and appropriation, see Schofield 1995: 193–9.

[209] *Fin.* 3.68, trans. Annas and Woolf 2001.

[210] Note again the theme of 'consistency' (*consentaneum ... naturae*), here ascribed to humans following gods in defending others.

[211] See *Fin.* 3.65 (also 3.64–5, 68) and 3.20. On the similarity of these features with the 'appropriate actions' of *Off.* 1.50–9, see text to n. 196; on the combination of appropriate actions and selection of indifferents in stage 2, see text to nn. 99–101.

in the first discussion. These points are suggestive even though the underlying rationale for the specific content and organization of 3.62–8 is not provided by the developmental sequence of 3.16–22 but, rather, the three-fold framework underlying the idea of appropriation as a whole, used here to analyse other-directed motivation.[212]

The combination of the two discussions of appropriation in *On Ends* 3 carries an important implication for interpreting the second discussion as well as the first. A complete account of social appropriation depends on recognizing the significance of the developmental sequence of 3.16–22 as well as of the points made explicitly in 3.62–8. For instance, the presence of the second primary motive (for social engagement and a sense of human community), identified in 3.62–3, depends on the emergence of rationality, together with the shaping of motivation by rationality, that constitutes the first of the three-stage (rational) sequence in 3.20–22, following the basic stage in 3.16.[213] Also, the movement from the basic motive (parental love, shared with other animals) in 3.62–3, to the benevolence and justice of Hercules or the wise person (3.66, 68) rests on the intermediate process of 'selection between indifferents' and performance of appropriate actions outlined in stage 2 of the developmental schema of 3.20 (and in *On Duties* 1).[214] To put the point in more general terms, simply having socially directed motives or carrying out socially beneficial actions is not enough by itself to provide a pathway towards developing virtue (or happiness) even as regards the treatment of other people. What is also needed is progress in learning how to select indifferents appropriately and how to develop an understanding of what virtue involves, especially recognizing the crucial distinction between the value of virtue (and virtue-based happiness) and that of preferable indifferents. In other words, to express other-directed motivation *correctly* we need not just the motives and actions described in 3.62–8 but also the step-by-step process in ethical learning set out in 3.16–22.[215] Thus, we need to combine the two discussions not just to give a complete account of appropriation overall but also to make sense of each of the two strands, considered separately.

4.6 Cicero and Stoic Social Ideals

The preceding section brings to a close the main argument of this chapter, on Stoic thinking on ethical development, as expressed in their thinking on appropriation

---

[212] See para. following n. 173.

[213] See *Fin.* 3.62–3 (also text to nn. 175–9) and 3.20 (also text to nn. 96–8). On the whole sequence, see text to n. 72.

[214] On the role of stage 2 in this respect (and for comparison with *Off.* 1), see text to nn. 99–102, also text to nn. 82–5.

[215] For an analogous account of the outcome of the first strand in appropriation, set out in 3.16–22, see text to 133–9.

of oneself and others. In this final section, which forms a kind of appendix to the chapter, I take up a question which arises out of the Ciceronian evidence discussed here. In *On Ends* 3.62–8, especially 3.63–4, Cicero presents the ideas of the community of humankind and of engagement with localized interpersonal and social relationships as social ideals which are compatible and on the same ethical level. How does this view relate to Stoic social thinking more generally? It is sometimes supposed that the community of humankind (or cosmopolitanism) is not only a distinctive Stoic idea[216] but is their primary and central ideal in social relations, and one that involves giving a lower value to conventional relationships.[217] A corollary of this view is that ethical development is conceived, in its social aspect, as progress from conventional relationships (in the first instance, parental love) towards recognition of the significance of the value of the community of humankind, with a correlated devaluation of conventional relationships. On this view, appropriation of others, like appropriation of oneself, follows a developmental sequence, with the relative valuation of the two kinds of relationship forming the beginning and end of the sequence.

On Ends 3.62–8, however, suggests a quite different picture. In 3.64–6, there is no sign of differentiation in ethical level between other-benefiting acts performed for family and country and for humankind in general. High value is attached to the acts of exceptional benefaction performed by outstanding figures (or heroes such as Hercules) on behalf of humankind (3.66). But high value is also attached to the wise person's readiness to engage in family life and politics in his own community (3.68). As noted earlier, these two examples are explicitly linked with the expression of virtue, and thus, by implication, with the culmination of the developmental sequence in *On Ends* 3.20–2. Also, as discussed earlier, the second primary motive (which is the rational offshoot of parental love) is presented in ambiguous or broad terms. While the community of humankind is clearly indicated (and reinforced by mention of the community of gods and humans), so too is the idea that human beings are naturally disposed to form communities, of a conventional kind (3.63–4). This two-fold emphasis is maintained throughout the account. Actions performed within a conventional framework are sometimes presented as expressing a broader benevolence towards human beings in general. This seems to imply that we can express concern for humanity as a community, in part at least, by showing concern for the specific people with whom we are involved.[218] *On Duties* 1.50–9 deploys the two ideas in a slightly different way.

---

[216] Although the idea of the community of humankind was not unique to Stoicism (it was adopted by Antiochus and Arius Didymus; see Gill 2016a: 232; Tsouni 2019: 157–66), it was recognized in antiquity as a distinctive, and sometimes controversial, Stoic thesis.

[217] For this view, see Annas 1993: 265–75; Nussbaum 2001: 359–60. However, Reydams-Schils 2005: ch. 2 sees the two ideals (community of humankind and engagement in specific communities) as co-existing in Stoic thought. See also ref. in n. 227.

[218] See *Fin.* 3.64–5; also text to nn. 196–8.

In the first part (1.50–3), recognizing the significance of the community of humankind is presented as wholly compatible with marking the validity of more restricted (conventional) groupings.[219] In the second part (1.54–8), the series of relationships set out as providing a basis for determining appropriate (generous) acts does not include the community of humankind.[220] Neither discussion lends support to the idea that recognizing the significance of the community of humankind, rather than that of conventional groupings, constitutes the conclusion of ethical development.

This raises the question how far the position taken on the relationship between these two ideas is representative of Stoic thought more generally or is restricted to Cicero. A full examination of this question would be a large and complex one, since the evidence for Stoic social and political thought raises several important interpretative and conceptual problems.[221] However, I offer here a brief statement, designed to address the (relatively specific) question whether Cicero's position in *On Ends* 3.62–8, and *On Duties* 1.50–9, is out of line with most Stoic thought on this topic or not.

Stoic thought, from the earliest period onwards, deploys ideal norms for social relationships, framed in universal terms. These are the community of the wise, of gods and humans (often described as the cosmic city), and of humankind.[222] The community of gods and humans and perhaps all three ideals reflect the Stoic providential worldview, outlined earlier in this book. The universe as a whole is presented as rational or at least shaped by rationality; it is also divine or shaped by immanent divinity. Human beings, alone among terrestrial animals, possess rationality; in this sense human beings and gods (that is, the rational element in the universe) form a community.[223] Human beings, or at least human adults, also share rationality (and sociability, informed by rationality) with each other; and in this sense they too can be regarded as a community. The wise embody the perfection of rationality, that is, rationality which has developed fully towards virtue and happiness. Hence, the wise can be seen as constituting another, more restricted, community.

---

[219] Recognition of the community of humankind is presented as leading to acts of (small-scale) charity, that are, explicitly, limited by the need to allow scope for generosity to those close to us (*Off.* 1.51–2).

[220] See also text to nn. 84–5.

[221] See Schofield 1999 (more briefly Schofield 2000: 443–53), stressing discontinuity in Stoic thought on this topic; Vogt 2008a, who sees a unified theory underlying at least early Stoic ideas; also Gill 2000b, on later Stoic writing.

[222] On these ideals, see (community of the wise) Schofield 1991: 22–56; (community of gods and humans or cosmic city) Schofield 1991: 57–92; and Vogt 2008a: 111–60: (community of humankind) Vogt 2008a: 65–110.

[223] See Cic. *N. D.* 2.16–18, 33–7, 46–7, 133–4; LS 54 A–B, E–H, N. See also Ch. 1, text to nn. 83–95; Ch. 3, text to nn. 145–6.

Obviously, these ideal communities are in some ways different from conventional social groupings (states, friendship groups, and families, for instance);[224] so the question arises of the relationship between these two types of community. If the universal communities represent ethical ideals or norms, what are the implications for the ethical validity of social life lived in conventional frameworks? Zeno seems not to have addressed this question. His *Republic* centres on characterizing an ideal community, that of the wise.[225] Our (limited) evidence suggests that this work was strongly influenced by Cynicism, a philosophical movement that stressed the radical difference between what is natural (and good) and what is conventional.[226] His successors seem to have gone further than Zeno in trying to bridge the gap between affirming the significance of ideal communities and engaging in relationships in conventional social contexts. Chrysippus, for instance, both deployed the ideal of the cosmic city (the community of gods and humans) and offered practical advice on ethically valid ways of life, or social institutions, as lived in conventional societies.[227] We lack reports of how, exactly, he understood the relationship between these two forms of community, although, since he was such an influential thinker, his views may underlie surviving Stoic discussions.

In Stoic writings from Cicero onwards, we find various ways in which this gap is bridged, some at least reflecting ideas in Hellenistic Stoicism, and these can be compared with Cicero's approach in *On Ends* 3 (and *On Duties* 1). For instance, we find in Seneca and Marcus Aurelius the idea that we are members (or citizens) of two kinds of community, the ideal (cosmic) one and the local, conventional one in which we live our lives. Although these two thinkers refer to the same idea, they highlight rather different implications. Seneca uses it, in the first instance, to refer to the contrast between leading a life of political action and one of philosophical theory, including understanding the nature and ethical significance of the universe. Seneca argues that both forms of life constitute valid options, on Stoic principles. However, he also insists that, if this two-fold ideal is to be fulfilled, each type of activity must be conducted virtuously, and in a way that benefits other

---

[224] On the difference between them (e.g. the conventional communities have a single location), see LS 67 I–J, L.

[225] D.L. 7.32–3 (LS 67 B); Plu. *Mor.* 329 A–B (LS 67 A) also ascribes to Zeno the idea of the community of humankind, though this is often seen as a misreport; however, Vogt 2008a: 86–90 thinks the report is correct.

[226] See LS 67 B–G (also on Chrysippus' *Republic*); and Schofield 1991: 3–56. However, the view of Zeno's *Republic* as Cynic-style utopianism is challenged by Vander Waerdt 1994; Vogt 2008a: 20–64.

[227] On these two aspects of Chrysippus' thought, see Schofield 1991: 67–9, 85–6, 110, 143–4; and 18–19, 120–1, 124, respectively. See also LS 67 R–S (and Schofield 1995: 205–9), on Chrysippus' thinking on natural law; and LS 67 V–W on practical advice on living in conventional societies. Jedan 2009: 146–7 suggests that the attempt to bridge ideal norms and involvement in conventional societies may go back to Zeno.

people. He cites the early Stoic heads as people who used philosophy to benefit 'the whole human race...people of all nations, both present and future'.[228] Marcus' usage of this idea is rather different, as indicated here: 'As Antoninus [his family name], my city and fatherland is Rome, as a human being it is the universe. It is only what benefits these cities which is good for me'.[229] What Marcus seems to have in view is, on the one hand, practising his specific, Roman, role (as emperor) in a fully engaged way, and holding in view the best Roman models of doing this, notably his adoptive father, Antoninus Pius.[230] On the other hand, he also aims to live by universal standards of ethical conduct, characterized in terms of the cosmic city, as here, or the community (or brotherhood) of human beings, or natural (rational) law.[231] Doing so has a significant effect on his actions, as he views the matter;[232] but he also sees this as compatible with playing his specific, locally framed, social role.[233]

In Marcus' use of the idea of 'dual citizenship', reference to the ideal community does not involve revision of normal standards of good practice in one's own community, though it is used to encourage one to live up to those standards and to view them in a broader perspective. However, in some other cases, the ideal is used in a more revisionist way, though without making a clear break with conventional ethical thinking. For instance, Cicero, in On Duties 3, records what he presents as a debate between the two Stoic heads after Chrysippus, Diogenes and Antipater, about the ethics of buying and selling. Diogenes is described as arguing for a legalistic approach, in which the seller discloses to the buyer only the information he is legally required to provide and does not take the initiative in conveying all the facts relevant to the sale which are unknown to the buyer. Antipater, on the other side, argues that the seller should disclose everything relevant to the sale known to him, even when this means he is likely to get a lower price for the goods sold. In doing so, he appeals to the ideals of the fellowship of human beings in general, the law of nature (a closely related Stoic theme), and the idea that the common benefit is identical with your own benefit. In doing so, Antipater is presented as advocating higher than normal standards of conduct towards others, though not as calling into question the ethical validity of buying and selling in general.[234] His approach has in common with the others considered here the aim of correlating the idea of an ideal community (that of humankind) with

---

[228] Seneca, On Leisure 4.1 (two communities) (LS 67 K); also 4.4–6, quotation from 4.6, trans. Fantham et al. 2014: 227; see also Griffin 2000: 555–8. For the stress on using knowledge to benefit as many people as possible, see Cic. Fin. 3.65–6.

[229] M. A. 6.44.5, trans. Gill 2013a.

[230] See M. A. 2.5.1, 3.5.2; 1.16, 6.30 (on Antoninus as model); also 9.29.5, dismissing utopian idealism.

[231] See M. A. 3.11.2, 4.4.

[232] For instance, in promoting action which is both humane and just, M. A. 2.1.4–5, 3.11.4–5.

[233] See Gill 2000b: 613, 2013a: xlv–i.

[234] Cic. Off. 3.50–7, esp. 52–3. See Schofield 1995:199–201; Annas 1997; also Ch. 2, text to nn. 229–33.

engagement in one's specific community and its practices; but it does so in a way that also involves some revision of what those practices should be.

The final example is also one that involves some revision of practice, though without calling into question the validity of conventional relationships altogether. This (well-known) example is ascribed to the late Stoic thinker, Hierocles, though not forming part of his main (partly surviving) work on the elements of ethics.[235] He presents social relationships as forming a series of concentric circles, centred on oneself: the occupants of the circles are one's immediate family, more distant relatives, local residents, fellow-members of one's tribe (a Greek ethnic group), fellow-citizens, people from other states, and, finally, the human race in general. He advocates drawing the circles inwards, so that, for instance, we treat those in the third circle as though they are those in the second circle. The aim is not to draw the circles inwards to the point where we treat any given human being as if they were members of our immediate family. The aim is the more modest one of reducing (by one circle) the distance between ourselves and members of each of the circles of relationship. One method advocated for doing this is calling people by the names used for the circle nearest to theirs, for instance, calling cousins brothers and sisters, and calling uncles and aunts fathers and mothers. This is, explicitly, revisionist, but in a limited degree, marking the fact that, as Hierocles puts it, 'the greater distance in blood will remove some affection' in the case of more extended family members. The human race, the community of humankind, as they are called elsewhere, figure here, and are treated as recipients of our concern (like those in other relationships), but they are still placed at the outer limit of this concern.[236] Thus, Hierocles' discussion, like that of other Stoic thinkers considered here, gives a role to the community of humankind, and invites us to see this larger community as less remote to us than we might otherwise have assumed. However, he does so, while assuming the validity of conventional relationships and their primary role in our concerns.

Although this review of Stoic thinking on this topic is not exhaustive,[237] it provides the basis for gauging whether Cicero's approach in On Ends 3.62–8 is broadly in line with other Stoic treatments. All the material discussed, with the exception of Zeno's Republic, like Cicero's account, treats the ideals of universal community as ones which should be used to inform a life of engagement in the conventional social contexts of family, friendship, or political state. The

---

[235] On Hierocles' *Elements of Ethics*, centred on appropriation, see Long 1996: ch. 11; Ramelli 2009; Gourinat 2016.

[236] Hierocles in Stob. 4.671.7–673.11 (LS 57 G), esp. (6), cited in the text. See also Ramelli 2009: 125–8, reviewing earlier scholarship in this topic.

[237] Brown 1997 (unpublished), which I have not seen, discusses Stoic cosmopolitanism as a whole and in different periods. According to an on-line summary, both Chrysippus (ch. 3) and Cicero's *On Duties* (ch. 4) are seen as presenting the ideal of cosmopolitanism as compatible with engagement in specific states, though Cic. *Off.* differs in recognizing special obligations for citizens. A published version (Brown forthcoming) is announced.

approaches of Antipater, as reported by Cicero, and Hierocles both involve some revision of conventional standards or practices, though without calling into question the validity of the social frameworks involved. The treatment of the idea of 'dual citizenship', especially as deployed by Marcus, seems closest to the approach found in On Ends 3.62–8. Both Cicero and Marcus regard participation in the cosmic community as fully compatible with engagement in specific relationships. Put differently, fulfilling one's specific role by acting in line with the highest possible standards is seen as a means of expressing participation in the community of humankind as well as one's local community.[238] Cicero and Seneca also regard aiming to benefit as many people as possible by communicating one's knowledge or understanding as a way of expressing this participation.[239] Although it is difficult to say if the views found in these discussions accurately reflect those of Chrysippus, it is possible that they do.[240] In any case, Cicero's approach is close enough to other Stoic treatments, including that of one Stoic head, Antipater, to say that it represents a valid Stoic interpretation of this theme.

[238] See text to nn. 218, 229–33.   [239] See Cic. Fin. 3.65–6; Sen. On Leisure 4.6; also n. 228.
[240] See text to n. 227.

5

Emotional Development

5.1 Emotional and Ethical Development

The theme of this second part of the book is 'learning how to live naturally'. Although the term 'learning' may suggest a purely rational or intellectual process, the Stoics, like other ancient thinkers, believe that ethical development has a significant emotional dimension.

Stoic thinking on emotion has sometimes been seen, in antiquity and modern times, as over-intellectualized and psychologically implausible.[1] But recent scholarship on the topic, some of which has underlined the parallels with modern cognitive theories of emotion and psychotherapy, has done much to correct this impression.[2] In this section, I consider how Stoic thinking about emotion is connected with their theory of appropriation, discussing especially links with the first strand of appropriation, centred on care of oneself and the development of ethical understanding. In the next two sections (5.2–3), I focus on the relationship between emotional development and the social strand in appropriation. I challenge the view of some scholars that the Stoics regard the function of emotional development, or the 'therapy' of emotions, as being to promote a state of (individual) self-sufficiency and detachment from other people.[3] Overall, I aim to show that Stoic thinking on emotional development reflects the same ethical framework as the theory of appropriation and represents another aspect of moving towards realization of 'the life according to nature'.

In seeing emotional development as an integral part of ethical development, the Stoics adopt an approach also found in Plato and Aristotle. They take up especially the idea found in both these thinkers that the development of virtue brings with it a high degree of psychological harmony or cohesion. However, the Stoic version of this theme is distinctive in certain ways which reflect broader differences from Plato and Aristotle. As highlighted earlier, Plato and Aristotle subdivide ethical development into two phases, one of preliminary social habituation, especially in

---

[1] Galen is an important source, but also a partial and polemical one; he criticizes Chrysippus' theory, especially, on this ground, followed, to some extent, by Sorabji 2000: parts 1–2. For the main primary evidence, see LS 65.

[2] See Brennan 1998, 2003: 269–79; Price 1995: ch. 4; Graver 2007; on Stoicism and cognitive theories of emotion, see Nussbaum 2001: ch. 1; on Stoicism and cognitive psychotherapy, see Ch. 8, text to nn. 115–23. On the relationship between Galen and Stoicism regarding psychology, see Gill 2006: 238–44; 2010a: 168–88.

[3] For this view, see text to nn. 77–80.

Learning to Live Naturally: Stoic Ethics and its Modern Significance. Christopher Gill, Oxford University Press.
© Christopher Gill 2022. DOI: 10.1093/oso/9780198866169.003.0006

childhood or youth, and a second phase, based on the first, which completes ethical development through the acquisition of ethical understanding or knowledge.[4] In both thinkers, the first, habituative phase, is seen as bringing with it one kind of psychic harmony, in which beliefs, attitudes, and emotions are brought into line, or 'harmonized', with social norms.[5] Plato also presents the fully developed, and wholly virtuous, person as psychologically cohesive or harmonized in a way that reflects her further degree of (philosophically based) ethical understanding.[6] The Stoics do not subdivide ethical development in this way, and do not present complete ethical development as depending on a prior phase of childhood emotional habituation.[7] Their focus is on adult life; and they present adult ethical development, in its various aspects, as a single, progressive movement towards virtue and happiness.[8] However, the Stoics too see the achievement of virtue as bringing with it a high degree of psychological cohesion or harmony, by contrast with the incoherence and internal conflict that they regard as characteristic of defective ethical states.[9]

A further point of difference relates to the psychological model involved. Plato and Aristotle conceive virtue-based harmony as involving a relationship of authority or control between separate psychic 'parts', seen as distinct and potentially conflicting sources of motivation. These are, in Plato's *Republic*, the rational, spirited, and appetitive parts, and in Aristotle, the rational and non-rational (or partly rational) parts, the latter being the seat of emotion and desire.[10] The Stoics do not accept the existence of psychological parts in this sense. They adopt an innovative psychological model in which emotions and desires are shaped directly by beliefs and reasoning. In their terms, the 'assent' of the mind to a 'rational impression' necessarily generates a 'motive' corresponding to the impression, a pattern illustrated shortly. In this respect, the Stoic psychological framework is highly unified or holistic. Hence, psychological harmony, in their view, does not consist in agreement between distinct and potentially conflicting (rational or emotional) parts. It consists in the internal cohesion of the beliefs ('rational impressions' or 'reasons') and of the correlated emotions or desires ('motives')

---

[4] See Introd. to Part II, text to nn. 11–15; also Gill 2006: 134–45.

[5] See Pl. *Rep.* 400d–402d; Arist. *NE* 1.13, 1102b25–1103a10, 2.1, esp. 1103b17–25.

[6] See Pl. *Rep.* 485d–e, 486a–b, 586e–587a); Gill 1985b, 1996: 245–60, 1998b: 193–214. Aristotle, while sometimes demarcating a higher level of virtue, e.g. in his distinction between moderation and self-restraint (*NE* 1.13, 1102a25–8, 7.1) does not link this higher level with theory (though he presents theoretical understanding as bringing the highest form of human happiness, *NE* 10.7–8).

[7] Posidonius, a late Hellenistic Stoic, may have adopted this view (Galen, *PHP* 5.5.32–5). But it is also possible that Galen overstates Posidonius' differences from Chrysippus on this point; see Tieleman 2003: 220–30; Gill 2006: 287–9.

[8] See the discussions of (adult) appropriation in 4.3–5; also Sen. *Ep.* 75, on stages of emotional development.

[9] See, on virtue as marked by structure and order, LS 60 Q, 61 A, 63 L–M, 65 W; also Ch. 1, text to nn. 185–200. On passions as internally conflicted, see LS 65 A, G, J; also Gill 2006: 94–5, 222–3, 254–5; on Medea, text to nn. 63–8.

[10] See Pl. *Rep.* 435e–443e; Arist. 1.13, 1102a32–1103a10; also Gill 1996: 245–60.

present in the mind at any one time or over time. Though less familiar than the Platonic-Aristotelian idea of psychic harmony, this conception is coherent and psychologically credible, and prefigures some modern ('cognitive') theories.[11]

I begin by illustrating the Stoic (unified) psychological account of emotion, before turning to the relationship between their ideas about emotion and about ethical development. The Stoic analysis of motivation applies, broadly, to humans and other animals. In both cases, motivation is analysed as a response to the impression (*phantasia*) that a certain action (or reaction) is 'appropriate' (*kathēkon*). However, the two patterns differ in that (adult) human impressions are rational in the sense that their content can be expressed in linguistic form. Also, the human being needs to 'assent' to the impression before it generates a 'motive' (*hormē*) to act or react. More precisely, the assent is given to the propositional content of the impression (such as 'this act is appropriate') whereas the motive is directed specifically towards the predicate ('is appropriate').[12] The overall point of this analysis is to bring out the fact that (adult) human motivation is informed by rationality, understood in terms of the capacities for language and communication, logical inference, and judgement formation.[13] The analysis also brings out the point that the motivating effect depends directly on the judgement formed, such as 'this act is appropriate'.[14] This framework explains why Stoics, typically, define emotions in two ways, in terms of belief (that is, the impression which gains assent) and the motive which is the outcome of the assent. These are inseparable aspects of an emotion and are causally linked, in that the belief causes the motive. This linkage comes out in the Stoic definitions of the emotions, considered shortly, which specify both the relevant belief and the motive (or emotional reaction) which is triggered by the belief.[15] The motives are sometimes described as reaching out for things or avoiding them. They are also described as being 'elated' or 'contracted' by the presence or absence of the object of the emotion or the prospective presence or absence of this object. While the Stoics

---

[11] See LS 53 G–K, and LS, vol. 1, p. 321, LS 65, esp. G. See also Inwood 1985: ch. 5; Nussbaum 2001: ch. 1; Gill 2006: 75–100, 244–66; Graver 2007: chs. 1–2. The term *hormē* is generally translated as 'impulse', but I think 'motive' fits the meaning of the Greek term better.

[12] See LS 53 A(4–5), Q; also LS 33 C–D, I; also Inwood 1985: 51–66; Brennan 1998: 28–9, 2003: 265–9; Gill 2006: 138–44.

[13] This does not mean that all human motivation takes the form of conscious articulation in language of the content of the process involved. The Stoic analysis spells out this content, but the person involved does not normally do so; see Gill 1991: 186–8. The idea that rationality involves the development of these capacities explains why the Stoics see children as not yet rational; see Inwood 1985: 72–80; Gill 2006: 140–1.

[14] See Brennan 2003: 265–9.

[15] The following account of Stoic thinking on emotions is based on our evidence for Chrysippus' thought. Galen claimed that Chrysippus' theory was substantively different from that of Zeno (LS 65 D), but this claim is now widely rejected; see Gill 2006: 247–9; Graver 2007: 32–4.

emphasize the importance of belief as the causal determinant of emotions, they also recognize the affective or 'feeling' dimension of emotions. This is sometimes characterized in psychophysical terms, such as those just noted, being 'elated' or 'contracted', referring to the functions of the 'leading part' (hēgemonikon) of the psyche, which is regarded as located in the heart. Beliefs and knowledge are also conceived in psychophysical terms.[16] Hence, while the Stoic theory of emotions is 'cognitive', in the sense that it stresses the role of beliefs (whether conscious or implied) in determining emotions, it also reflects a physicalist conception of psychology.[17]

I now turn to the question of the relationship between the Stoic theory of emotion and ethical development, beginning with their definitions of emotions. The Stoics distinguish between bad or defective emotions (sometimes called 'passions' by modern scholars, though the Stoics simply use the standard Greek term for emotions, namely pathē) and 'good emotions' (eupatheiai). Both types of emotion are presented as a matched set, with four generic bad emotions and three good ones, and numerous subdivisions,[18] a pattern also found in the Stoic accounts of the four cardinal virtues and their subdivisions.[19] The good emotions are those experienced by the virtuous or wise, that is, those who have completed ethical development. The bad emotions are those of the non-virtuous, that is, in Stoic terms, virtually all of us, though we are also all capable, in principle, of experiencing the good emotions if we develop ethically. Both sets of generic emotions are subdivided into those based on the belief that something is good and that we should go towards it and those based on the belief that something is bad and we should avoid it.

I cite, first, two ancient definitions of the four-fold set of bad emotions. Then I offer a reformulated version of the ancient definitions of both sets (bad and good emotions) which highlights certain key differences between them. First, then, two ancient accounts of the four generic bad emotions:

Appetite (epithumia) is an irrational stretching [desire], or pursuit of an expected good.

Fear (phobos) is an irrational shrinking [aversion] or avoidance of an expected danger.

Pleasure (hedonē) is an irrational swelling, or a fresh opinion that something good is present, at which people think it right to be swollen [i.e. elated].

---

[16] See LS 65 D, and 53 G–H. See also Graver 2007: 21–34; Gill 2010a: 87–103.

[17] See Tieleman 2003: chs. 3–4; Graver 2007: chs. 1–2. On the combination of cognitive psychology and physicalism in modern thought, see Nussbaum 2001: ch. 2; Gill 2010a: 333–50.

[18] On the generic emotions and their subdivisions, see Graver 2007: 53–9; on the two types of emotions, see Brennan 1998: 30–9, 2003: 269–72.

[19] On the four generic virtues, see LS 61 H (also LS 61 B–D).

Distress (*lupē*) is an irrational contraction, or a fresh opinion that something bad is present, at which people think it right to be contracted [i.e. distressed].[20]

Desire (*epithumia*) is a reaching out which is disobedient to reason, and its cause is believing that a good is in prospect in the presence of which we will flourish, the belief itself including a disorderly and [fresh] motive element [as to that being genuinely a thing to reach for].

Fear (*phobos*) is a withdrawing which is disobedient to reason, and its cause is believing that a bad thing is in prospect, the belief itself including a disorderly and fresh motive element as to that being genuinely a thing to avoid.

Pleasure (*hēdonē*) is an elevation of psyche which is disobedient to reason, and its cause is a fresh believing that some good is present towards which [it is appropriate] to be elevated.

Distress (*lupē*) is a contraction of psyche which is disobedient to reason, and its cause is a fresh believing that some bad thing is present at which it is appropriate to [be contracted].[21]

Also, here are definitions of both generic sets (bad and good emotions), based on ancient formulations but modified to bring out salient differences between the two types of emotion:[22]

Bad emotions:

Desire (or appetite) (*epithumia*) is a (mistaken) belief that a future thing is good, such that we (irrationally) reach out for it.

Fear (*phobos*) is a (mistaken) belief that a future thing is bad, such that we (irrationally) avoid it.

Pleasure (*hēdonē*) is a (mistaken) belief that a present thing is good, such that we are (irrationally) elated at it.

Pain (or distress) (*lupē*) is a (mistaken) belief that a present thing is bad, such that we are (irrationally) contracted (or depressed) by it.

Good emotions:

Wishing (*boulēsis*) is a (correct) belief that a future thing is good, such as that we (rationally) reach out for it.

[20] Andronicus, *On Passions* 1 (LS 65 B), LS additions in square brackets; order of emotions rearranged to match the third set.

[21] Stob. 10b, 2.90.7–18, trans. Graver 2007: 42, her additions in square brackets based on supplements by editors of the Greek text (see Graver 2007: 229, n. 13). For alternative translations, see Pomeroy 1999: 59; IG: 138–9. The order has been slightly rearranged to match the third set of emotions.

[22] These definitions are based on Andronicus, *On Emotions* 1 (LS 65 B), already cited, and D.L. 7.115 (LS 65 F). See also Gill 2016b: 144; Brennan 1998: 30–1, 34–5.

Caution (*eulabeia*) is a (correct) belief that a future thing is bad, such that we (rationally) avoid it.

Joy (*chara*) is a (correct) belief that a present thing is good, such that we are (rationally) elated about it.

These sets of definitions bring out certain features common to the two types of emotion: both types combine belief and motive and involve attitudes regarding what is good or bad in the future or present.[23] However, there are two important differences, which come out most clearly in the last set of definitions. The bad emotions are based on a mistaken understanding of what is good and bad, whereas the good emotions are based on a correct understanding of good and bad. I consider shortly the nature of these mistaken or correct beliefs. Secondly, the bad emotions are irrational in a whole series of ways, whereas the good emotions are rational. This contrast (between rationality and irrationality) is a normative or evaluative one; it co-exists with the fact that both sets of emotions are rational in the sense that they reflect the distinctively human (adult) forms of rationality.[24] The irrationality is underlined especially in the second set of definitions cited. The bad emotions are 'disobedient to reason'; the belief that good or bad is in prospect includes 'a disorderly and fresh motive element'.[25] These features correspond to aspects highlighted elsewhere in the Stoic accounts of bad emotions. Bad emotions are presented as intense or overwhelming and as marking an abnormal state of the person, like running legs as compared with walking ones. They constitute a 'rejection of reason' in that they fail to match the person's best judgement, and sometimes do so even at the moment of extreme emotion.[26] There is no equivalent for this feature in the case of the good emotions, which are described as being in line with the person's best judgement and which lack the disruptive or disorderly character of bad emotions. Hence, the motives of 'avoidance' and 'elation' which figure as part of the definitions of good emotions, as in those of bad emotions, are not described as irrational but as rational or 'well-reasoned'.[27]

I discuss this contrast between the two types of emotion further before considering the Stoic ideas about development that underlie their conception of

---

[23] However, there is no equivalent for distress in the good emotions since the virtuous person is never in the presence of what is truly bad (her own ethical badness).

[24] On human rationality and emotions, see text to nn. 11–17. On the contrast between the two senses of 'rationality', see Gal. *PHP* 4.2.10–18 (LS 65 J); this can be characterized as contrast between 'functional' and 'normative' rationality; see Gill 2006: 251–3.

[25] See text to n. 21.

[26] See Stob. 10–10a, 2.88.8–2.90.6 (excerpts in LS 65 A, esp. (1, 6–8)); Gal. *PHP* 4.2.10–18 (LS 65 J); Plu. *Virt. Mor.* 446 F–447A (LS 65 G).

[27] See D.L. 7.115, LS 65 F, cited earlier. The good emotions are described by Cicero as 'stable states' or 'consistencies' (*constantiae*) (*Tusc.* 4.12–15), by contrast with the disorderly bad emotions; see Graver 2007: 51–3.

emotions. How, more precisely, does the belief-content of bad emotions differ from that of good emotions? Both types are described as reactions to the supposed goodness or badness of certain states of affairs. However, the bad emotions involve mistaken judgements whereas the good emotions involve correct judgements or knowledge. The judgements centre, it seems, on the question of what kind of things properly count as good or bad. As brought out earlier in this book, the Stoic understanding of good (and bad) differs from that of Aristotle, for instance, in regarding as good only virtue (and virtue-based happiness and things that depend on virtue) but not the Aristotelian bodily and external goods which the Stoics called preferred indifferents.[28] The person experiencing bad emotions mistakenly regards as good or bad what are properly understood as preferred or dispreferred indifferents, whereas the good emotions involve correct recognition and application of this distinction.[29] We do not need to suppose that the belief-content of emotions, on this view, is formulated only in terms of goodness and badness and the distinction between these qualities and the value-status of indifferents. However, the belief-content, crucially, includes, or rests on, this kind of (correct or mistaken) understanding.[30] Nor should we suppose that the distinction between these two types of emotion involves attaching no value or disvalue to indifferents. On a mainstream Stoic view, preferred indifferents have real (natural) value and constitute valid grounds, in principle, for action (or 'selection').[31] Even so, good emotions, but not bad ones, register the appropriate distinction between virtue and indifferents in terms of value.

This distinction emerges more clearly from the Stoic definitions of the specific emotions of each type than from the generic definitions; it is especially evident in the specific good emotions. These definitions show that the person experiencing these emotions recognizes that the good is constituted by virtue or activity in line with virtue. For instance, the subdivisions of the generic good emotion 'joy' include 'cheerfulness' (*euphrosunē*) 'in response to the actions of a moderate (*sōphrōn*) person'. The subdivisions of the generic emotion 'caution' consist in 'shame' (*aidōs*), defined as 'caution about justified criticism', and 'reverence' (*hagneia*), that is, 'caution about wrong actions regarding the gods'. The subdivisions of wish include 'good will' (*eunoia*), defined as 'wishing someone else good things for his own sake'. The positive or negative responses identified here are directed at things falling within one's own or someone else's agency and are in line with the exercise of the virtues.[32] By contrast, the bad emotions are, typically, directed at states of affairs which fall outside one's agency, and they are responses

---

[28] See Ch. 1, text to nn. 29–37, Ch. 2, text to nn. 24–8.
[29] See also Brennan 1998: 36, 54–7; Graver 2007: 46–53.
[30] The definitions of specific emotions (good and bad), discussed shortly, give us a better indication of the agent's thought processes.
[31] See Ch. 2, text to nn. 18–23, 27–8.
[32] Andronicus, *On Passions* 6 (*SVF* 3.432); see also Graver 2007: 58; Gill 2016b: 146–7.

which are not, or not necessarily, in line with the virtues. For instance, under pleasure, we find 'spite' (*epichairekakia*), defined as 'pleasure at someone else's misfortunes'. Under distress, we find 'rivalry' (*zēlos*), 'pain at someone else getting what one desires oneself and not getting it oneself'. Subdivisions of fear include 'fear of failure' or 'fear of defeat', while 'shame' (*aischunē*) is 'a fear of bad reputation' (contrast the good emotion of 'shame' (*aidōs*), namely 'caution about justified criticism').[33] The definitions of the bad emotions correspond to formulations we find in various philosophical and other sources; the good emotions are less familiar, at least as definitions of emotions, though the ideas expressed are intelligible in terms of Greek ethical thought in general and not just Stoic thought.[34] The underlying distinction between the two types of emotion, at the specific as well as the generic level, is that the good emotions express an understanding of the difference in value between indifferents (preferable and dispreferable) and virtues or vices, whereas the bad emotions confuse or conflate these. The bad emotions express the mistaken belief that our happiness in life depends on acquiring preferable indifferents and avoiding dispreferable ones, rather than on developing and exercising the virtues and thereby living 'the life according to nature'.[35]

The Stoics believe that virtually all human beings, since they fall short of complete virtue, experience the bad emotions. However, they also think that human beings are constitutively capable of experiencing the good emotions and should aspire to do so. More precisely, they should aspire to lead the kind of life that brings with it the experience of these emotions.[36] Stoics also believe that certain features of the bad emotions, those linked earlier with the 'irrationality' of these emotions,[37] indicate recognition of the defectiveness of these emotions and also suggest scope for experiencing good emotions. What features of Stoic thinking about development make sense of this set of ideas about emotions? These views are best explained by reference to the theory of appropriation, discussed in Chapter 4, when taken alongside Stoic ideas about the causes of human corruption, discussed shortly. A key premise underlying the theory of appropriation is that 'all human beings have the starting-points of virtue' (LS 61 L) and that they retain these throughout their lives, even if they are never fully developed. These starting-points consist, in part, in the in-built capacity to form ethical notions ('preconceptions') and to apply them correctly.[38] They also consist in the primary

---

[33] See Stob. 10c, esp. 2.91.20, 2.92.7–8, 2.92.3–4; trans. based on IG: 139; see also Graver 2007: 56.

[34] E.g. the Stoic definition of anger as 'a desire to take revenge on someone who appears to have wronged you contrary to what is appropriate' (Stob. 10c, 2.91.10–11) is close to Arist. *Rh.* 2.2, 1378a31–3; and the definition of good will (cited in text to n. 32) is close to one of the key marks of friendship in Arist. *NE* 8.2, 1155b31. On this feature of Stoic thinking, see also Brennan 1998: 38–9; Graver 2007: 57–8.

[35] On the link between virtue and happiness in Stoic ethics, see 1.4.

[36] On the significance of this point, see text to nn. 90–1, also text to nn. 109–13.

[37] See text to nn. 24–6, 56–7.   [38] See Introd. to Part II, text to nn. 17–18.

motives, to care for oneself and others of one's kind which are also in-built in human nature (4.2). As set out by Cicero in *On Ends* 3.16–22, in the first strand of appropriation, the basic motive of care for oneself is realized fully by a sequence in which the instinctive attraction to 'things according to nature' develops into rational selection of these things, and this selection, in turn, forms the basis for the development of virtue (4.3–4). Implied here, as elsewhere in Stoic ethics, is the idea that virtue is a form of knowledge or expertise in selecting between indifferents in a way that realizes 'the life according to nature'.[39] The final stage of this process combines an understanding of the radical distinction in value between virtue, or virtue-based happiness, and 'things according to nature' (preferred indifferents) with continued selection between indifferents based on a correct understanding of their value.[40]

Cicero's account of this strand of appropriation is formulated not only in terms of the activities involved, such as selection and gaining understanding, but also of motives, and change in motivation;[41] and emotions, in Stoic theory, form a subcategory of motives.[42] Hence, although Cicero does not refer explicitly to emotions in *On Ends* 3.16–22, it is clear that a by-product of the final stage would be that one has good emotions rather than bad ones. The person who has developed complete virtue selects between indifferents in a way that is informed by virtue (expertise in selection) and does so with an understanding of the distinction in value between indifferents and what is genuinely good. These are, precisely, the features that differentiate good from bad emotions. The affective reactions that form part of happiness or 'the life according to nature' consist in the generic good emotions of wish, caution, and joy, and their specific subcomponents.[43] In this respect, experiencing good emotions forms an integral part of the realization, for human beings as rational animals, of the basic motives of care for oneself and others of one's kind that makes up the two strands of appropriation.

However, in practice, this realization occurs very rarely, because of the prevalence of human corruption. The Stoics couple their positive theory of development with an analysis of the causes of ethical corruption, and this analysis shares certain features in common with the theory of successful development. Central to this analysis is the idea that there is a 'two-fold cause' of corruption; the factors are, in one account, 'the persuasiveness of things from without' and the 'teaching (or "influence") of our associates'.[44] The first point is the more important one. The idea, put very broadly, is that 'the things according to nature' (preferable

---

[39] See Ch. 2, text to nn. 74–83.   [40] See Cic. *Fin.* 3.21–2; also Ch. 4, text to nn. 105–13.

[41] See Cic. *Fin.* 3.20: 'the first appropriate act ... is to seize hold of the things according to nature and to banish their opposites ... 3.22: [right action] stimulates us to desire it far more strongly than we are stimulated by all the earlier objects' (LS 59 D (3, 6)).

[42] On this point, see Stob. 10, 2.88.8–12; also Brennan 2003: 265–74.

[43] On good emotions as part of happiness, see Ch. 1, text to nn. 120–31, esp. n. 127.

[44] D.L. 7.89, trans. Graver 2007: 154. In another version, we find 'the persuasiveness of impressions' (or 'the very nature of things') and 'the conversation of many people': Gal. *PHP* 5.5.14, 19.

indifferents), have a natural appeal for us, and generate a kind of pleasure that leads us to over-value them and regard them, wrongly, as good things, in the Stoic sense. This specious but natural appeal is described as the 'persuasiveness' (*pithanotēs*) of 'things from without', that is, of our experiences, which can also be described in Stoic terms as our 'impressions' (*phantasiai*), rather than our in-built nature.[45]

In the fullest account, by the late writer, Calcidius, this process is traced back to birth. The experience of birth involves pain, because of the transition from the warm and moist womb to coldness and dryness; the warm bath provided by the midwife produces a contrasting sensation of pleasure. This, in turn, creates 'a kind of natural belief that everything sweet and pleasurable is good, and that what brings pain is bad and to be avoided', a belief reinforced by later experience of the contrast between hunger and satisfaction, and between punishments and caresses. Subsequently, this evolves into the belief that everything 'appealing' (*blandum*) is good, and what is 'troublesome' (*laboriosum*) is bad. This leads, in turn, to an over-valuation of things that produce pleasure, including wealth, glory, and power, that is, broadly, preferred indifferents rather than virtue, which is the only basis for happiness. The formation of this mistaken set of beliefs is reinforced by what we hear from other people from childhood on, and by the judgements built into literature and other cultural media.[46] Calcidius' treatment is confirmed by two Ciceronian discussions which deploy similar ideas. In *On Laws* 1, Cicero identifies six factors which have a natural appeal (or are naturally unappealing), and which draw us to attach goodness or badness to them, namely, pleasure and pain, life and death, honour and disrepute. As in Calcidius, the mistaken judge-ments we form about these things are reinforced by social influences, from childhood onwards.[47] In *Tusculans* 3, Cicero focuses on a pair of contrasts which also appears in Calcidius' account: between popular renown, however misconceived, and glory based on genuine merit, and between honour and right actions, of which honour is the appropriate accompaniment. There is a natural tendency, even for the best of us, to misidentify these related factors; and, again, we are told that this mistake is confirmed by family and social influences, going back to early childhood.[48]

This strand in Stoic thinking on development might seem to bring their theory close to the Platonic-Aristotelian one, particularly as regards the significance of family and social influence on action-guiding beliefs, pleasure and pain, and

---

[45] See Gal. *PHP* 5.5.14–15, 19–20, criticizing the Stoic theory; also Graver 2007: 155. D.L. 7.89 contrasts 'the persuasiveness of things from outside' (i.e. our experience and our reactions to them), and 'the starting-points (*aphormai*) which nature provides'.

[46] Calcidius (4th cent. AD), commentary on Plato's *Timaeus*, 165–6 (*SVF* 3.229), quotations trans. Graver 2007: 156.

[47] Cicero, *On Laws* 1.31–2, 47; also Graver 2007: 158–61. Although this point is not explicitly ascribed to the Stoics, it is very close to their ideas.

[48] Cic. *Tusc.* 3.3–4; also Graver 2007: 161–3.

emotions.[49] However, Stoic thinking on this topic makes best sense when correlated with Stoic accounts of successful development and seen as identifying things that can go wrong in that process. For instance, in one account of appropriation, Diogenes Laertius points out that pleasure is 'a by-product (*epigennēma*), which supervenes when nature itself, on its own, seeks out and acquires what is suitable to [the animal's] constitution'.[50] Thus, the corruption of attitudes described by Calcidius stems from cases when, as with the midwife's bath, the pleasurable by-product, rather than the restoration of one's natural constitution, is taken to be the primary object to pursue. In Cicero's account of one strand in appropriation in *On Ends* 3.20–1, attraction to 'things according to nature' (preferred indifferents) and selection between them is presented as forming an integral part in natural human development and a key element in making progress towards virtue and happiness. However, here too there can occur a misidentification of value, in which the preferred indifferents, such as wealth and honour, are taken to be good things in themselves. The role of these indifferents in producing pleasure promotes this mistake, building on the earlier error about the value of pleasure.[51] Cicero's discussion in *On Duties* 1 of the core human inclinations underlying the development of the virtues includes a desire for independence and 'mastery' (*principatus*), which, if properly developed, leads to the virtue of greatness of mind (magnanimity), in which one rises above adversity with a view to performing worthwhile actions.[52] Calcidius' account highlights a desire for power (*potestas*), in itself, as a misguided expression of this natural human motive. Cicero's *On Duties* 2 brings out how the desire for honour can form part of a virtuous set of attitudes. In *Tusculans* 3, however, Cicero also points out that this desire can easily lead to a misguided desire for popular renown, as does Calcidius.[53] These various forms of error can all be seen as examples of 'the persuasiveness of things from without', which are also reinforced by 'the influence of our associates'.[54] They also make good sense as mistaken or failed versions of the process of ethical development which is seen as a natural expression of human nature, and in this sense they fit coherently with the distinctively Stoic view of this process, while marking a deflection from the standard pattern. Also, in *Tusculans* 4, Cicero discusses the (defective) patterns of reaction or 'predispositions' (*euemptosiai*) that make different people liable to be drawn to one or other preferred indifferent and hence susceptible to one or other bad emotion.[55] Cicero does not explicitly highlight the

---

[49] See Introd. to Part II, text to nn. 11–14.

[50] D.L. 7.86, IG: 113 (IG's inserted words in square brackets). The Stoic view is contrasted to the Epicurean view that pleasure is the primary object of motivation for animals (D.L. 7. 85, see also Cic. *Fin.* 1.29–30).

[51] See Calcidius' account (refs. in n. 46).   [52] Cic. *Off.* 1.13, 66; also Ch. 1, text to n. 163.

[53] See Cic. *Tusc.* 3.3–4, Calcidius, commentary on Plato's *Timaeus*, 166. On Stoic thinking on glory and Cicero's presentation of their ideas, see Long 1995: 224–33, and Ch. 2, text to nn. 183–94.

[54] See text to nn. 44–5.

[55] See Cic. *Tusc.* 4.24–76; Stob. 10e, 2.93.1–13; also Gill 2006: 261–6; Graver 2007: 164–7.

linkage between the emergence of bad emotions and the first strand of appropriation, as presented in *On Ends* 3.16–22. However, conceptually, the accounts of successful ethical development (as appropriation) and the two-fold cause of corruption are closely linked; and, taken together, they provide an explanatory framework for the two types of emotion and their role in human life.

These two forms of development also provide an explanatory framework for one of the most distinctive and suggestive features of the Stoic theory. This is the idea that bad emotions are 'irrational' and 'unnatural' and constitute a 'rejection' or 'disobedience of reason' of an exceptional kind.[56] The idea that—at least certain—emotions are intense and overwhelming is, of course, a commonplace one, which the Stoics incorporate in their theory. However, the Stoics also stress the further point that, in bad emotions, people sometimes 'reject' reason consciously and deliberately. They do so, in some cases, even when the reason that they reject is their own better judgement, and not only that of other people advising them.[57] This too is a recognizable feature of human experience, though a rather puzzling or paradoxical one. The Stoics underline this feature, and present it as characteristic of bad emotions, because, I think, they see it as an implicit acknowledgement of the misguided or mistaken character of bad emotions, even though those emotions also involve beliefs endorsed by the person concerned.[58]

This feature of Stoic thinking on emotion also makes good sense in the light of the combination of their ideas about appropriation and the two-fold cause of corruption. The process of corruption generates the mistaken valuation of indifferents that forms part of the belief-content of bad emotions; and these emotions, as a result, overwhelm the person concerned and lead her to reject reason. However, the person's own awareness of this rejection does not derive from this process of corruption. This awareness derives from the 'uncorrupted starting-points' which 'nature provides';[59] that is, from the 'preconceptions' of ethical notions which we all possess but fail to develop into full ethical understanding.[60] They also derive from the in-built motives to take care of ourselves and others of our kind which we also possess (4.2). Typically, we fail to express these motives in a way which would fulfil our human nature as rational and sociable and would provide the basis for achieving virtue and happiness. The process by which those starting-points are properly developed is that of appropriation. Although we fail to carry this process through to its conclusion, this process remains for us, according to Stoic theory, the full and normal expression of our human nature, viewed in the

---

[56] See text to nn. 24–6.

[57] See Stob. 10a, 2.89.4–90.6; Gal. *PHP* 4.2.10–12 (LS 65 J(1–4)). See also Gal. *PHP* 4.6.24–7, 29–34, 4.6.38–41. On this feature in Stoic thought, see Tieleman 2003: 170–8.

[58] This feature is often associated with *akrasia* (weakness of will). Thus, in effect, the Stoics see all bad emotions as, in this respect, akratic; see Inwood 1985: 162–5; Price 1995: 163–7; Gill 2006: 256–7.

[59] D.L. 7.89; also Stob. 5b8, 2.65.8 (LS 61 L): 'All human beings have the starting-points of virtue'.

[60] See Introd. to Part II, text to nn. 17–18.

context of nature as a whole.[61] This point, I think, underlies not just the Stoic characterization of bad emotions as 'irrational' and 'unnatural' but also the idea that our experience of these emotions constitutes a 'rejection of reason'. Although we lack a full-scale ancient psychological analysis of this 'rejection of reason', it is explicable in terms of the combination of the two forms of development, successful and failed, that our sources do discuss in some detail.[62]

A poetic exemplar often deployed by Stoic thinkers to illustrate their conception of bad emotion as the rejection of reason is Euripides' Medea. The Stoics are especially fascinated by the monologue of internal self-division (1021–80) that leads Medea to reinforce her decision to kill her children as a way of taking vengeance on her husband, Jason, for his abandonment of her and marriage to the daughter of the king of Corinth. A special focus of interest, for Chrysippus in particular, are the lines closing this monologue: 'I understand that what I am about to do to is bad (kaka), but anger (or "spirit", thumos) is master of my plans, anger which is responsible for the worst things in human life'.[63] The fascination of these lines for the Stoics does not only derive from the ethical misjudgement embodied in Medea's anger: as Epictetus puts it, she regarded taking vengeance as 'more beneficial' than saving her children's lives.[64] In addition, the lines vividly exhibit the 'irrational' and 'unnatural' character of (bad) emotion and the way that this can overwhelm someone's better judgement and lead her to 'reject reason', including her own. What is particularly striking is that Medea herself, even while powerfully affected by anger, recognizes this feature of her emotion. The preceding monologue (1021–77) powerfully conveys the fact that Medea is strongly activated by parental love (in Stoic terms, philostorgia, an emotion compatible with virtue) which co-exists, and conflicts, with her anger-driven desire for vengeance.[65] This maternal love underlies her recognition that her vengeance plan is 'bad', meaning bad for her, as well as for the children and her husband, and that anger is the greatest source of human troubles. From a Stoic standpoint, the internal conflict in the monologue and the articulation of this in the final lines bring out the irrational and unnatural character of bad emotion and of the rejection of reason it involves.[66] In developmental terms, it shows that, despite

---

[61] See 4.4, text to nn. 144–8; also Introd. to Part II, text to nn. 52–5.

[62] See Gill 2006: 257–8. On 'rejection of reason', see also Tieleman 2003: 170–8.

[63] Eur. Med. 1078–80; the second line is more often translated 'anger overcomes my reasonings' (and may have been understood in this way by Chrysippus); the final line means, literally, 'responsible for the greatest bad things for human beings'.

[64] Epict. Diss. 1.28.7.

[65] Philostorgia is, more precisely, love of philoi, 'friends or loved ones', especially one's relatives; but parental love is a central instance of this emotion. Parental love is also taken by Stoics as a prime example of the core motive to take care of others (see Ch. 4, text to nn. 47–56). Philostorgia is not listed among ancient Stoic specific 'good emotions' (Graver 2007: 85), but it is similar to the good emotions listed under 'wish', and is presented positively by Stoic thinkers such as Epictetus and Marcus Aurelius. On Medea's internal conflict, see Gill 1987, 1996: 216–26.

[66] See Gill 1983, 2006: 259–60; Graver 2007: 70–2.

the extreme corruption of Medea's character, displayed by her actions within the play and in her mythical biography,[67] she retains the capacity for ethical understanding and the correlated emotional response. Even Medea, on the verge of killing her children, exemplifies the Stoic belief that 'all humans have the starting points of virtue'[68] and that they retain these starting-points throughout their lives. Hence, although she is very far from having developed these starting-points by completing the two strands of ethical development as appropriation, she is at some level aware of not having done so, and thus of not having fulfilled her nature as a human being, that is, as rational and sociable, and motivated to take care of herself and others of her kind.

It is significant that Chrysippus seems to have cited the example of Medea in connection with the idea of the 'therapy', or cure, of (bad) emotions; and Epictetus also discusses Medea as a potential subject for therapy.[69] This linkage might seem surprising; in Euripides' play, Medea, despite her powerful misgivings, goes on to kill her children and to glory in her brutal triumph over Jason.[70] However, the features of Medea just discussed must be those which underlie the connection with therapy. The fact that, even Medea, the poetic epitome of emotional and physical violence, recognizes that what she plans to do is bad is taken as showing that she, like all other human beings, is potentially capable of responding to therapeutic treatment. She is capable of engaging in the two strands of appropriation that constitute the means by which people complete the ethical development that realizes their nature as human beings.[71] It is also noteworthy that Chrysippus sees the possibility of internal conflict in people's attitude to grief as a factor that can promote the therapeutic treatment of what the Stoics see as a defective emotion. Specifically, he proposes persuading people that grieving is not something they are ethically required to do, even if they still regard death as something that is bad (two ideas that are normally linked in the minds of grieving people).[72] More generally, it is significant that Chrysippus, as well as the later Stoic Posidonius, shows a special interest in various forms of internal conflict, especially those relating to grief. On the face of it, such conflicts pose a challenge to the Stoic (unified or 'cognitive') psychological model, which assumes that emotions (good

---

[67] Within the play, Medea contrives a horrible death for Jason's new bride and her father as well as killing her children. Previously, she has cut up the body of her brother and scattered it in the sea to delay her father's pursuit of her, when she runs away with Jason.

[68] See text to nn. 59–60.

[69] See Tieleman 2003: 170–8, 326, on Chrysippus' 'therapeutic book' and Medea. On Epict. *Diss.* 1.28.7–10, see Long 1996: 277–80, 2002: 255–6.

[70] E. *Med.* 1270a–82, 1351–404.

[71] On appropriation as a means of therapy of emotions, see text to nn. 109–13.

[72] Cic. *Tusc.* 3.76–7; also Gill 2010a: 291–3.

or bad) express beliefs.[73] However, it seems likely that Stoic interest in such cases reflects their view that bad emotions are, typically, linked with internal conflict of a kind that indicates scope for ethical development. The development of virtue, on the Stoic view, brings with it inner cohesion, structure, and wholeness; and the internal conflict that marks bad emotions indicates scope for development towards that kind of cohesion or harmony.

I noted earlier that the Stoics resemble Plato and Aristotle in linking the topic of emotions closely with ideas about ethical development, and in presenting the formation of virtue as bringing with it a certain kind of psychological cohesion or harmony. However, the Stoic version of this theme has certain distinctive features. One, already discussed, is the fact that the Stoic unified psychological model enables a more complete form of internal cohesion than is possible for the Platonic-Aristotelian, part-based, approach.[74] In addition, Stoic thinking about ethical development or corruption carries with it further implications for the question of cohesion or incoherence, which mark points of difference from Aristotle, in particular. As just illustrated, in the Stoic view, the emotional life of the defective person is, typically, marked by internal conflict and incoherence, deriving from the fact that she has developed in a way that deflects from the patterns of appropriation that would realize the natural pathway of human development.[75] By contrast, Aristotle envisages the possibility of stable but defective ethical character, except in the special case of those who are susceptible to *akrasia* or weakness of will.[76] By the same token, the Stoics see the virtuous person as marked, to an exceptional degree, by psychological cohesion. This reflects their view that this person has completed the developmental sequence which matches human nature at its best, which brings about virtue as a kind of internal order, structure, and wholeness, and which enables 'the life according to nature'.[77] A similar line of thought underlies the Stoic belief that all human beings retain the capacity for ethical development throughout their lives, and are thus, in principle, open to the 'therapy' of emotions.[78] By contrast, Aristotle sometimes suggests that defective development of character can lead to a point where people are no longer able to improve, ethically, even if they want to.[79] Thus, the Stoics,

---

[73] Gal. *PHP* 4.7.12–17, 24–41 (extracts in LS 65 O–P); also Gill 2010a: 293–5. Galen presents Chrysippus' theory as unable to explain such cases and Posidonius as rejecting, and replacing, Chrysippus' psychological approach with a Platonic-Aristotelian one; but I think both claims are seriously misleading (see Tieleman 2003: 250–64, esp. 259–61; Gill 2006: 275–9).

[74] See text to nn. 4–11.   [75] See text to nn. 56–62; also Gill 2006: 261–4.

[76] For the contrast between (consistent) self-indulgence and (inconsistent) *akrasia*, see Arist. *NE* 7.8; however, *NE* 9.4 suggests that people of defective character are, necessarily, internally conflicted. For features of Platonic thought close to the Stoic view that the bad are internally conflicted, see Gill 2006: 318–21.

[77] See Ch. 1, text to nn. 183–200. On the Stoic ideal of (virtue-based) psychological unity, see LS 61 A, F, M; also Sen. *Ep.* 120,10–11, 19–21; more broadly, Gill 2006: 75–96.

[78] See text to nn. 36–43, 69–73, 109–13, 118–23.

[79] Arist. *NE* 3.5, 1114a3–21; also Gill 2006: 105–6.

while sharing to some degree the Platonic-Aristotelian framework of thought on these topics, reframe it in a way that involves some strikingly distinctive features. As brought out later, these features prefigure modern thinking regarding the cognitive approach to emotions and cognitive psychotherapy; they also have implications for the Stoic contribution to modern virtue ethical thinking about ethical development.[80]

5.2 Emotional and Social Development

So far, I have focused on the relationship between the Stoic theory of emotion and the first strand of appropriation, centred on care of oneself and the development of ethical understanding. Are there also links between emotion and the second strand of appropriation, on care of others? There are several well-marked points of connection, considered shortly. In discussing these links, I aim to counteract a rather prominent scholarly line of thought on this topic. In this line of thought, Stoic thinking on emotions, coupled with certain other Stoic ideas, expresses a certain kind of detachment from other people, rather than engagement with them or care for them. There are several elements making up this view. First, it is supposed that the Stoic belief that the welfare of other people constitutes a preferred indifferent rather than an external good (in Aristotelian terms), involves a devaluation of relationships with other people. Sorabji, for instance, says:

> I am against the Stoic thesis of indifference, and I find this an unattractive side of their philosophy. It is better to treat the welfare of our own loved ones as something very much more than rightly preferred even though the Stoics are right that this means incurring the risk of loss and desolation.[81]

A second strand is the belief that the Stoic distinction between good and bad emotions provides a less powerful and convincing framework for characterizing interpersonal relationships than the Aristotelian distinction between virtuous and vicious versions of emotions.[82] Third, it is supposed that the Stoics' innovative stress on the cosmopolitanism and the kinship of human beings is antithetical to giving value to close relationships between family members and friends. Nussbaum maintains:

---

[80] See Ch. 8, text to nn. 13–16, 44–53, 115–23.

[81] Sorabji 2000: 173. See also Sorabji 2000: 168–80; Nussbaum 1994: 370, 2001: 359–62, 371–4. For a more positive view of Stoic thinking on people and preferred indifferents, see Reydams-Schils 2005: 59–69.

[82] For Aristotle's thinking on emotion, see *NE* 2.5–6. For analysis of the two ancient views of emotion, see Annas 1993: 53–66 (Annas does not put forward the scholarly view I am challenging).

...the most shocking aspect of Stoic 'indifference'—the injunction not to be upset at the death of loved ones, including even one's own children—should be seen as closely linked to the Stoics' egalitarian cosmopolitanism.[83]

These three points, taken together, suggest that Stoic therapy of the emotions is self-centred, in being directed, primarily, at producing peace of mind (absence of disturbing emotions) for the person concerned. They also imply that Stoic ethical thought in this area aims at producing a kind of self-sufficiency in which the person is detached from emotional involvement with specific other people.[84]

These views have been offered by substantial scholars and a full response would require a long discussion, for which space is lacking.[85] However, I note certain features of Stoic thinking highlighted elsewhere in this book, which point in a different direction.[86] On the first point, the discussion of Cicero's On Duties in Chapter 2 has brought out the extent to which Stoic thinking on indifferents, in connection with practical deliberation, is fully compatible with full-hearted engagement with interpersonal and social relationships.[87] The treatment of Stoic emotions so far has indicated some of the implications for well (or badly) conducted personal relationships[88] and this theme is explored further shortly. The discussion of the social strand in appropriation in Chapter 4 has shown that, leaving aside the special case of Zeno's Republic, the Stoic ideal of cosmopolitanism is regularly combined with recognizing parental love as a basic human motive, and one that can, if fully developed, form part of a virtuous human life.[89] In response to the scholarly view of the aim of Stoic therapy just outlined, two points are worth emphasizing. First, in Stoic thinking, as contrasted with Epicurean, peace of mind or freedom from disturbance does not constitute the goal of human life. The goal is, typically, defined as the life according to nature, whereas freedom from bad emotions and the experience of good emotions are corollaries of achieving the goal.[90] As suggested shortly, according to the Stoics, the therapy of emotions is brought about by ethical development, conceived as appropriation, and so its overall objective is the same as appropriation, that is, achieving virtue and virtue-based happiness (the life according to nature). Second, Stoic ethics does not work towards producing the self-sufficiency of an individual person, regarded

---

[83] Nussbaum 2001: 359.

[84] See Nussbaum 1994: 364–5, 370–1, 376, 394–5, 400–1; for related points, see Sorabji 2000: 169, 173.

[85] For a subtle and complex study of Aristotelian and Stoic views on the significance of interpersonal relationships for happiness, see Russell 2012: part 3 (discussed in Gill 2016c: 349–51).

[86] See also Gill 2019a; and Graver 2007: ch. 8.

[87] See Ch. 2, text to nn. 137–47, 158–60, 234–48.   [88] See text to nn. 32–3, 59–66.

[89] See Cic. Fin. 3.62–4, 68; also Ch. 4, text to nn. 180–95. On the evidential and interpretative problems posed by Zeno's Republic, see Ch. 4, text to nn. 225–6.

[90] See LS 60 J–M, and 1.3, also 1.4, text to 120–31, esp. 127, on types of good, including good emotions, that are corollaries of virtue. Contrast the Epicurean view of the goal as pleasure, understood as freedom from pain in body (aponia) and freedom from disturbance (ataraxia) in mind (LS 21 A–B).

as detached from other people. It works towards achieving virtue, which is conceived as self-sufficient for happiness.[91] Also, both virtue and happiness, as conceived in Stoic thought, have fundamentally other-directed dimensions.[92] So, in Stoic terms, aiming at the self-sufficiency of virtue for happiness does not entail detachment from other people. The view of the goal of therapy that I am challenging could, more reasonably, be attributed to Cicero, in his role as the author of the *Tusculans*, an important source for this topic.[93] However, Cicero does not in that work attribute this view to the Stoics;[94] and elsewhere his discussion of Stoic ethics maintains the correct relationship between the goal of life and its emotional corollaries.[95] So the view of Stoic therapy outlined earlier can be challenged on several grounds.

What are the explicit aims of Stoic therapy, as I see them, and how do these relate to those of ethical development conceived as appropriation? It is worth noting, first, that the idea of philosophy as the therapy of emotions, though it has Platonic antecedents,[96] seems to have been adopted first, in a thoroughgoing way, by Epicurus and then the Stoics. Subsequently, it became a widespread idea in Hellenistic and post-Hellenistic thought, and was adopted also by Platonic and Aristotelian thinkers. In deploying this term, ancient thinkers were, deliberately, appropriating the medical language of sickness and cure for their own objectives; in the case of Epicureans and Stoics, this was linked with an innovative concept of emotions (more specifically, bad emotions) as sicknesses needing to be cured.[97] This reflected the fact that, in ancient medicine proper, the emphasis was on bodily illness, so that the domain of (what we call) 'psychotherapy' was, relatively, open.[98] Chrysippus' 'therapeutic' book, that is, Book 4 of *On Emotions*, was an important and influential Stoic work in this genre. Though lost, its main contents and ideas have been reconstructed by Teun Tieleman, and this evidence offers our best available guide to the Stoic conception of therapy.[99]

---

[91] On virtue as the sole basis (self-sufficient) for happiness, see Ch. 1, text to nn. 37–61, 105–31, and 2.2. On self-sufficiency and relationships with others in Stoic ethics, see Graver 2007: 182–5.

[92] Both can be defined in terms of the combination of rationality and sociability, and care for others as well as oneself; see Ch. 1, text to nn. 73–82, 96–104, 153–208.

[93] See Cic. *Tusc.* 4.63, 5.1, 5.4, 5.121 (on Cicero's personal aim in the work, to promote peace of mind, esp. his own). See 5.28, 5.41–2, 5.47, 5.52–3 (on the ideal of emotional invulnerability at which he aims, signalled by repeated use of the phrase 'we want').

[94] See Cic. *Tusc.* 5.33–4, also 5.40, 5.43, 5.45, 5.47, which maintains the correct distinctions.

[95] See Cic. *Fin.* 3.22–5, on the goal, and 3.28–9 on the emotional corollaries of achieving the goal. On the difference between the standpoints of the two Ciceronian works, see Gill 2020.

[96] See Pl. *Charm* 156e–157c., *Grg.* 477e–479c, *Sph.* 227c–230e.

[97] See Gill 2010a: 246–51; also Nussbaum 1994, esp. chs. 4, 10. On Epicurean thinking on emotions, see LS 21, esp. B(1); also Annas 1993: 190–5; Gill 2006: 112–14, 452–3 and 2010b; Tsouna 2007.

[98] On mental illness in antiquity, see Harris 2013; Thumiger and Singer 2018. On the interplay between philosophy and medicine, see Harris 2013: part 4; Thumiger and Singer 2018: part 3. On ancient psychotherapy, see (in outline) Gill 1985a; in Galen and Stoicism: Gill 2010a: 300–29.

[99] Tieleman 2003: ch. 4, also p. 326. Seneca's *On Anger* is the only surviving Stoic work of therapy; see Nussbaum 1994: ch. 11; Gill 2010a: 297–300.

The latter part of the 'therapeutic' book centres on certain practical techniques recommended by Stoic thinkers for dealing with people affected by (bad) emotions. These include the feature noted earlier, of discouraging people distressed by grief from thinking that grieving is something they should regard as right or required. Chrysippus also advises not tackling people when in the grip of intense emotion but waiting till they are less agitated, and 'dwelling in advance' (*proendemein*) on future disasters so as to be emotionally prepared for them.[100] One interesting feature of our evidence for this side of Chrysippus' thought is that his approach emerges as rather pragmatic, ready to respond in a flexible way to variations in people's emotional states over time and also prepared to work with people with non-Stoic ethical standpoints.[101] This aspect of Chrysippus' thought is of particular interest to Cicero, perhaps because it matches Cicero's own practically directed and non-doctrinaire approach in the *Tusculans*.[102] However, it is clear from the full range of our sources that this is, in fact, a relatively minor strand in Chrysippus' book and his overall conception of therapy. The first and larger section of the book seems to have centred on the analogy between medical (physical) and philosophical (psychological) therapy. This includes a contrast between psychological health, strength, and beauty, features correlated with the good emotions, and bad emotions, viewed as feverish states, which reflect longer-term weaknesses or susceptibilities (*euemptōsiai*) to emotional fever. Another theme, already noted here, is the idea of (bad) emotion or passion as a 'rejection of reason', including the Medea example, and as a type of 'madness' or psychological blindness.[103] The prominence of these themes makes good sense in the context of Stoic thinking on good and bad emotions in general; and in this respect the 'therapeutic' book seems to have constituted a resumé and elaboration of the theory set out in the preceding books of Chrysippus' work. However, it is not entirely obvious how such ideas constitute a form of therapy or cure for bad emotions or how they promote this cure; and Chrysippus was sometimes criticized on this ground in antiquity.[104]

I have suggested elsewhere that the larger part of Chrysippus' 'therapeutic' book had two main functions, those of persuasive re-description and promoting understanding of the nature of bad emotions. Bad and good emotions are, systematically, re-described in the medical terms of illness (especially fever) and health. This is coupled with an analysis, based on the preceding books of *On Emotion*, of bad and good emotions as phenomena reflecting defective or excellent states of human

---

[100] See Gal. *PHP* 4.7.2–11 (on Posidonius, but the method was also Chrysippean); Cic. *Tusc.* 3.28–31, 3.52, 3.76–7; also Sorabji 2000: 176–8, 235–8; Graver 2007: 197–200; Gill 2010a: 289–93.

[101] Cic. *Tusc.* 3.77, 4.60; Origen, *Against Celsus* 8.51; also Tieleman 2003: 166–70; Gill 2010a: 291–2. See further Gill 2010a: 293–5 on Gal. *PHP* 4.7.13–17.

[102] See text to nn. 93–5.

[103] See Tieleman 2003: 326 (outline of topics); also, on these topics, Tieleman 2003: 140–66, 170–90.

[104] See Cic. *Tusc.* 4.9; also Gill 2010a: 281–2.

beings as psychological agents.[105] In what sense do these features constitute therapy of emotions? They encourage the person concerned to see (bad) emotions, including her own, as sicknesses, or at least the expression of sicknesses,[106] and thus to want to be 'cured' of them. They also enable her to understand the distinctive psychological character of bad emotions, including their heightened intensity or 'feverish' character, and the puzzling phenomenon of the 'rejection of reason', including one's own reason. Also, when combined with the theory of corruption discussed earlier in *On Emotions*,[107] they enable her to understand how she and others have come to experience these 'diseased' emotions rather than healthy ones. However, the question remains, even if someone has acquired this new understanding of her emotional state, how does she set about trying to develop psychological health? The practical techniques recommended towards the end of Chrysippus' 'therapeutic' book offer some starting-points;[108] but they do not provide a sustained course of treatment.

In fact, the connections brought out earlier between the Stoic theory of emotions (good and bad) and ethical development and corruption provide the answer. What promotes good emotions, or psychological health, is the process of ethical development, as standardly presented in Stoic ethics, namely, the two strands of appropriation, taken in combination. These two strands do not only inform beliefs and understanding; they also shape the whole pattern of motivation, including emotions.[109] The growth in understanding of how to select between indifferents in a virtuous way, and how to recognize the distinction in value between virtue and indifferents, naturally brings with it a change in the overall pattern of desires and emotions.[110] The same is true of the social strand of appropriation, which, as argued in Chapter 4, is closely interlocked with the first strand.[111] Understanding how to express the primary human motive of care for others in a way that is in line with virtue naturally brings with it a shift from bad to good emotions. There is no need, or scope, for a wholly separate, emotion-centred, developmental pathway, in the Stoic view. This approach explains, on the one hand, the criticism sometimes made in antiquity that the Stoics do not offer a distinct type of guidance on emotional therapy.[112] It also explains why, in Stoic writings on practical ethics, the theme of therapy of the emotions is often combined and integrated with other genres of practical ethics, including 'protreptic' (encouragement to engage in

---

[105] See Gill 2010a: 283–8. See also text to n. 97.

[106] Strictly speaking, the underlying dispositional state (*euemptōsia*) constitutes the sickness, of which the (occurrent) bad emotion is an expression (see Brennan 1998: 39–44); but our sources do not always observe this distinction.

[107] See 5.1, text to nn. 44–55. This seems to have formed part of Book 2; see Tieleman 2003: 132–9.

[108] See text to nn. 100–2.

[109] This reflects the Stoic unified psychological model, see text to nn. 9–17; on the general point, see also Gill 2006: 138–45.

[110] On this point, see n. 43.   [111] See 4.3 and 4.5, text to nn. 202–15.

[112] See text to n. 104.

philosophy) and 'advice' or positive guidance on how to act. All three genres of
practical ethics, along with other such genres, are deployed by Stoic thinkers as
means of promoting ethical development as appropriation, a process that will, by
itself, generate the therapy of bad emotions and the production of good ones.[113]

I now discuss a series of passages in Stoic writings which bring out, in various
ways, the linkage between development in social relationships and different types
of emotion, good or bad. These passages confirm the idea that ethical development, as appropriation, constitutes, in essence, the Stoic therapy of (bad) emotions. My first example is one discussed already, namely Medea. So far, I have
underlined her role, in Chrysippus especially, as someone who exemplifies the
'rejection of reason', including her own reason, and who thus illustrates the
instability and internal conflict inherent in bad emotion. What is also important
is that the internal conflict is generated by tension between her anger, her desire
for vengeance against Jason, and her parental love for her children. This point is
forcefully underlined in all three Stoic treatments. Chrysippus focuses on the final
lines of the monologue which, powerfully, articulates this conflict.[114] Epictetus
spells the fact that Medea's internal conflict arises from the fact that she regards
taking vengeance as 'more beneficial' (*sumphorōteron*) than saving her children's
lives.[115] In Seneca's tragedy, Medea, presented for most of the play as an unequivocally malevolent figure, fastens on infanticide as the ultimate act of criminality
(924–6). However, even this version of Medea finds that the power of maternal
love, though not stressed in her presentation so far in this play, forces itself on her
(926–33), generating internal conflict and a kind of madness, in which she
performs the act of infanticide.[116] The stress on this theme in all three versions
reflects the fact that parental love is regarded in Stoic thought as a basic motive in
all human beings (and animals), and as a salient indicator of the care for others of
one's kind that is one of two primary human motives.[117] Although Medea's
decision to kill her children to achieve her vengeance marks an extreme corruption of character, her internal conflict brings out the universality of this core
human motive and also shows that it remains present in all human beings,
however ethically depraved they seem to be.

But how, more exactly, does the characterization of Medea make sense in terms
of Stoic thinking on development and therapy? It is significant that Medea,
presented in this way, seems to have figured in Chrysippus' 'therapeutic'
book.[118] Should we take it that, in Stoic terms, Medea is a potential candidate

---

[113] On genres of practical ethics, see Gill 2003: 40–4; on the combination of protreptic and therapy
in Stoic writings, see Graver 2007: 207–10; on protreptic and elenctic styles in Epictetus, see Long 2002:
52–66. On Stoic ethical guidance and development, see Introd. to Part 2, text to nn. 49–51.
[114] See text to nn. 63–8.   [115] Epict. *Diss.* 1.28.7.
[116] See Sen. *Med.* 926–57 (internal conflict), 958–977 (quasi-madness and infanticide). See also Gill
1987, 2006: 424–5, 428–9, 430–2, 433–5.
[117] See Ch. 4, text to nn. 51–64, 174–90.   [118] See Tieleman 2003: 170–8.

for ethical development and therapy? In a sense, the answer is 'yes', since she demonstrates, as suggested earlier, that 'all human beings have the starting-points of virtue' and retain them all their lives.[119] Accordingly, Epictetus, in his version, considers how we would, on Stoic principles, set about dealing with Medea and putting her on the right path. The proper response to someone in her state is not to be angry with her, but to show that she is mistaken in her judgements about what is 'more beneficial', and to urge her to examine her 'impressions' (assumptions or beliefs about value), since these are the factors that lead to bad emotions and the disastrous actions that flow from them. Epictetus' response reflects the Stoic unified psychological model as well as Stoic convictions about the universality of the scope for therapy and ethical development.[120] However, Stoic thinking on these topics also recognizes that Medea is an, exceptionally, hardened (or, in Stoic terms, 'callused') case of bad development,[121] as well as acknowledging the difficulty in applying therapy to someone while she is in the grip of intense (bad) emotion.[122] Hence, in effect, the main targets for therapy are the readers of Stoic writings on this subject, for whom Medea functions as an extreme, cautionary example. For an observer, Medea's condition, graphically, displays the negative features of bad emotions underlined in Chrysippus' 'therapeutic' book. These include the 'feverishness' and internal conflict, as well as the terrible actions, that constitute features that are bad for her as well as for others.[123] At the same time, in highlighting the fact that Medea is still subject to the basic motive of parental love, and that this generates intense conflict, these representations highlight a pathway towards a more normal and 'natural' form of human life that the observer can take; they also stimulate the desire to be 'purged' of Medea-like internal conflict. Thus, through a combination of negative, or cautionary, and potentially positive aspects, the Stoic presentations of Medea play a therapeutic role in promoting, by contrast, a developmental route towards virtue and virtue-based happiness, that is, the two strands of appropriation.

My second example is constituted by two versions of a contrast between bad and good emotions aroused by other people, a contrast which in each case implies Stoic thinking on social appropriation. The first version consists in a dialogue between Epictetus and the father of a sick daughter (1.11). The father is so upset by his daughter's illness that he feels he must leave home and go off elsewhere to

---

[119] See LS 61 L; and text to nn. 38–9.

[120] Epict. *Diss.* 1.28.8–9 (for this kind of response to wrongdoing, see also text to nn. 127–36). See also Long 1996: 277–80, 2002: 76–7. On Epictetus and Stoic unified psychology, see Brennan 2003: 265–9.

[121] For this image applied to dispositions to (bad) emotions (or pychological 'sicknesses'), see Epict. 2.18.8–10, Cic. *Tusc.* 4.24–5; also Graver 2007: 165–7. On this theme in Chrysippus' 'therapeutic' book, see Tieleman 2003: 186–7, 326.

[122] On this (Chrysippean) point, see Gal. *PHP* 4.7.28–31, Cic. *Tusc.* 4.78; also Gill 2010a: 289; Tieleman 2003: 130–1.

[123] See text to nn. 63–8.

ease his anxiety. When challenged by Epictetus, he defends himself by saying that his response is natural, given his fatherly concern. Epictetus, in a quasi-Socratic dialogue, persuades him that, on the contrary, the natural thing to do, the act that would best express his parental love (*philostorgia*), is to stay at his daughter's bedside, help to look after her, and encourage her recovery.[124] The discourse centres on the question of what kind of emotion counts as natural. The father presents as natural a rather panicky, and essentially self-directed, fear, that is, in Stoic terms, a bad (ethically misguided emotion). Although the father's response indicates the underlying basic human motive of parental love, it also shows a failure to express this motive in a mature and reasoned way that would benefit his daughter and the household generally, which is what Epictetus is urging him to do. Epictetus argues that the emotion which is natural in that situation is parental love expressed in a way that is consistent with virtuous, and with other-benefiting, actions and attitudes.[125] The exchange between them implies several features of Stoic thinking about ethical development as appropriation. As his bad emotion indicates, the father has failed to develop ethically, especially in the second, social strand of appropriation; but, since he, like all other human beings, can potentially do so, Epictetus uses the exchange to urge him to act in a way that would mark progress in this direction. The discourse can also be understood in therapeutic terms. Epictetus is aiming to 'purge' the father of the bad emotion he displays, and to promote a good emotion (properly expressed parental love). In each case, in line with Stoic theory, the emotion displayed depends on the beliefs underlying the emotion, which are also indicated in the actions of the person involved.[126]

The second version of this theme considered here is 2.1 of Marcus' *Meditations*. Marcus warns himself that during the day he will encounter people who are 'meddling, ungrateful, violent, treacherous, envious, and unsociable'.[127] A common reaction to such people (one that many people would regard as 'natural') would be to display what are sometimes called 'reactive attitudes', such as anger and resentment. However, Marcus urges on himself a different response.[128] This is to recognize that the behaviour and emotions of such people reflect misunderstanding of what is really good in human life, and what

[124] See Epict. *Diss.* 1.11.5–15, centred on the question of what is natural, and 1.16–26, explaining what is natural by reference to what expresses love of kin (see also Long 2002: 77–9). On *philostorgia*, i.e. affection esp. for one's kin, see n. 65.

[125] The focus on what is natural reflects the central role of nature in Stoic ethics (Ch. 3). Epictetus' view implies the standard Stoic idea that virtue enables 'the life according to nature' (combining rationality and sociability as well as care for oneself and others); it also implies that ethical development as appropriation is natural (in line with human nature at its best).

[126] On emotions and the Stoic unified psychological model, see text to nn. 10–17.

[127] M. A. 2.1.1, all translations from this passage taken from Gill 2013a: see also commentary in Gill 2013a: 88.

[128] Marcus refers to this kind of response in 2.1.3, 2.1.5. On 'reactive attitudes' such as anger and resentment, see Strawson 1974; for the idea that Stoicism recommends, in Strawson's terms, 'objective', rather than 'reactive' attitudes, see Gill 2013a: xlviii–xlix and refs. there.

constitutes real harm or wrongdoing.[129] The response recommended also acknowledges that these people, like all human beings, are fellow-members of the
brotherhood (or sisterhood) of humankind, and have a shared, constitutional
capacity for rationality and sociability.[130] Recognizing these two important points
is presented as counteracting anger or hatred directed at such people. Although
Marcus does not here specify the kind of good emotion that this response would
bring with it, in similar passages elsewhere, he urges himself to show *eumeneia*
('lasting good intent').[131] So in this passage too (and related passages),[132] we find a
clear contrast between two types of emotion, the bad one (anger and hatred) that
Marcus aims to counteract in himself, and the good emotion of good will or good
intent that he encourages. The occurrence of both types of emotion is presented as
dependent on beliefs and on the extent to which the person concerned has made
progress in ethical development in the two strands of appropriation. The response
that Marcus encourages in himself is one that depends on grasping two key
features of these strands. One is the recognition that what is good consists in
virtue, as expressed in right action, rather than preferred indifferents. This is the
type of ethical understanding that forms the culminating stage of the first strand in
appropriation, a stage that the people described (as 'meddling' and so on) have not
reached.[133] The other feature is the recognition that all human beings, as rational
and sociable, form part of a larger family or co-citizenship group, one of the main
features of the second, social, strand of appropriation.[134] The passage brings out
very clearly the Stoic view that the type of emotions we have depends on our
beliefs about value and human relationships, and on the level of ethical development reached, a level which is correlated with these beliefs.[135] The passage is also
typical of the kind of guidance offered in writings in Stoic practical ethics, in
aiming at promoting ethical development which carries with it a change in
patterns of emotional response.[136]

I now highlight a second feature of Marcus' *Meditations*, which is also relevant
to the linkage between emotions and ethical development. This feature falls within
the exceptional Book 1 of the *Meditations*. This book encapsulates, in seventeen
passages of varying length, the qualities that Marcus has learnt to value throughout his life from specific people (and the gods), which have contributed to his own

---

[129] M. A. 2.1.3, esp. 'the nature of the good and ... that it is the right ... I cannot be harmed by any of them, as no one will involve me in what is wrong'.
[130] M. A. 2.1.3, esp. 'he is related to me ... because he shares the same mind and portion of divinity'; 2.1.4: 'We were born for cooperation, like feet, like hands'.
[131] See M. A. 9.11, 9.42.4–5, 10.36.4, 6; also Gill 2016b: 158. For this good emotion, see Graver 2007: 58.
[132] See also M. A. 6.27, 11.18.15–23, and passages in n. 131. Epict. *Diss.* 1.28.8 expresses a similar idea (see also Long 2002: 250–2).
[133] See Cic. *Fin.* 3.21 (also 4.4, text to nn. 105–7).
[134] See Cic. *Fin.* 3.63–4 (also 4.5, text to nn. 174–88).   [135] See text to nn. 28–43.
[136] On M. A. and change in emotional patterns, see Gill 2013a: xlvii–xlix. See also Introd. to Part II, text to nn. 50–1.

ethical development. Although the book is unique in its format and in reviewing one's own life in this way, the idea that we acquire ethical understanding from observing, or interacting with, other people also plays a prominent role in Seneca's letter 120.[137] The feature underlined here is the place given to emotions in some of the passages, notably in two of the longer ones, reviewing the valuable qualities of certain philosophical teachers who have influenced Marcus' development.[138] The passages itemize briefly qualities that Marcus has learnt to value. Although the account is not analytic in form, Marcus' selection and juxtaposition of qualities has its own significance and suggestiveness, in the context of Stoic ethical thinking.

Three types of quality recur throughout Book 1. One type relates to ethical understanding or judgement; another type is of quality of interpersonal engagement. The third type is the quality of the pattern of emotional experience. Since the qualities are presented as admirable, the first two types can be considered as virtues, or, in some cases, virtuous (or virtue-like) forms of action.[139] The third type of quality consists in patterns of good emotion; these evoke emotional characteristics standardly valued in Stoic thought, and are sometimes close to the features highlighted in the main ancient source on specific good emotions.[140] The first two types of quality relate closely to the two strands of ethical development as appropriation. The third, emotional, type is conceived, in Stoic thought, as dependent on the first two; if someone develops in understanding and mode of social interaction, this carries with it a progressive change of emotional register. This point is implicit in the main accounts of appropriation and of (good and bad) emotions.[141] Marcus' passages do not present emotional qualities, systematically, as dependent on the other two types; but, in interweaving these three types of quality, Marcus implies a close linkage between them, and it seems likely that he presupposes the causal relationship between them that is standard in Stoic thinking.

Two of these passages can illustrate these points, those devoted to the influence of two Stoic teachers, Apollonius and Sextus.[142] The passage on Apollonius (1.8) begins with qualities of mind or judgement: 'leaving nothing to the dice of fortune' (1.8.1) and always taking 'as one's guide nothing but reason' (1.8.2). Then follow emotional qualities: 'to be always the same, in severe pain, at the loss of a child, during long illnesses' (1.8.3); and the recognition that 'the same person can be

---

[137] See Gill 2013a: lxxv–lxxxiv; Sen. *Ep.* 120.4–5, 8–9 (excerpts in LS 60 E(6–7)); also Inwood 2005: 283–96, 2007: 324–6.

[138] I focus here on M. A. 1.8–9, thought the features highlighted here appear in Book I more generally. See 1.14–15, for similar 'character-sketches' of politicians; also Gill 2013a: 61–3, 67–71, for commentary on these four passages.

[139] M. A. Book 1 combines admirable characteristics exhibited by specific individuals and descriptions of the characteristic behaviour of those individuals; see Gill 2013a: lxxv.

[140] See esp. M. A. 1.9.9 and n. 146.   [141] See text to nn. 32–43.

[142] On these figures, see Gill 2013a: 61–3; the following translations are based on Gill 2013a.

both very intense and yet also relaxed' (1.8.4). Finally, we have interpersonal qualities: patience 'in giving explanations' (as a teacher, presumably, 1.8.5); modesty as regards his intellectual expertise and skill in communication (1.8.7); nicely judged responses to favours from his friends (1.8.8). In Sextus' case (1.9), the focus is on interpersonal qualities. However, the opening points include 'the idea of living according to nature' (the Stoic conception of happiness 1.9.3); and the passage also includes 'a secure and methodical discovery and organization of the principles necessary for life' (1.9.8). Thus, an overarching ethical ideal ('the life according to nature') and qualities of mind and understanding play a significant role. The numerous comments on his interpersonal qualities sometimes have an emotional dimension.[143] One, striking, comment centres solely on his pattern of emotions: he never gave 'the impression of anger or any other passion but [was] at once completely free of passion (*apathestaton*) and yet full of affection for others (*philostorgotaton*)' (1.9.9).

The passages in Book 1, here and elsewhere, are not organized in a systematic or analytic way; some of the qualities or themes identified have a clear Stoic reson- ance, but not all of them.[144] However, the content of these passages takes on added significance in the light of Stoic thinking on the relationship between ethical development and emotions and can also contribute to our understanding of this relationship. The figures in 1.8–9 are presented as, though not Stoic wise people, illustrative of wise (or quasi-wise) characteristics.[145] They are presented as people who are well advanced in the two strands of ethical development as appropriation, in their understanding of value and their ability to express the primary human motive of care for others in a mature, rational, and socially engaged, benevolent, and perceptive way. The pattern of emotions whose importance they convey also reflects an advanced level of ethical development. Both figures are presented as free from (bad) emotions or passions, and as exhibiting attitudes similar to the good emotions (such as good will) included in the main ancient Stoic source for specific good emotions.[146] The seamless interlinking of these three kinds of quality and the consistency between the different aspects of characterization imply the

---

[143] See 1.9.4: 'seriousness without affectation'; (1.9.6) 'patience (*to anektikon*) with ordinary people…'; 1.9.7: 'his company was more pleasant' (*prosēnesteran*).

[144] On the exemplary style of M. A. Book 1, which combines Stoic and broader cultural connota- tions, see Gill 2013a: lxxix–lxxxi.

[145] For instance, 'secure and methodical discovery of the principles necessary for life' evokes the descriptions of the wise person's 'dialectical virtue' (D.L. 7.46–8, LS 31 B; also Giavatto 2008: ch. 2). The description of the interpersonal skill and charm of both people evokes similar characterization of the wise person (Stob. 11m, 2.108.5–11; also Gill 2013a: 62). On specific people, used as quasi-wise exemplars, see Inwood 2005: 286–7, 2007: 325–6 (Fabricius and Horatius Cocles), on Sen. *Ep.* 120.6–7.

[146] See M. A. 1.8.3; 1.9.9, cited in the preceding para. The positive, other-benefiting attitudes (1.8.5. 1.9.5, 1.9.7. 1.9.9–10, including 'full of affection for other people' (*philostorgotaton*), also evoke Stoic good emotions such as good intent or good will (Andronicus, *On Passions* 6, S.V.F. 3.432, Graver 2007: 58); see also text to nn. 32–5. On similarities between Marcus' vocabulary and that of the Andronicus passage, see Gill 2016b: 150–3.

standard Stoic view that emotions derive from judgements and that their quality reflects the degree of ethical development reached. In these ways, Marcus' exemplary character-sketches support and supplement the linkage accentuated here between ethical development, including the social strand, and good emotions, as well as freedom from bad ones.

5.3 Stoic Detachment?

So far, this discussion has found little evidence that supports the view outlined earlier, according to which the Stoic therapy of the emotions works towards producing (individual) self-sufficiency and detachment from other people.[147] However, there is one passage of Epictetus, in two versions, that has attracted widespread attention, and that seems to support this view. Here it is in the version given in the *Discourses* (3.24.88, trans. Hard 2014), presumably the original one:

> From now on, whenever you take delight in anything, call to mind the opposite impression: what harm is there in your saying beneath your breath as you're kissing your child, 'Tomorrow you'll die'? Or similarly to your friend, 'Tomorrow you'll go abroad, or I will, and we'll never see each other again'.
>
> 'But these are words of bad omen'.

As indicated by the final words, those of the interlocutor, the comment is, and is meant to be, troubling or shocking. This passage, or, more often, the version given in *Handbook* 3, is widely taken, on its own, as expressing an ethic of emotional detachment. However, I think that, if placed in the context of the whole discourse (3.24), and, more broadly, Stoic thinking of a similar kind, the passage makes sense as part of a framework of ideas which conveys a very different message. The main theme of this framework, as illustrated in the preceding section (5.2), is that ethical development, as expressed in the two strands of appropriation, naturally carries with it the 'therapy' of (bad) emotions and a pattern of good emotions, including well-judged good will or good intent towards others. I approach the interpretation of the passage in stages, first by highlighting parallel expressions of this strategy in Seneca and Marcus, and then by a reading of 3.24 as a whole. Even when contextualized in this way, the passage remains (like much else in Epictetus) challenging and provocative.[148] However, it makes better sense when considered as part of the broader Stoic ethical framework. This framework, as was widely recognized in antiquity, and as I have stressed here, is conspicuous for the

---

[147] See text to nn. 81–4.
[148] On Epictetus' teaching style, as expressed in the *Discourses*, see Long 2002: 52–66.

promotion of (virtue-based) interpersonal and social engagement, rather than detachment.[149]

I begin by outlining a set of Stoic ideas, linked with this overall framework, which underpin Seneca's dialogue, On Peace of Mind, as well as Epictetus, Discourses 3.24, and certain themes in Marcus' Meditations. There are three main, interconnected ideas. The first, very general, idea is that we should conceive our lives as a whole as a project of ongoing ethical development, towards virtue and virtue-based happiness. This conception of a properly conducted human life is one of the distinctive features of Stoic thinking about ethical development outlined earlier.[150] The second idea reformulates the first, general, one in a more specific form. The most fully worked-out version of this second idea is the theory of the four roles or personae in Cicero's On Duties. This theory presupposes the conception of one's life as a project in ethical development and adds that we should deploy the four roles as normative reference points for this project. The four roles are: (1) our common human nature, seen as constitutionally capable of developing and exercising the virtues; (2) our specific individual talents and inclinations; (3) our given social role or context; and (4) our chosen career or life-path. The overall advice is that we should aim to harmonize our performance of these four roles, in order to give our lives coherence and consistency as vehicles of working towards virtue and virtue-based happiness.[151] The third idea builds on the first two. This third theme is that, having selected a specific career or pathway, as a vehicle for ethical development, we should persist in maintaining this pathway, as far as possible, throughout our lives, in spite of contingent circumstances that draw us in competing directions. The claim is that doing so is crucial for achieving peace of mind or, put differently, freedom from bad emotions and a consistent pattern of good emotions. As already brought out here, what makes the difference between good and bad emotions is ethical development, as formulated in the two strands of appropriation.[152] What is contributed by the combination of the second and third ideas is the thought that ethical development can be taken forward most effectively by consistent adherence to a properly chosen career or pathway. Doing so enables us better to confront and surmount problems that all human lives are subject to, including the prospect or actuality of death (our own or that of others), without becoming liable to ethical misjudgements and correlated bad emotions.

---

[149] On this side of Stoic ethics, see esp. 2.4–5 and 4.5–6. The Epicureans, rather than the Stoics, were criticized on this ground in antiquity (not always fairly), especially because of their recommendation to avoid engagement in political life (LS 22, esp. 22 D(1) and Q(5)).

[150] See Introd. to Part II, text to nn. 52–4. For this view of one's life, see (in M. A.) Gill 2013a: xxxiv–xlix.

[151] See Cic. Off. 1.107–21; also Ch. 2, text to n. 133. For links with earlier Stoic ideas of this kind, see Tieleman 2007: 130–40; also Epict. 1.2, 2.10, and Gill 1988.

[152] See text to nn. 32–43.

Seneca's dialogue, *On Peace of Mind*, offers a clear expression of these themes. The first half is centred on the choice of a pathway for life, and the second half gives advice on responding to challenges, especially the prospect of death, with actions and attitudes that do not bring with them bad emotions and the associated internal conflicts and disturbances. The dialogue is presented as a therapeutic one, especially at the start, with Seneca, the main speaker, as the doctor, and Serenus, the (younger) interlocutor as the patient.[153] Serenus' emotional condition is one that makes good sense in the light of the themes just outlined. He is finding difficulty in determining, and carrying through, a pathway that can serve as a vehicle for a worthwhile life, one that can work consistently towards virtue. He finds himself drawn in competing directions, and experiences the emotional fluctuation and internal conflict that Stoics see as characteristic of bad emotions. In particular, he is conscious of his failure to stick to a pathway that would serve as a vehicle for virtue and hence confer good emotions.[154] The 'therapy' offered to Serenus takes the form of advice on a choice of pathway, designed to provide such a vehicle.[155] The advice offered by Athenodorus, another Stoic teacher, reported here, is that Serenus should aim at the public (political) career to which he is drawn, and which Stoic ethics, typically, recommends for those capable of it. If circumstances make this career dangerous or impossible, he should retreat to private life, but he should use this form of life as a way of playing a constructive, other-benefiting role, for instance as an ethical teacher.[156] Seneca's advice constitutes a modified version of this recommendation. Serenus should, as far as possible, stick to his original, political, aim; if forced by circumstances to retreat to private life, he should still use his private role as a way of expressing his public views and in that sense play a political role, as well as using his private role to benefit others. Seneca cites the conduct of Socrates, who engaged in a kind of passive resistance under the Thirty Tyrants in Athens, as an exemplar for this course of action.[157] In both types of advice, the importance of using the pathway chosen as a means of progress towards virtue is repeatedly underlined.[158]

The link with the theory of the four roles comes out especially in this comment: 'We must examine ourselves before all else (*inspicere ... nosmet ipsos*), then the business (*negotia*) we are going to tackle, then the people for whom or with whom we will take it on'. This passage refers to what are, in *On Duties*, the second role (one's individual talents and inclinations), and the fourth (the career or pathway,

---

[153] *De Tranquillitate Animi* (*TA*), 1.1, 1.17, 2.1–2, 2.5. On this work and the ancient therapy of emotions, see Gill 2013b: 354–7; viewed alongside other ancient writings on peace of mind, see Gill 1994: 4616–24.

[154] Sen. *TA* 1.3–17, 2.1–15.

[155] On the combination of therapy and advice in Stoic ethical guidance, see text to n. 113; also Gill 2013b: 356–7.

[156] Sen. *TA* 3.1–8 (on Stoic advice as, typically, to engage in public life, 1.10).

[157] Sen. *TA* 4.1–8, 5.1–3.   [158] Sen. *TA* 3.3, 3.6, 4.1, 4.4, 4.7.

here 'business' or project).[159] The importance of the first role (common human nature, as rational and sociable and potentially capable of virtue) has just been underlined, and the significance of one's social context (the third role) is implied throughout. As in *On Duties*, achieving consistency between these roles is presented as a precondition for maintaining coherence and stability in one's way of life, affecting both actions and emotions.[160] The other factor mentioned here, those benefited by the pathway we undertake, does not fall under the four Ciceronian roles but is discussed in *On Duties*, in connection with determining which 'appropriate action' is 'right' and in line with the virtues.[161] In the second half of the work (chapters 8–17), the theme of the importance of choice of pathway is less prominent, though it is not wholly absent.[162] The emphasis falls on the idea that, if we are to progress through life without emotional disturbance, we need to prepare ourselves for the disasters and contingencies that are potentially present in any human life, including loss of possessions, and, particularly for those who engage in politics under the Roman emperors in the first century AD, unpredictable, arbitrary, and brutal execution.[163] In this connection, we encounter themes common in Stoic discussions of emotional therapy and related topics, including mental preparation for disaster, wishing 'with reservation', and idealization of wise or quasi-wise figures who confront death without experiencing passion or bad emotions.[164]

There is also stress on self-sufficiency;[165] and it might seem that this part of the work lends support to the view outlined earlier with reference to Sorabji and Nussbaum. According to this view, Stoic therapy, and Stoic ethics generally, aim at emotional self-sufficiency, achieved in part by detachment from close relationships with other people, including one's own family.[166] However, on closer inspection, there is little here to support this view. Where detachment is encouraged, it is from things such as excessive wealth or political power, as objects aimed at for their own sake.[167] There is no parallel for the problematic Epictetus passage cited earlier and discussed shortly.[168] Although Seneca does not spell out at a general level the linkage between the two major themes of the work (choice of a

---

[159] Sen. *TA* 6.1, trans. Fantham in Fantham et al 2014; also *TA* 6.2–3; Cic. *Off.* 1.107–21.

[160] Sen. *TA* 6.2–3; Cic. *Off.* 1.110–14; on the linkage between achieving what is 'fitting' (*decorum*) and the proper management of emotions, see Cic. *Off.* 1.101–3.

[161] Sen. *TA* 7.1–6; Cic. *Fin.* 1.44–9; also Ch. 2, text to nn. 139–47.

[162] Sen. *TA* 12.1–7, esp. 12.1, 12.5, stressing the importance of focusing on a single, worthwhile project.

[163] Sen. *TA* 8–9, on wealth and its potential loss; on facing death, *TA* 11, esp. 11.3, including death at the hands of the emperor Gaius (Caligula), 11.10, 14.4–10, or Tiberius (11.11).

[164] Sen. *TA* 11.6–7 (preparation for disaster; also Cic. *Tusc.* 3.52); Sen. *TA* 13.2–3 (wishing with reservation; also Inwood 1985: 119–26); Sen. *TA* 11.3, 14.4–10 (exemplars of fortitude; also Gill 1994: 4617–18, 4619–20, 4622).

[165] Sen. *TA* 9.1–3, 11.1–3, 14.1–3, 14.10.   [166] See text to nn. 81–4.

[167] Sen. *TA* 8.1–9, 9.1–7 (wealth); 11.9–12 (wealth and power).

[168] Epict. *Diss.* 3.24.88 (or *Handbook* 3); see text to n. 147 and nn. 187–209.

pathway in life and facing disaster with equanimity),[169] this connection is implicit in his choice of exemplars. These include, as well as Socrates, figures such as Cato and Regulus. These are all figures whose deaths are presented in Stoic writings as (willingly accepted or chosen) consequences of carrying through consistently a specific type of socially beneficial and ethically justified role.[170] As brought out earlier, good emotions, as contrasted with bad ones, are presented in Stoic thought as a by-product of completing the two strands of ethical development as appropriation, leading to ethical understanding and to relationships that express care for others in the light of this understanding.[171] What is implied by the complex of themes in Seneca's *On Peace of Mind*, and especially by these exemplars, is a further element in this Stoic framework. Just as the social role is chosen as a vehicle for ethical development, so dying is accepted as a corollary, and in a sense a continuation, of carrying out the social role. Although these figures, like all human beings, have to face their own death for themselves and cannot share it,[172] their death is, none the less, conceived as part of the working through of a pathway that benefits others as well as themselves. This recognition contributes to the emotional quality of their response and underlies the fact that these figures experience good emotions or peace of mind, rather than passions based on ethical error.

Before turning to Epictetus, I refer briefly to Marcus' *Meditations*, since this work illustrates very clearly the features just highlighted in Seneca. Marcus conveys powerfully the idea of life as a project in ongoing ethical development and of one's specific pathway as a vehicle for this development. He also conveys the idea that facing one's own future or present death can represent a continuation and, in a sense, the culmination of this project.[173] Two further aspects of his attitude to his own death can be linked with this idea. Marcus aspires to confront death in a state of mind that includes two emotional responses not conventionally associated with dying: joy and good will, both of which count in Stoic thought as good emotions.[174] One of the forms of joy listed in our main ancient Stoic source for specific good emotions is 'joy in the progress and self-sufficiency of the whole' (that is, joy in the universe, viewed as a providential whole).[175] Marcus' reiterated stress on accepting the naturalness of death, as an expression of the providential workings of universal nature, reflects this idea.[176] Also, Marcus repeatedly couples his readiness for death with good will (*eumeneia*) towards those with whom he has shared his life and whom he has aimed to benefit, even those who are critical of

---

[169] For these themes as dominant in Sen. *TA*, see text to nn. 153–64.

[170] Sen. *TA* 5.13 (Socrates), 16.1–2 (Cato), 16.4 (Cato and Regulus). On Cato, see Cic. *Off.* 1.112, on Regulus, Cic. *Off.* 3.99–110 (also Ch. 2, text to nn. 234–48).

[171] See text to nn. 32–43; also, on the two strands of ethical development and their combination, 4.5, text to nn. 202–15.

[172] This point is brought out vividly by the death of Julius Canus in Sen. *TA* 14.4–10.

[173] See Gill 2013a: xxxv–xlvi, li–lii.   [174] On these good emotions, see D.L. 7.115 (LS 65F).

[175] Andronicus, *On Emotions* 6 (*SVF* 3.432); also Graver 2007: 58.

[176] M. A. 2.3, 2.11.1–2, 2.17.4, 5.4, 12.23, 12.36.; also Gill 2016b: 156.

him.[177] These emotional reactions are seen in Stoic ethics as corollaries of completing the two strands of ethical development as appropriation. Hence, Marcus' linkage between these forms of good emotion and the idea of viewing death as the culmination of his specific pathway in life makes sense in terms of the Stoic framework highlighted here.

These three passages illustrate aspects of this complex of ideas:

> At every hour, give your full concentration, as a Roman and a man, to carrying out the task in hand with a scrupulous and unaffected dignity and affectionate concern for others (*philostorgia*) and freedom and justice, and give yourself space from all other concerns. You will give yourself this if you carry out each act as if it were the last of your life, freed from all randomness and passionate (*empathous*) deviation from the rule of reason and from pretence and self-love and dissatisfaction with what has been allotted to you (2.5.1–2).

> Let the god within you be the overseer of a creature who is manly, mature, a statesman, a Roman, and a ruler who has taken up his post, waiting for the signal to quit life and ready to be released, without the need of an oath or someone else as a witness. Maintain an inner joy … (3.5.1–3)

> I am leaving the kind of life in which even those who were close to me, for whom I toiled, prayed and took so much care, even they want to see an end of me … [addressing himself] you must not, however, on that account, depart thinking less kindly (*eumenēs*) of them, but preserve your true character as one who is friendly, well-intentioned, and gracious (*philos, eunous, hileōs*) (10.36.4, 6).[178]

The first and second passages express the idea that one's specific, chosen pathway can serve as a vehicle for progress towards exercising the virtues and expressing these in one's relationships with other people. Both passages, along with the third, also convey the thought that one should prepare oneself for death in the conviction that it represents a continuation of this process. Dying and facing death are seen as a means of expressing the same virtues and attitudes towards others and the same state of mind, that is, the 'good emotions' of good will towards others and joyful acceptance of the place of one's finite, human life within the larger context of nature as a whole.

This complex of ideas also figures in Epictetus, *Discourses* 3.24, and forms the broader context for the lines about anticipating the death of your child, cited earlier (3.24.88).[179] 3.24 consists in a dialogue with a former student of Epictetus

---

[177] M. A. 3.16.4, 8.47.5, 10.36.4, 6; also Gill 2016b: 157–8.
[178] First two quotations trans. Gill 2013a; third quotation trans. Hard 2011.
[179] See text to n. 147.

from Athens, now based in Rome, where he is a senator for life and fully engaged in public affairs.[180] A recurrent theme is the concern of the interlocutor about leaving his home city in order to carry out his work. He is disturbed by the fact that friends and relatives (especially his mother) are upset at his absence; he worries that they might die while he is away; he also misses the sights and sounds of his home city.[181] Epictetus' advice, which is broadly similar to Seneca's advice to Serenus in *On Peace of Mind*, is that, assuming that the interlocutor's project in Rome is ethically justified, he should carry it through in a resolute attitude, and not be distracted by anxieties about family and friends at home or by the familiar appeal of his home city.[182] Epictetus underlines that the interlocutor's work in Rome constitutes a valid form of social engagement and enables him to play his part on behalf of his friends, family, country, and in a broader sense, the human race.[183] Epictetus uses as an exemplar for this idea Socrates, who fulfilled his mission and 'stood his ground' to the last, in the Athenian court which tried him in 399 BC, and was not distracted from this by family concerns, even though he was a loving father.[184] Epictetus also uses his typical alternative exemplar, Diogenes the Cynic, who was prepared to travel the world to help humanity (as Epictetus presents Diogenes' mission), and also, in the same mould, Odysseus and Heracles, heroes sometimes seen as wise people in Stoicism.[185] The attitude commended evokes the virtue of magnanimity or greatness of spirit, as presented in Cicero's *On Duties* 1. This involves 'disdain for things external', and not 'yielding to anyone, or agitation of spirit or fortune' in the pursuit of what is 'right and fitting'. It also involves (in the more socially directed side of the virtue) doing actions which are 'beneficial', even if they 'endanger both life itself and much that concerns life'.[186]

This advice forms the context for the passage cited earlier (3.24.88). This passage, and the words around it, respond especially to the interlocutor's concern about the effects of his absence on family and friends and his claim that he cannot show *philostorgia* (love of kin) if he is away working in Rome.[187] Epictetus challenges the interlocutor on this point, claiming that the attitude which the

---

[180] Epict. *Diss.* 3.24.36, 40, 44, 54, 73, 75, 78–81, 117. The following three paragraphs are close in content to parts of Gill 2019a: 280–3.

[181] See 3.24.4, 22, 27, 53, 58–9, 83.

[182] See 3.24.31–6, 95–102; also text to nn. 153–64 (on Sen. *TA*), and text to nn. 173–8 (on M. A.).

[183] 3.24.44, 47, 99; on social roles in Epictetus, see *Diss.* 1.2, 2.10, Gill 1988: 187–92; Long 2002: 232–44.

[184] 3.24.40, 60–1, 99. On Socrates' philosophical mission as a public benefit, see Pl. *Ap.* 28c–e, 29d–30e; on the significance of Socrates for Epictetus see Long 2002: ch. 3.

[185] 3.24.40, 64–73; also 3.24.13–20. On Socrates, Heracles and Odysseus as potential candidates for being wise people, see Brouwer 2014: 107–12 and ch. 4 (on Socrates); on Diogenes in Epictetus, see Long 2002: 58–61.

[186] Cic. *Off.* 1.66, trans. Griffin and Atkins 1991; on the two-fold presentation of virtues in Cic. *Off.* 1, see Ch. 1, text to nn. 169–77.

[187] See refs. in n. 181. For citation of 3.24.88, see text to n. 147.

interlocutor expresses, in which anxiety about losing other people prevents him from carrying out his chosen role in life, cannot be considered a proper form of *philostorgia* (3.24.83). Epictetus advocates training yourself to express your attachment to other people in a way that is combined with acceptance that they can be taken from you at any time. Hence, 'you should remind yourself that what you love is mortal, that what you love is not your own; it has been granted to you just for the present, not irrevocably, and not for ever, but like a fig or bunch of grapes for a particular season of the year, so that if you long for it in winter you're a fool'.[188] Then follow the words cited earlier (3.24.88), which the interlocutor describes as 'ill-omened' because of the reminder of the possible death of those one loves. Epictetus replies that words that are really ill-omened are accounts of vices such as 'cowardice and meanness of spirit' and that referring to things that are 'in the course of nature' is not ill-omened. Human travel, the cycle of the seasons, and death (our own and that of other people) form an integral part of the course of nature, so that referring to them is not ill-omened (3.24.89–93). We can accept that such things form part of the course of nature and still maintain our own pathway in life in a consistent way and one that benefits other people. Thus: 'A virtuous and good (*kalos kai agathos*) person, keeping in mind who he is, and where he has come from [that is, from nature]...concentrates on one thing alone, how he may fill his post in a well-ordered way (*eutaktōs*), remaining obedient to god'.[189]

The 'ill-omened' passage (3.24.88) is often taken as advocating a policy of emotional detachment from other people, notably your child or, in related passages, your brother or friend.[190] However, this is not what Epictetus is urging; nor would this advice be in line with Stoic ethics generally. He does not say we should stop loving our family and friends and expressing this in our actions and attitudes (that is, expressing *philostorgia*).[191] What he says is that we should continue to love them, while remaining aware that our relationship to them—or their relationship to us, of course, if we die first—may be terminated by death at any time.[192] Also, as stressed already, he urges us not to be distracted from our main project in life, which may involve working on behalf of family and friends as well as for our homeland, by anxieties about events which we cannot control, including the deaths of those we love, or our own death, while we are away.[193] In Stoic terms,

---

[188]   3.24.86, trans. Hard 2014.

[189]   3.24.95, trans. Hard 2014; for the image of staying at your post, see also Pl. *Ap.* 28d–e (Socrates at his trial).

[190]   See Sorabji 2000: 184, 216 (also 173, cited in text to n. 81); Nussbaum 1994: 370–1 (referring to *Handbook* 3), 2001: 359; Gloyn 2017: 21, 59, n. 34.

[191]   Epictetus shares the interlocutor's high valuation of *philostorgia* but argues for a different view about how this should be expressed (3.24.59–60, 83).

[192]   See 3.24.86–7, using *philein* ('love') and cognate terms repeatedly. See also 3.24.60, on Socrates' 'love' for his children. For this view, see also Long 2002: 249; Reydams-Schils 2005: 123; Gloyn 2017: 21, n. 21, 59, n. 34.

[193]   See text to n. 189. On this point, see also Graver 2007: 177–8.

we should act in line with the basic human motive of care for others (of which the paradigm is parental love), and aim at a way of life shaped by virtue, which carries with it good emotions such as good will and good intent and avoids bad emotions such as anxiety and fear.[194] Epictetus does not here suggest that the overall aim of the approach he recommends is to achieve one's own peace of mind at the expense of forming and maintaining close relationships. The main focus, as outlined earlier, is on maintaining in a consistent way one's chosen pathway in life as a basis for movement towards virtue.[195] Although Epictetus offers rather similar advice elsewhere to that found here,[196] this is the only passage which includes the disturbing image of whispering to one's child about his or her future death. This is in response, perhaps, to the interlocutor's stress on his worry about his absent relatives and the concern that travelling to carry out his work prevents him from expressing *philostorgia*. Epictetus wants to bring out as forcibly as possible the point that affection needs to be combined with awareness of the possibility of death; but he does so while maintaining that the affection is not therefore diluted or negated.[197]

So far, I have focused on the version of this passage found in *Discourses* 3.24.88. However, a second version of this idea, often cited, is *Handbook* 3, presumably based on the *Discourses* passage.[198]

> With regard to everything that is a source of delight to you, or is useful to you, or of which you are fond, remember to keep telling yourself what kind of thing it is, starting with the most insignificant. If you're fond of a jug, say, 'This is a jug I'm fond of', and then if it gets broken, you won't be upset. If you kiss your child or your wife, say to yourself that it is a human being that you're kissing. Then, if one of them should die, you won't be upset.[199]

Although most of the motifs here also occur in 3.24,[200] there are features of this passage that could give a rather misleading impression. For one thing, of course, the larger thematic context of 3.24 is missing, including the stress on the importance of maintaining one's pathway in life as a vehicle for ethical progress and benefiting others and the dispute with the interlocutor about the proper way to express *philostorgia*.[201] Also, the passage accentuates the jug-motif, rather than the naturalness and universality of death (including of course one's own death, not

---

[194] See 4.2, 4.5; also text to nn. 32–43.   [195] See text to n. 189, also text to nn. 182–6.
[196] See 3.3.14–19, 3.8.1–5, 4.1, 111–13.   [197] See text to n. 191–2.
[198] The *Handbook* or *Manual* (*Encheiridion*) is a collection of short passages, based, it seems, on the *Discourses* (not all of which survive). Both works were prepared by Arrian, reporting Epictetus' discussions with students and visitors to his school; see Long 2002: 8–9, 38–43.
[199] Trans. Hard 2014.   [200] See 3.24.84–6, 88.   [201] See text to nn. 183–6, 187, 191–3.

just other people's), which is the feature stressed more fully in 3.24,[202] and in Stoic advice on facing death more generally.[203] The jug-motif, at least as presented in *Handbook* 3, is potentially misleading. One might think that Epictetus is saying that your wife or child is no more valuable than a jug and is as easily dispensable or replaceable.[204] However, I do not think this is what he is saying, as is shown by a parallel passage in *Discourses* 4.1.111:

> [In preparing yourself for possible loss] Begin with the smallest and most fragile things, a pot or a cup, and then pass on to a tunic, a dog, a horse, a piece of land; and from there, pass on to yourself, to your body, and the parts of your body, and to your children, your wife, your brothers.[205]

What this passage shows is that the cup or jug is placed at a very low level of value, while family members are valued at a very high level, above one's own body, for instance.[206] The point of *Handbook* 3, then, is that family members, who are of great value and much loved by you, are similar to jugs in only one respect—you may lose them both.[207] Another potentially misleading point is that *Handbook* 3 ends by referring to avoidance of emotional disturbance (*ou tarachthēsēs*). This might seem to imply that the only reason for this strategy is to gain peace of mind, for you as an individual; or, more broadly, that peace of mind is the overall goal of life. From the full discussion in *Discourses* 3.24, we can tell that the main focus of Epictetus' advice is not on securing peace of mind, except viewed as a corollary of the fulfilment of one's overall life-project, including its social, other-benefiting dimension. The discussion of 3.24 is in line with the standard Stoic view that peace of mind is a corollary of achieving the goal of life, rather than being itself the goal.[208] In short, then, the version offered in *Handbook* 3 is a misleading, and in some ways untypical, version of Stoic advice, and not a passage to be treated, as it sometimes is, as encapsulating standard Stoic thinking on personal relationships and emotions.[209]

---

[202] On this theme (the naturalness and universality of death), see 3.24.86–8, 91–4. On facing one's own death (not that of a family member), see 3.24.94–101, linked closely with the theme of maintaining one's proper role in life. Marcus, interestingly, in alluding to Epict. *Diss.* 2.34.88, includes the naturalness of death but not the jug-motif (M. A. 11.34).

[203] See e.g. van Ackeren 2011: 163–4, 173–80; Gill 2013a: xlix–lii, on Marcus; Gloyn 2017: 21–5, on Senecan consolation.

[204] Nussbaum 1994: 370–1, seems to read the passage in this way.   [205] Trans. Hard 2014.

[206] It is still assumed that family members are, in Stoic terms, preferable indifferents; on this point, see text to n. 77 and nn. 87–8.

[207] See also text to n. 188 on this theme in 3.24.   [208] See text to nn. 90–5 and nn. 194–5.

[209] See Nussbaum 1994: 370–1; Sorabji 2000: 184, 216 (bracketing together *Handbook* 3 and *Diss.* 3.24.88).

PART III

STOIC ETHICS AND MODERN MORAL THEORY

6

Stoicism and Modern Virtue Ethics

6.1 Stoic Ethics and the Modern Philosophical Context

The aim of the first and second parts of the book has been to offer a fresh analysis of central ideas and claims in Stoic ethics, including ideas on development. The aim of this third part, building on the first two, is to give Stoic ethics more of a voice, as a contributor or challenger in current debates in moral philosophy, than it has at present. I begin by specifying the kind of modern debates to which Stoic ideas can make a significant and valuable contribution. Subsequently, I explain the kind of contribution that Stoicism can make. The area of modern theory to which Stoicism is best suited to contribute is what is sometimes called 'Neo-Aristotelian' virtue ethics, and most of this chapter is focused on the principal concerns and leading thinkers in this area. However, I begin by locating this approach in the broader framework of contemporary theory, outlining the origins of modern virtue ethics and distinguishing Neo-Aristotelian from non-Aristotelian virtue ethics.[1]

Modern thinkers sometimes distinguish between 'the theory of virtue', which is a longstanding feature of moral theory and not confined to any one approach, and 'virtue ethics', which gives to virtue the central role allocated in other types of theory to other ideas, such as doing your duty or maximizing human benefit.[2] The resurgence of virtue ethics was stimulated by pioneering discussions by Elizabeth Anscombe (1958), Alasdair MacIntyre (1985, first published in 1981), and Bernard Williams (1985). These discussions were highly critical of most modern moral theories including consequentialist ones, especially Utilitarianism, and deontological ones, especially Kant's; and their criticisms shaped much subsequent debate. These modern theories were criticized for failing to give proper weight to the agent's perspective in ethical reflection, notably her legitimate desire to live a life of happiness, however this was understood. They were also criticized for failing to give proper weight to what are, in lived experience, crucial sources of ethical attitudes, namely motivational, including emotional, responses linked with engagement with other individuals or communities. Put differently, the claim was that these theories neglected the role of virtues as dispositions, that is, patterns of

---

[1] For recent surveys of virtue ethics, see Russell 2013a; van Hooft 2013. Snow 2018a takes the broader topic of theory of virtue, but includes virtue ethics.

[2] See Snow 2018b: 321.

Learning to Live Naturally: Stoic Ethics and its Modern Significance. Christopher Gill, Oxford University Press.
© Christopher Gill 2022. DOI: 10.1093/oso/9780198866169.003.0007

motivational responses underpinning our lives as moral agents. These theories were also criticized for trying to ground moral theory by reference to general underpinning principles, without also acknowledging the crucial role of the agent's perspective and dispositions. As Williams, memorably, put the idea, these principles were used as 'Archimedean' points, designed to lever commitment to morality into a life that lacked the essential psychological and interpersonal basis for this commitment.[3] MacIntyre presented as a (failed) Enlightenment project the attempt to ground ethics 'from the outside', rather than from ethical dispositions and a community capable of developing and sustaining these dispositions.[4] A related criticism, made forcefully by Williams, is that these theories were unduly focused on a narrow set of claims or reasons for action which were characterized as 'moral', at the expense of other important aspects of human life.[5]

These thinkers were concerned to clear the ground, one might say, for a new form of ethics (new, at least in the modern context), virtue ethics, as it came to be called. Subsequent thinkers were thus enabled to assume that this could be treated as an independent, valid mode of ethical theory, alongside, for instance, deontology and consequentialism.[6] Later thinkers in this vein have tended to take a less critical or polemical stance towards other forms of moral theory. Many leading figures in this movement are, or have been, experts in ancient philosophy or are at least highly familiar with this area. Aristotle, taken by the pioneers of virtue ethics as their paradigm, has continued to function as the main ancient exemplar. Hence, one important strand in this movement is sometimes described as 'Neo-Aristotelian' virtue ethics. Nancy Snow, reviewing this strand of thought (2018c), cites Rosalind Hursthouse's *On Virtue Ethics* (1999) as an important programmatic work in this vein, and Daniel Russell's *Practical Intelligence and the Virtues* (2009) as a study of a major dimension of virtue, approached from this standpoint. Annas's *Morality of Happiness* (1993), while taking the form of a survey and analysis of Aristotelian and Hellenistic ethical theory, also constituted, in effect, an exploration of key ideas and arguments in virtue ethics, a project to which Annas has also contributed independently.[7] However, not all recent work in virtue ethics views itself in a post-Aristotelian framework. The writings of Michael Slote, Christine Swanton, Linda Zagzebski, and Robert Adams fall into this non-Aristotelian category. Slote and Swanton look for inspiration in

---

[3] Williams 1985: ch. 2, esp. 28–9.   [4] MacIntyre 1985: chs. 4–5.
[5] Williams 1985: ch. 10. On the emergence of modern virtue ethics, see Gill 2004a, 2005b: 1–4; also Snow 2018c: 322; Solomon 2018.
[6] Important ground-clearing work was also done by Philippa Foot, criticizing contemporary non-cognitivism and prescriptivism; see Solomon 2018: 305–7.
[7] In her monograph, *Intelligent Virtue* (2011), and numerous articles.

eighteenth-century thinkers such as Francis Hutchinson or Hume, and, in Swanton's case, Nietzsche, while Adams's approach is Neo-Platonic.[8]

Can we identify a clear point of differentiation between Neo-Aristotelian and non-Aristotelian thinkers in this area? For both types of theorist, the notion of virtue is central. However, for Neo-Aristotelian thinkers, virtue is, typically, correlated with the idea of happiness or flourishing (*eudaimonia*), and, in so far as virtue is seen as directed towards happiness, the framework is goal-directed or 'teleological'. Also, at least for some modern philosophers, as for Aristotle, the teleological character is linked with a conception of human nature. Hence, this vein of modern theory can be described not just as virtue ethics, but also eudaimonism, and sometimes, as involving ethical naturalism, in the sense of an ethical conception of human nature.[9] In the alternative, non-Aristotelian, framework, virtue is not correlated with happiness or viewed teleologically, but conceived independently. Michael Slote's *From Morality to Virtue* (1992) served as an important programmatic work for this approach, in a way comparable to the role of Hursthouse's *On Virtue Ethics* (1999) for writings in an Aristotelian mode. He has developed a theory often characterized as 'agent-based' or 'agent-prior', in treating the qualities of the virtuous agent as fundamental, defined without reference to a conception of human flourishing. Swanton, similarly, adopts a non-eudaimonistic framework. Her conception of virtue can be described as 'target-centred'; virtue is seen as responding, in a directed way, to a specific kind of demand. More precisely, Swanton defines virtues by reference to a combination of their field of operation, mode of responsiveness, basis of moral acknowledgement, and target.[10] A further feature of this strand of theory, shared by Slote, Zagzebski, and to some extent Swanton, is stress on the emotional or affective dimension of virtue and the idea that virtues are derived from (natural human) primary emotional responses to others. To this extent, this strand of theory can be described as naturalistic, though not in a form linked with teleology; the eighteenth-century term 'Sentimentalism' is sometimes used to characterize this side of their approach, which can be contrasted with the Kantian idea that rationality is fundamental for properly moral responses.[11]

A second general feature of the later period of virtue ethics is a less combative attitude towards other, more longstanding, modern theories, such as Kantianism and Utilitarianism. In their enthusiasm to clear the ground for a new ethics focused on virtue, pioneering figures such as Anscombe, MacIntyre, and

---

[8] Some key works in this area: Slote 1992, 2001, 2009; Swanton 2003, 2015; Zagzebski 1996; Adams 2006 (for an earlier important modern Neo-Platonic approach to virtue, see Murdoch 1970 (2001), discussed by Clarke 2018).

[9] See Snow 2018c: 321. On modern ethical naturalism and human nature, see 7.1–2.

[10] See Pettigrove 2018: 360–1, 367–8.

[11] Pettigrove 2018: 361–2, 362–5, 367. On Kant, rationality, and the properly moral response, see Gill 1996: 246–8.

Williams seemed to want virtue-centred theory to replace the other methods they criticized so vigorously.[12] However, subsequent thinkers have tended to present virtue ethics as one, valid, method of moral theory among others. They have sometimes stressed the presence of shared concerns and objectives among all moral theorists, while also underlining differences in methodology and conceptual framework. This is a marked feature of Hursthouse's programmatic study of virtue ethics,[13] and of Annas's 1993 book. Annas highlights what she sees as the structural contrast between eudaimonistic theory, which starts from the agent's perspective and thought about her life as a whole, and other types of theory, notably deontological and consequentialist, which offer a unified and architectonic framework based on certain general principles. However, she also accentuates shared concerns between these approaches, including what she called 'making room for other-concern', common ground flagged in her book-title, *The Morality of Happiness*, which gives prominence to a term ('morality') sometimes avoided by virtue ethical thinkers.[14] This period has been marked, especially, by the exploration of common ground between virtue ethicists and followers of Kant. The conceptions of virtue adopted by Aristotle and Kant have been examined by both virtue ethical theorists and Kantian thinkers for this purpose, along with related topics.[15] In this kind of discussion, typically, each type of theory has been regarded as valid and independent but also mutually informing. However, another type of approach has treated the relationship between the idea of virtue and modern moral theory in a more asymmetrical way. For instance, some thinkers (not those so far mentioned) have argued that the concept of virtue can be deployed most effectively to support at least some versions of Utilitarianism or deontology, by providing an analysis of ethical motivation to supplement theories sometimes held to lack such an analysis.[16] In such discussions, although the concept of virtue ethics is employed, the approach of virtue ethics as a distinct and independently valid form of theory is not adopted.

My aim here is to explore ways in which Stoic ideas can contribute to modern debate. Which of the strands of modern theory just reviewed is most relevant for this exercise and what kind of contribution do I have in view? Although Stoic ideas may have a generalized interest for any type of modern moral theory, in principle, the scope for closer engagement is most obvious in the case of Neo-Aristotelian virtue ethics. This is because the two types of theory are of the same general type,

---

[12] See text to nn. 2–5.   [13] See Hursthouse 1999: 1–8, 25–39.
[14] See Annas 1993: chs. 10 and 22. For a negative view of 'morality', from the standpoint of virtue ethics, see text to n. 5.
[15] See Engstrom and Whiting 1996; Sherman 1997 (Aristotle and Kant on virtue); Korsgaard 2009: chs. 6–8, Platonic and Aristotelian ideas on psychological unity viewed in the context of a Neo-Kantian project.
[16] See Crisp 1992: 154–60; Oakley 2013: 65–7, on virtue deployed to support a Utilitarian approach; also Driver 2001: ch. 4 on virtue and consequentialism. See McNaughton and Rawling 2006: 453–4; Crisp 2015, on virtue used to support deontology.

more so than, for instance, Kantian deontology or Utilitarian consequentialism, or, indeed, non-Aristotelian modern virtue ethics. Stoicism, although not an Aristotelian (or Peripatetic) theory in the strict sense, emerged and developed in the post-Aristotelian period; and Aristotelian, along with Platonic, influences seem to have played a significant role in the formation and consolidation of its ideas.[17] Hence, I think, Stoic ideas have most to offer when brought into close engagement with a type of modern theory (namely virtue ethics, particularly when combined with eudaimonism and ethical naturalism), which is inspired by Aristotle and has the same general scope and conceptual framework as his theory. However, I hope that Stoic ideas, if appropriately explained, may also be of interest to exponents of non-Aristotelian virtue ethics, and, to some extent, other modern moral theories.

How far is my discussion informed by, or anticipated by, previous treatments? Annas's 1993 analysis of central themes in Aristotelian and later ancient ethical theory brings out fully the importance of Stoic ethical theory in its own right and in the Hellenistic and post-Hellenistic thought-world. She also explores the relative strengths and weaknesses of Stoic and Aristotelian thinking on key topics, including the virtue-happiness relationship.[18] Another relevant and illuminating study is Russell's *Happiness for Humans* (2012). This anticipates my discussion here in juxtaposing ancient and modern thinking on virtue and happiness and in focusing on the Aristotle-Stoics comparison. However, our approaches differ in that Russell, overall, favours the Aristotelian position, as he understands this, while recognizing the cogency and appeal of the Stoic framework.[19] Lawrence Becker's *A New Stoicism* (1998/2017), at first glance, prefigures my work even more closely, in making the case for Stoicism as the philosophical paradigm for modern ethical theory and analysing Stoic ideas on virtue and happiness from that standpoint. However, there are certain features of Becker's book which make it very different from my treatment here. Becker's presentation of Stoic ethics, though highly original and powerfully argued, is sharply divergent, in methodology and sometimes content, from the main currents of scholarship on Stoic ethics; it is also not based explicitly on the primary ancient evidence. Although Becker does refer to Stoic scholarship and primary evidence, he does so in a set of 'commentaries', which are rather loosely related to his own main argument. It is sometimes open to question whether the ideas he presents are, indeed, distinctively Stoic or, rather, characteristic of ancient ethical theory more generally, including Aristotelian thinking. Also, and perhaps more surprisingly for a

---

[17] See Introd., text to nn. 14–15; also Gill 2006: 16–22.
[18] See Annas 1993, esp. chs 18–19 and 21. Her independent study of virtue (2011) is also strongly informed by Stoic, alongside Aristotelian, ideas. Irwin 2007: also gives a significant role to Stoic ideas (chs. 12–13) in the first volume of an analysis of ethics up the present (see Darwall's 2011 review of Irwin 2007–8).
[19] See Russell 2012, esp. parts 2–3.

contemporary moral theorist, he does not correlate his approach closely with that of other modern ethical thinkers.[20] Hence, although his work is philosophically arresting and has, I know, been inspirational for some readers, including those interested in Stoicism as a guide for practice,[21] it is difficult to correlate his arguments closely with other scholarship, including my discussion here.[22] Finally, Martha Nussbaum, in a wide-ranging study of emotions, presents Stoic ideas as prefiguring her own ('cognitive') approach, to some extent, at least. However, in the same study, she is strongly critical of the ethical dimension of Stoic thinking on emotion, presenting is as part of an 'anti-compassion' tradition which she sets out to confront, a view I do not adopt.[23]

What are the claims to be made here, as regards Stoicism and modern theory? My main claim is that, while Aristotle has played a valuable role in stimulating modern forms of ethical theory (virtue ethics, eudaimonism, ethical naturalism), Stoic ideas can be more helpful in taking forward this dialogue between ancient and modern ethics. Stoic ethics has many of the features that drew the attention of pioneers of virtue ethics such as Anscombe, MacIntyre, and Williams, to Aristotle. As underlined in the first part of this book, Stoicism deploys a similar type of framework, centred on the ideas of virtue and happiness, and allocates a similar importance to the agent's perspective and to the interpersonal and communal dimension of ethics. Also, as brought out in the second part, Stoicism gives a similar significance to questions of human psychology and emotion, and to the role of development in ethics. Stoicism, like Aristotle, but unlike much modern moral theory, is 'naturalistic', in several senses, explored fully here.[24] In all these respects, Stoic ethics is as appropriate as Aristotle as an ancient paradigm or interlocutor for modern virtue ethics. In addition, in certain ways, Stoic ethics can take us further than Aristotle, especially given the current state of debate in modern moral theory. Pioneers of modern virtue ethics, as noted earlier, were concerned to make the case, or clear the ground, for what was then an uncharted type of contemporary theory. They stressed large-scale differences between this approach and longstanding modern theories such as Kantian-style deontology, Utilitarianism, and contractualism.[25] Now that virtue ethics has a well-established

---

[20] See further Gill 2016c: 347–8.

[21] E.g. Massimo Pigliucci and Piotr Stankiewicz, authors of books on life-guidance based on Stoicism (Pigliucci 2017; Stankiewicz 2019, 2020). On Stoic ethics and modern life-guidance, see 8.2.

[22] Also worth noting are recent resumés of Stoic thinking on virtue in handbooks on virtue or virtue ethics, by Sharpe (2013), Becker (2018), and Gill (2021), the last highlighting links with modern virtue ethics.

[23] Nussbaum 2001, chs. 1–2, and pp. 358–86. See further on her criticisms and for some responses to them, 5.2–3, esp. text to n. 83. For fuller discussion of the works noted in this para, see Gill 2016c: 346–53.

[24] On Stoicism, ethics and nature, see Ch. 3; on Stoicism and modern ethical naturalism, see 7.1–2; on Stoicism and modern environmental ethics, see 7.3–4.

[25] See text to nn. 3–5.

status and exponents, the focus has shifted to more fine-grained examination of the core concepts and their interrelationship.[26]

Here, Stoic ethics can be of special value. In a whole series of ways, the Stoic ethical framework is more fully worked out, more systematic in conception and presentation, and more consistent. This point applies to the key concepts, including virtue and happiness (the goal of life), and their interrelationship. Aristotle's framework, for instance, as presented in the *Nicomachean Ethics*, is more provisional or exploratory, with a number of loose ends, ambiguities and internal tensions or inconsistencies, on quite major points.[27] This difference comes out, for instance, in their treatments of virtue, happiness, and the contribution of other valuable things, and of the relationship between practical and theoretical forms of virtue and happiness.[28] This feature of Aristotelian ethics raises difficulties for specialist interpretation of Aristotelian theory; but it also causes problems for modern theorists of virtue ethics offering their own analysis of these ideas, while doing so within a broadly Aristotelian framework. Stoic ethics, by contrast, though also operating within the same Aristotelian framework, offers more fully worked-out and consistent positions on these and related topics. In this respect, Stoic ethics can be more helpful for modern virtue theorists.

These differences between the two ancient theories reflect several further differences between them. One relates to the transmission of the two ideas. Aristotle's 'works', as we call them now, are actually lecture notes, by Aristotle or his students,[29] and have many of the characteristic features of this mode of expression, including provisionality and looseness of structure. The main sources for Stoic ethics are (relatively late) discursive discussions, for instance, by Cicero or Seneca, and handbook summaries of doctrines. Both types of writing were prepared after centuries of debate within the school and with other philosophical approaches.[30] Also, though Aristotle may appear to moderns to have an authoritative standing in ancient ethics, he was in many respects an innovator or pioneer. Although his writing is informed especially by Socratic-Platonic theory, he was the first thinker to produce writings on 'ethics', treated as a distinct subject, and to

---

[26] For instance, see recent discussion of the virtue-happiness relationship, text to nn. 55–62.

[27] Aristotle's other main ethical work, the *Eudemian Ethics*, is more unified and systematic, but does not, I think, differ fundamentally on the points discussed here. On the relationship between the two works, see Kenny 1978/2016. The third work ascribed to Aristotle, the *Magna Moralia*, is now often seen as post-Aristotelian (see Inwood 2014: 30–3). In the reception of Aristotle, the *NE* has been the most widely read work (Miller 2012) and is the one mainly referred to here.

[28] For discussion of *NE* 1.8–10 and 10.7–8 and analogous Stoic discussions illustrating this point, see 6.2.

[29] Aristotle also published (more general) writings, but these are largely lost, whereas the school-texts have survived. On the early stages of the transmission of Aristotle's school-texts, see Barnes 1997.

[30] See Introd., text to nn. 6–13; also Schofield 2003: 236–53. For discussion of the summaries of ethics (esp. on the topic of ethics and nature), see 3.3.

map out the parameters of this subject.[31] Zeno, the founder of Stoicism, formulating his philosophy at the start of the third century BC, thus inherited a subject-matter that had already been worked on and debated by several major thinkers. Zeno and his Hellenistic successors, especially Chrysippus, developed their theory into the elaborated and systematic framework that has been passed down to us.[32] A further factor is what one might call philosophical idiom or temperament. All major ancient philosophers after Socrates aim at logical and conceptual consistency. However, Aristotle is also committed to taking note of widely held or strongly maintained pre-existing beliefs on the subject, including, in ethics, conventional opinions as well as preceding philosophical views.[33] Thus, on the question of the virtue-happiness relationship, he takes account, at key moments, of conventional beliefs on the basis for happiness, as well as Platonic-style ideas on the highest form of happiness. He does so even though, on both occasions, arguably, this threatens the internal consistency and coherence of his theory.[34] The Stoics also maintain that their ethical theory matches what they call 'preconceptions', that is, widespread human beliefs or assumptions.[35] However, they are more prepared than Aristotle to maintain positions which are consistent with their theory as a whole, even if these differ markedly, at least at first sight, from conventional or earlier philosophical ideas. To rephrase this point, they are prepared to 'follow the argument (logos) wherever it leads', as Plato's Socrates often puts it, even if this leads to apparently paradoxical or unfamiliar results.[36]

The consistency and systematic character of Stoic ethics does not depend only on presenting Aristotelian-style ideas in a more tidy-minded and fully articulated form. It also depends on putting forward innovative ideas, such as 'indifferents', which define new conceptual categories. Also, the Stoics take up innovative positions within well-established areas of Platonic-Aristotelian controversy, such as that concerning the best form of human happiness or the relationship between practical and theoretical wisdom.[37] The same point applies to Stoic ideas on ethical development, including emotional development, as brought out in the second part of this book. In antiquity, these innovative Stoic ideas often generated critical responses, particularly from Aristotelian (or Platonic-Aristotelian) thinkers, though this criticism was sometimes combined with adoption of the Stoic innovations, albeit in a modified form.[38] A recurrent criticism was that the

---

[31] Strictly speaking, Aristotle sees the branch of knowledge as ethics plus politics (see NE 1.2, 10.9). In this, as in much else, Aristotle builds on the approach of Plato's Republic and Laws.

[32] On the early history of the school, see Sedley 2003: 9–18.

[33] See Arist. NE 7.1, 1145b2–7; also 1.5, 1.8, 1098b9–29; also Nussbaum 1986: 240–63.

[34] On Arist. NE 1.8–10, 10.7–8, see 6.2.   [35] See LS 40 N–T; also Irwin 2007: 312–13.

[36] For the idea that Stoic thought is characterized by a combination of naturalism (and holism) and Socratic logical and ethical rigour, even if the combination leads to paradoxical conclusions, see Gill 2006: xvi–xix, 81–100.

[37] See text to nn. 118–38.

[38] On this kind of response by other ancient theories, see Gill 2012: 36–51; Gill 2017: 109–17.

Stoic ideas, even if internally consistent, ran counter to what was widely seen as credible or in line with human nature.[39] However, arguably, these Stoic ideas are not only self-consistent, in some cases more so than their Aristotelian analogues, but also consistent with a credible view of human nature, which is sometimes placed in the context of nature as a whole. In these ways, Stoic ideas meet one of the demands of the pioneers of modern virtue ethics, that is, for a form of ethics more compatible with a credible account of human nature and psychology.[40]

The point can be put more broadly. The value of Stoicism for modern ethics does not consist only in its offering a more internally consistent and systematic version of the Aristotelian framework already adopted by some modern virtue ethical theorists. Stoic ethics also has substantive philosophical strengths in its own right, which provide the basis for engagement with several modern moral positions, especially, but not only, Neo-Aristotelian virtue ethics. For one thing, as was widely recognized in antiquity, Stoicism is marked by ethical or moral rigour, in its theory of value and associated ideas regarding ethical motivation and action. Moral rigour, in modern theory, is a quality associated more closely with theories other than virtue ethics or eudaimonism, for instance with Kantian deontology or (certain types of) Utilitarianism. Indeed, the idea of moral rigour (or 'morality', more broadly) has sometimes been regarded negatively by some modern virtue ethicists.[41] However, Stoicism shows that ethical rigour can coherently form part of a virtue ethical and eudaimonistic framework and one that has other features characteristic of modern virtue ethics. In Stoic theory, this rigour consists in their central claim that only virtue (and virtue-based happiness, and other things dependent on virtue) count as good, that is, objects of value in the full sense. Other things often regarded as good, such as health, property and social status are classed, by comparison with virtue, as 'matters of indifference', though they are also, in mainstream Stoic ethics, regarded as being of positive value and as significant, though not decisive, factors in determining action.[42] This position on value carries implications for properly ethical motivation and action. Hence, for instance, the Stoics hold that virtue is inherently good and worthy of choice in a way that is consistent with regarding happiness as the overall goal of life, since both of them count as good in ways that 'preferred indifferents' are not.[43] Also, properly conducted practical deliberation is directed at what is 'right', meaning in line with the virtues, while at the same time properly taking account of the preferability of factors relevant to the decision.[44]

---

[39] Cicero seems to reach this conclusion after the extended debate between Stoic and Platonic-Aristotelian ethical approaches in Cic. *Fin.* 3–5; see *Fin.* 5.77–86, and Gill 2016a: 242–3.

[40] For the demand for a more 'naturalistic' approach to ethics, in various senses, see text to nn. 3–5. On Stoic ethics and nature, see Ch. 3; on Stoicism and modern versions of ethical naturalism, see Ch.7.

[41] See text to n. 5.   [42] See Ch. 1, 2.2–3.

[43] See 6.3.   [44] See 2.4–5.

As just noted, moral rigour, in modern ethical theory, is often associated with positions other than virtue ethics and eudaimonism and is sometimes, though not always, viewed critically by modern virtue ethicists.[45] However, in Stoicism, this rigorous position is combined, in a coherent way, with other features that modern virtue ethicists as well as other theorists might recognize as philosophical strengths. These include rich and inclusive (but also cohesive and unified) conceptions of both virtue and happiness. The virtues are defined as forms of knowledge or expertise. However, knowledge is conceived broadly, as expertise in living as well as a form of understanding and also as expertise that shapes motivation generally, including emotions and desires.[46] Also, the expertise of virtue consists in two, interrelated aspects, as skill in selecting between indifferents and as skill in leading a happy life, with the first type of expertise shaped by the second.[47] Happiness (*eudaimonia*) consists primarily in a form of life (the life 'according to nature' or 'according to virtue'); and this life includes factors such as actions, practices, and emotions based on virtue. Hence, Stoic 'happiness' includes some of the features that could also form part of a conventional modern (or ancient) view of happiness, such as congenial pastimes and the emotion of joy.[48] Further, Stoic ideas about both virtue and happiness are informed by a rich and credible type of ethical naturalism, including an understanding of the qualities of human nature at its best and of features shared by human nature and nature as a whole, and of their significance for ethics.[49] In addition, Stoic ethics gives a prominent place to ideas about ethical development in three interrelated aspects, namely development in ethical understanding, in relationships with other people and communities, and in patterns of emotions. Stoic thinking on development is closely integrated both with their thinking on core ethical ideas about virtue and happiness and also on nature in its various aspects.[50] Finally, Stoic thinking offers distinctive insights on self-other relationships, centred on their conception of human nature as both rational and sociable and their view that the desire to care for others of one's kind is a basic or primary motive on the same level as care for oneself.[51] These are all, I think, substantive strengths of Stoicism as an ethical theory, and they are integrated with their distinctive version of ethical or moral rigour, as brought out in the previous chapters of this book.

I have suggested that these features of Stoic ethics are strong points in themselves and also ones that offer, in principle, the basis for engagement with modern ethical theory and an alternative, or at least supplementary, prototype for modern virtue ethics. As already suggested, the scope for philosophical dialogue is greatest

---

[45] On differences on this point within modern virtue ethics, see text to nn. 5, 13–15. For a positive view of ethical rigour in modern virtue ethics, see Annas 2011: ch. 7; Hursthouse 1999: ch. 7.

[46] See LS 61 B–H, 65 F; also 1.4, 5.1.   [47] See 2.1, 2.3, esp. text to nn. 74–95.

[48] See 1.3, 2.1–2; also on 'goods' other than virtue (but dependent on virtue), see LS 60 J–M (Ch. 1, text to nn. 12–42); Graver 2007: 145–8.

[49] See 1.3–4.   [50] See Chs. 4–5, esp. 4.2, 4.4–5; also 8.1.   [51] See 1.3–4, 4.2, 4.5; also 6.4.

STOIC ETHICS AND THE MODERN PHILOSOPHICAL CONTEXT 259

with Neo-Aristotelian ethics, in part because this type of modern theory combines virtue ethics with eudaimonism and also, in some cases, with ethical naturalism, centred on ideas of human nature or the natural environment. Hence, in this chapter and the next, I focus on topics relevant for those theories, as well as Stoicism. These topics are, in this chapter, the virtue-happiness relationship, and in the next chapter, questions relating to the ethical significance of human nature and the natural environment. In this chapter, my concern is to clarify how Stoic thinking on these concepts relates to Aristotle's ideas, which form the typical starting-point for modern virtue ethical thinking of this kind. I argue that Stoic thinking is more internally consistent and systematic than Aristotelian and that, in this sense, taken with its other philosophical merits, it forms a better basis for modern theory on this subject than is offered by Aristotle.[52] In the following chapter, I aim to correlate Stoic thinking on ethical naturalism with some modern theories, taking up, first, the role of the idea of human nature in ethics and, second, the contribution of virtue ethics to environmental debates. I suggest that Stoic ideas can add significantly to both these strands of thought in contemporary Neo-Aristotelian virtue ethics. Finally, in Chapter 8, I argue that Stoic thinking on ethical development and guidance can significantly enhance modern virtue ethical thinking on this subject, as well as contemporary life-guidance.

Although the discussion of these chapters is centred on topics which are of most relevance for Neo-Aristotelian virtue ethics, I do not wish to suggest that Stoic ethics is only of potential interest or importance for this type of modern theory. It is my hope that the strengths of Stoic ethical theory just outlined may also arouse interest, or heightened interest, in other modern moral approaches. I think the subsequent comparison of the virtue-happiness relationship in Stoicism and Aristotle may help to commend Stoic theory to non-Aristotelian virtue ethicists. The Stoic analysis of the virtue-happiness relationship, in which happiness is, exclusively, *virtue-based* happiness, may go some way towards addressing the reservations of exponents of this approach about making the idea of happiness central to their theories. Stoicism brings out, more effectively than Aristotle, how an idea of happiness can be consistent with ethical rigour, conceived in virtue ethical terms.[53] Also, as I bring out later, Stoic thinking on self-other relationships offers a defence against the charge that eudaimonistic virtue ethics is egoistic (or at least, 'foundationally egoistic') and does so more

---

[52] Several modern virtue ethicists put forward theories which can be seen as philosophical variations or extensions of the Aristotelian, rather than Stoic, position on the contribution of goods other than virtue to happiness. See Williams (1981: ch. 2) on 'moral luck'; Nussbaum (1986: ch. 11) on 'the fragility of goodness'; Hursthouse (1999: ch. 3) on 'tragic dilemmas'; and Russell (2012: parts 2–3) on the contrast between formalistic and embodied conceptions of happiness. I do not attempt to engage with these views from a Stoic standpoint here, which would be a complex and substantial project in its own right, though a worthwhile one; for some comments on Russell 2012, see Gill 2016c: 349–51.
[53] For non-Aristotelian virtue ethics, see text to nn. 8–11, and for reservations about incorporating a concern with happiness, see text to n. 140.

convincingly than Aristotle. The features of Stoicism just mentioned, may also serve to commend virtue ethics to exponents of other approaches, such as Kantian or Utilitarian ones, at least to those adherents of these approaches who are open to recognizing, in principle, the philosophical merits of virtue ethics. Ethical rigour, standardly, is more closely associated with these approaches. Hence, an analysis which brings out the conceptual coherence of an ethically rigorous virtue ethical position (that of Stoicism) may hold philosophical interest for such theorists, regardless of whether it leads to modifications of their own approach.

6.2 The Virtue-Happiness Relationship

As highlighted earlier, it is a mark of Neo-Aristotelian modern virtue ethics (though not its non-Aristotelian equivalent) to give a central role to happiness, understood in broadly ancient terms, as *eudaimonia*, as well as to virtue.[54] This gives rise to the question how to analyse the relationship between virtue and happiness. I suggest that, although Aristotle is helpful in providing a broad framework, Stoic ideas can take us further in exploring this relationship in some depth. Aristotle's discussion is less explicit and elaborated; also, his treatment includes qualifications and complications on certain key points that threaten the overall consistency of his account. The Stoic discussion of this relationship, examined in Chapter 1, is more fully thought out, and avoids the gaps and complications in Aristotle's analysis. In this respect, the Stoic treatment is more useful as a paradigm for modern virtue ethical treatments of this subject.

In modern philosophy, there has been a greater readiness to adopt the broadly Aristotelian conception of virtue than that of happiness (*eudaimonia*). Some virtue ethicists have not adopted it at all, and even within the Neo-Aristotelian strand of virtue ethics, deployment and examination of this concept has been less whole-hearted and extensive than that of virtue.[55] Some thinkers have highlighted the conceptual and semantic difference between (Aristotelian-style) *eudaimonia* and 'happiness', as used both in conventional and theoretical modern discourse. It is pointed out that 'happiness' in English, like its analogues in other European languages, has connotations such as 'welfare', 'good mood', and 'pleasure' which are not central, at least, for Aristotelian *eudaimonia*.[56] It is less often pointed out that, as explained in Chapter 1, the same is true of conventional ancient ideas of *eudaimonia*. The presentation of *eudaimonia* as closely, even inseparably, linked

---

[54] See text to nn. 9–10.

[55] Typically, in recent handbooks or monographs on virtue ethics, there are one or two chapters on 'happiness' or '*eudaimonia*'. Influential early works in this area, esp. MacIntyre 1985 and Williams 1985, focused more on virtue than happiness. However, Russell 2012 takes happiness as his main subject.

[56] See Baril 2013: 18–20; LeBar 2018: 470–1, 475–7; also Annas 2011: ch. 8; Russell 2012: ch. 2.

with virtue, reflects revisionist arguments to this effect, from Socrates onwards.[57] Ancient theorists adopting this line of thought (Plato, Aristotle, the Stoics) are also sometimes at pains to argue that their virtue-centred conception of *eudaimonia* carries with it some at least of the more conventional connotations, for instance those of pleasure' or 'contentment'.[58] Hence, the conception of *eudaimonia* we encounter in Aristotle and other ancient thinkers depends not only on accepting that this term has a certain meaning or usage but also on making substantive philosophical claims about the nature and basis of happiness. Put simply, the core claim is that real human happiness (happiness worth the name) depends on virtue, even if it brings other benefits with it.

A second tendency sometimes found in modern virtue ethical thinkers, particularly those who are not also specialists in ancient philosophy, is this. While adopting the ancient philosophical move of making a strong connection between virtue and happiness, they sometimes analyse this relationship in ways that reflect the alternative (non-virtue ethics) approach that is still dominant in modern moral philosophy. A salient feature of this approach is the idea that a moral theory needs to be grounded in a normative principle of some sort. Standard examples of such principles are, within the duty-centred (deontological) tradition, Kant's principle of universalization, or, within the consequentialist tradition, that of maximizing human benefit.[59] Such principles are seen as providing the moral force of obligation or as underpinning moral rules or requirements.[60] In line with this approach, happiness (or *eudaimonia*) is sometimes presented, like modern moral norms, as grounding virtue, or as providing criteria for what should count as virtues in the full sense. For instance, in some recent discussions, happiness is presented as constituting a 'standard' for virtue, or, in another formulation, as 'an unconditioned condition' for virtue.[61]

Although one can see the rationale for this kind of move, it represents a misinterpretation of the virtue-happiness relationship, at least if the aim is to adopt an Aristotelian, or, more broadly, ancient, approach to this relationship. As Annas points out, in the ancient framework, it is not a matter of using one concept (*eudaimonia*), which is taken to have a highly determinate meaning, to define or regulate another (virtue) which is taken to be indeterminate in significance. Nor is it a matter of treating one concept (*eudaimonia*) as providing the moral grounding or foundation for another (virtue) which requires this grounding for its moral

---

[57] See Ch. 1, text to nn. 3–8.

[58] See Ch. 1, text to nn. 17–19, 53. Stoics also present 'good emotions' (*eupatheiai*) as good, i.e. part of happiness (LS 60 K(1)).

[59] See Paton 1948: 84–6 (Kant, Prussian Academy edn., vol. 4, 421–3); Mill 1993: 7. See also on such modern moral norms Gill 2005a: 16–19.

[60] On this central theme in modern moral theory, see Korsgaard 1996: chs. 1–4; also Darwall 2011, 2012, discussing Irwin 2007–8, and distinguishing this approach from that centred on virtue and happiness.

[61] See Baril 2013: 24–5; LeBar 2018: 472–4; also Annas 2011: 154, criticizing this type of view.

force. Rather, the two concepts, taken as an interconnected pair, are subject to a process of reflection directed both at determining both their semantic meaning and their substantive philosophical content and significance. This applies to ethical reflection at the personal or individual level, in which the agent thinks about her life as a whole, as Annas puts it. It also applies to reflection regarded as part of a (typically collective) process of ethical theorizing or debate.[62]

However, even with these clarifications, the question how best to understand the virtue-happiness relationship in modern ethical theory of an Aristotelian type remains rather open. Aristotle provides a broad framework, which holds good for much later ancient theory, including Stoicism, and which is also widely accepted by modern theorists of virtue ethics and eudaimonism working in an Aristotelian mode.[63] This framework sets certain general criteria for what should count as happiness (*eudaimonia*), namely being complete, self-sufficient, and constituting the overall goal or end (*telos*) of a human life.[64] This still leaves open the question what conception of happiness meets these criteria, a subject on which ancient thinkers after Aristotle differ widely.[65] Aristotle's own definition of happiness is 'an activity of the psyche according to virtue'. This is presented as an 'outline' definition;[66] and it is, indeed, very broad, though the argumentation preceding this definition brings some clarification of its meaning. Aristotle reaches this definition by analysing happiness as the specifically human good; and human beings are presented as, distinctively rational.[67] In the course of setting out his criteria for happiness, Aristotle also comments that human beings constitute a 'naturally sociable (or 'political') animal' (*politikon zōon*); so we can infer that human beings are conceived as distinctively rational and sociable.[68] Aristotle also stresses that, in his view, happiness constitutes a form of activity, and not a state; hence, happiness involves the active exercise of rationality (and perhaps also sociability).[69] In formulating his definition, and subsequently, Aristotle adds certain qualifications to his 'outline'. These include the requirement that the activity must last 'not just for a random period of time but throughout a complete life'.[70] This point brings out Aristotle's conception of happiness as not just an occurrent activity but as constituting a certain kind of life (the best possible human life). Aristotle's idea of happiness seems to have exercised a broad influence on later ancient thought, though some later thinkers, notably the Epicureans, take a sharply different view

---

[62] Annas 2011: 150–2, 160–3: also, on thinking about one's life as a whole (in ancient theory), Annas 1993: ch. 1. On ancient thinking about reflection as, typically, communal or 'objective-participant' in approach, see Gill 1996: 9–10, 275–87, 2006: 389–91, 403–7.

[63] For modern discussions adopting this broad framework, see Annas 2011: ch. 9; Russell 2012: ch. 3, 2013b; Baril 2013; LeBar 2018.

[64] Arist. *NE* 1.7, 1097a15–1097b21.   [65] See Annas 1993: part 4.

[66] Arist. *NE* 1.7, 1098a16–17, 20–2.   [67] Arist. *NE* 1.7, 1097b24–1098a8.

[68] Arist. *NE* 1.7, 1097b8–11.   [69] Arist. *NE* 1.7, 1098a5–8, 1.8, 1098b30–1099a7.

[70] Arist. *NE* 1.10, 1101a16; also 1.7, 1098a18: 'in a complete life'. For his other qualification in 1.7, on the question of which virtue is best and most complete or perfect, (1.7, 1098a17–18), see text to n. 92. Further qualifications follow in 1.8–10, discussed in text to nn. 78–88.

on key points.[71] The Stoics adopted, or reached independently, a similar overall conception of happiness involving most of these points. For instance, they share his view that happiness constitutes living a certain kind of life, though not necessarily a 'complete life', in Aristotle's sense.[72] Modern virtue ethicists who are also eudaimonists tend to adopt the main features of Aristotle's account. To this extent, Aristotle sets a broad framework for understanding happiness (conceived as *eudaimonia*), which is largely accepted by modern virtue ethics working in the ancient mould.

Aristotle is also influential in modern virtue ethics in making virtue central for happiness.[73] In fact, this view is common ground for a series of ancient thinkers, from Socrates onwards (though not for all ancient philosophers),[74] but Aristotle has been the main ancient source used for this idea. This is understandable, given his well-marked definition of happiness by reference to virtue in *NE* 1.7. However, there are certain difficulties in taking Aristotle as the primary ancient model for this view. For one thing, Aristotle is rather inexplicit both in his analysis of the relationship between virtue and happiness and in his justification of the close linkage he claims between them. His account of happiness simply presents this as 'according to' (in line with) 'virtue' (1098a16–17), and this generalized statement is not analysed further, at least in 1.7. Also, the rationale for the central role of virtue is rather undeveloped. The main relevant point made in 1.7 is that if happiness is the human work or function, this function must be excellently carried out, and it is assumed, without further argument, that this means performance that is virtuous.[75] In addition, in sharp contrast with the Stoics, he does not explore the idea that the close linkage between virtue and happiness reflects a structural similarity in the core characteristics of both virtue and happiness. Aristotle's failure to do this is the more marked because his theory contains the materials for arguing for a structural similarity of this kind between virtue and happiness. Indeed, the materials are, in part, the same as those deployed by the Stoics for this purpose. The idea that human beings are, distinctively, rational and sociable, figures in the argument leading to his definition of happiness as 'according to virtue' (in *NE* 1.7);[76] and these characteristics form a prominent part of his analysis of virtue, particularly ethical (character-based) virtue.[77] But Aristotle does

---

[71] The Epicureans identify pleasure (as they conceive this notion) as the goal of life (LS 21); also Annas 1993: chs. 7, 16.
[72] See 1.3. On the Stoic view that happiness is not increased by greater length of life, see Cic. *Fin.* 3.46, 3. 76; also Gill 2006: 88.
[73] See refs. in n. 63.   [74] See Ch. 1, text to nn. 5–8.
[75] Arist. *NE* 1.7, 1098a7–18.   [76] See text to nn. 68–9.
[77] See Arist. 1.13, 1102b21–1103a10 (ethical virtue is located in the non-rational part of the psyche but is directed by reason); 2.6, 1107a1–2 (ethical) virtue 'is determined by reason and as a person of practical wisdom would determine it'); 6.12, 1144a20–1144b1 (ethical virtue and practical wisdom are interdependent). Sociability is assumed throughout Aristotle's account of ethical virtue.

not formalize this linkage in the way that some Stoic sources do nor does he use it to justify and explain the close linkage he claims between virtue and happiness.

Aristotle's fullest treatment of the virtue-happiness relationship comes, in fact, not when he is setting out his initial definition of happiness by reference to virtue in *NE* 1.7, but when he is qualifying this definition in 1.8–10, and pursuing the question what counts as the highest form of happiness in 10.7–8. In 1.8–10, following a finely balanced line of argument, he reaches the conclusion that happiness requires not just virtue but also an 'adequate' supply of external goods, and that throughout 'a complete life'.[78] Some virtue ethicists take a positive view of Aristotle's qualifications in 1.8–10 and use them as the basis for their own conception of happiness and the virtue-happiness relationship.[79] However, the corollary is that happiness is no longer, straightforwardly, 'according to virtue'; and Aristotle's move introduces complication, and arguably, internal tension or ambiguity into his account of this relationship.

On this point, the Stoic account is clearly defined and consistently worked out whereas Aristotle's treatment is more provisional and open-ended. This point applies with special force to the line of reasoning that leads Aristotle, in *NE* 1.8–10, to qualify his initial definition of happiness solely by reference to virtue (1.7) by adding the further requirement of an adequate supply of external goods throughout a complete life.[80] This discussion is remarkable for its dialectical attention to competing considerations. Put less positively, it juxtaposes contrasting or opposed ideas, without resolving the contrast or opposition between them. There are two sets of contrasting or opposed ideas. One is between (a) the idea that bodily and external goods are valuable and contribute to happiness as instruments of the exercise of virtue, and (b) the idea that they are inherently valuable.[81] The second contrast is between (c) the idea that virtue can overcome the loss of such things (and, by inference at least, retain happiness) and (d) the idea that the loss of such things, at least if sufficiently great, inevitably affects happiness.[82] Idea (c) is strongly marked, in fact, in *NE* 1.10, though not unequivocally. It is, then, surprising that Aristotle concludes, rather abruptly, that happiness requires an adequate supply of external goods throughout a complete life.[83] While

---

[78] Arist. *NE* 1.10, 1101a15–16.

[79] See Nussbaum 1986: ch. 11, illustrating 'the fragility of goodness' (i.e. virtue and happiness); Russell 2012: ch. 5, used as the basis for his 'embodied' conception of the self and of correlated ideas about virtue and happiness.

[80] Contrast *NE* 1.7, 1098a12–18 with 1.10, 1101a14–16; the requirement of a complete life is already indicated in 1.7, 1098a18–20. See also Ch. 1, text to nn. 29–34.

[81] *NE* 1.8: instruments of virtue (1099a15–b2); independent contributors or 'adornments' (1099b2–19). *NE* 1.9: instruments (1099b27–8); independent contributors (?) (1100a5–9). 1.10: not specified but seem to be independent contributors (1100b8–9, 25–30). Cooper 1985: 195–6 argues that Aristotle's position is only that of idea (a); but for (effective) counterarguments, see Annas 1993: 378–81.

[82] The first idea (c): 1.10: 1100b12–22, esp. 20–2, b30–1101a7; the second idea (d): 1.9, 1101a5–9, 1.10: 1100b22–30, 1101a6–13.

[83] Arist. *NE* 1.10, 1101a14–16. Russell 2012: 109 notes the abruptness.

highlighting these competing ideas, Aristotle does not make it clear precisely how the competition or tension between them should be resolved. Although his concluding position requires a combination of virtue and external (and presumably bodily) goods,[84] he does not provide any overall account of the way that these two factors should be weighed against each other to determine whether someone is or is not happy.[85] It is understandable, then, that Annas characterizes Aristotle's conception of happiness as, by contrast with the Stoic one, an 'unstable' one.[86] Russell too acknowledges these internal tensions, though he is sympathetic to Aristotle's overall or final position.[87] In the later Aristotelian tradition, these difficulties tend to persist (especially the lack of a worked-out analysis of how to weigh the two factors in relation to each other), despite some evident attempts to resolve the tensions in Aristotle' discussion.[88]

The Stoic theory, though differently formulated, has a clearly defined position on each of these questions. On the second contrast in Aristotle, the Stoics, unequivocally, adopt idea (c), rather than (d). They claim that virtue can be exercised under any circumstances, however unfavourable: in the famous image, the wise person is happy on the rack of torture. This happiness is not qualified by the amount or scale of loss of bodily or external advantages (by contrast with Aristotle's idea (d)); and the difference between the two approaches on this point is underlined towards the close of Cicero's debate between them in *On Ends* 3–5.[89] The Stoic position is also clear (though quite complex) on the first contrast in Aristotle's discussion. The Stoics adopt neither of Aristotle's ideas (a and b). Indifferents do not contribute to happiness, that is, they do not form 'parts' of happiness, under either of Aristotle's headings. The 'parts' of happiness are virtue and the other goods, such as good actions and emotions, that depend directly on the exercise of virtue.[90] Put differently, happiness is determined, solely by the exercise of virtue. However, the Stoics have ideas which are analogous to, though not identical with, Aristotle's ideas (a and b). They believe that preferred indifferents have positive value (*axia*): they are 'naturally' or objectively preferable, and this is independent of the virtue or vice of the person involved. Also, the expertise of the virtuous person consists, in part, in recognition of the preferability or dispreferability of the indifferents relevant on each occasion. In this sense, indifferents form 'the material' of virtue, as Chrysippus puts it; and, to this degree,

---

[84] For the three types of good, see *NE* 1.8, 1098b12–16; bodily goods are noted in 1.8, 1099b3–4, though not in the concluding formulation, 1.10, 1101a14–16.

[85] Aristotle sometimes suggests that a certain degree or amount of loss of bodily or external goods will prevent happiness; it will 'weigh down the scales of life' 1.10, 1100b24–5, trans. Barnes 1984. See 1.9, 1100a5–9; 1.10, 1100b22–30. But Aristotle offers no account of how this amount is to be determined, and what kind of 'weight' should be allocated to each kind of good.

[86] Annas 1993: 378–84.

[87] Russell 2012: 108–17. Nielsen 2012: 22–4 also underlines this tension.

[88] For this view, see Annas 1993: 385–8, 413–18; Russell 2012: 117–27. On this topic, see also Sharples 2007, 2010: ch. 18 (primary sources); Inwood 2014: esp. chs. 1, 3, 4.

[89] See Cic. *Fin.* 5.79–86; also Gill 2016a: 242–3.   [90] See Ch. 2, text to nn. 120–31.

virtue, and happiness, can be defined, in part at least, in terms of 'selection' of indifferents.[91] Hence, there is an analogue, at least, in Stoic theory to Aristotle's idea (b), that bodily and external goods contribute to happiness as instruments of virtue as well as (a), that they contribute by their inherent value. Overall, then, Aristotle's discussion, though reaching a determinate conclusion, is, for the most part, even-handed (or ambivalent) in its consideration of competing ideas on this question. The Stoic position, by contrast, is clear-cut and fully worked out. The clarity of the Stoic position does not depend simply on adopting one of Aristotle's alternatives in each case and rejecting the other. They do adopt (c) and reject (d); but this depends on their independently formulated theory of virtue, happiness, and indifferents (examined in Chapters 1 and 2). Their theory also offers analogues for Aristotle's ideas (a) and (b), which enable them to adopt versions of both ideas, but accommodated within a new, and coherent, framework. Hence, on this topic, as on the virtue-happiness question in general, the Stoic theory offers a fully elaborated analysis, whereas Aristotle's treatment is provisional, open-ended, or ambiguous.

Another context in which Aristotle explores rather fully the virtue-happiness relationship comes much later in the *Nicomachean Ethics* (10.7–8), anticipated in his earlier discussion of the relationship between practical and theoretical wisdom (6.5, 6.12–13). In *NE* 1.7, in offering his general definition of happiness as 'an activity of the psyche according to virtue', he adds the qualification that, 'if there are several virtues, according to the best and most perfect' (or 'complete', *teleiotatē*) virtue'.[92] In *NE* 10.7–8, he seems to return to the question left open in 1.7, that is, which virtue should be considered most perfect or complete. The two candidates considered are the combination of activity based on ethical (character-based) virtue and practical wisdom, on the one hand, and activity based on theoretical wisdom, on the other. His discussion, as in 1.8–10, is finely balanced and dialectical; and he accepts that a full life should contain both elements.[93] However, his conclusion is, decisively, that activity based on theoretical wisdom counts as the highest and most perfect form of happiness, whereas that based on ethical virtue combined with practical wisdom represents a lesser or secondary grade.[94] One of the grounds for this preference is that theoretical activity constitutes a 'divine' kind of happiness (shared with the gods), whereas practical activity constitutes a 'human' one.[95] Aristotle's move there has been much debated by

---

[91] For these ideas, see LS 58 A–E (indifferents and positive or negative value), LS 59 A (indifferents as 'material' of virtue), and LS 58 K (happiness, and, by inference, virtue, defined or characterized, by reference to 'selection' of indifferents). See Ch. 2, text to n. 8, nn. 16–23, nn. 37–42, nn. 60–2. As stressed in Ch. 2, text to nn. 69–72, the expertise of virtue does not consist solely in assessment of preferability, but takes account of this. On the factors involved in virtuous decision-making, see Ch. 2, text to nn. 73–5.

[92] Arist. *NE* 1.7, 1098a16–18.   [93] Arist. *NE* 10.8, 11788a9–14, 1178b5–7.

[94] Arist. *NE* 10.7, 1177a17–1178a8, 10.8, 1178a9–b7.

[95] Arist. *NE* 10.7, 1177b26–1178a2, 10.8, 1178a9–b7, 1178b8–32.

specialist scholars of Aristotle; and it has sometimes been maintained that it is inconsistent with his overall ethical theory.[96] I am not convinced that Aristotle is formally inconsistent on this point; the move is anticipated in *NE* 1.7 and Book 6.[97] However, it runs counter to the strong emphasis on ethical virtue, combined with practical wisdom, in earlier books of the *Nicomachean Ethics*, which is not there presented as linked with a secondary grade of happiness. Also, the use of the idea of 'human' (and 'divine' happiness) in 10.7–8 contrasts with the more inclusive use of 'human' in his definition of happiness as the 'human' function in 1.7. The move in 10.7–8 is sometimes seen as a reversion to a Platonic preference for philosophical contemplation rather than practical activity,[98] which is out of line with Aristotle's, generally, more balanced or inclusive approach.[99]

For these reasons, Aristotle's theory has serious limitations as a model for modern virtue ethicists aiming to produce a consistent and fully elaborated account of the virtue-happiness relationship. Stoic theory, by contrast, does offer this kind of account (though within a broadly Aristotelian framework), and one that avoids internal tension or incoherence, precisely on the points where Aristotle encounters this. I have already indicated how the Stoics avoid the tension that arises in *NE* 1.8–10, through their innovative idea of 'indifferents' (text to nn. 90–1). They also avoid the tension generated in *NE* 10.7–8, by rethinking the relationship between theoretical and practical wisdom. Both points are brought out fully in the following section.

The consistency and worked-out character of the Stoic account can also be illustrated by reference to other central features of their theory. These include a feature discussed fully in Chapter 1: the structural similarity between the core (good-making) characteristics of happiness and virtue, which underlies the Stoic claim that virtue forms the sole basis for happiness. One such pair of characteristics, rationality and sociability, is presented by Stoics as characteristic of human nature. As indicated earlier, these features also figure in connection with Aristotle's definition of happiness (conceived as the distinctively human function) and his, separate, discussion of virtue. However, in Aristotle's treatment, their role as a pair of distinctively human features, and as core characteristics of virtue and happiness, is not formalized or underlined, as it is in Stoic accounts of ethics, notably, that of Stobaeus, thought to reflect closely the framework of

---

[96] See Wilkes 1980: 350–1; Nussbaum 1986: 373–7.

[97] Arist. *NE* 10.7, 1177a12–18 seems to refer back to the question left open in 1.7, 1098a16–18. Book 6 also places a higher value on theoretical than practical wisdom: see 6.7, 1141a20–1141b8, 6.12, 1143b17, 6.13, 1145a6–11.

[98] For this preference, see Pl. *Rep.* 519c–521b, *Tht.* 172c–177c.

[99] For a review of a range of interpretations, see Gill 1996: 370–83; also White 2002: 244–62; Russell 2012: 77. Aristotle's *EE* is sometimes presented as offering a more consistent view of happiness (e.g. Kenny 1978/2016: 91–6, 1992: 93–102); however, the key relevant text there (*EE* 1249b16–22) is ambiguous and hard to interpret, as Kenny concedes (1978/2016: 96, 1992: 95–6).

Chrysippus.[100] A similar point applies to the second pair of characteristics closely associated in Stoic thought with both virtue and happiness, and associated with universal nature, namely the combination of structure, order, and wholeness, and care for oneself and for others of one's kind. This combination is not formalized in quite the same way as the other pair in the Stoic summaries of ethical doctrines. However, both sets of ideas form recurrent motifs of Stoic treatment of virtue and happiness, and also of universal nature; and Cicero's account of 'appropriation' in *On Ends* 3.16–22, 62–8, includes both features and highlights the linkage with the Stoic claim about the virtue-happiness relationship, especially in 3.20–2.[101] In this respect, Stoicism provides detailed points of correspondence between key markers of virtue and of happiness, and thus justifies and explains the idea that virtue is central for happiness in a way that goes beyond Aristotle's more sketchy and provisional account in *NE* 1.7.[102] Also, whereas Aristotle goes on to qualify and complicate the link between virtue and happiness, in ways just outlined, Stoicism embeds the link in various aspects of ethical theory, including the account of personal and social development and guidance on 'appropriate actions'.[103] In this respect, Stoic theory offers resources for modern virtue ethicists wanting to explore and substantiate the idea of virtue as central for happiness, and it does so in a fuller and less qualified form than we find in Aristotle.

6.3 Acting Virtuously for Its Own Sake

The advantages of the Stoic theory, in comparison with Aristotle's, emerge if we consider a question that has sometimes been posed about Aristotle's theory, but which can also arise in any modern theory that combines virtue ethics with eudaimonism. Aristotle sometimes stresses the idea that a virtuous action is performed 'for its own sake' (of 'for the sake of the fine', these ideas seemingly taken to be identical). At the same time, he presents happiness as the overall or ultimate goal of a human life.[104] This raises the question how these two ideas are to be correlated or squared with each other. Is virtue conceived as inherently or intrinsically good or worthwhile, and choiceworthy for its own sake, or is it valuable only (or in addition) as instrumental for achieving happiness? Although Aristotle's theory gives rise to this question, he does not address it explicitly;[105] and scholars have examined, for instance, his discussions of practical

---

[100]   See Ch. 1, text to nn. 72–8, 153–7, Ch. 3, text to nn. 79–91, on these Stoic ideas. See also text to nn. 76–7, on parallel ideas in Aristotle.

[101]   See Ch. 1, text to nn. 87–91, 96–101, 183–208; also 4.4.   [102]   See text to nn. 74–7.

[103]   See (on development) Ch. 4, text to nn. 106–7, 206–15; (on appropriate actions) Ch. 2, text to nn. 118–24.

[104]   See Arist. *NE* 2.4, 1105a31–2, 3.7, 1115b22–3; also 1.1–2, 1.7, 1097a15–1097b6.

[105]   On this point, see Annas 1993: 371–2.

deliberation with a view to finding an implicit answer.[106] It might be argued that, given Aristotle's general view of happiness (as stated in *NE* 1.7, for instance), this question does not identify a serious problem in his thinking. If happiness is defined as being 'according to virtue', then acting in a virtuous way 'for its own sake' and aiming, ultimately, at living a life 'according to virtue' are, either identical or at least fully compatible, however the process of virtuous deliberation is conceived. But at this point, the qualifications that Aristotle builds into his account of the virtue-happiness relationship take on special significance. In *NE* 1.8–10, it becomes clear that happiness depends not only, for Aristotle, on virtue, crucial though this is, but also on 'an adequate' supply of external goods, across the length of 'a complete life'.[107] Thus, by inference, aiming at the overall goal of happiness cannot just consist in performing virtuous acts 'for their own sake', but needs to take account of the additional objective of securing external goods throughout one's life; and these two aims need to be correlated in some way.[108] Also, there is the further qualification made, with some emphasis, in *NE* 10.7–8, presenting theoretical activity as the highest possible form of human happiness, with practical activity at a secondary level, even though a full human life should include both elements.[109] This second qualification has implications for this question. It means that performing a practical (virtuous) act 'for its own sake', does not, by itself, work towards the goal of achieving the highest form of human happiness. These and related questions have, of course, been addressed by Aristotelian scholars; and various expansions of his analysis have been proposed to provide a consistent and credible theory.[110] However, the extent of this scholarly exegesis only underlines the fact that Aristotle himself does not provide an explanatory framework that accommodates these points.

Stoic theory also formulates, in various ways, the idea that the virtuous act is performed 'for its own sake' (or is inherently choiceworthy),[111] as well as the idea that happiness (typically, conceived as 'the life according to nature') constitutes the overall goal for the virtuous person.[112] However, if the question is raised how these ideas are to be reconciled, the answer is, for several reasons, much more

---

[106] A further difficulty is that Aristotle's main discussion of deliberation (*bouleusis*) (*NE* 3.3) defines this rather narrowly, as focused on means not ends (on this much-debated point, see Annas 1993: 87–9; Russell 2009: 27–30). Hence, it is difficult to place within Aristotle's own psychological framework the activity we find in *NE* Book 1 and 10.7–8, that of examining candidates for the end or goal of life. See also refs. in n. 110.

[107] Arist. 1.10, 1101a15–16; also text to n. 67.

[108] Annas 1993: 380–3, underlines the difficulties for Aristotle raised by this point; see also text to nn. 78–87.

[109] See text to nn. 92–9.

[110] On Aristotelian practical deliberation, with reference to these questions, see Price 2005, 2011: 189–250, including full discussion of recent scholarship on this topic.

[111] See esp. Cic. *Fin.* 3.21–2; 'choice' (*hairesis*) of a virtuous act is distinguished from 'selection' (*eklogē*) (of indifferents) partly on this basis (see Inwood 1985: 205–14).

[112] See 1.3–4.

straightforward than in Aristotle's case. In the first instance, as brought out in Chapter 1, Stoic theory offers a more fully worked-out analytic framework than Aristotle, and the virtue-happiness relationship is more explicitly defined. The status of virtue, along with happiness, as 'good', by contrast with 'preferred indifferents', is fundamental to the analysis.[113] The virtues are, explicitly, presented as both 'instrumental and final goods. For they both generate happiness and they complete it, since they are parts of it'. The other 'parts' are not the 'preferred indifferents' but things such as good emotions and (perfectly) right actions, which are features of a life shaped by virtue.[114] The virtues are also explicitly presented as directed at the goal of achieving happiness, and as forms of expertise in leading a happy life, with different cardinal virtues playing distinct but co-ordinated roles in this objective.[115] It is not only in general analysis of the key concepts that Stoic theory achieves consistency and comprehensiveness. As just highlighted, the Stoics ascribe the same core characteristics to both virtue and happiness: rationality and sociability, structure, order, and wholeness, and care for oneself and others. As illustrated in Chapter 1, these characteristics are worked out in detailed elaboration of the ideas of virtue and happiness.[116] The shared possession of these characteristics explains why virtue can be seen as, in itself, an inherent or intrinsic good, and also as a means of realizing these same qualities in the form of happiness. The concepts of virtue and happiness play different roles within the theory (as qualities of the agent and the life lived by the agent);[117] but, at each level, and in a co-ordinated way, the shared characteristics ensure consistency between them.

Also, Stoic theory adopts several innovative concepts and positions that ensure that the problems or tensions associated in Aristotle with external goods (*NE* 1.8–10) and with the relationship between theory and practice (*NE* 10.7–8) do not arise in Stoic theory. Hence, the Stoic account of the relationship between virtue and happiness, just outlined, applies consistently. On the first point, the relevant Stoic doctrine has already been fully discussed here. The account of 'indifferents' recognizes the positive value of (what Aristotle calls) 'bodily and external goods',[118] while maintaining that happiness is determined wholly by virtue. Although preferability constitutes a basis, in principle, for action, selection between indifferents, for the virtuous person, is not based solely on the criterion of preferability, but on what is right, that is, in line with virtue. The implications of this theory for practical deliberation are worked out fully in Cicero's *On Duties*. As Cicero stresses in Book 3, there is no situation where the virtuous person will select preferable indifferents *despite* this selection not being right and in line with

---

[113] This is brought out clearly in Stob. 5a, 6b, 6e.
[114] See Stob. 5g, 2.72.4–6 (LS 60 M), and LS 60 J–L; also Ch. 1, text to nn. 111 and 120–31.
[115] See Ch. 1, text to nn. 132–57.   [116] See Ch. 1, text to nn. 72–91, 153–211.
[117] See Ch. 1, text to nn. 113–15.   [118] Arist. *NE* 1.8, 1098b12–17.

virtue. Hence, while happiness can be defined, or at least characterized, by reference to selection between indifferents,[119] it is also made clear that happiness does not depend on securing preferable, rather than dispreferable, indifferents.[120] Thus, the difficulties, or ambiguities, regarding the relationship between virtue and happiness that arise from Aristotle's position on external goods in *NE* 1.8–10, do not arise, not because they are ignored but because Stoic theory evolves new ideas which accommodate them.

The Stoic innovations regarding indifferents are well-known and fully recognized by scholars of ancient philosophy.[121] Less well recognized are certain features of Stoic thinking that avoid the complications and, arguably, inconsistencies arising from Aristotle's preference for theoretical, rather than practical, activity as an expression of the highest human happiness (*NE* 10.7–8). There are three main significant moves made in Stoic theory bearing on this question. First, the Stoics do not introduce into their conception of virtue the subdivisions that underpin Aristotle's position in *NE* 10.7–8, namely between ethical ('character-based') and intellectual virtue, and, within intellectual virtue between practical and theoretical (or contemplative) wisdom.[122] The Stoic concept of virtue is understood in a broad, holistic, way that accommodates the strands allocated by Aristotle to different types of virtue.[123] It is worth noting that in this respect, the Stoic theory matches the kind of unified view adopted by several modern virtue ethicists regarding virtue, notably Zagzebski, against those modern theorists who argue for a more Aristotelian, subdivided, account of virtue.[124] Hence, Aristotle's presentation of activities, or lives, based on the difference between the expression of theoretical wisdom and practical wisdom (combined with ethical virtue), as substantive ethical alternatives,[125] does not have an equivalent place or significance in Stoic theory.

Further, the Stoics, conspicuously, avoid taking a position on the Platonic-Aristotelian question whether the happy (or happiest) life is that of theory or practice. In one source, their view is reported in this form: 'There being three ways of life, the theoretical, the practical, and the rational (*logikos*), they say the third is to be chosen; the rational animal has been equipped (*epitēdes*) by nature for theory and action'.[126] The Stoics refuse to treat the difference between the theoretical and practical lives as fundamental. The presentation of the best kind of life as 'rational', coupled with the comment on our nature as a rational animal, evokes the idea of happiness as 'a life according to nature', and also suggests the view of

---

[119]   See Stob. 6a, 2.76.9–15 (LS 58 K); also Ch. 2, text to nn. 60–2.
[120]   See Ch. 2, esp. text to nn. 42–5, 197–201.   [121]   See 2.2–3.
[122]   For these distinctions, see Arist. *NE* 1.13, 1103a3–10; *EE* 2.1, 1220a4–12; *NE* 6.1, 1138b34–1139a17.
[123]   On the Stoic (unified) conception of virtue, see Ch. 1, text to nn. 132–40.
[124]   See Zagzebski 1996: 139; also Brady 2018, reviewing the unified view in recent virtue ethics. For a more subdivided modern view, closer to Aristotle's, see Baehr 2018: 800–2; Sim 2018.
[125]   See text to nn. 92–9.   [126]   D.L. 7.130, IG: 124.

virtue as a mode of expertise that enables us to live a happy life.[127] Both spheres of activity are presented as being, in principle, appropriate ones for realizing our nature and, by implication, for achieving the happy life.[128] The choice between them, or the combination of them adopted, should depend on the same considerations that are generally considered as valid in Stoic deliberation, namely selection between indifferents directed at determining what is right, that is, in line with virtue.[129]

On these two topics, the Stoics avoid the problems encountered by Aristotle, in providing a consistent view of the relationship between virtue and happiness, by framing the concepts (of virtue and happiness) at a higher or broader level than he does, at least in *NE* 10.7–8.[130] As Annas stresses, in a eudaimonistic framework, happiness consists in how we lead our lives overall, and cannot be formulated effectively in terms of specific types of activities.[131] A third way in which the Stoics avoid the difficulties generated by Aristotle's discussion consists in their understanding of the relationship between practical and theoretical wisdom. On the face of it, Aristotle's treatment in *NE* 10.7–8 presents practical and theoretical activity as clear-cut alternatives, considered as vehicles for the expression of the highest human happiness. However, he is sometimes interpreted as allowing scope for a more nuanced relationship between them. For instance, Aristotle's idea of *theoria* ('theory' or 'contemplation') has been understood as meaning, or at least including, the reflective dimension of a practical life. As Amélie Rorty puts it: 'There is nothing about the practical life which prevents it also being contemplative, and even enhanced by being contemplated . . . Properly conceived, *theoria* completes and perfects the practical life'.[132] Sarah Broadie too argues that *theoria* signifies there not so much purely theoretical activity but rather the reflective dimension of a fully developed human life; she also maintains that the proper use of such reflection is to 'celebrate' or 'crown' the fineness of practical wisdom and ethical virtue.[133] Although these readings, especially that of Broadie, are argued for with much philosophical sophistication and subtlety, I have to say they strike me as re-interpretations of Aristotle, designed, in part, to avoid the charges of inconsistency or internal tension sometimes directed at this aspect of his theory.[134]

However, a view close to that proposed by Rorty and Broadie could, more plausibly, be attributed to the Stoics. One of the outcomes of Stoic theory is to provide a broader perspective from which to understand practical, as well as theoretical, activities as, in principle, valid expressions of human virtue and

---

[127] For these ideas, see Ch. 1, text to nn. 63–8, 105–6, 132–57.

[128] See Bénatouïl and Bonazzi 2012: 8–9; Graver 2012.

[129] See also LS 66 J, 67 V–W; Bénatouïl 2007: 1–13.

[130] Aristotle's initial definition of happiness in *NE* 1.7 *is* pitched at a general level (though it is then subject to qualifications in 1.8–10); but, when he turns to the question of highest happiness (10.7–8), he does so in terms of specific types of activities.

[131] Annas 2011: 143–5.   [132] Rorty 1980: 377.   [133] Broadie 1991: 410–16.

[134] This interpretative aim is indicated in Broadie 1991: 414.

happiness. In Chapter 3, I suggest that Stoic theology is viewed as offering a vantage-point, from which to locate the best possible human characteristics in a broader framework, that of other natural kinds and universal nature, and to bring out the ethical significance of this framework.[135] One of the human characteristics 'celebrated' in this way (to use Broadie's term) is rationality, also seen as embodied in natural processes as a whole. As presented in Cicero's *On the Nature of the Gods*, Book 2, practical as well as theoretical expressions of human rationality are validated in this way, as one would expect, from Stoic thinking in general about the relationship between these two forms of rationality.[136] By contrast, in *NE* 10.7–8 and 6.7, Aristotle places practical wisdom on a lower level of value than intellectual wisdom. In 6.7, he explicitly rules out the idea that the special status of human beings within nature might lead us to qualify this valuation. He argues that the highest kind of knowledge is that of nature as a whole, and notably that of the heavenly bodies, seen as more valuable than human beings.[137] In effect, then, he rules out the possibility of using theoretical knowledge of nature as a whole to validate human practical rationality, in the way that the Stoics do.

In these ways, we can see Stoic theory as avoiding the difficulties, as regards consistency of theory, which arise in Aristotle's case because of his adoption of contemplative, rather than practical, activity as the highest expression of human virtue and happiness. By the same token, Stoic theory avoids the difficulty that arises in Aristotle's case of reconciling the idea that practical virtuous action is performed 'for its own sake' with the idea that it serves as a means of realizing happiness (or, at least, the highest form of human happiness).[138] Aristotle's underlining in *NE* 10.7–8 of the second-class status of practical action as an expression of highest happiness makes it more difficult to reconcile these two ideas. However, the Stoic ideas about virtue, happiness, and the relationship between theory and practice make this reconciliation possible and do so within an ethical framework that is, in other respects, more self-consistent and systematic in approach.

6.4 Self-Other Relationships

So far, in discussing the virtue-happiness relationship, I have highlighted questions that arise within ancient ethics, but which, I have suggested, are also relevant for constructing modern versions of the combination of virtue ethics and eudaimonism. I have argued that, for this purpose, Stoicism provides richer resources

---

[135] See 3.4, esp. text to nn. 142–8.
[136] Cic. *N. D.* 2. 147–53, on human reason, including practical uses of this (2.148, 150–2) as well as uses combining theory and practice (153); see also text to nn. 126–9.
[137] Arist. *NE* 6.7, 1141a33–1141b8.   [138] See text to nn. 98–9.

than Aristotle, because of its more consistent and systematic account of the virtue-happiness relationship, although Aristotle plays a valuable role in setting up the framework for this enquiry. In doing so, I have not generally made close reference to modern virtue ethical discussions and their distinctive concerns. However, I close this chapter by considering a question which is sometimes raised in modern treatments, but which has no obvious equivalent in ancient ethical debate. Modern virtue ethicists, as well as moral theorists of other types, sometimes object to giving (one's own) happiness a central role in ethical theory at all, on the grounds that doing so implies an egoistic or self-centred standpoint which is antithetical to the overall objectives of ethics (or of 'morality', as it is sometimes put).[139] This concern, partly at least, explains why some modern virtue ethicists are unwilling to give happiness a central role in their theories. It also goes some way towards explaining why some other modern thinkers see the concept of virtue as valuable primarily as a way of providing motivational support for other moral norms, notably maximizing human benefit or doing one's moral duty, rather than linking virtue with happiness.[140]

I consider two main forms of response to this objection. For both responses, although Aristotle provides relevant material, I suggest that Stoic ethics can take us further in the resources it offers. The first response (which assumes, in principle, the validity of the objection) is that the key consideration is how happiness is understood. If happiness is conceived, as it sometimes is, in modern (and ancient) conventional thinking, as consisting in, or including, one's own welfare or pleasure,[141] then the objection has some force. However, if virtue is conceived as central to happiness, then, to the extent that virtue is other-directed, aiming at happiness is not egoistic.[142] From this standpoint, as well as others, the Stoic theory has advantages, in comparison with the Aristotelian, in part because of its more self-consistent and systematic framework. The qualifications built into Aristotle's core thesis (that happiness is an activity 'according to virtue') have significant implications for the extent to which happiness is conceived as including other-directed virtuous activity. This point applies to Aristotle's conclusion in *NE* 1.10 that happiness requires some external goods as well as virtue, and his ranking of practical action (including the expression of other-benefiting virtues such as justice and courage) below theoretical activity in *NE* 10.7–8.[143] However, it

---

[139] On this concern, within virtue ethics, see LeBar 2018: 478–82, reviewing recent discussions; also Annas 2011: 152–63. 'Morality' is sometimes, but not always, associated in modern discussions with non-virtue ethical (e.g. deontological) approaches: see text to n. 5.

[140] I am referring here to (1) non-Aristotelian virtue ethicists (text to nn. 10–11) and (2) thinkers such as Crisp and Oakley who see the idea of virtue as supporting Utilitarian or deontological principles (text to n. 16).

[141] See text to nn. 56–7.

[142] As Annas points out in 1993: part 3, esp. 223–6, 322–5, all ancient forms of virtue ethics and eudaimonism 'find room for other-concern'. For a similar view, see LeBar 2018: 479–80.

[143] Arist. *NE* 10.8, 1178a9–14.

has also been argued that theoretical activity is conceived by Aristotle, as by other Greek thinkers, as shared and collective, closely linked with 'friendship' (*philia*), and hence not solely benefiting oneself.[144] Also, in *NE* 1.8–10, the 'external goods', whose loss detracts from happiness, include the welfare of others, for instance, family members, as well as our own welfare.[145] To this extent, Aristotle's position on these points allows for more concern for others than is immediately obvious.

None the less, the Stoic theory has a significantly less qualified approach to this question. Happiness is tied more closely to virtue; and both happiness and virtue are conceived in terms that include an other-benefiting dimension. The core characteristics, in both cases, are being sociable as well as rational, and caring for others as well as oneself. These core characteristics, as brought out already, are not limited to the general definition of these concepts; they are also embedded in the detailed working out of the theory, including its ideas about ethical development.[146] Also relevant is the fact that the unity (or at least interdependence) of the virtues is very firmly built into Stoic theory. Aristotle holds a version of this theory, in maintaining that the ethical (character-based) virtues are unified by the operation of practical wisdom.[147] However, although this bare claim appears in his work, its full implications are not worked out. By contrast, the unity or interdependence of the virtues is fully articulated in Stoic ethical sources.[148] Correspondingly, there is a much closer link in Stoic theory between virtues with an other-benefiting dimension, namely courage and justice, and the other virtues. In all these respects, the Stoic theory allows for a more cohesive and unqualified response to this objection. Stoic happiness, as well as Stoic virtue, has evident other-directed or other-benefiting dimensions; and Stoic happiness is uniformly tied to Stoic virtue.

However, both the objection and the response can be located at a deeper level and can give rise to more searching questions about the relationship between ancient and modern ethical frameworks. It is sometimes maintained that presenting happiness as the overall goal of life is egoistic in itself or 'foundationally egoistic', regardless of the way that happiness is conceived or of how virtue is

---

[144] On this point, see Kraut 1989: 74, 170–8, 182–4, referring to Arist. *NE* 9.9, 1170b11–14, 9.12, 1172a5 (in discussing friendship), 10.7 (1177a33–b1). The interpretations of Rorty and Broadie noted earlier (text to nn. 131–4) can also be seen as ways of mitigating the apparently egoistic dimension of Arist. *NE* 10.7–8. See also Gill 1996: 374–5 for an alternative response to this problem: for Aristotle to mount the argument found in 10.7–8 is, in itself, an other-benefiting action, since it brings out a profound human truth, which, if recognized, brings benefit to anyone.

[145] See Arist. *NE* 1.8, 1099a17–1099b6, 1.10, 1100a20–6 (the welfare of our family after our death); loss of life of our children is a theme especially relevant for the case of Priam, who lost virtually all his many children (1.10, 1101a7–8).

[146] See Ch. 1, text to nn. 72–91, 153–77, 201–8; also Ch.4.

[147] Arist. *NE* 6.13, 1144b30–1145a6. See also Russell 2009: 335–73.

[148] On the contrast between Aristotle and the Stoics on this point, see Annas 1993: 76–83: see also Ch. 1, text to nn. 133–46.

understood (assuming that virtue is fundamental for happiness).[149] Stoic ethics offers an effective response, and in some ways a more effective one than is enabled by Aristotle. In the first instance, assuming that the criticism is valid, Stoicism is more defensible against it than most other ancient theories, including Aristotle's. For instance, Aristotle presents as a key marker of friendship wishing the friend well 'for the other's sake', a feature realized most effectively in the best type of friendship, one based on virtue.[150] This idea is often interpreted by scholars as an ideal of 'altruistic' friendship. However, in three subsequent chapters (*NE* 9.4, 8, 9), he argues that exercising this kind of friendship also, at a deeper level, benefits the friend himself. Acting as an altruistic friend benefits oneself by enabling one to realize and express 'what each of us is' (our best self) and also provides an extension of our own happiness. The basis and validity of Aristotle's further moves have been much debated by scholars.[151] In the light of the modern criticism just noted, Aristotle's position can plausibly be seen as one which, while commending an altruistic friendship, does so in a way that is 'foundationally egoistic', in laying weight on the idea that such friendship is valuable because it contributes to the agent's own happiness.

Stoic thinking, on the other hand, is more defensible against this criticism. Although we find in Epictetus a line of thought close to the Aristotelian moves in *NE* 9.4, 8, 9,[152] in general Stoicism adopts a different approach to self-other relations. As stressed in Chapter 4, the Stoic theory of appropriation is based on the idea that the motive to benefit others is built into human nature as fundamentally as the motive to benefit oneself. Indeed, this motive is part of the make-up (or 'constitution') of other animals too; but in human beings this motive is developed through our distinctive rationality, leading us, among other things, to recognize human beings as such as potential objects of care and concern.[153] In these respects, the Stoics present ideas which are highly comparable to the modern ideal of altruism; as in some modern versions of altruism, the Stoics extend this concern to human beings in general. As just noted, Aristotle also presents as the best type of friendship one we might describe as an altruistic one (wishing the friend well for the friend's own sake) but then adds the qualification that this type of friendship also benefits the person herself at a deep level. The Stoics, however, do not make this further move. In texts such as Cicero *On Ends* 3.62–8 and *On Duties* 1.50–9, there is no attempt to show that (in modern terms) 'altruistic' relationships serve a 'foundationally egoistic' aim in expressing oneself (one's best self) at a deep level. Rational ethical development is, certainly, conceived as

---

[149] See Annas 2011: 154, referring to Hurka 2001: ch. 8; also LeBar 2018: 481, citing Hare 2000: 38.
[150] Arist. *NE* 8.2, 1155b31, elaborated in 8.3, 1156b6–12, as part of the account of best type of friendship, i.e. that based on virtue.
[151] See Kraut 1989: 78–154; Annas 1993: 249–62; Gill 1996: 346–70.
[152] See Epict. *Diss.* 1.9.11–15, 2.22.19–21; also Magrin 2018: 322–31.
[153] See esp. Cic. *Fin.* 3.62–3; also discussion in 4.2, 4.5.

realizing our nature as human beings and as an integral part of nature as a whole.[154] However this form of realization is not characterized in terms of 'self' versus 'others'; our concern for others as well as ourselves forms an integral part of our human nature as sociable as well as rational, and our concern for others of our kind as well as ourselves expresses a pattern built into nature as a whole. Hence, Stoic ethics provide little basis for the modern criticism that the theory is 'foundationally egoistic'.

Although the modern objection can be met in this way, as regards Stoicism, there are also grounds for questioning the validity of this objection, both in the modern context and as applied to ancient thought. Annas, for instance, challenges its cogency in the context of modern virtue ethics. She argues that, in eudaimonistic theories, raising the question of the nature of happiness, that is, of our overall goal, is, in the first instance at least, simply a way of reflecting on our life as a whole. This procedure, like making decisions on our own behalf (or indeed, living one's own life), is a function of being a rational agent or an individual human being, and is not, in itself, egoistic or self-centred in an ethically negative sense.[155] Annas also raises questions about the coherence and credibility of certain modern theories that present themselves as foundationally altruistic, citing Utilitarianism, in particular, which is based on the principle of maximizing benefit for other people. This theory, she argues, involves a radical, and puzzling, asymmetry between one's attitude to others and to oneself. The moral agent is required to act, consistently, so as to maximize the benefit (conceived as welfare or pleasure) of other people. But neither the agent herself nor the other person benefited is expected to be concerned with her own benefit.[156] So, if this is an example of a theory that is foundationally altruistic, it highlights the problem of making sense of the view of human motivation and action offered in the theory.

The objection can also be seen as problematic when applied to ancient ethics (or perhaps any non-modern or non-Western framework). The objection seems to presuppose that the egoism-altruism contrast is the only valid way of analysing our relations with other people. However, I have argued elsewhere that ancient culture deploys norms other than the egoism-altruism contrast for this purpose, including those of (proper forms of) reciprocity and 'the shared life'. These norms are sometimes used to validate actions and attitudes that we might class as altruistic, but the overall framework is differently conceived.[157] A further way of characterizing the typical approach of thinkers such as Aristotle and the Stoics is this. These thinkers assume that it is morally acceptable, and a normal part of a human life, both to take care of oneself and of others, and that these motives are

---

[154] See 4.3–5, esp. Ch. 4, text to nn. 140–8, 174–88.   [155] Annas 2011: 155–6, 160–3.

[156] Annas 2011: 157–8; for these criticisms of Utilitarianism, as being (damagingly) 'split-level', see also Williams 1985: 108–10.

[157] Gill 1996: 334–43.

not, in themselves, in conflict with each other, though they may give rise to actions or attitudes which conflict with each other. Virtue and happiness are both seen as including, or enabling, ethically valid ways of taking care of oneself and others, and of combining these forms of care, whereas vice and misery fail to do so in a valid way. This mode of analysing our relations with other people can be applied both to Aristotle and the Stoics, although in Aristotle's case, as on other questions, there are certain qualifications and complications.[158] In Stoicism, this view matches key features of their theory of development as appropriation as well as their conceptions of virtue and happiness.[159] It can also be correlated with their ideas about human and universal nature, which are themselves closely integrated with their ethical theory.[160] As with ancient ideals of reciprocity and the shared life, this framework of ideas provides an evaluative and motivational basis for actions and attitudes we (moderns) might class as altruistic, but within a different conceptual framework. In the light of these points, interpreting the Stoic theory in terms of the egoism-altruism contrast is problematic in two ways. It is problematic because it does not match Stoic modes of conceiving and evaluating self-other relationships. Also, doing so prevents us from recognizing and engaging intellectually with a framework that offers a potentially valuable alternative to the egoism-altruism contrast. Thus, overall, a further advantage of the Stoic ethical framework, in comparison with Aristotle, is that its account of self-other relationships provides more effective defences, of various kinds, against the modern charge of egoism.

---

[158] Some qualifications derive from the points already made about the virtue-happiness relationship (see text to nn. 78–88, 92–9). Further qualifications arise from Aristotle's way of correlating benefit to oneself and to others in friendship: see refs. in n. 151.

[159] For the idea that the motives of care for oneself and others are not seen by the Stoics as, in themselves, opposed, see also Ch. 4, text to nn. 27–9.

[160] See text to nn. 146–8, 154.

7

Stoic Ethics, Human Nature, and the Environment

7.1 Human Nature in Modern Virtue Ethics

In this chapter, I focus on a different, though related, way in which Stoic ethics can make a significant contribution to modern virtue ethics, namely on the role of nature in ethics, in two respects. First (7.1–2), I discuss some striking parallels between certain strands in Stoic thought and modern virtue ethics on the significance of the idea of human nature. I suggest that, in certain respects, Stoic thought explores this idea more thoroughly than modern theorists have done and that it can inform contemporary debate on this question. Second (7.3–4), I consider recent moves in modern virtue ethics to provide philosophical support for an effective response to the climate emergency. I suggest that Stoic ideas can also contribute to this debate, partly by offering new insights on the place of humanity within nature as a whole.

The question whether the idea of nature (human or universal) can play a useful role in ethical philosophy is one on which ancient and modern approaches have been, until recently, sharply divergent. In ancient philosophy, the idea played a prominent role, though one characterized in varying ways. Notably, a series of philosophers, from Plato to the Stoics and beyond, claimed that happiness, the goal of life, conceived as based on virtue, could be understood as the highest realization of human nature.[1] In modern philosophy, from the eighteenth century onwards, there was a strong reaction against this kind of approach. Influential theories such as Kantian deontology and Utilitarianism set aside questions about human nature, and focused on grounding moral principles such as the Categorical Imperative or the maximization of happiness.[2] In the twentieth century, G. E. Moore, in an influential study (1903), argued that the concept of good was, fundamentally, 'non-natural', and that the attempt to ground ethics in ideas such as human nature constituted the 'naturalistic fallacy'. Moore's move, among other factors, initiated what is sometimes called 'the linguistic turn', in which the

---

[1] See Ch. 1, text to nn. 10–28, 48–52, and Ch. 3. See also n. 12 (in this chapter) on Antiochus' version of this idea.
[2] See Ch. 6, text to n. 59. On these 'sources of normativity' (viewed from a Kantian standpoint), see Korsgaard 1996: chs. 1–2.

Learning to Live Naturally: Stoic Ethics and its Modern Significance. Christopher Gill, Oxford University Press.
© Christopher Gill 2022. DOI: 10.1093/oso/9780198866169.003.0008

focus moved to the language or logic of moral claims or reasoning. Moral statements were interpreted as a mode of giving commands ('prescriptivism') or of promoting a positive emotional attitude towards certain actions ('emotivism'). A related common claim was that there was a fundamental difference between 'facts' and 'values' or between statements about 'is' and 'ought'. The idea that moral reasoning might reflect core features of human nature or psychology was ignored or rejected by such theories.[3]

One of the distinctive features of the modern virtue ethics movement, from Anscombe's seminal article (1958) onwards, has been a call for renewed attention to questions about human nature and psychology. Theorists have focused not just on ethical principles, of certain kinds, but on features of human life that make those principles important and the ways in which people become psychologically motivated to respond to these principles.[4] In this respect, modern theorists have regarded themselves as reviving the ancient approach to ethics, though this has sometimes been combined with debate about how far this approach is compatible with modern conceptions of human nature.[5] Partly as a result, a more naturalistic standpoint has become more widespread, particularly in virtue ethics, both Neo-Aristotelian and non-Aristotelian, and also, to some extent, more generally. Non-Aristotelian virtue ethicists such as Slote and Driver have adopted and developed the eighteenth-century idea of 'Sentimentalism' (that virtue is grounded in natural human sympathy); Driver has also underlined the significance of this idea as an influence on Mill's Utilitarianism.[6] Korsgaard's study, *Self-Constitution* (2009), while Kantian in its overall conception, gives a more substantial role to questions about the psychology of ethical motivation than is normal in the Kantian approach. Korsgaard also draws extensively on Platonic and Aristotelian ideas about ethical psychology, though reoriented to her Kantian standpoint.[7] An indication of this shift towards a more naturalistic approach in ethics is a heightened interest in modern psychological research and its implications. For instance, there has been much recent debate about whether human actions are determined by long-term character traits or by the stimulus of specific situations.[8]

The last point, while illustrating the revival, in ethics, of the ancient focus on human nature and psychology, also raises the question how far modern thinkers can still adopt wholeheartedly ancient ideas on this topic. I pursue this topic, in this section, by outlining a debate on this question among virtue ethicists, centred on Aristotle's use of the idea of human nature and its characteristic work or

---

[3] For (critical) discussion of Moore and these modern philosophical movements, see MacIntyre 1985: 6–35; Williams 1985: 120–31; Foot 2001: 5–8.

[4] Notably, through the development of ethical dispositions; see Ch. 6, text to nn. 3–4.

[5] On the latter question, see n. 15.   [6] See Slote 2009; Oakley 2013; Driver 2015.

[7] See Korsgaard 2009, esp. chs. 6–8.

[8] On this debate, see Russell 2009: chs. 8–10; Annas 2011: 172–4; Snow 2013; Bates and Kleingeld 2018.

function (*ergon*) to define happiness (*NE* 1.7). Next (7.2), I discuss points of contact between Stoic thinking on human nature in ethics and the version of ethical naturalism offered in the closing chapters of Hursthouse's study, *On Virtue Ethics* (1999), which is partly based on Foot's work on this topic. I suggest that certain strands in Stoic thought, while closely parallel to Hursthouse's line of thought, explore it in more depth in certain respects. This illustrates my view that Stoic thinking on human nature can play a valuable role in informing contemporary virtue ethical debate on this subject, despite changes over time in conceptions of human psychology.

As highlighted earlier, a series of ancient thinkers use the idea of human nature, understood in various ways, to specify and support a specific conception of virtue-based happiness. In broad terms, this represents a response to longstanding debate in Greek thought about the relationship between 'nature' (*phusis*) and 'convention' or 'law' (*nomos*). Fifth-century BC thinkers sometimes deploy the idea of nature to support immoralist positions, whereas a series of later ancient thinkers use it to strengthen the case that happiness depends, wholly or in large measure, on virtue.[9] Plato, for instance, in the *Republic*, argues that virtue (more precisely, justice) can be understood as a structural arrangement of the parts of the psyche or the political state that constitutes the best condition of psyche and state (their harmony or health) and thus also their flourishing or happiness (*eudaimonia*).[10] Aristotle, in *NE* 1.7, uses the idea of human nature and its distinctive function to define happiness, based on virtue, as discussed earlier.[11] The idea of nature is deployed extensively in Stoic ethical theory, for different purposes and in various senses, as brought out in Chapter 3. However, it is used especially, and conspicuously, in connection with the specification of happiness or the goal of life, defined with reference to human or universal nature or both together.[12]

My main concern is with Stoic thought on this subject and its relationship to recent virtue ethical discussions. However, I begin by outlining an earlier scholarly debate (conducted mainly in the 1980s and 1990s) about Aristotle's use of the idea of human nature for this purpose, since this debate also has implications for the modern significance of Stoic thought. The chief point at issue is how, exactly, we should interpret Aristotle's procedure on this topic. In *NE* 1.7, Aristotle's definition of happiness is preceded by a brief taxonomic survey of natural kinds and their distinctive psychological capacities or functions. This paves the way for his definition of happiness as 'an activity of the psyche according to virtue'; this is

---

[9] See Guthrie 1969: ch. 4; Gill 1995: ch. 5; also Ch. 3, text to nn. 4–14.
[10] For a fuller summary, see Ch. 1, text to nn. 9–19; on the soul-state analogy, see Annas 1981: ch. 5; Ferrari 2003; Blössner 2007.
[11] See Ch. 6, text to nn. 63–70, 73–7; also Ch. 6, text to nn. 92–9, on his use in *NE* 10.7–8 of the ideas of human and divine to specify the highest form of happiness.
[12] See LS 63 A–C and Stob. 5b1, 5b3, 6; see also 1.3 and 3.3. Antiochus' theory of happiness, as the realization of human nature, based on Platonic, Aristotelian, and Stoic ideas, forms a continuation of this line of thought; see Cic. *Fin.* 5; Inwood 2014: 67–72; Gill 2016a.

presented as an 'outline' which best fulfils the criteria for happiness set out earlier in the chapter, namely constituting an end in itself, completeness, and self-sufficiency.[13] In locating the distinctively human function (rationality) in a broader survey of natural kinds, and in using this survey to define human excellence or virtue and happiness, Aristotle is, clearly, making a move that is marked as somewhat different from the rest of this discussion. But how different is it? Is he, for a short while at least, going outside ethical theory, as so far conducted by him, and taking up the standpoint of natural philosophy, which he adopts in other works, or adopting some kind of 'meta-level' viewpoint, embracing various fields of enquiry?[14] And, if so, does he suppose that the insight conferred by this new standpoint provides an authoritative basis for settling the question how to define happiness, that is, a question raised within ethical discourse? Or does Aristotle regard this section as a linear continuation of his normal ethical enquiry, though referring, in a generalized way, to what he understands as empirical facts about different natural kinds, for the purposes of specifying distinctively human happiness?

On this question, Williams adopted the first option and formulated his view in clear and striking terms, which aroused considerable debate. He maintained that, in the human function argument. Aristotle takes up a view 'outside' his normal ethical standpoint, with the aim of confirming his 'inside' standpoint, as an ethical agent. Aristotle aims to support his ethical convictions on the basis of 'an absolute understanding of nature', or 'the best possible theory of humanity and its place in the world'.[15] However, a number of other thinkers, also virtue ethicists, including McDowell, Annas, and Nussbaum, argued strongly for the second option.[16] They accepted that Aristotle's discussion in *NE* 1.7 is notable in locating human capacities in a broader spectrum of natural kinds and using this as the basis for supporting a specific conception of happiness, namely as being 'according to virtue'. (However, it is not unusual, in the context of ancient theory, to deploy

---

[13] See *NE* 1.7, 1097a24–1097b21 (criteria for happiness), 1097b22–1098a20 (the human function argument), including his definition of happiness in 1098a16–17.

[14] Aristotle was a pioneer in biology and the study of animal behaviour (*Parts of Animals, History of Animals*) as well as in ethical enquiry, as a distinct branch of philosophy (coupled with politics). For Aristotle, metaphysics or 'first philosophy' is the most general kind of enquiry, though whether he considered this as 'meta-level' and superordinate to other enquiries is more open to question.

[15] Williams 1985: 52. Williams's reading of Aristotle's move was influenced by a second controversial claim: that Aristotle's view of the harmony between the contents of the 'inside' and 'outside' view is one we can no longer accept, because, broadly put, we do not believe that the moral standpoint corresponds to the scientific understanding of human nature. On this second point, and on a related view of MacIntyre's, see Gill 1996: 430–43; also, challenging Williams's view, Hursthouse 1999: 256–65. In later discussions, Williams concedes that he may have overstated Aristotle's position on the first question (the one discussed here) (1995c: 200), while restating in strong terms his second claim (1995b: 109–11).

[16] See McDowell 1986 (reviewing Williams 1985), also McDowell 1980; Annas 1988; Nussbaum 1995.

this kind of argument for ethical purposes.[17]) On the other hand, these modern thinkers were sceptical that this signals a move from 'inside' Aristotle's normal ethical outlook to an 'outside' perspective. Aristotle, in this passage, as elsewhere, underlines that he assumes in his audience a shared understanding of the ethical 'facts', that is, the kind of thing that constitutes appropriate action and virtuous character.[18] The function argument depends on accepting that the proper performance of rational action consists in virtuous action, understood in the normal (ethical) sense of 'virtue' and not some special neutral ('scientific') sense.[19] Williams, admittedly, did not suggest that Aristotle's argument constituted what he calls an 'Archimedean' one, that is, one designed to convince *anyone*, even an immoralist, that they have objective reasons to want to become virtuous.[20] However, even the claim that Aristotle is appealing to an 'absolute understanding of nature', understood as going 'outside' the normal scope of ethical discourse, seems overstated.[21] Of course, Aristotle's argument differs, fundamentally, from that of those modern theorists for whom moral language is, necessarily, 'non-natural' or purely normative (consisting in 'ought'-language).[22] But this does not make Aristotle's move here as exceptional as Williams suggests either within ancient or modern ethical theory.

On this question, I share the views of those challenging Williams's position, rather than Williams himself.[23] However, the debate has a broader significance, since it raises questions that bear on any attempt to combine virtue ethics and eudaimonism with substantive claims about nature, as well as on the relationship between ancient and modern thinking on this topic. Indeed, the debate has a special relevance for my main claim here, that Stoic ideas can usefully inform modern virtue ethical theory. Stoic theory has often been taken as advancing very strong claims about the significance of nature (especially cosmic nature) for ethics, and ones that are very difficult for modern thinkers to accept. It is widely supposed that Stoic ethics is, systematically, grounded on ideas about cosmic nature, conceived in strongly teleological terms. Put differently, it is believed that the core principles of Stoic ethical theory depend on Stoic ideas about nature as a whole that are established by Stoic physics (theory of nature), which includes theology, as understood in Stoicism.[24] The Stoic approach, on this account, fits

---

[17] See e.g. Pl. *Smp.* 206c–207d, *Rep.* Book 1, 352d–353e (another 'function' argument); D.L. 7.85–6 (LS 57 A), Cic. *Fin.* 3.62–3 (LS 57 F(1–2)).
[18] On 'the facts' of ethics, see Arist. *NE* 1.4, 1095b4–7, 1.7, 1098b2–8; also Burnyeat 1980: 71–3; Gill 1996: 273–4.
[19] Arist. *NE* 1.7, 1098a7–17; also Gill 1990: 140–1.
[20] On 'Archimedean' arguments, see Williams 1985: 22–9. Obvious examples are Plato's *Gorgias*, directed in part at the immoralist Callicles, which Williams discusses, and Plato's *Republic*, directed (esp. in Book 1) at Thrasymachus.
[21] Williams 1985: 52.   [22] See text to n 3; also Williams 1985: 120–31.
[23] See Gill 1990: 138–43, 152–5; and Gill 1996: 430–43.
[24] For this scholarly view, see 3.2, text to nn. 17–20; and for primary evidence that seems to support this view, see 3.4, text to nn. 116–19.

Williams's interpretation of Aristotle, in supporting the 'inside' viewpoint of the ethical agent by going 'outside' ethics, and confirming ethical principles 'from an absolute understanding of nature'.[25] Indeed, the Stoic position, as thus understood, goes beyond (Williams's) Aristotle, in referring to cosmic or universal nature as well as human, and in seeing this reference as grounding, as well as confirming, Stoic ethical principles. It was unease about the philosophical credibility of this view that led Becker, in his updated version of Stoic ethics, first published in 1998, to remove the appeal to cosmic nature and to replace this with reference to human psychology, as understood in contemporary theory, which he called 'following the facts'.[26]

However, earlier in this book (Ch. 3), I have argued for a rather different, and more complex, understanding of Stoic thinking on the ethical significance of the idea of nature. We need to take account, first, of the fact that the Stoics subdivide philosophical knowledge into three main branches (logic or dialectic, ethics, and physics), even though they also see these branches as mutually supporting and as enabling an overall, synthesizing understanding.[27] Within Stoic ethical theory, as presented in the three main ancient summaries, the core concepts and principles are stated and supported, in the first instance, in their own terms (especially those of virtue, happiness, indifferents, and their interrelationship), which I described as type (1) ethical discourse; in this sense, ethics is free-standing or self-supporting. However, in all three summaries, these ethical concepts and principles are also supported by reference to certain ideas of nature. These ideas, which appear in varying degrees in the different ancient summaries, are: (type 2) human nature, (type 3) human nature viewed alongside animal nature as part of nature as a whole, (type 4) cosmic or universal nature.[28] These ideas of nature are closely integrated with discussion framed in standard ancient ethical terms. Although reference to nature, in these various senses, provides support for core ethical theses (such as that virtue is the sole basis for happiness), these theses are also stated, and argued for, independently; in this respect, these claims are not presented as grounded on, or derived from, ideas of nature.[29] Stoic physics, or, more specifically, theology (seen as a sub-branch of physics), is sometimes presented in ancient sources as authoritative for ethics in its account of nature, thus seeming to confirm the common scholarly view noted earlier.[30] However, as I have argued, the evidence, if more closely examined, suggests the following, more nuanced, picture. Theology is authoritative for ethics in the sense that it provides a comprehensive overall account of the types of nature in the universe (especially cosmic or universal and human). It also discusses the ethical status of those types of nature and their interrelationship; above all, claims are made about the

---

[25] Williams 1985: 52.   [26] See Becker 1998/2017: 6, 12–13: ch. 5. See also Ch. 6, text to n. 20.
[27] See LS 26 A–E; 3.4, text to nn. 109–14.   [28] For this numbering scheme, see 3.3, first para.
[29] See 3.3, esp. text to nn. 62–77.   [30] See 3.4, text to nn. 116–19; also 3.2, text to nn. 17–20.

goodness of the universe, as expressed, for instance, in its structure, order, and wholeness and its providential care for the component parts of the universe.[31] Although theology is presented as authoritative for ethics in this respect, there is no attempt, within Stoic theology, to argue for the core Stoic ethical claims, such as that virtue is fundamental for happiness or that virtue differs fundamentally in value from 'preferred indifferents', or to derive these claims from accounts of nature.[32] Although ideas such as good and virtue sometimes appear in theological writings, they are not examined or analysed there, but rather in writings on ethics. In this sense, Stoic theology is dependent, for its ethical content, on ethical theory; and this matches the fact that Stoic theology is sometimes presented as the 'culmination' (*teletai*) of a philosophical curriculum consisting of logic, ethics, and physics.[33] So overall, although ideas of nature, including cosmic or universal nature, are closely integrated, in various ways, with ethics, both in ethical theory and in theology, the relationship is more complex than that of the dependence of ethics on physics (specifically theology). Theology and ethics are better understood as mutually supporting, in this respect. In considering the relationship between Stoic thinking on nature (human and universal) and modern virtue ethics, it is this, more complex, picture that I am assuming.

7.2 Stoicism and Modern Ethical Naturalism

Within modern Neo-Aristotelian virtue ethics, I focus on those thinkers who have most explicitly adopted a naturalistic position, namely Anscombe, Foot, and Hursthouse.[34] The strands in Stoic ethical thought that are closest to their approach are those listed earlier as types (2) and (3), centred on the idea of human nature, taken either on its own or in connection with other forms of life within a broader view of nature. Stoic type (4) discourse, in which universal nature functions as an ideal for human beings, and Stoic theology, are less relevant for this purpose, though I discuss them in connection with modern environmental ethics. My main focus in this section is on a line of argument in Hursthouse's 1999 book (chs. 8–11), taken in conjunction with analogous Stoic ideas. However, I begin by outlining salient features of the ethical naturalism which is shared by Anscombe, Foot, and Hursthouse, and which Foot especially sets out in her programmatic book, *Natural Goodness* (2001).

---

[31] See 3.4, text to nn. 141–50.
[32] See 3.4, text to nn. 122–40, drawing a contrast, in this respect, with Christian theology and some modern moral theories.
[33] See Plu. *Sto. Rep.* 1035 A (LS 26 C); and 3.4, text to nn. 151–60, esp. n. 154.
[34] On virtue ethics and naturalism, see Annas 2005; Hamilton 2013; Solomon 2018 (on naturalism in early modern virtue ethics).

Foot's approach is presented as a sustained challenge to the claim of Moore, which underpins much subsequent modern moral theorizing, that 'good' is a non-natural property.[35] On the contrary, Foot argues, the goodness of human beings, like that of plants and non-human animals, is best understood in the context of the needs and activities that are characteristic of the relevant species or life-form. Of course, human beings are differentiated from other animals and plants by the fact that their actions are informed by rationality, which also differentiates one human being from another, in their actions and objectives, in ways that do not apply in the case of other species. However, the goodness of those actions and objectives makes best sense when correlated with the characteristic needs and aims of the human being as a species.[36] Promising, for instance, is taken as a prime example because it reflects distinctively human capacities and needs: the capacity for language, for giving and receiving commitment over a life-span, for structured social relationships, and the need for reliable help and support from others. Someone who keeps her promises and undertakings is appropriately described as 'good' because doing so enables her to participate fully in the co-operative activities characteristic of human beings.[37] The significance of the virtues and of what we can call 'flourishing' and 'happiness' also make best sense when correlated with characteristically human patterns of living.[38] On the basis of this line of argument, Foot maintains that goodness, for human beings as well as other species, is best understood as a 'natural', rather than 'non-natural' property, and that 'facts', rather than being radically different in kind from 'values', enable us to make sense of what is valuable in human life.[39] Moral reasoning also makes best sense when treated not as radically different from other kinds of practical reasoning, but when it is seen as reasoning which achieves the aims and fulfils the needs characteristic of a full human life.[40]

Hursthouse develops this approach in two main ways. On the one hand, she presents in a more structured and comprehensive way the parallel between goodness in human beings and in other animals that is central for the kind of ethical naturalism adopted by Anscombe and Foot.[41] On the other hand, she embeds this naturalism in a broader argument about virtue, happiness, and human nature, outlined shortly. In both respects, I suggest, her approach can be usefully compared with Stoic ideas, and also, potentially, informed and taken further by those Stoic ideas.

---

[35] See text to n. 3.
[36] See Foot 2001: 5–9, 16–17, 26–7, 34–5, 44–5, 66–7. See also Anscombe 1981: 29. Foot 2001: 27–31, also cites Thompson 1995 as a major influence on her view.
[37] Foot 2001: 15–16, 45–51; also Anscombe 1981: 18, 100–2.   [38] Foot 2001: 93–9.
[39] Foot 2001: 24, 51.   [40] Foot 2001: 52–66, 68–80.
[41] Hursthouse 1999 (the relevant chapters are chs. 8–11) was published before Foot's most comprehensive statement of her view (2001). But Hursthouse bases her naturalistic approach on several articles already published by Foot (Hursthouse 1999: 195–7).

On the first point, whereas Foot talks in a rather generalized way about the needs and aims of human beings and other forms of life, Hursthouse formalizes this idea by identifying four ends characteristic of social animals, including human beings. Thus:

> ...a good social animal... is one that is well fitted or endowed with respect to (i) its parts, (ii) its operations, (iii), its actions, and (iv) its desires and emotions; whether it is well fitted or endowed is determined by whether these four aspects well serve (1) its individual survival, (2) the continuance of its species, (3) its characteristic freedom from pain and characteristic enjoyment, and (4) the good functioning of its social group—in the ways characteristic of the species.[42]

Hursthouse presents this framework as 'objective', indeed 'scientific', to the extent that it matches the typical formulations of botanists or ethologists. However, she also maintains that it provides a basis that we (human beings) can use to evaluate ourselves as good or not. This framework is thus crucial for the kind of ethical naturalism that she adopts, like Foot, and for the broader argument she constructs, based on this naturalism.[43] Hursthouse summarizes her overall argument as consisting in these three theses:

(1) The virtues benefit their possessor. (They enable her to flourish, to be, and live a life that is, *eudaimon*.)
(2) The virtues make their possessor a good human being. (Human beings need the virtues in order to live well, to flourish *as* human beings, to live a characteristically good, *eudaimon*, human life.)
(3) The above two features of the virtues are interrelated.[44]

The claim that the happy or flourishing life is one that is based, solely or mainly, on virtue is, of course, a familiar one in ancient ethics and in modern virtue ethics based on the ancient model.[45] What is distinctive about her approach is that the link between virtue and happiness is based on the idea of being human, and that human nature is explicated, in the first instance at least, in terms of the four ends. How, in broad terms, does she deploy these ideas for the purpose?

---

[42] Hursthouse 1999: 102.
[43] Hursthouse 1999: ch. 9, esp. 201–6. On these four ends and their place in Hursthouse's argument, see also Annas 2005: 13–17.
[44] Hursthouse 1999: 167. These three theses are discussed in chs. 8, 9–10, and 11, respectively, of her book.
[45] Hursthouse 1999: 167 describes her argument as a response to 'Plato's requirement on the virtues', referring, in general terms, to the argument of Pl. *Rep.* (on which see Ch. 1, text to nn. 10–19). However, there are obvious points of comparison with Aristotle, and the Stoics, as well as modern virtue ethicists (e.g. Annas 2011: ch. 9).

She does so by maintaining, first, that the virtues (such as temperance, courage, generosity, honesty, justice) enable human beings to live in a way that fulfils the four ends, in a form that is characteristic of human beings.[46] She then acknowledges that her account thus far is incomplete in failing to incorporate the most obviously distinctive feature of human beings, namely rationality. What difference does rationality make to her framework? She considers, but rejects, the suggestion that the possession of rationality requires her to posit a fifth end, such as worshipping God and preparing for the afterlife or theoretical contemplation. She proposes, rather, that the possession of rationality informs the way in which human beings achieve the four ends; in particular, rationality enables human beings to fulfil these aims, in themselves and in their interrelationship, in a wide variety of (valid) ways.[47] The virtues, then, are presented as those qualities that enable a human being to achieve those ends, rationally, in divergent but valid ways.[48] Happiness or flourishing is also analysed on similar lines, as the (rational) realization of the four ends in a form characteristic of human beings. Further, she argues that the virtues provide the best possible basis for enabling someone to live a good human life, that is, one that fulfils the four ends, in their interrelationship, in a coherent and internally harmonious way.[49]

I have suggested that certain strands in Stoic ethics are similar in approach to Hursthouse's type of ethical naturalism and that, in some respects, they take this approach further. One relevant strand is what I have described as type (2) presentation, in which Stoic ethical claims are supported by reference to human nature.[50] The other is type (3) presentation, in which Stoic ethical claims are supported by reference to human beings, located, along with other animals, in a broader natural framework, as in Stoic accounts of development as 'appropriation'.[51] I explore the linkage between Hursthouse and Stoic theory in three stages. First, I highlight points of resemblance between Stoic thinking and Hursthouse's approach, and, second, respects in which Stoic theory takes these connections further than she does. Finally, I indicate features of Stoic thought that diverge from her views but still fall within the naturalistic approach shared by both theories, and I consider how far they are compatible with her view, or at least that of modern virtue ethics.

The most obvious and striking parallel is between Stoic thinking on the core motives of 'appropriation' and the four ends that are central for Hursthouse's account of human (and animal) nature. The Stoics identify two motives that are fundamental for making sense of animal, including human, behaviour: these are, in a basic form, the motives of self-preservation and the desire for procreation and

---

[46] Hursthouse 1999: 208–11.   [47] Hursthouse 1999: 218–22.
[48] Hursthouse 1999: 226–38.   [49] Hursthouse 1999: ch. 11, esp. 247–52.
[50] See 3.3, text to nn. 78–91; Stobaeus' ethical summary is especially relevant, taken with comparable features of Cic. *Off.*
[51] See 3.3, text to nn. 92–7; Cic. *Off.* 1.11–15, Cic. *Fin.* 3.17–22, 62–8, are especially relevant.

parental love. Viewed in a broader context, these motives can be analysed as the desire to take care of oneself and to take care of others of one's kind.[52] These motives are similar to the first two and the fourth of Hursthouse's four ends; like Hursthouse, the Stoics see these motives as shared by human beings and other animals.[53] Also, like Hursthouse, the Stoics see rationality (the distinctively human capacity) not as a wholly distinct function, but one which informs the motives of caring for oneself and others that are shared with other animals.[54] These are two notable features of the naturalistic framework that Hursthouse and the Stoics deploy in connection with their ethical theory, a theory which is based in both cases on the ideas of virtue and happiness. The Stoics, like Hursthouse (and Foot), also chart close links between this naturalistic framework and the ethical theory. Foot and Hursthouse stress the idea that goodness, human and animal, are best understood by reference to this framework; Hursthouse also uses it to analyse the role of the virtues in human life, and also the idea that human happiness is grounded in the virtues.[55]

The Stoics work out these links in full, complex, and suggestive ways; and the depth of their analysis is, I think, one of the contributions they can make to informing the kind of ethical naturalism found in Hursthouse, Foot, and Anscombe. The Stoic elaboration also supports the connections claimed in their theory, and in these versions of modern virtue ethics, between human nature (or nature more broadly), virtue, and happiness. In Stoicism, these links are spelled out especially in connection with their accounts of development as appropriation. In one version of this theory, the two core animal motives (to care for oneself and for others of one's kind) are analysed as providing, in their rational (human) version the motivational basis for the four cardinal or generic virtues, which are themselves seen as mapping the four main areas of human experience.[56] Each of those virtues can themselves be conceived as combining rational and sociable dimensions, thus expressing the core distinctive features of human nature (as rational and sociable).[57] In another version of the theory, the whole process of development as appropriation is subdivided into rational and sociable strands, in the course of which the core, basic animal motives are progressively transformed, thereby enabling the developing human being to understand the special value (goodness) of virtue and virtue-based happiness, and to express this in her care for

---

[52] See D.L. 7.85–6 (LS 57 A), Cic. *Fin.* 3.62 (LS 57 F(1)); Cic. *Off.* 1.11–12; see also 4.2.

[53] Pleasure and avoidance of pain are not given the same importance in Stoic ethics as in Hursthouse's account, though they are not wholly ignored (see D.L. 7.85–6 (LS 57 A(3)), Sen. *Ep.* 121.6–15 (LS 57 B). On Hursthouse's four ends, see text to n. 42.

[54] See Ch. 4, esp. 4.3 and 4.4, text to nn. 95–7, Ch. 5, text to nn. 10–17.

[55] See text to nn. 36–49.

[56] See Cic. *Off.* 1.15 (also 1.11–14), Stob. 5b3 (also Ch. 1, text to nn. 155–68).

[57] On this feature of the account of the virtues in Cic. *Off.* Book 1, following the summary account of appropriation in 1.11–15, see Ch. 1, text to nn. 169–77.

herself and for others of her kind.[58] The close linkages established in this way between the idea of human nature (characterized by the combination of rationality and sociability), virtue, and happiness,[59] underpin the core Stoic claim that virtue constitutes the sole basis for happiness, and support (in part) the characterization of happiness as 'the life according to nature'.[60] Of course, I cannot claim that Hursthouse or the other virtue ethicists who deploy a naturalistic approach would in fact accept (or would have accepted) each or any of the specific components of the Stoic analysis, though Stoicism and these modern theories have several important common elements. But I think the Stoic theory offers a cogent account of the way in which value notions and natural factors can be closely integrated, in a non-reductive way, that also supports central doctrinal claims such as the Stoic thesis on virtue and happiness.[61]

In making this proposal, I am not overlooking the fact that the Stoic theory and Hursthouse's diverge on certain important points, while still sharing a naturalistic approach to ethics. I note three salient differences. While these are, indeed, points of divergence, I think they constitute differences within a shared naturalistic approach. It would be worth considering how much of the Stoic view on these points could be incorporated in a theory such as Hursthouse's (though I do not attempt to do that here).[62] The Stoics, of course, regard not just human nature but also universal nature as ethically significant. Although this idea does not form part of Hursthouse's approach, it is linked, in Stoic theory, with ideas that she could accept. These are the ideas that care of oneself and others of one's kind form basic animal (and human) motives and that virtue (and happiness) constitute a type of structure, order, and wholeness.[63] It would be worth considering further which Stoic ideas about universal nature are or are not compatible with modern versions of ethical naturalism. Secondly, the Stoics diverge from Hursthouse in the scope recognized for human rationality vis-à-vis the four ends, or in the Stoic case, the core basic motives. Although Hursthouse allows scope for rationality to inform the fulfilment of these ends in diverse but valid ways, this scope is still limited by the nature of those ends.[64] Stoic theory, on the other hand, envisages human rationality as capable of transforming the core motives and their objectives. For instance, in the theory of development as appropriation, the nature of care of

---

[58] See Cic. *Fin.* 3. 16–22, 62–8; for a full analysis see 4.4–5.

[59] See Stob. 5b1, 6; also 3.3, text to nn. 78–91.

[60] For this definition, see LS 63 A–C. See also Ch. 1, text to nn. 73–82, 153–77.

[61] In other words, as Foot puts it, facts are not contrasted with values, but used to bring out what is valuable in human life (see text to n. 39).

[62] Here, I simply flag relevant points which I hope to explore more fully in another context.

[63] On these ideas, linked in Stoic thought with the idea of universal or cosmic nature, see Ch. 1, text to nn. 83–91, 183–209. The first idea evokes the first two and fourth of Hursthouse's four ends (text to nn. 42, 52–3); the second idea matches a feature (internal harmony and cohesion) that she sees as an essential feature of our conception of virtue and happiness and also (she argues, against Williams) one that is consistent with objective (scientific) accounts of human nature: see Hursthouse 1999: 247–65.

[64] Hursthouse 1999: 217–26.

oneself is progressively transformed as the human being recognizes the radical difference in value between virtue and virtue-based happiness, seen as good, and other things recognized as valuable. Analogously, the nature of care for others is transformed by the recognition that the basic motive of parental love forms part of a more general care for others of one's kind, which extends, in principle, to any given human being.[65] It would, again, be worth considering how far Hursthouse's theory could accommodate this enlarged role for rationality while retaining its naturalistic framework.[66] The third point relates to the concept of goodness. Hursthouse, like Foot and Anscombe, stresses that goodness can be ascribed equally, though on somewhat different grounds, to animals, and plants, as well as human beings, and Hursthouse links goodness closely with fulfilling the four ends.[67] The Stoics also ascribe goodness to the natural universe as a whole, and, in a secondary way, parts of the universe, especially human beings.[68] However, their analysis of goodness is not tied in the same way to the fulfilment of in-built natural ends or motives. Goodness is analysed in terms of benefit; and, on this basis, the Stoics ascribe goodness, in human beings at least, primarily to virtue and virtue-based happiness, as distinct from other valuable things.[69] In doing so, the Stoics are not, like Moore, defining goodness as a 'non-natural' property; on the contrary, the goodness of happiness and the value of preferred indifferents are both defined in terms of their being 'according to nature' in different senses.[70] However, the Stoic theory posits a more complex relationship between the definition of goodness and the naturalistic framework; and it would, again, be worth considering how far this conception could be accommodated in a modern theory of ethical naturalism such as Hursthouse's.

Finally, I return briefly to the question raised earlier, in connection with Williams's characterization of Aristotle's deployment of human nature.[71] Is it right to describe Hursthouse or the Stoics, on these points, as stepping 'outside' the ethical standpoint and aiming to support ethics from an 'absolute understanding of nature'. In both cases, I think, their approach matches the interpretation of Aristotle offered by Williams's critics, rather than Williams himself. Foot and Hursthouse state explicitly that their naturalistic theories are maintained from within an ethical outlook, that is, one that assumes the rightness and wrongness of

---

[65] See Cic. *Fin.* 3.20–22, 62–8: also 4.4–5. The second point leads the Stoics to adopt a form of (what Hursthouse calls) 'impersonal benevolence' that she might find more acceptable than the version she discusses in P. Singer's work: Hursthouse 1999: 224–5.

[66] For a comparable, but more fully developed, version of this point, also citing Stoic thought as a potential model, see Annas 2005: 17–28.

[67] See text to nn. 36, 41, 43.

[68] See Cic. *N. D.* 2.16, 37–9 (LS 54 E, H), taken with Ch. 3, text to nn. 135–8; also LS 60 I, Sen. *Ep.* 124.13–14 (60 H).

[69] On good as benefit, see S. E. *M.* 11.22–6 (LS 60 H); also Vogt 2008b: 158–60. On the virtue-indifferents distinction, based on the idea of goodness, see D.L. 7.101–3 (LS 58 A); also 2.2.

[70] Brüllmann 2015: ch. 3, esp. 99–138, stresses this point (see Ch. 3, text to n. 37–8).

[71] See text to nn. 13–22.

certain kinds of action and the ethical validity of certain virtues (the standard ones). As Hursthouse especially stresses, their theories are not designed to provide motivating reasons for ethically good actions, or to convert the immoralist or the moral sceptic.[72] However, this does not mean that their theories are conceived as purely internal to ethics. Their accounts of nature are presented as objective, and as corresponding to those of scientific experts on animal and human behaviour. What Hursthouse and Foot are discussing is the ethical significance of the facts given in those accounts, and their theory is naturalistic in this sense.[73] The same point applies, broadly speaking, to the Stoic theory; but we need to distinguish the standpoint of Stoic ethics (as expressed in the ancient summaries) and Stoic theology. In the summaries, claims which are also analysed in purely ethical terms are stated and supported by reference to human or universal nature or human nature viewed as part of a broader natural pattern.[74] Stoic theology does offer an account from 'an absolute understanding of nature' in the sense that it offers a comprehensive and authoritative account of the types of nature relevant to ethics, and also discusses the ethical significance of those natures (the goodness of the universe as well as that of human beings, as a natural kind). However, Stoic theology does not purport to analyse or explain the ethical categories deployed for this purpose and is in this respect dependent on ethics (and not authoritative).[75] So, overall, in both ethics and theology, what we find in Stoicism, as in these modern virtue ethical theories, is a combination of (allegedly) objective facts about human and other natures and discussion of their ethical significance, from a determinate ethical standpoint. The aim is not, in either case, to go 'outside' the ethical standpoint and to confirm it from an independent (fact-based) standpoint. To this extent, it is the same kind of ethical naturalism that is in involved, and their approaches can be fruitfully correlated.

7.3 Stoicism and Environmentalism in Modern Virtue Ethics

So far, I have explored the relationship between the kind of ethical naturalism found in Stoicism and certain thinkers in modern Neo-Aristotelian virtue ethics. On the Stoic side, the key relevant idea is that happiness constitutes a realization of the life according to nature, meaning according to human nature, conceived as constitutively rational and sociable. However, the Stoics also conceive happiness as the life according to universal nature, with certain qualities seen as shared by universal nature and human beings at their best. This idea, like that related to human nature, is firmly embedded in their thinking about happiness, virtue, and

---

[72] Hursthouse 1999: 165–6, 187–91, 228–31, 234–42.
[73] See Foot 2001: 24, 27; Hursthouse 1999: 195–7, 202–5, 206.
[74] See 3.3, first para.   [75] See 3.4, text to nn. 149–61.

ethical development.[76] Is this idea also one that has resonance, or could have resonance, for modern virtue ethics? The obvious answer might seem to be 'no', for several reasons. For one thing, there are major differences between the Stoic worldview, or any other ancient worldview, and ours.[77] For another, the idea of universal nature or nature or a whole does not, for the most part, play a substantial role in modern virtue ethics, by contrast with the idea of human nature, leaving aside religious versions of modern virtue ethics. Hence, we might conclude, this marks one major limitation in the extent to which Stoic ideas can inform modern ethics.

However, this conclusion may be too quick. There is one area in modern virtue ethics, and ethics generally, that is concerned with nature as a whole and the place of human beings in nature, namely environmental ethics. Can Stoic thinking on universal nature contribute to this, relatively new, dimension of modern virtue ethics? I explore this topic in two stages. First, in this section, I suggest that Stoic ethical thinking, especially the ideas about virtue and happiness, provides a conceptually powerful framework for formulating an appropriate ethical response to environmental concerns, as well as other ethical concerns. For this purpose, I reformulate Hursthouse's virtue ethical discussion of environmental ethics (2007) in terms of the Stoic framework. At this stage, I set aside the question of the relationship between the Stoic worldview and modern environmental ideas, though I refer to the Stoic use of the idea of universal nature in connection with happiness. Subsequently (7.4), turning to Stoic thinking on nature as a whole and the place of human beings, especially as presented in Stoic theology, I consider how to analyse their position from the standpoint of modern environmental ethics. I suggest that certain strands in their thinking match with, and could reinforce, leading ideas in modern environmental ethics (ideas associated with the terms 'biocentric' and 'ecocentric'). There are also strands in Stoic thinking (which we might be inclined to call 'anthropocentric') which are problematic from a modern environmental standpoint. I consider how far these strands can be reconceived or reconfigured, though consistently with Stoic thinking generally, in a way that renders them less problematic and enables Stoic ideas to contribute positively to this important and developing area of modern debate.[78]

What environmental concerns do I have most in view here? In much modern philosophical discussion, the focus has been on human treatment of other animals.[79] Questions about the value of animal life and welfare have been central for this topic. More recently again, the looming threat of climate breakdown, with greenhouse gas emissions the main likely cause, and of catastrophic damage to the

---

[76] See 1.3–4.
[77] Hence, Becker (1998/2017) eliminates it from his modernized version of Stoic ethics (see n. 26).
[78] See text to nn. 128–35. On the terminology used here ('anthropocentric, biocentric, ecocentric'), see text to n. 105 and references in n. 105.
[79] This is the focus in Hursthouse 2007, discussed shortly.

natural environment, human beings, and all other forms of life, has emerged as, far and away, the most serious and urgent problem of our time. Both these topics can also involve other environmental concerns, for instance, about the impact on other animals of the massive increase in the human population throughout the world, about loss of animal species and their habitats, and the environmentally damaging effects of the overwhelming focus in world agriculture on meat production. Of these problems, my main concern here is with climate breakdown, and the associated environmental damage, rather than human treatment of other animals (in so far as these can be separated). It is in connection with the effect of human action on the natural environment as a whole that reference to Stoic ideas can, I think, make a useful contribution, rather than on human-animal relations.[80] My concern here is not with the scientific analysis of these problems or with specific practical and political responses to them. My focus is on the question of the theories, ancient and modern, that can help us to make sense of these problems from an ethical standpoint and respond appropriately to them. It is obvious from the outline of topics that these are modern problems, for which human beings since the Industrial Revolution have been responsible. When Stoic or other ancient theorists reflected on the place of human beings in the world, or universe, they had in mind a very different picture of the power of human beings to affect or control, in a positive or negative way, other animals or parts of nature. This does not mean that reference to Stoic ideas is irrelevant to this topic. However, this difference needs to be borne in mind when we correlate Stoic thinking about the place of human beings in nature and modern environmental ideas, as I do later (7.4).

I begin with a different, though related, topic. I suggest that the Stoic ethical framework can be used to inform modern virtue ethical thinking on environmental questions. I take as my starting point a discussion by Hursthouse (2007) which reflects recent virtue ethical thinking more generally on this subject.[81] Hursthouse addresses the question how far virtue ethics need to be modified for this purpose from the normal use for purely human concerns; she also considers the merits of adopting a virtue ethical approach to this topic, as distinct from other modern moral standpoints. She discusses, for instance, whether environmental ethics require us to recognize new virtues or only to interpret the standard set of virtues in an environmentally relevant way. The virtues she considers as especially relevant are appropriate humility before nature and proper respect for nature, activated by a sense of wonder at natural beauty or vitality.[82] Nussbaum has also explored this theme, though from a different theoretical standpoint. Nussbaum

---

[80] As already indicated, Stoic thinking on human-animal relations is potentially problematic from a modern environmental standpoint; see text to nn. 119–21. On climate change (viewed as 'the defining environmental challenge of our time'), see Gardiner and Thompson 2017: part vii.

[81] See the review of recent work of this kind by Sandler 2017 and Kawall 2018.

[82] Hursthouse 2007: 155–62.

suggests that the response of wonder at nature (for instance, at the in-built artistry or 'striving' of life-forms) provides the starting-point, at least, for working out what constitutes justice in our relationships with other animals.[83] A further dimension of environmental ethics accentuated by Hursthouse is the central importance of the idea that nature, at least in the sense of living things, has intrinsic value apart from any value it holds for human beings.[84] However, she also stresses that if this idea is to play an effective role in shaping our actions and lives, it needs not only to be accepted as a general proposition but also embedded in our character and motives. In other words, the idea needs to be integrated with the formation of virtues and with our developing understanding of what constitutes happiness (*eudaimonia*). She sees the recognition of this point as one of the main contributions of virtue ethics to debate on environmental ethics.[85]

I now offer a reformulation of Hursthouse's virtue ethical approach, stated in terms of the Stoic framework. I consider first Stoic ideas on virtue and ethical development and then on happiness. I am assuming at this stage that the Stoic ethical framework can be deployed for this purpose and take up later the question of the relationship between Stoic and modern ideas on this topic.

Hursthouse, like some other recent virtue ethicists, identifies a specific virtue, respect for nature, which embodies, in motivational and practical terms, a recognition of the intrinsic value of nature.[86] Stoic ethics offer a different way of conceiving the role of virtue in this respect. Although we sometimes find, in Stoic writings, the idea that each of the four cardinal virtues has a distinct sphere of action,[87] the point generally emphasized is that, in any given situation, the virtuous person exercises all four virtues, or their subdivisions, in a co-ordinated way, even if one of the four is most salient.[88] I sketch what is involved schematically, using 'e-' to mean 'relevant to environmental concerns'. For example, a virtuous person might exercise good judgement (wisdom) regarding what counts as an e-act (for instance, not booking a mini-break winter holiday flight to the Azores). This same act might express justice, in giving what is due to all those concerned, including those affected by the environmental impact of her act. The same act might express temperance or self-control in moderating the desire for something desirable (the short vacation in a warm and scenic location) that has a

---

[83] Nussbaum 2006: ch. 6, esp. 347–8, referring to Arist. *Part. An.* 1.5, 645a1–25; see also Nussbaum 2008. Empathy or compassion is presented as mediating between wonder and justice. Nussbaum's approach is conceived not as virtue ethics but as part of her 'capabilities' theory shared with Amartya Sen. For helpful discussion of her view, see Bendik-Keymer 2014, 2017.

[84] Hursthouse takes Taylor 1981, 1986 as her main representative for this idea. According to Taylor 1986: 44, every living thing has intrinsic worth 'as a member of Earth's community of Life'; see also Hursthouse 2007: 163, 165. In terms discussed shortly, Taylor's view is biocentric, though Hursthouse indicates her attachment to a more ecocentric view (2007: 165–7). On these terms, see text to n. 105.

[85] Hursthouse 2007: 163–72.

[86] See Kawall 2018: 662–4; also Pianalto 2013, on environmental 'humility'.

[87] Cic. *Off.* 1, for instance discusses the cardinal virtues one by one; see Ch. 1, text to nn. 169–77.

[88] See Ch. 1, text to nn. 141–6.

significant e-impact. The same act might involve courage in giving up this option in the face of sceptical or disappointed reactions from family or friends.[89] In this example, whereas Hursthouse sees an e-action as the result of a specific e-virtue (respect for nature), the Stoic framework suggests that an e-action is the result of the whole virtue-set, exercised in an e-way. What are the advantages of the Stoic formulation? The Stoic account gives a fuller picture of how e-virtue works, by examining the component aspects of e-virtue and their interconnection. The Stoic analysis conveys more effectively what is, in many cases, involved in e-action, especially in responding as an individual to the complex demands of climate breakdown. What is required is the expression of a co-ordinated set of virtues, mapping the different aspects of human action and experience, but working to a single overall objective, in this respect at least.[90]

A second point made by Hursthouse relates to ethical development. She stresses that, for an effective response to environmental concerns, what is needed is not just adopting a proposition, for instance, about the intrinsic value of nature, in a purely intellectual way. The idea needs to have become integrated with the person's characteristic set of attitudes and dispositions and embodied in an e-virtue (respect for nature). She describes the formation of virtue in a typically Aristotelian way, by reference to the formation of beliefs and feelings in childhood by habituation.[91] The Stoic framework also emphasizes the importance of ethical development; however, the focus is on adult development, especially in the process that Stoics call 'appropriation'.[92] Their thinking on this topic is quite complex; but I highlight a few points to show how the Stoic pattern, apart from its general cogency, has a special relevance for the development of a coherent set of virtues focused in an e-way. The Stoics sometimes subdivide appropriation into two main strands, one centred on growth in ethical understanding and the other centred on social relationships, correlated with growth in ethical understanding. A salient feature of the first strand is coming to understand that happiness depends solely on virtue, and that other things normally considered good are, relatively, 'matters of indifferents'. A salient feature of the second strand is integrating this growing understanding with one's whole pattern of relationships (interpersonal and social); one aspect of this process is recognizing that other human beings, as such, are objects of ethical concern, alongside family, friends, and community.[93] Both features can be seen as relevant for exercising virtue in an e-way. The person

---

[89] For this kind of courage, see Kawall 2018: 664.

[90] I am assuming that the virtuous person may have several objectives but that these need to be integrated with each other in a way that enables the exercise of e-virtue.

[91] Hursthouse 2007: 163–72. See also Arist. *NE* 2.3, 1104b11–13, 1105a1–5, 10.9. On the role of habituation, in some Platonic and Aristotelian thinking about ethical development, see Introd. to Part II, text to nn. 11–15.

[92] On the main distinctive features of Stoic thinking on ethical development, see Introd. to Part II; on appropriation, see Ch. 4.

[93] See Cic. *Fin.* 3.20–2, 62–8 (LS 59 D and 57 F); also 4.4–5.

recognizes that her happiness (that is, leading the best possible human life) depends on expressing e-virtue, among other expressions of virtue. By comparison, other things that might otherwise seem desirable components of her life are regarded as 'matters of indifference'. This idea is relevant, of course, to many dimensions of human life; but it has a special relevance to the current situation, where responding effectively to the challenge of climate breakdown requires us to give up features of modern life otherwise considered desirable, such as the mini-break in the Azores. The same point could, no doubt, be conceptualized in terms of other ethical frameworks, including the Aristotelian;[94] but the Stoic framework formulates this idea with special force, because of the radical contrast that the Stoics draw between the value of virtue and preferred indifferents.[95] In the second strand of appropriation, the fact that ethical development includes reference to human beings in general has a special relevance to the exercise of virtue in an e-way.[96] Working out what counts as an appropriate response to climate breakdown is not just a matter of considering what is due to family, friends, and community, but also of taking account of the effect of one's actions on human beings in general (since all of us are affected negatively by climate breakdown).[97] Thus, the Stoic framework for ethical development incorporates Hursthouse's point that what is required ethically is not just the intellectual acceptance of the validity of an idea but also making it integral to one's character and understanding, that is, making it into a virtue.[98] Also, the Stoic analysis brings with it at least two significant features (the virtue-indifferents relation and the community of humankind) that have a special relevance for people trying to live their lives in an environmentally committed and effective way.[99]

Hursthouse's virtue ethical account envisages not only the formation of an e-virtue, respect for nature, but also the view that this virtue is shaped by an over-arching idea (Taylor's idea that nature has intrinsic value).[100] In ancient ethical theory, the idea of happiness (*eudaimonia*) functions as a key organizing one, as the overall end or goal of life, often conceived in Stoicism as the life according to nature (human or universal, or both), taken to be identical with the life according to virtue.[101] At this point, I leave open the question of the

---

[94] For instance, the point could be framed in terms of temperance or moderation, see Arist. *NE* 3.10–12.

[95] On this distinction, see 2.2. On the contrast with Aristotelian ethics, which present bodily and external goods as contributors to happiness, see Ch. 1, text to nn. 29–34, and Ch. 6, text to nn. 80–91.

[96] See Cic. *Fin.* 3.62–4, Cic. *Off.* 1.50–3; also 4.5.

[97] The Stoic theory provides an ethical framework relevant for action at the individual level (as in the mini-break example) and also for involvement in public or political activities expressing e-concerns.

[98] Hursthouse 2007: 163–72.

[99] Whiting et al. 2018: sections 2, 3.3, also suggest that these features of Stoic ethics are especially relevant to modern environmental ethics.

[100] See text to n. 84.   [101] See 1.3.

relationship between Stoic thinking on universal nature and modern environmental ideas. However, the fact that the Stoic ethical framework gives an important role, as a formulation of happiness, to *an* idea of universal nature, alongside that of human nature, is a further feature that makes Stoicism potentially serviceable for modern environmental ethics. To put the point in very broad terms, Stoic ethics suggest that living a happy life is not just a matter of living the best possible human life, but also doing so in a way that reflects the place of human beings in the larger natural world. More precisely, as brought out in Chapter 3, locating human nature in a broader natural framework is one of the ways in which Stoic ethics characterizes happiness and the development towards happiness.[102] This idea, by itself, renders the Stoic ethical framework helpful for modern environmental concerns.

The relevance of Stoic thinking on happiness for this purpose comes out more clearly if we anticipate, in broad terms, the conclusions of the following discussion of the relationship between the Stoic worldview and modern environmental ideas. Some of the principal connotations of the Stoic idea of universal nature are ones that are especially relevant for modern environmental concerns. These connotations, which link the Stoic worldview and their conception of human happiness, include those of structure, order, and wholeness.[103] Although modern environmentalists are unlikely to see the world as ordered precisely in the way the Stoics did, they may well be inclined to see climate breakdown as marking an interruption or collapse in relatively stable natural patterns (that is, as a breakdown of natural order). Also, they are likely to see environmental action as designed to counteract or mitigate this state of disorder or at least to adapt to this collapse.[104] A modern environmentalist wants to do everything in her power to promote natural structure, order or wholeness, of a kind which is currently under threat, in large measure as a result of human action. Considered in this light, the Stoic conception of happiness as the life according to universal nature is useful for modern environmental concerns in two ways. It is helpful because, as just noted, it establishes a link between human happiness and our understanding of the place of human beings in the natural world. It is also helpful for this purpose because universal nature is analysed in terms (structure, order, and wholeness) that bear relevantly on modern environmental objectives. Thus, combining Stoic and modern environmental ideas, we can say that the happy life is one in which human beings aim to live in line with universal nature (marked by structure, order, and wholeness) and to do everything in their power to restore the original order of the natural environment. In these respects, Stoic theory provides a conceptual

---

[102] In my terms, presentation type (3); see Ch. 3, text to nn. 92–7.

[103] See Ch. 1, text to nn. 87–101.

[104] For the distinction between mitigating the effects of climate breakdown and adapting to its effects, see Thompson and Bendik-Keymer 2012: introduction.

framework, framed in terms of virtue and happiness, that meets the ethical needs of modern environmentalists.

7.4 The Stoic Worldview and Modern Environmental Ethics

I develop this line of thought by addressing the question of the relationship between the Stoic worldview, especially as presented in Stoic theology, and modern environmental ideas. At first sight, the Stoic worldview represents what is, from a modern environmental standpoint, a paradoxical combination of biocentric (or ecocentric) and anthropocentric strands. Thus, on the face of it, the Stoic framework combines some elements which are, and others which are not, congenial to modern environmental thinking. However, on further analysis, the biocentric (or ecocentric) and anthropocentric strands derive from a single, and distinct, conceptual standpoint, the logocentric or reason-centred one. This standpoint, though less familiar in modern ecological discussion, has its own significance for this question. On the Stoic view, rationality, regarded as a valuable quality, is not, as we might have expected, confined to human beings, but is seen as present, and present to a greater extent, in nature as a whole. Thus, the Stoic worldview offers a perspective on nature that is highly suggestive for modern environmental concerns. There remains, however, the problem of Stoic anthropo-centrism, particularly the attitude towards other animals (an attitude linked with their logocentrism). However, on this point, I suggest that Stoic theory could consistently accommodate a modified account of human-animal relations, which would enable their thinking, taken as a whole, to make a positive contribution to modern ecological debate.

In the first instance, I ask whether the Stoic worldview reflects a biocentric, ecocentric, or anthropocentric viewpoint. I am assuming that an anthropocentric viewpoint is one that attaches intrinsic value only to human beings; that a biocentric viewpoint attaches intrinsic value to all living things; and that an ecocentric viewpoint attaches intrinsic value to all things that form part of nature, whether or not they are living. First, we need to be aware of features of Stoic thought that make it difficult to say whether its adherents adopt a biocentric or an ecocentric viewpoint; these features also have a broader interest for this whole question. Stoic accounts of the world sometimes distinguish between inanimate objects, such as stones, and living things, including plants and animals. However, Stoics see all natural entities, both animate and inanimate, as shaped and informed by god as an immanent agency (sometimes identified with fire or 'breath', *pneuma*) operating on matter.[105] This idea is sometimes expressed in the form

---

[105] See LS 46 A, 47 A–B; also Bénatouïl 2009: 25–8. On the terminology used here, see Thompson 2017 (anthropocentric), Palmer 2017 (biocentric), Kawall 2017: 17–19, Callicott 2017 (ecocentric).

of a *scala naturae* (spectrum of natural kinds) in which different types of entity are presented as constituting different degrees of 'tension' (*tonos*) of *pneuma*. This spectrum runs from material objects (such as stones or logs, and bones in bodies), unified by *hexis*, which 'holds them together', to entities, such as plants, which are unified by 'nature' (*phusis*, or 'life') and which are capable of movement of some kind. The sequence continues with entities (animals) unified by *psuchē*, and capable of psychological functions, in Stoic terms, 'impression' and 'motive'. The sequence is sometimes continued by rationality, which is also seen as a kind of 'tension' which shapes the functions of rational animals, such as adult human beings; and sometimes the sequence marks degrees of rationality, as human beings are more or less unified by virtue or wisdom.[106] What emerges from this line of thought is that the distinction between living and not living, while marked on the spectrum, is not signalled as a major dividing point, since all natural entities constitute modes of 'tension', or structured physical existence, shaped by divine agency. It is also noteworthy that entities, including human beings, do not figure on this schema primarily as species or natural kinds but as degrees of tension or modalities of divine agency or 'breath'. A second feature of Stoic thought that makes the biocentric-ecocentric distinction difficult to draw relates to its conception of the universe or the world. We might be inclined to see the universe or world, taken as a whole, as a 'thing' or material entity. But, for the Stoics, both universe and world are organic entities, or 'animals', which have an internal source of animation and activity, and which form a coherent complex of functions.[107] Also, conceived as wholes, they exhibit complex and advanced functions, and are described as having qualities such as rationality and goodness or virtue, as illustrated shortly. This, again, is a feature that makes it difficult to determine whether we should classify the Stoic worldview as biocentric or ecocentric.

Leaving this point aside, what reason do we have for regarding the Stoic approach as biocentric/ecocentric, rather than anthropocentric, on the question of what has intrinsic value? Stoic theology focuses on two central claims, which occupy the first three-quarters of Cicero's account in *On the Nature of the Gods* 2 and figure prominently in related sources. One is that the universe or world, taken as a whole, is good, indeed better than anything else, including human beings, or the best of things. However, it is not good by definition or postulate; its goodness, like that of other things, notably human beings, derives, in part at least, from its being rational, in a sense explained shortly.[108] The goodness of nature as a whole is also shown by its providential care for all elements within it, including animals and plants, but also inanimate things such as air and sea.[109] These elements are not

---

[106] See LS 47 N–S, D.L. 7.86 (LS 57 A(4–5)); also Gill 2006: 31–4; Bénatouïl 2009: 32–6.
[107] LS 47 C, O.   [108] See Ch. 1, text to nn. 85–95, Ch. 3, text to nn. 135–8, 144–5.
[109] Cic. *N. D.* 2.77–81 (more broadly, 2.73–153, including 2.100–1 on sea and air). On goodness and providential care, see Mansfeld 1999b: 465–9; D. Frede 2002: 100–5.

said to be good or rational in the same way; but they are, by implication, presented as valuable, as objects of providential care by nature as a whole. I consider shortly the rationale for these claims and the connection between them. However, an evident implication is that the natural world, including animate and inanimate entities, is seen as having intrinsic value. Although human beings are presented as being on a higher level than other animals or plants, it is reiterated that they are on a lower level than the universe or world as a whole (or the gods, with whom the universe or world are largely identified).[110] Thus far, the Stoic viewpoint is in line with the biocentric/ecocentric approach.

What is the rationale for these value judgements about the goodness of nature? The goodness of nature is explained by its being rational, presented as a mark of goodness. (This is one of the reasons that the Stoic viewpoint is sometimes characterized by modern scholars as 'logocentric' or reason-centred.)[111] However, the rationality of the universe and to some extent, the world[112] is taken to be shown by the fact that it exhibits structure, order, and wholeness. Features highlighted include the regular patterns of planetary movements in (what we call) the solar system; also the lunar cycle and the tides affected by this; the cycle of day and night, and the seasons throughout the year, all of which are taken as indications of rationality.[113] Structure and order are most obvious in these features; however, they also indicate wholeness, in that they reflect the fact that the universe and world constitute coherent wholes, or unified and self-sustaining systems.[114] This explains why rationality, expressed in this way, is taken as a mark of goodness. Goodness is defined, in Stoic thought, in terms of 'benefit';[115] and these features are seen as benefiting the universe or world, enabling them to maintain their character in a stable and coherent way. The same line of thought explains why the goodness of nature is shown by its providential care for all the elements within it. This providential care is beneficial for those elements and thus for the universe or world which is made up by those elements.[116] Also, nature's providential care enables those elements to maintain their role as integral parts of a coherent, interdependent, and self-sustaining system. Hence, while the component elements are not presented as good in themselves, their existence and, where relevant, their activity contribute to the goodness of the whole world or universe or natural system.

---

[110] Cic. N. D. 2.33–4, 2.36, 2.37–9. On the relationship between Zeus, god or gods, and the universe, see LS 43 F, 45 H, 46: also Ch. 1, text to nn. 92–5.

[111] See Stephens 1994: 278, 285; Whiting and Konstantakos 2019: 4–5; Whiting et al. 2022: 56–8; Shogry 2021: 399–400 (by implication).

[112] Despite some indications of a two-level hierarchy in this respect, with the heavenly bodies at a higher level of rationality than the world (Cic. N. D. 2.17, 39–43), both universe and world are generally seen as shaped by divine activity and rationality (Bénatouïl 2009: 31–6).

[113] Cic. N. D. 2.15, 19, 43, 49–56, 115–120; see also Ch. 1, text to nn. 85–9.

[114] On Stoic thinking on the 'sympathy' or interconnectedness of the natural world, see also Brouwer 2015: 22–8; Protopapadakis 2012: 293–5 (focused on Posidonius).

[115] See LS 60 G., I; also Vogt 2008b: 158–60; and Ch. 2, text to nn. 34–6.   [116] See text to n. 109.

I think it is clear why the Stoic worldview, as thus far explained, might be congenial to modern environmentalists (leaving aside the obvious conceptual differences between the modern scientific worldview and the ancient Stoic one).[117] The Stoic viewpoint ascribes intrinsic value (goodness) to the universe and world, taken as wholes; it also ascribes value to the elements within the universe and world, in so far as they form integral parts of these wholes (in Stoic terms, they are objects of nature's providential care). In particular, the Stoic worldview reinforces the standpoint of those modern environmentalists who emphasize the importance of maintaining existing, but threatened, natural systems, involving different but interdependent forms of natural entity. Thus, reference to the Stoic worldview can support the idea of placing value on bio-diversity, or maintaining ecosystems, and of doing so for their own sake, not just for human use.[118] The Stoic standpoint also has an obvious relevance for current concern about climate breakdown. There are, of course, many grounds for this concern, most obviously, the threat posed to the future existence and welfare of human beings. However, reference to the Stoic worldview offers another perspective on this problem, which represents a reversal or collapse of what the Stoics present as goodness in nature. Stoicism stresses precisely those features of the natural environment (regular natural patterns and cycles, including those of climate, interdependent ecosystems, the coherence and interconnectedness of the natural world) that are thrown into danger by climate breakdown. To this extent, reference to the Stoic worldview and its conception of what is valuable in nature can lend conceptual and visionary support to those arguing for a response to this crisis that matches its intensity and magnitude.

However, there are other aspects of Stoic thought that may well strike us as anthropocentric, that is, as placing intrinsic value only on human beings. For instance, we find in Stoic thought the idea that the universe, and world, are shaped for the benefit of human beings, rather than other animals or plants.[119] We also find the idea that there is an in-built hierarchy in nature, and that human beings are therefore entitled to use other animals as well as other natural resources for their own benefit.[120] A further Stoic idea is that, although human beings should act justly towards any other human being, including those falling outside our own

---

[117] On links between the Stoic worldview and modern environmentalist ethics, see also Whiting and Konstantakos 2019 and Whiting et al. 2022, who argue that this linkage is not invalidated by the religious dimension of the Stoic worldview. For this point, see also Levine 1994 (discussing a number of types of pantheism, including Spinoza's Neo-Stoicism). See too Protopapadakis 2012, comparing Posidonius and Arne Naess; also, though with more qualifications, Stephens 1994, Shogry 2021: 397–9.

[118] In these respects, the Stoic worldview supports an ecocentric, rather than anthropocentric, approach: for these terms, see text to n. 105.

[119] See Cic. N. D. 2.133, 154; also Sedley 2007: 231–8.

[120] See Cic. N. D. 2.37, 156–62. A striking (and offensive) idea is ascribed to Chrysippus; the pig's life has been given to it as a kind of salt to preserve it for human use (Cic. N. D. 2.160; also Sedley 2007: 235–8).

community, considerations of justice have no place in our relationships with other animals.[121] These features, taken on their own, seem to point to a markedly anthropocentric outlook, which we would not now want to adopt from the standpoint of environmental ethics.

How should we respond to these aspects of Stoic thought, and how far do they negate the other, more ecologically positive, aspects? First, how far are the two sides of Stoic thought consistent? As brought out earlier, the Stoic approach to nature as a whole can be characterized as logocentric (reason-centred); given the Stoic understanding of 'reason', this carries with it a positive valuation of order, structure, and wholeness in nature as a whole as well as in human beings.[122] Similarly, human beings are not allocated a special status by Stoics because the human species, as such, is considered exceptional, but because human beings are rational. Although the Stoics see human beings as unique among terrestrial animals in this respect, they regard rationality as present, and to a greater extent, in the universe, the world, and other heavenly bodies (sometimes described, collectively as 'gods').[123] Hence, their view, more precisely stated, is that the universe is shaped for the benefit of human beings and gods, that is, for rational animals, viewed collectively.[124] It is relevant too that the Stoics conceive rationality, seen as a feature of human life at its best, not just as constituting a certain kind of cognitive function but as a whole set of types of coherent and ordered system. These types of system include those of language, logical reasoning, social organization, as well as forms of character, understanding, and life (that is, virtue and happiness).[125] Hence, the Stoic view on the special status of human beings (and, at a higher level, gods) can be seen as restating in a different way their positive valuation of structure, order, and wholeness within the universe.

Regarded in this way, the Stoic view of the special place of human beings within nature is, at least broadly, consistent with their general outlook. However, we may still have reservations about accepting the specific claims made and their practical implications, from a modern environmental standpoint. The problem is not so much that of the practices that they assume as normal. To judge from Cicero's account in *On the Nature of the Gods* 2, what they see as validated by their theory are simply the standard practices of traditional farming methods.[126] Although these are problematic for those opposed to eating meat or dairy products, they may seem vastly preferable to modern agricultural processes, including factory farming, battery chickens, a massive concentration on meat production, especially beef, with consequential widespread destruction of natural habits, including

---

[121] Cic. *Fin.* 3.67, ascribed to Chrysippus. The relevant Stoic idea as regards human beings is that of the brotherhood of humankind or 'cosmopolitanism'. See also Shogry 2021: 401–3.
[122] See text to nn. 111–14.   [123] See text to n. 110.   [124] Cic. *N. D.* 2.37–8, 2.154.
[125] See Gill 2006: 140–1, 151, 253–4; also, on language as a rational system, Inwood 1985: 72–80. For relevant texts, see Cic. *Off.* 1.11–14, D.L. 7.46–8 (LS 31 B), Sen. *Ep.* 76.9–10 (LS 63 D).
[126] Cic. *N. D.* 2.151, 156, 158–60.

woodlands, and loss of biodiversity. However, the more serious problem is that the principles embraced by the Stoics, that human beings are entitled to use other animals and natural resources for their own benefit and that justice has no place in the relationship between humans and other animals,[127] open the door to these and other features of modern practice that are objectionable from the standpoint of modern environmental ethics.

Should we conclude that these aspects of Stoic thought mean that we cannot use its ideas to inform modern environmental ethics, despite the otherwise positive features of their framework? An alternative move is to adopt a modified version of their approach, which stays as close as possible to their thinking, with its distinct-ive insights, while still eliminating elements that have become problematic to us, from our own experience of the disastrous outcomes of the belief in human superiority and exceptionalism. It is worth pointing out that Stoic thinking on this topic is, arguably, not wholly consistent. On the Stoic view, the rationale for human superiority is our (alleged) distinctive rationality.[128] However, the features presented as validated on this basis are not limited to activities which are, in various ways, specifically rational, but include the broader exercise of domination over other animals and the natural environment and their use for the convenience for human beings as a species, in practices such as farming and mining.[129] So I think there is a positive case, regarding the interpretation of Stoic theory in its own terms, for adopting a modified version of their thought on this topic.

What modifications in the Stoic framework would render their thought self-consistent in this respect and enable us to benefit from the environmentally positive features of their worldview and ethics? It is not enough for this purpose to qualify the sharp Stoic distinction between rational (humans) and non-rational (animals), as Nussbaum does in a partly parallel discussion, although this move is justifiable on certain grounds.[130] What is needed is also the thought that the possession of rationality, to the extent that human beings have this distinctively,[131] confers special responsibilities within the broader economy of nature. Human beings, we might say, have a special responsibility for maintaining the eco-system in a sustainable and coherent way, to enable it to have its natural

---

[127] See text to nn. 119–21.

[128] Cic. N. D. 2.33–4, 2.133, 152–3. On Stoic thinking on human beings as constitutively rational, see Inwood 1985: ch. 2. The Stoics tend to overstate the difference between human beings and animals in this respect, setting aside their own observation of animal rationality (the so-called 'dialectical dog'). See S. E. PH 1.69 (LS 36 E); also Sorabji 1993: 20–8, 43, 89.

[129] Thus, Cic. N. D. 2.146–62 combines stress on human rationality (through divine or natural providence) (2.146–50, 153, 155) with human domination of other animals and the natural environ-ment for our own convenience (2.151–2, 156–62).

[130] Nussbaum 2001: ch. 1 adopts a 'Neo-Stoic' view of emotions, which is progressively modified in subsequent chapters, e.g. in ch. 2, on the Stoic distinction between humans and other animals as regards rationality. See also Shogry 2021: 406–7.

[131] On this point, see n. 128. This idea is sometimes described in modern environmental ethics as that of human 'stewardship' for nature as a whole; see Passmore 1974: 28–40.

structure, order, and wholeness. They also have a special role in promoting the welfare and flourishing of other forms of life and the stability of the inanimate elements in the eco-system, such as air and sea.[132] In Stoic terms, human beings as rational animals have a special role in putting into effect universal nature's providential care for all the elements within the universe and world. Indeed, to the extent that we have distinctive rationality, we have special responsibilities to do this for non-rational animals and the broader natural environment.[133] Also, in the modern context, our responsibility in this regard is greatly intensified by the extent to which human beings have, in recent years, done terrible damage to other forms of life and the environment as well as to ourselves. Although this proposed account of the place of human beings in the Stoic worldview, certainly, represents a modification of the Stoics' stated view, it also builds on well-marked aspects in their thinking. These include our status as distinctively rational animals, as well as the Stoic picture of the world (and universe) as a coherent structure or system, and one in which all the elements are objects of the providential care of universal nature.[134] Also implied is the motive, seen as in-built in all human beings, to exercise care for others (in principle, all human beings), in a rational way, though in my account, this has been widened to include other elements in nature.[135] With these modifications, I think, the Stoic worldview, including its view of human-animal relationships and its picture of nature as an eco-system, could play a constructive role for us moderns as a suggestive ancient ideal.

Earlier, I suggest that the Stoic ethical framework has distinctive advantages as a way of framing modern environmental principles in virtue ethical terms.[136] These advantages derive from certain general features of Stoic ethics accentuated in this study, in comparison with the Aristotelian framework. These features consist in their highly integrated and coherent conception of virtue and the virtue-happiness relationship, which is further integrated with a well worked-out account of (adult) ethical development.[137] Another relevant feature, for the present topic, is the Stoic definition of happiness in terms of universal, as well as human, nature. In discussing this idea earlier, I referred to their conception of universal nature as marked by structure, order, and wholeness, which they also see as characteristics of human happiness. I also suggested that this view of universal nature (as marked

---

[132] For these elements, see Cic. *N. D.* 2.100–1, which forms part of 2.81–153 (see text to n. 109).

[133] In fact, we do find this idea in M. A. 6.23: 'In the case of irrational animals and objects and things in general, treat them with generosity of spirit and freedom of mind, since you have rationality and they do not' (trans. Gill 2013a), though this is exceptional. The passage is also noted by Shogry 2021: 405.

[134] See text to nn. 111–16.

[135] For human (rational) care for human beings in general, see Cic. *Off.* 1.60–3, *Fin.* 3. 62–4. The idea that Stoic cosmopolitanism should be extended in this way, for the purposes of modern environmental ethics, is also proposed by Whiting et al. 2018: section 3.3, Whiting and Konstantakos 2019: 4, Whiting et al. 2022: 59–60, and, with more qualifications, by Shogry 2021: 406–7.

[136] See text to nn. 86–99.

[137] For these features, see 6.2–3; also 4.3–5 (on adult human development).

by structure, order, and wholeness) also marks a point of contact between Stoics and modern environmentalists.[138] The preceding discussion of the relationship between the Stoic worldview, as expressed in Stoics' theology, and modern environmental thought has borne out this connection. Hence, a modern environmentalist, might conceive happiness, as well as virtue, in quasi-Stoic terms. That is, she might see the happy life (the 'life according to nature') as giving a central place to the project of promoting (or trying to repair) the structure, order, and wholeness of nature. She might see the happy life not just as one that realizes the best possible qualities of a good human life, but also one that brings human life into line with nature as a whole. This means a life that gives a central role to living in an environmentally sustainable way and that helps to repair the damaging impact of human life on the environment. Thus, the Stoic theory, taken as a whole, including its ideas of virtue, happiness, and the linkage between these ideas and universal nature, offers a highly suggestive framework for a virtue ethical account of environmental ethics.

[138] See text to nn. 111–16.

8

Stoic Development and Guidance, and Modern Thought

8.1 Stoic Ideas and Modern Virtue Ethics

This final discussion takes up another aspect of the contribution of Stoic ethical thinking to modern thought. The topic is the relationship between Stoic ideas on ethical development and guidance (the subject of Part II of this book) and modern thinking. Although this discussion is closely linked with the rest of the book, it differs in two respects. As well as considering modern ethical theory, especially in virtue ethics, I also discuss (in 8.2) what is often called 'life-guidance', aimed at a broad public audience, and its conceptual background in modern thought. In this context I examine the actual influence of Stoic ideas, rather than their potential contribution to modern thought, which is my focus elsewhere. I also explore, to some extent, the significance of these two areas of modern thought for each other, and the overall implications for the potential, or continuing, contribution of Stoic ideas to modern thought.

I begin, however, by considering approaches to development and guidance in modern moral theory. Prior to the contemporary revival of virtue ethics, there was a very marked difference between modern and ancient theory in the importance attached to ethical development. Modern moral theory, broadly speaking, focused on specifying rules, or setting criteria for rules, to determine what should count as right action. Moral theorists supported this project by constructing, or deploying, normative frameworks, including deontological or consequentialist ones, designed to underpin the rules or criteria set.[1] The topic of ethical development played little role in this kind of theory. The focus was on the question of the rules governing right action, rather than the ethical quality of agents and the question how agents develop those qualities. In ancient ethics, by contrast, the emphasis lay on the ethical qualities of agents, their virtue and happiness, rather than the specification of right action.[2] Hence, the questions how those qualities developed and what were the optimal conditions for such development were central ones for ancient thought. However, the revival of modern virtue ethics brought with it renewed

---

[1] On ideas underpinning morality, or 'sources of normativity', in modern theory, see Korsgaard 1996.

[2] On this contrast, see Annas 1993: 4–11.

Learning to Live Naturally: Stoic Ethics and its Modern Significance. Christopher Gill, Oxford University Press.
© Christopher Gill 2022. DOI: 10.1093/oso/9780198866169.003.0009

interest in development, notably, as regards the formation of dispositions and the interpersonal or socio-political preconditions for this process. Although this shift in focus is evident from the beginning of modern virtue ethics, close and detailed treatment of this topic, from this standpoint, has not taken place until quite recently.[3] There has also been much engagement, including disagreement, with study of development in the social sciences, which became the main sphere for work on this subject, during the period when modern moral theory mostly addressed other questions.[4]

As in modern virtue ethics in general, Aristotle has been the most influential ancient prototype for ideas about development.[5] However, as brought out earlier, Aristotle's thought on this subject reflects a broader (Platonic-Aristotelian) pattern, with significant differences from Stoic ideas on development.[6] For instance, the Platonic-Aristotelian pattern presents the development of virtue as dependent on the shaping of dispositions in an appropriate kind of familial and communal context. Aristotle characterizes this process as grasping 'the that' (or 'the facts') of ethical life as a precondition for effective reflection on 'the why' (or 'the reason') for those facts.[7] MacIntyre and Williams can be seen as adopting versions of this idea. MacIntyre stresses that, for the development of the virtues, what is needed is a culture in which the virtues are widely recognized, and in which the social practices underlying the virtues are embodied in communal forms of life and in a tradition of thought and social behaviour.[8] Williams emphasizes the importance of social context in another way, underlining, for instance, the significance of the diversity of background and situation (the 'moral luck') that renders people very unequally placed as regards meeting ethical demands and matching expectations regarding right action. Also, he has accentuated the importance of what he calls 'thick' (culture-specific) values in forming ethical attitudes, by contrast with the more generalized ('thin') moral ideas such as 'right' and 'good' emphasized by most modern theories.[9]

A related Aristotelian idea is that emotional habituation in appropriate kinds of belief, attitude, and action forms a necessary basis for the development of the

---

[3] For collected volumes on this topic, see Snow 2015; Harrison and Walker 2018. Interest in the developmental aspect of ethics is not confined to modern virtue ethics but also sometimes forms part of other contemporary theories, including Utilitarianism (Driver 2015) and Kantian theory (Cureton and Hill 2015: 97–100; Korsgaard 2009: chs. 6–7).

[4] For virtue ethical responses to work by psychologists on the relationship between character and situation; see Russell 2009: part 3; Snow 2013; Narvaez 2015; Slingerland 2015; Thompson 2015.

[5] See Athanassoulis 2013, 2018; McAdams 2015; Russell 2015.

[6] See Introd. to Part II, text to nn. 9–15. As noted there (text to n. 9), the Socratic view, as normally understood, differs from the Platonic-Aristotelian one and prefigures the Stoic approach.

[7] Arist. NE 1.4, 1095b3–8, 1.7, 1098a33–b4, 10.9; also Burnyeat 1980: 71–3; Sherman 1989: 196–7; Gill 1996: 272–5.

[8] See MacIntyre 1985: 187–203, 222–5.

[9] See Williams 1981: ch. 2, 1985: 143–5; also, on Aristotle, Williams 1985: 30–53.

dispositions (*hexeis*) that make up 'ethical', as distinct from 'intellectual', virtue.[10] This idea has been widely adopted in modern virtue ethics, often coupled with the assumption that this kind of habituation needs to take place during childhood and early youth as a basis for the formation of stable adult ethical character. Hursthouse, particularly, emphasizes the importance of this dimension of ethical development.[11] A further Aristotelian idea is that the ethical learner needs to 'practise' or 'rehearse' right actions before she has developed a fully formed ethical disposition and understanding. Annas, in taking up this idea, uses the suggestive image of someone learning to play the piano, and practising to do so before she becomes a fully expert musician.[12] These are all features of the Aristotelian pattern of thinking about ethical development, which do not figure, at least in this form, in Stoic theory. To this extent, it may seem questionable whether Stoic thinking on ethical development is well placed to contribute to modern virtue ethical ideas.

The features of Aristotelian influence on modern virtue ethics just outlined mostly relate to childhood development, viewed as a basis for adult life, and to the effect of familial and social shaping of attitudes and ethical character. Although these factors are not wholly ignored in Stoic theory of development,[13] the focus is different. The central concern of Stoic thinking is with ethical development in adult life, coupled with the assumption that all human beings, in principle, have in-built capacities and motives enabling such development. Analogously, Stoics believe that ethical development can take place, in principle again, in any socio-political context and that it can be enabled by life experience, as well as, or instead of, philosophical education.[14] These assumptions underpin the two main innova-tive Stoic contributions to the ancient theory of ethical development, their accounts of appropriation, in its two related strands, and emotional development, seen as closely integrated with appropriation.[15] These Stoic ideas also explain their extensive writings on ethical guidance, especially guidance to adults on how to promote their own ethical development, which goes beyond anything we can find in Aristotle on this subject.[16] The Stoic theories of development, along with their innovative focus on ethical guidance, have substantial points of interest for various strands in modern thought, including psychotherapy and life-guidance, as brought out later.[17] However, they also offer an alternative ancient prototype to Aristotle on certain aspects of ethical development that are important for virtue ethics.

---

[10] See Arist. *NE* 2.1; also 1.13, esp. 1103a2–10. On emotional habituation in Aristotle, see Sherman 1989: 176–84, 1997: 75–83, 241–3.

[11] Hursthouse 1999: 38–9, 60–2, 113–16, 175–7, 183–6.

[12] Arist. *NE* 2.1; Annas 2011: 12–15, 17–24, 29–30.

[13] They are considered as part of the causes of corruption (Ch. 5, text to n. 44–8). Posidonius, exceptionally, seems to have had a special interest in development from early childhood (Gal. *PHP* 5.5.32–5; see also Ch. 5, n. 7).

[14] See Introd. to Part II, text to nn. 20–39.   [15] See Chs 4–5.

[16] See Introd. to Part II, text to nn. 49–51.   [17] See 8.2.

Why should modern virtue ethical thinkers take any special interest in Stoic ideas on this subject? The first reason is that Stoic writings on ethical development and guidance are much more extensive and fully explored than their Aristotelian equivalents. Despite the influence of Aristotelian ideas on development on modern virtue ethics, the scope of his actual writings on this topic is relatively modest. In the *Nicomachean Ethics*, his most influential work, this is limited to rather brief comments on the formation of ethical ('character-based') virtue and more generalized discussion of the basis of ethical development in the final chapter of the work, linking ethics and politics.[18] Aristotle seems to presuppose the existence, and validity, of Plato's much more extensive treatment of childhood ethical development in the *Republic* and *Laws*.[19] Also, there is very little that we can identify as ethical guidance, as such, going beyond brief comments on the practical implications of theoretical topics and questions.[20] The absence of guidance makes good sense in the light of his view that to engage effectively in ethical theory, you need already to have grasped the ethical 'facts' (or the 'that'), through habituative upbringing in appropriate beliefs and attitudes before reflecting on the 'why' or analysis of ethics.[21]

In Stoic theory, by contrast, the subject of development is treated much more fully, especially in connection with the theory of appropriation. My main concern in this book has been with advanced, rational development, especially as presented in Cicero, *On Ends* 3.16–22, 62–8 and *On Duties* 1.11–15. However, there are other Stoic writings centred on the early, more basic, phases of appropriation, shared by human beings and other animals.[22] Stoics also discuss the sources of corruption, or failed ethical development, in connection with the formation of (defective) emotions.[23] Their treatments of development, successful and failed, add up to a body of material which is more substantial than that offered by Aristotle. If we turn to the topic of ethical guidance, the contrast with Aristotle is yet more striking. Among the Stoic writings discussed here, Cicero's *On Duties*, taken as a whole, constitutes an extended treatment of Stoic guidance on practical deliberation, directed at enabling ethical progress in carrying out such deliberation. I have also considered, in Chapter 5, writings on guidance, of different kinds, on emotional development, including Seneca's dialogue, *On Peace of Mind*.[24] These works represent a rather small selection out of a much larger body of Stoic writings, by thinkers including Cicero, Seneca, Epictetus, and Marcus Aurelius, directed at offering ethical guidance for shaping one's pattern

---

[18] See Arist. *NE* 2.1–4, 10.9; also text to nn. 10–12, and Burnyeat 1980.

[19] See Arist. *NE* 2.3, 1104b11–13; also Introd. to Part II, text to nn. 10–13.

[20] A rare example of such guidance: Aristotle urges his listeners, in aiming at the 'mean', to counteract the motive towards the extreme that is more contrary to the mean, or the extreme to which we are, individually, more drawn (*NE* 2.9, 1109a30–1109b6).

[21] See text to n. 7.

[22] See Ch. 4; on the more basic phases, see 4.2; also LS 57 A–D; Gill 2006: 37–46.

[23] See Ch. 5, text to nn. 44–55.   [24] See 2.4–5, 5.2–3.

of actions, relationships, or emotions.[25] The emergence of this large corpus of writings on development and guidance reflects structural features in Stoic thought. Stoic writing on ethical development is centred on progress within adult life; and the works on guidance, taken as a whole, are directed at promoting adult development. This reflects the assumptions noted earlier: that all human beings have 'the starting-points of virtue' (LS 61 L), and that there is scope for ethical development and progress during adult life (*any* adult life), despite the pervasive influence of sources of corruption in human existence. These assumptions also underlie the emergence of the three-topic programmes of ethical development (in adult life) outlined earlier, which represent a distillation of the forms of guidance worked out in detail in these writings.[26]

Of course, the sheer quantity of Stoic writings on development and guidance does not, by itself, guarantee that they can make a valuable contribution to contemporary virtue ethics. However, there are several reasons for supposing that this is the case. First, I suggest, Stoic thinking on development, taken as a whole and viewed in its own terms, is coherent and cogent. Second, Stoic ideas on this subject, especially on appropriation, form part of a pattern of ethical thinking, which, as argued in Chapters 6–7, can contribute positively to modern (Neo-Aristotelian) virtue ethics. Since Stoic thinking on development is integrally linked with ideas which can inform contemporary virtue ethics, this provides a further reason to take account of their thinking on development. Third, Stoic ethical guidance, when taken with their thinking on development, is both extensive and potentially valuable for promoting the growth of the virtues, as conceived in contemporary virtue ethics. I explore these points first in general terms and then with specific reference to the writings of certain modern virtue ethicists.

First, then, I suggest that the Stoic approach to ethical development, considered as a whole, is wide-ranging but coherent and psychologically credible. Their thinking stresses both the importance of basic human motives (the instincts to take care of oneself and others of one's kind) and the scope for the rational expression and extension of these motives during full (adult) development.[27] Adult development, in turn, is analysed in terms of three distinct, but interconnected, pathways. The first two consist in development in the understanding of value, notably of the respective values of virtue and indifferents, and in forming relationships with other people and within communities of different kinds.[28] The third pathway, which depends on the first two, is development in motivation, especially the overall pattern of emotion.[29] All three strands are conceived broadly in the sense that the focus is on general human capacities and activities which can,

---

[25] See also Gill 2003: 40–4. This dimension of Stoic writing has attracted much scholarly attention in recent years; see Nussbaum 1994; P. Hadot 1998; Sorabji 2000: part 2; Brunt 2013; Griffin 2013.
[26] See Introd. to Part II, text to nn. 17–27, 43–51.   [27] See 4.2 and 4.3–5, respectively.
[28] See 4.3–5; on the interconnections, see 4.3 and 4.5, text to nn. 202–15.   [29] See 5.1.

in principle, be expressed in a wide range of social, cultural, and intellectual contexts. There is a marked contrast, in this respect, with the contrasting Platonic-Aristotelian account of ethical development which presupposes the need for more restricted or tightly defined social and intellectual contexts.[30] A further, Stoic feature is the combination and integration of ideas about value (notably about the virtue-happiness and virtue-indifferents relationships) and about nature, both human and universal. This point applies to Stoic ethical theory in general and also forms part of their ideas on ethical development.[31] The breadth, combined with coherence, of the Stoic framework is not always appreciated. However, it is one of the features I have aimed to bring out in Chapters 4–5, and one that renders their theory a conceptually powerful one, when considered in its own terms.

Second, Stoic thinking on development, especially their theory of appropriation, forms part of, and lends crucial support to, the ideas presented, in Chapters 6–7, as potential contributions to modern virtue ethics, and as, in some respects, more suitable for this purpose than the analogous Aristotelian ideas. The argument of Chapters 6–7 is not presented as being primarily about conceptions of development. However, it is a corollary of that argument that it lends support to the claim made here, that the Stoic conception of ethical development is cogent and credible.

I have argued, for instance, that the Stoic understanding of the virtue-happiness relationship is more internally coherent than the Aristotelian, because of differences between Stoic and Aristotelian ideas on the contribution of valuable things other than virtue to happiness and the relationship between practical and theoretical wisdom. Partly for this reason, the Stoic theory is better placed than the Aristotelian theory to inform modern virtue ethical thought on the virtue-happiness relationship.[32] Stoic thinking on development is integrally linked with this set of ideas. Thus, for example, the first strand of appropriation, as presented in Cicero's On Ends 3.16–22, presents the progressive understanding of the relationship between virtue (and virtue-based happiness) and indifferents as central for ethical development.[33] Also, by contrast with the ideal educational programme in Plato's Republic and similar ideas in Aristotle's Nicomachean Ethics, the Stoic conception of development does not present theoretical wisdom as a qualitatively higher and more valuable type of wisdom than practical wisdom and as the culmination of an ideal developmental sequence.[34] Similarly, I have suggested that Stoic thinking on self-other relations provides a valid alternative to the modern egoism-altruism contrast, and is, in certain respects, more suitable for

---

[30]   On this contrast, see Introd. to Part II, text to 16–39.
[31]   On this point, see (in Stoic ethical theory in general) Ch. 3, esp. 3.3; (in Stoic theory of development) Ch. 4, esp. 4.2, 4.4, text to nn. 123–65, 4.5, text to nn. 174–83.
[32]   See 6.2–3.   [33]   See esp. Cic. Fin. 3.16–22; see also 4.4.
[34]   Contrast Pl. Rep. Books 6–7, Arist. NE 10.7–8; see also Introd. to Part II, text to nn. 11–13, 28–39.

this purpose than Aristotelian thinking.[35] Stoic thinking on self-other relationships also underpins the Stoic theory of appropriation, which presupposes that care for others is a primary motive like care for oneself and that ethical development involves the rational fulfilment of both motives. In both these respects, the Stoic theory of development supports, and is integrally linked with, ideas which can contribute substantially to modern virtue ethics; and this provides a supplementary argument for seeing the Stoic theory of development as meriting serious consideration from this standpoint.

I have also argued, in Chapter 7, that the Stoic theory of appropriation, by integrating ideas about value with those about nature (human and universal) enables Stoic thinking to contribute positively to two other features of modern (Neo-Aristotelian) virtue ethical theory. One is the idea of ethics as, crucially, human ethics, an idea developed by Anscombe, Foot, and Hursthouse. As stressed throughout this book, the achievement of virtue and virtue-based happiness is conceived in Stoicism as the fullest realization of human nature (alongside the best qualities of universal nature); and this idea is also implied in the Stoic theory of appropriation.[36] As suggested earlier, the theory of appropriation offers a more fully elaborated account of the ethically relevant features of human nature and motivation identified by Hursthouse.[37] In this way, the Stoic theory suggests that ethical development can include deepening one's understanding of what it means to be human and correlating this understanding with an improved grasp of ethical notions such as virtue and happiness. In addition, as argued in Chapter 7, Stoic ethical theory can help us to construct an effective virtue ethical response to climate breakdown. It does so by providing a framework linking the understanding of virtue or happiness with that of universal nature (including the natural environment) as well as that of human nature. In this respect, Stoic theory goes beyond Aristotle, who focuses on the linkage between happiness and human nature.[38] The Stoic theory helps us to formulate the idea that the natural environment has inherent value and to recognize the connection between order (and breakdown of order) in the natural environment and in human character and understanding. Also, we can now add, the Stoic theory helps us to see the force of the idea that, for moderns, ethical development should give a central place to developing a response to climate breakdown that matches the scale of the problem.[39] So in both respects, regarding human and cosmic nature, Stoic theory provides the basis for an enlarged view of what ethical development involves, in a way that is coherently related to a virtue ethical framework.

The points made so far relate to Stoic thinking on appropriation and modern virtue ethical thinking on development: what about the Stoic ideas on emotional

---

[35] See 6.4, esp. text to nn. 149–60.   [36] See 1.3–4, 3.3, 4.3–4; also Cic. *Off.* 1.11–15, *Fin.* 3.16–22.
[37] See 7.2, esp. text to nn. 52–61.   [38] See Arist. *NE* 1.7; also 7.2, text to nn. 12–33.
[39] See 7.3, text to nn. 103–4, 7.4, text to nn. 108–18, 137–8.

development discussed in Chapter 5? Can they also make a constructive contribution to modern virtue ethical thinking? The position on this topic is rather more
complex or contested. Broadly speaking, from its beginning, modern virtue ethics
defined its approach as that of giving greater weight to the emotional dimension
of ethical life than most current theories. For instance, virtue ethics emphasized
the importance of emotions in the formation of ethical motivation and ethical
dispositions. Virtue ethical theorists, particularly Williams, also accentuated the
crucial role in ethical life of close interpersonal relationships as a basis for strong
other-directed emotions. By contrast, Kantian deontology and Utilitarianism, for
instance, tended to be seen as excessively rationalistic in their conception of moral
motivation and the moral life in general.[40] In this respect, as in others, Aristotle
has often been taken as the exemplar.[41] This kind of contrast has sometimes
recurred in discussion of Stoicism by virtue ethicists or scholars writing on
theories of emotion. Stoicism, sometimes compared or associated with Kant, has
been presented as overly rationalistic, by contrast with Aristotle, mainly because of
the Stoic advocacy of the 'extirpation' of (defective) emotions.[42] This criticism is
sometimes coupled with the claim that Stoicism advocates detachment from close
interpersonal relationships, a stance seen as linked with the idea of the self-
sufficiency of virtue for happiness and the contrast between virtue and 'preferred
indifferents, including the welfare of other people.[43] From this standpoint, it might
seem, Stoic thinking on emotional development does not present itself as a
promising contributor to modern virtue ethical thinking.

However, there has a gradual shift in the view taken on Stoic thinking on
emotions among those writing from a virtue ethical perspective. Recent treatments have tended to be less critical and either more even-handed or positive.
Sherman, for instance, whose earlier work stressed Stoic rationalism and associated Stoic views with Kantian ones, has moved progressively towards a more
sympathetic or positive stance towards the Stoic framework.[44] Russell's book on
happiness, while generally favouring the Aristotelian approach to the role of
emotions in ethical life, brings out the conceptual and ethical force of the Stoic
position.[45] Nussbaum, in a major study of emotion, adopts a version of the Stoic
(cognitive) psychological framework, while remaining critical of what she sees as
the Stoic 'anti-compassion' ethical stance.[46] Various factors underlie this shift in

---

[40] See Williams 1981: 14–19 on interpersonal relationships. See Williams 1985: 54–70, critical of the
Kantian focus on rationality; Williams 1985: 106–10, critical of the Utilitarian conception of ethical
motivation.
[41] See text to nn. 5–7; also Sherman 1997: 24–98; Hursthouse 1999: 108–20.
[42] See Nussbaum 1994: chs. 3, 9–10, 2001: ch. 7; Sherman 1997: ch. 3; Sorabji 2000: chs. 10, 12–13.
[43] See Ch. 5, text to nn. 81–3.
[44] Contrast Sherman 1997: ch. 3 with Sherman 2005 and 2021. However, she retains some
'Aristotelian' reservations about certain features of Stoic thinking on emotions.
[45] Russell 2012: parts 2–3; see also Gill 2016c: 349–51.
[46] Nussbaum 2001: chs. 1 and 7; see also Gill 2016c: 351–4.

the evaluation of Stoic thinking on emotions among those writing from a virtue ethical standpoint.[47] One set of factors, discussed in the following section, is the emergence within contemporary theory of mind, psychology, and psychotherapy, of cognitive theories and methods much closer to the Stoic, than the Aristotelian, framework. These movements have, in turn, contributed to the pervasive use of Stoic ideas in contemporary life-guidance. A related factor has been the adoption of Stoic ideas, among other ancient ideas, as a basis for the reflective management of one's own life (including emotional life), notably by prominent thinkers such as Michel Foucault and Pierre Hadot.[48]

A further important factor has been the emergence, within specialist scholarship on Stoicism, of treatments which bring out the psychological and ethical credibility, complexity, and coherence of the Stoic theory of emotion. Graver's study of Stoic emotions is a good example of this tendency. She presents the Stoic psychological framework as unified or holistic, rather than narrowly rationalistic.[49] Graver also brings out the point that the Stoic theory advocates the integration of emotions with ethical life more generally, rather than aiming at the complete elimination of emotions. Hence, she underlines the importance of Stoic thinking on good emotions (*eupatheiai*), the emotions of the virtuous or 'wise', as well as defective ones.[50] She also accentuates the emotional dimension of ethical development and the linkage with well-conducted interpersonal and social relationships.[51] The treatment of emotional development offered earlier in this book (in Chapter 5) proceeds on similar lines. As I suggest, emotional development, as conceived in Stoicism, forms part of an integrated view of ethical development, including making progress in understanding value and engaging in interpersonal or communal relationships in a virtuous way. I have also argued against the view sometimes adopted, that the Stoic theory advocates a kind of self-sufficiency based on a (fundamentally egoistic) form of emotional detachment from other people.[52] As so interpreted, the Stoic theory of emotional development, as well as their ideas about appropriation, can make a positive and significant contribution to modern virtue ethical thinking about what constitutes a complete and worthwhile form of ethical development. Indeed, as just noted, there are already indications that Stoicism is already contributing in this way.[53]

Similar points can be made about the potential contribution of Stoic guidance to modern (Neo-Aristotelian) virtue ethics. As underlined earlier, ethical guidance plays a much larger and more significant role in Stoic ethics than in Aristotelian

---

[47] A related movement has been the increasing readiness, among those writing from a virtue ethical standpoint, to recognize in Kantian or Utilitarian theory a significant and positive role for emotions: see Sherman 1997: ch. 4; Hursthouse 1999: ch. 4; Driver 2015.

[48] See Foucault 1990; P. Hadot 1994, 1998: also Gill 2013a: xxi–xxxi; Bénatouïl 2016b: 367–71.

[49] Graver 2007: chs. 1–2; also Gill 2006: 75–100.

[50] Graver 2007: 51–60; also 143–8. See also Graver 2016; Gill 2016b.   [51] Graver 2007: chs. 7–8.

[52] See 5.2–3, esp. text to nn. 81–4.   [53] See text to nn. 44–6.

ethics, and this reflects salient differences in their respective conceptions of ethical development.[54] Stoic guidance can inform modern virtue ethical thinking in two ways. First, Stoicism offers examples of guidance (from a virtue ethical standpoint) on determinate areas of life such as practical deliberation or emotional self-management or more localized and particularized questions.[55] This dimension of Stoic ethical writing is particularly significant since specific forms of guidance, especially on practical deliberation, are more often associated in modern moral theory with deontological or consequentialist approaches, and virtue ethics is sometimes criticized for being ill-equipped to provide guidance.[56] Second, Stoicism is exceptional in its focus on guidance designed to promote ethical development, understood as development towards virtue and virtue-based happiness. The three-topic programmes of ethical guidance, outlined earlier, represent a striking example of this pattern, though such guidance is also incorporated, in various forms, in much practically oriented Stoic ethical writing.[57] This mode of guidance expresses the virtue ethical view that, in order to understand how to act (and feel) properly in a given situation, what is needed is not just instruction of various kinds but also, and crucially, ethical understanding and character. The Stoic programmes of ethical guidance are devoted to helping people to carry forward the process of ethical development that can help them to move towards this kind of understanding and character.

These general observations on the potential value of Stoic thinking on development and guidance for modern virtue ethics can be supplemented by reference to specific points of connection between the two areas. I refer to Annas and Hursthouse, two exponents of the Neo-Aristotelian approach. Earlier I noted Annas's adoption of the Aristotelian idea that we become virtuous by performing virtuous actions, an idea she compares with playing the piano as a way of developing the skill of playing the piano.[58] However, two other, interconnected ideas stressed by Annas evoke, rather, Stoic thinking. One is what she calls 'the need to learn'; and the other is 'the drive to aspire'. Annas argues that, for effective ethical development, the agent should feel the force of both these motives, which need to inform her life as a whole, and not only during childhood and youth.[59] Annas's stress on the need to learn matches her presentation of virtue as a skill that needs to be acquired, partly by teaching, over time. The idea of virtue as a skill

[54] See text to nn. 20–1, 24–6.

[55] On Stoic guidance on appropriate actions, see 2.4–5 (also on Seneca's comparable guidance on providing benefits, see Sen. *Ben.*, and Griffin 2013). On Stoic guidance on emotions (or 'therapy'), see 5.2, text to nn. 96–113; also Tieleman 2003: ch. 3 on Chrysippus' 'therapeutic book', ch. 6 on Cic. *Tusc.* 3–4; Gill 2010a: 280–300 (on Chrysippus). Seneca's essays and dialogues cover numerous areas of practical life.

[56] On this point, see Hursthouse 1999: 35–42.

[57] On the three-topic programmes, see Introd. to Part II, text to nn. 49–51; on Stoic guidance, see text to nn. 22–6 in this section.

[58] See text to n. 12.   [59] Annas 2011: 16–32, esp. 22, 25.

or expertise was widely adopted in ancient thought (though not by Aristotle); it is one that Annas shares with some other modern virtue ethical thinkers.[60] Annas's stress on the (ongoing) need to aspire is more exceptional in modern virtue ethics; but she makes a strong case for its importance.[61] The Stoic account of development provides a comprehensive framework for working out the implications of these ideas in a way that is closely interlocked with other key ethical concepts and a coherent theoretical framework. As highlighted earlier, the Stoics stress both the role of the wise person as a paradigm of virtue and virtue-based happiness and the scope for all human beings to make progress towards this goal. They also present appropriation, in its two, interrelated strands, coupled with emotional development, as routes in this direction. In this way, the Stoics accentuate the need to learn (if we are to develop virtue and virtue-based happiness) and also specify a clear set of pathways for fulfilling this need. They also highlight the importance of conceiving one's life as a whole as one of ongoing progress or aspiration towards virtue, if the learning process that is essential for the development of virtue is to be realized.[62] In these respects, the Stoic theory of ethical development intersects with at least one modern virtue ethical approach, that of Annas; it also offers resources for working out her ideas more fully, by reference to ideas about virtue, happiness, and their development which are, in general, compatible with contemporary (Neo-Aristotelian) virtue ethics and eudaimonism.

My second example centres on modern virtue ethics and guidance, rather than development. I discuss the relationship between the kind of Stoic ethical guidance offered by Cicero in *On Duties*, especially Book 1, and Hursthouse's virtue ethical account of guidance. I suggest, again, that the two theories have common ground, and can therefore inform each other, though I accentuate the role of the Stoic theory in, potentially, enhancing the modern one.

At the start of this section, I have contrasted the interest of modern virtue ethics in the development of the virtuous agent with the tendency in most modern moral theories to focus on specifying rules for right action and offering theoretical justification for the type of rules offered.[63] A consequence of this contrast has been the criticism by some modern thinkers that virtue ethics fails to do what other moral theories do, namely, provide guidance for right action. In response, Hursthouse argues that virtue ethics does, indeed, provide such guidance, though framed in terms appropriate for virtue ethics. In her account, a right action is what a virtuous agent would characteristically do in the relevant circumstances, combined with a specification of what is meant by 'virtuous' and 'virtues'. She

---

[60] On virtue as skill or expertise in ancient ethics, see Annas 1993: 67–73; for this idea in modern virtue ethics, see Stichter 2018; also Annas 2011: ch. 3.

[61] Annas 2011: 16, 18, 22, 25.

[62] See Introd. to Part II, text to nn. 51–5; also 4.4–5 on the two strands of appropriation, 5.2–3 on emotional development as therapy.

[63] See text to nn. 1–2.

describes guidance of this type as 'V-rules', thus highlighting the link with the form of guidance that is standard in, for instance, deontological and consequentialist theories.[64] Hursthouse does not suppose that V-rules, taken by themselves, necessarily provide all that is needed for guidance on right action. The other main factor consists of reference to the type of reasons for which a virtuous agent, typically, chooses a virtuous action. These reasons can be specific considerations bearing on the action in question or more general ideas, such as duty or benefit, identifying the principle that leads someone to regard an action as characteristic of a particular virtue. As she puts it, the virtuous agent does a V act (one characteristic of a virtuous person) for X reasons.[65] Hursthouse's proposal has generated considerable interest among virtue ethicists and produced differing responses. One possible criticism is that she over-assimilates virtue ethical guidance to that of other theoretical approaches. However, Annas, among others, argues that her analysis offers a highly credible form of guidance on right action, while consistently maintaining a virtue ethical framework.[66]

My concern is with the relationship between Hursthouse's proposals and Stoic thinking on guidance. In Chapter 2, discussing Stoic guidance on practical deliberation, especially as presented by Cicero in On Duties, I distinguish my view of Stoic guidance from the interpretations offered by Barney and Brennan. A shared feature of their approach is scepticism about the idea that reference to the notion of virtue can play a useful role in Stoic deliberation or in guidance on this subject.[67] They present Stoic deliberation as conceived either wholly in terms of indifferents (Barney) or indifferents qualified by reference to consideration of justice and the benefit of the community (Brennan).[68] These scholars are concerned to make sense of the ancient evidence for Stoic deliberation, rather than to analyse the form of guidance appropriate to virtue ethics (ancient and modern). However, Hursthouse's account, while directed at modern virtue ethics, has an indirect relevance for scholarly debate about the form of Stoic deliberation. Hursthouse brings out how reference to the idea of virtue can provide a basis for analysing, or, at a practical level, guiding, deliberation about actions within a virtue ethical framework. Hursthouse's treatment shows that an analysis of this kind can avoid the defects of circularity or vacuousness that these scholars ascribe to use of the idea of virtue in the context of Stoic deliberation.[69] Also, Hursthouse's

---

[64] Hursthouse 1999: 28–30.

[65] Hursthouse 1999: 126–36. Hursthouse explains in this way the Aristotelian idea of doing something 'for its own sake' (on which see Ch. 6, text to n. 104); on this idea see also Williams 1995a and Hursthouse 1995.

[66] Annas 2011: 32–51, esp. 36, 39, 41. See also Russell 2009: chs. 2–4, for another virtue-centred approach to right action; Kawall 2013, reviewing recent debate on virtue ethics and right action.

[67] Barney 2003: 317–19, 330–2; Brennan 2005: 183–91, 210–12, 216–18.

[68] See further on their interpretations, Ch. 2, text to nn. 70–1, 145–55. It should be noted that their aim is to reconstruct early Stoic (or at least Chrysippean) theory of deliberation, and not to analyse the approach we find in Cicero, On Duties.

[69] See refs. in n. 67.

account is, strikingly, similar to the type of guidance which Cicero offers in *On Duties* and which, I have suggested, is in line with Stoic theory more generally. The primary guidance he offers, especially in Book 1, for choosing which 'appropriate acts' to perform is based on behaviour presented as typical of one or other of the four cardinal virtues (compare Hursthouse's 'what a virtuous agent would characteristically do in these circumstances').[70] In explaining the kind of behaviour he has in mind, Cicero refers both to specific factors in the relevant situation, justifying acts of generosity, for instance, and also general ones. The general ones may be either aspects of the virtue in question or broader considerations (about the nature and basis of human association, for instance), whose relevance to the specific act or virtue involved is explained by Cicero. These two types of consideration are similar to those that Hursthouse sees as supporting virtuous deliberation, when she says that the virtuous agent does a V act for X reasons.[71] From this standpoint, Hursthouse's analysis can usefully inform interpretative debate about Stoic ethical guidance on practical deliberation, by highlighting the credibility of an approach that makes good sense within a virtue ethical framework, ancient or modern.[72]

So far, I have stressed ways in which reference to Hursthouse's ideas can inform interpretation of Stoic guidance, as presented in *On Duties*. How, turning the tables, can reference to the Stoic parallel contribute to modern consideration of the validity of Hursthouse's account? In the first instance, this comparison lends support to her framework by highlighting similarities with a prominent ancient ethical theory, and one that is distinct from the Aristotelian one that she generally takes as her prototype.[73] Second, this parallel offers alternatives to some of the concepts she deploys in her analysis, which are taken from modern moral theories other than virtue ethics. Neither Cicero nor (I think) Stoic theory refer to 'rules' in this connection. Cicero refers to what Seneca, in a comparable discussion, presents as a combination of 'doctrines' (*decreta*) (such as accounts of the virtues and of types of 'nature') and 'instructions' or 'guidance' (*praecepta*). The Stoic guidance offered does not aim at the qualities, such as codification, comprehensiveness, and authoritative or definitive character, typically associated in modern thought with rules.[74] Similarly, there is no exact analogue in Cicero's treatment for the modern notion of 'right action'. The Stoic project is that of offering guidance on

---

[70] See Cic. *Off.* 1.15–17, 20, 152 (LS 59 P); and Ch. 2, text to nn. 118, 122, 130–4; also Hursthouse 1999: 28–30.

[71] See Cic. *Off.* 1.45, 47, 49 (specific factors guiding generosity), 1.50–9 (general considerations of human association, guiding specific decisions). See Ch. 2, text to nn. 146–7, 156–60. See also Hursthouse 1999: 126–36.

[72] See also Gill forthcoming (a), which refers to Hursthouse's approach in connection with interpretation of Stoic (and Ciceronian) practical deliberation.

[73] On her 'Neo-Aristotelian' approach, see Hursthouse 1999: 8–16.

[74] See Inwood 1999, arguing against the view sometimes advanced (on the basis of Stoic ideas about 'natural law') that Stoic ethics is rule-based. See Ch. 2, text to nn. 166–77, on the similarities between Senecan thinking on guidance and Cicero's treatment in *Off.*

performing 'appropriate actions', that is, actions which have a prima facie justi-fication, but not ones which are claimed to have the definitive rightness which belongs only to actions determined by the ideal wise person.[75] For related reasons, Stoic guidance on deliberation is conceived as having an educational function, that of helping the person guided to 'make progress' towards the kind of understand-ing and character that enables the performance of 'right actions' in the Stoic sense.[76] Some of these differences from Hursthouse's analysis might be regarded as peculiar to Stoicism. However, the comparison with Stoicism can suggest an alternative conceptual vocabulary to that of Hursthouse, one which is, arguably, more suited to her approach, or perhaps that of any virtue ethical framework. It might be better to talk in terms of 'V-guidance' than 'V-rules'; and to define criteria for informing the choice of 'appropriate actions' (in the Stoic sense), rather than 'right actions'.[77] Also, the Stoic conceptual language is linked with another idea that also applies to modern virtue ethics. Such guidance, as well as aiming to provide the basis for well-grounded decision-making, has an educational function, in promoting the project of ongoing ethical development that forms part of the life of any well-motivated ethical agent. In Annas's terms, noted earlier, such guidance underlines the importance of 'the need to learn' how to deliberate well and the significance of 'the drive to aspire', as an ongoing feature of adult ethical life.[78] Admittedly, these proposed modifications would not advance Hursthouse's aim of showing that virtue ethics can carry out a project which is typical of deontological and consequentialist theories, namely defining rules for right action.[79] However, these suggestions encourage reflection on virtue ethical alternatives to that project, and on ideas that can make a distinct and positive contribution to enabling people to work towards living a good human life.

There is one further feature of Cicero's treatment in *On Duties* whose relevance for modern moral theory is worth exploring further. This can be seen as an aspect of a broader characteristic of Cicero's account. Not only does he discuss, more fully than Hursthouse, the topic of the virtuous person's reasons, both general and specific, for regarding an action as right, that is, in line with virtue. He also explores in more detail the relationship between general and specific factors. For instance, as noted earlier, he discusses the relationship between the nature and grounds of human association and the specific connections we have with other people to provide criteria to determine what counts as a generous action in a given case.[80] In Book 3, as illustrated earlier, there is a series of such discussions, notably

---

[75] See Cic. *Off.* 1.7–8, 3.13–16; also, on the distinction between 'appropriate acts' and 'perfectly correct acts' (those of the wise person), see LS 59 B(4).

[76] See Ch. 2, text to nn. 102–11, 116, 126–8; also Introd. to Part II, text to nn. 49–51.

[77] On the question of the best kind of conceptual vocabulary for describing right action in virtue ethical theory see Russell 2009: 37–9; Kawall 2013: 137–40.

[78] On virtue ethical guidance as directed at promoting ethical development, see Annas 2011: 36–40; also text to nn. 58–61.

[79] See text to nn. 63–4.   [80] See refs. in n. 71.

Cicero's (controversial) use of the idea of the human and political community as an organic body to justify tyrannicide in the Roman context, and Antipater's citation of the idea of the community of humankind to support a particular course of action in business dealings.[81] This dimension of Cicero's treatment, which reflects Stoic thinking more broadly, can be seen as a strong point in the Stoic approach and, again, a potential contribution to modern virtue ethics.

There is one example of this general point that is especially worth noting for its potential significance for modern virtue ethics and, indeed, for other forms of moral thinking; this is the Stoic idea, already noted in this book, that all of us have four interconnected roles (*personae*).[82] This idea explores the interplay between general and specific factors in several respects. First, it represents a general framework for decision-making that all of us can deploy in ways that take account of the specific features of our lives. Second, the framework itself includes and co-ordinates general and specific factors. The general one, underpinning the whole pattern, is our shared human role as rational and sociable and as capable of expressing the virtues and achieving virtue-based happiness. The other three roles are specific in different ways: they are our individual talents and inclinations or personal style, our given or inherited role in society, and the role or life-project we choose, if we have scope for doing this.[83] Cicero's guidance focuses on the idea that, in making long-term or short-term decisions, we should aim to achieve consistency between the claims of these four roles, with a view to carrying out actions which are 'right', that is in line with the virtues.[84] The underlying idea is that the three specific roles represent ways in which we can coherently express our common human role, not that they constitute wholly independent and potentially competing sources of value.[85] This framework is one that is compatible with, but which also contributes to, Hursthouse's virtue-based model of ethical guidance. The idea of acting as a virtuous agent acts (the first role) is explored more fully by highlighting factors that need to be taken account of, and co-ordinated, in virtue-based deliberation. Put differently, the three specific roles provide reasons for acting in a certain way (hence, in Hursthouse's terms, the V-act is done for X reasons).[86] More broadly, the theory provides a framework for accommodating several ideas stressed by different virtue ethicists regarding practical deliberation. These ideas include the importance of giving weight to one's specific individuality

---

[81] See Cic. *Off.* 3.26–8, 32, 53; also Ch. 2, text to nn. 206–7, 225–8, 230.

[82] See Cic. *Off.* 1.107–21; also Ch. 2, text to n. 133, Ch. 5, text to nn. 151, 159–60.

[83] Cic. *Off.* 1.107 (cf. 105–6) (first role), 107–8, 112–14 (second role), 115–21 (third and fourth roles). See also on these roles Gill 1988: 173–87, and on the Stoic background Tieleman 2007: 130–40.

[84] On this emphasis, see Cic. *Off.* 1.110–11, 119, 120. The four-role theory is introduced as an illustration of the fourth virtue (fittingness, *decorum*, 1.93–6), and Cicero refers back to this virtue repeatedly in this connection (1.107, 110–11, 119, 120). For 'right' (*honestum*) as determined by what is in line with the virtues, see Ch. 2, text to nn. 129–34.

[85] On this point, see Gill 2008: 41–5, 2010b: 137–43, arguing against Sorabji, who gives greater weight to the ethical claim of the second (individual) role.

[86] See text to nn. 64–5.

(Nietzsche), one's own major or 'ground' projects (Williams), or factors particular to the context of decision-making (Price).[87] However, the Stoic theory does so while maintaining the focus on the expression of the virtues (the first role) and stressing the importance of preserving ethical consistency between these factors.

Finally, it is worth noting that the Stoic theory of the four roles is suggestively similar to Korsgaard's proposal that, in determining what is right, we make reference not just to universalizable considerations, or to the idea of 'a person' as a normative concept, but also to our specific 'practical identity', that is, our particular social roles and projects in life. Korsgaard's proposal constitutes a modification of the typically Kantian appeal to universalizable criteria, though it has also generated interest among modern virtue ethicists.[88] Korsgaard's 'practical identity' overlaps, in the first instance, with the third and fourth of the Stoic roles (our social context and chosen project). However, Korsgaard also suggests that this kind of identity can be viewed as a way of expressing our shared humanity, that is, in Stoic terms, the first human role. Hence, her Kantian version of this idea combines general and specific elements in a way that is parallel to the Stoic pattern.[89] The theory of the four roles, or some aspect of this, is also deployed by Stoic thinkers such as Epictetus and Seneca in the context of ethical guidance on decision-making.[90] Taken in the light of Korsgaard's deployment of a related idea within a Kantian approach, it indicates that Stoic ethical guidance, exemplified in Cicero's discussion, may have a broad range of application in modern moral theory, going beyond the limits of contemporary Neo-Aristotelian theory.

8.2 Stoicism and Modern 'Life-Guidance'

In this final section of the book, I widen the scope of modern areas of thought discussed to include contemporary Stoic life-guidance, located, to some extent, against the background of modern cognitive theory and psychotherapy. Life-guidance, along with cognitive theory of mind and psychotherapy, constitutes an area where Stoicism has already had significant influence; and this influence confirms the view that Stoicism has considerable modern resonance. Also, in discussing life-guidance, I highlight several respects in which modern practice lends support to Stoic ideas about ethical development or guidance, by contrast, to some extent, with the Aristotelian approach. These points reinforce the claim made in the preceding section that Stoicism is well-equipped to inform modern virtue ethical thinking on development and guidance.

---

[87] For these ideas, see Gill 1996: 110–11, referring to Nietzsche 1974: 290; Williams 1981: ch. 1; Price 2011: 226–35 (on Aristotle), more broadly Price 2008.
[88] Korsgaard 1996: 102–3, 105–7, 239–40.   [89] Korsgaard 1996: 120–5, 128–30.
[90] Epict. *Diss.* 1.2, 2.10; Sen. *TA* 6–7, *Ben.* 2.15.3–17; also Gill 1988: 187–93; Griffin 2013: 194–5.

A striking phenomenon in recent years has been the emergence of books and online resources on what is sometimes called 'life-guidance' or the pursuit of happiness through the way one manages one's life. This feature has coincided with, and is, surely, linked to, the waning influence, particularly in Western culture, of traditional sources of ethical guidance, namely churches, the family, and to some extent political and other communal groups. Resources on life-guidance offer a framework for living, and in this sense, represent an alternative source of ethical authority, while leaving it up to individuals which form of guidance to adopt and how to put it into practice. Much earlier writing on this subject drew heavily on Eastern philosophy; and Buddhism, in a Westernized form, remains a strong influence and has promoted a widespread interest in 'mindfulness'. However, more recently, applied Stoicism has become a major strand of life-guidance, with increasing number of books and other resources gaining a broad public audience.[91] The prominence of Stoicism, rather than Aristotle, in this movement, despite Aristotle's importance as an ancient proto-type for modern virtue ethics, is not surprising if one takes into account the general characteristics of Stoic ethical guidance highlighted already. As already explained, guidance forms a more substantial part of Stoic, than Aristotelian, ethical writing. Indeed, there are extensive and eloquent Stoic writings devoted, primarily, to this purpose, derived from Epictetus, Seneca, and Marcus Aurelius, especially, which have provided rich material for modern life-guidance.[92] Also, Stoic thought on development focuses, almost wholly, on adult life. A central theme in Stoicism is the idea of life (primarily adult life) as a project of ongoing ethical development or 'progress', involving the shaping of one's life as a whole towards the goal of virtue-based happiness.[93] This conception of development, rather than the competing Platonic-Aristotelian one,[94] offers a framework that is highly suitable for adults in the modern world looking for life-guidance. Also important is the fact that Stoic thinkers set out programmes of ethical develop-ment that people can work on for themselves. For instance, Epictetus' version of the three-topic programme of ethical progress, especially as mediated by Pierre Hadot, has become one of the most widely used features in Stoic-based life-guidance.[95]

Since 2012, I have been closely involved in a project, 'Modern Stoicism', designed to present Stoic ethical ideas to a broad public audience for the purpose

---

[91] For applied Stoicism, see Irvine 2008; Robertson 2013; Holiday 2014; Pigliucci 2017; Stankiewicz 2019, 2020; Sellars 2020; Sherman 2021; also, covering several Greek philosophies, Evans 2012.

[92] See also text to nn. 24–5, and Introd. to Part II text to nn. 43–51.

[93] See Introd to Part II, text to nn. 51–5; also text to nn. 59–61 in this chapter on links with Annas's virtue ethical approach.

[94] On the contrasting approaches, see Introd. to Part II, text to nn. 9–21.

[95] See Epict. *Diss.* 3.2.1–5; also Introd. to Part II, text to n. 50. See P. Hadot 1995: 191–202, 1998 43–7; Sellars 2003: 133–46.

of life-guidance.[96] This project represents a collaboration between scholars of ancient philosophy, writers of popular books on philosophy, psychotherapists, and life-guidance counsellors. From the beginning, we have focused on three main activities. These are (1) an annual online course, 'Stoic Week' (subsequently extended to a four-week version); (2) an annual public event on putting Stoic principles into practice, now called 'Stoicon'; (3) a blog 'Stoicism Today' for articles on applied Stoicism. Though originally set up in the UK, those most heavily involved are now from several countries, especially the USA.[97] The success of this project has helped to stimulate related activities in applied Stoicism. These include smaller annual public events in different locations or online (Stoicon-x); also Stoic fellowships, that is, groups meeting on a regular basis, which aim to put Stoic principles into practice. They also include two other organizations, the Stoic Gym, which produces a monthly magazine, *The Stoic*,[98] and the Aurelius Foundation, directed especially at younger people, especially in business.[99] In considering the broader implications of this movement, I concentrate on the core Modern Stoicism activities, especially the online courses.

The overall aim of these courses is to enable those using them to embed Stoic ethical ideas and practices into their daily living and the overall management of their lives. The Stoic week course handbook can serve to illustrate how the course is directed at this end. The handbook contains, as part of its introduction, summary of key Stoic ethical ideas, on topics such as virtue, happiness, ethical development, emotions, and nature. These ideas include, for instance, the Stoic claim that happiness depends not on external things such as wealth and social success (preferable indifferents, a term we explain), but, rather, on developing the virtues. They also include the Stoic view that all human beings are capable of developing towards virtue and happiness through the two strands of appropriation; and the Stoic contrast between good (virtue-based) emotions and other (defective) emotions. Also discussed is the ethical significance of the idea of nature, both human nature and cosmic nature. In short, the handbook summarizes, in the introduction and elsewhere, a similar set of ideas to those examined in this book, though obviously presented in a briefer and more straightforward way suitable for a broad public audience.

In the Stoic Week programme, each day is centred on one of these themes, which is presented partly though discussion relating this theme to practical life,

---

[96] See https://modernstoicism.com, home of Stoic Week, Stoicism Today and Stoicon. On the emergence of 'Modern Stoicism' in 2012, see Chakrapani 2019: 15, 35–43.

[97] Those currently most involved include: (scholars) Gabriele Galluzzo, Massimo Pigliucci, John Sellars; (psychotherapists and life-guidance counsellors) Tim LeBon, Greg Lopez, Brittany Polat, Eve Riches, Donald Robertson, Greg Sadler, Andi Sciacca. For books on applied Stoicism by members of this group (and others), see n. 91. Scholars who have given talks at the annual Stoic conferences include J. Annas, M. Graver, A. Hobbs, K. Ieradiakonou, A. A. Long, N. Sherman, R. Sorabji.

[98] Editor and organizer, Chuck Chakrapani; see https://TheStoic@TheStoicGym.com.

[99] Founder Justin Stead: see https://Aureliusfoundation.com.

and partly through quotations from Stoic thinkers, including Epictetus, Seneca, and Marcus Aurelius. These quotations also serve as the basis for morning and evening reflections, centred on the same overall theme. A further feature is an exercise for the day (designed for a lunchtime break or some other convenient time). The use of exercises, along with particularized examples of the themes discussed, reflects especially the contribution of the psychotherapists and counsellors in the group, and some of the exercises, such as 'values-clarification', are also widely used in psychotherapy and counselling. However, the aim of the exercises is explicitly linked with Stoic ideas;[100] and the exercises themselves are mostly based on those found in Stoic works of guidance. These exercises include 'the dichotomy of control', based on Epictetus' recurrent theme of the importance of distinguishing what is and is not within our control. They also include the exercise recommended by Hierocles of contracting the circles of our relationship with a view to expanding the scope of those who are seen as objects of concern, extending, in principle, to all human beings. Other such exercises, again taken directly from ancient sources, are those of preparing for (what is generally seen as) disaster by imagining this in advance; and adopting a 'view from above', from a cosmic perspective, to place one own's experience in a wider context. This exercise is also used to reinforce the idea that all human beings form part of nature, to promote heightened awareness of the need to respond effectively to the current environmental crisis.[101] In each case, the connection between these exercises and the Stoic ideas illustrated is explained:[102] these exercises supplement the exploration of Stoic ethical themes and do not replace it.

I now analyse the approach of the courses more closely, with a view to showing how this reflects distinctive features of Stoic thinking on development and guidance (in some cases contrasted with Aristotelian ideas) and thus supports the claim made in this book that such ideas can have considerable power and resonance for modern audiences. These features, in bare outline, are these: (1) the courses are directed at adults; (2) they are designed to contribute to ongoing ethical progress or development; (3) the courses underline the ethical basis of the attitudes and practices encouraged; (4) the methods presuppose a cognitive psychological approach. I explore each of these points and discuss evidence gathered through the courses that supports the effectiveness, in the contemporary context, of this kind of approach to development and guidance.

---

[100] For instance, 'values-clarification' is sometimes used in the courses as a way of bringing out the significance of the Stoic distinction between virtue and preferred indifferents.

[101] For the sources of these exercises, see Epict. *Handbook* 1, LS 57 G, Cic. *Tusc.* 3.52, M. A. 7.48, 9.30, 12.24.

[102] E.g. the contraction of circles of relationship is linked with the Stoic stress on the importance of a sense of community with others and the kinship of all human beings, the 'view from above' with the idea of human beings as integral parts of nature as a whole.

First, the courses, and the other activities of Modern Stoicism, are directed at adults; questionnaire results suggest that users of the courses fall, roughly equally, within all adult age-groups from 18 to 55+.[103] This feature of the courses might seem quite self-evident; any online vehicle which is not otherwise targeted to specific age-groups is likely to attract a broad adult audience. However, in our case, this reflects a deliberate policy and set of assumptions; we are presupposing the standard Stoic view that adults at any stage of their life are, in principle, capable of taking forward their own ethical development, and we are offering guidance for doing so. There is an instructive contrast in this respect with the approach of the Jubilee Centre for Character and Virtues, based at Birmingham University.[104] Although the activities of the Jubilee Centre are also directed at a broad public (adult) audience, there is a special focus on incorporating virtues-centred ethical values in the education of children and young adults. Their approach reflects the Aristotelian view, rather widely adopted by modern virtue ethicists, that childhood habituation in appropriate beliefs and attitudes plays a crucial, even indispensable, role in the development of a virtuous character, a process which is assumed to be largely complete on becoming adult. Although Modern Stoicism has recently developed a version of the Stoic week course for teenage children,[105] this is a deliberate extension of methods designed for a broad adult audience and based on Stoic assumptions about the general capacity of human beings to shape their self-direction throughout their lives.

A second, and related, feature is that the courses provide resources to help people to take forward their own personal and ethical development, and to do so, in principle, on an ongoing (life-long) basis. There are several components of this process of self-managed development: acquiring or exercising a sense of personal agency or direction of one's life; adopting a reflectively based approach to living; applying this approach in the various aspects of life, including daily actions and longer-term objectives, emotional responses, and interpersonal and communal relationships. The guidance offered by the courses is, in essence, guidance on taking forward this process of self-development, and is designed to enable people to apply their developing insights in these various sectors of living. In this respect, the courses reflect the three-topic programmes of ethical guidance provided by Seneca, Epictetus, and Cicero, outlined earlier.[106] Epictetus' version of this programme, especially as mediated by Pierre Hadot, and described as constituting three types of 'discipline' or 'spiritual exercise',[107] is an influential framework for this process, though the Modern Stoicism courses are not based on a single model of this type. As in Stoic practically oriented writings generally, the overall aim is to

---

[103] See n. 132.
[104] See https://jubilee.centre.ac.uk: character education is a key strand of their activities.
[105] See https://modernstoicism.com: under 'courses'.
[106] See Introd. to Part II, text to nn. 49–50.   [107] See text to n. 95.

enable people to 'make progress' in ethical development. The courses, and the questionnaires linked with the courses, offer indications of what constitutes progress in change of attitudes or types of behaviour. Also, the frameworks adopted (Stoic week and the month-long course) presuppose the scope for change within those timescales.[108] However, we are not pretending to set up a quasi-institutional framework of levels in ethical development, which the person herself and her guides or fellow learners can, unambiguously, recognize and apply. The guiding assumption, as in ancient Stoic thinking on this subject, is that progress towards virtue and virtue-based happiness (or 'wisdom') is a life-long project, even if we have a sense of making determinate changes in our attitudes and actions within specific periods. We are also assuming, in line with Stoic (though not Aristotelian) thought that such progress is possible for human beings as such, whatever their upbringing, background, or social situation, even if we have been hampered in this respect by features of our past life and by what the Stoics call the 'sources of corruption'.[109]

A third key feature of the courses is that they are designed to enable progress within a specific (Stoic) ethical framework, and they presuppose the core claims of Stoic ethics. As outlined earlier, the Stoic week handbook summarizes central Stoic ideas, such as that happiness depends on virtue and not 'indifferents', and the daily exercises help people to try to apply these ideas, and work out their implications, in different contexts. The point can be brought out clearly as regards emotion. Many of those who turn to life-guidance courses are looking for help in managing their emotional responses, and some do so as a result of deeply distressing or disturbing experiences. The Stoic Week course and, even more, the month-long course on Stoic Mindfulness and Resilience Training (SMRT), offers the prospect of positive change as regards emotion and includes change in emotional patterns as one of the indicators of progress in the self-assessment questionnaires. Also, as noted earlier, one of the exercises used is a version of the Stoic one of preparing for (what is normally seen as) disaster by imagining it in advance.[110] However, we also build into these courses the Stoic view that emotional change depends on ethical development more generally, involving understanding of value as well as increasing depth in one's interpersonal and social relationships. This progress carries with it an altered understanding of what counts as 'bad', and 'disastrous' in human life. This point is conveyed, for instance, by emphasizing the key Stoic ideas that happiness depends on virtue and on development towards virtue, or by the organization of the order of topics within

---

[108] A more extended course of this kind has now been created by Eve Riches for the Aurelius Foundation.

[109] See Introd. to Part II, esp. text to nn. 16–27, 49–54; Ch. 5, text to nn. 44–55 (on sources of corruption).

[110] See Cic. *Tusc.* 3.52.

the week or month.[111] Also, while underlining the benefits of Stoic guidance for psychological wellbeing, we avoid giving the impression that achieving tranquillity or peace of mind is the overall or dominant aim of Stoic ethics. As stressed in this book, the Stoic conception of the goal of life or happiness is a certain kind of life (the life 'according to virtue' or 'according to nature'), and not a certain mood or state of mind, even if achieving this life carries with it an altered emotional pattern, including the occurrence of 'joy' as part of this pattern.[112] On this point, the obvious point of contrast, within ancient philosophy, is with Epicureanism for which peace of mind is a key component of the goal of life.[113] However, this presentation of emotions also differs from the account of the role of emotions (in habituative training, for instance) in Aristotelian thinking on development and reflects the contrasting Stoic approach to development.[114]

The fourth feature, the cognitive approach to psychology is, potentially, the most complex; however, I simply outline the relevant background and highlight the cognitive dimension of the courses. A significant point of contact sometimes discussed is that between modern cognitive theory, in philosophy of mind and experimental psychology, and Stoic thinking on emotions and human psychology in general. The salient common feature is the idea that emotions and desires reflect beliefs, reasoning, and assumptions ('cognitions', in contemporary terms), rather than forming a distinct source of motivation. Hence, bringing about change is a matter of identifying and articulating the underlying cognitions (or 'impressions', in Stoic terms) and modifying or correcting them. On this point, Stoic thought differs from the Platonic-Aristotelian view, which also has modern analogues, that emotions and desires derive from an independent, and potentially conflicting, non-rational part of the psyche.[115] Nussbaum, for instance, analysing emotions as 'cognitive-evaluative' responses, presents her theory as 'Neo-Stoic' as well as informed by contemporary cognitive theory.[116] A further important point of connection is that between Stoicism and cognitive psychotherapy. In the second half of the twentieth century, CBT (cognitive-behavioural therapy) emerged

---

[111] E.g. in the 2020 version of the Stoic Week Handbook, 'progress', 'happiness' and 'virtue' formed the topics for Monday–Wednesday while 'emotions' and 'resilience' formed the topics for Friday–Saturday; similarly, 'resilience' falls within week 4 of the month-long SMRT course. This order reinforces the Stoic view that peace of mind depends on ethical development and understanding. See also Gill 2015: 39–44.

[112] See 1.3, and 1.4, text to nn. 120–31, esp. n. 127.

[113] The Epicurean goal is a combination of freedom from pain in the body and freedom from disturbance (*ataraxia*) in the mind; see LS 21 B(1).

[114] See text to nn. 10, 13–17.

[115] On the contrast between Platonic-Aristotelian and Stoic psychological models, see Ch. 5, text to nn. 10–11. For a survey of modern theories of emotion, both cognitive and non-cognitive, see Deigh 2010.

[116] See Nussbaum 2001: 3–5; her approach is informed both by cognitive theory of mind (1–14), and neurophysiology (114–19). See also Gill 2010a: 333–50 on parallels between these modern theories and those of Galen and Stoicism; and Gill 2018a on parallels between Stoic psychology and 'enactivism', one of the modern theories associated with 'extended' or 'distributed' cognition.

alongside, or in place of, Freudian psychoanalysis, as a widely used mode of psychotherapy. Psychoanalysis aims to bring to consciousness the unconscious roots of psychological disorders, often supposed to derive from infant traumas. By contrast, CBT focuses on beliefs or assumptions of a kind that can readily be brought to consciousness and on deliberate efforts that the client can make for herself to understand and improve her psychological state and to change her behaviour or situation by these efforts. In this respect, CBT is much closer than psychoanalysis to the forms of ancient philosophical guidance sometimes described, in antiquity, as the 'therapy' of emotions, including Stoic guidance.[117]

In fact, Stoic thought, especially as presented by Epictetus, exercised direct influence on the pioneers of CBT, Albert Ellis, founder of REBT (rational-emotive behaviour therapy) in the 1950s, and Aaron Beck, founder of cognitive therapy in the 1970s. Epictetus' comment, 'We are disturbed not so much by events as by our beliefs about events' was taken as encapsulating the belief-based (cognitive) conception of emotions underlying both Stoic guidance and the Ellis-Beck approach to psychotherapy.[118] Donald Robertson, a CBT therapist with a strong and sustained interest in Stoicism, identifies ten points on which REBT reflects Stoic ethical ideas or therapeutic methods,[119] though these were not all presented by Ellis himself as based directly on Stoicism. Beck's cognitive therapy, though less explicitly, also reflects the influence of Stoic ideas. This method is centred on a quasi-Socratic challenge to the client, inviting her to examine and, potentially, reject the beliefs underlying her emotional problems.[120] From the 1990s onwards, several (partly) new versions of CBT have emerged, including ACT (acceptance and commitment therapy).[121] Although practitioners of ACT do not generally refer to Stoic ideas in the way that Ellis and Beck did, I think we can identify certain parallels between ACT and the Stoic guidance offered by Epictetus. Notably, we can see links between Epictetus' stress on the importance of 'examining impressions' (including thoughts and assumptions underlying emotional responses) and the 'cognitive distancing' and 'values-clarification' that forms part of the ACT method. Another point of contact is between the stress on the importance of the commitment to change attitudes and behaviour (in ACT) and Epictetus' emphasis on agents' exercising their power of 'decision' (*prohairesis*) or agency, in putting into practice the outcome of their 'examination of

---

[117] On modern psychotherapy and the Stoic therapy of the emotions, see Gill 2010a: 350–63, 2018c: 278–84. In 1985a, I compare ancient psychotherapeutic methods (including philosophical ones) with that of Anthony Storr, based on Freudian and Jungian approaches. On the ancient (esp. Stoic) therapy of the emotions, see Gill 2010a: ch. 5. See also Ch. 5, text to nn. 96–113.

[118] Epict. *Handbook* 5. See also Epict. *Diss.* 1.18.1–2; Brennan 2003: 265–74. On the influence of Epictetus' comment, see Robertson 2010: 5–9, 2016: 378–9, 382–3.

[119] Robertson 2016: 377–93: Stoic features with REBT equivalents include the ideas of wishing with reservation and preparation for future disaster.

[120] Robertson 2010: chs. 1–2. On cognitive therapy, see also Herbert and Forman 2011: 26–56.

[121] These are sometimes described as 'third-wave' therapies, the two previous waves being behaviourist and cognitive therapies. On ACT, see Hayes et al. 1999; Herbert and Forman 2011.

impressions'.[122] In these respects, the Stoic belief-based approach to emotions and guidance has played a significant role in shaping, directly or indirectly, what has become the most widely used form of modern psychotherapeutic method (CBT).[123]

The Modern Stoicism courses reflect cognitive assumptions about psychology and psychotherapy in several ways. As noted earlier, some of the members of this collaborative project are CBT therapists, and some of the exercises used, for instance, values-clarification, are similar to those used in therapeutic contexts. Also, more broadly, the courses adopt an overall approach comparable to that used in cognitive therapy. The courses presuppose, and promote, the capacity to adopt a critical and reflective attitude towards the underlying beliefs and assumptions shaping actions, emotions, and relationships. They assume, and encourage, the capacity for self-management, and for bringing about change in these beliefs and the resulting actions and emotional response. In these respects, the courses match, and build on, the three features already discussed: that the courses are directed to adults; that they promote self-managed progress; and that they encourage living within a determinate framework of ideas, those of Stoic ethics. Thus, characterizing the courses as cognitive in approach sums up several leading features of the courses and their underlying approach.

Does it follow from these points of influence and resemblance that Stoic guidance, sometimes presented as the therapy of emotions, represents the ancient equivalent of modern (CBT) psychotherapy? Can Stoic guidance be treated as an ancient prototype for modern psychotherapeutic practice, in the way that, I have suggested elsewhere in this book, Stoic ethics can be taken, alongside or in place of Aristotle, as a prototype for modern virtue ethical theory? To claim this is, I think, to overstate the similarity between the two approaches. The relationship between Stoic psychotherapy (or, in their terms, the 'therapy of emotions') and medical practice more generally, both in antiquity and the modern era, is a complex and sometimes controversial one.[124] However, I think we can say that modern (CBT) psychotherapy is appropriately described as 'medical' in a more straightforward sense than Stoic guidance. Modern psychotherapy aims to address and treat, or enable clients to treat, emotional disturbances which are preventing them from living what the clients themselves regard as a normal and fulfilling life. Stoic guidance, like other forms of ancient therapy of the emotions, can also be presented as having this function.[125] However, Stoic guidance is, in principle,

---

[122] On these features, see Epict. *Handbook* 1.5, *Diss.* 1.4.18–21; also Gill 2006: 372–83. On the parallels with ACT, see Gill 2018c: 284–9.

[123] At least in the UK and USA, although I believe psychoanalysis remains strong in Germany; also widely used in all these countries is 'psychodynamic' therapy, similar in format to CBT but based on psychoanalytic principles.

[124] On the relationship between Stoic therapy and ancient medicine, see Gill 2010a: 300–29, 2013(b), 2018(b).

[125] See e.g. Sen. *TA* 1.1–2, Gal. *Aff. Dig.*, V.37; also Gill 2018(c): 281–2.

addressed to anyone, whether or not they see themselves as suffering from disabling psychological problems; and it offers the prospect of achieving a better life, regardless of the person's current state of mind. Broadly put, Stoic guidance is ethical, rather than, or as well as, therapeutic, and also revisionary, in aiming to provide a new understanding of what it means to live a fulfilling human life (the life 'according to nature', in Stoic terms) and to enable someone to 'make progress' towards this goal.[126] Also, although Stoic guidance is sometimes presented as therapy, the core project of Stoic therapy is to promote ethical development, conducted not in the therapeutic context, but by living out in one's life the two strands of 'appropriation'.[127] Even so, and while taking all these differences into account, there remain suggestive analogies between Stoic guidance and modern (CBT) psychotherapy.[128] These points of resemblance offer scope for further exploration of the way in which Stoic guidance can inform modern psychotherapeutic practice.[129] But what is involved is interaction and influence between two practices conceived in significantly different ways.

Do these Modern Stoicism courses actually work, in the sense of providing those who use them with the kind of life-guidance looked for? The large number of those taking these courses each year or participating in the other activities linked with the project is, certainly, a strong indicator that they are found worthwhile.[130] In addition, from the beginning, the courses have been combined with questionnaires, asking participants to assess their effectiveness in promoting a sense of wellbeing. We have used three standard scales (on life satisfaction, positive and negative emotions, and flourishing); these show significant improvement (12–15 per cent) as a result of the one-week course and greater improvement (15–20 per cent) after the four-week course, results which have been consistent over several years and are maintained in a follow-up questionnaire. We have also devised a Stoic attitudes and behaviour scale (SABS) designed to identify and measure the extent to which the courses promote a specifically Stoic approach to life. The results on this scale correlate closely with the results of the other scales.[131] We are aware of the limitations of these findings: they are based on self-reporting questionnaires, which are not triangulated with other evidence; the sample is self-selecting and likely to be responsive to Stoic ideas and courses of this kind; and there is no randomized control group. However, positive features of this data

---

[126] On the overall objectives of Stoic guidance, see Introd. to Part II, text to nn. 49–55.

[127] See Ch. 5, text to nn. 105–13.

[128] See further on the relationship between Stoic and modern psychotherapy Gill 2010a: 350–63, 2013b: 357–60, 2018c.

[129] Exploring this scope is part of the focus of psychotherapists such as Donald Robertson and Tim LeBon who are involved in the Modern Stoicism project.

[130] Some examples: about 7,000 people registered for Stoic week in 2017; over 1,500 people attended the on-line Stoicon in 2020; about 30,000 views per month for the blog, 'Stoicism Today'.

[131] Full data and analysis in the Stoic Week reports for recent years by Tim LeBon; see https://modernstoicism.com/research; also n. 132.

include the large number of people involved, the wide range of ages and national contexts (and both genders), and the consistency of the results in successive years.[132] Also, we are working with other collaborators and researchers to address these limitations and build on the findings so far. In fact, a recent paper, published in a social science journal, based on an experiment including a control group, has gone some way towards confirming the findings of the Modern Stoicism questionnaires.[133]

How far can we say that the positive response of participants to these courses also supports the Stoic, rather than the Aristotelian, conception of ethical development and of the role of guidance in promoting such development? As brought out earlier, Stoic thinking on development involves several strong, universalizing claims. Stoics maintain that all human beings are fundamentally capable of ethical development, regardless of their upbringing and social or political context, and that this capacity persists throughout their lives. The Stoic view can be contrasted in this respect with the Aristotelian approach, which stresses the importance of childhood habituation (the 'that' of ethical life), and which sometimes suggests that ethical character may become too ingrained in adult life to be modified.[134] The Modern Stoicism project cannot, of course, by itself verify Stoic claims on the possibility of life-long change or the credibility of the Stoic, as distinct from Aristotelian, view on ethical development. That would require a much more in-depth and multi-strand type of assessment than we have attempted so far. However, the breadth of the appeal across ages, gender, and national context of these courses, which are designed to enable ethical development on Stoic lines, offers some support for these claims about the universality of the scope for change.[135] Also, we can claim that the assessment methods show that people respond positively to courses which presuppose the possibility of life-long ethical and personal development, understood in Stoic terms.[136] Also, the week-long and month-long courses are explicitly presented as introductory and as pointing towards a journey to be undertaken by the person herself throughout her life, if she chooses to do so.

---

[132] There are detailed reports on Stoic week each year and on SMRT, when this is run, with part 1 on demographics. Tim LeBon is a psychotherapist, and author of books on counselling and positive psychology. Typically, the highest percentage of participants in Stoic week is from the USA (about 40 per cent) and UK (about 20 per cent) with some participation in all continents (listed by country in the most recent reports). The male-female ratio is usually 2/3 to 1/3. All adult age-groups are roughly equally represented (from 18 to 55+). Exact figures are given in the reports.

[133] MacLellan and Derakshan 2021; the abstract lists among the results: 'significant effects of Stoic training [of the type used by Modern Stoicism] on rumination [worrying] and self-efficacy'. The paper also notes the correlation between adoption of Stoic attitudes and behaviour (as measured on the SABS scale) and beneficial effects on negative and positive emotions and self-efficacy. Further research and publication of this type is planned, involving Tim LeBon from the Modern Stoicism team.

[134] See Introd. to Part II, text to nn. 9–27; also text to nn. 7, 13–17, 26 in this chapter. For the idea that adult character may become too ingrained to be modified, see Arist. *NE* 3.5, 1114a3–21.

[135] See figures in nn. 130, 132.   [136] See text to nn. 106–9.

Overall, the success of the Modern Stoicism project, taken as a whole, alongside many other indications of interest in applied Stoicism, gives strong support to my general claims in this book. I have argued not only that Stoic thinking presents a powerful and coherent ethical framework, including their ideas on development and guidance, but also that their approach speaks strongly to contemporary thought and can inform modern thinking, especially cognate types of ethical theory. The Modern Stoicism project lends support, in particular, to the claim of the contemporary appeal of Stoic ideas on development and guidance, and to some extent of the whole ethical framework. On a more personal note, I have been impressed by the sustained collaborative character and commitment of those most closely involved in the project, as well as of the participants, in widely different contexts, trying sincerely to live a life based on Stoic principles. In this small but not insignificant way, the project has reflected the Stoic ideal of the community of humankind, as rational and sociable animals. It has also brought out the continuing power of the Stoic aspiration to learn to live a life according to nature.

References

Ackeren, M. van (2011), *Die Philosophie Marc Aurels*, 2 vols., Berlin.

Adams, R. (2006), *A Theory of Virtue: Excellence in Being for the Good*, Oxford.

Algra, K. (2003), 'Stoic Theology', in B. Inwood (ed.), *The Cambridge Companion to the Stoics*, Cambridge: 153–78.

Annas, J. (1981), *An Introduction to Plato's Republic*, Oxford.

Annas, J. (1988), 'Naturalism in Greek Ethics: Aristotle and After', *Proceedings of the Boston Area Colloquium in Ancient Philosophy* 4: 149–71.

Annas, J. (1993), *The Morality of Happiness*, Oxford.

Annas, J. (1994), 'Virtue as the Use of Other Goods', in T. Irwin and M. C. Nussbaum (eds), *Virtue, Love, and Form: Essays in Memory of Gregory Vlastos*, Edmonton (= *Apeiron* Special Issue 26.3–4): 53–66.

Annas, J. (1995), 'Reply to Cooper', *Philosophy and Phenomological Research* 55: 599–610.

Annas, J. (1997), 'Cicero on Stoic Moral Philosophy and Private Property', in M. Griffin and J. Barnes (eds), *Philosophia Togata 1: Essays on Philosophy and Roman Society*, rev. edn., Oxford: 151–73.

Annas, J. (2005), 'Virtue Ethics: What Kind of Naturalism?', in S. M. Gardiner (ed.), *Virtue Ethics: Old and New*, Ithaca: 11–29.

Annas, J. (2007a), 'Carneades' Classification of Ethical Theories', in A. M. Ioppolo and D. N. Sedley (eds), *Pyrrhonist, Patricians, Platonizers: Hellenistic Philosophy in the Period 155–86 BC*, Naples: 187–223.

Annas, J. (2007b), 'Ethics in Stoic Philosophy', *Phronesis* 52: 58–87.

Annas, J. (2011), *Intelligent Virtue*, Oxford.

Annas, J. and Betegh, G. (2016) (eds), *Cicero's De Finibus: Philosophical Approaches*, Cambridge.

Annas, J. and Woolf, R. (2001), *On Moral Ends*, ed. and trans., Cambridge.

Anscombe, E. (1958), 'Modern Moral Philosophy', *Philosophy* 33: 1–19.

Anscombe, E. (1981), *Collected Papers*, vol. 3, Minneapolis.

Arnim, von., H. (1903–5) (ed.), *Stoicorum Veterum Fragmenta*, 4 vols., Leipzig (repr. Munich, 2004).

Athanassoulis, N. (2013), 'Educating for Virtue', in S. van Hooft (ed.), *Handbook of Virtue Ethics*, Durham: 440–50.

Athanassoulis, N. (2018), 'Acquiring Aristotelian Virtue', in N. Snow (ed.), *The Oxford Handbook of Virtue*, Oxford: 415–31.

Baehr, J. (2018), 'Intellectual Virtues and Truth, Understanding, Wisdom', in N. Snow (ed.), *The Handbook of Virtue*, Oxford: 800–19.

Baril, A. (2013), 'Eudaimonia in Contemporary Virtue Ethics', in S. van Hooft (ed.), *Handbook of Virtue Ethics*, Durham: 17–27.

Barnes, J. (1984), *The Complete Works of Aristotle: the Revised Oxford Translation*, 2 vols., Oxford.

Barnes, J. (1997), 'Roman Aristotle', in J. Barnes and M. Griffin (eds), *Philosophia Togata II: Plato and Aristotle at Rome*, Oxford: 1–69.

Barney, R. (2003), 'A Puzzle in Stoic Ethics', *Oxford Studies in Ancient Philosophy* 24: 303–24.

Bates, T. and Kleingeld, P. (2018), 'Virtue, Vice, and Situationism', in N. Snow (ed.), *The Oxford Handbook of Virtue*, Oxford: 524–45.

Becker, L. (1998/2017), *A New Stoicism*, Princeton.

Becker, L. (2018), 'Stoic Virtue', in N. Snow (ed.), *The Handbook of Virtue*, Oxford: 132–52.

Bénatouïl, T. (2007), 'Le débat entre Platonisme et Stoïcisme sur la vie scolastique: Chrysippe, La Nouvelle Académie et Antiochus', in M. Bonazzi and C. Helmig (eds), *Stoic Platonism—Platonic Stoicism: The Dialogue between Platonism and Stoicism in Antiquity* (Leuven), 1–31.

Bénatouïl, T. (2009), 'How Industrious can Zeus be? The Extent and Objects of Divine Activity in Stoicism', in R. Salles (ed.), *God and Cosmos in Stoicism*, Oxford: 23–45.

Bénatouïl, T. (2016a), 'Structure, Standards and Stoic Moral Progress in *De Finibus* 4', in J. Annas and G. Betegh (2016) (eds), *Cicero's De Finibus: Philosophical Approaches*, Cambridge: 198–220.

Bénatouïl, T. (2016b), 'Stoicism and Twentieth-Century French Philosophy', in J. Sellars (ed.), *The Routledge Handbook of the Stoic Tradition*, Abingdon: 360–73.

Bénatouïl, T. and Bonazzi, M. (2012) (eds), *Theoria, Praxis, and the Contemplative Life After Plato and Aristotle*, Leiden.

Bendik-Keymer, J. D. (2014), 'From Humans to All of Life: Nussbaum's Transformation of Dignity', in F. Comim and M. C. Nussbaum (eds), *Capabilities, Gender, Equality: Towards Fundamental Entitlements*, Cambridge: 175–91.

Bendik-Keymer, J. D. (2017), 'The Reasonableness of Wonder', *Journal of Human Development and Capabilities* 18.3: 337–55.

Betegh, G. (2003), 'Cosmological Ethics in the *Timaeus* and Stoicism', *Oxford Studies in Ancient Philosophy* 24: 273–302.

Blössner, N. (2007), 'The City-State Analogy', in G. R. F. Ferrari (ed.), *The Cambridge Companion to Plato's Republic*, Cambridge: 345–85.

Blundell, R. (1990), 'Parental Nature and Stoic *oikeiosis*', *Ancient Philosophy* 10: 221–41.

Bobzien, S. (1998a), *Determinism and Freedom in Stoic Philosophy*, Oxford.

Bobzien, S. (1998b), 'The Inadvertent Conception and Late Birth of the Free-Will Problem', *Phronesis* 43: 133–75.

Bobzien, S. (1999), 'Chrysippus' Theory of Causes', in K. Ieradiakonou (ed.), *Topics in Stoic Philosophy*, Oxford: 196–242.

Boeri, M. D. (2009), 'Does Cosmic Nature Matter? Some Remarks on the Cosmological Aspects of Stoic Ethics', in R. Salles (ed.), *God and Cosmos in Stoicism*, Oxford: 173–200.

Brady, M. S. (2018), 'Moral and Intellectual Virtues', in N. Snow (ed.), *The Handbook of Virtue*, Oxford: 783–99.

Brennan, T. (1998), The Old Stoic Theory of Emotions', in J. Sihvola and T. Engberg-Pedersen (eds), *The Emotions in Hellenistic Philosophy*, Dordrecht: 21–70.

Brennan, T. (2003), 'Stoic Moral Psychology', in B. Inwood (ed.), *The Cambridge Companion to the Stoics*, Cambridge: 257–94.

Brennan, T. (2005), *The Stoic Life: Emotions, Duties, and Fate*, Oxford.

Brennan, T. (2014), 'The *Kathekon*: A Report on Some Recent Work at Cornell', *Philosophie Antique* 14: 41–70.

Brittain, C. (2016), 'Cicero's Sceptical Methods: the Example of *De Finibus*', in J. Annas and G. Betegh (2016) (eds), *Cicero De Finibus: Philosophical Approaches*, Cambridge: 12–40.

Broadie, S. (1991), *Ethics with Aristotle*, Oxford.

Broadie, S. (2005), 'On the Idea of the *summum bonum*', in C. Gill (ed.), *Virtue, Norms, and Objectivity: Issues in Ancient and Modern Ethics*, Oxford: 41–58.

Brouwer, R. (2014), *The Stoic Sage: The Early Stoics on Wisdom, Sagehood and Socrates*, Cambridge.

Brouwer, R. (2015), 'Stoic Sympathy', in E. Schliesser (ed.), *Sympathy: A History*, Oxford: 15–35.

Brown, E. (1997), 'Stoic Cosmopolitanism and the Political Life', University of Chicago PhD thesis (unpublished).

Brown, E. (forthcoming), *Stoic Cosmopolitanism*, Cambridge.

Brüllmann, P. (2015), *Grounding Ethics in Nature: A Study of Stoic Naturalism*, Habilitation, LMU, Munich (unpublished).

Brunschwig, J. (1986), 'The Cradle Argument in Epicureanism and Stoicism', in M. Schofield and G. Striker (eds), *The Norms of Nature*, Cambridge: 113–44.

Brunt, P. A. (2013), *Studies in Stoicism*, ed. M. Griffin and A. Samuels, Oxford.

Burnyeat, M. (1980), 'Aristotle on Learning to be Good', in A. O. Rorty (ed.), *Essays on Aristotle's Ethics*, Berkeley: 69–92.

Burnyeat, M. (2000), 'Plato on Why Mathematics is Good for the Soul', in T. Smiley (ed.), *Mathematics and Necessity: Essays in the History of Philosophy. Proceedings of the British Academy*, Oxford: 1–81.

Callicott. J. B. (2017), 'How Ecological Collectives are Morally Considerable', in S. Gardiner and A. Thompson (eds), *The Oxford Handbook of Environmental Ethics*, Oxford: 113–24.

Čelkytė, A. (2017), 'The Stoic Definition of Beauty as *summetria*', *Classical Quarterly* 67: 88–105.

Čelkytė, A. (2020), *The Stoic Theory of Beauty*, Edinburgh.

Chakrapani, C. (2019), *The Stoic Atlas: A Reference Book for Modern Stoics* (no place of publication listed).

Chappell, T. (2005), '"The Good Man is the Measure of All Things"', in C. Gill (ed.), *Virtue, Norms, and Objectivity: Issues in Ancient and Modern Ethics*, Oxford: 233–55.

Cherniss, H. (1976), *Plutarch Moralia* 13.2, ed. and trans., Cambridge, Mass.

Clarke, B. (2018), Virtue as a Sensitivity', in N. Snow (ed.), *The Handbook of Virtue*, Oxford: 35–56.

Colombetti, G. (2014), *The Feeling Body: Affective Science meets the Enactive Mind*, Cambridge, Mass.

Cooper, J. M. (1985), 'Aristotle and the Goods of Fortune', *Philosophical Review* 94: 173–97.

Cooper, J. M. (1995), 'Eudaimonism and the Appeal to Nature in the Morality of Happiness: Comments on Julia Annas, *The Morality of Happiness*', *Philosophy and Phenomenological Research* 55: 118–37.

Cooper, J. M. (1999), *Reason and Emotion: Essays on Ancient Moral Psychology and Ethical Theory*, Princeton.

Crisp, R. (1992), 'Utilitarianism and the Life of Virtue', *Philosophical Quarterly* 42.167: 139–60.

Crisp, R. (2015), 'A Third Method of Ethics?', *Philosophy and Phenomenological Research* 90.2: 257–73.

Cureton, A. and Hill, T. E. (2015), 'Kant on Virtue and the Virtues', in N. Snow (ed.), *Cultivating Virtue: Perspectives from Philosophy, Theology, and Psychology*, Cambridge: 87–109.

Damasio, A. (1994), *Descartes' Error*, London.

Darwall, S. (2011), Review of T. Irwin, *The Development of Ethics*, vols. 1–2, *British Journal of the History of Philosophy* 19.1: 131–47.

Darwall, S. (2012), 'Grotius at the Creation of Modern Moral Philosophy', *Archiv für die Geschichte der Philosophie* 94: 296–325.

Deigh, J. (2010), 'Concepts of Emotions in Modern Philosophy and Psychology', in P. Goldie (ed.), *The Oxford Handbook of the Philosophy of Emotion*, Oxford: 1–40.

Dorandi, T. (2013), *Diogenes Laertius: Lives of Eminent Philosophers*, ed. with introduction, Cambridge.

Dover, K. J. (1974), *Greek Popular Morality in the Age of Plato and Aristotle*, Oxford.

Driver, J. (2001), *Uneasy Virtue*, Cambridge.

Driver, J. (2015), 'Mill, Moral Sentimentalism, and the Cultivation of Virtue', in A. Snow (ed.), *Cultivating Virtue: Perspectives from Philosophy, Theology, and Psychology*, Cambridge: 49–63.

Dyck, A. W. (1996), *A Commentary on Cicero, De Officiis*, Ann Arbor.

Engberg-Pedersen, T. (1990), *The Stoic Theory of Oikeiosis: Moral Development and Social Interaction in Early Stoic Philosophy*, Aarhus.

Engstrom, S. and Whiting, J. (1996) (eds), *Aristotle, Kant, and the Stoics: Rethinking Happiness and Duty*, Cambridge.

Evans, J. (2012), *Philosophy for Life*, London.

Fantham, E., Hine, H. M., Kerr, J., Williams, G. D. (2014), trans. *Lucius Annaeus Seneca: Hardship and Happiness*, Chicago.

Ferrari, G. R. F. (2003), *City and Soul in Plato's Republic*, St Augustin.

Foot, P. (2001), *Natural Goodness*, Oxford.

Foucault, M. (1990), *Care of the Self*, trans. R. Hurley, London.

Frede, D. (2002), 'Theology and Providential Care in Stoicism', in D. Frede and A. Laks (eds), *Traditions of Theology: Studies in Hellenistic Theology, its Background and Aftermath*, Leiden: 85–117.

Frede, D. (2003), 'Stoic Determinism', in B. Inwood (ed.), *The Cambridge Companion to Stoicism*, Cambridge: 179–205.

Frede, M. (1996), 'Introduction', in M. Frede and G. Striker (eds), *Rationality in Greek Thought*, Oxford: 1–28.

Frede, M. (1999), 'On the Stoic Conception of the Good', in K. Ieradiakonou (ed.), *Topics in Stoic Philosophy*, Oxford: 71–94.

Gardiner, S. and Thompson, A. (eds.) (2017), *The Oxford Handbook of Environmental Ethics*, Oxford.

Giavatto, A. (2008), *Interlocutore di se stesso: La dialettica di Marco Aurelio*, Hildesheim.

Gill, C. (1983), 'Did Chrysippus Understand Medea?', *Phronesis* 28: 136–49.

Gill, C. (1985a), Ancient Psychotherapy', *Journal of the History of Ideas* 46: 307–25.

Gill, C. (1985b), 'Plato and the Education of Character', *Archiv für Geschichte der Philosophie* 67: 1–26.

Gill, C. (1987), 'Two Monologues of Self-Division: Euripides *Medea* 1021-89 and Seneca *Medea* 893-977', in M. Whitby, P. Hardie, and M. Whitby (eds), *Homo Viator: Classical essays for John Bramble*, Bristol: 25–37.

Gill, C. (1988), 'Personhood and Personality: The Four-*Personae* Theory in Cicero, *De Officiis* 1', *Oxford Studies in Ancient Philosophy* 6: 169–99.

Gill, C. (1990), 'The Human Being as an Ethical Norm', in C. Gill (ed.), *The Person and the Human Mind: Issues in Ancient and Modern Philosophy*, Oxford: 137–61.

Gill, C. (1991), 'Is There a Concept of Person in Greek Philosophy?', in S. Everson (ed.), *Psychology: Companions to Ancient Thought* 2, Cambridge: 166–93.

Gill, C. (1994), 'Peace of Mind and Being Yourself: Panaetius to Plutarch', in W. Haase and H. Temporini (eds), *Aufstieg und Niedergang der römischen Welt*, II.36.7, Berlin: 4599–4640.

Gill, C. (1995), *Greek Thought*, New Surveys in the Classics No. 25, Oxford.

Gill, C. (1996), *Personality in Greek Epic, Tragedy, and Philosophy: The Self in Dialogue*, Oxford.

Gill, C. (1998a), 'Did Galen Understand Platonic and Stoic Thinking on Emotions?', in J. Sihvola and T. Engberg-Pedersen (eds), *The Emotions in Hellenistic Philosophy*, Dordrecht: 113–48.

Gill, C. (1998b), 'Ethical Reflection and the Shaping of Character: Plato's *Republic* and Stoicism', *Proceedings of the Boston Area Colloquium in Ancient Philosophy* 12: 193–225.

Gill, C. (2000a), 'Protreptic and Dialectic in Plato's *Euthydemus*', in T. M. Robinson and L. Brisson (eds), *Plato: Euthydemus, Lysis, Charmides*, St Augustin: 133–43.

Gill, C. (2000b), 'Stoic Writers of the Imperial Era', in C. J. Rowe and M. Schofield (eds), *The Cambridge History of Greek and Roman Political Thought*, Cambridge: 597–615.

Gill, C. (2003), 'The School in the Roman Imperial Period', in B. Inwood (ed.), *The Cambridge Companion to the Stoics*, Cambridge: 33–58.

Gill, C. (2004a), 'The Impact of Greek Philosophy on Contemporary Ethical Philosophy', in L. Rossetti (ed.), *Greek Philosophy in the New Millennium: Essays in Honour of Thomas M. Robinson*, St Augustine: 209–26.

Gill, C. (2004b), 'The Stoic Theory of Ethical Development: In What Sense is Nature a Norm?', in J. Szaif and M. Lutz-Bachmann (eds), *Was is das für den Menschen Gute? Menschliche Natur und Güterlehre: What is Good for a Human Being? Human Nature and Values*, Berlin: 101–25.

Gill, C. (2005a), 'In What Sense are Ancient Ethical Norms Universal?', in Gill, C. (ed.) *Virtue, Norms, and Objectivity: Issues in Ancient and Modern Ethics*, Oxford: 15–40.

Gill, C. (2005b) (ed.), *Virtue, Norms, and Objectivity: Issues in Ancient and Modern Ethics*, Oxford.

Gill, C. (2006), *The Structured Self in Hellenistic and Roman Thought*, Oxford.

Gill, C. (2007), 'The Good and Mathematics', in D. Cairns, F.-G. Hermann, and T. Penner (eds), *Pursuing the Good: Ethics and Metaphysics in Plato's Republic*, Edinburgh: 251–74.

Gill, C. (2008), 'The Ancient Self: Issues and Approaches', in P. Remes and J. Sihvola (eds), *Ancient Philosophy of the Self*, New York: 35–56.

Gill, C. (2010a), *Naturalistic Psychology in Galen and Stoicism*, Oxford.

Gill, C. (2010b), Particulars, Selves, and Individuals in Stoic Philosophy', in R. Sharples (ed.), *Particulars in Greek Philosophy*, Leiden: 127–45.

Gill, C. (2010c), 'Stoicism and Epicureanism', in P. Goldie (ed.), *The Oxford Handbook of the Philosophy of Emotion*, Oxford: 143–65.

Gill, C. (2012), 'The Transformation of Aristotle's Ethics in Roman Philosophy', in J. Miller (ed.), *The Reception of Aristotle's Ethics*, Cambridge: 31–52.

Gill, C. (2013a), *Marcus Aurelius Meditations Books 1–6*, trans. with introduction and commentary, Oxford.

Gill, C. (2013b), 'Philosophical Therapy as Preventive Psychological Medicine', in W. Harris (ed.), *Mental Disorders in the Classical World*, Leiden: 339–60.

Gill, C. (2015), 'Building Resilience Today: How Can Ancient Stoicism Help?' in T. M. Ostrowski, I. Sikorska, and K. Gerc (eds), *Resilience and Health in a Fast-Changing World*, Kraków: 33–45.

Gill, C. (2016a), 'Antiochus' theory of *oikeiōsis*', in *Cicero's De Finibus: Philosophical Approaches*, J. Annas and G. Betegh (eds), Cambridge: 221–47.

Gill, C. (2016b), 'Positive Emotions in Stoicism: Are They Enough?', in R. R. Caston and R. A. Kaster (eds), *Hope, Joy, and Affection in the Classical World*, Oxford: 143–60.

Gill, C. (2016c), 'Stoic Themes in Contemporary Anglo-American Ethics', in J. Sellars (ed.), *Routledge Handbook of the Stoic Tradition*, Abingdon: 346–59.

Gill, C. (2017), '*Oikeiōsis* in Stoicism, Antiochus and Arius Didymus', in T. Engberg-Pedersen (ed.), *From Stoicism to Platonism: The Development of Philosophy 100 BCE–100 CE*, Cambridge: 100–20.

Gill, C. (2018a), 'Enactivism and Embodied Cognition in Stoicism and Plato's *Timaeus*' in M. Anderson, D. Cairns, and M. Sprevak (eds), *Distributed Cognition in Classical Antiquity*, Edinburgh: 150–68.

Gill, C. (2018b), 'Philosophical Psychological Therapy: Did it Have any Impact on Medical Practice?', in C. Thumiger and P. N. Singer (eds), *Mental Illness in Ancient Medicine*, Leiden: 365–80.

Gill, C. (2018c), 'The Psychology of Psychotherapy: Ancient and Modern Perspectives', in J. Lauwers, H. Schwall, and J. Opsomer (eds), *Psychology and the Classics*, Berlin: 278–92.

Gill, C. (2019a), 'Stoic Detachment – is this a Myth?', *Philosophia* 49: 271–86.

Gill, C. (2019b), 'Stoic Magnanimity', in S. Vasalou (ed.), *The Measure of Greatness: Philosophers on Magnanimity*, Oxford: 49–71.

Gill, C. (2020), 'Questions and Answers: *De Finibus* 3 and *Tusculans* 5', in G. Müller and J. Müller (eds), *Cicero Ethicus: Die Tusculanae disputationes im Vergleich mit De finibus bonorum et malorum*, Heidelberg: 113–34.

Gill, C. (2021), 'Stoicism and Modern Virtue Ethics', in C. Halbig and F. Timmermann (eds), *Handbuch Tugend und Tugendethik (Handbook of Virtue and Virtue Ethics)*, New York.

Gill, C. (forthcoming a), 'Cicero's *De Officiis* on Practical Deliberation', in R. Woolf (ed.), *Cambridge Companion to Cicero's De Officiis*, Cambridge.

Gill, C. (forthcoming b), 'Virtue and Happiness', in J. Sellars (ed.), *Cambridge Companion to Marcus Aurelius*, Cambridge.

Gloyn, L. (2017), *The Ethics of the Family in Seneca*, Cambridge.

Gourinat, J.-B. (2014), 'Comment se determine le *kathekon*?', *Philosophie Antique* 14: 13–40.

Gourinat, J.-B. (2016) (ed.), *L'éthique du stoïcien Hiéroclès (Philosophie Antique Hors-Série)*, Villeneuve d'Asq.

Graver, M. (2007), *Stoicism and Emotion*, Chicago.

Graver, M. (2012), 'Seneca and the *contemplatio veri*: De Otio and Epistulae Morales', in T. Bénatouïl, and M. Bonazzi (eds), *Theoria, Praxis, and the Contemplative Life After Plato and Aristotle*, Leiden: 75–100.

Graver, M. (2016), 'Anatomies of Joy: Seneca and the *Gaudium* Tradition', in R. R. Caston and R. A. Kaster (eds), *Hope, Joy, and Affection in the Classical World*, Oxford: 123–42.

Griffin, M. (1976), *Seneca: A Philosopher in Politics*, Oxford.

Griffin, M. (1986), 'Philosophy, Cato, and Roman Suicide I and II', *Greece and Rome* 33: 64–77, 192–202.

Griffin, M. (1995), 'Philosophical Badinage in Cicero's Letters to his Friends', in J. G. F. Powell (ed.), *Cicero the Philosopher*, Oxford: 325–46.

Griffin, M. (2000), 'Seneca and Pliny', in C. J. Rowe and M. Schofield (eds), *The Cambridge History of Greek and Roman Political Thought*, Cambridge: 532–58.

Griffin, M. (2007), 'Seneca's Pedagogic Strategy: Letters and *De Beneficiis*', in R. Sorabji and R. W. Sharples (eds), *Greek and Roman Philosophy 100 BC–200 AD (Bulletin of the Institute of Classical Studies*, Supplement 94, London) vol. 1: 89–113.

Griffin, M. (2013), *Seneca on Society: A Guide to De Beneficiis,* Oxford.

Griffin, M. and Atkins, E. M. (1991), *Cicero: On Duties,* trans. with introduction and notes, Cambridge.

Guthrie, W. K. C. (1969), *A History of Greek Philosophy,* vol. 3, Cambridge.

Hadot, I. (2014), 'Getting to Goodness: Reflections on Chapter 10 of Brad Inwood, *Reading Seneca*', in J. Wildberger and M. L. Colish (eds), *Seneca Philosophus,* Berlin: 9–41.

Hadot, P. (1995), *Philosophy as a Way of Life: Spiritual Exercises from Socrates to Foucault,* trans. M. Chase, Oxford.

Hadot, P. (1998), *The Inner Citadel: The Meditations of Marcus Aurelius,* trans. M. Chase, Oxford.

Hamilton, R. (2013), 'Naturalistic Virtue Ethics and the New Biology', in S. van Hooft (ed.), *Handbook of Virtue Ethics,* Durham: 42–52.

Hard, R. (2011), *Marcus Aurelius: Meditations,* trans., ed. C. Gill, Oxford.

Hard, R. (2014), *Epictetus: Discourses, Fragments, Handbook,* trans., ed. C. Gill, Oxford.

Hare, J. (2000), 'Scotus on Morality and Nature', *Medieval Philosophy and Theology* 9: 15–38.

Harris, W. V. (2013) (ed.), *Mental Disorders in the Classical World,* Leiden.

Harrison, T. and Walker, D. I. (2018) (eds), *The Theory and Practice of Virtue Education,* London.

Hawton, K., Salovskis, P., Kirk, J. and Clark, D. (1989) (eds), *Cognitive Behaviour Therapy for Psychiatric Problems: A Practical Guide,* Oxford.

Hayes, S., Strosahl, K., and Wilson, K. (1999) (eds), *Acceptance and Commitment Therapy: An Experiential Approach to Behavior Change,* New York.

Herbert, J. and Forman, E. (2011) (eds), *Acceptance and Mindfulness in Cognitive Behavior Therapy: Understanding and Applying the New Therapies,* Hoboken.

Hooft, S. van (2013) (ed.), *Handbook of Virtue Ethics,* Durham.

Holiday, R. (2014), *The Obstacle is the Way: The Timeless Art of Turning Trials into Triumph,* London.

Hurka, T. (2001), *Virtue, Vice, and Value,* Oxford.

Hursthouse, R. (1995), 'The Virtuous Person's Reasons: A Reply to Bernard Williams', in R. Heinaman (ed.), *Aristotle and Moral Realism,* London: 24–33.

Hursthouse, R. (1999), *On Virtue Ethics,* Oxford.

Hursthouse, R. (2007), 'Environmental Virtue Ethics', in R. L. Walker and P. J. Ivanhoe (eds), *Working Virtue: Virtue Ethics and Contemporary Moral Problems,* Oxford: 155–72.

Ieradiakonou, K. (1993), 'The Stoic Division of Philosophy', *Phronesis* 38: 57–74.

Inwood, B. (1983), 'Comments on H. Görgemanns, "*Oikeiōsis* in Arius Didymus"', in W. W. Fortenbaugh (ed.), *On Stoic and Peripatetic Ethics: The Work of Arius Didymus,* New Brunswick: 190–201.

Inwood, B. (1985), *Ethics and Human Action in Early Stoicism,* Oxford.

Inwood, B. (1995), Review of J. Annas, *The Morality of Happiness, Ancient Philosophy* 15: 647–65.

Inwood, B. (1999), 'Rules and Reasoning in Stoic Ethics', in K. Ieradiakonou (ed.), *Topics in Stoic Philosophy,* Oxford: 95–127.

Inwood, B. (2005), *Reading Seneca: Stoic Philosophy at Rome,* Oxford.

Inwood, B. (2007), *Seneca's Philosophical Letters,* trans. with introduction and commentary, Oxford.

Inwood, B. (2009), 'Why Physics?', in R. Salles (ed.), *God and Cosmos in Stoicism,* Oxford: 201–23.

Inwood, B. (2013), 'How Unified is Stoicism Anyway?', in R. Kamtekar (ed.), *Virtue and Happiness: Essays in Honour of Julia Annas*, Oxford Studies in Ancient Philosophy Supplementary volume, Oxford: 224–41.

Inwood, B. (2014), *Ethics After Aristotle*, Cambridge, Mass.

Inwood, B. (2016), 'The Voice of Nature', in J. Annas and G. Betegh (eds), *Cicero's De Finibus: Philosophical Approaches*, Cambridge: 147–66.

Inwood, B. (2018), *Stoicism: A Very Short Introduction*, Oxford.

Inwood, B. and Gerson, L. (2nd edn. 1997), *Hellenistic Philosophy: Introductory Readings*, Indianapolis.

Inwood, B. and Gerson, L. (2008), *The Stoics Reader: Selected Writings and Testimonia*, Indianapolis.

Inwood, B. and Donini, P. (1999), 'Stoic Ethics', in K. Algra, J. Barnes, J. Mansfeld, and M. Schofield (eds), *The Cambridge History of Hellenistic Philosophy*, Cambridge: 675–738.

Irvine, W. B. (2008), *A Guide to the Good Life: The Ancient Art of Stoic Joy*, Oxford.

Irwin, T. (1986), 'Stoic and Aristotelian Conceptions of Happiness', in M. Schofield and G. Striker (eds), *The Norms of Nature: Studies in Hellenistic Ethics*, Cambridge: 205–44.

Irwin, T. (2007), *The Development of Ethics: vol. 1: From Socrates to the Reformation*, Oxford.

Irwin, T. (2008), *The Development of Ethics: vol. 2: From Suarez to Rousseau*, Oxford.

Jackson-McCabe, M. (2004), 'The Stoic Theory of Implanted Preconceptions', *Phronesis* 49: 323–47.

Jedan, C. (2009), *Stoic Virtues: Chrysippus and the Religious Character of Stoic Ethics*, New York.

Johnson, M. R. (2005), *Aristotle on Teleology*, Oxford.

Kawall, J. (2013), 'Qualified Agent and Agent-based Ethics and the Problem of Right Action', in S. van Hooft (ed.), *The Handbook of Virtue Ethics*, Durham: 130–40.

Kawall, J. (2017), 'A History of Environmental Ethics', in S. Gardiner and A. Thompson (eds), *The Oxford Handbook of Environmental Ethics*, Oxford: 13–26.

Kawall, J. (2018), 'Environmental Virtue Ethics', in N. Snow (ed.), *The Oxford Handbook of Virtue*, Oxford: 659–79.

Kenny, A. (1978/2016), *The Aristotelian Ethics*, Oxford.

Kenny, A. (1979), *Aristotle's Theory of Will*, London.

Kenny, A. (1992), *Aristotle on the Perfect Life*, Oxford.

Kerferd, G. B. (1978), 'What Does the Wise Man Know?', in J. M. Rist (ed.), *The Stoics*, Berkeley: 125–36.

Kerferd, G. B. (1981), *The Sophistic Movement*, Cambridge.

Klein, J. (2015), 'Making Sense of Stoic Indifferents', *Oxford Studies in Ancient Philosophy* 49: 227–81.

Klein, J. (2016), 'The Stoic Argument from *oikeiosis*', *Oxford Studies in Ancient Philosophy* 50: 143–50.

Korsgaard, C. M. (1996), *The Sources of Normativity*, Cambridge.

Korsgaard, C. M. (2009), *Self-Constitution: Agency, Identity, and Integrity*, Oxford.

Kosman, A. (2007), 'Justice and Virtue: The *Republic*'s Inquiry into Proper Difference', in G. R. F. Ferrari (ed.), *The Cambridge Companion to Plato's Republic*, Cambridge: 116–37.

Kraut, R. (1989), *Aristotle on the Human Good*, Princeton.

LeBar, M. (2018), in N. Snow (ed.), *Oxford Handbook of Virtue*. Oxford: 470–87.

Levine, M. P. (1994), 'Pantheism, Ethics and Ecology', *Environmental Values* 3: 212–38.

Lloyd, G. E. R. (1966), *Polarity and Analogy: Two Types of Argumentation in Early Greek Thought*, Cambridge.

Long, A. A. (1995), 'Cicero's Politics in *De Officiis*', in A. Laks and M. Schofield (eds), *Justice and Generosity: Studies in Hellenistic Social and Political Philosophy*, Cambridge: 213–40.

Long, A. A. (1996), *Stoic Studies*, Cambridge.

Long, A. A. (1999), 'The Socratic Legacy', in K. Algra, J. Barnes, J. Mansfeld, and M. Schofield (eds), *The Cambridge History of Hellenistic Philosophy*, Cambridge: 617–41.

Long, A. A. (2002), *Epictetus: A Stoic and Socratic Guide to Life*, Oxford.

Long, A. A. and Sedley, D. N. (1987), *The Hellenistic Philosophers*, Cambridge.

Long, A. G. (2013a) (ed.), *Plato and the Stoics*, Cambridge. (N.B. References in this book to 'Long' are to A. A. Long unless specified as 'A. G. Long'.)

Long, A. G. (2013b), 'Subtexts, Connections and Open Opposition', in A. G. Long (ed.), *Plato and the Stoics*, Cambridge: 106–27.

McAdams, D. P. (2015), 'Psychological Science and the *Nicomachean Ethics*: Virtuous Actors, Agents, and Authors', in N. Snow (ed.), *Cultivating Virtue: Perspectives from Philosophy, Theology, and Psychology*, Oxford: 307–36.

McCabe, M. M. (2002), 'Indifference Readings: Plato and the Stoa on Socratic Ethics', in T. P. Wiseman (ed.), *Classics in Progress: Essays on Ancient Greece and Rome*, Oxford: 363–98.

McDowell, J. (1980), 'The Role of *Eudaimonia* in Aristotle's Ethics', in A. O. Rorty (ed.), *Essays on Aristotle's Ethics*, Berkeley: 359–76.

McDowell, J. (1986), Review of B. Williams, *Ethics and the Limits of Philosophy*, Mind 95: 377–86.

MacIntyre, A. (1981/1985), *After Virtue: A Study in Moral Theory*, London.

MacLellan, A. and Derakshan, N. (2021), 'The Effects of Stoic Training and Adaptive Memory Working Training on Emotional Vulnerability in High Worriers', *Cognitive Therapy and Research*, Springer. https://doi.org/10.1007/510608-020-10183-4 (first published 1 January 21; last accessed 21 May 2021).

McNaughton, D. and Rawling, P. (2006), 'Deontology', in D. Copp (ed.), *The Oxford Handbook of Ethical Theory*, Oxford: 424–58.

Magrin, S. (2018), 'Nature and Utopia in Epictetus' Theory of *oikeiosis*', *Phronesis* 63: 293–350.

Mansfeld, J. (1999a), 'Sources', in K. Algra, J. Barnes, J. Mansfeld, and M. Schofield (eds), *The Cambridge History of Hellenistic Philosophy*, Cambridge: 3–30.

Mansfeld, J. (1999b), 'Theology', in K. Algra, J. Barnes, J. Mansfeld, and M. Schofield (eds), *The Cambridge History of Hellenistic Philosophy*, Cambridge: 452–78.

Menn, S. (1995), 'Physics as a Virtue', *Proceedings of the Boston Area Colloquium in Ancient Philosophy* 11: 1–45.

Meyer, S. S. (2009), 'Chain of Causes: What is Stoic Fate?', in R. Salles (ed.), *God and Cosmos in Stoicism*, Oxford: 71–90.

Mill, J. S. (1993), *Utilitarianism*, etc., ed. G. Williams, London.

Miller, J. (2012) (ed.), *The Reception of Aristotle's Ethics*, Cambridge.

Moore, G. E. (1903), *Principia Ethica*, Cambridge.

Morel P.-M. (2009), 'Epicurean Atomism', in J. Warren (ed.), *The Cambridge Companion to Epicureanism*, Cambridge: 65–83.

Murdoch, I. (1970/2001), *The Sovereignty of Good*, London.

Narvaez, D. (2015), 'The Co-Construction of Virtue: Epigenetics, Development, and Culture', in N. Snow (ed.), *Cultivating Virtue: Perspectives from Philosophy, Theology, and Psychology*, Oxford: 251–77.

Nielsen, K. M. (2012), 'The *Nicomachean Ethics* in Hellenistic Philosophy: a Hidden Treasure?', in J. Miller (ed.), *The Reception of Aristotle's Ethics*, Cambridge: 5–30.

Nietzsche, F. (1974), *The Gay Science*, trans. W. Kaufman. New York.

Nussbaum, M. C. (1986), *The Fragility of Goodness; Luck and Ethics in Greek Tragedy and Philosophy*, Cambridge.

Nussbaum, M. C. (1994), *The Therapy of Desire: Theory and Practice in Hellenistic Ethics*, Princeton.

Nussbaum, M. C. (1995), Aristotle on Human Nature and the Foundations of Ethics', in R. Harrison and J. E. J. Altham (eds), *World, Mind, and Ethics*, Cambridge: 86–131

Nussbaum, M. C. (2001), *Upheavals of Thought: The Intelligence of Emotions*, Cambridge.

Nussbaum, M. C. (2006), *Frontiers of Justice: Disability, Nationality, Species Membership*, Cambridge, Mass.

Nussbaum, M. C. (2008), 'Human Dignity and Political Entitlement', in *Human Dignity and Bioethics*, Essays commissioned by the President's Council on Bioethics, Washington, D. C.: 351–81.

Oakley, J. (2013), 'Virtue Ethics and Utilitarianism', in S. van Hooft (ed.), *The Handbook of Virtue Ethics*, Durham: 64–75.

O'Keefe, T, (2009), 'Action and Responsibility', in J. Warren (ed.), *The Cambridge Companion to Epicureanism*, Cambridge: 142–57.

Palmer, C. (2017), 'Living Individuals: Biocentrism in Environmental Ethics', in S. Gardiner and A. Thompson (eds) (2017), *The Oxford Handbook of Environmental Ethics*, Oxford: 101–12.

Passmore, J. (1974), *Man's Responsibility for Nature: Ecological Problems and Western Traditions*, London.

Paton, H. J. (1948), *The Moral Law: Kant's Groundwork of the Metaphysic of Morals*, translated and analysed, London.

Pembroke, S. (1971), 'Oikeiosis', in A. A. Long (ed.), *Problems in Stoicism*, London: 114–49.

Pettigrove, G. (2018), 'Alternatives to Neo-Aristotelian Virtue Ethics', in N. Snow (ed.), *The Handbook of Virtue*, Oxford: 359–76.

Pianalto, M. (2013), 'Humility and Environmental Virtue Ethics', in M. Austin (ed.), *Virtues in Action: New Essays in Applied Virtue Ethics*, New York: 132–49.

Pigliucci, M. (2017), *How to be a Stoic: Ancient Wisdom for Modern Living*, London.

Pohlenz, M. (1940), 'Die Oikeiosis', in *Grundfragen der Stoischen Philosophie*, Göttingen: 1–81.

Pohlenz, M. (2nd edn. 1959), *Die Stoa: Geschichte einer geistigen Bewegung*, 2 vols., Göttingen.

Pomeroy, A. J. (1999) (ed.), *Arius Didymus: Epitome of Stoic Ethics*, Atlanta.

Powell, J. G. F. (1995) (ed.), *Cicero: The Philosopher*, Oxford.

Price, A. W. (1995), *Mental Conflict*, London.

Price, A. W. (2005), 'Aristotelian Virtue and Practical Judgement', in C. Gill (ed.), *Virtue, Norms, and Objectivity: Issues in Ancient and Modern Ethics*, Oxford: 233–78.

Price, A. W. (2008), *Contextuality in Practical Deliberation*, Oxford.

Price, A. W. (2011), *Virtue and Reason in Plato and Aristotle*, Oxford.

Protopapadakis, E. (2012), 'The Stoic Notion of Cosmic Sympathy in Contemporary Environmental Ethics', *Antiquity, Modern World and Reception of Ancient Culture*, The Serbian Society for Ancient Studies, Belgrade: 290–305.

Radice, R. (2000), *'Oikeiosis': Ricerche sul fondamento del pensiero Stoico e sulla sua genesi*, Milan.

Ramelli, I. (2009), trans. D. Konstan, *Hierocles the Stoic: Elements of Ethics, Fragments, and Excerpts*, Atlanta.

Reydams-Schils, G. (2005), *The Roman Stoics: Self, Responsibility, and Affection*, Chicago.

Robertson, D. (2010), *The Philosophy of Cognitive-Behavioural Therapy (CBT): Stoic Philosophy as Rational and Cognitive Therapy*, London.

Robertson, D, (2013), *Stoicism and the Art of Happiness*, London.

Robertson, D. (2016), 'The Stoic Influence on Modern Psychotherapy', in J. Sellars (ed.), *The Routledge Handbook of the Stoic Tradition*, Abingdon: 374–88.

Rocca, J. (ed.) (2017), *Teleology in the Ancient World: Philosophical and Medical Approaches*, Cambridge.

Rorty, A. O. (1980), 'The Place of Contemplation in Aristotle's *Nicomachean Ethics*', in A. O. Rorty (ed.), *Essays on Aristotle's Ethics*, Berkeley: 377–94.

Roskam, G. (2005), *On the Path to Virtue: The Stoic Doctrine of Moral Progress and its Reception in (Middle-) Platonism*, Leiden.

Russell, D. C. (2009), *Practical Intelligence and the Virtues*, Oxford.

Russell, D. C. (2012), *Happiness for Humans*, Oxford.

Russell, D. C. (2013a) (ed.), *Cambridge Companion to Virtue Ethics*, Cambridge.

Russell, D. C. (2013b), 'Virtue Ethics, Happiness, and the Good Life', in D. C. Russell (ed.), *Cambridge Companion to Virtue Ethics*, Cambridge: 7–28.

Russell, D. C. (2015), Aristotle on Cultivating Virtue', in N. Snow (ed.), *Cultivating Virtue: Perspectives from Philosophy, Theology, and Psychology*, Cambridge: 17–48.

Schmitz, P. (2014), *Cato Peripateticus: Stoische und Peripatetische Ethik im Dialog*, Berlin.

Schofield, M. (1983), 'The Syllogisms of Zeno of Citium', *Phronesis* 28: 31–58.

Schofield, M. (1991), *The Stoic Idea of the City*, Cambridge.

Schofield, M. (1995), 'Two Stoic Approaches to Justice', in A. Laks and M. Schofield (eds), *Justice and Generosity: Studies in Hellenistic Social and Political Philosophy*, Cambridge: 191–21.

Schofield, M. (1999), 'Social and Political Thought', in K. Algra, J. Barnes, J. Mansfeld, and M. Schofield (eds), *The Cambridge History of Hellenistic Philosophy*, Cambridge: 739–70.

Schofield, M. (2000), 'Epicurean and Stoic Political Thought', in C. Rowe and M. Schofield (eds), *The Cambridge History of Greek and Roman Political Thought*, Cambridge: 435–56.

Schofield, M. (2003), 'Stoic Ethics', in B. Inwood (ed.), *The Cambridge Companion to the Stoics*, Cambridge: 233–56.

Schofield, M. (2013), 'Cardinal Virtues: A Contested Socratic Inheritance', in A. G. Long (ed.), *Plato and the Stoics*, Cambridge: 11–28.

Schofield, M. (2021), *Cicero: Political Philosophy*, Oxford.

Sedley, D. N. (1997), 'The Ethics of Brutus and Cassius', *Journal of Roman Studies* 87: 41–53.

Sedley, D. N. (2003), 'The School, from Zeno to Arius Didymus', in B. Inwood (ed.), *The Cambridge Companion to the Stoics*, Cambridge: 7–32.

Sedley, D. N. (2007), *Creationism and its Critics in Antiquity*, Berkeley.

Sellars, J. (2003), *The Art of Living: The Stoics on the Nature and Function of Philosophy*, Aldershot.

Sellars, J. (2020), *Lessons in Stoicism: What Ancient Philosophers Teach us about How to Live*, London.

Sellars, J. (2021), *Marcus Aurelius*, Abingdon.

Sharpe, M. (2013), 'Stoic Virtue Ethics, in S. van Hooft (ed.), *Handbook of Virtue Ethics*, Durham: 28–41.

Sharples, R. W. (2007), 'Peripatetics on Happiness', in R. W. Sharples and R. Sorabji (eds), *Greek and Roman Philosophy 100 BC–200 AD*, vol. 2, London: 627–37.

Sharples, R, W. (2010), *Peripatetic Philosophy 200 BC to AD 200: An Introduction and Collection of Sources in Translation*, Cambridge.

Sheffield, F. (2012), 'The *Symposium* and Platonic Ethics: Plato, Vlastos, and a Misguided Debate', *Phronesis* 57: 117–141.

Sherman, N. (1989), *The Fabric of Character: Aristotle's Theory of Virtue*, Oxford.

Sherman, N. (1997), *Making a Necessity of Virtue: Aristotle and Kant on Virtue*, Cambridge.

Sherman, N. (2005), *Stoic Warriors: The Ancient Philosophy behind the Military Mind*, Oxford.

Sherman, N. (2021), *Stoic Wisdom: Ancient Lessons for Modern Resilience*, Oxford.

Shogry, S. (2021), 'Stoic Cosmopolitanism and Environmental Ethics', in K. Arundsen (ed.), *Routledge Handbook of Hellenistic Philosophy*, Abingdon: 397–409.

Sim, M. (2018), 'The *Phronimos* and the Sage', in N. Snow (ed.), *The Handbook of Virtue*, Oxford: 190–205.

Slingerland, E. (2015), 'The Situationist Critique and Early Confucian Virtue Ethics', in N. Snow (ed.), *Cultivating Virtue: Perspectives from Philosophy, Theology, and Psychology*, Oxford: 135–69.

Slote, M. (1992), *From Morality to Virtue*, Oxford.

Slote, M. (2001), *Morals from Motives*, Oxford.

Slote, M. (2009), *Moral Sentimentalism*, Oxford.

Snow, N. (2013), Situationism and Character: New Directions', in S. van Hooft (ed.), *Handbook of Virtue Ethics*, Durham: 430–9.

Snow, N. (2015) (ed.), *Cultivating Virtue: Perspectives from Philosophy, Theology, and Psychology*, Oxford.

Snow, N. (2018a) (ed.), *The Handbook of Virtue*, Oxford.

Snow, N. (2018b), 'Introduction', in N. Snow (ed.), *The Handbook of Virtue*, Oxford: 1–6.

Snow, N. (2018c), 'Neo-Aristotelian Virtue Ethics', in N. Snow (ed.), *The Handbook of Virtue*, Oxford: 321–42.

Solomon, W. D. (2018), 'Early Virtue Ethics', in N. Snow (ed.), *The Handbook of Virtue*, Oxford: 303–20.

Sorabji, R. (1993), *Animal Minds and Human Morals*, London.

Sorabji, R. (2000), *Emotion and Peace of Mind*, Oxford.

Spinelli, E. (2012), 'Philosophy and *Praxis* in Sextus Empiricus', in T. Bénatouïl and M. Bonazzi (eds), *Theoria, Praxis, and the Contemplative Life After Plato and Aristotle*, Leiden: 101–17.

Stankiewicz, P. (2019), *Does Happiness Write Blank Pages? On Stoicism and Artistic Creativity*, Wilmington, Delaware.

Stankiewicz, P. (2020), *Manual of Reformed Stoicism*, Wilmington, Delaware.

Stephens, W. O. (1994), 'Stoic Naturalism, Rationalism, and Ecology', *Environmental Ethics* 16: 275–84.

Stichter, M. (2018), 'Virtue as Skill', in N. Snow (ed.), *The Handbook of Virtue*, Oxford: 57–81.

Strawson, P. E. (1974), 'Freedom and Resentment, in *Freedom and Resentment and Other Essays*, London: 1–25.

Striker, G. (1996), *Essays on Hellenistic Epistemology and Ethics*, Cambridge.

Swanton, C. (2003), *Virtue Ethics: A Pluralistic View*, Oxford.

Swanton, C. (2015), *The Virtue Ethics of Hume and Nietzsche*, Hoboken.

Taylor, P. W. (1981), 'The Ethics of Respect for Nature', *Environmental Ethics* 1: 197–218.

Taylor, P. W (1986), *Respect for Nature*, Princeton.

Thompson, A. and Bendik-Keymer, J. (eds) (2012), *Ethical Adaptation to Climate Change: Human Virtues of the Future*, Cambridge, Mass.

Thompson, M. (1995), 'The Representation of Life', in R. Hursthouse, G. Lawrence, and W. Quinn (eds), *Virtues and Reasons*, Oxford: 247–96.

Thompson, R. A. (2015), 'The Development of Virtue: A Perspective from Developmental Psychology', in N. Snow (ed.), *Cultivating Virtue: Perspectives from Philosophy, Theology, and Psychology*, Oxford: 279–306.

Thumiger, C. and Singer, P. N. (2018) (eds), *Mental Illness in Ancient Medicine*, Leiden.

Tieleman, T. (2003), *Chrysippus' On Affections: Reconstruction and Interpretation*, Leiden.

Tieleman, T. (2007), 'Panaetius' Place in the History of Stoicism with Special Reference to his Moral Psychology', in A. M. Ioppolo and D. N. Sedley (eds), *Pyrrhonists, Patricians, Platonizers: Hellenistic Philosophy in the Period 155–86* BC, Naples: 103–42.

Tsouna, V. (2007), *The Ethics of Philodemus*, Oxford.

Tsouni, G. (2019), *Antiochus and Peripatetic Ethics*, Cambridge.

Ussher, P. (2016) (ed.), *Stoicism Today: Selected Writings* II (no place of publication listed).

Vander Waerdt, P. A. (1994), 'Socrates and Stoic Natural Law', in P. A. Vander Waerdt (ed.), *The Socratic Movement*, Ithaca, NY: 272–308.

Veillard, C. (2014), 'Comment définer son devoir? Le *peri kathekontos* de Panétius', *Philosophie antique* 14: 71–109.

Vogt, K. M. (2008a), *Law, Reason, and the Cosmic City: Political Philosophy in the Early Stoa*, Oxford.

Vogt, K. M. (2008b), 'The Good as Benefit: On the Stoic Definition of the Good', *Boston Area Colloquium in Ancient Philosophy* 14: 155–74.

Vogt, K. M. (2014), 'Taking the Same Things Seriously and not Seriously: A Stoic Proposal on Value and the Good', in D. R. Gordon and D. B. Suits (eds), *Epictetus: His Continuing Influence and Contemporary Relevance*, Rochester, NY: 55–75.

Vogt, K. M. (2017), 'The Stoics on Virtue and Happiness', in C. Bobonich (ed.), *The Cambridge Companion to Ancient Ethics*, Cambridge: 183–99.

Wachsmuth, C. and Hense, O. (1884–1912, repr. 1958) (eds), *Ioannis Stobaei: Anthologium*, 5 vols. Berlin.

Walsh, P. G. (1998), *Cicero, The Nature of the Gods*, trans. with introduction and notes, Oxford.

White, N. P. (1979), 'The Basis of Stoic Ethics', *Harvard Studies in Classical Philology* 83: 143–78.

White, N. P. (1985), 'The Role of Physics in Stoic Ethics', *The Southern Journal of Philosophy* 23 (Supplement: Proceedings of the Spindel Conference): 57–74.

White, N. P. (2002), *Individual and Conflict in Greek Ethics*, Oxford.

Whiting, K., Konstantakos, L., Carrasco, A., and Carmona, L. G. (2018), 'Sustainable Development, Wellbeing and Material Consumption: A Stoic Perspective', *Sustainability* 10. 2: 474.

Whiting, K. and Konstantakos, L. (2019), 'Stoic Theology: Revealing or Redundant?', *Religions* 10.3: 193.

Whiting, K., Dinucci, A., Simpson, E, and Konstantakos, L. (2022), 'The Environmental Battle Hymn of the Stoic God', *Symposion* 9.1: 51–68.

Wilkes, K. (1980), 'The Good Man and the Good for Man in Aristotle's Ethics', in A. O. Rorty (ed.), *Essays in Aristotle's Ethics*, Berkeley: 341–76.

Williams, B. (1981), *Moral Luck: Philosophical Papers 1973–1980*, Cambridge.

Williams, B. (1985), *Ethics and the Limits of Philosophy*, London.

Williams, B. (1995a), 'Acting as the Virtuous Person Acts', in R. Heinaman (ed.), *Aristotle and Moral Realism*, London: 13–23.

Williams, B. (1995b), *Making Sense of Humanity*, Cambridge.

Williams, B. (1995c), 'Replies', in J. E. J. Altham and R. Harrison (eds), *World, Mind, and Ethics*, Cambridge: 185–224.

Winterbottom, M. (1994) (ed.), *Cicero: De Officiis*, Oxford.

Woolf, R. (2015), *Cicero: The Philosophy of a Roman Sceptic*, London.

Zagzebski, L. (1996), *Virtues of the Mind*, Cambridge.

Index of Ancient Passages

(This index includes references to Long and Sedley, *Hellenistic Philosophers*, in cases where the ancient sources are not also cited.)

General Index